D1592961

**Hermeneia
—A Critical
and Historical
Commentary
on the Bible**

Philippians

A Commentary

by Paul A. Holloway

Edited by
Adela Yarbro Collins

**Fortress
Press**   Minneapolis

Philippians
A Commentary

Cover and interior design by Kenneth Hiebert
Typesetting and page composition by
The HK Scriptorium

Library of Congress cataloging-in-publication data is available

Print ISBN: 978-0-8006-6096-3

eISBN: 978-1-5064-3843-6

The paper used in this publication meets the mini-
mum requirements of American National Standard
for Information Sciences—Permanence of paper for
Printed Library Materials, ANSI Z329.48–1984.

Manufactured in the U.S.A.

■ *For Melissa, and for Chap, Abby, Callie, and Lillian*

The Author

Paul A. Holloway (Ph.D., University of Chicago, 1998) lives in Old Salem, Tennessee, with his family and an assortment of domestic livestock, including a small herd of prize milk goats. He enjoys traditional carpentry and especially the continued restoration of his family's circa 1800 Federalist farmhouse and outbuildings. He is University Professor of Classics and Ancient Christianity in the University of the South in nearby Sewanee. Prior to coming to "Sewanee" he was Senior Lecturer in the Department of Theology and Religious Studies in the University of Glasgow, Scotland. The present commentary builds on his published dissertation, *Consolation in Philippians* (SNTSMS 112; Cambridge: Cambridge University Press, 2001). He has also written *Coping with Prejudice: 1 Peter in Social-Psychological Perspective* (WUNT 244; Tübingen: Mohr Siebeck, 2009), as well as numerous articles on Judaism and early Christianity for such journals as *Byzantinische Zeitschrift, Early Christianity, Harvard Theological Review, Journal of Biblical Literature, New Testament Studies, Novum Testamentum, Vetus Testamentum,* and *Zeitschrift für die neutestamentliche Wissenschaft.* He is currently preparing a commentary on 1 Corinthians for the International Critical Commentary (ICC) series.

Endpapers

Endpapers show a leaf from $\mathfrak{P}^{46}$, dated c. 180–200 CE, containing Philippians 1:30—2:12; Chester Beatty Library, BP II, folio 84v. Reprinted courtesy of the Chester Beatty Library.

Contents
Philippians

■ Back Matter

The name *Hermeneia,* Greek ἑρμενεία, has been chosen as the title of the commentary series to which this volume belongs. The word *Hermeneia* has a rich background in the history of biblical interpretation as a term used in the ancient Greek-speaking world for the detailed, systematic exposition of a scriptural work. It is hoped that the series, like its name, will carry forward this old and venerable tradition. A second, entirely practical reason for selecting the name lies in the desire to avoid a long descriptive title and its inevitable acronym, or worse, an unpronounceable abbreviation.

The series is designed to be a critical and historical commentary to the Bible without arbitrary limits in size or scope. It will utilize the full range of philological and historical tools, including textual criticism (often slighted in modern commentaries), the methods of the history of tradition (including genre and prosodic analysis), and the history of religion.

Hermeneia is designed for the serious student of the Bible. It will make full use of ancient Semitic and classical languages; at the same time, English translations of all comparative materials—Greek, Latin, Canaanite, or Akkadian—will be supplied alongside the citation of the source in its original language. Insofar as possible, the aim is to provide the student or scholar with full critical discussion of each problem of interpretation and with the primary data upon which the discussion is based.

Hermeneia is designed to be international and interconfessional in the selection of authors; its editorial boards were formed with this end in view. Occasionally the series will offer translations of distinguished commentaries which originally appeared in languages other than English. Published volumes of the series will be revised continually, and eventually, new commentaries will replace older works in order to preserve the currency of the series. Commentaries are also being assigned for important literary works in the categories of apocryphal and pseudepigraphical works relating to the Old and New Testaments, including some of Essene or Gnostic authorship.

The editors of *Hermeneia* impose no systematic-theological perspective upon the series (directly, or indirectly by selection of authors). It is expected that authors will struggle to lay bare the ancient meaning of a biblical work or pericope. In this way the text's human relevance should become transparent, as is always the case in competent historical discourse. However, the series eschews for itself homiletical translation of the Bible.

The editors are heavily indebted to Fortress Press for its energy and courage in taking up an expensive, long-term project, the rewards of which will accrue chiefly to the field of biblical scholarship.

The editor responsible for this volume is Adela Yarbro Collins of Yale University.

Peter Machinist　　*Harold W. Attridge*
For the Old Testament　For the New Testament
Editorial Board　　　Editorial Board

The commentary by Paul A. Holloway contains a fresh
translation of the letter to the Philippians that reflects his
exegetical decisions. Texts from the rest of the New Testament are his translations as well, unless otherwise noted.
Passages from the Hebrew Bible are usually quoted from
the New Revised Standard Version. Quotations from
Greek and Latin authors are generally his translations
and follow standard critical editions.

Writing a critical commentary on Paul's letter to the Philippians, one of the foundational texts of Western culture, and one that puts on clear display the imprisoned apostle's deep humanity and courage, has been both a challenge and a joy, and I would like to thank the New Testament editors of the Hermeneia commentary series for inviting me to do so. The commentary that follows builds on my University of Chicago dissertation, published in 2001 by Cambridge University Press, and countless times over the course of writing I have had occasion to recall with gratitude the expert and collegial instruction I received at Chicago, especially from my *Doktormutter,* Prof. Adela Yarbro Collins, whose "maternal" duties have now been extended to include serving as the present volume's editor. Three other of my teachers at Chicago whose instruction is reflected on the pages of this book are Prof. Elizabeth Asmis, who taught me to take seriously the various schools of Hellenistic and Roman philosophy; Prof. John J. Collins, who showed me the importance of ancient Judaism and instilled in me a desire to know as much about it as possible; and Prof. Richard Saller, who insisted that I learn to reason critically and historically about the social realities of the eastern provinces of the Roman Empire. I first became interested in Philippians in 1989 when I prepared a seminar paper on the letter for Prof. Werner Kelber at Rice University. It was with some effort that Werner awakened me from my dogmatic slumbers and launched me on an academic career, and for that I will always be grateful.

In producing this commentary I have been aided by two scholars in particular. In all things Pauline, I have been instructed by my good friend Prof. Christopher Mount of DePaul University. My understanding of Paul's religious thought would be much impoverished where it not for Chris's profound insights, frequently and generously communicated to me. I have also been helped by my colleague at Sewanee, Dr. James Dunkly. Jim is Sewanee's recently retired theological librarian, an excellent stylist and editor, and a New Testament scholar in his own right. In addition to being thoughtful conversation partners, both Chris and Jim read and commented on portions of the commentary. I am in their debt—and so are my readers! I would also like to thank Dr. Sandra Bingham of the University of Edinburgh, who brought *Vindolanda Tablet* 2.154 to my attention; Prof. Brent Shaw of Princeton University, who sent me the page proofs of his article "The Myth of the Neronian Persecution," *JRS* 105 (2015) 73–100; Prof. Cédric Brélaz of the University of Strasbourg, who kept me from erring in a matter of Latin epigraphy; Prof. Michael Cover of Marquette University, who shared a draft of his award-winning paper "The Death of Tragedy: The Form of God in Euripides' *Bacchae* and Paul's *Carmen Christi*," *HTR* (forthcoming); and Dr. Romulus Stephanut, Sewanee's new theologian librarian and a gifted scholar of Alexandrian Judaism, who kindly helped me with a question I had about Philo. I am also grateful to Maurya Horgan and Paul Kobelski of the HK Scriptorium for their expert and patient copyediting and typesetting of a challenging manuscript.

Although I have been thinking about and writing about Philippians for over a decade, I was able to bring this commentary into its final form thanks to a generous sabbatical for the academic year 2015–16. I am grateful to Sewanee provost Prof. John Swallow for this time to write and for his continuing interest in my scholarship.

I dedicate this volume to my much-loved wife and life partner Melissa Coulter Holloway, and to our four much-loved children, Chap, Abby, Callie, and Lillian. A keen observer of human nature, a searing cultural critic, and a selfless interlocutor, Melissa's fingerprints are on virtually every page of this book.

A note on language. When writing in my own voice I have used inclusive language; when translating Paul I have not done so for historical reasons. Paul repeatedly refers to the Philippian Christ-believers as "brothers" (ἀδελφοί) even though he means to include in this women such as Euodia and Syntyche (4:2). I have consistently translated ἀδελφοί as "brothers" and in each instance attached a footnote clarifying Paul's usage. Paul's use of the noun πνεῦμα presents special problems. Suffice it to say that in expressions like πνεῦμα θεοῦ ("spirit of God") or πνεῦμα Χριστοῦ ("spirit of Christ") I have not capitalized "spirit." When, however, the divine πνεῦμα is mentioned without a modifier I have capitalized "Spirit" to avoid confusion with other uses, e.g., πνεῦμα as substance.

Reference Codes

1. Sources and Abbreviations

AAR	American Academy of Religion
AB	Anchor Bible
ABD	*The Anchor Bible Dictionary*, ed. David Noel Freedman (6 vols.; New York: Doubleday, 1992).
ABRL	Anchor Bible Reference Library
ABV	J. D. Beazley, *Attic Black-Figure Vase-Painters* (Oxford: Oxford University Press, 1956).
AClass	*Acta classica*
Act. Paul.	*Acts of Paul*
Act. Paul. et Thecl.	*Acts of Paul and Thecla*
Act. Thom.	*Acts of Thomas*
AÉ	*L'Année Épigraphique*
Aeg	*Aegyptus*
Aelianus	
Var. hist.	*Varia historia*
Aesop	
Fab.	*Fabulae*
AGJU	Arbeiten zur Geschichte des antiken Judentums und des Urchristentums
AJA	*American Journal of Archaeology*
AJPh	*American Journal of Philology*
ALGHJ	Arbeiten zur Literatur und Geschichte des hellenistischen Judentums
Ambrose	
De exc. Sat.	*De excessu fratris sui Satyri*
Ep.	*Epistulae*
Hexam.	*Hexameron*
Obit. Theod	*De obitu Theodosii*
Obit. Valent.	*De obitu Valentiniani*
AMNG	*Antiken Münzen Nord-Griechenland*
AnBib	Analecta biblica
AncW	*The Ancient World*
ANF	Ante-Nicene Fathers
ANRW	*Aufstieg und Niedergang der römischen Welt*, ed. Hildegard Temporini and Wolfgang Haase (New York/Berlin: de Gruyter, 1972–).
ANTF	Arbeiten zur neutestamentlichen Textforschung
Anth. Graec.	*Anthologia Graeca*
Antoninus Liberalis	
Metam.	*Metamorphoses*
APF	Archiv für Papyrusforschung
Aphthonius	
Prog.	*Progymnasmata*
Apoc. Abr.	*Apocalypse of Abraham*
Apollonius of Rhodes	
Argon.	*Argonautica*
Apollonius of Tyana	
Ep.	*Epistulae*
Appian	
Bell. civ.	*Bellum civile*
Apuleius	
Metam.	*Metamorphoses*
Aristides	
Or.	*Orationes*
Aristophanes	
Eccl.	*Ecclesiazusae*
Eq.	*Equites (Knights)*
Ran.	*Ranae (Frogs)*
Vesp.	*Vespae (Wasps)*
Aristotle	
EN	*Ethica ad Nicomachum*
Rhet.	*Ars rhetorica*
ASC	altered state(s) of consciousness
Asc. Isa.	*Ascension of Isaiah*
Asclepius	*Asclepius (Hermetica)*
Athenaeus	
Deip.	*Deipnosophistae*
Augustine	
Ep.	*Epistulae*
In Psalm.	*Ennarationes in Psalmos*
Serm.	*Sermones*
Spir. et litt.	*De spiritu et littera*
AV	Authorized Version
AYB	Anchor Yale Bible
BAK	Beiträge zur Altertumskunde
2 Bar.	*2 Baruch*
Basil	
Ep.	*Epistulae*
BBR	*Bulletin for Biblical Research*
BCH	*Bulletin de correspondance hellénique*
BCHSup	Bulletin de correspondance hellénique Supplements
BDAG	Walter Baur, *A Greek-English Lexicon of the New Testament and Other Early Christian Literature*, ed. William F. Arndt, F. Wilbur Gingrich (3rd ed. rev. by Frederick W. Danker; Chicago: University of Chicago Press, 2000).
BDF	F. Blass and A. Debrunner, *A Greek Grammar of the New Testament and Other Early Christian Literature*, ed. and trans. Robert W. Funk (Chicago: University of Chicago Press, 1961).
BEThL	Bibliotheca ephemeridum theologicarum lovaniensium
BFCTh	Beiträge zur Förderung christlicher Theologie
BGU	*Aegyptische Urkunden aus den Königlichen Staatlichen Museen zu Berlin, Griechische Urkunden* (15 vols.; Berlin: Weidmann, 1895–1937).

Bib	*Biblica*
BibInt	*Biblical Interpretation*
BJRL	*Bulletin of the John Rylands University Library of Manchester*
BN	*Biblische Notizen*
BNTC	Black's New Testament Commentary
Boios	
Ornith.	*Ornithogonia*
BTB	*Biblical Theology Bulletin*
BZ	*Byzantinische Zeitschrift*
BZAW	Beihefte zur Zeitschrift für die alttestamentliche Wissenschaft
BZNW	Beihefte zur Zeitschrift für die neutestamentliche Wissenschaft
Callimachus	
Hym. Dem.	*Hymn 6, To Demeter* (*In Cererem*)
Hym. Dionys.	*Hymn 7, To Dionysus* (*In Bacchum*)
Cassius Dio	
Hist.	*Historia romana*
Catullus	
Carm.	*Carmina*
CBET	Contributions to Biblical Exegesis and Theology
CbNT	Commentaire biblique: Nouveau Testament
CBQ	*Catholic Biblical Quarterly*
C.C.	Maxime Collignon and Louis Couve, *Catalogue des vases peints du Musée national d'Athènes* (3 vols.; Paris: Fontemoing, 1902–4).
CCSL	*Corpus Christianorum series latina*
Chariton	
Chaer. et Call.	*De Chaerea et Callirhoe*
Cicero	
Ad Att.	*Ad Atticum*
Ad Brut.	*Ad Brutum*
Ad fam.	*Ad familiares*
De amic.	*De amicitia*
De clem.	*De clementia*
De fin.	*De finibus*
De off.	*De officio*
De orat.	*De oratore*
De prov.	*De providentia*
De sen.	*De senectute*
Mur.	*Pro Murena*
Pro Mil.	*Pro Milone*
QFr.	*Ad Quintum fratrem*
Resp.	*De republica*
Top.	*Topica*
Tusc.	*Tusculanae disputationes*
Ver.	*In Verrem*
CIJ	*Corpus inscriptionum judaicarum*, ed. Jean-Baptiste Frey (2 vols.; Rome: Pontifical Biblical Institute, 1936–52).
CIL	*Corpus inscriptionum latinarum* (Berlin: G. Reimer, 1862–).
CIPh	Cédric Brélaz, *Corpus des inscriptions grecques et latines de Philippes* (Athens: École française d'Athènes, 2014).
1 Clem.	*1 Clement*
CNT	Commentaire de Nouveau Testament
Corp. Herm.	*Corpus Hermeticum*
CP	*Classical Philology*
CPJ	*Corpus Papyrorum Judaicarum*, ed. Victor A. Tcherikover (3 vols.; Cambridge, MA: Harvard University Press, 1957–64).
CPSSup	Cambridge Philological Society Supplements
CSCO	Corpus Scriptorum Christianorum Orientalium
CSEL	*Corpus scriptorum ecclesiasticorum latinorum*
CSP	Colectánea San Paciano (Barcelona)
Cyprian	
De mort.	*De mortalitate*
Demetrius	
Eloc.	*De elocutione*
Dio Chrysostom	
Or.	*Orationes*
Diodorus Siculus	
Bib. hist.	*Bibliotheca historica*
Diogenes Laertius	
Vit.	*Vitae philosophorum*
Dionysius of Halicarnassus	
Ant.	*Antiquitates Romanae*
Rhet.	*Ars rhetorica*
DSD	*Dead Sea Discoveries*
EB	Études biblique
EBR	Christine Helmer et al., *Encyclopedia of the Bible and Its Reception* (Berlin: de Gruyter, 2009–).
EC	*Early Christianity*
ECL	Early Christianity and Its Literature
EHPhR	Études d'histoire et de philosophie religieuses
EKK	Evangelisch-Katholischer Kommentar
EM	*Etymologicum Magnum*, ed. T. Gaisford (Oxford, 1848)
Ennius	
frag.	fragmenta
Med.	*Medea*
1 Enoch	*1 Enoch* (*Ethiopic Enoch*)
2 Enoch	*2 Enoch* (*Slavonic Enoch*)
3 Enoch	*3 Enoch* (*Hebrew Enoch*)
Epictetus	
Diss.	*Dissertationes*
Ench.	*Enchiridion*
Epicurus	
frag.	fragmenta
Sent. Vat.	*Sententiae Vaticanae*
Epiphanius	
Pan.	*Panarion* (*Adversus Haereses*)

EPRO	Études préliminaires aux religions orientales dans l'empire romain
ET	English Translation
EThSt	Erfurter theologische Studien
Euripides	
Alc.	*Alcestis*
Andr.	*Andromache*
Bacch.	*Bacchae*
frag.	fragmenta
Hec.	*Hecuba*
Hel.	*Helena*
Her.	*Hercules*
Iph. Aul.	*Iphigenia Aulidensis*
Med.	*Medea*
Phoen.	*Phoenissae*
Suppl.	*Supplices*
Eusebius	
Praep. Ev.	*Praeparatio Evangelica*
Hist. Eccl.	*Historia Ecclesiastica*
EvQ	*Evangelical Quarterly*
ExpTim	*Expository Times*
Ezekiel the Tragedian	
Exag.	*Exagoge*
Favorinus	
De exil.	*De exilio*
frag.	fragmenta
FGrH (= FrGrHist)	Felix Jacoby, *Die Fragmente der griechischen Historiker* (Berlin: Weidmann, 1923–).
FPhGr (= FPG)	F. W. A. Mullach, *Fragmenta philosophorum Graecorum* (3 vols.; Paris: Didot, 1860–81).
FRLANT	Forschungen zur Religion und Literatur des Alten und Neuen Testaments
Fronto	
Ad Verum Imp.	*Ad Verum Imperatorem*
De nep. am.	*De nepote amisso*
Gaius Gracchus	
frag.	fragmenta
Galen	
De indol.	*De indolentia*
De plac.	*De placitis Hippocratis et Platonis*
George of Alexandria	
Vit. Chrys.	*Vita Chrysostomi*
George Syncellus	
Chronographia	*Ecloga chronographica*
Glotta	*Glotta: Zeitschrift für griechische und lateinische Sprache*
Gosp. Pet.	*Gospel of Peter*
GRBS	*Greek, Roman, and Byzantine Studies*
Gregory of Corinth	
Περὶ τροπ.	Περὶ τροπῶν ποιητικῶν
Gregory of Nyssa	
Flac.	*Oratio funebris in Flacilliam imperatricem*
Melet.	*Oratio funebris in Meletium episcopum*
Pulch.	*Oratio consolatoria in Pulcheriam*
Gregory Nazianzen	
Ep.	*Epistulae*
Or.	*Orationes*
Gregory Thaumaturgus	
Pan. Orig.	*In Originem oratio panegyrica*
GThA	Göttinger theologische Arbeiten
HABES	Heidelberger althistorische Beiträge und epigraphische Studien
HBS	Herders biblische Studien
HDR	Harvard Dissertations in Religion
Hermas (Shepherd of Hermas)	
Sim.	*Similitudes*
Vis.	*Visiones* (in *Pastor Hermae*)
Hermes	*Hermes: Zeitschrift für klassische Philologie*
Hermogenes	
Inv.	*De inventione*
Prog.	*Progymnasmata*
Herodotus	
Hist.	*Historiae*
Himerius	
Or.	*Orationes*
Hippocrates	
Mul.	*De mulierum affectibus*
Hippolytus	
Ref.	*Refutation omnium haeresium*
HNT	Handbuch zum Neuen Testament
Hom. Clem.	*Pseudo-Clementinae homiliae*
Homer	
Il.	*Iliad*
Od.	*Odyssey*
Horace	
Carm.	*Carmina*
HSCP	*Harvard Studies in Classical Philology*
HThKNT	Herders theologischer Kommentar zum Neuen Testament
HTR	*Harvard Theological Review*
HTS	Harvard Theological Studies
HWPh	J. Ritter, *Historisches Wörterbuch der Philosophie* (Darmstadt: Schwabe, 1971–2007).
Hyginus	
Fab.	*Fabulae*
ICC	International Critical Commentary
IG	*Inscriptiones Graecae* (Berlin: de Gruyter, 1924–).
IGLS	*Les inscriptiones grecques et latines de la Syrie*
Ignatius	
Eph.	*Ad Ephesios*
Mag.	*Ad Magnesios*
Rom.	*Ad Romanos*
Smyrn.	*Ad Smyrnaios*
Trall.	*Ad Trallianos*
IGR	*Inscriptiones Graecae ad Res Romanas Pertinentes*

ILS	*Inscriptiones Latinae selectae*	
IPerg	*Die Inschriften von Pergamon*, ed. Max Fränkel (2 vols.; Berlin: W. Spemann, 1890–95).	
Isocrates		
Nic.	*Nicocles* (orat. 3)	
Phil.	*Ad Philippum*	
JAC	Jahrbuch für Antike und Christentum	
JBL	*Journal of Biblical Literature*	
Jerome		
Ep.	*Epistulae*	
Vir. ill.	*De viris illustribus*	
JJS	*Journal of Jewish Studies*	
John Chrysostom		
Ad Stag.	*Ad Stagirium a daemone vexatum*	
De incomprehen.	*De incomprehensibili dei natura*	
Ep. ad Olymp.	*Epistulae ad Olympiadem*	
Hom. Act.	*Homiliae in Acta apostolorum*	
In Epist. ad Thess.	*Homiliae in epistulam ad Thessalonicenses*	
In Phil.	*Homiliae in epistulam ad Philippenses*	
Laud. Paul.	*De laudibus sancti Pauli apostoli*	
Quod nemo laed.	*Quod nemo laeditur nisi a se ipso*	
Josephus		
Ap.	*Contra Apionem*	
Ant.	*Antiquitates Judaicae*	
Bell.	*De bello Judaico*	
JQR	*Jewish Quarterly Review*	
JRASup	Journal of Roman Archaeology Supplements	
JRS	*Journal of Roman Studies*	
JSNT	*Journal for the Study of the New Testament*	
JSNTSup	Journal for the Study of the New Testament: Supplement Series	
JSOTSup	Journal for the Study of the Old Testament: Supplement Series	
JSPSup	Journal for the Study of the Pseudepigrapha Supplements	
JTC	*Journal of Theology and Church*	
JTS	*Journal of Theological Studies*	
Jub.	*Jubilees*	
Julian		
Ep.	*Epistulae*	
Justin		
1 Apol.	*Apologia*	
2 Apol.	*Apologia secunda*	
Juvenal		
Sat.	*Satires*	
KEK	Kritisch-exegetischer Kommentar über das Neue Testament	
LAB	*Liber Antiquitatum Biblicarum*	
L.A.E.	*Life of Adam and Eve* (*Apoc.* = Greek version; *Vita* = Latin version)	
Laod.	*Laodicians* (Pseudo-Paul)	
LCL	Loeb Classical Library	
LEC	Library of Early Christianity	
Leo VI Philosophus		
Or.	*Orationes*	
Libanius		
Ep.	*Epistulae*	
Or.	*Orationes*	
Livy		
Ab urb.	*Ab urbe condita libri*	
LNTS	Library of New Testament Studies	
LSJ	Henry George Liddell, Robert Scott, and Henry Stuart Jones, *A Greek-English Lexicon* (9th ed. with revised supplement; Oxford: Clarendon, 1940; reprinted 1966).	
Lucian		
Cal.	*Calumniae non temere credendum*	
Icar.	*Icaromenippus*	
Tox.	*Toxaris vel amicitia*	
Lucretius		
De re. nat.	*De rerum natura*	
LXX	Septuagint	
Macrobius		
In somn. Scip.	*Commentarii in somnium Scipionis*	
Maj	Majority Text	
Manetho		
frag.	fragmenta	
Mara bar Serapion		
Ep.	*Epistula*	
Marcus Aurelius		
Med.	*Meditationes*	
Martial		
Epig.	*Epigramata*	
Martin (Martinius 1 papa)		
Narr. de exil.	*Narrationes de exilio*	
Mart. Pion.	*Martyrium Pionii*	
Menander Rhetor		
Περὶ ἐπιδεικ.	Περὶ ἐπιδεικτικῶν	
MIFAO	Mémoires publiés par les members de L'Institut français d'archéologie orientale du Caire	
MM	James Hope Moulton and George Milligan, *The Vocabulary of the Greek Testament* (Grand Rapids: Eerdmans, 1949).	
MMA	Metropolitan Museum of Art (used in reference to item catalogue numbers)	
Mnemosyne	*Mnemosyne* (Bibliotheca classica Batava)	
Moschus		
Eur.	*Europa*	
Musonius		
frag.	fragmenta	
MT	Masoretic Text	
NCE	*New Catholic Encyclopedia*	
Neot	*Neotestamentica*	

NewDocs	*New Documents Illustrating Early Christianity*, ed. G. H. R. Horsley and S. Llewelyn (North Ryde, New South Wales: Ancient History Documentary Research Centre, Macquarie University, 1981–).	Ovid	
		Agam.	*Agamemnon*
		Am.	*Ars amatoria*
		Ex Pont.	*Ex Ponto*
		Her.	*Heroides*
		Med.	*Medea*
NHC	Nag Hammadi Codex	*Metam.*	*Metamorphoses*
NHS	Nag Hammadi Studies	Papyri	
NIB	*New Interpreter's Bible*, ed. Leander E. Keck (12 vols.; Nashville: Abingdon, 1994–2004).	*P. Berol.*	*P. Berolinensis*
		P. Cair. Masp.	*Papyrus grecs d'epoque byzantine* (ed. J. Maspéro)
Nicander		*P. Cair. Zen.*	Zenon Papyri (Musée du Caire)
Hetero.	*Heteroeoumena*	*P. Congr.*	*Actes du Congrès International de Papyrologie*
NICNT	New International Commentary on the New Testament	*P. Elephant.*	Elephantine Papyri
Nicolaus		*P. Flor.*	*Papiri Fiorentini*
Prog.	*Progymnasmata*	*P. Giss.*	Papyri in the Museum des ober-hessischen Geschichtsvereins zu Giessen
NIGTC	New International Greek Testament Commentary		
NKZ	*Neue kirchliche Zeitschrift*	*P. Hamb.*	Griechische Papyri der Staats- und Universitätsbibliothek Hamburg
NPNF	*Nicene and Post-Nicene Fathers*		
n.s.	new series		
NTD	Das Neue Testament Deutsch	*P. Lond.*	Greek Papyri in the British Museum
NTG	*Novum Testamentum Graece*		
NTOA	Novum Testamentum et Orbis Antiquus	*P. Louvre*	*Papyrus Mimaut* (Louvre inv. 2391; *PGM* 3)
NTS	*New Testament Studies*	*P. Mert.*	Papyri in the Collection of Wilfred Merton
NTT	*Nederlands Theologisch Tijdschrift*		
NTTS	New Testament Tools and Studies	*P. Mich.*	Michigan Papyri
NovT	*Novum Testamentum*	*P. Ness.*	Nessana Papyri (ed. Kraemer)
NovTSup	Novum Testamentum Supplements	*P. Oxy.*	Oxyrhynchus Papyri
		P. Petr.	Flinders Petrie Papyri
NRSV	New Revised Standard Version	*P. Polit. Jud.*	*Urkunden des Politema der Juden von Herakleopolis*
NTApoc	Edgar Hennecke and Wilhelm Schneemelcher, *New Testament Apocrypha* (rev. ed.; 2 vols.; Louisville: Westminster John Knox, 1991).		
		P. Princ.	Papyri in the Princeton University Collection
		P. RainerCent.	*Corpus Papyrorum Raineri*
NW	Udo Schnelle, *Neuer Wettstein* (Berlin: de Gruyter, 1996).	*P. Ross. Georg.*	*Papyri russischer und georgischer Sammlungen*
Od. Sol.	*Odes of Solomon*	*PSI*	*Pubblicasioni della Società Italiana: Papiri Greci e Latini I–IX*
OLD	P. G. W. Glare, *Oxford Latin Dictionary* (Oxford: Clarendon, 1982).	*P. Vat.*	see UPZ
		P. Wisc.	*Wisconsis Papyri* (ed. Sijpesteijn)
O. Mon. Epiph.	W. E. Crum and H. G. Evelyn White, ed., *The Monastery of Epiphanius at Thebes: Coptic Ostraca and Papyri* (Milan: Cisalpino, 1977).	*P. Yale*	Papyri in the Beinecke Rare Book and Manuscript Library (Yale)
		Palaephatus	
		Incred.	*De incredibilibus*
		Paulinus of Nola	
OPA	Les oeuvres de Philon d'Alexandrie	*Carm.*	*Carmina*
		Ep.	*Epistulae*
Origen		Pausanias	Pausanias, *Graeciae Descriptio*
Cel.	*Contra Celsum*	*PG*	*Patrologiae cursus completus: Series Graeca*, ed. J.-P. Migne (162 vols.; Paris, 1857–86)
In Ioann.	*In Ioannem*		
OTP	*The Old Testament Pseudepigrapha*, ed. James H. Charlesworth (2 vols.; Garden City, N.Y.: Doubleday, 1983–85).	*PGL*	G. W. H. Lampe, ed., *A Patristic Greek Lexicon* (Oxford: Clarendon, 1961)
OTS	*Oudtestamentische Studiën*		

PGM	*Papyri Graecae Magicae. Die grieschen Zauberpapyri.* Vol. 1, ed. and trans. Karl Preisendanz, revised by Albert Heinrichs (2nd ed.; Munich and Leipzig: Saur, 2001; 1st ed. 1928)

Philo

Abr.	*De Abrahamo*
Conf.	*De confusione linguarum*
Congr.	*De congressu eruditionis gratia*
De cher.	*De cherubim*
De migr. Abr.	*De migratione Abrahami*
Det.	*Quod deterius potiori insidiari soleat*
Fug.	*De fuga et inventione*
Her.	*Quis rerum divinarum heres sit*
Jos.	*De Josepho*
Leg.	*Legum allegoriae II*
Leg. Gai.	*Legatio ad Gaium*
Mos.	*De vita Mosis*
Op.	*De opificio mundi*
Plant.	*De plantatione*
Post.	*De posteritate Caini*
Praem.	*De praemiis et poenis*
Prob.	*Quod omnis probus liber sit*
Q. Gen.	*Quaestiones in Genesim*
Sac.	*De sacrificiis Abelis et Caini*
Spec.	*De specialibus legibus*
Virt.	*De virtutibus*

Philodemus

De mort.	*De morte*
Rhet.	*Rhetorica*

Philostratus

Vit. Apoll.	*Vita Apollonii*

Philostratus of Lemnos

Imag.	*Imagines*
PL	*Patrologiae cursus completus: Series Latina,* ed. J.-P. Migne (217 vols.; Paris, 1844–64)

Plato

Apol.	*Apologia Socratis*
Ion	*Ion*
Lys.	*Lysis*
Menex.	*Menexenus*
Phaedo	*Phaedo*
Polit.	*Politicus*
Resp.	*Respublica*

Plautus

Mer.	*Mercato*
Pers.	*Persae*

Pliny

Ep.	*Epistulae*

Plutarch

Ad ux.	*Ad uxorem*
Caes.	*Caesar*
Cato mai.	*Cato maior*
Comm. not.	*De communibus notitiis adv. Stoicos*
Cor.	*Marcius Coriolanus*
De coh. ir.	*De cohibenda ira*
De exil.	*De exilio*

De Is. et Os.	*De Iside et Osiride*
De rect. aud.	*De recta ratione audiendi*
De tran. an.	*De tranquilitate animi*
De vir. mor.	*De virtute morali*
Fab.	*Fabius Maximus*
Marc.	*Marcellus*
Phil.	*Philopoemen*
Praec. ger. reip.	*Praecepta gerandae reipublicae*
Quom adul.	*Quomodo adulator ab amico internoscatur*
Superst.	*De superstitione*
PMS	Patristic Monograph Series of the North American Patristic Society

Polycarp

Phil.	*Epistula ad Philippenses*

Porphyry

Nymph.	*De antro nympharum*

Priscianus

Praeex.	*Praeexercitamina*

Proclus

In Plat. Resp.	*In Platonis rem publicam*

Propertius

El.	*Elegiae*
Pr. Thank.	*Prayer of Thanksgiving* (Nag Hammadi)

Pseudo-Apollodorus

Bibl.	*Bibliotheca*
Epitom.	*Epitome*

Pseudo-Demetrius

Typoi epist.	τύποι ἐπιστολικοί (*Formae epistolicae*)

Pseudo-Libanius

Char. epist.	*Characteres epistolici*

Pseudo-Lucian

Asin.	*Asinus*

Pseudo-Ovid

Cons. ad Liv.	*Consolatio ad Liviam* (*Epicedion Drusi*)

Pseudo-Phalaris

Ep.	*Epistulae*

Pseudo-Phocylides

Sent.	*Sententiae*

Pseudo-Plato

Ax.	*Axiochus*
Eryx.	*Eryxias*

Pseudo-Plutarch

Ad Apoll	*Ad Apollonium* (*consolatio*)
PSI	*Papiri greci e latini* (Società Italiana per la Ricerce dei Papiri Greci e Latini in Egitto)
Pss. Sol.	*Psalms of Solomon*
PVTG	Pseudepigrapha Veteris Testamenti Graece
PW	Pauly Wissowa, *Real-Encyclopädie der classischen Altertumswissenschaft*
Q	Synoptic Sayings Source (*Quelle*)
QD	Quaestiones Disputatae

Quintilian

Inst.	*Institutio oratoria*

Qumran writings		
1Q, 4Q, etc.	Qumran Cave 1, 4, etc.	
1Q28a	1QSa	
1QHª	Hodayot (cited according to the edition of Donald W. Parry and Emanuel Tov, *The Dead Sea Scrolls Reader* [2nd ed., revised and expanded; 2 vols.; Leiden/Boston: Brill, 2014])	
1QM	War Scroll	
1QS	Rule of the Community	
1QSa	Messianic Rule (Appendix A to 1QS)	
4Q171	4QpPs37 (pesher on Psalm 37)	
4Q174	Florilegium (Midrash on Eschatology)	
4Q374	Moses Apocryphon A	
4Q471	4QSelf-Glorification Hymn	
4QMMTª	*Miqsat Ma'ase ha-Torahª*	
4QpPs37	Commentary on Psalm 37	
4QShirShabb	Songs of the Sabbath Sacrifice	
11QMelch	Melchizedek	
11QPsª	Psalms Scroll of Cave 11 (= 11Q5)	
CD	Cairo (Geniza) Damascus Document	
Rabbinic writings		
b. Sanh.	Babylonian Talmud Tractate *Sanhedrin*	
m. 'Abot	Mishnah, Tractate *'Abot*	
m. Sanh.	Mishnah Tractate *Sanhedrin*	
Mekh. Exod.	*Mekhilta on Exodus*	
Sifre Deut.	*Sifre Deuteronomy*	
Sifre Num.	*Sifre Numbers*	
t. Sanh.	*Tosefta Sanhedrin*	
y. Sanh.	Jerusalem Talmud Tractate *Sanhedrin*	
RAC	*Reallexikon für Antike und Christentum*	
RasT	*Rassegna di Teologia*	
RB	*Revue biblique*	
REA	*Revue des études anciennes*	
REL	*Revue des études Latines*	
RevQ	*Revue de Qumran*	
RevScRel	*Revue de sciences religieuses*	
Rhet. ad Alex.	*Rhetorica ad Alexandrum*	
Rhet. ad Her.	*Rhetorica ad Herrenium*	
RPC 1	*Roman Provincial Coinage,* vol. 1: *From the Death of Caesar to the Death of Vitellius* (London: British Museum; Paris: Bibliothèque Nationale, 1992; reprinted with corrections, 1998).	
RPT	Religion in Philosophy and Theology	
Rufinus of Antioch		
De comp.	*De compositione*	
Rutilius Namatianus		
De red.	*De reditu suo*	

RVV	Religionsgeschichtliche Versuche und Vorarbeiten
SAWW	*Sitzungsberichte des österreichischen Akademie der Wissenschaften* (Akademie der Wissenschaften in Wien).
SB	*Sammelbuch griechischer Urkunden aus Aegypten,* ed. Friedrich Preisigke et al. (Wiesbaden: Harrassowitz, 1915–2002).
SBLDS	Society of Biblical Literature Dissertation Series
SBLRBS	Society of Biblical Literature Resources for Biblical Study
SBLSBS	Society of Biblical Literature Sources for Biblical Study
SBLSCS	Society of Biblical Literature Septuagint and Cognate Studies
SBLSP	Society of Biblical Literature Seminar Papers
SBLSymS	Society of Biblical Literature Symposium Series
SBLWGRW	Society of Biblical Literature Writings from the Greco-Roman World
SBS	Stuttgarter Bibelstudien
SC	Sources chrétiennes
SCHNT	Studia ad Corpus Hellenisticum Novi Testamenti
SEG	*Supplementum Epigraphicum Graecum*
SelPap	*Select Papyri* (LCL)
Seneca	
Ad Helv.	*Ad Helviam*
Ad Marc.	*Ad Marciam*
Ad Poly.	*Ad Polybium*
Agam.	*Agamemnon*
De benef.	*De beneficia*
De brev. vit.	*De brevitate vitae*
De clem.	*De clementia*
De prov.	*De providentia*
De tran. an.	*De tranquillitate animi*
De vit. beat.	*De vita beata*
Ep.	*Epistulae morales*
Herc.	*Hercules*
Med.	*Medea*
Seneca Rhetor	
Contr.	*Controversiae*
Suas.	*Suasoriae*
Sextus Empiricus	
Adv. math.	*Adversus mathematicos*
Pyrrh.	*Pyrrhoniae hypotyposes*
SHCT	Studies in the History of Christian Traditions
SHR	Studies in the History of Religions
Sib. Or.	*Sibyline Oracles*
*SIG*³	*Sylloge Inscriptionum Graecarum*³, ed. Wilhelm Dittenberger (4 vols.; Leipzig: Hirzel, 1915–24).

SJLA	Studies in Judaism in Late Antiquity	*Ann.*	*Annales*
		Dial.	*Dialogus de oratoribus*
Smyth	Herbert Weir Smyth, *Greek Grammar* (revised by Gordon M. Messing; Cambridge, MA: Harvard University Press, 1984).	*Hist.*	*Historia*
		TANZ	Texte und Arbeiten zum neutestamentlichen Zeitalter
		TAPA	*Transactions of the American Philological Association*
SNG ANS	*Sylloge Nummorum Graecorum,* American Numismatic Society		
		Tatian	
SNG Cop.	*Sylloge Nummorum Graecorum,* Copenhagen	*Or.*	*Oratio ad Graecos*
		TDNT	*Theological Dictionary of the New Testament,* ed. G. Kittel and G. Friedrich; trans. and ed. Geoffrey W. Bromiley (10 vols.; Grand Rapids: Eerdmans, 1964–76).
SNG Evelp.	*Sylloge Nummorum Graecorum,* Réna H. Evelpidis	
SNG Tüb.	*Sylloge Nummorum Graecorum,* Tübingen	
SNTSMS	Society for New Testament Studies Monograph Series	
Sophocles		*TDOT*	*Theological Dictionary of the Old Testament,* ed. G. J. Botterweck et al.; trans. D. E. Green et al. (Grand Rapids: Eerdmans, 1974–).
Ajax	*Ajax*	
Phil.	*Philoctetes*	
Soranus		
Gynaec.	*Gynaeciorum libri*	Teles	
SR	*Studies in Religion/Sciences Religieuses*	frag.	fragmenta
		Tertullian	
ST	*Studia Theologica*	*Adv. Marc.*	*Adversus Marcionem*
STA	Studia et Testimonia Antiqua	*Apol.*	*Apologeticum*
STAC	Studien und Texte zu Antike und Christentum	*Scap.*	*Ad Scapulam*
		Themistius	
Statius		*Or.*	*Orationes*
Ach.	*Achilleis*	Theognis	
Silv.	*Silvae*	*El.*	*Elegiae*
STDJ	Studies on the Texts of the Desert of Judah	Theon	
		Prog.	*Progymnasmata*
		ThF	Theologische Forschung
Stesichorus		ThHKNT	Theologischer Handkommentar zum Neuen Testament
Palin.	*Palinode*	
Stobaeus		*ThPh*	*Theologie und Philosophie*
Ecl.	*Eclogae*	Thucydides	
Flor.	*Florilegium*	*Hist.*	*Historiae*
StPatr	*Studia Patristica*	*ThZ*	*Theologische Zeitschrift*
StudLit	*Studia Liturgica*	Tibullus	
Suetonius		*El.*	*Elegiae*
Aug.	*Augustus*	Trag. Graec. Frag.	
Claud.	*Claudius*	(= *TrGF*)	*Tragicorum Graecorum Fragmenta* (ed. Nauck)
Dom.	*Domitian*	
Ner.	*Nero*	*TRE*	*Theologische Realenzyclopädie*
Tib.	*Tiberius*	TSAJ	Texte und Studien zum antiken Judentum
Suidas	*Suidae Lexicon, Graece et Latine*	
s.v.	*sub voce*	TU	Texte und Untersuchungen zur Geschichte der altchristlichen Literatur
Symeon Metaphrastes		
Vit. Chrys.	*Vita Chrysostomi*	
T. Abr.	*Testament of Abraham*	*TynBull*	*Tyndale Bulletin*
T. Ben.	*Testament of Benjamin*	UNT	Untersuchungen zum Neuen Testament
T. Job	*Testament of Job*	
T. Jos.	*Testament of Joseph*	*UPZ*	*Urkunden der Ptolemäerzeit* (ed. Wilken)
T. Levi	*Testament of Levi*	
T. Mos.	*Testament of Moses*	UTB	Uni-Taschenbücher
T. Reub.	*Testament of Reuben*	*VC*	*Vigiliae Christianae*
T. Sol.	*Testament of Solomon*	*Vind. Tab.*	*Vindolanda Tablet*
Tacitus		Virgil	
Agr.	*Agricola*	*Aen.*	*Aeneid*

v.l.   *varia lectio* (variant reading)
VT   *Vetus Testamentum*
WBC   Word Biblical Commentary
WMANT   Wissenschaftliche Monographien
                zum Alten und Neuen Testament
WUNT   Wissenschaftliche Untersuchun-
                gen zum Neuen Testament
WZJena   *Wissenschaftliche Zeitschrift der
                Friedrich-Schiller-Universität* (Jena)
Xenophon
   Apol.   *Apologia Socratis*
   Cyropaed.   *Cyropaedia*
   Mem.   *Memorabilia*
Xenophon of Ephesus
   Eph.   *Ephesiaca*
ZNW   *Zeitschrift für die neutestamentliche
                Wissenschaft*
ZPE   *Zeitschrift für Papyrologie und
                Epigraphik*
ZThK   *Zeitschrift für Theologie und Kirche*

2. Short Titles

Abel, *Bauformen*
   Karlhans Abel, *Bauformen in Senecas Dialogen: Fünf
   Strukturanalysen: dial. 6, 11, 12, 1 und 2* (Biblio-
   thek der klassischen Altertumswissenschaften 18;
   Heidelberg: Winter, 1967).

Aichele and Walsh, "Metamorphosis"
   George Aichele and Richard Walsh, "Metamorphosis, Transfiguration and the Body," *BibInt* 19 (2011)
   253–75.

Alexander, "Hellenistic Letter-Forms"
   Loveday Alexander, "Hellenistic Letter-Forms
   and the Structure of Philippians," *JSNT* 37 (1989)
   87–101.

Aletti
   Jean-Noël Aletti, *Saint Paul, Épître aux Philippiens:
   Introduction, traduction et commentaire* (EB n.s. 55;
   Paris: Gabalda, 2005).

Ambrosiaster
   Ad Filippenses, CSEL 81.3:129–63; ET: Gerald Bray,
   trans. and ed., *Commentaries on Galatians–Philemon.
   Ambrosiaster* (Ancient Christian Texts; Downers
   Grove, IL: IVP Academic, 2009).

Anger, *Laodocenerbrief*
   Rudolf Anger, *Über den Laodicenerbrief: Eine
   biblisch-kritische Untersuchung* (Leipzig: Gebhardt &
   Reisland, 1843)

Aquinas
   Thomas Aquinas, *Commentaria in omnes D. Pauli
   Apostoli Epistolas* (Paris: Larouse, 1874) 2:318–55.
   ET: Fabian R. Larcher and Michael Duffy,
   trans., *Commentary on St. Paul's First Letter to the
   Thessalonians and the Letter to the Philippians* (Aqui-
   nas Scripture Series 3; Albany: Magi Books, 1969).

Arband, "Gefangenschaft"
   S. Arband, W. Macheiner, and C. Colpe,
   "Gefangenschaft," *RAC* 9:318–45.

Arnold, *Christ as the* Telos
   Bradley Arnold, *Christ the Telos of Life: Moral
   Philosophy, Athletic Imagery and the Aim of Philippians*
   (WUNT 2/371; Tübingen: Mohr Siebeck, 2014).

Arzt, "Epistolary Introductory Thanksgiving"
   Peter Arzt, "The 'Epistolary Introductory Thanksgiving' in the Papyri and in Paul," *NovT* 36 (1994)
   29–46.

Ashton, *Religion*
   John Ashton, *The Religion of Paul the Apostle* (New
   Haven/London: Yale University Press, 2000).

Avery-Peck and Neusner, *Judaism in Late Antiquity*
   Alan J. Avery-Peck and Jacob Neusner, eds., *Judaism
   in Late Antiquity*, Part 4: *Death, Life-After-Death,
   Resurrection and the World-To-Come in the Judaisms of
   Antiquity* (Handbuch der Orientalistik 55; Leiden:
   Brill, 2000).

Baillet, *Inscriptions*
   Jules Baillet, *Inscriptions grecques et latines des tombeaux des rois ou syringes à Thèbes* (MIFAO 42; Cairo:
   L'Institut français d'archéologie orientale du Caire,
   1926).

Barclay, *Gift*
   John M. G. Barclay, *Paul and the Gift* (Grand Rapids:
   Eerdmans, 2015).

Barclay and Gathercole, *Agency*
   John M. G. Barclay and Simon J. Gathercole, eds.,
   *Divine and Human Agency in Paul and His Cultural
   Environment* (LNTS; London/New York: T&T
   Clark, 2006).

Barth
   Karl Barth, *Epistle to the Philippians* (Richmond:
   John Knox, 1962).

Beard, *Religions of Rome*
   Mary Beard, John North, and Simon Price, *Religions
   of Rome* (2 vols.; Oxford: Oxford University Press,
   1998).

Beare
   F. W. Beare, *A Commentary on the Epistle to the
   Philippians* (3rd ed.; BNTC; London: A. & C. Black,
   1973).

Bengel
   Johann Albrecht Bengel, *Gnomon Novi Testamenti*
   (1742; 3rd ed.; Stuttgart: J. F. Steinkopf, 1855).

Berger, *Formgeschichte*
   Klaus Berger, *Formgeschichte des Neuen Testaments*
   (Heidelberg: Quelle & Meyer, 1984).

Betz, *Galatians*
   Hans Dieter Betz, *Galatians: A Commentary on Paul's
   Letter to the Churches in Galatia* (Hermeneia; Phila-
   delphia: Fortress Press, 1979).

Betz, *Greek Magical Papyri*
   Hans Dieter Betz, ed., *The Greek Magical Papyri in
   Translation, Including the Demotic Spells*, vol. 1: *Texts*
   (2nd ed.; Chicago: University of Chicago Press,
   1992).

Betz, *Studies*
   Hans Dieter Betz, *Studies in Paul's Letter to the Philippians* (WUNT 343; Tübingen: Mohr Siebeck, 2015).

Bingham, *Praetorian Guard*
Sandra Bingham, *The Praetorian Guard: A History of Rome's Elite Special Forces* (London: I. B. Tauris, 2013).

Bittasi, *Gli esempi*
Stephano Bittasi, *Gli esempi necessari per discernere: Il significato argomentativo della struttura della lettera di Paolo ai Filippesi* (AnBib 153; Rome: Pontifical Biblical Institute, 2003).

Blenkinsopp, *Isaiah 56–66*
Joseph Blenkinsopp, *Isaiah 56–66: A New Translation with Introduction and Commentary* (AB 19B; New York: Doubleday, 2003).

Boardman, *Black Figure Vases*
John Boardman, *Athenian Black Figure Vases* (New York: Oxford University Press, 1974).

Boardman, *Red Figure Vases*
John Boardman, *Athenian Red Figure Vases in the Archaic Period* (New York: Oxford University Press, 1979).

Bockmuehl
Marcus Bockmuehl, *The Epistle to the Philippians* (BNTC 11; London: A. & C. Black; Peabody, MA: Hendrickson, 1998).

Bockmuehl, "Form"
Marcus Bockmuehl, "'The Form of God' (Philippians 2:6): Variations on a Theme of Jewish Mysticism," *JTS* n.s. 48 (1997) 1–23.

de Boer, "Paul and Apocalyptic Eschatology"
M. C. de Boer, "Paul and Apocalyptic Eschatology," in *The Encyclopedia of Apocalypticism*, vol. 1: *The Origins of Apocalypticism in Judaism and Christianity*, ed. John J. Collins (New York: Continuum, 2000) 345–83.

Bonhöffer, *Epiktet*
Adolf F. Bonhöffer, *Epiktet und das Neue Testament* (RVV 10; Giessen: Töpelmann, 1911).

Bonner, *Declamation*
Stanley Bonner, *Roman Declamation in the Late Republic and Early Empire* (Liverpool: University Press of Liverpool, 1949).

Bonnard
P. Bonnard, *L'épître de saint Paul aux Philippiens* (CNT 10; Neuchâtel: Delachaux & Niestlé, 1950).

Bormann, *Philippi*
Lukas Bormann, *Philippi: Stadt und Christengemeinde zur Zeit des Paulus* (NovTSup 78; Leiden: Brill, 1995).

Bornkamm, "Briefsammlung"
Günther Bornkamm, "Der Philipperbrief als paulinische Briefsammlung," in *Neotesamentica et Patristica: Eine Freundesgabe Herrn Professor Dr. Oscar Cullmann* (NovTSup 6; Leiden: Brill, 1962) 192–202.

Brélaz, *Corpus des inscriptions*
Cédric Brélaz, *Corpus des inscriptions grecques et latines de Philippes,* vol. 2: *La colonie romaine,* part 1: *La vie publique de la colonie* (Études Épigraphiques 6; Athens: École française d'Athènes, 2014).

Bruce
F. F. Bruce, *Philippians* (NICNT 11; San Francisco: Harper & Row; Peabody, MA: Hendrickson, 1989).

Bruce, "St. Paul in Macedonia 3"
F. F. Bruce, "St. Paul in Macedonia 3: The Philippian Correspondence," *BJRL* 63 (1981) 260–84.

Bultmann, *Stil*
Rudolf Bultmann, *Der Stil der paulinischen Predigt und die kynisch-stoische Diatribe* (FRLANT 13; Göttingen: Vandenhoeck & Ruprecht, 1910; repr., 1984).

Buresch, "Historia critica"
Carl Buresch, "Consolationum a Graecis Romanisque scriptarum historia critica," *Leipziger Studien zur classischen Philologie* 9 (1886) 1–170.

Buxton, *Forms of Astonishment*
Richard Buxton, *Forms of Astonishment: Greek Myths of Metamorphosis* (Oxford: Oxford University Press, 2009).

Calvin
Commentarius in Epistolam ad Philippenses, Corpus Reformatorum, *Joannis Calvini opera quae supersunt omnia*, 52:5–76; ET: *The Epistles of Paul the Apostle to the Galatians, Ephesians, Philippians, and Colossians* (Edinburgh: Oliver & Boyd, 1965) 225–95.

Carroll, *When Prophecy Failed*
Robert P. Carroll, *When Prophecy Failed: Reactions and Responses to Failure in the Old Testament Prophetic Traditions* (New York: Seabury, 1979).

Chapa, "Consolatory Patterns?"
Juan Chapa, "Consolatory Patterns? 1 Thes 4,13.18; 5,11," in *The Thessalonian Correspondence*, ed. Raymond F. Collins (BEThL 87; Leuven: Leuven University Press, 1990) 220–28.

Chapa, *Letters of Condolence*
Juan Chapa, *Letters of Condolence in Greek Papyri* (Papyrologica Florentina 29; Florence: Gonnelli, 1998).

Charlesworth, "Portrayal"
James H. Charlesworth, "The Portrayal of the Righteous as an Angel," in *Ideal Figures in Ancient Judaism: Profiles and Paradigms*, ed. George W. E. Nickelsburg and John J. Collins (SBLSCS 12; Chico, CA; Scholars Press, 1980) 135–51.

Chrysostom
Johannes Chrysostomus, *In Epistolam ad Philippenses*, PG 62:177–298. Frederick Field, ed., *Ioannis Chrysostomi Interpretatio omnium Epistolarum Paulinarum* (7 vols.; Oxford: Parker, 1859–62) 5:1–171, 499–530 (notes). Cited according to the edition of Pauline Allen, *John Chrysostom, Homilies on Paul's Letter to the Philippians* (SBLWGRW 36; Atlanta: Society of Biblical Literature, 2013).

Collange
Jean-François Collange, *The Epistle of Saint Paul to the Philippians* (translated from the 1st French edition by A. W. Heathcote; London: Epworth, 1979).

Collart, *Philippes*
Philippe Collart, *Philippes, ville de Macédoine, depuis ses origins jusqu'à la fin de l'époque romaine* (2 vols.; Paris: Boccard, 1937).

Collins, "Angelic Life"
John J. Collins, "The Angelic Life," in *Metamorphoses: Resurrection, Body and Transformative Practices in Early Christianity*, ed. Turid Karlsen Seim and Jorunn Økland (Ekstasis 1; Berlin/New York: de Guyter, 2009) 291–310.

Collins, "Apocalyptic Eschatology"
John J. Collins, "Apocalyptic Eschatology and the Transcendence of Death," *CBQ* 36 (1974) 21–43.

Collins, *Daniel*
John J. Collins, *Daniel: A Commentary on the Book of Daniel* (Hermeneia; Minneapolis: Fortress Press, 1993).

Collins, *Encyclopedia*
John J. Collins, ed., *The Encyclopedia of Apocalyticism*, vol.1: *The Origins of Apocalytpicism in Judaism and Christianity* (New York: Continuum, 2000).

Collins, "From Prophecy to Apocalypticism"
John J. Collins, "From Prophecy to Apocalypticism: The Expectation of the End," in *The Encyclopedia of Apocalypticism*, vol. 1: *The Origins of Apocalypticism in Judaism and Christianity* (New York: Continuum, 2000) 129–61.

Collins, "Heavenly Representative"
John J. Collins, "The Heavenly Representative: The 'Son of Man' in the Similitudes of Enoch," in *Ideal Figures in Ancient Judaism: Profiles and Paradigms*, ed. George W. E. Nickelsburg and John J. Collins (SBLSCS 12; Chico, CA: Scholars Press, 1980) 111–33.

Cover, "Death of Tragedy"
Michael Cover, "The Death of Tragedy: The Form of God in Euripides' *Bacchae* and Paul's *Carmen Christi*" (forthcoming in *HTR*).

Dalton, "Integrity"
W. J. Dalton, "The Integrity of Philippians," *Bib* 60 (1979) 97–102.

De Wette
W. M. L. De Wette, *Kurze Erklärung der Briefe an die Colosser, an Philemon, an die Ephesier und Philipper* (Leipzig: Weidmann, 1847).

Dibelius
Martin Dibelius, *An die Thessalonicher II: An die Philipper* (3rd ed.; HNT 11; Tübingen: Mohr, 1937).

Dibelius, *Paulus*
Martin Dibelius, *Paulus: Eine kultur- und religionsgeschichtliche Skizze* (Tübingen: Mohr Siebeck, 1911).

Dirkse and Brashler, "Prayer"
Peter Dirkse and James Brashler, "The Prayer of Thanksgiving. VI,7:63,33–65,7," in *Nag Hammadi Codices V,2-5 and VI, with Papyrus Berolinensis 8502*, ed. Douglas M. Parrott (Coptic Gnostic Library; Leiden: Brill, 1979) 378–87.

Doering, *Ancient Jewish Letters*
Lutz Doering, *Ancient Jewish Letters and the Beginnings of Christian Epistolography* (WUNT 298; Tübingen: Mohr Siebeck, 2012).

Dunn, *New Perspective*
James D. G. Dunn, *The New Perspective on Paul* (rev. ed.; Grand Rapids: Eerdmans, 2008).

Dunn, *Theology*
James D. G. Dunn, *The Theology of Paul the Apostle* (Grand Rapids: Eerdmans, 1998).

Eliade, *Shamanism*
Mircea Eliade, *Shamanism: Archaic Techniques of Ecstasy* (London: Routledge and Kegan Paul, 1964).

Engberg-Pedersen, *Cosmology*
Troels Engberg-Pedersen, *Cosmology and Self in the Apostle Paul: The Material Spirit* (Oxford: Oxford University Press, 2010).

Engberg-Pedersen, *Paul and the Stoics*
Troels Engberg-Pedersen, *Paul and the Stoics* (Edinburgh: T&T Clark, 2000).

Erasmus
Desiderius Erasmus, *Adnotationes in Epistolam Pauli ad Philippenses*, in *Opera Omnia* (Basel: Froben, 1518) 6:861–80; facsimile reprint, Anne Reeve, ed., *Erasmus' Annotations on the New Testament: Galatians to the Apocalypse* (Leiden: Brill, 1993) 619–32.

Esteve-Forriol, *Trauer- und Trostgedichte*
José Esteve-Forriol, *Die Trauer- und Trostgedichte in der römischen Literatur* (Munich: Schubert, 1962).

Evaristus, *Consolations of Death*
Mary Evaristus, *The Consolations of Death in Ancient Greek Literature* (Washington, DC: National Capital Press, 1917).

Fairweather, *Seneca the Elder*
Janet Fairweather, *Seneca the Elder* (Cambridge Classical Studies; Cambridge: Cambridge University Press, 1981).

Favez, *Consolation latine chrétienne*
Charles Favez, *La consolation latine chrétienne* (Paris: J. Vrin, 1937).

Favez, *L. Annaei Senecae Dialogorum liber XII*
Charles Favez, *L. Annaei Senecae Dialogorum liber XII Ad Helviam matrem de consolatione, texte latin publié avec une commentaire explicatif* (Lausanne/Paris: Payot, 1918).

Fern, *Latin Consolatio Mortis*
Mary E. Fern, *Latin Consolatio Mortis as a Literary Type* (St. Louis: Saint Louis University Press, 1941).

Fitzgerald, *Friendship*
John T. Fitzgerald, ed., *Friendship, Flattery, and Frankness of Speech: Studies on Friendship in the New Testament World* (NovTSup 82; Leiden: Brill, 1996).

Fitzmyer
Joseph A. Fitzmyer, "Philippians," In *Jerome Biblical Commentary*, ed. Raymond E. Brown, Joseph A. Fitzmyer, and Roland E. Murphy (Englewood Cliffs, NJ: Prentice Hall, 1968) 2:247–53.

Fitzmyer, "Ἐφ' Ὧ"
  Joseph A. Fitzmyer, "The Consecutive Meaning of
  Ἐφ' Ὧ in Romans 5:12," *NTS* 39 (1993) 321–39.
Fitzmyer, "Qumran Angelology"
  Joseph A. Fitzmyer, "A Feature of Qumran Angelol-
  ogy and the Angels of 1 Cor 11:10," in *Paul and
  the Dead Sea Scrolls*, ed. Jerome Murphy-O'Connor
  and James H. Charlesworth (New York: Crossroad,
  1990) 31–47.
Forbes Irving, *Metamorphosis*
  P. M. C. Forbes Irving, *Metamorphosis in Greek Myths*
  (Oxford: Oxford University Press, 1990).
Fowler, "Rhetoric"
  R. L. Fowler, "The Rhetoric of Desperation," *HSCP*
  91 (1987) 5-38.
Frede, *Epistulae*
  Hermann Josef Frede, ed., *Epistulae ad Philip-
  penses et ad Colossenses* (Vetus Latina: Die Reste der
  altlateinischen Bibel - 24.2; Freiburg im Breisgau:
  Herder, 1966–71).
Fredriksen, "Mandatory Retirement"
  Paula Fredriksen, "Mandatory Retirement: Ideas
  in the Study of Christian Origins Whose Time Has
  Come to Go," *SR* 35 (2006) 231–46.
Frey and Schliesser, *Philipperbrief*
  Jörg Frey and Benjamin Schliesser, eds., *Der Philip-
  perbrief des Paulus in der hellenistisch-römischen Welt*
  (WUNT 353; Tübingen: Mohr Siebeck, 2015).
Friedrich
  Gerhard Friedrich, *Der Brief an die Philipper* (15th
  ed.; NTD 8; Göttingen: Vandenhoeck & Ruprecht,
  1981).
Friesen, *Reading Dionysus*
  Courtney Friesen, *Reading Dionysus: Euripides'
  Bacchae and the Cultural Contestations of Greeks, Jews,
  Romans, and Christians* (STAC 95; Tübingen: Mohr
  Siebeck, 2015).
Funk, *Language*
  Robert Funk, *Language, Hermeneutic, and Word of
  God: The Problem of Language in the New Testament
  and Contemporary Theology* (New York: Harper &
  Row, 1966).
Gamble, *Textual History*
  Harry Gamble, *The Textual History of the Letter to the
  Romans* (Grand Rapids: Eerdmans, 1977).
Garland, "Composition and Unity"
  David Garland, "The Composition and Unity of
  Philippians: Some Neglected Literary Features,"
  NovT 27 (1985) 141–73.
von Gemünden, "Freude"
  Petra von Gemünden, "Der 'Affekt' der Freude im
  Philipperbrief und seiner Umwelt," in *Der Philip-
  perbrief des Paulus in der hellenistisch-römischen Welt*,
  ed. Jörg Frey and Benjamin Schliesser (WUNT 353;
  Tübingen: Mohr Siebeck, 2015) 223–53.
Gieschen, *Angelomorphic Christology*
  Charles A. Gieschen, *Angelomorphic Christology:
  Antecedent and Early Evidence* (AGJU 42; Leiden:
  Brill, 1998).

Gnilka
  Joachim Gnilka, *Der Philipperbrief* (3rd ed.;
  HThKNT 10.3; Freiburg: Herder, 1980).
Goodspeed, *Problems*
  Edgar J. Goodspeed, *Problems of New Testament
  Translation* (Chicago: University of Chicago Press,
  1945).
Gregg, *Consolation Philosophy*
  Robert C. Gregg, *Consolation Philosophy: Greek
  and Christian Paideia in Basil and the Two Gregories*
  (Patristic Monograph Series 3; Cambridge, MA:
  Philadelphia Patristic Foundation, 1975).
Grollios, *Seneca's Ad Marciam*
  Constantin Grollios, *Seneca's Ad Marciam: Tradition
  and Originality* (Athens: Christou, 1956).
Grollios, Τέχνη ἀλυπίας
  Constantine C. Grollios, Τέχνη ἀλυπίας: κοινοὶ
  τόποι τοῦ Πρὸς Πολύβιον τοῦ Σενέκα καὶ πηγαὶ
  αὐτῶν (Ἑλληνικά, παράρτημα 10; Athens: Chris-
  tou & Son, 1956).
Gundry Volf, *Perseverance*
  Judith M. Gundry Volf, *Paul and Perserverance:
  Staying In and Falling Away* (WUNT 2.34: Tübingen:
  Mohr Siebeck, 1990).
Gunkel, *Influence*
  Hermann Gunkel, *The Influence of the Holy Spirit:
  The Popular View of the Apostolic Age and the Teaching
  of the Apostle Paul* (Philadelphia: Fortress Press,
  1979; orig., 1888).
Hani, "Consolation"
  Jean Hani, "La consolation antique," *REA* 75 (1973)
  103–10.
Harrisville, "ΠΙΣΤΙΣ ΧΡΙΣΤΟΥ"
  R. A. Harrisville III, "ΠΙΣΤΙΣ ΧΡΙΣΤΟΥ: The Wit-
  ness of the Fathers," *NovT* 36 (1994) 233–41.
Hays, *Faith*
  Richard B. Hays, *The Faith of Jesus Christ: The Nar-
  rative Substructure of Galatians 3:1–4:11* (2nd ed.;
  Grand Rapids: Eerdmans, 2002).
Heinrici, "Hellenismus"
  C. F. Georg Heinrici, "Zum Hellenismus des
  Paulus," in idem, *Der zweite Brief an die Korinther*
  (KEK 6.8; Göttingen: Vandenhoeck & Ruprecht,
  1900) 436–58.
Himmelfarb, *Ascent*
  Martha Himmelfarb, *Ascent to Heaven in Jewish and
  Christian Apocalypses* (New York/Oxford: Oxford
  University Press, 1993).
Himmelfarb, "Revelation"
  Martha Himmelfarb, "Revelation and Rapture:
  The Transformation of the Visionary in the Ascent
  Apocalypses," in *Mysteries and Revelations: Apocalyp-
  tic Studies after the Uppsala Colloquium*, ed. John J.
  Collins and James H. Charlesworth (JSPSup 9;
  Sheffield: JSOT Press, 1991) 79–90.

Hofius, *Christushymnus*
Otfried Hofius, *Der Christushymnus Philipper 2:6-11: Untersuchungen zu Gestalt und Aussage eines urchristlichen Psalms* (WUNT 17; Tübingen: Mohr Siebeck, 1991).

Holloway, "*Alius Paulus*"
Paul A. Holloway, "*Alius Paulus*: On Paul's Promise to Send Timothy in Phil 2.19-24," *NTS* 54 (2008) 542-56.

Holloway, "*Bona Cogitare*"
Paul A. Holloway, "*Bona Cogitare*: An Epicurean Consolation in Phil 4:8-10," *HTR* 91 (1998) 89-96.

Holloway, "*Commendatio*"
Paul A. Holloway, "*Commendatio aliqua sui*: Reading Romans with Pierre Bourdieu," *EC* 2 (2011) 356-83.

Holloway, *Consolation*
Paul A. Holloway, *Consolation in Philippians: Philosophical Sources and Rhetorical Strategy* (SNTSMS 112; Cambridge: Cambridge University Press, 2001).

Holloway, "Consolation"
Paul A. Holloway, "Consolation: II. Greco-Roman Antiquity; III. New Testament; IV. Judaism: Second Temple and Hellenistic Judaism," *EBR* 5:669-73.

Holloway, *Coping with Prejudice*
Paul A. Holloway, *Coping with Prejudice: 1 Peter in Social-Psychological Perspective* (WUNT 244; Tübingen: Mohr Siebeck, 2009).

Holloway, "Deliberating"
Paul A. Holloway, "Deliberating Life and Death: Paul's Tragic *Dubitatio* in Philippians 1:22-26," (forthcoming in *HTR*).

Holloway, "Enthymeme"
Paul A. Holloway, "The Enthymeme as an Element of Style in Paul," *JBL* 120 (2001) 329-39.

Holloway, "Hellenistic Philosopher"
Paul A. Holloway, "Paul as Hellenistic Philosopher: The Evidence of Philippians," in *Paul and the Philosophers*, ed. Ward Blanton and Hent de Vries (New York: Fordham University Press, 2014) 52-68.

Holloway, "Laodiceans"
Paul A. Holloway, "The Apocryphal *Epistle to the Laodiceans* and the Partitioning of Philippians," *HTR* 91 (1998) 321-25.

Holloway, "Left Behind"
Paul A. Holloway, "Left Behind: Jesus' Consolation of His Disciples in John 13-17," *ZNW* 96 (2005) 1-34.

Holloway, "*Nihil inopinati accidisse*"
Paul A. Holloway, "*Nihil inopinati accidisse*– 'Nothing unexpected has happened': A Cyrenaic Consolatory Topos in 1 Pet 4:12ff.," *NTS* 48 (2002) 433-48.

Holloway, "Paul's Pointed Prose"
Paul A. Holloway, "Paul's Pointed Prose: The *Sententia* in Roman Rhetoric and Paul," *NovT* 40 (1998) 32-53.

Holloway, "Thanks for the Memories"
Paul A. Holloway, "Thanks for the Memories: On the Translation of Phil 1.3," *NTS* 52 (2006) 419-32.

Hooker
Morna D. Hooker, "The Letter to the Philippians," in *The New Interpreter's* Bible, ed. Leander E. Keck (Nashville: Abingdon, 2000) 11:467-549.

Horbury, *Cult of Christ*
William Horbury, *Jewish Messianism and the Cult of Christ* (London: SCM, 1998).

van der Horst, *Epitaphs*
Pieter W. van der Horst, *Ancient Jewish Epitaphs: An Introductory Survey of a Millennium of Jewish Funerary Epigraphy (300 BCE–700CE)* (CBET 2; Kampen: Kok Pharos, 1991).

Hultin, "Rhetoric of Consolation"
N. Hultin, "The Rhetoric of Consolation: Studies in the Development of the 'Consolatio Mortis'" (Ph.D. diss., Johns Hopkins University, 1965).

Jerome
Commentarii in Epistolam ad Philippensis, PL 30:879-92.

Jewett, "Conflicting Movements"
Robert Jewett, "Conflicting Movements in the Early Church as Reflected in Philippians," *NovT* 12 (1970) 362-90.

Jewett, *Romans*
Robert Jewett, *Romans: A Commentary* (Hermeneia; Minneapolis: Fortress Press, 2006).

Johann, *Trauer und Trost*
H. T. Johann, *Trauer und Trost: Eine quellen- und strukturanalytische Untersuchung der philosophischen Trostschriften über den Tod* (STA 5; Munich: Fink, 1968).

Käsemann, "Kritische Analyse"
Ernst Käsemann, "Kritische Analyse von Phil. 2,5-11," *ZThK* 47 (1950) 313-60; ET: "A Critical Analysis of Philippians 2:5-11," *JTC* 5 (1968) 45-88.

Kassel, *Konsolationsliteratur*
Rudolf Kassel, *Untersuchungen zur griechischen und römischen Konsolationsliteratur* (Zetemata 18; Munich: Beck, 1958).

Koester, "Experiment"
Helmut Koester, "1 Thessalonians—Experiment in Christian Writing," in *Continuity and Discontinuity in Church History*, ed. F. F. Church and T. George (SHCT 19; Leiden: Brill, 1979) 33-44.

Koester, "Purpose"
Helmut Koester, "The Purpose of the Polemic of a Pauline Fragment (Philippians iii)," *NTS* 8 (1961-62) 317-32.

Koskenniemi, *Studien*
Heikki Koskenniemi, *Studien zur Idee und Phraseologie des griechischen Briefes bis 400 n. Chr.* (Helsinki: Kirjakauppa; Wiesbaden: Harrassowitz, 1956).

Koukouli-Chrysanthaki, "Colonia"
    Chaido Koukouli-Chrysanthaki, "Colonia Iulia
    Augusta Philippensis," in *Philippi at the Time of
    Paul and after His Death*, ed. Charalambos Bakirtzis
    and Helmut Koester (Harrisburg, PA: Trinity Press
    International, 1998) 5–35.
Krause, *Gefängnisse*
    Jens-Uwe Krause, *Gefängnisse im Römischen Reich*
    (HABES 23; Stuttgart: Franz Steiner, 1996).
Kremydi-Sicilianou, *Multiple Concealments*
    Sophia Kremydi-Sicilianou, *Multiple Concealments
    from the Sanctuary of Zeus Olympios at Dion: The
    Roman Provincial Coin Hoards* (Meletemata 35; Ath-
    ens: Boccard [Paris], 2004).
Kremydi-Sicilianou, "*Victoria Augusta*"
    Sophia Kremydi-Sicilianou, "*Victoria Augusta* on
    Macedonian Coins: Remarks on Dating and Inter-
    pretation," Τεκμήρια 7 (2002) 63–84.
Kurth, *Senecas Trostschrift an Polybius*
    Thomas Kurth, *Senecas Trostschrift an Polybius,
    Dialogue 11: Ein Kommentar* (BAK 59: Stuttgart:
    Teubner, 1994).
Kyle, *Sport*
    Donald G. Kyle, *Sport and Spectacle in the Ancient
    World* (2nd ed.; Malden, MA/Oxford: Wiley Black-
    well, 2015).
Lampe, *From Paul to Valentinus*
    Peter Lampe, *From Paul to Valentinus: Christians at
    Rome in the First Two Centuries* (Minneapolis: For-
    tress Press, 2003).
Lattimore, *Themes*
    Richmond Lattimore, *Themes in Greek and Latin
    Epitaphs* (Illinois Studies in Language and Literature
    28.1-2; Urbana: University of Illinois Press, 1942).
Leonard and Löhr, *Literature or Liturgy?*
    Clemens Leonhard and Hermut Löhr, eds., *Litera-
    ture or Liturgy? Early Christian Hymns and Prayers
    in Their Literary and Liturgical Context in Antiquity*
    (WUNT 2/363; Tübingen: Mohr Siebeck, 2014).
Lightfoot
    J. B. Lightfoot, *St. Paul's Epistle to the Philippians: A
    Revised Text with Introduction, Notes, and Dissertations*
    (London: Macmillan, 1868).
Lightfoot, *Colossians*
    J. B. Lightfoot, *St. Paul's Epistle to the Colossians and
    to Philemon* (London: Macmillan, 1892).
Lillo Redonet, *Palabras contra el dolor*
    Fernando Lillo Redonet, *Palabras contra el dolor:
    La consolación filosófica latina de Cicerón a Frontón*
    (Madrid: Ediciones Clásicas, 2001).
Lohmeyer
    Ernst Lohmeyer, *Der Brief an die Philipper, an die
    Kolosser und an Philemon* (KEK 9.1; Göttingen:
    Vandenhoeck & Ruprecht, 1953).
Lohmeyer, *Kyrios Jesus*
    Ernst Lohmeyer, *Kyrios Jesus: Eine Untersuchung zu
    Phil 2,5-11* (Heidelberg: Winter, 1928).
Mach, *Entwicklungsstadien*
    Michael Mach, *Die Entwicklungsstadien des jüdischen
    Engelglaubens in vorrabbinischer Zeit* (TSAJ 34;
    Tübingen: Mohr Siebeck, 1992).

Mackay, "Further Thoughts"
    B. S. Mackay, "Further Thoughts on Philippians,"
    NTS 7 (1961) 161–70.
Mahé, "Prière"
    J. P. Mahé, "La Prière d'actions de graces du Codex
    VI de Nag-Hamadi et Le Discours parfait," *ZPE* 13
    (1974) 40–60.
Malherbe, "Exhortation"
    Abraham J. Malherbe, "Exhortation in First Thes-
    salonians," *NovT* 25 (1983) 238–56.
Malherbe, "Paul's Self-Sufficiency"
    Abraham J. Malherbe, "Paul's Self-Sufficiency
    (Philippians 4:11)," in *Friendship, Flattery, and
    Frankness of Speech: Studies on Friendship in the New
    Testament World*, ed. John T. Fitzgerald (NovTSup
    82; Leiden: Brill, 1996) 125–39.
Malherbe, *Thessalonians*
    Abraham J. Malherbe, *The Letters to the Thessalo-
    nians: A New Translation with Introduction and Com-
    mentary* (AB 32B; New York: Doubleday, 2000).
Malingrey, *Lettres à Olympias*
    Anne-Marie Malingrey, ed. and trans., *Jean
    Chrysostome: Lettres à Olympias; vie d'Olympias*
    (2nd ed.; SC 13; Paris: Cerf, 1968).
Malunowiczówna, "Les éléments stoïciens"
    Leokadia Malunowiczówna, "Les éléments stoïciens
    dans la consolation grecque chrétienne," *StPatr* 13.2
    (TU 116; Berlin: Akademie-Verlag, 1975) 35–45.
Martin, *Carmen Christi*
    Ralph P. Martin, *Carmen Christi: Philippians 2:5-11
    in Recent Interpretation and in the Setting of Early
    Christian Worship* (SNTSMS 4; Cambridge: Cam-
    bridge Univeristy Press, 1967; 3rd ed., Downers
    Grove, IL: InterVarsity, 1997).
Marxsen, *Introduction*
    Willi Marxsen, *Introduction to the New Testament: An
    Approach to Its Problems* (trans. G. Buswell; Oxford:
    Blackwell, 1968).
Matlock, "Detheologizing"
    R. Barry Matlock, "Detheologizing the ΠΙΣΤΙΣ
    ΧΡΙΣΤΟΥ Debate: Cautionary Remarks from a
    Lexical Semantic Perspective," *NovT* 42 (2000)
    1–24.
Matlock, "Rhetoric"
    R. Barry Matlock, "The Rhetoric of πίστις in Paul:
    Galatians 2.16, Romans 3.22, and Philippians 3.9,"
    JSNT 30 (2007) 173–203.
McGing, "Synkrisis"
    B. C. McGing, "Synkrisis in Tacitus' Agricola,"
    Hermathena 132 (1982) 15–25.
Meeks, "Man from Heaven"
    Wayne A. Meeks, "The Man from Heaven in Philip-
    pians," in *The Future of Early Christianity: Essays
    in Honor of Helmut Koester*, ed. Birger A. Pearson
    (Minneapolis: Fortress Press, 1991) 329–36.
Meeks, *Urban Christians*
    Wayne A. Meeks, *The First Urban Christians: The
    Social World of the Apostle Paul* (New Haven: Yale
    University Press, 1983).

Meinel, *Verbannung*
Peter Meinel, *Seneca über seine Verbannung: Trost-schrift an die Mutter Helvia* (Bonn: Habelt, 1972).

Melanchthon
Philip Melanchthon, *Argumentum Epistolae Pauli ad Philippenses*, Corpus Reformatorum, *Philippi Melanchthonis opera quae supersunt omnia*, 15:1283-94.

Meyer
H. A. W. Meyer, *Kritisch-exegetisches Handbuch über die Briefe an die Philipper, Kolosser und an Philemon* (KEK 9; Göttingen: Vandenhoeck & Ruprecht, 1859).

Michaelis
Wilhelm Michaelis, *Der Brief des Paulus an die Philipper* (ThHKNT 11; Leipzig: Deichert, 1935).

Michaelis, "Die Gefangenschaftsbriefe"
Wilhelm Michaelis, "Die Gefangenschaftsbriefe des Paulus und antike Gefangenenbriefe," *NKZ* 36 (1925) 586-95.

Miller, "Exigence"
Arthur Miller, "Rhetorical Exigence," *Philosophy & Rhetoric* 5 (1972) 111-18.

Mitchell, "Consolatory Letters"
Jane F. Mitchell, "Consolatory Letters in Basil and Gregory Nazianzen," *Hermes* 96 (1968) 299-318.

Montefiore, *Jewish and Greek Encouragement*
C. G. Montefiore, *Ancient Jewish and Greek Encouragement and Consolation* (Bridgeport, CT: Hartmore House, 1971).

Morray-Jones, "Transformational Mysticism"
Christopher Morray-Jones, "Transformational Mysticism in the Apocalyptic-Merkabah Tradition," *JJS* 43 (1992) 1-31.

Moss, "Transfiguration"
Candida R. Moss, "The Transfiguration: An Exercise in Markan Accommodation," *BibInt* 12 (2004) 69-89.

Mount, "Gullibility"
Christopher Mount, "Belief, Gullibility, and the Presence of a God in the Early Roman Empire," in *Credible, Incredible: The Miraculous in the Ancient Mediterranean*, ed. Tobias Nicklas and Janet E. Spittler (WUNT 321; Tübingen: Mohr Siebeck, 2013) 85-106.

Mount, "Religious Experience"
Christopher Mount, "Religious Experience, the Religion of Paul, and Women in the Pauline Churches," in *Women and Gender in Ancient Religions: Interdisciplinary Approaches*, ed. Stephen P. Ahearne-Kroll, Paul A. Holloway, and James A. Kelhoffer (WUNT 263; Tübingen: Mohr Siebeck, 2010) 23-47.

Mount, "Spirit Possession"
Christopher Mount, "1 Corinthians 11:3-16: Spirit Possession and Authority in a Non-Pauline Interpolation," *JBL* 124 (2005) 313-40.

Müller
Ulrich B. Müller, *Der Brief des Paulus an die Philipper* (1993; 2nd ed.; ThHKNT 11.1; Leipzig: Evangelische Verlagsanstalt, 2002).

Müller-Bardorff, "Frage"
J. Müller-Bardorff, "Zur Frage der literarischen Einheit des Philipperbriefes," *WZJena* 7 (1957-58) 591-604.

Nickelsburg, *1 Enoch 1*
George W. E. Nickelsburg, *1 Enoch 1: A Commentary on 1 Enoch, Chapters 1-36; 81-108* (Hermeneia: Minneapolis: Fortress Press, 2001).

Nickelsburg, "Judgment"
George W. E. Nickelsburg, "Judgment, Life-After-Death, and Resurrection in the Apocrypha and Non-Apocalyptic Pseudepigrapha," in *Judaism in Late Antiquity*, Part 4: *Death, Life-After-Death, Resurrection and the World-To-Come in the Judaisms of Antiquity*, ed. Alan J. Avery-Peck and Jacob Neusner (Handbuch der Orientalistik 55; Leiden: Brill, 2000) 141-62.

Nickelsburg, "Religious Exclusivism"
George W. E. Nickelsburg, "Religious Exclusivism: A World View Governing Some Texts Found at Qumran," in *Das Ende der Tage und die Gegenwart des Heils: Begegnungen mit dem Neuen Testament und seiner Umwelt. Festschrift für Heinz-Wolfgang Kuhn zum 65. Geburtstag*, ed. Michael Becker and Wolfgang Fenske (AGJU 44; Leiden: Brill, 1999) 45-67.

Nickelsburg, *Resurrection*
George W. E. Nickelsburg, *Resurrection, Immortality, and Eternal Life in Intertestamental Judaism and Early Christianity* (HTS 56; expanded ed.; Cambridge, MA: Harvard University Press, 2007).

Nickelsburg and Collins, *Ideal Figures*
George W. E. Nickelsburg and John J. Collins, eds., *Ideal Figures in Ancient Judaism: Profiles and Paradigms* (SBLSCS 12; Chico, CA: Scholars Press, 1980).

Nickelsburg and VanderKam, *1 Enoch 2*
George W. E. Nickelsburg and James C. VanderKam, *1 Enoch 2: A Commentary on 1 Enoch, Chapters 37-82* (Hermeneia; Minneapolis: Fortress Press, 2011).

Noth, "Holy Ones"
Martin Noth, "The Holy Ones of the Most High," in idem, *The Laws of the Pentateuch and Other Studies* (London: Oliver & Boyd, 1966) 215-28.

Oakes, *Philippians*
Peter Oakes, *Philippians: From People to Letter* (SNTSMS 110; Cambridge: Cambridge University Press, 2001).

O'Brien
Peter T. O'Brien, *The Epistle to the Philippians: A Commentary on the Greek Text* (NIGTC; Grand Rapids: Eerdmans, 1991).

O'Brien, *Introductory Thanksgivings*
Peter T. O'Brien, *Introductory Thanksgivings in the Letters of Paul* (NovTSup 49; Leiden: Brill, 1977).

Ogereau, *Paul's Koinonia*
Julien M. Ogereau, *Paul's Koinonia with the Philippians: A Socio-Historical Investigation of a Pauline Partnership* (WUNT 2/377; Tübingen: Mohr Siebeck, 2014).

Parrott, *Nag Hammadi Codices V,2-5 and VI*
 Douglas M. Parrott, ed., *Nag Hammadi Codices V,2-5 and VI, with Papyrus Berolinensis 8502* (NHS 11; Leiden: Brill, 1979).

Pelagius
 Expositio in Philippenses, in Alexander Souter, *Pelagius's Expositions of Thirteen Epistles of St. Paul* (2 vols.; Texts and Studies 9; Cambridge: Cambridge University Press, 1926) 2:387–416.

Pervo, *Acts*
 Richard I. Pervo, *Acts: A Commentary* (Hermeneia; Minneapolis: Fortress Press, 2009).

Peterlin, *Disunity*
 Davorin Peterlin, *Paul's Letter to the Philippians in Light of the Disunity in the Church* (NovTSup 79; Leiden: Brill, 1995).

Pilhofer, *Philippi*
 Peter Pilhofer, *Philippi*, vol. 1: *Die erste christliche Gemeinde Europas;* vol. 2: *Katalog der Inschriften von Philippi* (WUNT 87, 119; Tübingen: Mohr Siebeck, 1995, 2000).

Pitta
 Antonio Pitta, *Lettera ai Filippesi: Nuova versione, introduzione e commento* (Milan: Paoline, 2010).

Rabbow, *Seelenführung*
 Paul Rabbow, *Seelenführung: Methodik der Exerzitien in der Antike* (Munich: Kösel, 1954).

Rahtjen, "Three Letters"
 B. D. Rahtjen, "The Three Letters of Paul to the Philippians," *NTS* (1959–60) 167–73.

Räisänen, *Rise of Christian Beliefs*
 Heikki Räisänen, *The Rise of Christian Beliefs: The Thought World of Early Christians* (Minneapolis: Fortress Press, 2010).

Rankov, "Governor's Men"
 Boris Rankov, "The Governor's Men: The *Officium Consularis* in Provincial Adminstration," in *The Roman Army as a Community, Including Papers of a Conference Held at Birkbeck College, University of London, on 11–12 January 1997*, ed. Adrian Goldsworthy and Ian Haynes (JRASup 34; Portsmouth, RI: Journal of Roman Archaeology, 1999) 15–34.

Rapske, *Roman Custody*
 Brian Rapske, *The Book of Acts and Paul in Roman Custody* (Grand Rapids: Eerdmans; Carlisle: Paternoster, 1994).

Reed, "Paul's Thanksgivings"
 Jeffrey T. Reed, "Are Paul's Thanksgivings 'Epistolary'?" *JSNT* 61 (1996) 87–99.

Reumann
 John Reumann, *Philippians: A New Translation with Introduction and Commentary* (AYB 33B; New Haven: Yale University Press, 2008).

Reumann, "Church Office"
 John Reumann, "Church Office in Paul, Especially in Philippians," in *Origins and Method: Towards a New Understanding of Judaism and Christianity*, ed. B. H. McLean (JSNTSup 86; Sheffield: JSOT Press, 1993) 82–91.

Rolland, "La structure littéraire"
 P. Rolland, "La structure littéraire et l'unité de l'Epître aux Philippiens," *RevScRel* 64 (1990) 213–16.

Sanders, *Paul and Palestinian Judaism*
 E. P. Sanders, *Paul and Palestinian Judaism: A Comparison of Patterns of Religion* (Philadelphia: Fortress Press, 1977).

Sanders, *Paul, the Law, and the Jewish People*
 E. P. Sanders, *Paul, the Law and the Jewish People* (Philadelphia: Fortress Press, 1983).

Sandnes, *Belly and Body*
 Karl Olav Sandnes, *The Belly and the Body in the Pauline Epistles* (SNTSMS 120; Cambridge: Cambridge University Press, 2002).

Scanlon, *Eros*
 Thomas F. Scanlon, *Eros and Greek Athletics* (Oxford: Oxford University Press, 2002).

Schäfer, *Hidden*
 Peter Schäfer, *Hidden and Manifest God: Some Major Themes in Jewish Mysticism* (Albany: State University of New York Press, 1992).

Schäfer, *Origins*
 Peter Schäfer, *The Origins of Jewish Mysticism* (Princeton: Princeton University Press, 2011).

Schenk
 Wolfgang Schenk, *Die Philipperbriefe des Paulus: Kommentar* (Stuttgart: Kohlhammer, 1984).

Schmithals, "False Teachers"
 Walter Schmithals, "The False Teachers of the Epistle to the Philippians," in idem, *Paul and the Gnostics* (Nashville: Abingdon, 1972) 65–122.

Schnelle, *Gerechtigkeit*
 Udo Schnelle, *Gerechtigkeit und Christusgegenwart: Vorpaulinische und paulinische Tauftheologie* (GThA 24; Göttingen: Vandenhoeck & Ruprecht, 1983).

Schnelle, *History*
 Udo Schnelle, *The History and Theology of the New Testament Writings* (Minneapolis: Fortress Press, 1998).

Schoonhoven, *Ad Liviam*
 Henk Schoonhoven, *The Pseudo-Ovidian AD LIVIAM DE MORTE DRUSI (Consolatio ad Liviam, Epicedium Drusi): A Critical Text with Introduction and Commentary* (Groningen: Forsten, 1992).

Schubert, *Form and Function*
 Paul Schubert, *Form and Function of the Pauline Thanksgivings* (BZNW 20; Berlin: Töpelmann, 1939).

Schweitzer, *Mysticism*
 Albert Schweitzer, *The Mysticism of Paul the Apostle* (Baltmore: Johns Hopkins University Press, 1998; orig., 1930).

Scourfield, *Consoling Heliodorus*
 J. H. D. Scourfield, *Consoling Heliodorus: A Commentary on Jerome 'Letter 60'* (Oxford: Clarendon, 1993).

Segal, *Paul the Convert*
Alan F. Segal, *Paul the Convert: The Apostolate and Apostasy of Saul the Pharisee* (New Haven: Yale University Press, 1992).

Seim and Økland, *Metamorphoses*
Turid Karlsen Seim and Jorunn Økland, eds., *Metamorphoses: Resurrection, Body and Transformative Practices in Early Christianity* (Ekstasis 1; Berlin/New York: de Gruyter, 2009).

Sellew, "Laodiceans"
Philip Sellew, "*Laodiceans* and the Philippians Fragments Hypothesis," *HTR* 87 (1994) 17–28.

Sevenster, *Paul and Seneca*
J. N. Sevenster, *Paul and Seneca* (NovTSup 4; Leiden: Brill, 1961).

Shantz, *Paul in Ecstasy*
Colleen Shantz, *Paul in Ecstasy: The Neurobiology of the Apostle's Life and Thought* (Cambridge: Cambridge University Press, 2009).

Shaw, "Myth"
Brent Shaw, "The Myth of the Neronian Persecution," *JRS* 105 (2015) 73–100.

Sherwin-White, *Roman Society and Roman Law*
A. N. Sherwin-White, *Roman Society and Roman Law in the New Testament* (Oxford: Clarendon, 1963).

Smith, "Pauline Worship"
Morton Smith, "Pauline Worship as Seen by Pagans," *HTR* 73 (1980) 241–49.

Sommer, *Bodies of God*
Benjamin D. Sommer, *Bodies of God and the World of Ancient Israel* (Cambridge: Cambridge University Press, 2009).

Sorensen, *Possession*
Eric Sorensen, *Possession and Exorcism in the New Testament and Early Christianity* (WUNT 2/157; Tübingen: Mohr Siebeck, 2002).

Speidel, *Guards*
Michael Speidel, *Guards of the Roman Imperial Armies: An Essay on the Singulares of the Provinces* (Antiquitas 1; Bonn: Habelt, 1978).

Standhartinger, "Letter"
Angela Standhartinger, "Letter from Prison as Hidden Transcript: What It Tells Us about the People at Philippi," in *The People beside Paul: The Philippian Assembly and History from Below*, ed. Joseph A. Marchal (ECL; Atlanta: SBL Press, 2015) 107–40.

Stendahl, "Introspective Conscience"
Krister Stendahl, "Paul and the Introspective Conscience of the West," *HTR* 55 (1963) 199–215.

Stowers, "Friends"
Stanley K. Stowers, "Friends and Enemies in the Politics of Heaven: Reading Theology in Philippians," in *Pauline Theology*, vol. 1, ed. Jouette M. Bassler (Minneapolis: Fortress Press, 1991) 105–21.

Stowers, *Rereading*
Stanley K. Stowers, *A Rereading of Romans: Jews, Justice, and Gentiles* (New Haven: Yale University Press, 1994).

Taatz, *Frühjüdische Briefe*
Irene Taatz, *Frühjüdische Briefe: Die paulinischen Briefe im Rahmen der offiziellen religiösen Briefe des Frühjudentums* (NTOA 16; Fribourg: Universitätsverlag; Göttingen: Vandenhoeck & Ruprecht, 1991).

Taylor, "From Faith to Faith"
John W. Taylor, "From Faith to Faith: Romans 1.17 in the Light of Greek Idiom," *NTS* 50 (2004) 337–48.

Theodore of Mopsuestia
Theodore Mopsuestia, *In Epistolam B. Pauli ad Philippenses*, in H. B. Swete, *Theodori Episcopi Mopsuesteni in Epistolas B. Pauli Commentarii: The Latin Version with Greek Fragments* (2 vols.; Cambridge: Cambridge University Press, 1880) 1:197–252. ET: Rowan A. Greer, *Theodore of Mopsuestia: The Commentaries on the Minor Epistles of Paul* (SBLWGRW 26; Atlanta: Society of Biblical Literature, 2010) 290–361.

Theodoret
Theodoret, *In Epistolam ad Philippenses*, in *Theodoreti Episcopi Cyri Commentarius in omnes B. Pauli Epistolas*, ed. Charles Marriott, completed by Philip E. Pusey (2 vols.; Oxford: Parker, 1870) 2:45–67. ET: Robert C. Hill, *Theodoret of Cyrus: Commentary on the Letters of St. Paul* (2 vols.; Brookline, MA: Holy Cross Orthodox Press, 2001) 2:64–83.

Vincent
Marvin R. Vincent, *A Critical and Exegetical Commentary on the Epistles to the Philippians and to Philemon* (ICC; Edinburgh: T&T Clark, 1897).

Vollenweider, "Metamorphose"
Samuel Vollenweider, "Die Metamorphose des Gottessohns," in *Das Urchristentum in seiner literarischen Geschichte: Festschrift für Jürgen Becker zum 65. Geburtstag*, ed. Ulrich Mell and Ulrich B. Müller (BZNW 100; Berlin/New York: de Gruyter, 1999) 109–31.

Vollenweider, "Raub"
Samuel Vollenweider, "Der 'Raub' der Gottgleichheit: Ein religionsgeschichtlicher Vorschlag zu Phil 2.6(-11)," *NTS* 45 (1999) 413–33.

Vollenweider, "Waagschalen"
Samuel Vollenweider, "Die Waagschalen von Leben und Tod: Zum antiken Hintergrund von Phil 1,21-26," *ZNW* 85 (1994) 93–115.

Wansink, *Chained*
Craig S. Wansink, *Chained in Christ: The Experience and Rhetoric of Paul's Imprisonments* (JSNTSup 130; Sheffield: Sheffield Academic Press, 1996).

Watson, "Rhetorical Analysis"
Duane F. Watson, "A Rhetorical Analysis of Philippians and Its Implications for the Unity Question," *NovT* 30 (1988) 57–88.

Weaver, *Familia Caesaris*
P. R. C. Weaver, *Familia Caesaris: A Social Study of the Emperor's Freedmen and Slaves* (Cambridge: Cambridge University Press, 1972).

Weaver, *Plots of Epiphany*
John B. Weaver, *Plots of Epiphany: Prison Escape in the Acts of the Apostles* (BZNW 131; Berlin: de Gruyter, 2004).

Wedderburn, "Some Observations"
A. J. M. Wedderburn, "Some Observations on Paul's Use of the Phrases 'in Christ' and 'with Christ,'" *JSNT* 25 (1985) 83–97.

Weiss
Bernhard Weiss, *Der Philipper-Brief ausgelegt und die Geschichte seiner Auslegung kritisch dargestellt* (3rd ed.; Berlin: Hertz, 1859).

White, "Introductory Formulae"
John L. White, "Introductory Formulae in the Body of the Pauline Letter," *JBL* 90 (1971) 91–97.

White, *Light*
John L. White, *Light from Ancient Letters* (Philadelphia: Fortress Press, 1986).

White, "Morality"
  L. Michael White, "Morality between Two Worlds: A Paradigm of Friendship in Philippians," in *Greeks, Romans, and Christians: Essays in Honor of Abraham J. Malherbe*, ed. D. L. Balch, E. Ferguson, and Wayne A. Meeks (Minneapolis: Fortress Press, 1990) 201–15.

White, *Cicero in Letters*
  Peter White, *Cicero in Letters: Epistolary Relations of the Late Republic* (Oxford: Oxford University Press, 2010).

Wilcox, "Sympathetic Rivals"
  Amanda Wilcox, "Sympathetic Rivals: Consolation in Cicero's Letters," *AJPh* 126 (2005) 237–55.

Wiles, *Paul's Intercessory Prayers*
  Gordon P. Wiles, *Paul's Intercessory Prayers* (SNTSMS 24; Cambridge: Cambridge University Press, 1974).

Wrede, *Paul*
  William Wrede, *Paul* (London: Green, 1907).

Yarbro Collins, "Philippians 2:6-11"
  Adela Yarbro Collins, "Psalms, Philippians 2:6-11, and the Origins of Christology," *BibInt* 11 (2002) 361–72.

Zahn, *Introduction*
  Theodor Zahn, *Introduction to the New Testament* (trans. John Moore Trout et al. from 3rd German ed.; 3 vols.; Edinburgh: T&T Clark, 1903).

Zeller, "Menschwerdung"
  Dieter Zeller, "Die Menschwerdung des Sohnes Gottes im Neuen Testament und die antike Religionsgeschichte," in *Menschwerdung Gottes–Vergöttlichung von Menschen*, ed. Dieter Zeller (NTOA 7; Freiburg, Schweiz: Universitätsverlag; Göttingen: Vandenhoeck & Ruprecht, 1988) 141–76.

Zeller, "New Testament Christology"
  Dieter Zeller, "New Testament Christology in Its Hellenistic Reception," *NTS* 47 (2001) 312–33.

Zimmermann, "Philosophie als Psychotherapie"
  Bernhard Zimmermann, "Philosophie als Psychotherapie: Die griechisch-römische Consolationsliteratur," in *Stoizismus in der europäischen Philosophie, Literatur, Kunst und Politik: Eine Kulturgeschichte von der Antike bis zur Moderne*, ed. Barbara Neymeyr, Jochen Schmidt, and Bernhard Zimmermann (2 vols.; Berlin: de Gruyter, 2008) 1:193–213.

1. Some Prefatory Remarks on Ancient Consolation

Since I will argue over the course of the following commentary that Philippians is a "letter of consolation" (ἐπιστολὴ παραμυθητική; Pseudo-Demetrius, *Typoi epist.* 5), and since modern Western notions of consolation differ in significant ways from ancient notions, it will be helpful to begin with a description of ancient consolation that anticipates its relevance to the interpretation of Philippians.[1] Most of what we know about ancient consolation comes from Greek and Roman sources, which have long been an object of critical study.[2] Ancient Hebrew and Jewish consolation, on the other hand, has received very little scholarly attention.[3] This is unfortunate, since these sources, though eventually influenced by Greek and Roman theory and practice, also preserve important ancient Mesopotamian and Levantine traditions. The ear-liest Christians, of course, drew upon both Greco-Roman and Jewish consolation. For purposes of description, I will treat Greco-Roman consolation and ancient Hebrew and Jewish consolation separately. I will conclude with a few comments on early Christian consolation as witnessed in the New Testament. It is common to include later "patristic" sources in discussions of Greek and Roman consolation since these elite thinkers were educated in that tradition, and I will follow that practice here.

a. Greek and Roman Consolation

Ancient Greek and Roman consolation differs from modern Western consolation in at least two important ways. First, while modern usage generally restricts the terms "grief" and "consolation" to occasions of bereavement,[4] the ancients imagined grief (λύπη, πένθος, *dolor, aegritudo*) and consolation (παράκλησις, παραμυθία, *solacium*) more broadly to include all forms of mental distress and their

---

This section epitomizes much of my earlier writing on consolation, especially: *Consolation in Philippians: Philosophical Sources and Rhetorical Strategy* (SNTSMS 112; Cambridge: Cambridge University Press, 2002) 55–83; *Coping with Prejudice: 1 Peter in Social-Psychological Perspective* (WUNT 244; Tübingen: Mohr Siebeck, 2009) 86–112; and "Consolation, II: Greco-Roman Antiquity; III: New Testament; IV: Judaism: Second Temple and Hellenistic Judaism," in *EBR* 5:669–73.

1   My concern here is to offer a broad working description of ancient consolation. I will say more about the specific consolatory arguments that Paul deploys in Philippians in a series of excursuses over the course of the commentary.

2   The most authoritative study remains Rudolf Kassel, *Untersuchungen zur griechischen und römischen Konsolationsliteratur* (Zetemata 18; Munich: Beck, 1958); cf. Carl Buresch, "Consolationum a Graecis Romanisque scriptarum historia critica," *Leipziger Studien zur classischen Philologie* 9 (1886) 1–170. Insightful surveys include Jean Hani, "La consolation antique," *REA* 75 (1973) 103–10; Franz-Bernhard Stammköter, "Trost," in *HWPh* 10 (2002) 1523–27; and Bernhard Zimmermann, "Philosophie als Psychotherapie: Die griechisch-römische Consolationsliteratur," in *Stoizismus in der europäischen Philosophie, Literatur, Kunst und Politik: Eine Kulturgeschichte von der Antike bis zur Moderne*, ed. Barbara Neymeyr, Jochen Schmidt, and Bernhard Zimmermann (2 vols.; Berlin: de Gruyter, 2008) 1:193–213. For the Latin tradition, now see Fernando Lillo Redonet, *Palabras contra el dolor: La consolación filosófica latina de Cicerón a Fronto* (Madrid: Ediciones Clásicas, 2001); for the medieval tradition, see Peter von Moos, *Consolatio: Studien zur mittellateinischen Trostliteratur über den Tod und zum Problem der christlichen Trauer* (4 vols.; Munich: Fink, 1971–72).

3   The only general survey is a century-old set of popular lectures by Claude G. Montefiore, *Ancient Jewish and Greek Encouragement and Consolation in Sorrow and Calamity* (Bridgeport, CT: Hartmore House, 1971; privately printed in 1917), and my own efforts in *Coping with Prejudice*, 86–112 and "Consolation," 672–73; cf. Charles A. Muenchow, "Consolation: An Old Testament Perspective" (Ph.D. diss., Yale University, 1983); Carol Newsom, "'The Consolations of God': Assessing Job's Friends across a Cultural Abyss," in *Reading from Right to Left: Essays on the Hebrew Bible in Honor of David J. A. Clines*, ed. J. Cheryl Exum and H. G. M. Williamson (JSOTSup 373; Sheffield: Sheffield Academic Press, 2003) 374–58; Gwen Sayler, "*2 Baruch*: A Story of Grief and Consolation," *SBLSP* 21 (1982) 485–500. Several consolatory inscriptions are discussed in Pieter W. van der Horst, *Ancient Jewish Epitaphs: An Introductory Survey of a Millennium of Jewish Funerary Epigraphy (300 BCE–700 CE)* (CBET 2; Kampen: Kok Pharos, 1991).

4   This no doubt explains Ben Witherington III's anachronistic assertion that Philippians cannot be a letter of consolation because "[n]o one has died" (*Paul's Letter to the Philippians: A Socio-rhetorical Commentary* [Grand Rapids: Eerdmans, 2011] 75 n. 13).

remedies.[5] In *Tusc.* 3.34.81, Cicero mentions handbook treatments of death, poverty, exile, life without honors, the destruction of one's country, slavery, illness, and blindness. Dio Chrysostom offers a similar list in *Or.* 16.3. This range of subject matter is reflected in the surviving corpus of consolatory writings.[6]

Second, whereas modern practice tends to equate consolation with sympathy, ancient consolers generally distinguished between these two concepts. They often began their letters or speeches with words of sympathy,[7] but they quickly moved to consolation proper, which typically took the form of a series of rational arguments against grief supplemented with exhortations to responsible behavior and bits and pieces of practical advice.[8]

Thucydides has Pericles express this distinction in his famous funeral oration: "I am not here to lament with you; I am here to console you" (*Hist.* 2.44).[9] Aelianus attributes a similar remark to Aristippus: "I have not come to share your grief, but to end it" (*Var. hist.* 7.3). Plutarch takes it for granted that consolation is a form of moral instruction: "in difficult circumstances we have no need of those who like the chorus in some tragedy weep and wail with us, but of those who speak frankly and instruct us that grief and self-abasement are always useless" (*De exil.* 599b). [10]

The goal of consolation was to defeat grief, one of the four cardinal passions,[11] and to replace it as far as possible with its contrary, joy (χαρά, *gaudium*, *laetitia*).

---

5   Pseudo-Demetrius (*Typoi epist.* 5) defines the consolatory letter broadly as composed for someone grieving "because something hard to bear [δυσχεροῦς] has happened"; cf. *P. Hamb.* 4.254 for a similar model letter.

6   Death was by far the most common misfortune treated (Mary E. Fern, *The Latin* Consolatio Mortis *as a Literary Type* [St. Louis: Saint Louis University Press, 1941]; Mary Evaristus, *The Consolations of Death in Ancient Greek Literature* [Washington, DC: National Capital Press, 1917]), followed by exile (Alfred Giesecke, *De philosophorum veterum quae de exilium spectant sententiis* [Leipzig: Teubner, 1891]; Heinz-Günther Nesselrath, "Later Greek Voices on the Predicament of Exile: From Teles to Plutarch and Favorinus," in *Writing Exile: The Discourse of Displacement in Greco-Roman Antiquity and Beyond*, ed. Jan Felix Gaertner [Mnemosyne Supplements 283; Leiden: Brill, 2007] 87–108). Other misfortunes included destruction of one's country (Seneca, *Ep.* 91.9; cf. Cicero, *Tusc.* 3.22.54), poverty (Cicero, *Tusc.* 3.24.57; Seneca, *Ad Helv.* 10–13; Diogenes Laertius, *Vit.* 2.34), illness (Pseudo-Jerome, *Ep.* 5; Gregory Nazianzen, *Ep.* 31.4), blindness (Jerome, *Ep.* 76.2), old age (Diogenes Laertius, *Vit.* 5.24 [Theophrastus]; 9.20 [Demetrius of Phalerum]; Cicero, *De sen.*; Favorinus, frags. 9–17 Barigazzi), legal difficulties (Cicero, *Ad fam.* 5.18; Seneca, *Ep.* 17; 24), financial setbacks (Cicero, *Ad fam.* 5.13; 16; 17; Seneca, *Ep.* 21), an ungrateful client (Seneca, *Ep.* 81), a runaway slave (Seneca, *Ep.* 107), fraud (Juvenal, *Sat.* 13). Galen's recently discovered *De indolentia* (Περὶ ἀλυπίας) treats among other things the loss of a personal library (see Véronique Boudon-Millot, Jacques Jouanna, and Antoine Pietrobelli, eds., *Galien, Oeuvres*, vol. 4: *Ne pas se chagriner* [Paris: Belles Lettres, 2010] esp. xxix–lviii).

7   Kassel, *Konsolationsliteratur*, 51–52, 91 n. 1; Charles Favez, "Le sentiment dans les consolations de Sénèque," in *Mélanges Paul Thomas: Recueil de mémoires concernant la philosophie classique dédié à Paul Thomas* (Bruges: Sainte Catherine, 1930) 262–70; J. H. D. Scourfield, *Consoling Heliodorus: A Commentary on Jerome, Letter 60* (Oxford Classical Monographs; Oxford: Clarendon, 1993) 80–81; cf. Pseudo-Demetrius, *Typoi epist.* 5; Menander Rhetor, περὶ ἐπιδεικ. 2.9. Sympathy as well as consolation was the duty of friends: Aristotle, *EN* 9.11.1171a35–b4; Stobaeus, *Flor.* 4.48.16–31.

8   Christoph Jedan, "Troost door argumenten: Herwaardering van een filosofische en christelijke traditie," *NTT* 68 (2014) 7–22. I will return to this aspect of consolation below when I discuss the letter's disposition. Cicero's often pointed letters of consolation offer an interesting case study; see Amanda Wilcox, "Sympathetic Rivals: Consolation in Cicero's Letters," *AJPh* 126 (2005) 237–55; cf. Hubert Zehnacker, "*Officium Consolantis*: Le devoir de consolation dans le correspondance de Cicéron, de la bataille de Pharsale à la mort Tullia," *REL* 63 (1985) 69–86.

9   Cf. Plato, *Menex.* 247c–d. Epicurus is characteristically more humane: "We should share in our friends' pain not by lamenting with them, but by caring for them" (*Sent. Vat.* 66). According to Gregory Nazianzen (*Ep.* 165), sympathy was itself a form of consolation.

10 Cf. Pseudo-Plutarch, *Ad Apoll.* 118a, which equates consolation with "noble and sober encouragement" (ἡ γενναῖα καὶ σεμνὴ παρηγορία).

11 The other cardinal passions were "fear" (φόβος), "desire" (ἐπιθυμία), and "pleasure" (ἡδονή). Theories of consolation varied depending on one's view of the passions. Stoics, for example, sought to eradicate

Indeed, to experience joy in difficult circumstances was synonymous with being consoled.[12] Nowhere is this more obvious than in Paul himself. "I am filled with consolation [παρακλήσει]," he writes to the Corinthians; "I am overflowing with joy [χαρᾷ] in the midst of all our affliction" (2 Cor 7:4; cf. 7:13).[13] Similarly, the exiled Seneca assures his mother that he is "happy" (*beatus*) and has found "joy" (*gaudium*) in circumstances that would make others miserable (*Ad Helv.* 4–5). Further, inasmuch as "joy" was the characteristic disposition or εὐπάθεια ("good emotion") of the sage,[14] a person's ability to rejoice in the face of hardship could be read as a measure of his or her progress toward wisdom and virtue. "He has made it to the top," Seneca writes, "who understands what is to be the proper object of joy" (*Ep.* 23.2).[15] And again: "to the degree that you lack joy, to that degree you lack wisdom"

(*Ep.* 59.14). In Phil 1:25, Paul intuitively links moral progress with joy: εἰς τὴν ὑμῶν προκοπὴν καὶ χαρὰν τῆς πίστεως ("for your *progress* and *joy* in the faith").[16] Joy is a key motif in Philippians, where in one form or another it appears sixteen times.[17] The commentary tradition has yet to come to grips with Paul's use of this important term.[18]

As a form of moral instruction, ancient consolation argued by way of both precept and example.[19] Stock examples of legendary or famous persons who had suffered similar hardships were popular.[20] Sometimes consolers pointed to themselves as examples of those who overcame grief in an effort to spur or even shame their readers into heeding their advice.[21] Exhortation also had a prominent place in ancient consolation.[22] It could stand by itself as a distinct section within a consolatory

---

grief completely; Peripatetics, simply to lessen it; Epicureans, to distract the mind from it. I will say more about this below. See further Marcus Wilson, "The Subjugation of Grief in Seneca's Epistles," in *The Passions in Roman Thought and Literature*, ed. Susanna Morton Braund and Christopher Gill (Cambridge: Cambridge University Press, 1997) 48–67.

12 E.g., Seneca, *Ad Marc.* 3.4; *Ad Poly.* 10.6; *Ep.* 99.3; Plutarch, *De tran. an.* 469d; Ambrose, *De exc. Sat.* 1.3; Jerome, *Ep.* 60.7; John Chrysostom, *Ep. ad Olymp.* 9.3.60-67; 12.1.44, 136; 16.1.12 (Malingrey). According to *Corp. Herm.* 13.8, just as, when "knowledge" (γνῶσις) comes, "ignorance" (ἄγνοια) is expelled, so also when "joy" (χαρά) comes "grief" (λύπη) will "flee" (φεύγειν).

13 "Joy" and "consolation" are equated elsewhere in Paul; see Phil 1:18, 25-26; 2:17-18, 27-28; 3:1; 4:4. For joy in affliction, see 2 Cor 6:10; 7:4; 8:2; 1 Thess 1:6; Phlm 7; for joy as the antithesis of grief, see esp. Phil 2:28 ("that you might rejoice [χαρῆτε] and I might be less grieved [ἀλυπότερος]"); for joy as the antithesis of weeping, see Rom 12:15 ("weep with those who weep and rejoice with those who rejoice").

14 Stoics were particularly keen to distinguish between the εὐπάθειαι, or "good emotions," and the πάθη, or "passions." The first were rational dispositions characteristic of the sage, while the latter were always irrational and excessive. Thus, the sage felt "joy" (χαρά) but not "pleasure" (ἡδονή), "caution" (εὐλάβεια) but not "fear" (φόβος), "wishing" (βούλησις) but not "desire" (ἐπιθυμία). There was no rational analogue to "grief," since grief occurs in the presence of perceived misfortune and for the Stoics the only possible perceived misfortune of the sage was vice, all else being a matter of indifference.

15 Cf. *Ep.* 23.3: "This you must do before all else, my dear Lucilius: learn how to rejoice [*disce gaudere*]"; 23.4: "Believe me, true joy [*verum gaudium*] is a serious matter [*res severa*]!"; in *Ep.* 66.5 he calls it the *primum bonum*. Philo says that "joy is the noblest of the good emotions" (ἡ εὐπαθειῶν ἀρίστη χαρά; *Abr.* 156), and he agrees with Seneca that it is the "goal" (τέλος; *Her.* 315); cf. *Praem.* 32; *Det.* 135; *Plant.* 138.

16 In this regard it is noteworthy that both "progress" and "joy" are governed by the same article (τήν) and the same genitive (ὑμῶν). See my comments on Phil 1:25 in the commentary below.

17 Phil 1:4, 18 (twice), 25; 2:2, 17 (twice), 18 (twice), 28, 29; 3:1; 4:1, 4 (twice), 10.

18 But see Petra von Gemünden, "Der 'Affekt' der Freude im Philipperbrief und seiner Umwelt," in *Der Philipperbrief des Paulus in der hellenistisch-römischen Welt*, ed. Jörg Frey and Benjamin Schliesser (WUNT 353; Tübingen: Mohr Siebeck, 2015) 223–53.

19 Favorinus, *De exil.* 96.2 (Barigazzi 376.25–377.1): "not only through argument [λόγῳ] but personal example [παραδείγματι]."

20 Seneca, *Ad Marc.* 2-4; *Ad Poly.* 5.4; 14.1-16.3; 17.3-6; Cicero, *Tusc.* 3.23.56; Ovid, *Ex Pont.* 1.3.27, 61. Of course, for Paul Christ is a preeminent example of one who suffered (Phil 2:8; 3:10).

21 Wilcox, "Sympathetic Rivals." For grief as shameful, see the biting comments by Cicero, *Tusc.* 4.16.35. Paul offers himself as an example of one who endured suffering similar to the Philippians in Phil 1:30; cf. Epaphroditus in 2:29-30.

22 Juan Chapa, *Letters of Condolence in Greek Papyri* (Papyrologica Florentina 29; Florence: Gonnelli, 1998) 38–43; for exhortation to oneself in ancient

discourse, or it could be interspersed throughout the argument.[23] Seneca goes so far as to classify consolation as a "type" or *genus* of exhortation (*Ep.* 94.39; cf. 23.1).[24] In difficult cases exhortation might turn to rebuke, which was typically indirect, but not always: "You want words of comfort. Have a scolding instead. You are taking your son's death like a sissy [*molliter*]!" (*Ep.* 99.2; cf. 99.32).[25] The most common exhortation was to accept consolation and return to responsible behavior, on the assumption that grief, if left unchecked, caused one to shirk one's duties.[26] Another frequent exhortation was not to complain against God.[27] Both of these exhortations occur in Philippians (1:27 and 2:14, respectively).

Consolation was a topic of considerable interest to philosophers (e.g., Dio Chrysostom, *Or.* 27.9; Plutarch, *Superst.* 168c). Each major philosophical school developed its own approach based on such things as its view of the soul, its doctrine of good and evil, and its theory of the passions.[28] Cicero summarizes these approaches in *Tusc.* 3.31.76:[29]

> Some, like [the Stoic] Cleanthes, believe that the consoler's only task is to convince the person afflicted

with grief that the alleged "evil" is not an evil at all. Others, like the Peripatetics, argue that the evil in question is not great. Others, like the Epicureans, try to avert our attention away from evil things to good things. Others, like the Cyrenaics, think that it is sufficient to show that nothing unexpected has happened. Chrysippus, however, believes that the most important thing in consoling others is to disabuse them of their opinion that it is right to feel grief or that grief is somehow their duty.

Cicero goes on to observe, however, that in practice consolation was eclectic and school lines were frequently crossed.[30]

Three of the theories listed by Cicero—the Stoic theory of Cleanthes, Epicurean theory, and Cyrenaic theory—appear in Philippians and may be briefly elaborated here. (I will have more to say about each of these over the course of the commentary.[31]) Cleanthes's theory that consolation lies in convincing the afflicted person that no actual evil has occurred turns on the familiar Stoic distinction between things that matter and things that do not.[32] The assumption is that grief is due to mistaking

---

consolation, see Zimmermann, "Philosophie als Psychotherapie," 195–200.

23 Pseudo-Demetrius (*Typoi epist.* 5) gives the impression that exhortation formed a separate section (Stanley K. Stowers, *Letter Writing in Greco-Roman Antiquity* [LEC 5; Philadelphia: Westminster, 1986] 144); similarly, Gregory Nazianzen, *Ep.* 165 (Marcel Guignet, *Les procédés épistolaires de Saint Grégoire de Nazianze comparés a ceux de ses contemporains* [Paris: Picard, 1911] 80–82, but see Jane F. Mitchell, "Consolatory Letters in Basil and Gregory Nazianzen," *Hermes* 96 [1968] 299–318, esp. 303).

24 On the relation of consolation and parenesis, see Abraham J. Malherbe, "Exhortation in First Thessalonians," *NovT* 25 (1983) 238–56.

25 See also Cicero, *Ad Brut.* 1.9.1; *Ad fam.* 5.14.2; 5.16.6; *Ad Att.* 13.6.3; Cassius Dio, *Hist.* 38.18. Examples of indirect rebuke include *Ad Marc.* 2–3, where Seneca, who is convinced that Marcia has become self-indulgent, rails not against her but against Octavia, who was known to have been excessive in her grief for Marcellus; or Chrysostom, *Ep. ad Olymp.* 8.3.11–13 (Malingrey), where, instead of rebuking Olympias for her stubborn grief, Chrysostom imagines a scenario in which he might need to rebuke her: "and if you say, 'I can't take it!' then I'll say, 'Excuse and

pretense!'" (cf. *Ep. ad Olymp.* 17.4.32–43; Jerome, *Ep.* 39.3–4; Ambrose, *Ep.* 39). I will argue below that Phil 1:22-26 contains an indirect rebuke.

26 Cicero, *Ad Brut.* 1.9.2; Seneca, *Ep.* 94.39; *Ad Poly.* 5–6. In *Ad Helv.* 18.7–8, Seneca not only urges his mother to do her duty but argues that doing one's duty brings a consolation of its own.

27 Seneca, *Ad Marc.* 10.2; *Ad Poly.* 2.2; 4.1; *Ep.* 107.9; Plutarch, *Ad ux.* 610e–f; 611b; see Richmond Lattimore, *Themes in Greek and Latin Epitaphs* (Illinois Studies in Language and Literature 28.1-2; Urbana: University of Illinois Press, 1942) 147–58, 183–84; Albert B. Purdie, *Some Observations on Latin Verse Inscriptions* (London: Christophers, 1935) 44–48.

28 For a recent discussion, see Christopher Gill, *The Structured Self in Hellenistic and Roman Thought* (Oxford: Oxford University Press, 2006).

29 I discuss each of these theories in more detail in *Consolation*, 65–74.

30 Cicero, *Tusc.* 3.31.76; cf. *Ad Att.* 12.14.3. This eclectism was practical and should not be overemphasized, as Stowers has recently pointed out in his "Paul and the Terrain of Philosophy," *EC* 6 (2015) 141–56.

31 See esp. the excursuses after 1:3a, 10, 28b-30 and 4:8-9.

32 Maximillian Forschner, *Die stoische Ethik: Über den*

the latter for the former.[33] To realize that a presenting hardship—say, exile or, as in Paul's case, imprisonment—does not really matter is to be consoled.[34] I shall argue that Paul's prayer in Phil 1:10 that the Philippians learn to identify "the things that really matter" (τὰ διαφέροντα) evokes this theory.

As a philosophical hedonist, Epicurus could not deny that "pain" in any form, including grief, was an evil. But he could allow that a person in pain might be distracted from it by recalling past pleasures. Here is how Cicero summarizes Epicurean consolation: "calling the mind away from [avocatione] thinking about the things that distress us and calling the mind back to [revocatione] the contemplation of past pleasures."[35] Cicero was offended by the emphasis on pleasure and so modified the technique to focus instead on such moral goods as virtue.[36] The technique was popular in its original form,[37] but a

few instances of its modified form have also come down to us.[38] Paul deploys the technique in its unaltered form in Phil 1:3-4, where he reports that he is grateful to God for pleasant memories of the Philippians, which give him "joy." He later employs it in its modified form in 4:8-9 when he urges the Philippians to contemplate "virtue" and its corollaries.

According to Cyrenaic theory, grief is caused not by every misfortune but by misfortune that—like the surprise attack of an enemy or a fast-moving storm at sea[39]—strikes unexpectedly (Tusc. 3.13.28; 3.22.52-54).[40] To avoid being caught off guard, the Cyrenaics advocated meditating on possible future calamities, the so-called praemeditatio futuri mali.[41] For individuals already afflicted with grief, they claimed that comfort could be found in the thought that misfortunes are a normal part of human existence and so "nothing unexpected has happened" (Tusc. 3.23.55),[42]

Zusammenhang von Natur-, Sprach-, and Moralphilosophie im altstoischen System (Stuttgart: Klett-Cotta, 1981) 160–82; e.g., Seneca, *Ep.* 13.4; *Ad Helv.* 4–5.

33 In other words, grief always derives from the judgment "X is an evil," when the correct judgment would have been "X does not matter"; see Cicero, *Tusc.* 3.11.24; 4.7.14; 4.38.82; Epictetus, *Ench.* 5; Galen, *De plac.* 4.3.2.

34 Seneca, *Ad Helv.* 5.1; Teles, frag. 3, 22.1-2; 29.2-3 (Hense); Musonius, frag. 9.42.6; 9.50.9–10 (Hense); Plutarch, *De exil.* 599d; Cassius Dio, *Hist.* 38.26.2; Dio Chrysostom, *Or.* 13.8; Favorinus, frag. 22.22.44–48 (Barigazzi); cf. Peter Meinel, *Seneca über seine Verbannung: Trostschrift an die Mutter Helvia* (Bonn: Habelt, 1972) 56–72; Charles Favez, *L. Annaei Senecae Dialogorum liber XII Ad Helviam matrem de consolatione, texte latin publié avec une commentaire explicatif* (Lausanne: Payot, 1918) xlii–xliii, 10; Leokadia Malunowiczówna, "Les éléments stoïciens dans la consolation greque chrétienne," in *Papers Presented to the Sixth International Conference on Patristic Studies, Held in Oxford, 1971*, ed. Elizabeth A. Livingstone (3 vols.; StPatr 11–14; TU 115–17; Berlin: Akademie-Verlag, 1975–76) 2:35–45, esp. 35.

35 Cicero, *Tusc* 3.15.33; cf. 5.26.73–74; *De fin.* 1.57; Epicurus, *Sent. Vat.* 55; Philodemus, *De mort.* 38.21. I discuss this technique at length in "*Bona Cogitare*: An Epicurean Consolation in Phil 4:8-10," *HTR* 91 (1998) 89–96; and "Thanks for the Memories: On the Translation of Phil 1.3," *NTS* 52 (2006) 419–32; cf. Kassel, *Konsolationsliteratur*, 31–32; and now von Gemünden, "Freude," 236–38.

36 Cicero, *Tusc.* 3.16.35–17.37; *De fin.* 2.96–98.

37 Seneca makes extensive use: *Ad Poly.* 5-8; 12–13; *Ad Helv.* 18–19; *Ad Marc.* 2.3-4; 4.3–5.6; 21.1-4; *Ep.* 63.4; 99.3–5; *De ira* 3.39.4; *De brev. vit.* 10.2-4; *De vit. beat.* 6.1-2; *De benef.* 3.4.1; as does Plutarch: *De tran. an.* 468f–469d; *Ad ux.* 608a-b; 610a; cf. Pseudo-Plutarch, *Ad Apoll.* 116a-b. In early Christian literature, see Ambrose, *De exc. Sat.* 1.3; Jerome, *Ep.* 60.7.3; 108.1.2; 118.4.2; Basil, *Ep.* 5.2; 269.2; Paulinus of Nola, *Ep.* 13.6.

38 Seneca uses the modified technique in *Ad Poly.* 18.8; *Ad Marc.* 24.1-4; cf. Jerome, *Ep.* 60.7.3.

39 For two favorite Cyrenaic analogies, see Cicero, *Tusc.* 3.13.28; Seneca, *Ad Helv.* 5.3; *Ep.* 47.4; *De prov.* 4.6, 13; *De clem.* 1.7.3; Pseudo-Plutarch, *Ad Apoll.* 112d; John Chrysostom, *Ep. ad Olymp.* 15.1 (Malingrey).

40 Constantin Grollios, *Seneca's Ad Marciam: Tradition and Originality* (Athens: Christou, 1956) 44–51; Kassel, *Konsolationsliteratur*, 66–67.

41 The *praemeditatio* was not unique to Cyrenaic theory; see Kassel, *Konsolationsliteratur*, 66; Paul Rabbow, *Seelenführung: Methodik der Exerzitien in der Antike* (Munich: Kösel, 1954) 160–79; H. T. Johann, *Trauer und Trost: Eine quellen- und strukturanalytische Untersuchung der philosophischen Trostschriften über den Tod* (STA 5; Munich: Fink, 1968) 63–84. See now Galen's newly discovered Περὶ ἀλυπίας. The technique is parodied in Juvenal, *Sat.* 13, for which see Susan Morton Braund, "Grief and Anger in Juvenal satire 13," in *The Passions in Roman Thought and Literature*, ed. Susanna Morton Braund and Christopher Gill (Cambridge: Cambridge University Press, 1997) 68–88.

42 Cf. Pseudo-Plato, *Ax.* 364b; 370a; Pseudo-Ovid, *Cons.*

supported by the observations that others have suffered similar things.[43] Some such technique must underlie Phil 1:28-30, where Paul urges the Philippians not to be "frightened" by their enemies, since such opposition is to be expected as part of the apocalyptic plan of God, and since they have themselves been witnesses to Paul's similar suffering both now and in the past.

In addition to these more theoretical arguments, ancient consolers also made use of a number of popular arguments. These are too numerous to list here, but at least three of them appear in Philippians: (1) that in some circumstances "to die is gain" (Phil 1:21); (2) that one can often find a replacement or surrogate for a lost or absent loved one, especially in that loved one's "child" (Phil

2:19-22); and (3) that suffering endured leads to moral betterment (Phil 3:8-11; cf. 1:28).[44]

Finally, it should be said that the evidence for ancient Greek and Roman consolation is quite good and that the above description rests on solid evidentiary grounds. Because consolation was one of the primary duties of friendship,[45] the consolatory letter is very well attested.[46] Several longer letter-essays also survive,[47] as well as a number of consolatory poems.[48] Funerary inscriptions and private funeral orations also contain elements of consolation,[49] as do departure speeches (λόγοι συντακτικοί) and literary speeches of those about to die.[50] As I have already indicated, a number of elite patristic sources from the third to the fifth centuries also witness to

ad Liv. 397–400; Seneca, Ad Marc. 9.2; Ad Helv. 5.3; Ad Poly. 11.1; Ep. 63.14; 107.4; Plutarch, De tran. an. 476a–d; Pseudo-Plutarch, Ad Apoll. 112d.

43 See esp. Seneca, Ep. 107.2–9; cf. Ad Marc. 2.1–5.6; Ad Poly. 14.1–17.6; Constantine C. Grollios, Τέχνη ἀλυπίας: κοινοὶ τόποι τοῦ Πρὸς Πολύβιον τοῦ Σενέκα καὶ πηγαὶ αὐτῶν (Ἑλληνικά, παράρτημα 10; Athens: Christou and Son, 1956) 67–71; Thomas Kurth, Senecas Trostschrift an Polybius, Dialogue 11: Ein Kommentar (BAK 59: Stuttgart: Teubner, 1994) 26–34, 167–216.

44 Other popular arguments not listed here include the following: grief does not benefit the dead; the dead do not want the living to grieve; life is a gift from God to be surrendered without complaint; an early death preempts future suffering and temptation; time heals all grief; grief is unhealthy; and grief accomplishes nothing. See Fern, Latin Consolatio Mortis; Evaristus, Consolations of Death; N. Hultin, "The Rhetoric of Consolation: Studies in the Development of the 'Consolatio Mortis'" (Ph.D. diss., Johns Hopkins University, 1965); Stobaeus, Flor. 4.51.1–32.

45 E.g., Euripides, Alc. 369–70; Iph. Aul. 408; Zimmermann, "Philosophie als Psychotherapie," 193–95.

46 E.g., Cicero, Ad fam. 4.5; 5.16; 5.18; Ad Att. 12:10; 15:1; Ad Brut. 1.9; Seneca, Ep. 63, 93, 99; Pliny, Ep. 1.12; 3.21; 5.19; 8.1; 9.9; Fronto, De nep. am. 1; 2; Ad Verum Imp. 2.9; 2.10; Apollonius of Tyana, Ep. 55; 58; Julian, Ep. 69; 201; Libanius, Ep. 344; 1473; cf. Pseudo-Phalaris, Ep. 10; 103. Papyrus letters include P. Oxy. 1.115; 16.1874; 55.3819; 59.4004; SB 14.11646; 18.13946; BGU 3.801; P. Wisc. 84.1; P. Ross. Georg. 3.2; PSI 12.1248; P. Princ. 2.102; P. RainerCent. 70; see Chapa, Letters of Condolence.

47 Seneca, Ad Marc., Ad Poly., and Ad Helv.; Plutarch, De exil. and Ad ux.; and Pseudo-Plutarch, Ad Apoll.;

cf. Teles, frag. 8 (Hense); Cicero, De sen.; Musonius, frag. 9 (Hense).

48 The most substantial verse consolation from this period is Pseudo-Ovid, Cons. ad Liv., an elegy of almost 475 lines on the death of Drusus. Other consolatory poems include Catullus, Carm. 3; 96; Horace, Carm. 2.9; Ovid, Am. 3.9; Ex Pont. 1.9; 4.11; Propertius, El. 2.1; 2.6; 2.13; 3.18; 5.5; Statius, Silv. 2.1; 2.4; 2.6; 2.7; 3.3; 5.1; 5.3; 5.5; Martial, Epig. 1.88; 1.101; 5.34; 5.37; 6.28; 6.29; 6.85; 7.40; 9.74; 10.61; 11.91; cf. Lucretius, De re. nat. 3.830–1094; see further José Esteve-Forriol, Die Trauer- und Trostgedichte in der römischen Literatur (Munich: Schubert, 1962).

49 For inscriptions, see Lattimore, Themes, 215–65. Private funeral orations with consolatory themes include Dio Chrysostom, Or. 28 and 29; Aristides, Or. 31; and Libanius, Or. 17 and 18; cf. Himerius, Or. 8 (Colonna); Themistius, Or. 20.

50 The departure speech (λόγος συντακτικός) is discussed at Menander Rhetor, περὶ ἐπιδεικ. 2.15.430.9–434.9 and the informal talk (συντακτικὴ λαλιά) at 2.4.393.31–394.31; examples include: Homer, Od. 13.38–41; Theognis, El. 11–14; Sophocles, Phil. 1452–71; Euripides, Hec. 445–83, Phoen. 625–35; Catullus, Carm. 46; Tibullus, El. 1.10; Propertius, El. 3.21; Virgil, Aen. 4.333–61; Juvenal, Sat. 3; Himerius, Or. 11 (Colona); Rutilius Namatianus, De red. 1–164; cf. Gregory Thaumaturgus, Pan. Orig. 16–19. Speeches of those about to die include Plato, Apol. 39e–42a; Phaedo; Xenophon, Apol. 27–28; Cyropaed. 7.6–28; Cicero, De sen. 22.79–81; Tacitus, Ann. 15.60–64; Agr. 46.1; Dio Chrysostom, Or. 30; cf. Epicurus's deathbed letters in Diogenes Laertius, Vit. 10.22, and Cicero, De fin. 2.96; Jesus's so-called farewell speech in John 13–17, for which see Paul A. Holloway, "Left Behind: Jesus' Consolation of His Disciples in John 13–17," ZNW 96 (2005): 1–34.

traditional arguments and practices.[51] A particularly rich resource that does not fall into any of these categories is Cicero's *Tusculan Disputations*, which repeats much of the research that went into his earlier *Consolation to Himself*, which he composed after the death of his daughter Tullia and as he watched the Republic slip into tyranny.[52]

b. Ancient Hebrew and Jewish Consolation

In Greco-Roman society consolation lay primarily with the philosopher and to a lesser degree with the orator. In Judaism it lay with the sage and the prophet and, after the advent of apocalypticism, with the seer. This led to three more or less distinct Jewish consolatory traditions, distinguished by their respective modes of knowing and the range of subjects each treated. The wisdom tradition focused on individual suffering and the prophetic tradition on national calamities, while the apocalyptic tradition spoke both to individual and communal concerns, though here the group in question was frequently not the nation as a whole but the apocalyptist's own religious circle or sect.[53]

Given the cosmopolitan scope of Jewish wisdom, it is not surprising that most of its consolatory arguments are similar if not identical to popular Greco-Roman consolation: that grief is useless (Sir 30:23); that grief is harmful to the mourner (Job 5:1-5; Sir 38:18); that suffering improves the sufferer (Job 5:17-26); that an early death exempts one from life's sorrows and temptations (Wis 4:11-14); that suffering is to be expected (Prov 3:11-12; Job 5:6-7; Qoh 5:8; Sir 6:18-37); and so on. A few consolatory topics characteristic of prophecy also appear in certain wisdom texts, such as the hope of vengeance (Prov 20:22; Job 8:20-22) and a concern for theodicy (Job; Sir 11:25-28).[54] Later wisdom texts such as the Wisdom of Solomon also incorporate a range of apocalyptic motifs, such as personal immortality, the preservation of the righteous in suffering, and the perfection of the righteous through suffering.[55]

Consolation appears in the prophetic tradition in response to the Babylonian conquest—less so the earlier Assyrian crisis—and the lingering problems of exile and promised restoration.[56] The prophetic voices that have come down to us from the Assyrian crisis contain little that is hopeful.[57] Foreign domination is deserved and will likely be permanent.[58] Looking back on this period, Jeremiah can claim that the mark of a true prophet has been

51 Sermons: Cyprian, *De mort.*; Gregory of Nyssa, *Melet.*; *Pulch.*; *Flac.*; Ambrose, *De exc. Sat.*; *Obit. Valent.*; *Obit. Theod.*; Augustine, *Serm.* 172; 173; Gregory Nazianzen, *Or.* 7; 18. Letters: Jerome, *Ep.* 23; 39; 60; 66; 75; 77; 79; 108; 118; 127; Augustine, *Ep.* 92; 259; 263; Paulinus of Nola, *Carm.* 31; 33; *Ep.* 13; Basil, *Ep.* 5; 6; 28; 29; 31; 140; 238; 247; 256; 257; 301; 302; Ambrose, *Ep.* 15; 39. See Robert C. Gregg, *Consolation Philosophy: Greek and Christian Paideia in Basil and the Two Gregories* (PMS 3; Cambridge, MA: Philadelphia Patristic Foundation, 1975); Scourfield, *Consoling Heliodorus*; Charles Favez, *La consolation latine chrétienne* (Paris: J. Vrin, 1937), which should be supplemented by idem, "Les Epistulae 92, 259 et 263 de S. Augustin," *Museum Helveticum* 1 (1944) 65–68; cf. Juan Chapa, "Consolatory Patterns? 1 Thes 4,13.18; 5,11," in *The Thessalonian Correspondence*, ed. Raymond F. Collins (BEThL 87; Leuven: Leuven University Press, 1990) 220–28.

52 See his comments on Tullia's death and the demise of the Republic at *Ad fam.* 4.6.

53 John J. Collins, "Apocalyptic Eschatology and the Transcendence of Death," *CBQ* 36 (1974) 21–43, here 30; George W. E. Nickelsburg, *1 Enoch 1: A Commentary on 1 Enoch , Chapters 1–36; 81–108* (Hermeneia: Minneapolis: Fortress Press, 2001) 147–

48, 447–48; Nickelsburg and James C. VanderKam, *1 Enoch 2: A Commentary on 1 Enoch, Chapters 37–82* (Hermeneia; Minneapolis: Fortress Press, 2011) 46–47.

54 See James L. Crenshaw, "The Problem of Theodicy in Sirach: On Human Bondage," *JBL* 94 (1975) 47–64.

55 For immortality, see Wis 3:1, 4; for preservation, see Wis 3:9; 4:17; for perfection, see Wis 3:5-6; 11:8-10; 12:20-22; 16:3-6, 11; 18:20; cf. 2 Macc 6:12-16; 7:33.

56 This was already noted by Max Weber, *The Sociology of Religion* (Boston: Beacon Press, 1963) 51; cf. Robert P. Carroll, *When Prophecy Failed: Reactions and Responses to Failure in the Old Testament Prophetic Traditions* (New York: Seabury, 1979) 157–83.

57 There were, of course, dissenting voices, but these have not survived (see Mic 2:6-7; 3:11; Jer 7:4). Later postexilic editors will bring these texts into line with contemporary optimism: Hos 14:1-7; Amos 9:11-15; Mic 7:8-20.

58 Amos 5:2, 18-20; 8:9-14; Isa 13:9-13; Zeph 1:7, 14-16; Joel 2:1-2. Hosea holds out the possibility that the destruction of the nation might not be complete: 2:14-15; 11:1-11; 14:1-8 (MT 14:2-9).

to preach "war, famine, and pestilence" (Jer 28:8).[59] To the degree that these early oracles offered any comfort at all, it was that the destruction of the nation might not be complete (Zeph 2:8) and that God would eventually take vengeance on the nation's enemies, a topos that would become increasingly popular (e.g., Isa 10:7, 15-16; 33:1).[60]

But with the sacking of Jerusalem in 586 BCE things begin to change. Ezekiel is a pivotal figure. He promises a time when Jerusalem will again believe in the justice of God (14:22-23) and when "a new heart and a new spirit" will animate the nation's obedience.[61] Second Isaiah (chaps. 40–55) is even more explicit that the nation has paid fully for its sins and that salvation is at hand.[62] Such enthusiasm was short-lived, however, as it quickly became apparent that these promises would not be fulfilled. This realization made for a different, more long-term set of problems for which new solutions had to be developed.[63] These included a deemphasizing of the political for the spiritual, a projection of salvation onto an ideal eschatological future, and a reimagining of the people of God as a smaller group of the righteous.[64] Each of these strategies was taken up *mutatis mutandis* in apocalypticism, through which they were eventually mediated to early Christianity.

Promises of salvation and vengeance take on new meaning in the apocalyptic tradition, which imagines a time beyond death in which God can still act to bring about justice (*1 Enoch* 98:12). Apocalyptists were particularly anxious to explain what they perceived to be the suffering of the righteous few at the hands of the unrighteous many, who now included unrighteous Jews as well as gentiles.[65] They theorized that the suffering of the righteous was according to a divine plan crafted to accomplish two objectives in the eschatological justice of God: first, to seal the fate of the unrighteous, who would be condemned without mercy in the final judgment, and, second, to guarantee the salvation of the righteous, who were being perfected by their suffering.[66] In support of this theory, apocalyptists also taught that God was even now actively strengthening the righteous so that they might persevere in their sufferings, a doctrine made possible by Ezekiel's prophecy of "a new spirit."[67] Paul uses each of these consolatory themes in his letter to the Philippians: the sealing of the fate of the unrighteous (1:28; 2:15; 3:18-19), the perfecting of the righteous through the suffering of the last days (1:28-30),[68] and the preserving of the righteous by the "spirit of Jesus Christ" (1:6; 2:13).[69]

A final apocalyptic consolatory motif that had significant influence on Paul was belief in an eschatological redeemer who even before the end would serve as a kind of heavenly patron for the people of God. This motif has its origins in the "one like a son of man" figure in Daniel 7, whose fate both parallels and effects the fate of "the people of the holy ones of the Most High." It takes definitive shape, however, in the Righteous and Chosen One/Messiah/Son of Man of the Parables of Enoch (*1 Enoch* 37–71), who unambiguously functions as the heavenly

59 Again, there were dissenting voices (6:14 and 8:11).

60 Nahum 1:15 (MT 2:1) calls the destruction of Nineveh "glad tidings," a term Second Isaiah will apply to Babylon's demise (40:9).

61 Ezek 36:26-28; cf. 11:19-20; 18:31; Jer 31:31-34 (probably a later addition); Isa 44:3. The guarantee that salvation will be permanent is an important theme in apocalypticism: *1 Enoch* 5:8; 10:16, 20, 22; 91:17; 92:5; 1QS 4:18-26, for which see Nickelsburg, *1 Enoch 1*, 162–64.

62 Here see esp. Isa 40:1-2; cf. 43:1-21; 44:24-26; 46:8-13 and passim. For the use of Isa 40:1-3 at Qumran, see Jesper Høgenhaven, "The Literary Character of 4QTanhumim," *DSD* 14 (2007): 99-123; idem, "4QTanhumin (4Q176): Between Exegesis and Treatise?" in *The Mermaid and the Partridge: Essays from the Copenhagen Conference on Revising Texts from Cave Four*, ed. George J. Brooke and Jesper Høgenhaven (STDJ 96; Leiden: Brill, 2011) 151–68.

63 Carroll, *When Prophecy Failed*, esp. 157–83.

64 Here see esp. Joseph Blenkinsopp, *Isaiah 56–66: A New Translation with Introduction and Commentary* (AB 19B; New York: Doubleday, 2003) 80–89; cf. John J. Collins, "From Prophecy to Apocalypticism: The Expectation of the End," in *The Encyclopedia of Apocalypticism*, ed. John J. Collins, vol. 1: *The Origins of Apocalytpicism in Judaism and Christianity* (New York: Continuum, 2000) 129–61; Stephen L. Cook, *Prophecy and Apocalypticism: The Post-Exilic Setting* (Minneapolis: Fortress Press, 1995).

65 At issue here is not human suffering in general—a pressing philosophical problem, to be sure—but the persecution of one's own religious group by outsiders.

66 Dan 11:35; *Pss. Sol.* 10:1-3; 13:8-10; 18:4; cf. 3:3-10.

67 *1 Enoch* 48:47; 1QHᵃ 17:32; Wis 3:9; 4:17.

68 Cf. Phil 1:6, 19; 2:15; 3:9-11, 19.

69 Cf. Phil 1:19; 3:15; 4:13, 19, 23.

counterpart to the "chosen righteous" on earth.[70] Christ is clearly such a figure for Paul, and especially so in Philippians, where undeserved suffering not only perfects believers but, because it recapitulates Christ's own suffering, gains for them a mystical and transformative "knowledge" of him (Phil 3:8). This knowledge begins to change the believer even now and, in the age to come, culminates in a radical metamorphosis that Paul describes as both a glorious physical transformation (3:21) and what he probably imagined as a kind of quasi-personal absorption: "that I might gain Christ and be found *in* him" (3:9).

c. Consolation in Earliest Christianity

Consolation played an important role in early Christian moral education (1 Thess 2:12). It is the principal objective in two New Testament documents, Philippians and Revelation, and is a major theme in at least three others: John (esp. chaps. 13–17, the so-called Farewell Discourse),[71] 1 Thessalonians (esp. 4:12-18),[72] and 1 Peter (esp. 1:1-12; 4:12–5:23),[73] and some would add portions of 2 Corinthians.[74]

Greco-Roman consolation predominates in Philippians, John 13–17, and 1 Pet 4:12–5:23. I have already intimated the various consolatory arguments that Paul employs in Philippians and will return to these frequently over the course of the commentary. The author of 1 Peter employs the Cyrenaic topos "nothing unexpected has happened" in 4:12, when he exhorts his readers, "Do not be surprised by the fiery ordeal now testing you, as if something unexpected has occurred." Jesus's post-factum prediction of suffering in John 16:1-4 probably conveyed a similar message to that Gospel's first readers.

Paul deploys the same topos in passing in 1 Thess 3:2-4: "we told you beforehand that we were about to suffer." Elsewhere in the Farewell Discourse Jesus consoles his followers that his death is for the good (John 16:6-7)[75] and that he will send the Spirit as his replacement ("another advocate"; John 14:16),[76] a role Timothy plays in Phil 2:19-24.[77]

Jewish consolation, especially as it was developed in the apocalyptic tradition, is found throughout the New Testament. Key texts include Rom 8:31-39; 1 Thess 4:12-18; 1 Pet 1:1-12; and Revelation. The correlative topics of personal salvation and the judgment of one's enemies dominate the book of Revelation. They are also present in 1 Pet 1:1-12, but in much more nuanced tones, where the readers' rewards have already been prepared and are being held in safekeeping, and where it is promised that the readers themselves are being preserved for their final reward (cf. 5:12; 1 Thess 5:23; Jude 24). The theme also appears briefly in Phil 1:28 and 3:18-21. 1 Thessalonians 4:12-18 offers a concrete hope of resurrection spelled out by means of a complicated apocalyptic timetable and urges its readers to "comfort one another with these words."

The belief that the Messiah is a heavenly being who already represents the faithful before the throne of God is particularly prevalent, for obvious reasons. It can be found most famously in Rom 8:31-39, but in one form or another dominates New Testament Christology. It is especially important for Paul, who claims not only that the exalted Christ is the believer's advocate in heaven but also that the promised eschatological spirit is actually "the spirit of Jesus Christ" that even now possesses

70 Here see esp. John J. Collins, "The Heavenly Representative: The 'Son of Man' in the Similitudes of Enoch," in *Ideal Figures in Ancient Judaism: Profiles and Paradigms*, ed. John J. Collins and George W. E. Nickelsburg (SCS 12; Chico, CA: Scholars Press, 1980) 111–33; cf. Nickelsburg and VanderKam, *1 Enoch 2*, 98–101, 113–23.

71 Holloway, "Left Behind."

72 Abraham J. Malherbe, *The Letters to the Thessalonians* (AB 32B; New York: Doubleday, 2000) on 1 Thess 4:12-18.

73 Paul A. Holloway, "*Nihil inopinati accidisse* – 'Nothing unexpected has happened': A Cyrenaic Consolatory Topos in 1 Pet 4.12ff.," *NTS* 48 (2002) 433–48; idem, *Coping with Prejudice*, 214–29.

74 Ben Kaplan, "Comfort, O Comfort, Corinth: Grief and Comfort in 2 Cor 7:5-13a," *HTR* 104 (2011) 433–45.

75 Klaus Berger, *Formgeschichte des Neuen Testaments* (Heidelberg: Quelle & Meyer, 1984) 81.

76 Holloway, "Left Behind," 24–25; cf. George L. Parsenios, *Departure and Consolation: The Johannine Farewell Discourse in Light of Greco-Roman Literature* (NovTSup 117; Leiden: Brill, 2005).

77 Paul A. Holloway, "*Alius Paulus*: On Paul's Promise to Send Timothy in Phil 2.19-24," *NTS* 54 (2008) 542-56.

all believers (Gal 4:6; Phil 1:19).[78] Taken together, these notions make possible Paul's famous "Christ-mysticism," in evidence, among other places, in Philippians 3 and 2 Corinthians 3–4.

2. Literary Integrity of Canonical Philippians

A generation ago most critical scholars were agreed that Philippians as it appears in the manuscript tradition is a composite document pasted together from two or three originally separate Pauline letters.[79] Today that view has largely been abandoned,[80] but there are complications. On the one hand, the ranks of those who reject the partitioning of the letter are swelled by a host of religiously conservative commentators whose conclusions one cannot help but suspect have been determined by theological commitments as well as historical judgments.[81] At the same time, there are still a number of important critical scholars who hold to some type of partition theory, though in this case it is noteworthy that most but not all of these scholars formed their opinions decades ago when source theories were much more in vogue than they are today.[82] Considerations such as these, while not wholly irrelevant, are notoriously difficult to assess and run the obvious risks of ad hominem argument, on the one hand, and appeals to authority, on the other. Thus, despite the present shift in opinion, it is still advisable to take the problem of the literary integrity of Philippians seriously, even if in the current climate to do so may strike some as pedantic.

---

78 Cf. the role of the Paraclete, who not only replaces the absent Jesus but in many ways is that Jesus in another form (Holloway, "Left Behind").

79 See my *Consolation*, 7–33 for a slightly fuller version of these arguments. The modern debate over the integrity of the epistle derives from four apparently independent studies published between 1957 and 1960: Walter Schmithals, "Die Irrlehrer des Philipperbriefes," *ZThK* 54 (1957) 297–341 (revised for *Paulus und die Gnostiker: Untersuchungen zu den kleinen Paulusbriefen* [ThF 35; Hamburg-Bergstedt: Herbert Reich, 1965] 47–87; citations hereafter are from the English translation: "The False Teachers of the Epistle to the Philippians," in idem, *Paul and the Gnostics* [Nashville: Abingdon, 1972] 65–122); J. Müller-Bardorff, "Zur Frage der literarischen Einheit des Philipperbriefes," *WZJena* 7 (1957–58) 591–604; B. D. Rahtjen, "The Three Letters of Paul to the Philippians," *NTS* (1959–60) 167–73; and F. W. Beare, *A Commentary on the Epistle to the Philippians* (BNTC; London: A. & C. Black, 1959; citations hereafter are from the 3rd ed.) 1–5, 24–29. Subsequent studies have added little to the case for partitioning; e.g., Helmut Koester, "The Purpose of the Polemic of a Pauline Fragment (Philippians III)," *NTS* 8 (1961–62) 317–32. On the early debate, see the helpful clarifications by David Cook, "Stephanus Le Moyne and the Dissection of Philippians," *JTS* 32 (1981) 138–42; Veronica Koperski, "The Early History of the Dissection of Philippians," *JTS* 44 (1993) 599–603.

80 Udo Schnelle, *The History and Theology of the New Testament Writings* (Minneapolis: Fortress Press, 1998) 135–38; Raymond E. Brown, *An Introduction to the New Testament* (ABRL; New York: Doubleday, 1997) 496–98; cf. Horst Balz, "Philipperbrief," *TRE* 26:504–13.

81 E.g., Gerald F. Hawthorne, *Philippians* (WBC 43; Waco, TX: Word, 1983; 2nd ed. revised and expanded by Ralph P. Martin [Nashville: Nelson Reference & Electronic, 2004]); Peter T. O'Brien, *The Epistle to the Philippians: A Commentary on the Greek Text* (NIGTC; Grand Rapids: Eerdmans, 1991); Moises Silva, *Philippians* (Baker Exegetical Commentary on the New Testament; Grand Rapids: Baker Academic, 1992; 2nd ed., 2005); Gordon D. Fee, *Paul's Letter to the Philippians* (NICNT; Grand Rapids: Eerdmans, 1995); Marcus Bockmuehl, *The Epistle to the Philippians* (BNTC; London: A. & C. Black; Peabody, MA: Hendrickson, 1998); Ben Witherington, *Paul's Letter to the Philippians: A Socio-rhetorical Commentary* (Grand Rapids: Eerdmans, 2011). There are, of course, many fine exegetical observations in some of these commentaries.

82 E.g., Hans Dieter Betz, *Studies in Paul's Letter to the Philippians* (WUNT 343; Tübingen: Mohr Siebeck, 2015) 9–10; Helmut Koester, *Introduction to the New Testament* (2nd ed.; 2 vols.; New York/Berlin: Walter de Gruyter, 1995, 2000) 2:136–38; John Reumann, *Philippians: A New Translation with Introduction and Commentary* (AYB 33B; New Haven: Yale University Press, 2008) 8–13. But see also Philip Sellew, "*Laodiceans* and the Philippians Fragments Hypothesis," *HTR* 87 (1994) 17–28; Lukas Bormann, *Philippi: Stadt und Christengemeinde zur Zeit des Paulus* (NovTSup 78; Leiden: Brill, 1995); Jean-Baptiste Edart, *L'Épître aux Philippiens: Rhétorique et composition stylistique* (EB 45; Paris: Gabalda, 2002).

Scholars who partition Philippians have typically understood it to be a composite of three separate letters,[83] the first two of which at least were written while Paul was in prison.[84] These are, in chronological order: Letter A (4:10-20), a short thank-you note sent immediately after the arrival of Epaphroditus with a gift from the Philippians; Letter B (1:1—3:1), a letter of reassurance sent with Epaphroditus upon his return; and Letter C (3:2—4:3), a polemical letter sent at some later date (perhaps after his release) when Paul had become more fully apprised of the theological debate at Philippi.[85] The remaining material in 4:4-9 and 4:21-23 is variously assigned, though usually 4:4-7 and 21-23 are assigned to Letter B.[86] Evidence adduced in support of this hypothesis falls into two categories: (1) external evidence suggesting that Philippians is a composite, and (2) internal

evidence variously pointing to 3:2—4:3 and 4:10-20 as fragments of separate letters.

a. External Evidence That Philippians Is a Composite

Four pieces of external evidence have been adduced in support of the theory that Philippians is a composite. Three of these support the more general claim that Paul wrote more than one letter to the church at Philippi and are of little direct consequence.[87] They are (1) the listing of Philippians twice in the *Catalogus Sinaiticus*,[88] (2) the mention of a "first epistle to the Philippians" in the *Chronographia* of the ninth-century Byzantine historian Georgius Syncellus,[89] and (3) a reference by Polycarp in *Ad Phil.* 3.2 to Paul's "letters" (ἐπιστολαί) to the Philippians.[90] Recently, however, Philip Sellew has introduced a fourth piece of external evidence that speaks more directly to the

---

83   The three-letter hypothesis is the more common. For the two-letter hypothesis, see Joachim Gnilka, *Der Philipperbrief* (3rd ed.; HThKNT 10.3; Freiburg: Herder, 1980) 7–10; Gerhard Friedrich, *Der Brief an die Philipper* (15th ed.; NTD 8; Göttingen: Vandenhoeck & Ruprecht, 1981) 126–28; cf. Jürgen Becker, *Paul: Apostle to the Gentiles* (Louisville: Westminster John Knox, 1993) 307–10. Gnilka: Letter A: 1:1–3:1a; 4:2-7, 10-23; Letter B: 3:1b–4:1, 8-9. Friedrich: Letter A: 1:1–3:1a; 4:10-23; Letter B: 3:1b–4:9; Becker: Letter A: 1:1–3:1; 4:1-7, 10-23; Letter B: 3:2-21; 4:8-9.

84   Jerome Murphy O'Connor argues that Letter A (4:10-20) may have been sent before Paul was imprisoned (*Paul: A Critical Life* [Oxford: Oxford University Press, 1996] 216–18).

85   F. F. Bruce is, to my knowledge, unique in arguing that "Letter C" was sent not after but before Paul's imprisonment ("St. Paul in Macedonia 3: The Philippian Correspondence," *BJRL* 63 [1981] 260–84, here 281).

86   See the table in Bormann, *Philippi*, 110.

87   Rahtjen, "Three Letters," 167–68. Rahtjen's evidence is typically relegated to the footnotes, even by those who partition the letter, e.g., Gnilka, p. 11 n. 57; Walter Schmithals, "The False Teachers of the Epistle to the Philippians," in Schmithals, *Paul and the Gnostics* (Nashbille: Abingdon, 1972) 65–122, here 81 n. 59.

88   A. S. Lewis, ed., *Catalogue of the Syriac MSS. in the Convent of S. Catherine on Mount Sinai* (Studia Sinaitica 1; London: C. J. Clay, 1894) 4–16.

89   W. Dindorf, ed., *Corpus Scriptorum Historiae Byzantinae* (Bonn: Weber, 1828) 12:651 (= 420.14

90

Mosshammer): "The Apostle [Paul] has also remembered this man [= Clement] saying in the first letter to the Philippians, 'with Clement and the rest of my coworkers.'" Ironically, this citation, if taken at face value, actually counts against the modern partition theory, since it assigns Phil 4:3, which is either from Letter B or from Letter C according to the critical reconstruction, to "the first letter to the Philippians [ἡ πρὸς Φιλιππησίους πρώτη ἐπιστολή]." Various explanations of the plural have been offered. J. B. Lightfoot suggests that it is used idiomatically for the singular (*The Apostolic Fathers* [London/New York: Macmillan, 1889] part 2, vol. 3:327, 348). Theodor Zahn proposes that it refers to an early collection of Paul's letters to Macedonia and thus includes 1 Thessalonians (*Introduction to the New Testament* [trans. John Moore Trout et al. from 3rd German ed.; 3 vols.; New York: Scribners, 1909] 1:535–36). Walter Bauer wonders, quite plausibly in my view, whether Polycarp has simply inferred an additional letter on the basis of 3:1 ("to write the same things [again] to you") (*Die Apostolischen Väter*, vol. 2: *Die Briefe des Ignatius von Antiochien und der Polykarpbrief* [HNT 18; Tübingen: Mohr Siebeck, 1920] 287). That this was a common reading of this verse can be seen in Theodoret, who feels it necessary to argue that this phrase does not imply another letter: οὐκ ἄλλην αὐτοῖς ἐπιστολὴν γέγραφεν ("he has not written another letter to them"). That Polycarp's comment derives from an interpretation of canonical Philippians is consistent with the fact that it may reflect Phil 1:27 (*Ad Phil.* 3.2: "and who [= Paul] when he was absent [ἀπών] wrote you letters"; cf. Phil 1:27: "or remain absent [ἀπών]").

issue of partitioning.[91] Finding that the pseudepigraphical *Epistle to the Laodiceans*,[92] which draws upon Philippians for both its content and its structure,[93] contains no reference either to Letter C (Phil 3:2–4:3 + 4:7-9) or Letter A (Phil 4:10-20) of the critical reconstruction, he concludes that the compiler of *Laodiceans* used a version of Philippians lacking both of these fragments and thus similar to Letter B (Phil 1:1–3:1 + 4:4-6 + 4:20-23).

This is an intriguing piece of evidence, and Sellew has done well to spot it. Nevertheless, there are, I believe, at least two problems with his analysis.[94] First, it is not at all clear, as Sellew must maintain, that *Laodiceans* contains no reference to the so-called *Kampfbrief* of Phil 3:2–4:3, since *Laod.* 13, which reads "rejoice [*gaudete*] in Christ and beware [*praecavete*] of those who have defiled themselves for profit," reproduces quite remarkably the trou-

bling χαίρετε . . . βλέπετε ("rejoice . . . beware") of Phil 3:1-2.[95] Second, there are some rather obvious explanations why the compiler of *Laodiceans* would have chosen to omit the bulk of Phil 3:2–4:3 along with Phil 4:10-20.

For instance, one might argue regarding the omission of material from so-called Letter C (3:2–4:3): (1) that *Laodiceans*, like its companion pseudepigraphon Colossians (cf. Col 4:15), purports to be written from prison, (2) that almost all the material in *Laodiceans* excerpted from Philippians pertains to Paul's imprisonment,[96] and thus (3) that Phil 3:2–4:2, which makes no explicit mention of Paul's imprisonment, was passed over en masse, with the possible exception of 3:2, as noted in the previous paragraph. Similarly, regarding the omission of so-called Letter A (4:10-20), one might reason that, just as those portions of so-called Letter B that focus on Paul's

91 Sellew, "*Laodiceans.*"

92 Originally composed in Greek, *Laodiceans* survives in Latin and several late vernaculars. A critical Latin text may be found in Rudolf Anger, *Über den Laodicenerbrief: Eine biblisch-kritische Untersuchung* (Leipzig: Gebhardt & Reisland, 1843) 155–65; J. B. Lightfoot, *St. Paul's Epistle to the Colossians and to Philemon* (London: Macmillan, 1892) 281–91. For an English translation of *Laodiceans*, see *NTApoc* (1992) 2:42–46.

93 Anger, *Laodicenerbrief*, 155–65; J. B. Lightfoot, *St. Paul's Epistle to the Philippians: A Revised Text with Introduction, Notes, and Dissertations* (London: Macmillan, 1868) 293–94; Adolf von Harnack, *Marcion: Das Evangelium vom fremden Gott; Eine Monographie zur Geschichte der Grundlegung der katholischen Kirche* (Darmstadt: Wissenschaftliche Buchgesellschaft, 1960; reprint of 2nd ed., 1924) Beilage 3, 140; cf. Sellew, "*Laodiceans*," 28.

94 For a more detailed discussion of these problems, see Paul A. Holloway, "The Apocryphal *Epistle to the Laodiceans* and the Partitioning of Philippians," *HTR* 91 (1998) 321–25, with response by Philip Sellew, "*Laodiceans* and Philippians Revisited: A Response to Paul Holloway," *HTR* 91 (1998) 327–29.

95 Anger (*Laodicenerbrief*, 162) calls *Laod.* 13b an allusion (*Anspielung*) to Phil 3:2 with an additional reference (*Rücksicht*) to 3:7-8; cf. Lightfoot, *Colossians*, 291; Karl Pink, "Die pseudo-paulinischen Briefe II," *Bib* 6 (1925) 179–200, here 190. This kind of synthesis is typical of *Laodiceans* (e.g., *Laod.* 6 [which conflates Phil 1:13 and 8]; *Laod.* 7 [Phil 1:19-20]; *Laod.* 9 [Phil 2:1-2]; *Laod.* 15-16 [Phil 4:8-9]). Sellew objects to this interpretation on the grounds that the Vulgate translates the βλέπετε of Phil 3:2

with *videte* not *praecavete* ("*Laodiceans*," 23 n. 17). But this is beside the point, (1) because the Latin text of *Laodiceans* frequently departs from both the Vulgate and the Old Latin versions of Philippians, and (2) because the Latin translator of the original Greek of *Laodiceans* almost certainly did not check his translation against the translation of the various sources in the Corpus Paulinum as identified in the modern critical analysis of the document—presumably he thought *Laodiceans* was authentic—but rendered them directly as he was able. Nevertheless, it is worth noting that at least one Old Latin version, Frede's Text Type I, derivable from Victorinus's commentaries on Ephesians, Philippians, and Colossians, translates with the cognate *caveo* (*cavete a canibus*), a reference no doubt to the common expression *cave canem*; see Hermann Josef Frede, *Epistulae Ad Philippenses et Ad Colossenses* (Vetus Latina 24.1; Freiburg im Breisgau: Herder, 1996–71) on Phil 3:2. A similar translation (*cavete canes*) is found in Ambrose (*Hexam.* 5.6 [*PL* 14:222A; CSEL 32.1.144.10]) and Augustine (*Ep.* 79 [*PL* 33:273.8; CSEL 34.2.346.12]; *In Psalm.* 67.32.4 [*PL* 36:833.18; CCSL 39:892]); cf. Donatien de Bruyne, *Préfaces de la Bible latine* (Namur: Godenne, 1920) 240: *admonet etiam ut caveant a pseudoapostolis.*

96 Of the nineteen or so verses excerpted from Philippians (1:2, 3, 12[?], 13, 18-21; 2:2, 12-14; 3:1-2[?]; 4:6, 8-9; 22-23), three of which are taken up with greetings and farewells (1:2; 4:22-23), at least seven directly pertain to Paul's imprisonment (1:12-13, 18-21; 2:12), while six others treat the readers' response to Paul's imprisonment (2:2 [cf. its rendering in *Laod.* 9], 13-14; 4:6, 8-9).

unique relationship with the Philippians were omitted by the compiler of *Laodiceans* (e.g., all of 2:19-30, which relates the plans regarding Timothy and Epaphroditus, is missing),[97] so also 4:10-20 was omitted as pertaining to the gift the Philippians had sent Paul. As intriguing as the evidence from *Laodiceans* is, it does not support a partitioning of Philippians.

b. Internal Evidence That Philippians 3:2—4:3 Is a Letter Fragment

The internal evidence for partitioning Philippians has always been where the major objections to reading the letter as an original unity lie. In discussing this evidence it will be important to distinguish between (1) evidence that points to 3:2—4:3 as a separate letter fragment and (2) evidence that points to 4:10-20 as a separate fragment. These two *independent* bodies of evidence cannot be added together to make a cumulative case for partitioning.[98]

The evidence pointing to 3:2—4:3 as a separate fragment may be grouped around three claims: (1) that 3:2—4:3 reflects a different set of circumstances than 1:1—3:1,[99] (2) that the travel plans described in 2:19—3:1

signal the end of a typical Pauline letter,[100] and, most influentially, (3) that the abrupt shift in tone between 3:1 and 3:2 marks a later editorial seam.

The first two claims founder on false assumptions. The first claim assumes that the "enemies" casually mentioned in 1:28 are the same as the teachers vehemently attacked as "dogs" in 3:2.[101] But, as 1:29-30 makes plain, the "enemies" of 1:28 are not teachers posing a theological danger to the community but political opponents threatening legal action and imprisonment.[102] The shift in Paul's mood between 1:28 and 3:2 is therefore to be explained not as a change in circumstances but as a change of subject. Similarly, the second claim, that the travel plans discussed in 2:19-30 indicate the end of a Pauline letter, assumes an ideal Pauline letter form[103] that does not fit the actual evidence of Paul's letters. Sometimes Paul mentions travel plans near the end of a letter (Rom 15:22-29; 1 Cor 16:5-12; Phlm 22),[104] and sometimes in the middle (1 Thess 2:17—3:13; Rom 1:10-15; 1 Cor 4:14-20). In the present instance, the sending of both Timothy and Epaphroditus is well placed as they continue the consolation of 1:12-26 + 2:17-18.[105]

---

97   Sellew is not unaware of this criterion. For instance, regarding the omission of Phil 2:25-30 he writes, "The discussion of Epaphroditus's illness at the end of Philippians 2 presumably had no relevance for the fictional audience in Laodicea" ("*Laodiceans*," 26). He simply does not apply it consistently to the composition of *Laodiceans*.

98   Contra Reumann, p. 9.

99   Schmithals ("False Teachers," 74) believes that the change lies with Paul, while Müller-Bardorff ("Frage," 591) feels that changes have also occurred at Philippi.

100   See Schmithals, "False Teachers," 70, and the literature cited there; also Beare, p. 95, but especially Robert W. Funk, *Language, Hermeneutic, and Word of God: The Problem of Language in the New Testament and Contemporary Theology* (New York: Harper & Row, 1966) 248–49, 257, 263û74. I discuss Funk at length in *Consolation*, 19–23. More generally, see W. G. Doty, *Letters in Primitive Christianity* (Guides to Biblical Scholarship; Philadelphia: Fortress, 1973); Terrence Y. Mullins, "Visit Talk in New Testament Letters," *CBQ* 35 (1973) 350–58.

101   Schmithals, "False Teachers," 69–70; Müller-Bardorff, "Frage," 592; Willi Marxsen, *Introduction to the New Testament: An Approach to Its Problems,* trans. G. Buswell (Oxford: Blackwell, 1968) 61.

102   Cf. 1 Thess 2:2; Acts 16:20-21. Even those who partition the letter on other grounds see the problem here: Günther Bornkamm, "Der Philipperbrief als paulinische Briefsammlung," in *Neotesamentica et Patristica: Eine Freundesgabe Herrn Professor Dr. Oscar Cullmann* (NovTSup 6; Leiden: Brill, 1962) 192–202, here 197–98; Gnilka, pp. 8, 99–100; Bormann, *Philippi*, 218–20. Bornkamm ("Briefsammlung," 197) and Gnilka (pp. 9, 13) have also pointed out that in 3:2—4:3 Paul makes no explicit mention of his imprisonment, a dominant motif in chaps. 1–2. This, however, is not so much an argument for partitioning as a consequence of it. There is nothing that required Paul to make repeated explicit mention of his imprisonment in Philippians. That being said, however, allusions to imprisonment may be found in Paul's references to having lost all things in 3:8, to the fellowship of Christ's sufferings in 3:10, to the cross of Christ in 3:18, and his final eschatological appeal in 3:20-21.

103   This was an elusive desideratum of a previous generation of Pauline scholars; see, e.g., Funk, *Language*, 250–74.

104   This was, of course, not a uniquely Pauline practice; cf. 2 John 12; 3 John 13-14.

105   Chrysostom (hom. 11.212.11-12); see the commentary below on Phil 2:19-30.

The principal argument for partitioning Philippians is the third claim—that an abrupt shift in tone between 3:1 ("rejoice!") and 3:2 ("beware!") indicates a later editorial seam.[106] Here is Edgar J. Goodspeed's frequently cited explanation:

> In 3:1 all is serene; [the Philippians] must not mind Paul's repeating himself, for it is for their own good. But in the next verse he breaks out against the Judaizers with an intensity unsurpassed even in Galatians. . . . This sharp change after 3:1 . . . raises the question whether our Philippians does not break at this point into two letters.[107]

Attempts to smooth this break have focused on 3:2 and have sought by one means or another to qualify its alleged unsurpassed intensity. They have been only marginally persuasive.[108] But as Goodspeed's explanation makes plain, Paul's "intensity" in 3:2 is problematic only because 3:1 has already been judged "serene."[109]

Scholars have consistently underestimated the seriousness of Paul's command to "rejoice in the Lord" in 3:1a.[110] Kirsopp Lake is characteristic when he asks, "Is it natural to say 'rejoice in the Lord always [sic]' and then suddenly say 'Beware of the dogs'?"[111] The answer, of course, is yes, provided one does not trivialize Paul's command to "rejoice in the Lord." It is telling in this regard that Lake misquotes Phil 3:1a, adding "always" as in 4:4. Lake's unstated assumption is clear: Paul's command to rejoice in the Lord in 3:1a is a piece of general parenesis—which Lake and most others of his generation also trivialized—and belongs with the other pieces of generic advice collected at the end of a Pauline letter.

The tendency among scholars to trivialize Paul's command to rejoice in 3:1 is symptomatic of the larger tendency to trivialize Paul's repeated use of "joy" and its cognates in the letter. J. Müller-Bardorff is typical in his repeated allusions to a "Grundton der Freude" in the first two chapters of Philippians, which he then contrasts to the utterly serious "Kampfbrief" of 3:2-21.[112] But this fails to take into account the purposive way in which Paul uses "joy" to confront the Philippians with a philosophical ideal and to urge them to behave in a manner "worthy of the gospel" (1:27).[113]

106 So Schmithals, "False Teachers," 68–72; Beare, pp. 3–4; Rahtjen, "Three Letters," 168; Müller-Bardorff, "Frage," 592; Gnilka, p. 7; Jean François Collange, *The Epistle of Saint Paul to the Philippians* (London: Epworth, 1979) 4.

107 Edgar J. Goodspeed, *An Introduction to the New Testament* (Chicago: University of Chicago Press, 1937) 90-91.

108 E.g., G. D. Kilpatrick, "ΒΛΕΠΕΤΕ in Phil 3:2," in *In Memoriam Paul Kahle*, ed. Matthew Black and Georg Fohrer (BZAW 103; Berlin: Töpelmann, 1968) 146–48, who argues unconvincingly that βλέπετε in 3:2 is to be translated "consider" and not "beware"; cf. BDF §149.

109 This point, which is obvious enough, has to my knowledge been universally overlooked by commentators. I do not know how to explain this oversight except to say that the initial formulation of the problem focused attention exclusively on 3:2 and ignored 3:1. At any rate, regarding the alleged break *between* 3:1 and 3:2, 3:1 is every bit as much a part of the equation as 3:2.

110 To some extent this is a question of translation. Thus Goodspeed renders "Good bye and the Lord be with you" (*Problems of New Testament Translation* [Chicago: University of Chicago Press, 1945] 174–75); cf. Beare, pp. 100, 145–46; Rahtjen, "Three Letters," 171. But prior to 3:1 Paul has used χαίρω and its cognates a total of eleven times, always with the sense of "rejoice," and it is only natural to continue to translate it "rejoice" here. To do otherwise requires that one has *already* decided on other grounds in favor of the partition theory.

111 Kirsopp Lake, "Critical Problems of the Epistle to the Philippians," *The Expositor* 8, no.7 (1914) 485.

112 Müller-Bardorff, "Frage," 591–92; cf. Bornkamm, "Briefsammlung," 194; Marxsen, *Introduction*, 63; Collange, p. 4; Rahtjen, "Three Letters," 170; Ulrich B. Müller, *Der Brief des Paulus an die Philipper* (ThHKNT 11.1; Leipzig: Evangelische Verlagsanstalt, 1993) 28, 136.

113 P. F. Aspan comes close to this insight when he writes, "Philippians is not a joyful letter, as is often suggested. Rather, the 'rhetoric of joy' represents a manifestation of the *Vollendungen* towards which the letter is exhorting the audience" ("Toward a New Reading of Paul's Letter to the Philippians in Light of a Kuhnian Analysis of New Testament Criticism" [Ph.D. diss., Vanderbilt University, 1990], 289). Johann A. Bengel's familiar summary of the letter makes much the same point: *Gaudeo, gaudete,* "I rejoice, now you do the same!" (*Gnomon Novi Testamenti* [3rd ed.; Stuttgart: J. F. Steinkopf, 1860; original, 1773] 766).

Paul models this ideal himself by his own "joyful" response to hardship. Like the philosopher whose happiness rests solely on "the things that really matter" (1:10)—or, as Seneca puts it, who has learned "that one must not rejoice in empty things" (*Ep.* 23:1)[114]—Paul's experience of joy remains undiminished even though he is in prison awaiting trial on capital charges (1:18; 2:17-18). This is significant for a number of reasons, not the least of which is that "joy," as we have already noted, can be read as the measure of a person's "progress" toward perfection and, for Paul, salvation. "He has made it to the top," Seneca writes, "who understands the proper object of joy [*qui scit, quo gaudeat*], who has not placed his happiness in the power of externals" (*Ep.* 23.2).[115] This is precisely the way Paul deploys the term in Philippians.[116]

I note that these similarities were not lost on Chrysostom, whose native understanding of Paul's Greek and its cultural connotations must be taken seriously. Here are his comments on Phil 1:18, which are worth quoting at length:

The great and philosophic soul is vexed by none of the grievous things of this life, not enmities, accusations, slanders, perils or plots. . . . And such was the soul of Paul. . . . That blessed man had not only the emperor

waging war against him, but many others attempting to grieve him in many ways, even with bitter slander. But what does he say? Not only "I am not hurt or overcome by these things," but "I rejoice and I will rejoice."[117]

Seneca makes a remarkably similar claim in *Ad Helv.* 4.2. Writing from exile, he consoles his mother that his deportation is really a matter of indifference (*nihil mihi mali esse*, "nothing bad has happened to me") and that his "joy" (*gaudium*) remains unaffected by it (*Ad Helv.* 4.2; cf. 4.1; 5.1). Far from something to be trivialized, therefore, a properly placed joy is for both Paul and Seneca "a matter of the utmost importance" (*res severa*).[118]

We will have occasion to return to the philosophical and consolatory topos of joy over the course of this commentary. It should be clear at this point, however, that Paul's command in 3:1a is anything but a moral cliché.[119] When this is duly noted, not only does the alleged shift in tone from 3:1 to 3:2 disappear, but also 3:1a becomes a natural introduction to the rest of chap. 3, where, having urged the Philippians to "rejoice in the Lord," Paul goes on to celebrate his "knowledge of Christ Jesus my Lord."[120]

---

114 Seneca, *Ep.* 23.1: "What is the foundation that you seek? That one must not rejoice in empty things. Did I say 'foundation'—it is the apex!"

115 Two sentences later Seneca exhorts Lucilius: "This do before anything else, my dear Lucilius, learn how to rejoice" (*Hoc ante omnia fac, mi Lucili: disce gaudere*), which calls back to mind Bengel's apt summary of Philippians: *Summa epistolae: gaudeo, gaudete*. For Seneca, of course, the object of joy was one's own virtue (*de tuo gaude*; *Ep.* 23.6), whereas for Paul it is the progress of the gospel (1:12-18b), the salvation of the confessing believer (1:18c-21), and ultimately that believer's knowledge of Christ (3:1–4:1). One of Paul's principal concerns in Philippians is to instruct the Philippians how to rejoice in these truly important things so as not to be grieved by the things that do not matter.

116 See esp. 1:25, where Paul explicitly links "progress" and "joy."

117 Hom. 4.58.7-17 Allen; cf. 1.6.11-13: "In the beginning of his letter Paul offers the Philippians much consolation [πολλὴν παράκλησιν] regarding his imprisonment, showing [by his own example] not

only that they should not be grieved, but that they should rejoice [χαίρειν]."

118 Seneca, *Ep.* 23.4: *Crede mihi, verum gaudium res severa est.*

119 See Peter Wick, *Der Philipperbrief: Der formale Aufbau des Briefs als Schlüssel zum Verständnis seines Inhalts* (BWANT 7/15; Stuttgart: Kohlhammer, 1994) esp. 61–63, 82–85; cf. P. Rolland, "La structure littéraire et l'unité de l'Epître aux Philippiens," *RevScRel* 64 (1990) 213–16.

120 See Bernhard Weiss, *Philipper-Brief ausgelegt und die Geschichte seiner Auslegung kritisch dargestellt* (3rd ed.; Berlin: Hertz, 1859) 214–57; Johann Christian Konrad von Hofmann, *Die Heilige Schrift des Neuen Testaments zusammenhängend untersucht*, Teil 4, 3. Abt., *Der Brief Pauli an die Philipper* (8th ed.; Nördlingen: Beck, 1872); Ernst Lohmeyer, *Der Brief an die Philipper, an die Kolosser und an Philemon* (KEK 9; Göttingen: Vandenhoeck & Ruprecht, 1953) 123–24; cf. Wayne A. Meeks, "The Man from Heaven in Philippians," in *The Future of Early Christianity: Essays in Honor of Helmut Koester*, ed. Birger A. Pearson (Minneapolis: Fortress Press, 1991) 332.

c. Internal Evidence That Philippians 4:10-20 Is a Letter Fragment

The evidence suggesting that 4:10-20 derives from a separate letter may also be grouped around three claims: (1) that Phil 2:25-30 presupposes communications between Paul and the Philippians notifying them of Epaphroditus's illness and in which Paul must have already thanked the Philippians for their gift, making the thank-you of 4:10-20 redundant in its present context;[121] (2) that 4:10-20, which conveys Paul's formal expression of thanks to the Philippians for their gift, comes unacceptably late in a letter specifically written to acknowledge that gift;[122] and (3) that 4:10-20 is a self-contained pericope loosely tied to the rest of the letter that may be read, if there is warrant to do so, as a separate thank-you note.[123]

These claims are of varying merit. For instance, it is simply not the case that 2:25-30 implies additional communication between Paul and the Philippians. It is clear from 2:26-27 that the Philippians did not know of the eventual severity of Epaphroditus's illness, indicating that any report they received about it told only of its initial stage, while 2:30 implies that Epaphroditus fell ill on the road and that it was in pressing on to Paul to deliver the Philippians' gift that he "drew near to death." Taken together, these two texts strongly suggest that it was someone passing Epaphroditus in the opposite direction that brought news of his developing condition to the Philippians, and that afterwards they had received no further

communication.[124] Further, we are not told how Epaphroditus learned of the Philippians' concern for him. Word may have gotten back to him—it could have arrived shortly after he did—or he may simply have assumed that they were worried, knowing that the individual who passed him on the road would tell them of his condition.[125]

Similarly, the claim that the thank-you note of 4:10-20 comes unacceptably late in a letter, whose primary purpose was to thank the Philippians for their gift, assumes that the primary purpose of Paul's letter was to express thanks.[126] But this assumption is by no means obvious. Given the difficulty of finding a suitable letter carrier and the delays this inevitably involved, it was often the case that ancient letters served several functions.[127] Further, if we accept the commonly held view that Paul communicates his primary concern in writing a given letter in his introductory prayer report,[128] then the overriding purpose of Paul's letter to the Philippians will have been to remind them of "the things that really matter" (1:10). Indeed, a major rhetorical hurdle facing Paul in corresponding with the Philippians was how to thank them for their gift while at the same time maintaining that such externals do *not* really matter.[129] This more than accounts for the placement of 4:10-20 after Paul's discussion of the things that matter in the body of the letter, as well as for Paul's jarring insistence on his own self-sufficiency (4:13-14) in the very act of expressing his appreciation.[130] Paul's so-called thankless thanks is difficult enough to under-

---

121 Schmithals, "False Teachers," 78; Rahtjen ("Three Letters," 169–70) also argues that the aorists of 2:25 and 28 are historical (not epistolary) aorists; but see B. S. Mackay, "Further Thoughts on Philippians," *NTS* 7 (1961) 161–70, here 165–66; David Garland, "The Composition and Unity of Philippians: Some Neglected Literary Features," *NovT* 27 (1985) 141–73, here 150 n. 34.

122 Collange, pp. 5–6; Schmithals ("False Teachers," 77) refers to the placement of 4:10-20 as a case of "unbelievable" forgetfulness.

123 Collange, p. 5.

124 There is no problem in this gap in communication, since finding a suitable letter carrier could be a problem even for someone of Cicero's status (*Ad Att.* 1.13.1; cited by Mackay, "Further Thoughts," 169).

125 C. O. Buchanan, "Epaphroditus' Sickness and the Letter to the Philippians," *EvQ* 36 (1964) 158-60; cf. Garland, "Composition and Unity," 151; F. F. Bruce, "St. Paul in Macedonia 3," 274–77.

126 Once we allow that to thank the Philippians was not Paul's primary purpose, then the positioning of 4:10-20 is altogether unproblematic; cf. Ignatius, *Smyrn.* 10.1–2.

127 Cf. Pseudo-Libanius, *Char. epist.* 41.

128 E.g., Paul Schubert, *Form and Function of the Pauline Thanksgivings* (BZNW 20; Berlin: Töpelmann, 1939) 62; Gordon P. Wiles, *Paul's Intercessory Prayers* (SNTSMS 24; Cambridge: Cambridge University Press, 1974) 156–229; Peter T. O'Brien, *Introductory Thanksgivings in the Letters of Paul* (NovTSup 49; Leiden: Brill, 1977) 39 and passim; Meeks, "Man from Heaven," 333.

129 See my comments below under "Rhetorical Situation."

130 Paul's so-called dankloser Dank (Martin Dibelius, *An die Thessalonicher I, II, An die Philipper* [3rd ed.; HNT 11; Tübingen: Mohr Siebeck, 1937] 74) is difficult to explain other than in its canonical context. For a different but compatible view, see Abraham J.

stand even after his discussion of the things that do and do not matter—how much more before it! This rhetorical hurdle also explains Paul's brief allusion to the gift in 1:3-5, and again in 2:25 and 30, but without dwelling on the subject.[131]

We are left, then, with the claim that 4:10-20 is a self-contained pericope loosely tied to its context and capable of being read as a separate thank-you note or receipt. This claim is at best half right: 4:10-20 reads like a post-scripted acknowledgment of goods received,[132] but there is much to link it to the rest of the letter, especially to 1:3-11, as W. J. Dalton has shown.[133] In addition, Paul's prayer in 1:10 that the Philippians learn to distinguish the things that matter from the things that do not is echoed in his claim to be "self-sufficient" (αὐτάρκης) in 4:11 and

the peristasis catalogue of 4:12.[134] Further, to read 4:10-20 as a prior thank-you note only exacerbates the problem of its "thankless thanks," as I have already indicated. In the context of the canonical letter, Paul's backhanded expression of thanks coupled with his insistence on self-sufficiency makes good sense: Paul has been exhorting the Philippians not to place too much value in things that do not matter, and now he must not be seen to be doing so himself. Removed from this context, however, Paul's extended discussion of how he did not actually need the Philippians' gift is unexplained and offensive.[135] These considerations suggest that 4:10-20 is an appended note of acknowledgment—perhaps in Paul's own hand[136]—composed after he had dictated 1:1—4:9 and continuing to express some of its themes.[137]

Malherbe, "Paul's Self-Sufficiency (Philippians 4:11)," in *Friendship, Flattery, and Frankness of Speech: Studies on Friendship in the New Testament World*, ed. John T. Fitzgerald (NovTSup 82; Leiden: Brill, 1996) 125–39; and, in the same volume, Ken L. Berry, "The Function of Friendship Language in Philippians 4:10-20," 111–16.

131 Cf. Gnilka, pp. 9–10.

132 See my comments below in the commentary on 4:10-20.

133 W. J. Dalton, "The Integrity of Philippians," *Bib* 60 (1979) 97–102, here 101: μετὰ χαρᾶς (1:4), ἐχάρην . . . μεγάλως (4:10); κοινωνία . . . εἰς (1:5), ἐκοινώνησεν εἰς (4:15); εἰς τὸ εὐαγγέλιον ἀπὸ τῆς πρώτης ἡμέρας (1:5), ἐν ἀρχῇ τοῦ εὐαγγελίου (4:15); φρονεῖν ὑπέρ (1:7), ὑπὲρ . . . φρονεῖν (4:10); ἔν τε τοῖς δεσμοῖς μου . . . συγκοινωνούς (1:7), συγκοινωνήσαντές μου τῇ θλίψει (4:14); πεπληρωμένοι καρπὸν δικαιοσύνης (1:11), τὸν καρπὸν τὸν πλεονάζοντα εἰς λόγον ὑμῶν (4:17); I have slightly augmented Dalton's list. Theodor Zahn (*Introduction*, 1:564) had already spoken of 4:10-20 as a "doublet" of 1:3-8. Cf. Schubert, *Form and Function*, 76–77; Robert Jewett, "The Epistolary Thanksgiving and the Integrity of Philippians," *NovT* 12 (1970) 40–53, here 53; Rolland, "La structure littéraire," 213; Duane F. Watson, "A Rhetorical Analysis of Philippians and Its Implications for the Unity Question," *NovT* 30 (1988) 57–88, here 77–79; D. A. Black, "The Discourse Structure of Philippians: A Study in Text Linguistics," *NovT* 37 (1995) 24–25.

134 According to both Cynic and Stoic traditions, one became self-sufficient by learning that the things conventionally understood to be good or evil do not matter. This self-sufficiency was advertised in

the peristasis catalogue, where conventional goods and evils are listed as indifferent things. See John T. Fitzgerald, *Cracks in an Earthen Vessel: An Examination of the Catalogues of Hardships in the Corinthian Correspondence* (SBLDS 99; Atlanta: Scholars Press, 1988) 45 and passim, and my comments below in the commentary on 4:11-12.

135 *Pace* Malherbe, whose learned note on "Paul's Self-Sufficiency" in the context of ancient friendship theory accounts for Paul's comment only if one assumes, wrongly in my view, that Paul's friendship with the Philippians is a significant subtext in Philippians.

136 Harry Gamble, *The Textual History of the Letter to the Romans* (Grand Rapids: Eerdmans, 1977) 94, 145–46.

137 John L. White argues that "I rejoiced greatly" in 4:10 is an introductory formula and marks the beginning of a letter (cf. *P. Giss.* 21.3: λίαν ἐχάρην ἀκούσασα ὅτι; *P. Elephant.* 13.2 [3rd cent. BCE]; *P. Lond.* 43.3 [2nd cent. BCE]; *P. Mich.* 483.3 [Reign of Hadrian]; cf. *P. Mert.* 1.12.4 [29 August 58 CE]; 2 John 4; 3 John 3) (White, "Introductory Formulae in the Body of the Pauline Letter," *JBL* 90 [1971] 94–95). Cf. Schubert, *Form and Function*, 177. But as Heikki Koskenniemi has shown, in some cases (e.g., *P. Elephant.* 13.2) the expression of joy seems to be simply an acknowledgment formula (= acknowledgment of a letter received) and not an introductory formula marking the beginning of the letter body (*Studien zur Idee und Phraseologie des griechischen Briefes bis 400 n Chr.* [Helsinki: Kirjakauppa; Wiesbaden: Harrassowitz, 1956] 75–77). Expressions of joy can appear elsewhere than at the beginning of a letter (e.g., *P. Yale* 42.11 [12 January 229 BCE]; *BGU* 2.632.10 [2nd cent. BCE]). White ("Introductory Formulae," 94–95) limits

d. Positive Evidence for the Integrity of Philippians

The debate over the integrity of Philippians has, understandably, focused on the various arguments for partitioning. However, a number of positive arguments for the unity of Philippians have been advanced. Particularly striking are the number of verbal and thematic parallels that run through the various alleged letter fragments.

We have already noted the parallels between 1:3-11 and 4:10-20. Scholars have long been impressed with the thematic and verbal parallels between 2:6-11 and 3:4-16,[138] but the most striking are between 2:6-11 and 3:20-21.[139] Neal Flanagan compiled these in a short note in 1959.[140] William Dalton offered a more extended analysis in 1979.[141] Here is Flanagan's list:

2:5-11	3:20-21
μορφῇ (v. 6), μορφήν (v. 7)	σύμμορφον (v. 21)
ὑπάρχων (v. 6)	ὑπάρχει (v. 20)
σχήματι (v. 7)	μετασχηματίσει (v. 21)
ἐταπείνωσεν (v. 8)	ταπεινώσεως (v. 21)

ἐπουρανίων (v. 10)	οὐρανοῖς (v. 20)
κύριος Ἰησοῦς Χριστός (v. 11)	κύριον Ἰησοῦν Χριστόν (v. 20)
δόξαν (v. 11)	δόξης (v. 21)

To which may be added:

πᾶν ὄνομα . . . πᾶν γόνυ . . . πᾶσα γλῶσσα (vv. 9-11)	τὰ πάντα (v. 21)

And if we extend the range of comparison to include 3:18-19:

ἐπιγείων (v. 10)	ἐπίγεια (v. 19)
σταυροῦ (v. 10)	σταυροῦ (v. 18)

Not all of these parallels are equally impressive,[142] but Dalton is no doubt correct to conclude that Paul wrote Phil 3:20-21 with "the thoughts and phrases of the Christ hymn still fresh in [his] mind."[143]

Other verbal and thematic parallels between 3:1—4:1 and 1:1—2:30 can also be found. Garland mentions the following:[144]

expressions of joy to conventional introductions but later changes his mind, writing that such phrases are "characteristic of the opening and closing of the letter" (*Light from Ancient Letters* [Philadelphia: Fortress Press, 1986] 201); cf. Loveday Alexander, "Hellenistic Letter-Forms and the Structure of Philippians," *JSNT* 37 (1989) 87–101, here 98; esp. Terence Y. Mullins, "Formulas in the New Testament Epistles," *JBL* 91 (1972) 386–88: "expressions of joy . . . might occur anywhere in the letter" (387); "it is not the nature of these forms [e.g., the joy expression, etc.] to introduce, but to punctuate . . . even the thanksgiving cannot be said to introduce the body of the letter apart from Paul's use" (388). For a similar critique of the "introductory" thanksgiving-period, see Peter Arzt, "The 'Epistolary Introductory Thanksgiving' in the Papyri and in Paul," *NovT* 36 (1994) 29–46; with response by Jeffrey T. Reed, "Are Paul's Thanksgivings 'Epistolary'?" *JSNT* 61 (1996) 87–99. *Pace* White ("Introductory Formulae," 94), Phlm 7 (χαρὰν γὰρ πολλὴν ἔσχον, "I had great joy") does not introduce the body of the letter, which begins in vv. 8-9 with the request formula (Διὸ . . . παρακαλῶ, "Therefore . . . I appeal [to you]").

138 Maurice Jones observes that Paul's "self-emptying" in chap. 3 closely parallels the "self-emptying" of Christ in chap. 2 (*The Epistle to the Philippians* [Westminster Commentaries; London: Methuen, 1918] xlvii); Pierre Bonnard speaks of the "dépouillement"

of Christ in 2:7-8 and of Paul in 3:4-11 (*L'épître de saint-Paul aux Philippiens* [CNT 10; Neuchâtel/Paris: Delachaux & Niestlé, 1950] 44, 66, 69); T. E. Pollard cites verbal parallels: ἡγεῖσθαι (2:6; 3:7, 8 [twice]), and εὑρίσκω (2:7; 3:9) ("The Integrity of Philippians," *NTS* 13 [1967] 57–66, here 58–59).

139 The claim that 3:20-21 derives from a pre-Pauline hymn is based on verbal parallels with 2:6-11 and obviously presupposes that 2:6-11 is itself a pre-Pauline hymn; see John Reumann, "Philippians 3.20-21—a Hymnic Fragment?" *NTS* 30 [1986] 593–609. On the genre of 2:6-11 and its likely Pauline composition, see the commentary below.

140 Neal Flanagan, "A Note on Philippians 3:20-21," *CBQ* 18 (1956) 8–9.

141 Dalton, "Integrity," 99–100; more recently, Jean-Noël Aletti, *Saint Paul, Épître aux Philippiens: Introduction, traduction et commentaire* (EB n.s. 55; Paris: Gabalda, 2005) 17–21.

142 The word δόξα, for example, is a common term in Paul and can be found elsewhere in Philippians four times.

143 Dalton, "Integrity," 100; cf. Andrew T. Lincoln, *Paradise Now and Not Yet: Studies in the Role of the Heavenly Dimension in Paul's Thought with Special Reference to His Eschatology* (SNTSMS 43; Cambridge: Cambridge University Press, 1981) 88.

144 Garland, "Composition and Unity" 160–62.

πολιτεύεσθε (1:27)	πολίτευμα (3:20)
στήκετε ἐν πνεύματι (1:27)	στήκετε ἐν κυρίῳ (4:1)
συναθλοῦντες τῇ πίστει τοῦ εὐαγγελίου (1:27)	ἐν τῷ εὐαγγελίῳ συνήθλησαν (4:3)
ἀπωλείας, σωτηρίας (1:28)	ἀπώλεια (3:19), σωτῆρα (3:20)
ἐπιποθῶ πάντας ὑμᾶς (1:8)	ἐπιπόθητοι (4:1)

Jewett cites the themes of χαρά and φρονεῖν, which are introduced in the thanksgiving-period and repeated thoughout the letter.[145]

Several scholars have recently pointed to friendship language as a unifying element.[146] The thesis advanced in this commentary, that the prayer report of 1:9-11 is programmatic for the argument of the whole letter, is further evidence for the integrity of Philippians.

3. Place and Date of Writing

While some ancient letters indicate the date when they were written—or, more correctly, the date when they were sent—and in a few instances the place,[147] Paul mentions neither of these in his letter to the Philippians.[148] He

does, however, describe his circumstances in some detail, especially in the report on "my situation" (τὰ κατ' ἐμέ) in 1:12-26 + 2:17-30. Scholars debate the degree to which these details reveal where and when Philippians was written.

a. Place of Writing

Here are the relevant facts regarding the place where Philippians was written.[149] Paul is in prison awaiting trial on potentially capital charges (Phil 1:12-14, 20; 2:17-18).[150] The city in which he is being held has an established community of Christ-believers (1:14; 4:22). Most of these are supportive of Paul (1:16), but a number are opposed to him. The latter, Paul claims, have stepped up their efforts at proclamation out of jealousy and spite, "hoping to make my imprisonment as hard as possible" (1:15a, 17). Paul has apparently been in prison for some time, since he complains that the Philippians have been slow in sending aid,[151] a delay of sufficient length to have caused offense were it not for the fact that they had "lacked opportunity,"[152] presumably meaning that they could not find an available and trustworthy carrier.[153] Part of the reason for the delay may also have been the

145 Jewett, "Epistolary Thanksgiving," 52–53 (χαρά: 1:4, 25; 2:2, 29; 4:1; χαίρω: 1:18 [twice]; 2:17, 18, 28; 3:1; 4:4 [twice], 10; συνχαίρω: 2:17, 18; φρονεῖν: 1:7; 2:2 [twice], 5; 3:15 [twice], 19; 4:2, 10 [twice]). Cf. κοινωνία (1:5; 2:1; 3:10) κοινωνέω (4:15) συγκοινωνέω (4:14) συγκοινωνός (1:7).
146 See my discussion of the genre of the letter below.
147 Peter White estimates that about 15 percent of Cicero's letters contain a dateline (*Cicero in Letters: Epistolary Relations of the Late Republic* [Oxford: Oxford University Press, 2010] 75–76), while Cicero himself observes (*Ad Att.* 3.23.1) that Atticus included a dateline in virtually all of his letters. According to Suetonius (*Aug.* 50), Augustus included not only the date but also the hour in which the letter was sent, for which see also, Ludwig Gurlitt, "Über das Fehlen der Briefdaten in den Ciceronischen Korrespondenzen," in *Festschrift zu Otto Hirschfelds sechzigsten Geburtstage* (Berlin: Weidmann, 1903) 16–29. The typical form may be illustrated from Cicero, *Ad fam.* 12.16, which concludes *D. VIII Kal. Iun. Athensis* ("Mailed [*Data*] May 25th in Athens"; or Cicero, *Ad fam.* 7.20, which simply ends: *XIII Kal. Sext. Velia* ("July 20th, from Velia").
148 In Rom 16:23 Paul speaks of being a guest in the house of a certain Gaius (cf. Acts 19:29), while in 1 Cor 16:8 he indicates a plan to "stay in Ephesus

until Pentecost." 1 Thessalonians was written after Paul had spent some time in Athens (see 1 Thess 3:1, 6) and had perhaps moved on to Corinth.
149 For a fuller description, see the next section of this introduction, "Rhetorical Situation."
150 Cf. 1:7, 30; 2:23, 27; 3:10; 4:14.
151 Prisoners in Roman custody typically paid for their own upkeep. For the conditions of Roman custody (*custodia*), see Jens-Uwe Krause, *Gefängnisse im römischen Reich* (HABES 23; Stuttgart: Steiner, 1996); S. Arband, W. Macheiner, and C. Colpe, "Gefangenschaft," *RAC* 9:318–45; cf. Brian Rapske, *The Book of Acts and Paul in Roman Custody* (Book of Acts in Its First Century Setting 3; Grand Rapids: Eerdmans; Carlisle: Pater Noster, 1994) 209–16; Richard J. Cassidy, *Paul in Chains: Roman Imprisonment and the Letters of St. Paul* (New York: Crossroad, 2001) 124–42.
152 Phil 4:10: "I rejoiced in the Lord greatly that now at last [ἤδη ποτέ] you revived your mindfulness of me"; cf. Chrysostom's comment (hom. 16.296.25 Allen): "The expression 'now at last' shows that a long time [χρόνον μακρόν] is passed."
153 The difficulty in finding a reliable carrier for a letter not to mention for money and other goods is well known; see, for instance, the evidence collected in White, *Light from Ancient Letters*, 215.

length and difficulty of the journey from Philippi, since Epaphroditus, the person finally charged with carrying the Philippians' gift, appears to have fallen ill along the way but pressed on, becoming critically ill in the process.[154] Epaphroditus has since recovered and Paul is sending him back with the present letter (2:25, 27). When he knows something more definite about his case, Paul will also send Timothy (2:19, 23), who is to report back to Paul on the status of the Philippians. Paul claims to be "confident in the Lord" that he will himself be free to visit Philippi in the near future (2:24).[155]

The traditional view is that Paul wrote Philippians in Rome,[156] but Caesarea Maritima is also a possibility. According to Acts, Paul was imprisoned awaiting trial in both of these cities, and while much of Acts is novelistic, there is good reason to accept these claims, since Paul in Roman custody does little to support the author of Acts' larger thesis that the gospel received a positive reception from gentiles.[157] Both Rome and Caesarea would

have required a substantial journey from Philippi, and there will also have been opposition to Paul from other Christ-believers in both of these locations, though perhaps the alleged motives of jealousy and spite fit better with a Roman provenance, where Paul was clearly an interloper.[158] Nevertheless, deciding between Rome and Caesarea makes little actual difference for the interpretation of Philippians, since in either case Philippians will be one of Paul's last letters, and since for all practical purposes Caesarea and Rome were merely two phases in the same lengthy incarceration beginning in Judea and ending in Rome.[159]

There is also a case to be made that Paul was imprisoned for a time in Ephesus and that Philippians was written there.[160] This has been a particularly attractive alternative to scholars who partition Philippians (e.g., Collange), since the more exchanges between Paul and the Philippians one assumes—Reumann manages to discover ten![161]—the more difficult it is to imagine Paul as far

---

154 According to Phil 2:27, 30 Epaphroditus's initial illness as well as its critical worsening were due to his efforts to reach Paul with the Philippians' gift, which suggests that Epaphroditus fell ill on the way and then continued on at some risk to his health. It is also noteworthy that, while the Philippians had received word of Epaphroditus's condition (2:26), they did not know just how bad it had become (2:27a), suggesting that someone traveling in the opposite direction had passed Epaphroditus on the road when he was in the initial stages of his illness and had brought news of this back to Philippi. This fact is important in determining the distance between Paul's location and Philippi. It is also important in calculating the number of implied trips between Paul and Philippi, as we shall see below.

155 Paul's plan to send Timothy may be taken at face value. However, his professed confidence in the Lord that he himself will be able to visit soon should be read as an echo of his earlier effort in 1:25-26 to allay the Philippians' fears that he may be executed: "and being confident of this, I know that I shall stay on etc." This assurance is immediately withdrawn in 1:27 and then explicitly contradicted in 2:17-18!

156 So, for instance, the so-called Marcionite prologues found in a number of Latin manuscripts; see Nils Dahl, "The Origin of the Earliest Prologues to the Pauline Letters," *Semeia* 12 (1978) 233–77.

157 Richard I. Pervo, *Acts: A Commentary* (Hermeneia; Minneapolis: Fortress Press, 2009) 552–53. Of

course, to accept these two imprisonments is not necessarily to accept Acts' account of them in all the details.

158 Rom 15:20: "lest I build on another's foundation."

159 The Philippians' considerable delay in sending to Paul's aid (4:10) nevertheless points to the latter phase.

160 The principal arguments for an Ephesian provenance were set forth at the beginning of the last century by Paul Feine, *Die Abfassung des Philipperbriefes in Ephesus mit einer Anlage über Röm 16,3-20 als Epheserbrief* (BFCTh 20; Gütersloh: Bertelsmann, 1916); Adolf Deissmann, "Zur ephesinischen Gefangenschaft des Apostel Paulus," in *Anatolian Studies presented to Sir William Mitchell Ramsey*, ed. W. H. Buckler and W. M. Calder (Manchester: Manchester University Press, 1923) 121–27; and G. S. Duncan, *St. Paul's Ephesian Ministry: A Reconstruction with Special Reference to the Ephesian Origin of the Imprisonment Epistles* (London: Hodder & Stoughton; New York: Scribners, 1930). While an Ephesian provenance is not impossible, the evidence for an Ephesian imprisonment remains circumstantial (1 Cor 15:32; 2 Cor 1:8-10; for the former, see Abraham Malherbe, "The Beasts at Ephesus," *JBL* 87 [1968] 71–80); for a recent discussion, see Paul R. Trebilco, *The Early Christians in Ephesus from Paul to Ignatius* (WUNT 166; Tübingen: Mohr Siebeck, 2004) 83–87.

161 Reumann, p. 7.

away as Rome or Caesarea. An Ephesian provenance also makes good sense of Paul's plan to send Timothy (2:19-24), who allegedly is to report back to him.[162] Further, at 2 Cor 2:8-11 Paul claims to have despaired of life when he was in Ephesus, which fits nicely his mental state when he wrote Philippians (see esp. 1:22-23).

There are, however, several considerations that count against Ephesus as the place from which Paul sent his letter. Even if one allows for a lengthy imprisonment in Ephesus, which must remain uncertain,[163] it is odd that Philippians contains no reference to the Jerusalem collection, which was foremost on Paul's mind during his stay in Ephesus and to which the Macedonian churches were to make a significant contribution.[164] The difficulty in finding a letter carrier and the resulting delay in sending to Paul's support also argue against an Ephesian provenance, as does the apparently arduous nature of Epaphroditus's journey. Other locations are theoretically possible, since Paul claims to have been jailed on multiple occasions (2 Cor 11:23), although it is doubtful that any of these was a lengthy imprisonment in anticipation of a capital trial, as Philippians requires.[165]

A key piece of evidence in determining the provenance of Philippians that I have not yet mentioned is Paul's boast in 1:13 that his witness has spread ἐν ὅλῳ τῷ πραιτωρίῳ, "in the whole πραιτώριον." The Greek πραιτώριον transliterates the Latin *praetorium*,[166] which was originally used to refer to a Roman general's tent or camp headquarters and then, by extension, to members of his staff such as his military council or personal bodyguard. In the late Republic the term also came to be used of a governor's residential compound or its guardsmen. Eventually it denoted the Imperial Guard in Rome established by Augustus.[167]

It has been suggested that πραιτώριον in Phil 1:13 refers to an official building, such as the residence of a provincial governor, as it does for instance in Acts 23:35.[168] If this is the case, then Philippians cannot have been written from Rome, since it is unthinkable that imperial buildings in Rome during the early Principate would have borne military names implying that Rome was an occupied city, something Augustus and the rest of the Julio-Claudians would have been anxious to avoid.[169] It is unlikely, however, that πραιτώριον here refers to a building. The whole expression reads ἐν ὅλῳ τῷ πραιτωρίῳ καὶ τοῖς λοιποῖς πᾶσιν, "in the whole πραιτώριον and all the rest," where "and all the rest," given Paul's usage elsewhere,[170] is most naturally inter-

---

162 It is unclear whether Paul actually expected Timothy to report back to him. Given the rhetoric of the letter at this point (1:25-26; 2:24), Paul must maintain the assumption that he will survive his current ordeal, the question being only whether he will return to Philippi (1:27). In truth, however, the outlook is not quite so optimistic (2:17-18). For an attempt to calculate the time it took to travel from Rome to Philippi, see Bockmuehl, p. 32.

163 The provenance of Philemon might help decide this matter, but, like Philippians, it remains uncertain, though Ephesus is a strong possibility.

164 1 Cor 16:1-4; 2 Corinthians 8–9; Gal 2:10; cf. Rom 15:25-28. Philippians was almost certainly written after the collection had been completed and thus not from Ephesus. For recent bibliography on the collection, see Ronald Charles, *Paul and the Politics of Diaspora* (Paul in Critical Contexts; Minneapolis: Fortress Press, 2014) 216–37.

165 Cf. Paul's short imprisonment in Acts 16 and Peter's in Acts 12.

166 BDF §5.1. On its own, πραιτώριον would most naturally refer to a building, since words ending in -(ε)ιον regularly refer to buildings. But πραιτώριον is a loanword, and the Latin term *praetorium*, which it transliterates, was not used in this limited sense.

167 *OLD*, s.v. *praetorium* 2; LSJ, s.v. πραιτώριον II. Still essential is Marcel Durry, *Les cohortes prétoriennes* (Paris: Boccard, 1938; 2nd ed., 1968), but now see Sandra Bingham, *The Praetorian Guard: A History of Rome's Elite Special Forces* (London: I. B. Tauris, 2013); cf. Lightfoot, pp. 99–104; Dibelius, pp. 97–98.

168 Cf. Matt 27:20; Mark 15:16; John 18:28, 33; 19:9.

169 Lightfoot, pp. 99–104. Augustus's and his heirs' anxieties not to offend against Republican sensitivities, as Caesar had, are well known. For a recent authoritative account, see J. A. Crook, "Augustus: Power, Authority, Achievement," in *The Cambridge Ancient History*, vol. 10: *The Augustan Empire, 43 B.C.–A.D. 69*, ed. Alan K. Bowman, Edward Champlin, and Andrew Lintott (2nd ed.; Cambridge: Cambridge University Press, 1996) 113–46.

170 1 Thess 4:13 ("that you not grieve as the rest [οἱ λοιποί]"); 5:6 ("let us not sleep as the rest [οἱ λοιποί]"); 1 Cor 7:8-12 ("to the unmarried and widows . . . to those married . . . to the rest [τοῖς λοιποῖς]"); 2 Cor 13:2 ("I warned those who sinned previously and all the rest [τοῖς λοιποῖς πᾶσιν]");

preted as a reference not to other buildings but to other personnel, something like "and everyone else."[171] This would imply that πραιτώριον similarly is a reference to personnel.[172] This interpretation makes excellent sense of 1:14, where Paul continues, "and the majority of the brothers in the Lord, etc." Taken together, vv. 13-14 would then describe the effect of Paul's imprisonment first on persons outside the church (v. 13) and then on persons inside (v. 14).

If one accepts this line of interpretation—that πραιτώριον in Phil 1:13 refers to military personnel and not to a building—then a Roman provenance becomes almost certain. For as Michael Speidel has shown, after the establishment of the Imperial Guard in Rome, provincial governors "were denied a praetorian cohort," which quickly became "an imperial prerogative."[173] Governors still retained a sizable bodyguard, but this guard was now drawn from auxiliary forces[174] and was referred to as their *singulares*.[175] To my knowledge this change in nomenclature has not been noted in the commentary

Rom 11:7 ("the elect obtained, but the rest [οἱ λοιποί] were hardened"); see Wilhelm Michaelis, *Der Brief des Paulus an die Philipper* (ThHKNT 11; Leipzig: Deichert, 1935) 51. But see 1 Cor 11:34; 15:37.

171 It must be said, however, that Chrysostom (hom. 3.40.21-22 Allen) understands both expressions locally. He first equates τὸ πραιτώριον with τὰ βασιλεία, assuming that someone of Paul's stature was detained in the "imperial palace," not in the *castra praetoria*, after which he must interpret καὶ τοῖς λοιποῖς πᾶσιν locally: οὐδὲ ἐν τῷ πραιτωρίῳ μόνον, ἀλλὰ καὶ ἐν τῇ πόλει . . . πάσῃ, "and not in the palace only, but also in all the *city*." By Chrysostom's day πραιτώριον had largely lost its military connotations and was used regularly to refer to any large house or estate (cf. *PGL*, s.v. πραιτώριον). Theodoret takes a similar view.

172 Similar expressions in which ὅλος ("whole"), which is often used of buildings, refers to people include "the whole Sanhedrin" (Matt 26:59; Mark 15:1); "the whole people" (Acts 2:47); "the whole church" (Acts 15:22; Rom 16:23; 1 Cor 14:23); "the whole inhabited world" (Rev 3:10; 12:9); "the whole household" (Heb 3:2-5; Titus 1:11); "the whole city" (Mark 1:33); "the whole world" (1 John 2:2; 5:19).

173 Michael Speidel, *Guards of the Roman Armies: An Essay on the* Singulares *of the Provinces* (Antiquitas 1.28; Bonn: Habelt, 1978) 5-6.

174 Because it was now made up of auxiliaries, a governor's guard no longer qualified as a *cohors* but was referred to less formally as a *numerus* or "contingent."

175 Early examples include *AÉ* 1923.33 (Germania inferior, first century CE); *CIL* 13.7709 (Germania inferior, first century CE); Brigitte Galsterer and Hartmut Galsterer, *Die römischen Steininschriften aus Köln* (Cologne: Greven & Bechtold, 1975) no. 260 (Germania inferior, 70–89 CE); *Vind. Tab.* 2.154 (Britannia, 92–97 CE); Jules Baillet, *Inscriptions grecques et latines des tombeaux des rois ou syringes*

à Thèbes (MIFAO 42; Cairo: L' Institut français d'archéologie orientale, 1926) 1688 (Egypt, early second century CE); *P. Lond.* 2851 (Moesia inferior, 105 CE). A *praetorianus* is mentioned in *CIL* 3.6085, 7135, and 7136 serving as a *stationarius* (police officer) near Ephesus, but this can simply mean that he was a *former* imperial guardsman (see F. F. Bruce, *Philippians* [NICNT 11; San Francisco: Harper & Row; Peabody, MA: Hendrickson, 1989] xxii); for a *singularis* similarly employed, see *AÉ* 1937.250. A slightly different conclusion is reached by Christopher J. Fuhrmann, *Policing the Roman Empire: Soldiers, Administration, and Public Order* (Oxford: Oxford University Press, 2011) 250, who interprets *ILS* 9072 (Africa) and *AÉ* 1981.344 (Italy) as examples of imperial praetorians dispatched to serve as *stationarii*; see also Kent J. Rigsby, "Graecolatina," *ZPE* 113 (1996) 249–52, here 252. For evidence that the term *praetorium* may have on occasion continued to be used for a governor's guards, see Speidel (*Guards*, 20 n. 97), who cites as the principal evidence for this *IG* 12.5.697: στρατιώτηρ ἐκ τῶν τοῦ πραιτωρίου τοῦ ἀνθυπάτου, "a soldier of those of the πραιτώριον of the governor (of Achaia)"; but see R. Egger, "Das Praetorium als Amtssitz und Quartier römischer Spitzenfunktionäre," *SAWW* 250 (1966) 13–29, here 26, who interprets this as a reference to the governor's residence. For *AÉ* 1933.56 (*princeps praetori[i]*), see Boris Rankov, "The Governor's Men: The *Officium Consularis* in Provincial Adminstration," in *The Roman Army as a Community: Including Papers of a Conference Held at Birkbeck College, University of London, on 11–12 January 1997*, ed. Adrian Goldsworthy and Ian Haynes (JRASup 34; Portsmouth, RI: Journal of Roman Archaeology, 1999) 15–34, here 19, for whom the expression refers to the centurion in charge of "headquarters." See further G. Lopuszanski, "La police romaine et les Chrétiens," *L' Antiquité Classique* 20 (1951) 5–46, esp. 18; and N. J. E. Austin and N. B. Rankov, *Exploratio: Military and Political Intelligence in the Roman World from the Second Punic*

tradition on Philippians. This change applied in both imperial and senatorial provinces.[176] Paul's claim in 1:13 would then be that his reputation has spread throughout "the whole Imperial Guard and all the rest," with "the rest" perhaps being other members of the imperial service. The hyperbolic rhetoric of 1:13—"in the *whole* πραιτώριον and *all* the rest," where both "whole" and "all" are emphatic by position—also supports a reference to the Imperial Guard, which by this time was at least six thousand.[177] Roman governors, on the other hand, typically had relatively small staffs.

The reference in 4:22 to "those of the household of Caesar" (οἱ ἐκ τῆς Καίσαρος οἰκίας) also favors a Roman provenance.[178] This is certainly the case if it refers to members of Nero's "family" (*familia* or *domus*), which by Roman standards would have included numerous household slaves and any dependent kin. But it also favors a Roman provenance if, as Lightfoot has argued, "household of Caesar" refers to members of the imperial service or so-called *familia Caesaris*, the majority of whom would have been stationed in Rome.[179]

Two common objections to a Roman provenance should be briefly noted: (1) the fact that Paul speaks of a return visit to Philippi upon his release (1:25-27; 2:24), which contradicts his plan to continue on to Spain announced in Rom 15:24 and 28, and (2) the fact that Rome's distance from Philippi makes problematic the number of trips required by the implied communications between Paul and the Philippians. Neither of these objections carries much weight. Paul's plan to go on to Spain from Rome was contingent upon his finding adequate support in Rome (Rom 15:24),[180] so that a mixed reception there, as would be implied in Phil 1:14-17—not to mention several years in prison—could easily have changed that plan. At any rate, Paul's plans were subject to change, even after he had announced them (2 Cor 1:15—2:1).[181]

The objection regarding distance is most convincing if one assumes that canonical Philippians is a compilation of letters. Apart from that, however, no more than one trip from the Philippians to Paul is actually required by the evidence, despite inflated claims to the contrary.[182]

War to the Battle of Adrianople (2nd ed.; London: Routledge, 1998) index, s.v. *singulares*. The term was simply transliterated in Greek as σινγουλαρίος, though Josephus (*Bell.* 3.120), speaking of Vespasian's military guard during the first phases of the Jewish–Roman war, translates ἐπίλεκτοι. Examples of the term in Greek include: *IG* 10.2.384, 495, 583; *IGR* 3.394; *AÉ* 1937.250; 1940.216 (= *IGLS* 4037); 1969–70.602; 1973.538; Baillet, *Inscriptions*, graffito 1473; *P. Oxy.* 20.2284; and *P. Ross. Georg.* 3.1 (collected by Speidel, *Guards*); see also Michael Speidel, "Two Greek Graffiti in the Tomb of Ramses V," *Chronique d'Égypte* 49 (1974) 384–86. (I would like to thank Dr. Sandra Bingham of the University of Edinburgh for discussing this topic with me over the course of several e-mails in 2013–14.)

176 Speidel, *Guards*, 15. For an authoritative discussion of provincial boundaries (with maps), see Stephen Mitchell, *Anatolia: Land, Men, and Gods in Asia Minor*, vol. 2: *The Rise of the Church* (Oxford: Oxford University Press, 1993) 151–63 (appendixes 1 and 2).

177 By the time of Nero the Praetorian Guard had grown to twelve cohorts of approximately five hundred each (*AÉ* 1978.286). The *castra* was built in 23 CE under Tiberius (Tacitus, *Ann.* 4.2; Suetonius, *Tib.* 37.1). According to Tacitus, *Hist.* 2.93.2, Vitellius strengthened the guard to sixteen cohorts of one thousand. See further *Brill's New Pauly: Antiquity*,

ed. Hubert Cancik and Helmuth Schneider, 16 vols. (Leiden: Brill, 2001–10) 11:773–76, s.v. Praetorians; cf. Bockmuehl, pp. 28–30, following Bruce.

178 See my comments on 4:22 below.

179 Paul R. C. Weaver, Familia Caesaris: *A Social Study of the Emperor's Freedmen and Slaves* (Cambridge: Cambridge University Press, 1972) 78–80; cited by Bockmuehl, pp. 30–31.

180 Rom 15:24b: "to be sent on my way [προπεμφθῆναι] by you"; cf. 1:10-13, 15; 15:28-29; Robert Jewett, *Romans: A Commentary* (Hermeneia; Minneapolis: Fortress Press, 2006) 925–26; Paul A. Holloway, "*Commendatio aliqua sui*: Reading Romans with Pierre Bourdieu," *EC* 2 (2011) 356–83.

181 Here see esp. Margaret M. Mitchell, "The Corinthian Correspondence and the Birth of Pauline Hermeneutics," in *Paul and the Corinthians: Studies on a Community in Conflict; Essays in Honour of Margaret Thrall*, ed. Trevor J. Burke and J. Keith Elliott (NovTSup 109; Leiden: Brill, 2003) 17–53; eadem, "Paul's Letters to Corinth: The Interpretive Intertwining of Literary and Historical Reconstruction," in *Urban Religion in Roman Corinth: Interdisciplinary Approaches*, ed. Daniel N. Schowalter and Steven J. Friesen (HTS 53; Cambridge, MA: Harvard University Press, 2005) 307–38.

182 I treat this problem above in some detail in my discussion of literary integrity.

News that Paul was being transferred from Caesarea to Rome (assuming Acts' basic story line) would likely have reached Philippi near or even before the time Paul reached Rome. Further, since Epaphroditus almost certainly became ill on the road (2:30), news of his illness could have been brought back to Philippi by someone traveling in the opposite direction, so that the Philippians would have received word of Epaphroditus's illness about the same time that he arrived in Rome. The fact that the Philippians knew of Epaphroditus's illness but not its eventual severity (2:26-27) is consistent with this interpretation. Epaphroditus, of course, would have known that news of his illness was being conveyed to his co-religionists back in Philippi, which would explain his anxiety reported in 2:26. Upon his recovery, Epaphroditus would then have been sent back to Philippi with Paul's letter, which explained among other things that Epaphroditus's illness had become more critical than the Philippians knew and commended him for his heroic efforts.

b. Date of Writing

This brings us to the question of date and with it to the well-known problem of Pauline chronology. It is beyond the scope of a commentary introduction to delve into this difficult problem in any detail.[183] If Paul did indeed write Philippians while in a Roman prison, then it is likely his last extant letter, with the possible exception of Philemon.[184] If beyond this we accept Acts' account of his imprisonment in Caesarea Maritima, and if we date the beginning of the procuratorship of Festus to 58 CE,

after which (according to Acts) Paul was sent to Rome, then Paul will have arrived in Rome sometime in 59 or 60. Allowing, then, for the time it took the Philippians to find an adequate carrier, and for the ailing Epaphroditus to reach Paul and afterwards recover enough for a return trip, Philippians could have been written no earlier than 61, but perhaps as late as 62 or even 63 CE. Since the author of Acts found it inconvenient to continue Paul's story after the first two years in Rome,[185] it is likely that Paul's trial ended in his execution, though if Philippians was not dispatched until, say, 63, then it is possible that Paul was put to death with the other Roman Christians allegedly scapegoated by Nero after the fire of 64.[186] Gerd Theissen has proposed that Paul's trial before Nero may well have brought the Christians in Rome to Nero's attention and convinced him that they were no longer a protected Jewish sect but a separate and newly concocted *superstitio*, and that this in turn led to the scandalous events of 64 CE.[187]

4. Rhetorical Situation

Paul's letters are targeted acts of communication designed to solve a set of perceived problems in one or more of his assemblies. It is not enough, therefore, simply to reconstruct so far as possible the historical occasion of a Pauline letter, as important as that is.[188] We must also try to describe the letter's "rhetorical situation,"[189] the exigence that invited Paul's act of communication in the first place, which ultimately means

183 For an introduction to the problem, see the discussion in Schnelle, *History*, 15–28.

184 Ibid., 144–45.

185 Paul A. Holloway, "Inconvenient Truths: Ancient Jewish and Christian History Writing and the Ending of Luke-Acts," in *Die Apostelgeschichte im Kontext antiker und frühchristlicher Historiographie*, ed. Jörg Frey, Clare Rothschild, and Jens Schröter (BZNW 162; Berlin: de Gruyter, 2009) 418–33; cf. Pervo, *Acts*, 688–90, 695–96.

186 Later tradition assumes this (e.g., Dionysius of Corinth apud Eusebius, *Hist. eccl.* 2.25.8; *Act. Paul.* 14; cf. *1 Clem.* 5.5), but see Brent Shaw, "The Myth of the Neronian Persecution," *JRS* 105 (2015) 73–100, which casts doubts not only on later legends of Paul's execution by Nero but on Nero's persecution of Christians altogether. (I would like to thank

Professor Shaw for sending me a draft of his article in advance of its publication.)

187 Gerd Theissen, "Paulus — der Unglücksstifter: Paulus und die Verfolgung der Gemeinden in Jerusalem und Rom," in *Biographie und Persönlichkeit des Paulus*, ed. Eve-Marie Becker and Peter Pilhofer (WUNT 187; Tübingen: Mohr Siebeck, 2005) 228–44.

188 See the distinctions drawn in Herbert A. Wichelns, "Some Differences between Literary Criticism and Rhetorical Criticism," in *Historical Studies of Rhetoric and Rhetoricians*, ed. Raymond F. Howes (Ithaca, NY: Cornell University Press, 1961) 217–24.

189 Lloyd Bitzer, "The Rhetorical Situation," *Philosophy & Rhetoric* 1 (1968) 1–14; idem, "Functional Communication: A Situational Perspective," in *Rhetoric in Transition: Studies in the Nature and Uses of Rhetoric*, ed. Eugene White (University Park: Pennsylvania

what Paul *perceived* to be problematic, his diagnosis as it were.[190] As one theorist has put it, the rhetorical situation exists as "a conclusion in the mind" of the author.[191]

a. Some Basic Observations

Let me begin with some basic observations, first about the city of Philippi and then about its assembly of Christ-believers and recent events in their ongoing relationship with Paul.[192] The story of Philippi will be familiar to many.[193] Originally known as Krenides after its "springs," in the first half of the fourth century BCE it was colonized by the Thasians to protect their mainland interests from Thracian tribes.[194] In 356 BCE, under pressure from Thrace, the Thasians aligned themselves with Philip II of Macedon, who fortified the city and renamed it Philippi. Little is known of Philippi during the Hellenistic period, but there is good reason to think that it fared well under Macedonian hegemony.[195] The Romans gained control of

State University Press, 1980) 21–38. Bitzer theorized that a rhetorical situation consists of three things: an exigence, an audience capable of remedying that exigence, and set of "constraints" (values, assumptions, prior commitments, etc.) by which a rhetor might move that audience to act. I am here emphasizing only the first and in my view most salient of these elements, the presenting exigence, for which see Arthur Miller, "Rhetorical Exigence," *Philosophy & Rhetoric* 5 (1972) 111–18.

190 Bitzer has been criticized for not allowing for a rhetor's own interpretation of events, for which see esp. Miller, "Exigence"; Richard Vatz, "The Myth of the Rhetorical Situation," *Philosophy & Rhetoric* 6 (1973) 154–61; J. H. Patton, "Causation and Creativity in Rhetorical Situations: Distinctions and Implications," *Quarterly Journal of Speech* 65 (1979) 36–55; Barbara A. Biesecker, "Rethinking the Rhetorical Situation from Within the Thematic of *Différance*," *Philosophy & Rhetoric* 22 (1989) 110–30.

191 Miller, "Exigence," 112. For the problems commonly associated with "authorial intent" that this sentence raises, see the helpful comments by G. O. Hutchinson in his *Cicero's Correspondence: A Literary Study* (Oxford: Clarendon, 1998) 1–24, esp. 22–23. Among other things, Hutchinson notes that the kind of formalist strictures imposed more or less willy-nilly by certain literary critics since the publication of William K. Wimsatt and Monroe Beardsley's famous essay on the interpretation of poetry ("The Intentional Fallacy," *Sewanee Review* 54 [1946] 468–88, republished with revisions in William K. Wimsatt, *The Verbal Icon: Studies in the Meaning of Poetry* [Louisville: University of Kentucky Press, 1954] 3–18) do not apply equally to all genres and especially not to letters.

192 I have already made some of these observations above in my discussion of the place of writing. It will be helpful to review them here from the perspective of the letter's rhetorical situation.

193 The standard history remains Philippe Collart's *Philippes, ville de Macédoine, depuis ses origins jusqu'à la fin de l'époque romaine* (2 vols.; Paris: Boccard,

1937), which for later materials can be supplemented by Paul Lemerle, *Philippes et la Macédoine orientale à l'époque chrétienne et byzantine* (Bibliothèque des Écoles Françaises d'Athènes et de Rome 158; Paris: Boccard, 1945), and, for a more general survey of the region, by Fanoula Papazoglou, *Les villes de Macédoine à l'époque romaine* (BCHSup 16; Athens: École française d'Athènes, 1998), esp. 385–413. For a brief history, see Chaido Koukouli-Chrysanthaki, "Philippi," in *Brill's Companion to Ancient Macedon: Studies in the Archaeology and History of Macedon, 650 BC–300 AD*, ed. Robin Lane Fox (Leiden: Brill, 2011) 437–52; Koukouli-Chrysanthaki, "Colonia Iulia Augusta Philippensis," in *Philippi at the Time of Paul and after His Death*, ed. Charalambos Bakirtzis and Helmut Koester (Harrisburg, PA: Trinity Press International, 1998) 5–35. The Philippian assembly itself has been discussed by Peter Pilhofer, *Philippi*, vol. 1: *Die erste christliche Gemeinde Europas* (WUNT 87; Tübingen: Mohr Siebeck, 1995); Bormann, *Philippi*; and Peter Oakes, *Philippians: From People to Letter* (SNTSMS 110; Cambridge: Cambridge University Press, 2001). Much of the material evidence has been collected by Philhofer, *Philippi*, vol. 2: *Katalog der Inschriften von Philippi* (WUNT 119; Tübingen: Mohr Siebeck, 2001). The École française d'Athènes is currently preparing what will eventually be the definitive collection of the inscriptional evidence regarding Philippi (including numerous *inedita*) in its forthcoming multi-volume *Corpus des inscriptions grecques et latines de Philippes* (CIPh). CIPh, vol. 2, part 1: *La colonie romaine: La vie publique de la colonie* by Cédric Brélaz has already appeared as Études épigraphiques 6 (Athens: École française d'Athènes, 2014).

194 Koukouli-Chrysanthaki, "Colonia," 6, pl. 1.1.

195 L. Missitzis, "A Royal Decree of Alexander the Great on the Land of Philippi," *Ancient World* 12 (1985) 9–14, Claude Vatin, "Lettre addressée à la cité de Philippes par les ambassadeurs auprès Alexandre," in Πρακτικά του Η΄ Διεθνούς Συνεδρίου Ελληνικής και Λατινικής Επιγραφικής (Αθήνα, 3–9 Οκτωβρίου 1982) (Athens: Ministry of Culture and Science, 1984) 1:259–70.

Macedonia in 148 BCE and shortly thereafter constructed the Via Egnatia, the principal land route connecting Rome to its eastern provinces, which necessarily ran through Philippi.[196] In 42 BCE Mark Antony and Octavian defeated the forces of Cassius and Brutus on the plain just west of Philippi (Appian, *Bell. civ.* 4.105–38). Antony refounded the city as *Colonia Victrix Philippensium*[197] and settled a number of military veterans there. In 30 BCE, the year after he defeated Antony at the Battle of Actium, Octavian renamed the city *Colonia Iulia Augusta Philippensis* and settled more veterans there, including possibly a number of Octavian's praetorian guardsmen.[198] In 44 CE, less than a decade before the Christian apostle Paul arrived, the emperor Claudius conquered Thrace, giving Philippi and Macedonia more generally its long sought-after "peace and safety."[199]

An account of Paul's initial visit to Philippi is given in Acts 16, but it is of almost no independent historical value. If, as now seems likely, the author of Acts knew Paul's letters and used them as sources,[200] then the Acts account of Paul's visit could have easily been constructed simply from evidence gleaned from Paul's letters,[201] enhanced by popular legend (e.g., Paul's miraculous prison escape),[202] the common knowledge that Philippi was a Roman colony (e.g., the city's duumviral form of government),[203] and the author's well-known theological agenda (e.g., that upon arrival in a new city Paul sought out its Jews). We are left, then, with Paul's letters and what can be discerned from them.

At the time of the writing of Philippians, Paul is in a Roman prison awaiting trial on potentially capital charges.[204] How he got there is not explained: Acts claims that he was originally arrested in Judea on charges related to the temple and eventually sent to Rome (Acts 21–26). Paul has received a gift from the church at Philippi to support him in his incarceration[205]—Roman prisoners were largely responsible for their own upkeep[206]—carried by one of its members, a man named Epaphroditus, who was charged with staying on and tending to Paul's needs (2:25-27; 4:18).[207] Epaphroditus had fallen critically ill during the journey, but he has since recovered (2:26-27, 30). It has been some time since Paul has heard from the Philippians (4:10), who have been among his most loyal supporters (1:5; 4:15-16), and so, as the conditions of Paul's custody and Epaphroditus's health permit, Epaphroditus brings Paul up-to-date on the circum-

---

196 Here see esp. Yannis Lolos, "Via Egnatia after Egnatius: Imperial Policy and Inter-regional Contacts," in *Greek and Roman Networks in the Mediterranean*, ed. Irad Malkin, Christy Constantakopoulou, and Katerina Panagopoulou (London: Routledge, 2009) 264–84.

197 *RPC* 1:1648 dating from this period carries the legend A(ntonii) I(ussu) C(olonia) V(ictrix) P(hilippensium).

198 *RPC* 1:1650 dating from during this period reads COL(onia) AUG(usta) IUL(ia) PHIL(ippensis) IUSSU AUG(usti).

199 Cf. 1 Thess 5:3: εἰρήνη καὶ ἀσφάλεια.

200 Richard I. Pervo, *Dating Acts: Between the Evangelists and the Apologists* (Santa Rosa, CA: Polebridge, 2006).

201 On this reading Paul's arrest and shameful beating (Acts 16:22-23) reflect 1 Thess 2:1-2; his stint in a Philippian jail (16:24), Phil 1:29-30; his enthusiastic reception first by Lydia (16:14-15, 40) and then by the Philippian jailor and his family (16:33-34), Phil 4:16-17; and his boldness before the city's hostile officials (16:36-39), Phil 1:20 and 28.

202 Here see esp. John B. Weaver, *Plots of Epiphany: Prison-Escape in Acts of the Apostles* (BZNW 131; Berlin: de Gruyter, 2004). Paul and Silas singing in prison recalls Socrates's composing paeans in prison in *Phaedo* 60d; cf. Diogenes Laertius, *Vit.* 2.42; Epictetus, *Diss.* 2.6.27.

203 Acts 16:20, 22, 38; cf. v. 21: "advocating customs it is not lawful *for us as Romans* to adopt or observe."

204 Phil 1:7, 13-14, 17, 21-22, 29-30; 2:17-18, 23; 4:14.

205 Phil 1:5; 2:25, 30; 4:10, 14, 18.

206 The conditions of imprisonment in the Roman world were harsh, and Luke's description of Paul in Roman custody in Acts 22–28 is part of his "triumphalism" and is not to be trusted (Pervo, *Acts*, 552–53). Papyrus letters from actual prisoners tell a very different story (e.g., *P. Yale* 42 [= White, *Light*, no. 28]; *P. Petr.* 3.36 verso). See further Krause, *Gefängnisse*, 271–304; Arband, "Gefangenschaft," 318–45; Rapske, *Roman Custody*. The actual conditions of prisoners is captured in the verisimilitude of Philo, *Ios.* 81–84, and Lucian, *Tox.* 29–33 (cited by Pervo, *Acts*, 552–53).

207 We may infer from the fact that Paul feels it necessary to explain why he is sending Epaphroditus back with the current letter that Epaphroditus was to stay on and take care of Paul, an explanation that would have been unnecessary if Epaphroditus had simply been charged with delivering the church's gift and then returning.

stances at Philippi. Based on these conversations, and in response to their gift, Paul dictates a letter to the church, which he now sends back by way of Epaphroditus.

Paul says nothing directly about the content of his conversations with Epaphroditus, other than that Epaphroditus was concerned that news of his illness will have gotten back to his already flagging co-religionists (2:26). But judging from Paul's letter, the two men must have talked at some length about at least three things:[208] (1) that the church, which remained very much invested in Paul and his mission, had been grieved to learn of Paul's imprisonment and possible execution;[209] (2) that certain local residents, perhaps those who opposed Paul in his first visit, had become more menacing in their opposition to the church and that this too was taking its toll;[210] and finally (3) that there was a mounting fractiousness among the members, most visible in a disagreement between two prominent women, Euodia and Syntyche (4:2-3), but also evident across the assembly as a whole, and that this was in turn giving way to a certain disaffectedness (1:27b; 2:2-4, 12-16). No doubt Epaphroditus's report was more nuanced than this short list implies, and no doubt as he recounted these and other items he did so from his own perspective. But none of this can be recovered. All that we have at this point is Paul's own perception of things—the "conclusions" he drew as a result of his conversations with Epaphroditus and his own prior knowledge of the

church—and that only insofar as it can be inferred from what he actually wrote in his letter.

b. Paul's Interpretive Framework

Before going further it will be helpful to describe briefly the ideological framework in which Paul will have interpreted Epaphroditus's report, a framework laden with myths and assumptions foreign to most modern readers of his letter. I will say more about this framework later in this introduction.[211] Here I call attention to three items.

First, essential to any informed reading of Paul is his self-understanding as God's chosen "apostle to the gentiles."[212] Messiah had come and gone and would come again very soon, and Paul understood himself to be tasked with recruiting gentiles for the eschatological people of God, gentiles who would go on to be the collegial "nations" predicted in the great biblical prophecies of restoration.[213] Paul cannot have viewed this as an easy assignment, however, since gentiles were by his account notorious "sinners" in acute need of "sanctification" if they were to have any hope of final "salvation" in the coming judgment of God.[214]

Two things made the sanctification of the gentiles and thus Paul's mission possible: (1) the suffering that was ordained to test and perfect the people of God in the last days, a popular piece of apocalyptic consolation traceable to the book of Daniel,[215] and (2) the "spirit of Christ" that

---

208 Some interpreters will be inclined to add the "evil workers" attacked in 3:2-4. I omit these here, however, since on my view these opponents are not actually at Philippi but are simply adduced as foils for Paul's comparative argument (his *synkrisis*). See my comments below on that passage.

209 Here see esp. 1:25-26 and 2:19, both of which are discussed below, but also 1:27; 2:12, 24. Prospects of Paul's demise will have been particularly distressing, if, like their near neighbors in Thessalonica (1 Thess 4:13-18), the Philippians had believed that Christ would return while they and Paul were still alive. Paul himself seems acutely aware of death in his letter.

210 Phil 1:28-30; cf. 1:7; 3:10-11; 1 Thess 2:2; See Nikolaus Walter, "Die Philipper und das Leiden: Aus den Anfängen einer heiden-christlichen Gemeinde," in *Die Kirche des Anfangs: Festschrift für Heinz Schürmann zum 65. Geburtstag*, ed. Rudolf Schnackenburg, Josef Ernst, and Joachim Wanke (EThSt 38; Freiburg: Herder, 1978) 417–43. If the fact that the Philippians now had formal leadership ("overseers and assistants"; 1:1) implies growth in the assembly, as

it likely does, then this increased visibility and the social threat it brought would explain a rise in social hostility against the group. Tertullian offers a similar explanation of social hostility against Christians in *Apol.* 1.7: "[Our opponents cry in alarm:] The State is filled with Christians! They are in the fields, in the city centers, on the islands!" (cf. 37.4; *Scap.* 2.10).

211 See part 7, "Key Religious Topoi," below.

212 Rom 1:5; 11:13; 1 Cor 1:1; 9:1-5; 15:9; 2 Cor 11:5; 12:11-12; Gal 1:1, 17; cf. 2 Cor 1:1; 1 Thess 1:1.

213 Paul offers a short litany of such texts in Rom 15:7-13; cf. Jer 16:9; Ps 22:28; Isa 42:5-9; 45:20-25; 49:1-6; 51:4; 55:5.

214 Gal 2:15 ("sinners"); 1 Thess 4:3-5 ("sanctification"); Phil 2:12 ("salvation"); and esp. the decline narrative of Rom 1:18-30.

215 Dan 11:35; 12:10 (for which see 4Q174); cf. 2 Macc 6:13-15; *2 Bar.* 13:1-12; 78.6; 4 Ezra 7:14; *Pss. Sol.* 3:3-4; 10:1-4; 13:6-11; Mark 13:19-20; Acts 14:22; Rom 8:18; 2 Cor 4:17; 1 Thess 3:4; 1 Pet 1:6; 4:17; 5:10; 1 John 2:18; Rev 2:22; 7:14, and, more generally, K. T. Kleinknecht, *Der leidende Gerechtfertigte:*

according to Paul's gospel possessed and empowered all believers,[216] a hopeful idea that began in somewhat different terms in Ezekiel[217] but was now radically transformed by Paul's spirit Christology.[218] Paul was optimistic, therefore, that his gentile converts, despite their deep-seated sinfulness, could make the "progress" necessary to accomplish their salvation—provided, of course, that they stayed the course.[219]

A second item influencing Paul's interpretation of the situation facing him at Philippi will have been his developing Christology and especially his so-called "Christ-mysticism."[220] By the time he wrote Philippians, Paul had come to imagine Christ as a preexistent divine being who, as a reward for his own suffering and death, had been elevated to the post of God's principal, Name-bearing angel, an important figure in emerging Jewish mysticism: "therefore God more highly exalted him and gave him the Name that is above every other name" (Phil 2:9).[221] This elevation did not distance Christ from his followers,

however, since Paul also imagined that in his resurrection Christ had become a $\pi\nu\epsilon\hat{v}\mu\alpha$ or "spirit"—"the second Adam became a spirit that gives life" (1 Cor 15:45)—in which form he now possesses all who believe in him: "if anyone does not have the spirit of Christ that one is not his" (Rom 8:9).[222]

These two propositions—that Christ's suffering led to his glorification and that all Christ-believers were now possessed by Christ's spirit—carried with them at least three important implications for Paul's theory of how gentiles were to be sanctified. First, Paul imagined sanctification specifically as the process of becoming increasingly Christlike: "until Christ be formed [$\mu o\rho\phi\omega\theta\hat{\eta}$] in you" (Gal 4:19).[223] Second, since Christ himself had been glorified, Paul imagined sanctification as a process of increasing glorification: "we are transformed [$\mu\epsilon\tau\alpha\mu o\rho\phi o\hat{v}\mu\epsilon\theta\alpha$] from glory to glory" (2 Cor 3:18),[224] ending in a final glorification in resurrection: "who will transform [$\mu\epsilon\tau\alpha\sigma\chi\eta\mu\alpha\tau\acuteι\sigma\epsilon\iota$] the body of our

---

Die alttestamentlich-jüdische Tradition vom "leidenden Gerechten" und ihre Rezeption bei Paulus (WUNT 2/13; Tübingen: Mohr Siebeck, 1984).

216 E.g., Rom 8:9; Gal 2:20. For Paul and spirit possession, see esp. Christopher Mount, "1 Corinthians 11:3-16: Spirit Possession and Authority in a Non-Pauline Interpolation," *JBL* 124 (2005) 313–40; idem, "Belief, Gullibility, and the Presence of a God in the Early Roman Empire," in *Credible, Incredible: The Miraculous in the Ancient Mediterranean*, ed. Tobias Nicklas and Janet E. Spittler (WUNT 321; Tübingen: Mohr Siebeck, 2013) 85–106; see also the classic study by Hermann Gunkel, *The Influence of the Holy Spirit: The Popular View of the Apostolic Age and the Teaching of the Apostle Paul* (Philadelphia: Fortress Press, 1979; German original, 1888).

217 Ezek 36:27: "I will put my spirit within you and make you follow my statutes." See Walther Zimmerli, *Ezekiel 2: A Commentary on the Book of the Prophet Ezekiel Chapters 25–48* (Hermeneia; Minneapolis: Fortress Press, 1983) on 36:25-27. The sequence is striking: purification or "sprinkling" (v. 25), followed by giving a "new (human?) spirit" (v. 26), followed by giving "my spirit" (v. 27), which empowers the beneficiary to "follow my statutes." See the later exegesis of this text in Isa 44:3 and possibly Jer 31:31-33, and then 1QS 4:20-23; cf. Jer 24:7; 32:39; 1 Bar 2:31; 1QHᵃ 21, esp. lines 10-14.

218 1 Cor 15:45; cf. Rom 8:9; Gal 4:6; Phil 1:19; 1 Cor 2:12; 2 Cor 3:17-18. See further my comments below in part 7b, "Paul's Spirit-Christ."

219 Phil 2:12-16 (cf. 1:6, 11, 19, 25-26, 27-30; 2:1-4; 3:15-18). Epaphroditus's report will have caused Paul to question whether the Philippians were in fact staying the course. Cf. Gal 6:9-10; Col 1:22-23.

220 Albert Schweitzer, *The Mysticism of Paul the Apostle* (Baltimore: Johns Hopkins University Press, 1998; German original, 1930). For the problem of definition, see Peter Schäfer, *The Origins of Jewish Mysticism* (Princeton: Princeton University Press, 2011) 1–9.

221 This is the point of Phil 2:6-11, for which see Markus Bockmuehl, "'The Form of God' (Phil. 2:6): Variations on a Theme of Jewish Mysticism," *JTS* 48 (1997) 1–23.

222 Mount, "Spirit Possession."

223 Paul no doubt imagined sanctification this way because he believed that a person possessed by a spirit would necessarily take on certain qualities of the possessing spirit, even to the point of identifying with that spirit: "I no longer live; Christ lives in me" (Gal 2:20).

224 See, e.g., Phil 2:15, where believers are said to shine like stars "in the world" and not only "in heaven" as in Dan 12:3 and *1 Enoch* 104:2. It was in this regard that Paul chose the term "holy ones" or "saints" to refer to his converts, terminology initially reserved for angels (see John J. Collins, *Daniel: A Commentary on the Book of Daniel* [Hermeneia; Minneapolis: Fortress Press, 1993] 313–17). See further my comment on 1:1 below.

humiliation to be conformed [σύμμορφον] to his glorious body" (Phil 3:20). And third, since it was precisely through suffering that one recapitulated Christ's *hieros logos*, or sacred story (see Phil 2:6-11; 1 Cor 15:3-8), and was progressively transformed into his likeness, the suffering of the righteous took on a particular salience for Paul: "that I might know him and the power of his resurrection and the fellowship of his suffering, being conformed [συμμορφιζόμενος] to his death, if somehow I might arrive at the resurrection of the dead!" (Phil 3:10-11). It will have been essential for Paul that the Philippians not lose sight of the role that Christlike suffering was to play in their transformation/sanctification. This insight would sustain them in their and Paul's present suffering and lead ultimately to their final salvation.[225]

Finally, Paul will have brought to Epaphroditus's report certain philosophical assumptions about the nature of grief, including its typical effects and possible cures. I have already described ancient consolation in some detail above. Here I simply recall the following points: (1) that in Paul's day grief was believed to be a destructive passion that caused one to neglect one's duties and—in the case of Stoicism—inhibited one's moral "progress";[226] (2) that consolation was generally understood to consist in finding "joy"[227] in the midst of grief; and (3) that, while every major philosophical school developed its own theory of consolation, actual consolation could be quite eclectic, with relief being sought wherever it might be found.[228] Taken together, these points explain how Paul could take grief to be the root problem facing the Philippians and thus the underlying cause of their other failings,[229] and why he does not hesitate to draw on a range of consolatory arguments in seeking to restore the Philippians to their former "progress" and "joy" (1:25).

c. Paul's Perception of Problems at Philippi

I now return to Paul's perception of the problems facing him at Philippi. The first thing to note is that, as I have already intimated, Paul interpreted the Philippians' response to his and their predicaments as "grief" broadly conceived and sought to console them accordingly. We see this most clearly at 2:19, when Paul expresses his desire to send Timothy to Philippi: "I hope in the Lord Jesus to send Timothy to you shortly, in order that *I too* (κἀγὼ) might be comforted when I know how things are with you." The implication is that Paul has informed the Philippians of his situation in order to console them (1:12-26), and now he wishes to hear of their situation that he too might be consoled.[230]

Paul interpreted the Philippians' grief over his imprisonment along Stoic lines as a failure to focus on the things that matter so as not to be grieved by the things that do not: "And this is what I am praying, . . . so that you can ascertain the things that really matter [τὰ διαφέροντα]" (1:9-10). Paul applies this distinction immediately in 1:12-26 when he attempts to shift the Philippians' focus from his imprisonment to the "progress" of the gospel and from his possible demise to his assured "salvation." He also takes it as his point of departure for the exhortation of 1:27—2:16: "whether I come and see you or remain absent" (i.e., neither matters).[231] Finally,

---

225 This is the point of Phil 3:1–4:1, where 3:1 implies that Paul had taught his Christ-mysticism to the Philippians earlier.

226 For "joy" as a measure of progress, see Seneca, *Ep.* 59.14: "To the degree that you lack joy [*gaudio*], to that degree you lack wisdom." And again at *Ep.* 23.2: "He has made it to the top who knows how to rejoice [*gaudeat*]." In *Ep.* 66.5 Seneca goes so far as to equate joy with moral perfection, calling it the *primum bonum*, a sentiment with which Philo would have agreed (*Her.* 315).

227 Holloway, *Consolation*, 78–83.

228 Cicero, *Tusc.* 3.31.76 (cf. *Ad Att.* 12.14.3), a claim borne out by the evidence.

229 In other words, the fundamental problem at Philippi was not disunity (contra Davorin Peterlin, *Paul's Letter to the Philippians in Light of the Disunity in the Church* [NovTSup 79; Leiden: Brill, 1995]) but grief, which to Paul's mind had led to disunity. Over the course of the letter Paul argues against grief and then exhorts unity.

230 See Chrysostom's comment on this passage (10.186.17-23 Allen). I discuss his remarks in the following section of the tntroduction (part 5, "Genre: Philippians as a Letter of Consolation") and in the commentary on 2:19. See also Alexander, "Hellenistic Letter-Forms." Paul's interpretation of the Philippians' response to his imprisonment as grief is evident also in 1:25-26, where Paul complains that his imprisonment and possible demise have robbed the Philippians of their "joy" and stalled their "progress" in faith. The letter's leitmotif of "joy" (= consolation) is also to be explained along these lines.

231 Paul here uses the correlatives εἴτε . . . εἴτε ("whether

the distinction is central to his autobiographical remarks in 3:1–4:1, where "the surpassing greatness of the knowledge of Christ" renders all else "table scraps."

Paul interprets the Philippians' grief over their own hardship in slightly different terms. In this case, it is not so much that they have failed to discern what matters—though he does reintroduce that theme in his discussion of suffering in 3:1–4:1—as it is that they have failed to prepare themselves mentally for the opposition they must inevitably face as the people of God in the last days: "and [that you are] in no way frightened [πτυρόμενοι, 'panicked'] by your enemies" (1:28). Here Paul incorporates into his apocalyptic theory of suffering the Cyrenaic claim that grief overpowers us when calamity takes us by surprise but is thwarted when we realize that calamities are to be expected: "it has been given to you . . . to suffer" (1:29; cf. 1 Thess 3:3-4). In a nutshell, then, Paul imagines the Philippians succumbing to grief (1) over his imprisonment because they have failed to recognize his imprisonment as a matter of indifference and (2) over their own suffering because they have failed to prepare themselves for such apocalyptic eventualities.

A second problem identified in Epaphroditus's report was the various disruptions taking place in the church. Two things are to be noted here. First, as already indicated, Paul links these disruptions to the Philippians' grief, especially their grief over his imprisonment and possible execution, which he euphemistically calls his "absence."[232] Second, he interprets these disruptions in theological terms as failures of mission: "I ask only that you act in a manner worthy of *the gospel* of Christ . . . contending side by side in one accord for the faith of *the gospel*" (1:27b). The latter point raises the stakes considerably, for if the Philippians fail in so basic an obligation, then it is doubtful that they are making the

necessary "progress" (1:25) to achieve their final "salvation" (2:12; cf. 1:11). It is imperative therefore that the Philippians overcome their grief, put aside any personal differences,[233] and begin to work together again for the advancement of the gospel.

This brings us to a third and final element of the situation facing Paul, namely, that the Philippians have sent him a gift for which he should thank them. Normally this would have been simple enough. In the case of Philippians, however, it has been significantly complicated by Paul's decision to present himself as someone unaffected by things that do not matter—which presumably includes the Philippians' gift! Paul is therefore faced with the problem of how to thank the Philippians for their gift without contradicting his larger "stoicizing" strategy.[234] The result is the letter's remarkable "thankless thanks"[235] awkwardly appended at 4:10-20, where Paul says in effect, "Thank you for your gift, though I did not really need it."[236]

Based on the above reflections I propose that, as Paul planned out and eventually began to dictate his letter to the Philippians, he imagined himself faced with the following "rhetorical situation":

1. that the Philippians' reported fractiousness was causing them to live "in a manner [un]worthy of the gospel," thus endangering their final "salvation";
2. that the root cause of this was their grief over his imprisonment and their own unexpected suffering;
3. that the first source of grief, his imprisonment, indicated a failure on Philippians' part to identify "the things that really matter";
4. that the second source of their grief, their own suffering, indicated a further failure to expect suffering as the apocalyptic people of God;

. . . or") to express indifference. He has already used them to that effect in 1:18 and 20. Cf. 1 Thess 5:9; 1 Cor 3:22; 12:13; 2 Cor 5:9; 12:2.

232 Phil 1:27: "whether I come and see you again or else remain absent [ἀπών]," and 2:12: "as you have always obeyed, not as in my presence only, but now even more so in my absence [ἀπουσία]." Paul prepares for this euphemism in 1:26 when his speaks of his survival in terms of his "presence" [παρουσία] again at Philippi, which presence would then provide for their renewed "progress and joy in faith."

233 Of course, not all these differences need have been

merely personal. But if this was so, Paul does not acknowledge it, labeling them ἐριθεία ("contentiousness," "jealous ambition") and κενοδοξία ("empty conceit," 2:3).

234 To repeat: this was a problem of his own making.

235 Lohmeyer on 4:10-20; cf. Marvin R.Vincent, *A Critical and Exegetical Commentary on the Epistles to the Philippians and to Philemon* (ICC; Edinburgh: T&T Clark, 1897) on 4:10-20, who attributes the expression to Holsten (*non vidi*). For a history of the problem, see Reumann, pp. 684–88.

236 This explanation is, of course, not available to those

5. and, finally, that while he had to thank the Philippians for their recent gift, he would need to do so without contradicting his claim that a person's material circumstances do not really matter.

Philippians is Paul's attempt to address this complex situation.[237]

5. Genre: Philippians as a Letter of Consolation

Genre is a complex phenomenon raising questions of form, content, and purpose. Historical development and social and cultural context are also important, since genres change over time and vary across social groups and cultures. Form and content have been emphasized in biblical studies for reasons unique to the discipline. That has changed recently, however, with the advent of rhetorical criticism and certain types of epistolary criticism, both of which tend to emphasize a text's purpose.[238] Genre analysis allows interpreters of Paul's letters to identify other ancient materials that might serve as legitimate sources for comparison.

Scholars are currently divided on how best to describe a Pauline letter. Should one be guided by the genre categories of ancient letter writing,[239] or should one deploy the categories of ancient rhetoric or oratory?[240] This ambivalence is due in part to the complex nature of Paul's letters, which, in addition to being sent as real letters, would have been read aloud to the assembled congregation. There is also a liturgical aspect to Paul's letters, though this is rarely examined.[241] The fact remains, however, that Paul's letters are letters and in any instance can be read as such, which will be the approach taken in this commentary.

At this point an important but often overlooked aspect of Paul's letters should be mentioned. Any historical account of the epistolary genre of a Pauline letter must not lose sight of the fact that insofar as they constitute the beginning of the "apostolic letter" tradition Paul's letters were in their day strictly speaking *sui generis*.[242] To

---

who see in 4:10-20 an earlier, separate thank-you note, in which case Paul's awkwardness remains unexplained.

237 A further source of grief for the church—news of Epaphroditus's nearly fatal illness—is answered not by the letter itself but by sending the recovered Epaphroditus back with the letter: "that upon seeing him again you might rejoice" (2:28).

238 There are two commonly accepted definitions of rhetoric extending back to antiquity: speaking *well* and speaking *persuasively*. The former tends to emphasize form and especially style, while the latter emphasizes purpose, since persuasion is always directed to some end. This distinction is frequently overlooked, and this has caused some confusion. A similar phenomenon occurs in epistolary criticism, which can focus on characteristic parts of an ancient letter, typical clichés, and so on, or on a letter's purpose, which is how the various letter types were classified in the ancient letter handbooks.

239 E.g., Pseudo-Demetrius, *Typoi epist.*; Pseudo-Libanius, *Char. epist.*; collected with translation and introduction in Abraham J. Malherbe, *Ancient Epistolary Theorists* (SBLSBS 19; Atlanta: Scholars Press, 1988).

240 Most scholars following this approach adopt the threefold division of Aristotle (*Rhet.* 1.3): deliberative, forensic, and epideictic. Thus, George A. Kennedy in his much read *New Testament Interpretation through Rhetorical Criticism* (Studies in Religion; Chapel Hill: University of North Carolina Press, 1984) regards Philippians as epideictic (p. 77), while Watson ("Rhetorical Analysis") describes it as deliberative. I do not find this kind of "macro" analysis very helpful, though in a few instances it can make a meaningful contribution, as when Paul's so-called εὐχαριστῶ-periods are read as hybrid versions of rhetorical proems. My own efforts at understanding the rhetorical element in Paul's letters have been at the "micro" level: Paul A. Holloway, "Paul's Pointed Prose: The *Sententia* in Roman Rhetoric and Paul," *NovT* 40 (1998): 32–53; idem, "The Enthymeme as an Element of Style in Paul," *JBL* 120 (2001) 329–39. Philip Melanchthon famously analyzed Paul's letters (esp. Romans) rhetorically in terms of their theological topoi, which formed the basis for his important *Loci communes rerum theologicarum seu hypotyposes theologicae*. I discuss contemporary consolatory topoi used by Paul in Philippians above in part 1 of this introduction and at various excursuses in the commentary. I discuss certain of Paul's religious topoi below in part 7.

241 The liturgical aspect of Paul's letters is rarely discussed, largely because of our ignorance of ancient liturgy. But one may reasonably ask, for instance, whether Paul's practice of beginning his letters with a thanksgiving prayer derives as much from his liturgical sensibilities as from epistolary practice.

242 Malherbe, *Thessalonians*, 101: "[Paul's] letters are *sui generis* as to their form and content"; cf. John L. White, "Saint Paul and the Apostolic Letter

be sure, this is not the whole story: new genres are not created out of whole cloth, and relevant comparisons can and should be made. And, of course, the apostolic letter developed far beyond anything Paul could have imagined. Nevertheless, the uniqueness of Paul's letters stands as a warning to interpreters not to force them woodenly into ancient genre categories and to note differences as well as similarities.[243]

a. Two Recent Proposals

Recent scholarship has tended to describe Philippians either (1) as a "letter of friendship" (ἐπιστολὴ φιλική) or (2) as a type of "family letter" (a genre not discussed in handbook tradition but in evidence in the papyri).[244] Much of the scholarship on Philippians and friendship has focused on various friendship themes and clichés in the letter.[245] There is little to object to here, as friendship language occurs at several points in Philippians, though perhaps not as frequently as some think.[246] A problem arises, however, when on the basis of this language one takes the additional step of classifying Philippians as a "letter of friendship."[247] In this case, the friendship expressed must by definition be between the writer and reader(s): "written by a friend to a friend" (ὑπὸ φίλου γράφεσθαι πρὸς φίλον).[248] Paul's use of friendship language in Philippians, however, does little to meet this requirement, since in almost every instance it refers not to Paul's relationship with the Philippians, as the genre demands, but to the Philippians' relationships with one another.

More promising is the claim advanced by Loveday Alexander that Philippians displays features and objectives characteristic of so-called family letters, especially letters sent by young military recruits to their anxious parents and siblings back home.[249] Drawing on earlier

---

Tradition," *CBQ* 45 (1983) 433–44; Helmut Koester, "1 Thessalonians—Experiment in Christian Writing," in *Continuity and Discontinuity in Church History: Essays Presented to George Huntston Williams on the Occasion of his 65th Birthday*, ed. F. Forrester Church and Timothy George (SHCT 19; Leiden: Brill, 1979) 33–44.

243 The following discussion will assume the integrity of the letter. If Philippians as we now have it is a compilation of two or three earlier letters, then the genre of each of these letters (or letter fragments) must be treated separately; see Betz, *Studies*, 133–54.

244 It is also possible to speak of Philippians as a generic "mixture" (following Pseudo-Libanius, *Char. epist.* 45); see David E. Aune, *The New Testament in Its Literary Environment* (LEC 8; Philadelphia: Westminster, 1987) 203, who maintains, not without reason, that all of Paul's letters are in fact "mixed."

245 E.g., L. Michael White, "Morality between Two Worlds: A Paradigm of Friendship in Philippians," in *Greeks, Romans, and Christians: Essays in Honor of Abraham J. Malherbe*, ed. David L. Balch, Everett Ferguson, and Wayne A. Meeks (Minneapolis: Fortress Press, 1990) 201–15; Stanley K. Stowers, "Friends and Enemies in the Politics of Heaven: Reading Theology in Philippians," in *Pauline Theology: Volume 1*, ed. Jouette M. Bassler (Minneapolis: Fortress Press, 1991) 105–21; John T. Fitzgerald, "Philippians, Epistle to the," *ABD* 5:218–26.

246 Alan C. Mitchell is particularly enthusiastic: "the richest treasure of Pauline friendship is his letter to the Philippians" ("'Greet the Friends by Name': New Testament Evidence for the Greco-Roman

Topos on Friendship," in *Greco-Roman Perspectives on Friendship*, ed. John T. Fitzgerald [SBLRBS 34; Atlanta: Scholars Press, 1997] 225–62, here 233); but see John Reumann, "Philippians, Especially Chapter 4, as a 'Letter of Friendship': Observations on a Checkered History of Scholarship," in Fitzgerald, *Friendship*, 83–106; and, more recently, Todd D. Still, "More Than Friends? The Literary Classification of Philippians Revisited," *Perspectives in Religious Studies* 39 (2012) 53–66. I find only two unambiguous friendship clichés in the letter: that friends are of "one soul" (1:27; 2:2; cf. 2:20), and that friends "think the same thing" (2:2; 4:2). It is a stretch to see in Paul's use of "partnership" (κοινωνία) a third cliché that "friends hold things in common" (κοινὰ τὰ φίλων). The motif that friends rejoice together is probably reflected in 2:17-18 but as a consolatory topos—it was the duty of friends to share one another's grief and joy and to console one another when necessary (e.g., Euripides, *Alc.* 369–70; *Iph. Aul.* 408; Xenophon, *Mem.* 2.4.6; Aristotle, *EN* 9.11.1171a35–b4; cf. Rom 12:15). See further Gottfried Bohnenblust, "Beiträge zum Topos Περὶ Φιλίας" (Inaugural Dissertation, University of Bern; Berlin: Gustav Schade [Otto Francke], 1905), esp. 39–44, and now von Gemünden, "Freude," 233–36.

247 *Pace* White, "Morality"; Stowers, "Friends."

248 Pseudo-Demetrius, *Typoi epist.* 1; cf. Pseudo-Libanius, *Char. epist.* 11.

249 Alexander, "Hellenistic Letter-Forms." An additional example is *Vind. Tab.* 2.311.

work by J. G. Winter, Heikki Koskenniemi, and John L. White,[250] Alexander isolates the following elements as characteristic of these letters: (1) "reassurance about the sender," followed by (2) a "request for reassurance about the recipients," followed by (3) "information about the movements of intermediaries" who will provide further opportunities for communication.[251] Alexander discerns a similar progression in Philippians 1-2: Paul writes first of himself (1:12-26), then of his desire to hear more about the Philippians (1:27–2:18), and then of his sending of Epaphroditus and of his plan to send Timothy (2:19-30).[252]

The parallels are suggestive, and I will return to them in my discussion of the disposition of Philippians in the following section. It is not clear to me, however, to what degree we can speak of a distinct subgenre here and, even if we can, whether the comparisons this invites are of first-order importance for the interpretation of Philippians. Seneca wrote a similar letter to this mother, Helvia, during his exile to Corsica, in which he likewise first reassures her of his own situation (4.2–13.8) and then advises her regarding hers (14.1–19.1). One could in principle, therefore, read the *Ad Helviam* as a "family letter" similar to the kind Alexander describes. But it is far more productive to interpret it as a letter of consolation sent by an exile to an anxious and grieving loved one and to compare it with other consolatory literature, which is, of course, the way the letter is universally read,[253] and how Seneca himself understood it (*Ad Helv.* 1.2).

b. Philippians as a Letter of Consolation

The view taken in this commentary is that, not unlike the *Ad Helviam*, Philippians is a "letter of consolation" (ἐπιστολὴ παραμυθητική; Pseudo-Demetrius, *Typoi epist.* 5) sent by Paul the prisoner to his grieving co-religionists. The merits of this view are best seen in a close reading of the letter, and I will offer that in the commentary that follows. But a prima facie case can be made by way of introduction. First, regarding the initial plausibility of reading Philippians as a letter of consolation, it should be noted that this is precisely how Philippians was understood by some of its earliest and most culturally attuned interpreters. According to Chrysostom, Paul wrote to the Philippians and would later send Timothy to them "to lift them from their despondency over his chains [ἀπὸ τῆς ἀθυμίας τῆς ἐπὶ τοῖς δεσμοῖς]."[254] And summarizing 1:18-22 he writes, "all these things he says for the consolation [πρὸς παραμυθίαν] of the Philippians."[255] Similarly, Theodoret: "[S]ince it was with great anxiety [λίαν μεριμνῶντες] that they sent the blessed Epaphroditus, he [Paul] consoles [ψυχαγωγεῖ] them."[256] And in the Latin tradition, Jerome writes, "[H]e consoles them regarding his own suffering [consolatur eos de sua tribulatione], since they had heard that he was being held in custody in Rome."[257] It is a puzzle why these important comments have been lost on modern interpreters.[258]

Second, if my earlier account of the "rhetorical situation" is correct, then the primary problem facing Paul will have been the Philippians' grief, in answer to which

250 J. G. Winter, "In the Service of Rome: Letters from the Michigan Papyri," *CP* 22 (1927) 237–56; Koskenniemi, *Studien*, 104–14; White, *Light*, 196–97.
251 Alexander, "Hellenistic Letter-Forms," 92–93.
252 Ibid., 94–96.
253 Favez, *L. Annaei Senecae Dialogorum liber XII*; Meinel, *Verbannung*.
254 Chrysostom, hom. 1.4.15 Allen; cf. 1.6.11-13 Allen. Similarly, according to John Calvin, Paul wrote to console the Philippians "lest they should be broken hearted [ne fractiore sint animo] on seeing him a prisoner and in danger of his life" (*In Epistolam ad Philippenses* [Corpus Reformatorum 52:5–76]; ET: *The Epistles of Paul the Apostle to the Galatians, Ephesians, Philippians, and Colossians* [Edinburgh: Oliver & Boyd, 1965] praef.).
255 Chrysostom, hom. 4.66.16 Allen. Chrysostom identifies further individual points of consolation in the letter at 9.182.24-25 (on 2:17-18); 10.186.7-8,

17-23 (on 2:19-21 but describing 1:12-26; 2:17-18); 11.212.11-13 (on 3:1 but summarizing 1:12-26; 2:19-30); 12.238.31-34 (on 3:9-11); 15.284.6-8 (on 4:5-6). Chrysostom also interprets 1:27–2:16 as Paul's request that the Philippians return the favor and console him by heeding his advice (hom. 6.98.7-100.11 Allen).
256 On Phil 1:12-13 (*PG* 82:564.2–3); cf. Theodoret on 2:17-18 and 4:22. Paul himself speaks of the Philippians' "anxiety" in 4:6.
257 On Phil 1:12-13 (*PL* 30:881.15).
258 But see Zahn, *Introduction*, 1:529: "Paul's used every means in his power to dispel this feeling [among the Philippians of grief and despair] and to make the Church rejoice." According to Zahn, the Philippians were "depressed" over Paul's imprisonment, his possible execution, the apparent stalling of the gospel mission, Epaphroditus's illness, and the disappointingly modest nature of their recent gift.

he naturally would have written to console them. As I have already noted, Phil 2:19 is especially instructive in this regard: "I hope in the Lord Jesus to send Timothy to you shortly, *in order that I too might be comforted* [ἵνα κἀγὼ εὐψυχῶ] when I know how things are with you." The clear implication is that Paul's earlier report concerning "my own situation" in 1:12-26 had been intended to serve a similar consolatory purpose with regard to the Philippians. Chrysostom (1.6.5-7 Allen) comes to the same conclusion: "The 'in order that I too' [ἵνα κἀγώ] here clearly means that just as you sent to know 'my own situation,' even so I am sending 'in order that I too might be comforted when I know how things are with you.'"[259]

A third piece of prima facie evidence in favor of reading Philippians as a letter of consolation is the number of striking similarities between it and Seneca's already noted letter of consolation to this mother, Helvia.[260] Two items in particular stand out: (1) the two letters' nearly identical circumstances and consolatory strategies, and (2) their programmatic use of the Stoic topos of things that do and do not matter. As to the first similarity, both Seneca and Paul are sufferers writing to others grieved at their misfortune:[261] Seneca is in exile writing to his mother, while Paul is in prison writing to some of his closest supporters. Not surprisingly, they adopt similar consolatory strategies, not the least of which is that each begins with a lengthy report

concerning his own emotional well-being.[262] Karlhans Abel perceptively observes that Seneca is "nicht nur ihr *consolator* sondern ihr *solacium*" ("not only her [= his mother's] consoler, but her consolation").[263] The same can be said in regard to Paul and the Philippians.[264]

A second similarity between Philippians and the *Ad Helviam* is that in crafting their respective consolations both Seneca and Paul appeal programmatically to the Stoic topos "the things that do not matter" (τὰ ἀδιάφορα) (Seneca, *Ad Helv.* 4.1; Phil 1:9-10).[265] This time, however, a slight difference emerges. Seneca deploys the topos in its traditional form, focusing on the things that do not matter: "External things are of slight importance and are of little effect in either direction [i.e., towards either happiness or grief]" (*Ad Helv.* 5.1).[266] Paul, on the other hand, stands the topos on its head focusing on the things that do matter: "so that you can ascertain the things that really matter [τὰ διαφέροντα]" (1:10a). The result is that Paul's approach is much more positive, emphasizing the *presence* of "joy" versus simply the *absence* of "grief." Chrysostom notes Paul's emphasis: "But what does Paul say? Not only 'I am not grieved or overcome by these things,' but 'I rejoice and I will rejoice.'"[267]

Based on these and other similarities to the *Ad Helviam*,[268] I would even go so far as to argue that Philippians is not simply a letter of consolation but a particular

---

259   For εὐψυχέω as "console," see *BGU* 4.1097.15; *P. Oxy.* 1.115; Hermas, *Vis.* 1.3.2, and the discussion in Chapa, *Letters of Condolence*, 62–63. Cf. Eph 6:22, a piece of verisimilitude that is in its own way a commentary on Phil 2:19 and through it on 1:12-26: "[Tychicus], whom I have sent for this very reason, that you might know our affairs [τὰ περὶ ἡμῶν] and that he might console [παρακαλέσῃ] your hearts." In funerary inscriptions εὐψυχέω is synonymous with "do not grieve" (μὴ λυπῇς; Chapa, *Letters of Condolence*, 36 n. 51). See also Bärbel Kramer and Dieter Hagedorn, eds., *Griechische Papyri der Staats- und Universitätsbibliothek Hamburg (P. Hamb. IV)* (APF 4; Stuttgart/Leipzig: Teubner, 1998) 98–99.

260   I have described these in more detail in "Paul as Hellenistic Philosopher: The Evidence of Philippians," in *Paul and the Philosophers,* ed. Ward Blanton and Hent de Vries (New York: Fordham University Press, 2014) 52–68.

261   Seneca notes the uniqueness of this situation in *Ad Helv.* 2–3.

262   Seneca, *Ad Helv.* 4.2–13.8; Philippians 1–2, esp. 1:12-26.

263   Karlhans Abel, *Bauformen in Senecas Dialogen: Fünf Strukturanalysen: dial. 6, 11, 12, 1 und 2* (Bibliothek der klassischen Altertumswissenschaften 18; Heidelberg: Winter, 1967) 54 (italics original). Abel uses the Latin terms *consolator* and *solacium*. The first simply means "consoler" and is easily translated. But the latter (*solacium*) can mean not only "consolation" but "consolatory argument." Read in its epistolary context, Seneca's account of his current situation is an "argument." Presumably Abel would say the same thing of Paul's account of "my situation" in Phil 1:12-30. Cf. Seneca, *Ad Poly.* 5.5.

264   Bengel's famous *Gaudeo, gaudete* may get at this: "I rejoice, *so now you also* rejoice."

265   See Abel, *Bauformen,* 48.

266   See Meinel, *Verbannung,* 22–25, 58.

267   Hom. 4.58.16-17 Allen (on 1:18).

268   For example, both Seneca and Paul go on to mix in other similar forms of consolation: the Cyrenaic

type of letter of consolation in which *a sufferer writes to console those grieved by the sufferer's own misfortune.*[269] Seneca is quick to note this difference in his letter to his mother: "Although I unrolled all the works that the most famous writers had composed for the purpose of repressing and controlling grief, not one instance did I find of a man who had offered consolation to his loved ones when he himself was bewailed by them" (*Ad Helv.* 1.2).[270] Other letters of this subtype would include Epicurus's death-bed letters of consolation to two of his disciples—Hermarchus of Mitilene, who would succeed him as head of his school,[271] and Idomeneus of Lampsacus[272]—and Mara bar Serapion's letter from prison to his son.[273] Chrysostom's letters of consolation from exile to his friend Olympias[274] stand at the head of a long tradition of exiled bishops writing back to console their supporters.[275] The so-called family letters by young recruits to their families back home adduced by Alexander might also be analyzed along these lines,[276] as might a number of Greco-Roman speeches of those about to die.[277]

c. Philippians as a Letter Sent by a Prisoner

In addition to being a letter of consolation, Philippians was also a letter from prison. Prison letters had not yet become a recognized genre by the time Philippians was written,[278] but a handful of these letters survive, and they offer several interesting points of comparison and contrast.[279] The most obvious feature of these letters is the writer's desperate need for clothes or food and his or

---

269 topos that misfortune is to be expected (*Ad Helv.* 5.3–5 and Phil 1:28-30), and the popular strategy of finding a replacement for an absent loved one (*Ad Helv.* 18.1–19.7 and Phil 2:19-24). For other similarities, see my "Paul as Hellenistic Philosopher" and the commentary below.

269 Recall Jerome on Phil 1:12-13 (*PL* 30:881.15): "he consoles them regarding his own suffering [*de sua tribulatione*]."

270 This oddity perhaps helps to explain why commentators have failed to describe Philippians as a letter of consolation.

271 Preserved in Latin translation at Cicero, *De fin.* 2.96 (= Usener frag. 122).

272 See Diogenes Laertius, *Vit.* 10.22 (= Usener frag. 138; Arrighetti frag. 52).

273 Mara's letter raises the question of whether Paul's letter might also be classified as a "letter from prison."

274 See Jean Chrysostome, *Lettres à Olympias; vie d'Olympias*, ed. and trans. Anne-Marie Malingrey (2nd ed.; SC 13; Paris: Cerf, 1968); see also Chrysostom's letter-essay *Quod nemo laed.* sent under similar circumstances (Jean Chrysostome, *Lettre d'exil à Olympias et à tous les fidèles*, ed. and trans. Anne-Marie Malingrey [SC 103; Paris: Cerf, 1964]).

275 See, e.g., Neil Bronwen, "From *tristia* to *gaudia*: The Exile and Martyrdom of Pope Martin," in *Martyrdom and Persecution in Late Antique Christianity: Festschrift Boudewijn Dehandschutter*, ed. J. Leemans (BETL 241; Leuven: Peters, 2010) 179–94, who cites the exiled Martin's fourth letter (*Narr. de exil.* 30), which begins, "We always have every desire to comfort you [*consolandi*] with our letters, beloved, and to relieve you of your anxiety [*solicitudine*] for us" (trans. Bronwen, modified; p. 186 n. 25).

276 Alexander herself comes close to this when she says that "reassurance" is the "functional centre" of these letters and of Philippians ("Hellenistic Letter-Forms," 95).

277 E.g., Plato, *Apol.* 39e–42a; *Phaedo*; Xenophon, *Apol.* 27–28; *Cyroped.* 7.6–28; Cicero, *De sen.* 22.79–81; *De fin.* 2.96; Tacitus, *Ann.* 15.60–64; *Agr.* 46.1; Dio Chrysostom, *Or.* 30; Diogenes Laertius, *Vit.* 10.22. Dio Chrysostom (*Or.* 30.6) specifically identifies these speeches as consolatory. I discuss these speeches in more detail in "Left Behind," 11–16. Consolation does not play a prominent role in the Jewish testamentary genre, where the emphasis is almost exclusively hortatory (as emphasized by Eckhard von Nordheim, *Die Lehre der Alten*, Band 1: *Das Testament als Literaturgattung im Judentum der hellenistisch-römischen Zeit* [ALGHJ 13; Leiden: Brill, 1980]) and predictive (so Enric Cortès, *Los discursos de adiós de Gn 49 a Jn 13–17: Pistas para la historia de un género literario en la antigua literatura judía* [CSP 23; Barcelona: Herder, 1976] esp. 486–88).

278 Roman elites were typically exiled, not imprisoned, and so the prison letter, unlike letters from exile, was slow to develop as a genre.

279 Müller, p. 51; cf. Wilhelm Michaelis, "Die Gefangenschaftsbriefe des Paulus und antike Gefangenenbriefe," *NKZ* 36 (1925) 586–95; and the recent assessment by Angela Standhartinger, "Letter from Prison as Hidden Transcript: What It Tells Us about the People at Philippi," in *The People beside Paul: The Philippian Assembly and History from Below*, ed. Joseph A. Marchal (ECL 17; Atlanta: SBL Press, 2015) 107–40. Michaelis and Standhartinger discuss the following papyrus letters from prison: *PSI* 4.416; 7.807; *P. Petr.* 3.36 recto; *P. Petr.* 3.36 verso; *P. Yale* 34; 42 (= White, *Light*, no. 28); *P. Oxy.* 56.3870; *P. Polit. Jud.*

her passionate plea for help,[280] which sometimes includes an appeal to a particular deity (*P. Yale* 42). The writer often complains of not having heard from the recipient for some time[281] and expresses his or her anxiety and requests news of the recipient's well-being (*P. Yale* 42). If the writer's situation is not completely desperate, which it almost always is, he or she might also seek to reassure the recipient regarding his or her (i.e., the writer's) own well-being (*P. Yale* 42).

P. Yale 42 is a good example of a prison letter that displays many of these features. It can be dated to the reign of Ptolemy Euergetes (247–221 BCE) and is from a certain Nechthosiris, the steward of the toparch Leon in Philadelphia. Nechthosiris and certain of Leon's slaves are being held in prison in Alexandria, possibly because of a dispute between Leon and the dioiketes Athenodorus. Nechthosiris begins by complaining that he has written repeatedly to Leon but has yet to receive a reply. In his "anxiety" (ἀγωνία) he has consulted the god Sarapis. News from Philadelphia has recently been brought by a certain Protolaos: "[W]hen Protolaos brought us word of how things are with you [τὰ κατά σε] I rejoiced greatly [λίαν ἐχάρην]." But there has still been no letter from Leon. Nechthosiris asks that Leon instruct his agent Dionysius to bring him and the others food and clothes when he next visits Alexandria. He then reassures Leon that so far his case (περὶ δὲ τῶν κατ᾽ ἐμέ) has gone well—the first hearing was favorable but the case is on appeal to Euergetes—and that should Apollonius (Leon's brother?) come to Alexandria his case will likely receive a favorable verdict, too. Nechthosiris urges Leon "not to be anxious" (μὴ ἀγωνία).

Like Alexander's so-called family letters,[282] *P. Yale* 42 offers a number of striking parallels to Philippians. Paul too is anxious about his readers' welfare (τὰ περὶ ὑμῶν, 1:27; 2:19), and he is quick to reassure them that

things are well with him (τὰ κατ᾽ ἐμέ, 1:12; cf. 2:23). He complains that he has not heard from them for a while—"now at last [ἤδη ποτέ] you revived your mindfulness of me" (4:10)—but reports that he "rejoiced greatly" (ἐχάρην . . . μεγάλως; 4:10) when their representative arrived. As occasion permits, Paul also discusses intermediaries (Timothy and Epaphroditus; 2:19-30). Paul's "need" (2:25; cf. 4:11) and "affliction" (4:14) are also addressed but only to thank his readers for having already sent assistance (4:10-20). Paul is careful to say that, despite conditions in prison, their gift has been more than adequate, and like Nechthosiris he urges them not to be anxious (μηδὲν μεριμνᾶτε; 4:6). It is noteworthy that, unlike Nechthosiris, Paul has no real assurance to offer about his trial as such[283] but only on its fortunate effects, such as the "progress" of the gospel and his "salvation" should he endure his ordeal without denying Christ (1:12, 19). It is also noteworthy that, even in the face of "hunger" and "deprivation" (4:12), Paul presents himself to the Philippians as a model of one who is "self-sufficient" (αὐτάρκης; 4:11) in all things.[284]

6. The Disposition of the Letter

If we allow that Paul composed Philippians pretty much as we now find it in the manuscript tradition, and if we agree that, regardless of whatever uniqueness it might possess as an early apostolic letter, Philippians can also be described as a letter of consolation—in the ancient sense of that term—then we are immediately met with the problem that ancient letters of consolation, fitted as they are to the specific situation of the sufferer,[285] differ significantly in terms of their overall structure or disposition.[286] The most that can be said is that they typically begin with a warm and friendly

---

2; *SB* 1.4301; *P. Cair. Masp.* 1.67020; cf. the sixth-century CE Coptic ostracon *O. Mon. Epiph.* 177 (ET in Roger S. Bagnall and Raffaela Cribiore, *Women's Letters from Ancient Egypt, 300 BC–AD 800* [Ann Arbor: University of Michigan Press, 2006] 246). For a letter to a prisoner, see Apollonius of Tyana's letter to Musonius Rufus at Philostratus, *Vit. Apoll.* 4.46.

280 *PSI* 4.416; *P. Petr.* 3.36 recto; *P. Petr.* 3.36 verso; *P. Oxy.* 56.3870; *O. Mon. Epiph.* 177.

281 *P. Petr.* 3.36 verso; *P. Yale* 42; *O. Mon. Epiph.* 177.

282 Alexander, "Hellenistic Letter-Forms."

283 For the nominal reassurance offered in 1:25-26, see

the commentary on 1:22-26 below, as well as my forthcoming (2017) "Deliberating Life and Death: Paul's Tragic *Dubitatio* in Philippians 1:22-26."

284 Michaelis, "Die Gefangenschaftsbriefe," 590.

285 Cicero, *Tusc.* 3.31.76: "one person is moved in one way, and another person in another way."

286 Ancient letters of consolation were distinguished by their purpose and content more than by their form. Here see esp. J. H. D. Scourfield, who demonstrates that form was far less important than "purpose" or "social function" in defining the genre ("Towards a Genre of Consolation," in *Greek and Roman Consola-*

greeting,[287] and then proceed more or less seriatim through an assortment of consolatory "arguments,"[288] pausing from time to time either to offer small pieces of practical advice also of a consolatory nature or to exhort the recipient not to shirk his or her obligations and duties.[289] On this analysis the reader of Philippians can probably do no better than to take stock of Paul's consolatory arguments, noting also where he stops to advise or exhort his readers.

John Chrysostom took this approach in his published homilies on Philippians, where over the course of his exposition he is careful to identify each of the letter's various consolatory arguments. Particularly helpful are the times that Chrysostom pauses to remind his audience of the arguments that have gone before, as at the beginning of Homily 11 (Allen) on Phil 3:1-3, where he interprets the τὸ λοιπόν ("Lastly") of 3:1 as introducing the last of the letter's consolatory arguments, which arguments on his reading began in 1:12 with Paul's report on the "progress" of the gospel. He reviews these arguments for a few sentences and then, speaking in Paul's voice and working backwards from 3:1, he exclaims, "You no longer have any grounds for dejection: you have Epaphroditus, for whom you were grieved [2:25-30]; you

have Timothy [2:19-24]; I am also coming [1:22-26; cf. 2:24]; the gospel is progressing [1:12-18b]—what more do you want! Rejoice!" (11.212.11-13).[290]

Chrysostom's reading has much to recommend it, not least its elegant solution to the long-standing problem of how 3:1—4:1 fits into the rest of the letter. It also accounts nicely for the mention of Timothy and Epaphroditus in 2:19-30, who are adduced as further points of consolation.[291] By attending, then, to the letter's various consolatory arguments we arrive at the following provisional outline:

First Argument (1:12-18b): Despite Paul's imprisonment the gospel is making "progress."

Second Argument (1:18c-21): Despite the possibility of Paul's execution the current ordeal should result in his "salvation."

Third Argument (1:22-26 + 2:17-18): Paul's death, should it occur, will be a sacrifice "poured out" in the service of the gospel.[292]

Fourth Argument (2:19-24): Timothy, Paul's "like-minded" "child," will soon come as a surrogate for the absent apostle.[293]

tions: Eight Studies of a Tradition and Its Afterlife, ed. Han Baltussen [Swansea: Classical Press of Wales, 2013] 1–36). Fernando Lillo Redonet takes a slightly different approach, focusing on characteristic rhetorical elements (Palabras contra el dolor: La consolación filosófica latina de Cicerón a Frontón [Madrid: Ediciones Clásicas, 2001]). The disposition of Philippians has always been a puzzle to commentators (e.g., Lightfoot, p. 67).

287 It is in these initial words that an expression of sympathy might be found; e.g., Cicero, Ad fam. 4.5.1; 5.16.1.

288 The arguments are sometimes grouped according to theme, sometimes not; see Abel, Bauformen. Cf. Cicero's "dispositio" for consolations at Tusc. 3.32.77 and the discussion by Zimmermann, "Philosophie als Psychotherapie," 202–5; Lillo Redonet, Palabras contra el dolor, 68–69.

289 For the disputatio or schola as the typical form of consolation, sce A. E. Douglas, "Form and Content in the Tusculan Disputations," in Cicero the Philosopher: Twelve Papers, ed. J. G. F. Powell (Oxford: Clarendon, 1995) 197–208, esp. 199–205. For a close reading of two of Seneca's letters of consolation, the Ad Marciam and the Ad Helviam, see Paul A.

Holloway, "Gender and Grief: The Consolation of Women in the Early Principate," in Women and Gender in Ancient Religions: Interdisciplinary Approaches, ed. Stephen Ahearne-Kroll, Paul A. Holloway, and James A. Kelhoffer (WUNT 263; Tübingen: Mohr Siebeck, 2010) 299–321.

290 Modern biblical scholars attuned to identifying the various parts and micro-genres of a Pauline letter should note that Chrysostom, who is here more concerned with function than form, does not hesitate to interpret all of 1:12-26 + 2:17–4:1 as a series of consolatory arguments. Zahn, as I have already noted, takes a similar view: "Paul used every means in his power to dispel this feeling [among the Philippians of grief and despair] and to make the Church rejoice" (Introduction, 1:529; emphasis added).

291 According to Chrysostom (hom. 1.4.15 Allen; cf. 9.182.24-26), Paul returns to consolation, after the digression of 1:27–2:16, in 2:17-18.

292 I say more about the connection between 1:22-26 and 2:17-18 below.

293 For this reading of 2:19-24, see my "Alius Paulus" and my comments below on 2:19-24.

Fifth Argument (2:25-30): Epaphroditus has recovered and is now returned.

Sixth Argument (3:1—4:1): And "lastly" (τὸ λοιπόν), suffering of the sort that both Paul and the Philippians are experiencing brings with it a mystical and ultimately saving "knowledge of Christ."

Obviously missing from this outline is the extended exhortation of 1:27—2:16. It can readily be fitted in, however, once we recall that exhortation was an integral part of ancient consolation, especially exhortation not to shirk one's duties, which is precisely the point of 1:27—2:16: "I only ask that you act in a manner worthy of the gospel, and so on."[294] A similar account can be offered for the exhortation and consolatory advice in 4:2-9, though here the matter is not as pressing, at least as regards the disposition of the letter, since Paul often ends his letters with a paragraph of hortatory material.

Mention should be made at this point of Loveday Alexander's proposal that Philippians be compared to certain papyrus letters from young, recently deployed recruits to their anxious families.[295] We have already observed in our discussion of genre that these letters are in their own way consolatory.[296] They also cast light on the structure of Philippians. Particularly illuminating is Alexander's observation that these letters are structured around the related topics of "reassurance about the sender" and the "request for reassurance about the recipients,"[297] for which there are parallels respectively in Phil 1:12-26 ("I want you to know . . . my situation")

and 1:27—2:18 ("that . . . I might hear how things are with you"). Alexander can also account for the notice about Timothy and Epaphroditus in 2:19-30, as this pertains to another feature of these letters, namely, "information about the movements of intermediaries."

There are, however, several shortcomings with Alexander's approach. The most obvious is its difficulty in accounting for 3:1—4:1, as Alexander herself admits.[298] Moreover, Alexander can only offer a rather thin description of Paul's comments regarding Timothy and Epaphroditus in 2:19-30, which do much more than simply convey information about the movements of intermediaries.[299] A further problem is that, while Paul clearly shifts topics from himself to the Philippians at 1:27, his primary concern in 1:27—2:16 is not to request reassurance about the Philippians but to exhort them to live "in a manner worthy of the gospel." Nevertheless, the claim that Paul's objective in 1:12-26 is to "reassure" (or console) the Philippians is a lasting insight,[300] as is the location of the notices about Timothy and Epaphroditus in 2:19-30. It should also be said that, while Paul's primary purpose in 1:27—2:16 is hortatory, at several points here and elsewhere in the letter Paul makes his own consolation or "joy" depend on the Philippians, much as Alexander's young recruits' continuing equanimity is tied to news from home.[301]

Reading Philippians as a letter of consolation also helps to clarify the relationship between 1:22-26 and 2:17-18, which bookend the hortatory material in 1:27—2:16. In the above outline, I interpret 2:17-18 as a resumption

---

294 It should also be noted in this regard that the exhortation of 1:27—2:16 develops out of the consolation of 1:12-26. Thus, the theme of Paul's "absence" introduced in 1:25-26 is continued in 1:27 (cf. 2:12), where it is again relativized to the gospel.

295 Alexander, "Hellenistic Letter-Forms."

296 It is noteworthy in this regard that Alexander proposes a reading of Phil 1:12-26 that is not unlike Chrysostom's: "[Paul's first concern is to reassure the Philippians] that the situation is 'all right' in three ways: *first*, because 'what has happened to me has really served to advance the Gospel' (1.12-18); *second*, because death, if it should come, is not to be feared (1.19-23); and *third*, and slightly contradictorily, because Paul will probably soon be released anyway (1.24-26)" ("Hellenistic Letter-Forms," 95; emphases original).

297 Ibid., 91–94. As in Phil 1:27—2:16, in the "request"

portion of these letters verbs in the imperative begin to appear.

298 Ironically, it is precisely this problem she set out to solve (ibid., 89).

299 Timothy and Epaphroditus offer further examples of the virtues of Christ extolled in 2:6-11. Most importantly in my view, however, they offer additional grounds for consolation. See my commentary below on 2:19-30.

300 Paul implies as much in Phil 2:19. Cf. Seneca's similar report in *Ad Helv.* 4.2–13.8. Like Seneca and Paul, these young recruits are both their family's consolers and their consolation.

301 Phil 1:5-7; 2:2, 19, 27-28; 3:18; 4:1. Here see esp. my introductory comments on 1:27—2:16 in the commentary below.

of the consolatory argument of 1:22-26, which has been broken off by the hortatory digression of 1:27—2:16.[302] Here are 1:25-26 and 2:17-18 read together without the intervening material:

> And being confident of this, I know that I shall stay on and be restored to you all for your progress and joy in the *faith* [πίστεως], in order that your boast in Christ might increase because of me by my presence again with you. . . . *But even if* [ἀλλὰ εἰ καί] I am poured out as a libation on top of the sacrifice and service of your *faith* [πίστεως], I rejoice [in my sacrifice] and rejoice with you [in yours]; likewise you rejoice [in your sacrifice] and rejoice with me [in mine].

The nominal assurance of 1:22-26 gives way to a more frank assessment and what amounts to a *consolatio mortis* in 2:17-18.[303] This arrangement carries with it a number of implications, not the least of which is that with 2:17-18 Paul returns to the consolation of 1:12-26.[304] This in turn implies that the notices about Timothy and Epaphroditus that follow in 2:19-30 were also intended to console the Philippians, as Chrysostom correctly saw.[305]

But this raises the question why Paul chose to interrupt the consolation of 1:12-26 + 2:17-30 with the hortatory digression of 1:27—2:16. Strictly speaking, this is a matter of interpretation, not disposition per se, and

can be treated properly only in the commentary below. Nevertheless, it will be helpful to anticipate my conclusions here. I take it that Paul's point in 1:22-26 + 2:17-18 (the third argument in the outline above) is that if he is executed the Philippians can take comfort in the fact that he died in the service of the gospel.[306] But this would be a distressing thought for the Philippians at this point in time, so Paul warms to the topic slowly. He first calms his readers with the nominal assurance that that they will see him again (1:25-26). He then pauses to exhort them at length to live "in a manner worthy of the gospel" whether they see him again or not (1:27—2:16; esp. 1:27; 2:12). Then finally, after these words of exhortation, he returns to the question of the outcome of his trial, but now he speaks more frankly about the possibility of his execution: "but even if I am poured out . . ." (2:17-18).[307] In a nutshell, then, 1:22—2:18 is Paul's attempt to break a piece of bad news to his already discouraged followers in the least painful manner possible.[308]

Based on these and other more familiar considerations, I propose the following reading outline of Philippians:

1:1-2   I.   Letter prescript
1:3-11   II.   Introductory thanksgiving-period with intercessory prayer report

---

302 Most current commentators read 2:17-18 as continuing 2:12-16, but the connection is far from clear, as Friedrich has noted. It is better, with Barth and Lohmeyer, to see a reference back to 1:25-26 (Calvin and Weiss also lean in this direction). W. M. L. de Wette recommended reading 2:17 "directly" (*unmittelbar*) after 1:26 (*Kurze Erklärung der Briefe an die Colosser, an Philemon, an die Ephesier und Philipper* [Leipzig: Weidmann, 1847]).

303 Cf. Pericles's famous funeral oration, which consoles the survivors of Athens's war dead that their loved ones died for a noble cause (Thucydides, *Hist.* 2.44). Betz (*Studies*, 153) comes close to the mark when he proposes that Philippians be read as a *praemeditatio mortis*. Betz's proposal ultimately fails as a genre description of the letter as a whole, but it accurately discerns Paul's sense of his impending demise, an important insight missed by the vast majority of commentators. Cf. Chrysostom, 5.84.2 (on 2:23): "[Paul is] persuading *himself* not to grieve [πείθων ἑαυτὸν μὴ ἀλγεῖν]."

304 In addition to Chrysostom, hom. 1.4.15 Allen,

noted above, see also his comments at 2:17-18 (hom. 9.182.24 Allen): "[Paul is here] consoling [παραμυθούμενος] the Philippians regarding his own death."

305 See hom. 11.212.12 Allen cited above. That the return of Epaphroditus is consolatory is clear from 2:28 and 29 where twice Paul speaks of the Philippians "joy" at Epaphroditus's recovery and return. That the sending of Timothy is consolatory is less obvious, but see my "*Alius Paulus*," as well as the excursus "Consolation by Means of a Surrogate" in the commentary below on 2:19-24.

306 This is where the argument ends up in 2:17-18.

307 Cf. Calvin on 2:17-18: "Paul had earlier said that death was gain [*lucro*, 1:21]; but his chief worry here is that his death not confound [*conturbet*] the Philippians. And so he denies that it should be a source of grief [*tristitiae*] but an occasion for rejoicing [*laetandum*]."

308 Paul will offer further nominal assurance in 2:24.

A Note on Paul's Paragraphing

A frequent feature of Paul's prose style that can help us in accurately paragraphing his letters is his use of *sententiae*, artful turns of phrase that range in form from the traditional maxim to the fashionable bon mot.[309] Like many public speakers in his day, Paul deployed *sententiae* throughout his discourse but especially to mark the end of a line of thought.[310] C. F. Georg Heinrici dubbed these Paul's "Schlusssentenzen."[311] The Latin term was *clausula*, from *claudere*, "to close." Quintilian complained that *clausulae* were used to excess and trivialized in the process:[312]

> But now they want . . . every thought at the end of a paragraph to strike the ear. Indeed, they think it shameful, almost criminal, to take a breath at a place that does not draw applause. The result is that our discourses today are strewn with tiny, affected, and far-fetched ditties. For there simply cannot be as many good *sententiae* as there must be *clausulae*. (*Inst.* 8.5.13–14)

There were as many types of *clausulae* as there were types of *sententiae*.[313] Four types particularly relevant to

---

309 Holloway, "Paul's Pointed Prose." Accomplished speakers were also able to produce metrical *clausulae*.

310 Quntilian *Inst.* 8.5.2: "But current custom . . . would have us reserve the term *sententia* for those striking statements that occur primarily at the end of a section of discourse [*in clausulis*], which were rare among the ancients but in our days are used without restraint"; cf. 9.3.38. Outside of Philippians, examples in Paul include Gal 2:21; 5:6; 6:10; 1 Cor 1:25; 3:17; 4:20; 6:20; 9:27; 10:31; 11:1, 31-32; 13:13; 14:20, 33, 40; 15:11, 58; 2 Cor 4:18; 5:21; 10:6, 11, 18; 12:10; Rom 2:28-29; 3:20; 6:23; 7:25b; 10:13, 17; 12:21; 14:23.

311 C. F. Georg Heinrici, "Zum Hellenismus des Paulus," in idem, *Der zweite Brief an die Korinther* (KEK 6.8; Göttingen: Vandenhoeck & Ruprecht, 1900) 454; cf. Johannes Weiss, "Beiträge zur Paulinischen Rhetorik," in *Theologische Studien: Herrn Wirkl. Oberkonsistorialrath Professor D. Bernhard Weiss zu seinem 70. Geburtstag*, ed. C. R. Gregory et al. (Göttingen: Vandenhoeck & Ruprecht, 1897) 165–247, here 189 n. 1: "die Clauseln [= *clausulae*], mit denen der Apostel grössere oder kleinere Abschnitte zu Ende führt"; Rudolf Bultmann, *Der Stil der paulinischen Predigt und die kynisch-stoische Diatribe* (FRLANT 13; Göttingen: Vandenhoeck & Ruprecht, 1910; repr., 1984) 94: "Paulus liebt es, in seine Erörterung scharf formulierte Sentenzen einzuflechten."

312 Quintilian is here caricaturing what is commonly referred to as the "*ardens* style" (*genus dicendi ardens et concitatum*, Seneca Rhetor, *Contr.* 3 pr. 7; Quintilian, *Inst.* 10.1.90; 12.9.3; Pliny, *Ep.* 1.16.2), for which see esp. Janet Fairweather, *Seneca the Elder* (Cambridge Classical Studies; Cambridge: Cambridge University Press, 1981) 200–214; Stanley Bonner, *Roman Declamation in the Late Republic and Early Empire* (Liverpool: University Press of Liverpool, 1949).

313 Quintilian gives a partial list in *Inst.* 8.5 (Jean Cousin, *Études sur Quintilien* [2 vols.; Paris: Boivin, 1935]

Paul were (1) the maxim or gnomic *sententia*, (2) the brief summary or *conclusio*, (3) the rhetorical flourish, and (4) the ἐπιφώνημα, or exclamation. Quintilian described the first of these, the maxim, as the oldest and most appropriate form of *sententia* (*Inst.* 8.5.3–8).[314] It was a complete thought succinctly expressed that could stand on its own as a memorable saying. Because these traditional *sententiae* involved not only verbal ingenuity but also substantial insight they were highly valued. Tacitus tells of young men from the provinces sent to study in Rome stealing the *sententiae* of the declaimers and including them in their letters home in an effort to show educational progress (*Dial.* 20). Paul includes a number of maxims in his letters, some of which serve as concluding thoughts.[315] One of his better known gnomic *clausulae* is Phil 1:21—"For to me to live is Christ and to die is gain"— which comes at the end of the letter's second consolatory argument (1:18c-21).[316]

A second type of *clausula* common in Paul is what Quintilian calls the *conclusio*.[317] As the name implies, it brings closure to a unit of discourse by drawing together certain of its themes or summarizing its main point. For this reason *conclusiones* tend not to be as pointed as most other *clausulae*. Paul uses *conclusiones* to round off a thought at least twice in Philippians. First at 1:18a-b: "So what really matters in this? Only that in every way, whether in pretense or in truth, Christ is proclaimed! And in this I rejoice." And again at 1:25-26: "And being confident of this, I know that I shall stay on and be restored to you all for your progress and joy in the faith, in order that your boast in Christ might increase because of me by my presence again with you."[318]

The third type of clausular sentence relevant to the reading of Paul is the rhetorical flourish, Quintilian's "tiny, affected, and far-fetched ditties." By the standards of the day Paul's clausular flourishes were modest and could even be substantive. Though not fully independent maxims, they are generally well fitted to their contexts and show a good amount of variety deploying such figures as wordplay,[319] antithesis,[320] paradox,[321] climax,[322] and what Quintilian calls doubling (*geminatio*).[323] *Inclusio* (repeating an expression from the beginning of a line of thought at its end) should probably also be included in this list,[324] as well as certain liturgical expressions.[325]

A fourth type of traditional concluding sentence not particularly common in Paul but used in Philippians is

1:423–25; D. M. Kriel, "Forms of the *Sententia* in Quintilian VIII.v.3-24," *AClass* 4 [1961] 80–89). The *sententia* was also the topic of Domitius Marus's *De urbanitate*, for which see E. Ramage, "The *De urbanitate* of Domitius Marus," *CP* 54 (1959) 250–55. A much more detailed treatment is the elder Seneca's *Oratorum et rhetorum sententiae divisiones colores*, for which see Michael Winterbottom, *The Elder Seneca: Declamations* (2 vols.; LCL; Cambridge, MA: Harvard University Press, 1974); cf. Henri Bornecque, *Les déclamations et les déclamateurs d'après Sénèque le père* (Lille: University of Lille Press, 1902); Fairweather, *Seneca the Elder*; eadem, "The Elder Seneca and Declamation," *ANRW* 3.32.1 (1984) 514–56.

314 Cf. Aristotle, *Rhet.* 2.21.1394a.19–1395b.20; Theophrastus apud Gregory of Corinth, Περὶ τροπ. 7.1154.23 (Walz); *Rhet. ad Alex.* 11.1430b.1-29; *Rhet. ad Her.* 4.17.24–25; Demetrius, *Eloc.* 9; Hermogenes, *Prog.* 4.24–27; Aphthonius, *Prog.* 4.67–72; Priscianus, *Praeex.* 3.11–14.

315 Holloway, "Paul's Pointed Prose," 49–50.

316 Phil 2:13 is a maxim used not as a *clausula* but as a rhetorical proof. Cf. Aristotle, *Rhet.* 2.20.1393a24–26.

317 Quintilian, *Inst.* 8.5.13; 5.10.2; 5.14.1, 20; cf. *Rhet. ad Her.* 4.30.41; Cicero, *Top.* 13.54; 14.56–57.

318 Phil 3:16 might also be classified as a *conclusio*.

319 E.g., Phil 4:9; cf. Rom 3:26; 1 Cor 9:23; cf. Quintilian, *Inst.* 8.5.20: *sententia a verbo*.

320 E.g., Phil 2:4; cf. 1 Cor 10:12; Rom 4:25; 12:21; cf. Quintilian, *Inst.* 8.5.9 (cf. 8.5.18): *sententia ex contrariis*; 8.5.5: γνώμη *ex diversis*, for which see Holloway, "Enthymeme," 329–39.

321 E.g., Phil 2:8; cf. Rom 1:32; 9:30-31. "Paradox" here is meant in the ancient sense of something surprising (Quintilian, *Inst.* 9.2.23: "παράδοξον . . . id est inopinatum").

322 E.g., Phil 3:10-11; Rom 10:17.

323 E.g., Phil 1:30; 2:4; 2:16; cf. Quintilian, *Inst.* 8.5.18, who quotes from a letter written by Seneca to be sent to the senate by Nero after the murder of Nero's mother: "I can neither believe nor rejoice [*nec credo nec gaudeo*] that I am safe." He prefers Cicero's "I have someone to flee, but someone to follow I have not" (*Habeo quem fugiam; quem sequar non habeo*; *Ad Att.* 8.7.2).

324 E.g., Phil 4:1 (cf. 3:1).

325 E.g., Phil 2:11; 4:20; cf. 1 Thess 3:11-13; Rom 11:33-36; and often elsewhere.

the ἐπιφώνημα, or "exclamation," in which an emotional crescendo is achieved.[326] Quintilian (*Inst.* 8.5.11) cites Virgil, *Aen.* 1.33: *Tantae molis erat Romanam condere gentem!* ("So great a toil it was to found the Roman race!"). A clear instance of this is the oath of Phil 1:8, which concludes the first part of his introductory paragraph in preparation for the prayer report of 1:9-11: "for God is my witness how I long for you all with the deepest affections of Christ!" Another possible ἐπιφώνημα is 3:11: "if somehow I might arrive at the resurrection from the dead!"[327]

7. Key Religious Topoi

Paul's letters stand at the head of what would become the Christian theological tradition, and it is tempting to imagine Paul as the first Christian theologian. This could be misleading.[328] Paul's letters do not yet bear witness to a body of carefully defined "doctrines" but rather to a set of ready-to-hand religious topoi, or "places," where Paul went to construct this or that argument or to press home this or that exhortation, always in support of some apostolic objective. In this regard Paul was not unlike a provincial orator with his collection of set themes, although in Paul's case these themes derived not so much from commonly held social and political ideals—although Paul made use of these too from time to time—as from his own distinctive constellation of religious myths and moral assumptions.[329]

a. Paul's Apocalyptic Heritage

Paul's principal concern in his letter to the Philippians, as in most of his letters, was with the eschatological salvation of his gentile readers. He imagined this salvation coming at the end of an arduous process of divine enablement and human effort.[330] In the case of the Philippians, he worried that this process had been interrupted by their grief over his imprisonment and their unexpected suffering and that, as a result, they were no longer living "in a manner worthy of the gospel" (1:27). He prayed that by the coming "Day of Christ"[331] they would be "filled with the fruit of righteousness to the glory and praise of God" (1:10-11).[332] He urged them to "work hard to accomplish [their] salvation" (2:12) so that he would not have "labored in vain" (2:16).[333]

As a Pharisee (Phil 3:5), Paul derived his theory[334] of salvation from Jewish apocalyptic speculation.[335] Late exilic and postexilic prophecy promised the salvation of the nation as a whole: the Jewish exiles in Babylon and elsewhere would return to their ancestral lands, Jerusa-

---

326 Quintilian, *Inst.* 8.5.11; Demetrius, *Eloc.* 2.106.

327 Cf. Karl Ludwig Bauer, *Rhetoricae Paullinae* (2 vols.; Halae: Impensis Orphanotrophei, 1782) 2:756–60, who also lists Rom 1:31; 7:24; 2 Cor 9:15.

328 William Wrede, *Paul* (London: Green, 1907) 74–84.

329 In the case of Philippians, Paul drew not only on the religious themes summarized below but on a number of popular and philosophical themes surrounding the problem of grief and its cure (consolation), which I have discussed in the first part of this introduction. For Paul's moral assumptions and religious taboos, which do not figure prominently in Philippians, see esp. Dale B. Martin, *The Corinthian Body* (New Haven: Yale University Press, 1999).

330 E.g., 2:12-13; cf. 1:6, 29; 2:29-30; 3:12-14. For the larger question of agency in Paul, see John M. G. Barclay and Simon J. Gathercole, eds., *Divine and Human Agency in Paul and His Cultural Environment* (LNTS 335; London: T&T Clark, 2006).

331 For "Day of Christ" and similar expressions denoting eschatological judgment, see the commentary below on 1:10b-11.

332 Cf. 1:6; 1 Thess 3:13; 5:23; 1 Cor 1:8; 2 Cor 11:2; Gal 5:5; Rom 15:16.

333 This phrase is one of several euphemisms in the letter, the reference in this case being to the Philippians' possible failure to achieve "salvation." Cf. 4:1; 1Thess 2:19; 3:5; 1 Cor 15:2; 2 Cor 6:1; Gal 4:11.

334 I use "theory" here with some hesitation. Paul's inherently mythological manner of thinking must not be overrationalized. Nevertheless, it seems to me that within his mythological framework Paul gave considerable thought to solving various types of problems—both speculative and practical—and that from his often conflicting myths he constructed a largely coherent account. I struggle to find a better word.

335 So Schweitzer, *Mysticism*; echoed by Ernst Käsemann, "The Beginnings of Christian Theology," in idem, *New Testament Questions Today* (London: SCM Press, 1969) 82–107; and, in the same volume, "On the Subject of Primitive Christian Apocalyptic," 108–37; cf. J. Christiaan Beker, *Paul the Apostle: The Triumph of God in Life and Thought* (Philadelphia: Fortress, 1980) 135–81; J. Louis Martyn, *Theological Issues in the Letters of Paul* (London: T&T Clark, 1997) 85–156. For Paul as Pharisee, see also Gal 1:14; Acts 22:3; 23:6.

lem would be rebuilt and Israel restored to its alleged former preeminence, and all the gentiles would either turn to the God of Israel and pay tribute to his people or be destroyed.[336] This of course did not happen. Israel as such was not reconstituted, and those Jews who did return from exile, along with those who were never deported, continued to be subjected to one form or another of imperial domination. Eventually, a new theory of salvation commonly referred to today as apocalypticism was developed that took these disappointments into account.[337]

The genius of apocalypticism was that it transferred traditional hopes of salvation from the present life, where failed predictions were the rule, to an ideal world to come that would soon be inaugurated directly by God or God's agent.[338] According to one influential strand of apocalyptic myth, this eschatological salvation would extend not to the Jewish nation as a whole but only to the "righteous" who steadfastly resisted the encroachments of foreign custom,[339] and possibly to any who converted to their cause in the last days.[340] In the world to come these righteous few and their followers would be resurrected and rewarded and their "unrighteous" detractors punished.[341] Presently, the righteous were being perfected by persecution,[342] in which they were sustained and transformed by special revelations and God's spirit.[343] This inherently sectarian theology found concrete expression in a number of apocalyptic groups, each of which imagined itself as the eschatological community of the suffering righteous.[344] We have firsthand knowledge of three of these groups: the evolving group behind the documents constituting *1 Enoch*;[345] the Essene assemblies revealed in

336 See, e.g., the texts collected in E. P. Sanders, *Judaism: Practice and Belief, 63 BCE – 66 CE* (London: SCM, 1992) 289–94.

337 Collins, "From Prophecy to Apocalypticism"; cf. Carroll, *When Prophecy Failed*, 204–13.

338 These "agents" were imagined in various ways depending on the amount of God's direct involvement. The greater the agency attributed to them, the more powerful they were imagined to be. In Daniel, for instance, the agent of God's salvation is the mighty archangel Michael, who for all practical purposes acts alone (12:1). For the otherworldliness of apocalyptic myth, see Collins, "Apocalyptic Eschatology."

339 We see this narrowing, for example, in the transformation of the biblical cliché "[the whole] congregation of Israel" (e.g., Exod 12:3, 47), which becomes at this time the "congregation of the righteous" (*1 Enoch* 38:1) or "the congregation of the chosen and holy" (*1 Enoch* 62:8); cf. *Pss. Sol.* 17:16 (18); 4QpPs37 [4Q171] 2:5; 11QPsᵃ [11Q5] 18:10; but see 1QSa [1Q28a] 1:1, where the term "congregation of Israel" is itself appropriated by the sect. Other texts indicating a sectarian shift include *1 Enoch* 91:10; 92:3-4; 93:10; 104:12-13; CD 1:3-12; 2:14–4:12; 5:20–6:11; 1QS 8–9; Patrick A. Tiller, "'The Eternal Planting' in the Dead Sea Scrolls," *DSD* 4 (1997) 313–35; George W. E. Nickelsburg, "Religious Exclusivism: A World View Governing Some Texts Found at Qumran," in *Das Ende der Tage und die Gegenwart des Heils: Begegnungen mit dem Neuen Testament und seiner Umwelt; Festschrift für Heinz-Wolfgang Kuhn zum 65. Geburtstag,* ed. Michael Becker and Wolfgang Fenske (AGJU 44; Leiden: Brill, 1999) 45–67; idem, *Ancient Juda-*

ism and Christian Origins: Diversity, Continuity, and Transformation* (Minneapolis: Fortress, 2003) 160–84; Nickelsburg and VanderKam, *1 Enoch 2*, 46–48.

340 For continued hopes of national salvation, see *1 Enoch* 90:34-38; *Jub.* 1:15-25; cf. *Pss. Sol.* 17:21-26 (cited by James D. G. Dunn, *The New Perspective on Paul* [rev. ed.; Grand Rapids: Eerdmans, 2008] 66).

341 Sometimes this post-mortem existence was imagined as otherworldly, sometimes as occurring on a renewed earth; and sometimes these conceptions were combined, as in Dan 12:2-3, where the righteous are raised to what appears to be a new earthly existence and the "wise," the visionary leaders of the movement, to a kind of astral immortality.

342 Dan 11:35; *Pss. Sol.* 3:3-10; 10:1-3; 13:8-10; 18:4; *2 Bar.* 13:1-2; 4 Ezra 7:14; cf. Jas 1:2-4; Rev 7:14. More generally, see 2 Macc. 6:12-17.

343 For speculation regarding the divine spirit in Second Temple Judaism, see John R. Levison, *Filled with the Spirit* (Grand Rapids: Eerdmans, 2009); and, more broadly, Jörg Frey and John R. Levison, eds., *The Holy Spirit, Inspiration, and the Cultures of Antiquity: Multidisciplinary Perspectives* (Ekstasis 5; Berlin: de Gruyter, 2014).

344 Wolfgang Kraus, *Das Volk Gottes: Zur Grundlegung der Ekklesiologie bei Paulus* (WUNT 85; Tübingen: Mohr Siebeck, 1996); for the emerging sectarian realities behind Isaiah 56–66, see esp. Isa 66:2, 5 and the comments on these verses in Blenkinsopp, *Isaiah 56–66*.

345 For a recent discussion of this group, see John J. Collins, "'Enochic Judaism' and the Sect of the Dead Sea Scrolls," in *The Early Enoch Literature,* ed. Gabriele

the sectarian writings from Qumran; and the early Christian assemblies established by Paul in such urban centers as Philippi, Thessalonica, and Corinth.[346]

Paul left much from his apocalyptic heritage intact: its belief in an eschatological community of the righteous,[347] its theory of redemptive suffering,[348] its emphasis on special revelations and endowments of God's spirit, its hope of resurrection and reward.[349] But there were new problems to be solved. Not the least of these was how to incorporate into the expectations of the last days the belief that the agent of God's salvation had *already* appeared in the person of Jesus of Nazareth and that,

rather than inaugurating a new era as apocalyptic myth predicted, he had been executed by the Romans and raised from the dead![350] Had the resurrection of the righteous begun?[351] Was the end about to arrive? Was it already taking shape?[352] A related problem was whether this turn of events had altered the status of gentiles. Did the old amorphous category of "God-fearer" still hold?[353] Or were gentiles who "turned to God from idols . . . to wait for his son from heaven whom he raised from the dead" (1 Thess 1:9-10) even now part of the eschatological people of God? And if so on what terms?[354] The second problem proved to be particularly thorny, not only

---

Boccaccini and John J. Collins (JSJSup 121; Leiden: Brill, 2007) 283–99.

346 It is unclear to what degree Enochic Judaism and the Essenes are to be understood as two phases in the same overall movement; see Florentino García Martínez and Adam S. van der Woude, "A 'Groningen' Hypothesis of Qumran Origins and Early History," *RevQ* 14 (1990) 521–41; Gabriele Boccaccini, *Beyond the Essene Hypothesis: The Parting of the Ways between Qumran and Enochic Judaism* (Grand Rapids: Eerdmans, 1998); Boccaccini, ed., *Enoch and Qumran Origins: New Light on a Forgotten Connection* (Grand Rapids: Eerdmans, 2005). For sectarianism at Qumran, see Eyal Regev, *Sectarianism in Qumran: A Cross-Cultural Perspective* (Religion and Society 45; Leiden: Brill, 2007); Nickelsburg, "Religious Exclusivism"; for early Christianity, see Nickelsburg, "Revealed Wisdom as a Criterion for Inclusion and Exclusion: From Jewish Sectarianism to Early Christianity," in *"To See Ourselves as Others See Us": Christians, Jews, "Others" in Late Antiquity*, ed. Jacob Neusner and Ernest S. Frerichs (Scholars Press Studies in the Humanities; Chico, CA: Scholars Press, 1985) 73–91.

347 Like the Essenes, this "community" was composed of various local assemblies, what Paul called ἐκκλησίαι.

348 Paul would eventually modify this to incorporate the fact that Jesus himself had suffered and that by suffering Christ-believers were not only perfected but also brought into a kind of mystical, imitative relationship with Christ. This becomes a key theme in Phil 3:1—4:1, for which see my comments on that passage in the commentary below.

349 For a general introduction to Paul's apocalypticism, see Martinus C. de Boer, "Paul and Apocalyptic Eschatology," in *Encyclopedia of Apocalypticism*, vol. 1: *The Origins of Apocalypticism in Judaism and Christianity*, ed. John J. Collins (New York: Continuum, 2000) 345–83.

350 In effect, this was another instance of failed prophecy. In the person of Jesus of Nazareth and in the beliefs circulating about him among his followers the seemingly nonfalsifiable promises of apocalypticism had themselves became subject to empirical falsification.

351 See Paul's innovations on this core belief in 1 Cor 15:20-28; cf. Col 1:18.

352 This question also arose among the sectaries at Qumran, though for different reasons. Here see esp. John J. Collins, "The Angelic Life" in *Metamorphoses: Resurrection, Body, and Transformative Practices in Early Christianity*, ed. Turid Karlsen Seim and Jorunn Økland (Ekstasis 1; Berlin/New York: de Gruyter, 2009) 291–310. In the so-called Apocalypse of Weeks (*1 Enoch* 93:1-10 + 91:11-17), the end of days was imagined as an extended period of time. The same was true in the sectarian documents from Qumran.

353 For the well-known problems and ambiguities associated with this term, see esp. Joyce M. Reynolds and Robert F. Tannenbaum, *Jews and God-Fearers at Aphrodisias: Greek Inscriptions with Commentary; Texts from the Excavations at Aphrodisias Conducted by Kenan T. Erim* (CPSSup 12; Cambridge: Cambridge Philological Society, 1987); cf. John J. Collins, *Between Athens and Jerusalem: Jewish Identity in the Hellenistic Diaspora* (2nd ed.; Grand Rapids: Eerdmans, 2000) 264–70.

354 Were the great biblical prophecies that spoke of nations submitting to the rule of Israel and worshiping Yahweh now in play (so Paul in Romans 11)? *1 Enoch* 90:37-38 imagines a radical restoration in which both Jews and gentiles are restored to primordial righteousness (Nickelsburg, *1 Enoch 1*, on *1 Enoch* 90:37-38). A further problem was the terms on which believing gentiles might be welcome. Would it be sufficient for them to observe certain food laws so as to share a common table (Peter's

because of ambiguities regarding the present status of gentiles in the apocalyptic plan of God but because many Jews, including Paul, were convinced that gentiles were "sinners" in desperate need of sanctification, without which they were unfit to be counted among the righteous either in this life or the life to come.[355]

b. Paul's Spirit-Christ

Apocalypticism brought with it robust speculation about the agent of God's eschatological salvation. For the author of Daniel, this agent was the angel Michael (12:1), "one like a son of man" (7:13),[356] who stood at the head of thousands of "holy ones" (7:18; cf. 8:13). Pious Jews were "the people of the holy ones" (7:27), which is to say those whose cause was supported by the angels.[357] Angels were also the agents of God's eschatological salvation in *1 Enoch*, and especially in the Parables of Enoch (*1 Enoch* 37–72), where speculation regarding an angelic hero now identified titularly as "that Son of Man" was merged with

earlier predictions of an anointed ruler or Messiah.[358] The result was a *heavenly* Messiah/Son of Man whose coming rule now included ascending to God's "throne of glory" to judge the world.[359] The Enochic Messiah/Son of Man figured prominently in early Christian attempts to solve the first problem above—how to imagine Jesus apocalyptically—and provides a striking analogy for Paul's heavenly Christ (cf. Phil 2:6-11).[360]

Particularly important for a historically informed reading of Paul is the fact that the Enochic Messiah/Son of Man was not simply a mighty patron and eventual savior of the righteous, as Michael had been in Daniel, but that he was in some sense their heavenly *Doppelgänger,* or double. In other words, not only could Enochic Jews look to their angelic Messiah/Son of Man for their eventual salvation, but even in this life they could identify with him as a kind of heavenly counterpart.[361] He was "the Chosen One," they were "the chosen ones"; he was "the Righteous One," they were "the righteous ones"; he was

---

and possibly James's view; Gal 2:12a)? Or would they have to convert and, if male, be circumcised (the view of the so-called circumcision party; Gal 2:12b)? Or did they merely have to give up their idolatry and lead morally upright lives (Paul's view; Gal 2:13-14; 1 Thess 1:9-10)? Here see the astute observations by Paula Fredriksen, "Mandatory Retirement: Ideas in the Study of Christian Origins Whose Time Has Come to Go," *SR* 35 (2006) 231–46, esp. 234–37.

355   Gal 2:15; cf. 1 Thess 4:5; 1 Cor 5:1; Rom 1:18-32. It is one of the great ironies of Paul's letters that, despite his self-understanding as "apostle to the gentiles" (e.g., Rom 11:13) and his conviction that Christ-believing gentiles should be fully incorporated into his assemblies, Paul remained deeply prejudiced against them. Subsequent history has shown that a desire for mission and a continuing prejudice against the missionized are not mutually exclusive.

356   For the "Son of Man" figure in Judaism and early Christianity, see Adela Yarbro Collins and John J. Collins, *King and Messiah as Son of God: Divine, Human, and Angelic Messianic Figures in Biblical and Related Literature* (Grand Rapids: Eerdmans, 2008) 75–100, 149–74.

357   Collins, *Daniel,* on 7:27.

358   Nickelsburg and VanderKam, *1 Enoch 2,* 113–23; and, more generally, the essays in *Enoch and the Messiah Son of Man: Revisiting the Book of Parables,* ed. Gabriele Boccaccini (Grand Rapids: Eerdmans, 2007).

359   *1 Enoch* 45:3; 55:4; 61:8; 62:2, 3, 5; 69:27, 29; 71:7; cf. 61:3.

360   See James A. Waddell, *The Messiah: A Comparative Study of the Enochic Son of Man and the Pauline Kyrios* (Jewish and Christian Texts in Context 10; London/New York: Bloomsbury T&T Clark, 2011). Like the Messiah/Son of Man of the Parables of Enoch, Paul's Christ would also to come as judge; see, e.g., 2 Cor 5:10; Rom 2:16; 14:10 *v.l.*; cf. *1 Enoch* 61:6–63:12. This same function is attributed to Christ in the so-called Synoptic Sayings Source (Q [= Luke] 12:40; 17:24, 26, 30; cf. Luke 6:22; 11:30; 12:8-9) and in the later Synoptic tradition, esp. Matt 19:28; 25:31, where Jesus as Son of Man sits on his "throne of glory." It is generally assumed that, while Paul was indebted to the Son of Man tradition, he avoided the title "Son of Man" because the expression would have been incomprehensible to his readers (Nickelsburg and VanderKam, *1 Enoch 2,* 74)—as it has been to many subsequent interpreters.

361   Collins, "Heavenly Representative"; see also Alan F. Segal, "Ruler of the World: Attitudes about Mediator Figures and the Importance of Sociology for Self-Definition," in *Jewish and Christian Self-Definition,* vol. 2, ed. E. P. Sanders, A. I. Baumgarten, and Alan Mendelson (Philadelphia: Fortress Press, 1981) 245–68.

"hidden" and so were they; he would be "revealed" triumphant in the last days and so would they.[362] Paul theorized that Jesus's suffering, death, and resurrection produced further points of contact between Christ-believers and their heavenly Christ. The result was a set of "realistic" tropes that came to characterize Paul's discourse regarding salvation: Christ-believers had died with Christ in baptism;[363] they presently suffer with him at the hands of the wicked;[364] they would soon be raised with him (1 Thess 4:13; Rom 6:5); even now the power of his resurrection was operative within them (Phil 3:10; cf. Rom 6:4).

Also important to Paul's Christ-myth was his understanding of resurrection. Like many of his Jewish contemporaries, Paul believed that those entering the world to come did so with a σῶμα, or "body."[365] However, Paul imagined this "body" not as an earthly, human body, a body still made of "flesh and blood" (1 Cor 15:50) but a "heavenly body," probably like the body of an angel.[366] In 1 Cor 15:44 Paul describes this body as a σῶμα πνευματικόν, or "body made of spirit."[367] In 1 Cor 15:45 he dispenses with the term "body" altogether and speaks of the resurrected person simply as a πνεῦμα ("spirit"),[368] which he is able to do, presumably, because, not unlike the Stoics, he imagined πνεῦμα as a very fine material substance.[369] Such a body would be able to bear the "weight of glory" and "inherit the kingdom of God" (2 Cor 4:17; 1 Cor 15:50).[370] This was the type of body that the righ-

---

362 The relevant texts are given and discussed in Nickelsburg and VanderKam, *1 Enoch 2*, 98–101, 113–20. For the hidden/revealed motif, see *1 Enoch* 38:1-2; 48:6-7; 53:6; 62:7; cf. 4 Ezra 7:28; 13:26. It is striking that one of the earliest interpretations of Paul's heavenly Christ makes explicit its connection to the hidden and revealed Enochic Messiah/Son of Man: "when Christ who is our life is revealed then you also will be revealed with him in glory" (Col 3:4). According to Adela Yarbro Collins (*Mark: A Commentary* [Hermeneia; Minneapolis: Fortress Press, 2007] 60–61, 69–70) this motif also lies behind Mark's so-called Messianic Secret.

363 Rom 6:3-4; Gal 2:19; 3:27; 5:24; cf. Col 2:12.

364 Rom 8:17; 2 Cor 4:10; cf. 2 Tim 2:3; 1 Pet 4:13. For Paul, suffering not only perfected the righteous (Rom 5:3-4) but insofar as it was imitative of Christ's own suffering produced in them a mystical γνῶσις Χριστοῦ, or "knowledge of Christ." See my comments on 3:7-11 in the commentary below.

365 E.g., 2 Macc 7:9; *2 Bar.* 50:2; cf. Josephus, *Bell.* 2.163; *Ant.* 18.14. For Paul, see esp. 1 Cor 15:35-49, where he explains in some detail "with what sort of body" (ποίῳ σώματι) the dead are raised; cf. Phil 3:21, where "the body [σῶμα] of our humiliation" is made to "conform" to the "body [σώματι] of his [Christ's] glory."

366 1 Cor 15:40: "heavenly bodies" (σώματα ἐπουράνια; cf. 15:48-49). For angels, see my comments in subsection 3 ("Paul's Metamorphic Myths") and in the commentary on 2:6.

367 Philo uses the adjective πνευματικός to describe the οὐσία, or substance, of angels in *Q. Gen.* 1.92: πνευματικὴ δὲ ἡ τῶν ἀγγέλων οὐσία ("But the substance of angels is spiritual"; for which see Françoise Petit, ed., *Philo: Quaestiones in Genesim et in Exodum:*

Fragmenta graeca [OPA 33; Paris: Cerf, 1978]); cf. *Abr.* 113, where the substance of both angels and prophets is said to be "spiritual."

368 Paul's position may be helpfully contrasted with that of *Jubilees*. For the author of *Jubilees*, the righteous dead leave their bodies behind and enter the world to come only with their "spirits" (*Jub.* 23:31), a belief sometimes referred to as the resurrection of the spirit. For Paul, however, the righteous dead are *transformed into* "spirits": "the last Adam *became* [ἐγένετο εἰς] a spirit" (1 Cor 15:45), a metamorphosis that applies to the living righteous also: "We shall not all sleep but we shall all be transformed [ἀλλαγησόμεθα]" (1 Cor 15:51; cf. Phil 3:21).

369 See Troels Engberg-Pedersen, *Cosmology and Self in the Apostle Paul: The Material Spirit* (Oxford: Oxford University Press, 2010), but see the review by John M. G. Barclay, *JSNT* 33 (2011) 406–14, who, among other things, resists Engberg-Pedersen's larger ontological claims regarding the graded relationship between God and the world.

370 For similar views of resurrection in Second Temple Judaism, see John J. Collins, *Apocalypticism in the Dead Sea Scrolls* (Literature of the Dead Sea Scrolls; London: Routledge, 1997) 112–13 (referring to Dan 12:1-3; *1 Enoch* 104:2, 4, 6; *Jub.* 23:30-31; cf. Pseudo-Phocylides, *Sent.* 103–8); Nickelsburg, *Resurrection* (expanded ed.), 141–62. According to *2 Bar.* 51:3 the righteous must "be changed into the light of their beauty, so that they will be able to acquire and receive the world that is promised to them," for which see the discussion in Matthias Henze, *Jewish Apocalpyticism in Late First Century Israel: Reading Second Baruch in Context* (TSAJ 142; Tübingen: Mohr Siebeck, 2011) 305–17.

teous would eventually possess.[371] More importantly, this is the type of body that Christ already possessed.[372]

Excursus: σῶμα πνευματικόν

The expression σῶμα πνευματικόν in 1 Cor 15:44 has proven difficult. It forms the second half of an antithesis the first part of which is σῶμα ψυχικόν: "[one] is sown a σῶμα ψυχικόν and raised a σῶμα πνευματικόν." Commentators typically assume they know what the first expression (σῶμα ψυχικόν) means and use it to interpret the latter (σῶμα πνευματικόν).[373] The reasoning goes like this: the ψυχή is a body's animating principle, therefore a σῶμα ψυχικόν is "a body animated by a ψυχή," therefore a σῶμα πνευματικόν is "a body animated by a πνεῦμα." One is buried with a body formerly animated by "soul" and raised with a body animated by "spirit," which in this case would be the Holy Spirit. This would make sense if Paul were here operating with the notion of ψυχή as animating principle. But he is not. For, as he goes on to say in the next sentence (1 Cor 15:45) quoting Gen 2:7 LXX, "The first man, Adam, became [ἐγένετο] a living ψυχή." Here ψυχή is not something that Adam *has*, it is what Adam *is*.[374] Similarly, continuing the sentence, "the last Adam [Christ] became a πνεῦμα

that gives life." Paul must be allowed to define his terms, and here he is explicit that in his resurrection Christ became a πνεῦμα. For Paul, then, a σῶμα πνευματικόν is a body made of "spirit."[375]

The understanding of resurrection as "spiritual" and Christ as a "spirit" had far-reaching implications for Paul's theory of salvation.[376] Much as an angel or demon might enter and control a human body, Paul believed that the spirit of Christ had entered his body and now possessed him.[377] "I no longer live," he writes to the Galatians, "Christ lives in me" (Gal 2:20).[378] Paul believed that the same was true for other Christ-believers: "if anyone does not have the spirit of Christ [πνεῦμα Χριστοῦ οὐκ ἔχει], this one does not belong to him" (Rom 8:9)—where "to have a spirit" (πνεῦμα ἔχειν) is a common expression denoting spirit possession.[379] For Paul, then, the spirit of God that according to apocalyptic myth sustained and transformed the righteous was none other than the resurrected Christ: "God has sent the spirit of his son into our hearts, the spirit that cries out, 'Abba!' which means father" (Gal 4:6).[380] The spirit of Christ entered a believ-

---

371 For the fate of the wicked, see the excursus in the commentary below at 1:28b, as well as my comments on 3:11. Paul did not believe that the wicked were raised.

372 1 Cor 15:45: "the last Adam became a spirit that gives life [πνεῦμα ζῳοποιοῦν]."

373 Hans Conzelmann, *1 Corinthians: A Commentary on the First Epistle to the Corinthians* (Hermeneia; Philadelphia: Fortress Press, 1975) on 15:44.

374 Elsewhere (e.g., 1 Thess 5:23) Paul uses both ψυχή and πνεῦμα as parts of a person prior to resurrection.

375 This is confirmed by 1 Cor 15:49, where resurrected believers "bear the image of the heavenly one [φορέσομεν καὶ τὴν εἰκόνα τοῦ ἐπουρανίου]," which is to say that they bear the image of the resurrected and therefore "pneumatic" Christ (cf. Phil 3:21).

376 See Martin Dibelius, *Paulus: Eine kultur- und religionsgeschichtliche Skizze* (Tübingen: Mohr Siebeck, 1911) 84–87.

377 Paul's much-discussed expression "in Christ" is probably to be explained along these lines: just as Christ-believers are "in the Spirit" (ἐν πνεύματι) because the spirit of God "dwells in" (οἰκεῖ ἐν) them (Rom 8:9), so they are "in Christ" (ἐν Χριστῷ) because Christ dwells in them (e.g., Gal 4:6). It is often noted that Paul uses the expressions "spirit of God" or πνεῦμα θεοῦ and "spirit of Christ" or πνεῦμα Χριστοῦ inter-

changeably (e.g., Rom 8:9); however, the expressions are not strictly parallel, since in the latter case the spirit in question does not in some sense *belong to* Christ but *is* Christ: "the spirit which is Christ" or even "the Christ spirit." See further my comments on 1:1-2 below.

378 See Hans Dieter Betz, *Galatians: A Commentary on Paul's Letter to the Churches in Galatia* (Hermeneia: Philadelphia: Fortress Press, 1979) on this verse. Cf. Gal 1:16: "reveal his son in [ἐν] me"; 4:6: "sent the spirit of his son into [εἰς] our hearts." It was a common belief that a possessing spirit replaced the mind of the possessed person. This typically took place in ecstatic worship (Plato, *Ion* 534a) and prophetic inspiration (Philo, *De migr. Abr.* 35; *De cher.* 27; *LAB* 28:5). Paul normalizes this experience for Christ-believers: Christ "lives in" the believer.

379 For the expression "to have a spirit," see Mark 3:30; 7:25; 9:17; Luke 4:33; 11:6; Acts 8:7; 16:16; 1 Cor 7:40; 2 Cor 4:13; cf. Mark 3:22 ("to have Beelzebul"); 5:15 ("to have Legion"); Matt 11:18; Luke 7:33; John 7:20; 10:20 ("to have a demon"). For other expressions in Paul indicating possession, see Eric Sorensen, *Possession and Exorcism in the New Testament and Early Christianity* (WUNT 2/157; Tübingen: Mohr Siebeck, 2002) 144–48.

380 Because the Galatians are crying out in ecstatic worship what Paul takes to be "Abba," it follows that the

er's body at baptism (1 Cor 12:13; Gal 3:26-27) and began a process of transformation impossible otherwise.[381] This was Paul's eventual answer to the second problem mentioned above, namely, the much-needed sanctification of gentile Christ-believers.[382]

c. Paul's Metamorphic Myths

Apocalypticism also brought increased speculation about the nature of angels and their relationship to humans.[383] Angels were imagined as luminous spirits who exhibited the glory of God to varying degrees depend-ing on their rank and proximity to the divine throne.[384] The most glorious could even be appointed to bear the divine "Name"[385] and to sit on God's throne as viceroy and judge.[386] In their dealings with humans, however, angels typically veiled their splendor and took humbler forms similar to the way the immortal gods of Greek and Roman metamorphic myths transformed themselves in order to interact with mortals.[387] In the *Testament of Job*, for instance, Satan transforms himself first into a pauper (6:4) and then into the likeness of the king of Persia (17:2). According to *T. Reub.* 5:6, the Watchers of

---

spirit possessing them is the spirit of God's son; see Wrede, *Paul*, 107–9. It is characteristic of Paul's ad hoc theologizing that he never fully reconciles his conclusion that the Christ-believer's possessing spirit is the "spirit of Christ" with his preexisting belief in a separate "spirit of God." Sometimes he equates the two (as here in Gal 4:6; cf. Rom 8:9); at other times he does not (e.g., 2 Cor 13:13; cf. Phil 2:1).

381 2 Cor 3:18: "we are metamorphosed into the same image [= the glory of the Lord] from glory to glory by the Lord who is the Spirit." In this regard the author of Colossians understood Paul's theology better than most: "Christ in you, the hope of glory" (Col 1:28). The disproportionality of the overwhelming power of the divine spirit to the problem of human, especially gentile, sinfulness is the topic of Romans 5–8, esp. 5:12-21.

382 The other commonly proposed source of transformation of gentile Christ-believers was Torah, which, it was claimed, had made the Jews a holy people; see Stanley K. Stowers, *A Rereading of Romans: Jews, Justice, and Gentiles* (New Haven: Yale University Press, 1994) 58–65. Paul, of course, famously opposed this view.

383 Michael Mach, *Die Entwicklungsstadien des jüdischen Engelglaubens in vorrabbinischer Zeit* (TSAJ 34; Tübingen: Mohr Siebeck, 1992) 132–255.

384 Seen most dramatically in the *Ascension of Isaiah*, a later Christian text with Jewish antecedents; see Mach, *Entwicklungsstadien*, 262–64. For Christ's intense reflection of the divine glory, see 2 Cor 3:18; 4:6.

385 At the head of this tradition is Exod 23:20-21. In the *Apocalypse of Abraham* the principal angel Yahoel is not only said to bear the divine name (10:3, 8), but his own doubly theophoric name, which clearly combines YAH and EL, would seem to make this assertion explicit. In *Conf.* 146 Philo describes the divine *logos* as an "archangel" (ἀρχάγγελος), "the most revered of the angels" (ὁ ἀγγέλων πρεσβύτατος),

who is sometimes called "God's name" (ὄνομα θεοῦ); in *Asc. Isa.* 7:2-4 Isaiah's glorious *angelus interpres* has an unknowable name; in *3 Enoch* 12:5 Metatron/ Enoch is called "Little YHWH"; cf. *b. Sanh.* 38b; Melchizedek has the divine name El applied to him twice at 11QMelch 2:7-14.

386 *1 Enoch* 45:3; 51:3; 55:4; 61:8; 62:2, 3, 5; 69:27, 29 (Messiah/Son of Man who sits on the "throne of glory" belonging to the Lord of Spirits; cf. Matt 19:28; 25:31). In this regard it is noteworthy that in *Apoc. Abr.* 10:4 Yahoel is said to be in the "likeness of a man," an allusion to the enthroned "likeness of a man" in Ezek 1:26 (Schäfer, *Origins*, 88); further allusion to the enthroned "Glory" in Ezekiel 1 lies in the descriptions of various principal angels that are often strikingly similar to the enthroned figure in Ezekiel. For an account of these angels, see Charles A. Gieschen, *Angelomorphic Christology: Antecedent and Early Evidence* (AGJU 42; Leiden: Brill, 1998) 124–50; cf. the wide-ranging essay by Martin Hengel, "Sit at My Right Hand!" in Hengel, *Studies in Early Christology* (Edinburgh: T&T Clark, 1995) 119–225.

387 Divine and human metamorphosis was a common theme in Greek and Roman mythology beginning with Homer. P. M. C. Forbes Irving offers a helpful historical survey (*Metamorphosis in Greek Myths* [Oxford: Oxford University Press, 1990]); for Hellenistic anthologies, see K. Sara Myers, *Ovid's Causes: Cosmogony and Aetiology in the Metamorphoses* (Ann Arbor: University of Michigan Press, 1994) 21–26. For the early Latin tradition, see Christian Zgoll's published Munich dissertation, *Phänomenologie der Metamorphose: Verwandlungen und Verwandtes in der augusteischen Dichtung* (Classica Monacensia 28; Tübingen: Gunter Narr, 2004). For a recent critical assessment, see Richard Buxton, *Forms of Astonishment: Greek Myths of Metamorphosis* (Oxford: Oxford University Press, 2009). See further the excursus "Metamorphosis in Greco-Roman and Jewish Myth" in the commentary below on 2:7-8.

Gen 6:1-6 had transformed themselves into men in their efforts to seduce women (cf. *1 Enoch* 86:3). According to *T. Sol.* 20:13 and Heb 13:2 angels have often appeared in human form (cf. Gal 1:8; 3:19; 4:3, 9).[388] The author of Hebrews (1:7) believed that it was an essential property of angels to change their form as necessary in executing the divine will. In *Apoc. Abr.* 15:7 the ascended Abraham participates in an angelic liturgy in which even in heaven angels are constantly changing form as part of their worship.[389]

Paul conceived of what is commonly referred to as Christ's incarnation as a kind of metamorphosis.[390] According to Phil 2:6-11 Christ was a mighty angel who originally existed "in the form [μορφῇ] of God."[391] For the sake of humans and in obedience to the divine will he took "the form [μορφήν] of a slave," changing himself into human "likeness" (ὁμοίωμα) and "appearance" (σχῆμα).[392] After his death on a cross,[393] God restored him to his original angelic form, but now as the even more glorious ruling angel who bears the divine Name

---

388 It was frequently the case that Greek and Roman gods transformed themseves in order to visit humans (cf. Acts 14:11-13 and the texts cited by Pervo, *Acts*, in his discussion of that passage). It is clear from Gen 19:1 that the two "men" of chap. 18 were "angels."

389 Abraham arrives in heaven in the midst of an angelic liturgy and finds the angels "all changing in aspect and shape, running and changing form and prostrating themselves and crying aloud words I did not know" (trans. Rubinkiewicz, *OTP*, 1:696). Abraham is instructed to join in the liturgy (17:4-6; cf *Asc. Isa.* 8:16-17) and is presumably himself transformed, as 30:1—"I was no longer in the glory in which I was above"—spoken upon Abraham's return to earth will later imply. See Martha Himmelfarb, *Ascent to Heaven in Jewish and Christian Apocalypses* (New York/Oxford: Oxford University Press, 1993) 61–66; Schäfer, *Origins*, 86–92. It would seem here that angels are imagined as "shape-shifters," for which see Forbes Irving, *Metamorphosis in Greek Myths*, 171–94. Cf. *2 Bar.* 51:10, where the resurrected righteous are "changed into any shape they wish, from beauty to loveliness, from light to the splendor of glory." For Christ as shape-shifter, see Paul Foster, "Polymorphic Christology: Its Origins and Development in Early Christianity," *JTS* 58 (2007) 66–99.

390 Dieter Zeller, "Die Menschwerdung des Sohnes Gottes im Neuen Testament und die antike Religionsgeschichte," in *Menschwerdung Gottes – Vergöttlichung von Menschen*, ed. Dieter Zeller (NTOA 7; Freiburg, Switzerland: Universitätsverlag; Göttingen: Vandenhoeck & Ruprecht, 1988) 141–76, esp. 160–63; Samuel Vollenweider, "Die Metamorphose des Gottessohns," in *Das Urchristentum in seiner literarischen Geschichte: Festschrift für Jürgen Becker zum 65. Geburtstag*, ed. Ulrich Mell and Ulrich B. Müller (BZNW 100; Berlin/New York: de Gruyter, 1999) 109–31. For a recent interpretation of the so-called transfiguration of Jesus in Mark 9:2-8 (the Greek is

μεταμορφώθη) as metamorphosis, see Candida R. Moss, "The Transfiguration: An Exercise in Markan Accommodation," *BibInt* 12 (2004) 69–89. On the reticence of Christian commentators to describe the "transfiguration" as metamorphosis, see George Aichele and Richard Walsh, "Metamorphosis, Transfiguration and the Body," *BibInt* 19 (2011) 253–75; C. B. Tzack, "Ovid, Jerome, and the Vulgate," *Studia Patristica* 33 (1997) 378–82; Gieschen, *Angelomorphic Christology*. Even Moss in her fine essay imagines Mark's use of metamorphosis as "accommodation" rather than as a constitutive element of his theology possibly inherited from Paul.

391 Cf. Philo, *Mos.* 1.66 for similar language: Moses sees a divine "form" (μορφή) in the bush, which Philo calls an "angel." For a historically sensitive reading of Phil 2:6-11, see Schäfer, *Origins*, 324–27; Jarl E. Fossum, "The Magharians: A Pre-Christian Jewish Sect and Its Significance for the Study of Gnosticism and Christianity," *Henoch* 9 (1987) 303–44, here 341–43. For Christ as angel, see William Horbury, *Jewish Messianism and the Cult of Christ* (London: SCM, 1998) 113.

392 Cf. *Asc. Isa.* 8:9-10, where the so-called incarnation is similarly imagined.

393 It remains one of the distinctive features of Paul's Christ-myth that it had to incorporate elements from the life of a historical person. Nevertheless, the notion that some legendary figures were in fact angels was not unknown in ancient Judaism. The parade example occurs in the *Prayer of Joseph* (frg. A), where the patriarch Jacob is revealed to be the angel Israel (see Jonathan Z. Smith, "The Prayer of Joseph," in *Religions in Antiquity: Essays in Memory of Erwin Ramsdell Goodenough*, ed. Jacob Neusner [SHR 14; Leiden: Brill, 1970] 253–94, reprinted with afterword in Jonathan Z. Smith, *Map Is Not Territory: Studies in the History of Religions* [SJLA 23; Leiden: Brill, 1978; repr., Chicago: University of Chicago Press, 1993] 24–66). Origen, to whom we owe this frag-

and shares the divine throne: "therefore God more highly exalted him [ὑπερύψωσεν] and gave him the Name that is above every other name [τὸ ὄνομα τὸ ὑπὲρ πᾶν ὄνομα], in order that in the name of Jesus every knee should bow . . . to the glory of God the Father."[394] Just as the Messiah/Son of Man of the Parables of Enoch would one day sit on God's "throne of glory,"[395] Paul believed that Christ would soon sit as eschatological judge on "God's throne of judgment."[396]

Many apocalyptists claimed that a type of metamorphosis also awaited the righteous—though in this case the transformation went the other way around, from human to angel.[397] Initially this destiny seems to have been reserved for a select few. According to Daniel, while all the righteous "who sleep in the dust of the earth shall awake," only the "wise" among them "who lead many to righteousness" will shine "like the stars forever and ever" (Dan 12:3).[398] It was soon extended, however, to include all "the righteous and pious," who "will shine like the stars of heaven" and to whom "the portals of heaven will be opened" (1 Enoch 103:9; 104:2; cf. T. Mos. 10:9). According to the Animal Vision of 1 Enoch 85–90, Noah and Moses had even been transformed into angels during their lifetime—Noah in order to build the ark and Moses in order to construct the tabernacle.[399] In a number of apocalypses the ascending seer himself undergoes a temporary "angelomorphic" transformation[400] in anticipation of the permanent angelification of the righteous after

ment, uses it to support his argument that John the Baptizer was himself an angel sent to bear witness to Jesus (Origen, In Ioann. 2:31; cf. PGM 4.1716–1870 ["The Sword of Dardanos"], lines 1735–36). The importance of Prayer of Joseph frg. A to Paul's Christology appears to have first been recognized by Hans Windisch, "Die göttliche Weisheit der Juden und die paulinische Christologie," in Neutestamentliche Studien: Georg Heinrici zu 70. Geburtstag (14 März 1914) dargebracht, ed. G. A. Deissman and H. Windisch (UNT 6; Leipzig: Hinrichs, 1914) 220–34, here 225; Morton Smith, "The Account of Simon Magus in Acts 8," in Harry Austryn Wolfson Jubilee Volume on the Occasion of His Seventy-fifth Birthday, ed. Saul Lieberman et al. (3 vols.; Jerusalem: American Academy for Jewish Research, 1969) 2:735–49; see also Gieschen, Angelomorphic Christology, 137–42 and 159–61 with further bibliography. Compare also the account of Moses in Ezekiel the Tragedian, Exag. 68–81, for which see Pieter van der Horst, "Moses' Throne Vision in Ezekiel the Dramatist," JJS 34 (1983) 19–29.

394 See Hengel, "'Sit at My Right Hand!'"

395 1 Enoch 45:3; 55:4; 61:8; 62:2, 3, 5; 69:27, 29; 71:7; cf. 61:3.

396 For Paul the βῆμα θεοῦ ("God's throne of judgment"; Rom 14:10) was also the βῆμα Χριστοῦ ("Christ's throne of judgment"; 2 Cor 5:10).

397 James H. Charlesworth, "The Portrayal of the Righteous as an Angel," in Ideal Figures in Ancient Judaism: Profiles and Paradigms, ed. George W. E. Nickelsburg and John J. Collins (SBLSCS 12; Chico, CA: Scholars Press, 1980) 135–51; Christopher Morray-Jones, "Transformational Mysticism in the Apocalyptic-Merkabah Tradition," JJS 43 (1992) 1–31; Mach, Entwicklungsstadien, 163–69; Himmelfarb, Ascent, 47–71; Gieschen, Angelomorphic

Christology, 152–83; John J. Collins, "A Throne in the Heavens: Apotheosis in Pre-Christian Judaism," in Death, Ecstasy and Other Worldly Journeys, ed. John J. Collins and Michael Fishbane (Albany: State University of New York Press, 1995) 43–58; Collins, "Angelic Life"; Schäfer, Origins, index s.v. "angelification"; cf. Wis 5:5; Matt 22:30.

398 See Collins, Daniel, on this passage. For angels as stars, see esp. 1 Enoch 18:12-16 (cf. 19:1); 86:1-3.

399 Noah (1 Enoch 89:9); Moses (1 Enoch 89:36; cf. Sir 45:1-5 [Greek]; Philo, Mos. 2.288; Ezekiel the Tragedian, Exag. 68–82; and possibly 4Q374, for which see Crispin Fletcher-Louis, "4Q374: A Discourse on the Sinai Tradition: The Deification of Moses and Early Christology," DSD 3 [1996] 236–52; for Moses as angel in Samaritan thought see Jarl E. Fossum, The Name of God and the Angel of the Lord: Samaritan and Jewish Concepts of Intermediation and the Origin of Gnosticism [WUNT 36: Tübingen: Mohr Siebeck, 1985] 123; also John Lierman, The New Testament Moses: Christian Perceptions of Moses and Israel in the Setting of Jewish Religon [WUNT 2/173; Tübingen: Mohr Siebeck, 2004] 237–47). The patriarchs are similarly transformed at T. Abr. 11 (Recension A), as is Adam in 2 Enoch 30:8-11. In 1 Enoch 71:11-14, Enoch is dramatically transformed into an angel immediately at the end of his earthly life.

400 E.g., Asc. Isa. 7:25: "the glory of my face [Slav. "spirit"] was being transformed as I went up from heaven to heaven"; 1 Enoch 39:14: "and my face was changed, for I was unable to see" (for which see Nickelsburg and VanderKam, 1 Enoch 2, 129, 327); cf. Apoc. Abr. 30:1; 4QSelf-Glorication Hymn. The parade example of this is 1 Enoch 71.11, which imaginatively portrays Enoch's experience of being changed into an angel as he enters the divine throne room: "I fell on my face, and all my flesh melted,

death that would enable them to join with the angels in worshiping God.[401] The sectaries at Qumran believed that they were already worshiping with the angels.[402]

According to Paul, Christ-believers undergo a similar angelomorphic transformation. This transformation takes place over time and is ideally permanent, and it occurs not as a result of ascent but as a result of possession.[403] It begins in earnest in this life and is completed on one's admission to the next. In 2 Cor 3:18 Paul describes how Christ-believers are progressively "metamorphosed [μεταμορφούμεθα] from glory to glory."[404] Similarly, in Phil 2:15 he promises the Philippians that

---

and my spirit was transformed, and I cried out with a loud voice, with a spirit of power, and I blessed and praised and exalted [God]." Two striking analogies are Apuleius, *Metam.* 3.24 and 11.13, where Lucius offers a first-person account of his being transformed into an ass and its reverse (cf. Pseudo-Lucian, *Asin.* 13).

401 See the discussion of the *Ascension of Isaiah* in Schäfer, *Origins*, 93–99; cf. W. Bousset, "Die Himmelsreise der Seele," *Archiv für Religionswissenschaft* 4 (1901) 136–69, 229–73, esp. 136; Martha Himmelfarb, "Revelation and Rapture: The Transformation of the Visionary in the Ascent Apocalypses," in *Mysteries and Revelations: Apocalyptic Studies since the Uppsala Colloquium*, ed. John J. Collins and James H. Charlesworth (JSPSup 9; Sheffield: JSOT Press, 1991) 79–90; Mach, *Entwicklungsstadien*, 216–40.

402 Cf. 1 Cor 11:10; 13:1. Peter Schäfer calls this a kind of *unio liturgica* (*The Hidden and Manifest God: Some Major Themes in Early Jewish Mysticism* [Albany: State University of New York Press, 1992] 165). See also Schäfer, *Origins*, 112–53 and index s.v. *unio liturgica*; Björn Frennesson, *"In a Common Rejoicing": Liturgical Communion with Angels in Qumran* (Studia Semitica Upsaliensia 14; Uppsala: Uppsala University Library, 1999); Mach, *Entwicklungsstadien*, 209–40. Collins ("Angelic Life," 296–97) notes that, according to 1QS 11:7-8 (cf. 1QHᵃ 11:23), the sectaries at Qumran considered their community (יחד) to include the angels. He also suggests (ibid., 301–2) that it was precisely because angels were present in the יחד that women (and children) were excluded, lest the angels be tempted as Gen 6:1-8 was interpreted to imply (e.g., *1 Enoch* 15; cf. 1 Cor 11:10).

403 The distinction between ascent and possession should not be pressed too hard. Both are "altered states of consciousness" (ASC) that construct the presence of a divinity. It remains the case, however, that ASC always happen under a description, which is to say that they are not brute facts but are from the beginning constituted at least in part by their interpretation, and that "ascent" and "possession," while perhaps physiologically indistinguishable, are different descriptions. Possession raises the question of *agency* in a way that ascent does not. Possession also evokes a degree of *permanence* not typically found in ascent accounts; and, of course, possession is not a journey but the *invasion* of the possessed person's body. Galatians 2:20a strikes all three of these notes: "I [= agency] no longer live [= permanence] but Christ [= again agency] lives in me [= invasion]." Paul goes on to say in v. 20b that it is his "faith" or "belief" that is the vehicle by which the continuing presence of Christ is maintained. Of course, from time to time Paul did imagine his ASC as ascents. The most famous account of these is 2 Cor 12:1-10, where he speaks in the plural of "revelations" (v. 7), language he uses of his conversion in Gal 1:12. Paul is emphatic that he has "seen the Lord" (1 Cor 9:1); he also insists that his converts have seen "the light of the knowledge of the glory of God in the face of Jesus" (2 Cor 4:6). It is interesting that Paul is undecided about the nature of his ascent experiences ("whether in the body or out of the body I cannot say"; 2 Cor 12:3; cf. Rev 1:10; 4:2; 17:3; 21:1; *Asc. Isa.* 6:6-12). For the nature of religious experience in Paul, see the incisive analysis by Christopher Mount, "Religious Experience, the Religion of Paul, and Women in the Pauline Churches," in *Women and Gender in Ancient Religions*, ed. Stephen P. Ahearne-Kroll, Paul A. Holloway, and James A. Kelhoffer (WUNT 263; Tübingen: Mohr Siebeck, 2010) 23–47. I am grateful to Professor Mount for a number of conversations over the years that have shaped my thinking on Paul's possession language.

404 This progressive metamorphosis is effected by the "spirit of the Lord" as Christ-believers "behold the glory of the Lord reflected [in Christ]." It is unclear how and when this vision takes place. Paul's assemblies regularly engaged in ecstatic worship, so much so that in Corinth at least he was worried that if an unbeliever were to wander into one of the group's meetings he or she might conclude that all there were possessed by a divine madness (1 Cor 14:23; Morton Smith, "Pauline Worship as Seen by Pagans," *HTR* 73 [1980] 241–49; reprinted in *Studies in the Cult of Yahweh*, ed. Shaye J. D. Cohen (2 vols.; Religions of the Greco-Roman World 130, 131; Leiden: Brill, 1996) 2:95–102; cf. Wilhelm Bousset, *Kyrios Christos: A History of the Belief in Christ from the Beginnings of Christianity to Irenaeus* [Nashville: Abingdon, 1970] 159). But Paul also speaks of "walking

if they submit to the discipline of God they will begin to "shine like stars" (φαίνεσθε ὡς φωστῆρες) even now, a clear allusion to the astral metamorphosis of the righteous in the afterlife in Dan 12:3 and *1 Enoch* 104:2. Believers who stay the course—as Paul hopes the Philippians will—will have Christ "formed" (μορφωθῇ) in them (Gal 4:19), with the result that at the final judgment they will be "found in him" possessing a perfect "righteousness that is from God" (Phil 3:9). When Christ returns, he will complete the metamorphosis and "transfigure" (μετασχηματίσει) the bodies of his followers to be σύμμορφος (lit. "of like form") to his own now supremely glorious body (Phil 3:21; cf. Rom 8:29). Those so transfigured will include both those who had died, who will be raised "incorruptible" (ἄφθαρτοι), and those still alive, who will also "be changed" (ἀλλαγησόμεθα; 1 Cor 15:51-52; cf. 1 Thess 4:17).

Paul imagined the Christ-believer's present metamorphosis as a primarily internal process, taking place in what he called ὁ ἔσω ἄνθρωπος or "the inner human being" (2 Cor 4:16; cf. Rom 7:22; Eph 3:16).[405] Paul did not mean by this, however, that the transformation of Christ-believers in this life was simply moral—an all-too-common rationalizing interpretation of Paul's thoroughly mythological thinking[406]—but rather that Christ-believers were becoming angels as it were from the inside out.[407] Whether Paul thought this transformation could be visibly observed before the believer's final transfiguration is unclear. The reference to "shin[ing] like stars" in Phil 2:15 suggests that he may have, as does the claim in 2 Cor 3:18 that Christ-believers who behold the glory of the Lord reflected in Christ are metamorphosed "into the same image [τὴν αὐτὴν εἰκόνα]." According to the apocryphal *Acts of Paul and Thecla*, at least Paul's own transformation had reached the point of being visible: "[Onesiphorus] saw Paul coming . . . full of grace. For sometimes he appeared as a human [ὡς ἄνθρωπος] and sometimes he had the face of an angel [ἀγγέλου πρόσωπον]" (*Act. Paul. et Thecl.* 3 [= *Act. Paul.* 3.3]).

d. Postscript: Justification

The preceding account of Paul's theory of salvation departs significantly from the traditional (Protestant) reading of Paul, which takes as its centerpiece justification by faith interpreted as a kind of legal fiction according to which Christ-believers have an alien righteousness (i.e., God's righteousness) imputed to them.[408] Most of what Paul has to say about justification is found in the

---

in the Spirit" and "being led by the Spirit" (e.g., Gal 5:16, 18, 25; Rom 8:4, 14), which may imply a kind of routinization of religious ecstasy. In commenting on 2 Cor 3:18, Victor Paul Furnish proposes that Paul here combines the apotheosis of the initiate in the Hellenistic mysteries, an apotheosis that occurs in this life and is effected by a vision of the deity (e.g., Apuleius, *Metam.* 11.23–24; *Corp. Herm.* 4.11b), and the eschatological transformation of the righteous in Jewish apocalypticism (*II Corinthians: Translated with Introduction, Notes, and Commentary* [AB 32A; Garden City, NY: Doubleday, 1984] 239–41). For the expression "from glory to glory," see John W. Taylor, "From Faith to Faith: Romans 1.17 in the Light of Greek Idiom," *NTS* 50 (2004) 337–48.

405 For Paul's concept of the inner human being, see esp. Walter Burkert, "Towards Plato and Paul: The 'Inner Human Being,'" in *Ancient and Modern Perspectives on the Bible and Culture: Essays in Honor of Hans Dieter Betz*, ed. Adela Yarbro Collins (Scholars Press Homage Series 22; Atlanta: Scholars Press, 1998) 59–82; Hans Dieter Betz, "The Concept of the 'Inner Human Being' (ὁ ἔσω ἄνθρωπος) in the Anthropology of Paul," *NTS* 46 (2000) 315–41; cf. Christoph

Markschies, "Innerer Mensch," *RAC* 18 (1997) 2660–312.

406 Speaking of Paul's realistic theory of transformation, E. P. Sanders writes, "This sort of question is one of the hardest to face the modern student of an ancient thinker" (*Paul: A Very Short Introduction* [Oxford: Oxford University Press, 2001] 83; cf. Sanders, *Paul: The Apostle's Life, Letters, and Thought* [Minneapolis: Fortress Press, 2015] index, s.v. "Transformation," and esp. 408–18).

407 Richard Reitzenstein, *Hellenistic Mystery-Religions: Their Basic Ideas and Significance* (Pittsburgh Theological Monograph Series 15; Pittsburgh: Pickwick, 1978) 454: "[I]n II Cor. 3:18 Paul describes that material transformation which must already here on earth have occurred with the Christian, so that he might be able to receive the σῶμα οὐράνιον."

408 For a nuanced account of this so-called Lutheran perspective, see Francis Watson, *Paul, Judaism, and Gentiles: Beyond the New Perspective* (rev. and expanded ed.; Grand Rapids: Eerdmans, 2007) 28–40; see also Stephen Chester, "It Is No Longer I Who Live: Justification by Faith and Participation in Christ in Martin Luther's Exegesis of Galatians,"

polemical chapters of Galatians and Romans, where he argues that Torah observance should not be required of gentile Christ-believers, whose sanctification is being accomplished independent of Torah by the spirit of Christ.[409] Torah observance is not a major theme in Philippians, but it is introduced as a kind of theological foil in 3:2-11, where in 3:9 Paul rehearses his central ideas on justification. Here as elsewhere Paul's justification language is formulaic and terse and is forced into a set of rhetorical antitheses.[410]

It is not immediately clear what Paul means by justification by faith.[411] In the sixteenth century, differing interpretations of justification divided Catholics and Protestants.[412] Today justification looms large in debates around the so-called New Perspective on Paul.[413] The Protestant reformers were right to insist that the Greek

verb typically translated "to justify" ($\delta\iota\kappa\alpha\iota o\hat{\upsilon}\nu$) implies a legal judgment.[414] What subsequent interpretation has generally failed to observe, however, is that Paul uses $\delta\iota\kappa\alpha\iota o\hat{\upsilon}\nu$ and its cognates to refer to two different and distinct judgments: (1) an initial judgment that pronounces the believer to be a member of the eschatological community of the "righteous,"[415] and (2) a final judgment that determines where one stands in the eschatological justice of God, which is to say whether one's end is "destruction" or "salvation."[416]

The first of these justifications, as is well known, is achieved by faith. From the perspective of the Christ-believer, it is a thing of the past and is accomplished by the death of Christ, which somehow—Paul never specifies—averts the wrath of God.[417] Paul uses the verb $\delta\iota\kappa\alpha\iota\acute{o}\omega$ in this sense in Rom 5:1a when he speaks of "hav-

NTS 55 (2009) 315–37; Jonathan A. Linebaugh, "The Christo-Centrism of Faith in Christ: Martin Luther's Reading of Galatians 2.16, 19-20," NTS 59 (2013) 535–44.

409 Wrede, Paul, 122–38.

410 Schweitzer has famously called justification a "subsidiary crater" in Paul's theology (Mysticism, 225). Wrede gets even closer to the mark when he treats it as "polemical doctrine" (Paul, 122–42, esp. 123).

411 The acid test for any interpretation of Paul's theory of justification is what to do with Rom 2:1-16, for which see Thomas Schreiner, "Did Paul Believe in Justification by Works? Another Look at Romans 2," BBR 3 (1993) 131–58, which contains a number of key insights.

412 Alister E. McGrath, Iustitia Dei: A History of the Christian Doctrine of Justification (3rd ed.; Cambridge: Cambridge University Press, 2005). McGrath's account of Luther (pp. 223–35) is especially to be recommended in light of the current scholarly trend of attributing to Luther what are essentially Rudolf Bultmann's much more simplistic views.

413 The bibliography is vast. See the review in Dunn, New Perspective, 1–97.

414 LSJ, s.v. δικαιόω; BDAG, s.v. δικαιόω: "to render a favorable verdict," "to acquit," "to pronounce righteous"; see John M. G. Barclay, Paul and the Gift (Grand Rapids: Eerdmans, 2015) 375–78.

415 Justification in this sense is what Sanders calls Paul's "transfer language" (Paul and Palestinian Judaism: A Comparison of Patterns of Religion [Philadelphia: Fortress Press, 1977] 470–72; Sanders, Paul, the Law and the Jewish People [Philadelphia: Fortress Press, 1983] 5–10); Dunn has proposed "conversion justifi-

cation" or "initial justification" (New Perspective [rev. ed.], 72 and 78, respectively). At first glance it is odd that Paul does not refer to Christ-believers as "the righteous ones" but as "the holy ones" or "saints." I discuss this in my comments on 1:1. It is, however, clear from 1 Cor 6:1, where "holy ones" is explicitly contrasted with "unrighteous ones," that for Paul "holy ones" denotes the eschatological community of the "righteous."

416 1 Cor 1:18; 2 Cor 2:15; Phil 1:28; cf. 1 Thess 5:9; Gal 6:8; 1 Cor 11:32; Rom 2:12; 9:22; Phil 3:19.

417 Paul never developed a coherent "theory" of Christ's death, which he approached not as the solution to a problem (e.g., sin) but as a problem itself—both a puzzle and an embarassment—in need of solution. For Christ's death as an apotropaism in the tradition of Euripides's Alcestis and Heracleidae, see Cilliers Breytenbach ("'Christus starb für uns': Zur Tradition und paulinschen Rezeption der sogenannten 'Sterbeformeln,'" in Breytenbach, Grace, Reconciliation, Concord: The Death of Christ in Graeco-Roman Metaphors [NovTSup 135; Leiden: Brill, 2010] 95–126), who cites Christina Eschner, Gestorben und hingegeben "für" die Sünder: Die griechischen Konzeption des Unheil abwendenden Sterbens und deren paulinische Aufname für die Deutung des Todes Jesu Christi (2 vols.; WMANT 122; Neukirchen-Vluyn: Neukirchener Verlag, 2010); cf. Klaus Wengst, Christologische Formeln und Lieder des Urchristentums (2nd ed.; Studien zum Neuen Testament 7; Gütersloh: Gerd Mohn, 1973); Sam K. Williams, Jesus' Death as Saving Event: The Background and Origin of a Concept (HDR 2; Missoula, MT: Scholars Press, 1975); Martin Hengel, The Atonement: A Study of the Origins of the Doctrine in the New Testament

ing been justified (δικαιωθέντες) by faith."[418] But, as he goes on to say in Rom 5:1b-2, this justification not only brings "peace with God," what he will a few verses later describe as "reconciliation" (Rom 5:10-11),[419] but also grants the Christ-believer access to God's empowering "grace,"[420] the principal expression of which is the gift of the divine "spirit" (Rom 5:5). This "spirit," which Paul identifies as "the spirit of Christ" (Rom 8:9), possesses and transforms[421] every Christ-believer, making possible justification in the second sense.

Justification in the second sense can be distinguished from justification in the first sense by the fact that it still lies in the future.[422] Thus, Paul can write to the Corinthians: "I know nothing against myself, but I am not thereby justified; the one who passes judgment on me is the Lord" (1 Cor 4:3-4), adding *Therefore let us not pass judgment ahead of time, until the Lord comes*" (1 Cor 4:5).[423] And in Rom 2:13: "For it is not the hearers of the law who are righteous before God, but the doers of the law *who will be justified*." Similarly, in Gal 5:4-5: "You who attempt to be justified by the law have fallen away from grace; for by the Spirit and in faith *we wait for the hope of righteousness*."

Yet not only does justification in the second sense take place in the future rather than the present, it is based on subsequent works rather than initial faith. Thus Rom 2:5-6: "the day of wrath and the revelation of the righteous judgment of God, who will give to each *according to his works*." Similarly, in 2 Cor 5:10: "for we must all appear before Christ's throne of judgment to be recompensed for *the things done while in the body, whether good or evil*." And to quote Rom 2:13 again: "it is . . . *the doers of the law who will be justified*." Paul insists that this final judgment will be based not on group membership but on actual righteousness, and that it will be exacting: "for there is no partiality with God" (Rom 2:11).[424] Paul promises, however, that Christ-believers who stay the course can hope to achieve that righteousness and receive a favorable judgment: "work hard to accomplish your own salvation . . . for God, as an expression of his goodwill, is the one producing in you both the ability to will [what is right] and to actually do [it]."

This leads to one final observation. Paul believes that justification in the first sense (by faith) initiates a divinely assisted process of transformation that makes not only possible but even *probable* justification in the second sense (by works): "he who began a good work in you will continue to perfect it until the day of Jesus Christ" (Phil 1:6; cf. Gal 3:3).[425] This observation is important for a

---

(London: SCM, 1981); Henk S. Versnel, "Making Sense of Jesus' Death," in *Deutungen des Todes Jesu im Neuen Testament*, ed. Jörg Frey and Jens Schröter (WUNT 181; Tübingen: Mohr Siebeck, 2005) 213–94.

418 Cf. Rom 5:9: "having now been justified by his blood [δικαιωθέντες . . . ἐν τῷ αἵματι αὐτοῦ] we shall be saved through him from the wrath [ἀπὸ τῆς ὀργῆς]" (5:9). For salvation from the wrath of God here and its relationship to the wrath of God in Rom 1:18-32, see my "*Commendatio*," 369–82.

419 See esp. Rom 5:10, where Paul substitutes "having been reconciled" (καταλλαγέντες) for the "having been justified" (δικαιωθέντες) of 5:9 (cf. 5:1). For the language of "reconciliation" here, see Cilliers Breytenbach, who has shown that Paul's concept of "reconciliation" derives from contemporary diplomatic language (*Versöhnung: Eine Studie zur paulinischen Soteriologie* [WMANT 60; Neukirchen-Vluyn: Neukirchener Verlag, 1989]).

420 Barclay could have given more attention to this central feature of grace in Paul (*Gift*, 499–500); see my comment on Phil 3:10 below.

421 For possession and sanctification, see Sorensen, *Possession*, 153–66; see also Emma Wasserman, *Death of the Soul in Romans 7: Sin, Death, and the Law in Light of Hellenistic Moral Philosophy* (WUNT 2/256; Tübingen: Mohr Siebeck, 2008) 136–43.

422 The commentary tradition often conflates the two; see, e.g., Peter Stuhlmacher, *Paul's Letter to the Romans: A Commentary* (Louisville: Westminster John Knox, 1991) 61–65.

423 Cf. 1 Cor 9:27, where Paul worries that he might be "disqualified" (ἀδόκιμος) in the final judgment.

424 Jouette M. Bassler, *Divine Impartiality: Paul and a Theological Axiom* (SBLDS 59; Chico, CA: Scholars Press, 1982).

425 More generally see Judith M. Gundry Volf, *Paul and Perseverance: Staying in and Falling Away* (WUNT 2/34: Tübingen: Mohr Siebeck, 1990); John M. G. Barclay, "Believers and the Last Judgment in Paul: Rethinking Grace and Recompense," in *Eschatologie = Eschatology: The Sixth Durham-Tübingen Research Symposium: Eschatology in the Old Testament, Ancient Judaism, and Early Christianity (Tübingen, September 2009)*, ed. Hans-Joachim Eckstein, Christof Landmesser, and Hermann Lichtenberger (WUNT 272; Tübingen: Mohr Siebeck, 2011) 195–208, esp. 203–8. The divine preservation of the righteous in the last days was a popular theme in Jewish apocalypticism;

number of reasons, not least of which is that it allows us to avoid a common confusion in interpreting Paul's justification language, a confusion for which Paul himself is largely to blame. For while it should be clear to the careful reader that Paul imagines salvation as a process consisting of both "faith" and "works," in the course of arguing against Torah observance Paul for rhetorical reasons often contrasts the two: "not by works of the law but by faith in Christ" (Gal 2:16). This contrast is not a problem in texts where initial justification (by faith) is in view. But it is a problem in a text like Phil 3:8-9, where the believer's final justification (by works) is in view and yet Paul still speaks of it as coming about through faith: "that I might gain Christ and be found in him, not having my own righteousness which is from the law, but the righteousness which is *through faith in Christ*, the righteousness that is from God *based on such faith*."[426] This contradiction is removed, however, once we realize that,

for purposes of drawing a contrast between his view and that of his opponents, Paul has engaged in a kind of rhetorical shorthand in which "faith" is a metonym for the process of faith *and works* that it effectively initiates.[427] It is commonly said that Paul oversimplifies to the point of caricature the views of his opponents. In this instance he has also oversimplified his own view. As is often the case with Paul, clarity is sacrificed for rhetorical advantage.

8. Text

The present commentary is based on the 28th edition of Erwin Nestle and Kurt Aland, *Novum Testamentum Graece* (*NTG*[28]).[428] The text of Philippians is largely problem free.[429] The apparatus of *NTG*[28] shows 102 textual variants, of which 4 are conjectural. Almost all of these, however, are easily accounted for. Most of these will be noted in the notes to the translation, and the more significant

---

see *1 Enoch* 1:8; 5:8-9; 22:3-5; 48:47; 100:4; *Jub.* 14:32; 1QH[a] 10:24-25, 35-36; 12:23, 31-32; cf. Jude 24; 1 Pet 1:5, 5:12; *Did.* 16.5. According to Eph 2:10, God has "created" good works for the righteous "to walk in." Commenting on 1QS 3:21-24 and 1QH[a] 17:32, Geza Vermes writes, "Not only is election itself owed to God's grace, but perseverance in the way of holiness cannot be counted on unless he offers his continuous help and support" (*The Complete Dead Sea Scrolls in English* [rev. ed.; London: Penguin, 2004] 74).

426 For the expression πίστις Χριστοῦ, which I have here and in the quotation of Gal 2:16 in the preceding sentence translated as "faith in Christ," see the excursus in the commentary below at 3:9.

427 For Paul, "works" is also a metonym for a life lived in submission to the Torah. In subsequent Christian interpretation, this was caricatured as legalism and the like to devastating effect. For a similar metonymic understanding of these terms, see Watson, *Paul, Judaism and Gentiles*, 11: "Such terms as 'law' and 'works' stood not for abstract theological principles but for a concrete form of social praxis associated with a specific minority community." Cf. Margaret M. Mitchell, "Rhetorical Shorthand in Pauline Argumentation: The Function of 'the Gospel' in the Corinthian Correspondence," in *Gospel in Paul: Studies on Corinthians, Galatians and Romans for Richard N. Longenecker*, ed. L. Ann Jervis and Peter Richardson (JSNTSup 108; Sheffield: Sheffield Academic Press, 1994) 63-88.

428 *NTG*[28] incorporates the text-critical insights from the *Novum Testamentum Graecum – Editio Critica*

Maior IV: The Catholic Letters (2nd rev. ed.; Stuttgart: Deutsche Bibelgesellschaft, 2012) for the Catholic Letters, but for the Pauline letters the text of *NTG*[28] is the same as *NTG*[27], though the textual apparatus for those letters has been revised to conform to the *NTG*[28] template. The textual history of Philippians is tied to the textual history of the *Corpus Paulinum*. For this larger question, see Günther Zuntz, *The Text of the Epistles: A Disquisition upon the Corpus Paulinum* (The Schweich Lectures of the British Academy 1946; London: British Academy and Oxford University Press, 1953); Hans Lietzmann, "Einführung in die Textgeschichte der Paulusbriefe," in Lietzmann, *An die Römer* (5th ed.; HNT 8; Tübingen: Mohr Siebeck, 1971) 1–18; Kurt Aland, "Die Entstehung des Corpus Paulinum," in Aland, *Neutestamentliche Entwürfe* (Munich: Kaiser, 1979) 302–50; Michael W. Holmes, "The Text of the Epistles Sixty Years After: An Assessment of Günther Zuntz's Contribution to the Text-Critical Methodology and History," in *Transmission and Reception: New Testament Text-Critical and Exegetical Studies*, ed. J. W. Childers and D. C. Parker (Piscataway, NJ: Gorgias, 2006) 89–113; David C. Parker, *An Introduction to the New Testament Manuscripts and the Texts* (Cambridge: Cambridge University Press, 2008) 246–82.

429 E.g., Bruce M. Metzger, *A Textual Commentary on the Greek New Testament: A Companion Volume to the United Bible Societies' Greek New Testament (Fourth rev. ed.)* (2nd ed.; Stuttgart: United Bible Societies, 1994) 544–51.

of them will be discussed. The principal witnesses for Philippians are as follows:[430]

Papyri[431]

$\mathfrak{p}^{16}$	*P. Oxy.* 1009 (3rd–4th cent.): 3:9-17; 4:2-8
$\mathfrak{p}^{46}$	*P. Chester Beatty II* (ca. 200 CE[432]): 1:1, 5-15, 17-28; 1:30—2:12, 14-27; 2:29—3:8, 10-21; 4:2-12, 14-23.
$\mathfrak{p}^{61}$	*P. Colt.* 5 (ca. 700 CE): 3:5-9, 12-16

Uncial Codices or Codex Fragments[433]

ℵ	(01)	Codex Sinaiticus (4th cent.): complete
A	(02)	Codex Alexandrinus (5th cent.): complete
B	(03)	Codex Vaticanus (5th cent.): complete[434]
C	(04)	Codex Ephraemi rescriptus (5th cent.): 1:23—3:4
D	(06)	Codex Claromontanus (6th cent.): complete
F	(010)	Codex Augiensis (9th cent.): complete
G	(012)	Codex Boernerianus (9th cent.): complete
I	(016)	Codex Freerianus (5th cent.): 1:1—4:11, 13, 20-23
K	(018)	Codex Moquensis (9th cent.): complete
L	(020)	Codex Angelicus (9th cent.): complete
P	(025)	Codex Porphyrianus (9th cent.): complete

Ψ	(044)	Codex Athous Laurae (9th–10th cent.): complete
048		(5th cent.): 1:8-23; 2:1-4, 6-8
075		(10th cent.): complete
0278		(9th cent.): 1:1—3:4; 4:2-13, 17-21
0282		(6th cent.): 2:22-24; 3:6-8

Important Minuscule Witnesses

33 (9th cent.): complete
81 (1044 CE): complete
104 (1087 CE): complete
365 (12th cent.): complete
630 (12th–13th cent.): complete
1175 (10th cent.): complete
1505 (12th cent.): complete
1506 (1320 CE): complete
1739 (10th cent.): complete
1881 (14th cent.): complete
2464 (9th cent.): complete

Versions

Philippians survives in Coptic translation in both the Sahidic (sa)[435] and Bohairic (bo)[436] dialects. It also survives in Syriac in the Peshitta (sy^p) and in the Harclean version (sy^h).[437] The Vulgate for the Pauline letters is

---

430 Kurt Aland, *Kurzgefasste Liste der griechischen Handschriften des Neuen Testaments* (ANTF 1; Berlin: de Gruyter, 1963); cf. Kurt Aland, ed., *Text und Textwert der griechischen Handschriften des Neuen Testaments*, part 2: *Die paulinischen Briefe* (4 vols.; Berlin: de Gruyter, 1991). For quotations in early Christian literature, see Jean Allenbach, ed., *Biblia patristica: Index des citations et allusions bibliques dans la littérature patristique* (7 vols.; Paris: Editions du Centre national de la recherche scientifique, 1975–2000).

431 See further, Klaus Wachtel and Klaus Witte, eds., *Das Neue Testament auf Papyrus*, vol. 2: *Die paulinischen Briefe, Teil 2: Gal, Eph, Phil, Kol, 1 u. 2 Thess, 1 u. 2 Tim, Tit, Phlm, Hebr* (ANTF 22; Berlin/New York: de Gruyter, 1994) 92–126.

432 But see Y. K. Kim, "Paleographic Dating of P⁴⁶ to the Later First Century," *Bib* 69 (1988) 248–57.

433 Readers familiar with *NTG*²⁷ will note that *NTG*²⁸ no longer distinguishes between first- and second-order uncial or minuscule witnesses (*NTG*²⁸, 48–49; cf. *NTG*²⁷, 50–51).

434 Generally judged to be less reliable in the Pauline letters than elsewhere; see Dirk Jongkind, "The Text

of the Pauline Corpus," in *The Blackwell Companion to Paul*, ed. Stephen Westerholm (Oxford: Blackwell, 2011) 216–31, here 221.

435 George William Horner, ed., *The Coptic Version of the New Testament in the Southern Dialect Otherwise Called Sahidic and Thebaic* (7 vols.; Oxford: Clarendon, 1911–24); H. Thompson, ed., *The Coptic Version of the Acts of the Apostles and the Pauline Epistles* (Cambridge: Cambridge University Press, 1932).

436 George William Horner, ed., *The Coptic Version of the New Testament in the Northern Dialect Otherwise Called Memphic or Bohairic* (4 vols.; Oxford: Clarendon, 1898–1905).

437 The Old Syriac version of the Pauline letters has not survived and can be reconstructed only partially from patristic quotations of the period, for which see Josef Kerschensteiner, *Der altsyrische Paulustext* (CSCO 315.37; Louvain: Secrétariat du CSCO, 1970). A critical edition of the Peshitta for the *Corpus Paulinum* is currently in preparation. Presently, the standard text remains J. Pinkerton and R. Kilgour, *The New Testament in Syriac* (London: British and Foreign Bible Society, 1920). The Harclean version

generally believed to be late, reflecting a Koine text type. The Old Latin (*Vetus Latina*) of Philippians is represented in the following manuscripts: [438]

ar (61) Codex Armachanus (9th cent.); Vulgate of NT but Old Latin text of the Pauline letters[439]

b (89) Codex Budapestiensis (8th–9th cent.)[440]

d (75) Codex Claromontanus (D) (5th cent.); Greek with Latin translation

f (78) Codex Augiensus (F) (9th cent.); Greek with Latin translation

r (64) Frisingensia Fragmenta (6th and 7th cent.): 1:1-20; 4:11–fin.[441]

t (t, 56) Liber Comicus, Lectionarius Toletanus (9th cent.): 2:5-11; 3:7-12; 3:17–4:9[442]

---

for Pauline letters may be found in Barbara Aland and Andreas Juckel, *Das Neue Testament in syrischer Überlieferung*, vol. 2: *Die paulinischen Briefe* (ANTF 14, 23, 32; Berlin/New York: de Gruyter, 1991–2002).

438 For the Old Latin of the Pauline letters, see Hermann Josef Frede, ed., *Vetus Latina: Die Reste der altlateinischen Bibel*, vol. 24.2: *Epistulae ad Philippenses et ad Colossenses* (Freiburg: Herder, 1966–71); Frede, *Altlateinische Paulus-Handschriften* (Freiburg: Herder, 1964).

439 John Wordsworth, Henry Julian White, eds., *Novum Testamentum Latine* (Oxford: Oxford University Press, 1905); J. Gwynn, *Liber Ardmachanus: The Book of Armagh* (Dublin: Hodges & Figgis; London: Williams & Norgate, 1913).

440 Hermann Josef Frede, *Ein neuer Paulustext und Kommentar* (2 vols.; Vetus Latina: Aus der Geschichte der lateinischen Bibel 7–8; Freiburg: Herder, 1973–74).

441 Donatien de Bruyne, ed., *Les Fragments de Freising* (Collectanea biblica latina 5; Rome: Bibliotèque vaticane, 1921).

442 Germain Morin, *Liber Comicus sive Lectionarius Missae, quo Toletana Ecclesia ante annos mille et ducentos utebantur* (Anecdota Maredsolana 1; Maredsous: In Monasterio S. Benedicti, 1893; repr., 1987); Justo Pérez de Urbel and Atilano González Ruiz-Zorrilla, *Liber Commicus* (2 vols.; Madrid: Escuela de Estudios Medievales, 1950-55).

Commentary

1

1/ **Paul and Timothy, slaves of Christ Jesus, to all the saints in Christ Jesus who are in Philippi, along with overseers[a] and assistants; 2/ grace and peace to you from God our father and the Lord Jesus Christ.**

a   Several witnesses (B[2] D[2] K P[vid] 075, 33, 1241, 1739, 1881 r; Cass[pt]) read συνεπισκόποις, "to fellow overseers," for σὺν ἐπισκόποις, "with overseers." On this reading, Paul designates the "overseers" in Philippi "fellow overseers," presumably along with himself and Timothy (cf. 1 Pet 5:1, where pseudo-Peter refers to himself as a "fellow elder," συμπρεσβύτερος). The reading is almost certainly the result of a simple transcriptional error from a manuscript written in *scriptio continua*. It is explicitly rejected by Theodore of Mopsuestia. On a similar use of σύν, see 1 Cor 1:2; 2 Cor 1:1.

Analysis

Ancient Mediterranean letters began with a brief notice identifying the sender and the intended recipient and conveying a personal greeting.[1] The typical Greek letter expressed this with the name of the sender in the nominative, the name of the recipient in the dative, and some verb conveying a greeting in the infinitive.[2] Semitic letters, insofar as they remained a distinct class,[3] conveyed this greeting in a separate noun clause expressing a wish or prayer for the reader's well-being.[4] Although Paul writes in Greek, his greeting "grace and peace to you" follows the Semitic form, to which he characteristically adds "from God our father and the Lord Jesus Christ."

Paul's letter prescripts differ widely in length and content, reflecting the circumstances at the time of writing, including Paul's anxieties about how his letter would be received. Romans has the longest prescript at 93 words, of which 72 are devoted to Paul's self-description.[5] Galatians has the second longest at 75 words. 1 Thessalonians has the shortest prescript at 19 words, and Philippians the second shortest at 32 words.[6] It is not surprising that Paul begins his letter to the Philippians with what was for him a relatively brief and simple prescript, since in writing to console them he would have intuitively adopted the stance of a friend—consolation was one of the primary duties of friendship[7]—and Greco-Roman custom encouraged friends to dispense with unnecessary formalities such as those sometimes found at the beginning and end of letters.[8] Consistent with this stance is Paul's avoidance of the title "apostle"—he and Timothy are simply "slaves of Christ Jesus"—and his making special mention

1   Seminal studies include F. X. L. Exler, *The Form of the Ancient Greek Letter: A Study in Greek Epistolography* (Washington, DC: Catholic University of America, 1923); Otto Roller, *Das Formular der paulinischen Briefe: Ein Beitrag zur Lehre vom antiken Briefe* (BWANT 58; Stuttgart: Kohlhammer, 1933); John L. White, "New Testament Epistolography in the Framework of Ancient Epistolography," *ANRW* 2.25.2 (1984) 1730–56.

2   E.g., χαίρειν ("greetings," lit., "to rejoice"); Judith M. Lieu suggests that this form goes back to an oral greeting carried by a third party: "A says for B to rejoice" ("'Grace to You and Peace': The Apostolic Greeting," *BJRL* 68 [1985] 161–78, here 163).

3   The χαίρειν greeting is used in 1 Macc 10:18, 25; 11:30; 12:6; 13:36; 14:20; 15:2, 16; 2 Macc 1:1 (with εἰρήνην ἀγαθήν, "good peace"), 10; 9:19; 11:16, 22, 27, 34; 1 Esdr 6:7; 8:9; Add Est 16:1; cf. Jas 1:1; Acts 15:23.

4   E.g., שלום ("peace"), חיים ("life"), רחם ("favor"); see

Irene Taatz, *Frühjüdische Briefe: Die paulinischen Briefe im Rahmen der offiziellen religiösen Briefe des Frühjudentums* (NTOA 16; Freiburg, Schweiz: Universitätsverlag; Göttingen: Vandenhoeck & Ruprecht, 1991); Lutz Doering, *Ancient Jewish Letters and the Beginnings of Christian Epistolography* (WUNT 298; Tübingen: Mohr Siebeck, 2012). The typical Latin letter was similar in form: e.g., *Cicero Attico salutem* [*dicit*], "Cicero [bids] health to Atticus," often abbreviated *s. d.* or *s. p. d.* (= *salutem plurimam dicit*); see White, *Cicero in Letters*; Michael Trapp, ed., *Greek and Latin Letters: An Anthology with Translation* (Cambridge: Cambridge University Press, 2003).

5   Holloway, "*Commendatio*," 358–60.

6   Of Paul's remaining letters, the prescript of 1 Corinthians has 55 words, 2 Corinthians has 41, and Philemon has 41.

7   E.g., Euripides, *Alc.* 369–70: "I will share in this grief with you as friend with friend [ὡς φίλος φίλῳ]."

8   Cf. Julius Victor *Ars rhet.* 27; Seneca, *Ep.* 75.

of the church's leadership ("overseers and assistants"), who have presumably arranged for the gift he has now received by way of Epaphroditus.

Comment

■ **1a** As in all his authentic letters, Paul identifies himself as Παῦλος ("Paul"),[9] the Greek form of the Roman *cognomen Paul(l)us*.[10] Acts alleges that Paul was also known as Σαῦλος ("Saul"), sometimes spelled Σαούλ,[11] from the Hebrew שאול.[12] This is certainly possible given Paul's Benjaminite roots.[13] But it is also consistent with Luke's agenda: the good Jew Saul is also the good Roman Paul.[14] It has traditionally been assumed that Paul was given the name Σαῦλος at birth and that he himself added the name Παῦλος at some point after his conversion.[15] But this is to read too much into Acts 13:9—Σαῦλος δέ, ὁ καὶ Παῦλος ("Saul, who was also called Paul")—which states only that in addition to Σαῦλος Paul was called Παῦλος without indicating how or when he acquired either name.[16] If Paul was born a Roman citizen[17]—and this is also uncertain—then he possessed from

---

9   Cf. Rom 1:1; 1 Cor 1:1 (also 1:10, 12, 13 [twice]; 3:4, 5, 22; 16:21); 2 Cor 1:1 (also 10:1); Gal 1:1 (also 5:2); 1 Thess 1:1 (also 2:18); Phlm 1 (also 9, 19). Also used of Paul in the Deutero-Pauline and Pastoral Letters (Eph 1:1; 3:1; Col 1:1, 23; 4:18; 2 Thess 1:1; 3:17; 1 Tim 1:1; 2 Tim 1:1; Tit 1:1); cf. 2 Pet 3:15: "our beloved brother Paul [Παῦλος] . . . in all his letters."

10   By the Augustan period, *Paul(l)us* had become a common *cognomen* for various *gentes*: the Aemilii, the Sergii, and the Vettenii (e.g., Lucius Sergius Paullus, the proconsul of Cyprus mentioned in Acts 13:7, for which see A. N. Sherwin-White, *Roman Society and Roman Law in the New Testament* [Oxford: Clarendon, 1963] 153–54). An ancient *praenomen*, it was also sometimes used as an elite *praenomen* for archaizing effect: e.g., Paullus Aemilius Lepidus (consul suffectus 34 BCE), Paullus Fabius Maximus (consul 11 BCE). See F. Münzer, "Paullus," PW 18.4:2362–63; Iiro Kajanto, *The Latin Cognomina* (Commentationes humanarum litterarum 36.2; Helsinki: Societas Scientiarum Fennica, 1965) 41, 243–44.

11   This form was uninflected, which is typical of transliterated loanwords, esp. names (e.g., Ἀβραάμ).

12   The inflected form Σαῦλος appears in Acts 7:58; 8:1, 3; 9:1, 8, 11, 22, 24; 11:25, 30; 12:25; 13:1, 2, 7, 9; the spelling Σαούλ (in Acts only in the vocative) occurs in 9:4, 17; 22:7, 13; 26:14; cf. 13:21.

13   See Phil 3:5; Rom 11:1; cf. 1 Sam 9:1-2, 21; 10:20-21; Acts 13:21.

14   Pervo, *Acts*, 326.

15   Jerome connected the change to the conversion of the proconsul Sergius Paulus in Acts 13:4-12 (*Vir. ill.* 5); Augustine assumed that Paul, who designated himself "the least of the apostles," chose Παῦλος out of humility because the Latin *paulus* means "little" (*Spir. et litt.* 7.12); Chrysostom linked the name change to Paul's commission (*Hom. Act.* 28.13; *PG* 60:209); cf. Plutarch, *Sera* 24.564c, where Aridaeus after a religious experience takes the name Thespesius; similarly, Aristides, *Or.* 50.53-54 (Keil),

tells how in a religious dream he acquired the name Theodorus. But Rufinus, in his postscript to the preface of Origen's commentary on Romans, assumes that Paul bore both names before his conversion; see H. Dessau, "Der Name des Apostels Paulus," *Hermes* 45 (1910) 347–68, here 349–50.

16   While ὁ/ἡ καί (Lat *qui/quae et*) typically links *cognomen* and *supernomen*, either name may be mentioned first, depending on the context; see M. Lambertz, "Zur Ausbreitung des Supernomen oder Signum im römischen Reiche," *Glotta* 4 (1913) 78–143, esp. 133 and 140; *Glotta* 5 (1914) 99–170; Iiro Kajanto, *Supernomina: A Study in Latin Epigraphy* (Commentationes humanarum litterarum 40.1; Helsinki: Societas Scientiarum Fennica, 1967). On the origins and use of double naming in the Hellenistic period, see Rita Calderini, "Ricerche sul doppio nome personale nell' Egitto greco-romano," *Aeg* 21 (1941) 221–60; *Aeg* 22 (1942) 3–45. Relevant NT examples are Acts 1:23 (Joseph/Justus); Acts 4:36 (Joseph/Barnabas); Acts 12:12, 25 (John/Mark; cf. 15:37); Acts 13:1 (Simon/Niger); Col 4:11 (Jesus/Justus). Unlike Paul, Ignatius wrote under his double name: Ἰγνάτιος ὁ καὶ Θεοφόρος ("Ignatius, also called Theophorus"); *Eph.* 1.1; *Mag.* 1.1; *Trall.* 1.1; etc.), for which see William R. Schoedel, *Ignatius of Antioch: A Commentary on the Letters of Ignatius of Antioch* (Hermeneia: Philadelphia: Fortress Press, 1985) 36; cf. "Simon Peter" (Mark 3:16 and often thereafter in the NT).

17   Acts 22:28; cf. 16:37; 22:25-28; 23:26-30; 25:11. On Paul's Roman citizenship, see Theodor Mommsen, "Die Rechtsverhältnisse des Apostels Paulus," *ZNW* 2 (1901) 81–96; Sherwin-White, *Roman Society and Roman Law*, 144–93; Gerd Lüdemann, *Early Christianity according to the Traditions in Acts: A Commentary* (London: SCM; Minneapolis: Fortress, 1989) 240–41; Martin Hengel, *The Pre-Christian Paul* (London: SCM, 1991) 1–17. Against Paul's citizenship, see W. Stegemann, "War der Apostel Paulus ein römischer Bürger?" *ZNW* 78 (1987) 200–229.

birth the requisite *tria nomina* (*praenomen*, *nomen*, and *cognomen*), of which either Παῦλος or Σαῦλος could have been the *cognomen*,[18] with the remaining name being added as a *supernomen* or nickname, possibly also at birth.[19] Of course, even if Paul was not a Roman citizen a nickname could have been added at any point.

Paul lists Timothy as a co-sender of his letter, as he does in 1 Thessalonians (along with Silvanus), 2 Corinthians, and Philemon. Paul often includes one or more of his close associates as the nominal co-senders of his letters.[20] His reasons for this practice vary. Sometimes it is to bolster his authority, as in Galatians, where he includes not one or two associates but "*all* the brothers with me."[21] Other times it may be because of the co-sender's relationship with the recipients: thus in 1 Corinthians Paul includes Sosthenes, who, according to Acts 18:17, was the president of the synagogue at Corinth.[22] In Philippians, Paul mentions Timothy, whom he will soon send to Philippi (2:19-24).[23] Paul's naming Timothy in the prescript does not mean that Timothy was an actual co-author of the letter, since Paul continues in the first person singular (1:3), and when he mentions Timothy again in 2:19-24 it is in the third person.

When designating co-senders, Paul is usually careful to distinguish himself from them, referring to himself as an "apostle" and the co-sender or co-senders as "the brother" or "the brothers."[24] In Philippians, Paul not only avoids the title "apostle"[25] but refers to both himself and Timothy as "slaves [δοῦλοι] of Christ Jesus." This lack of pretension is consistent with Paul's rhetorical stance as a friend, but it also serves to link Timothy closely to Paul in anticipation of Paul's plan to send Timothy as his surrogate.[26] Dale Martin has proposed that Paul uses "slave" (δοῦλος) as an honorific title, as in Rom 1:1, where it is linked appositionally with "called apostle."[27] But in Phil 1:1, where the expression anticipates the examples

---

18 In favor of Παῦλος being Paul's *cognomen*, see G. A. Harrer, "Saul Who Is Also Called Paul," *HTR* 33 (1940) 19–33; cf. C. J. Hemer, "The Name of Paul," *TynBull* 36 (1985) 179–83; T. J. Leary, "Paul's Improper Name," *NTS* 38 (1992) 467–69. The use of Semitic *supernomina* among Jews has been demonstrated by H. J. Leon, "The Names of Jews in Ancient Rome," *TAPA* 59 (1928) 205–24. *Cognomina* and ethnic *supernomina* often had similar sounds. On the names of famous personalities (e.g., King Saul) used as *supernomina*, see Kajanto, *Supernomina*, 18–19.

19 For double names given at birth, see *NewDocs* 1:89–96, which cites *AÉ* 1976 (1980) 419: "Paula or Eustatia" (from the epitaph of a child less than two years old); *CIJ* 1:108: "To Hermione . . . surnamed Barseoda" (from the epitaph of a child who lived eleven months and seven days).

20 Only in Romans does Paul not mention a co-sender; see Malherbe, *Thessalonians*, 86–89; and, more generally, Wolf-Henning Ollrog, *Paulus und seine Mitarbeiter: Untersuchungen zu Theorie und Praxis der paulinischen Mission* (WMANT 50; Neukirchen-Vluyn: Neukirchener Verlag, 1979).

21 This may also be the case in 1 Thessalonians, where Paul worries that he has scandalized the Thessalonians by leaving town quickly at the first sign of opposition. He mentions as co-senders both Timothy and Silvanus and begins his characteristic thanksgiving-period with the first person plural instead of the more typical first person singular.

22 Unless, of course, Luke's account of Sosthenes is itself based on 1 Corinthians. Sosthenes appears

to be a mere foil for the triumphalism of the Acts pericope (Pervo, *Acts*, on 18:17), and Luke's vignette when read in conjunction with 1 Cor 1:1 makes a great story of a Jew brought to his senses (i.e., converting to belief in Christ) by a beating from a Roman governor.

23 According to Acts, Timothy was with Paul during the foundation of the Philippian church (16:1, 13; 17:14), and he returned there once if not twice during Paul's so-called third missionary journey (19:22; 20:3-4). Timothy's previous contact with the church is confirmed by Phil 2:22, where the Philippians are said to have firsthand knowledge of Timothy's character. But again the question is whether Luke derives his knowledge of Timothy at Philippi from the letter to the Philippians or has independent information.

24 In Phlm 1 Paul refers to himself as a "prisoner of Christ Jesus."

25 Paul will use the term "apostle" of Epaphroditus in 2:25.

26 For consolation by means of a surrogate, see the excursus "Consolation by Means of a Surrogate" below at 2:20-22.

27 Dale B. Martin, *Slavery as Salvation: The Metaphor of Slavery in Pauline Christianity* (New Haven: Yale University Press, 1990) 51–60; see also Gerhard Sass, "Zur Bedeutung von δοῦλος bei Paulus," *ZNW* 40 (1941) 24–32, which draws on ancient Near Eastern sources. For the term in Rom 1:1, see Jewett, *Romans*, 100. Apart from Rom 1:1 and Phil 1:1, Paul refers to himself as a "slave" of Christ elsewhere only in Gal 1:10.

of both Christ ("taking the form of a slave [δούλου]"; 2:7) and Timothy ("he served as a slave [ἐδούλευσεν] with me"; 2:22), the servile connotations of "slave" should not be discounted.

■ **1b** Paul addresses his letter "to all[28] the saints in Christ Jesus who are in Philippi, with overseers and ministers." Three items call for comment: (1) the designation "saints," (2) the characteristically Pauline phrase "in Christ Jesus," which in one form or another appears a total of twenty-two times in the letter,[29] and (3) the unprecedented reference to "overseers and assistants."

Paul uses the substantive "the saints" (οἱ ἅγιοι, lit., "the holy ones") to refer to Christ-believers twenty-four times in his authentic letters.[30] The substantive appears elsewhere in the New Testament with any frequency only in later Pauline tradition and in Revelation,[31] which suggests that Paul was one of the first to apply the term to Christ-believers. E. P. Sanders has proposed that Paul decided on the expression "holy ones" versus, say, the more common "righteous ones" or "chosen ones" in order to emphasize the need for the sanctification of gentiles, who from Paul's point of view were "tainted with moral impurity."[32] This is a reasonable assumption given Paul's ethnic prejudices,[33] but it sheds little light on the fact that Paul also uses the term to refer to *Jewish* Christ-believers.[34] Further, it does not take into account the fact that in antecedent Jewish literature "holy ones" (קדשים/קדשין) is used almost exclusively of angels (a usage Paul retains in 1 Thess 3:13) and only by extension and then at first rarely of the members of an apocalyptic sect because of their close association with angels.[35] A better explanation is that, like other apocalyptic Jews, Paul chose the term

---

28 A number of commentators have proposed that emphasis be placed on the fact that Paul addresses his letter to "*all* [πᾶσιν] the saints" in Philippi as part of Paul's strategy to unite an obviously fractured congregation (e.g., Lightfoot on 1:4; see also Peterlin, *Disunity*, 19–30). In support of this, they note that Paul goes on to repeat the adjective πᾶς ("all") in v. 4 (πάντων ὑμῶν, "all of you"), v. 7 (twice: πάντων ὑμῶν, "all of you"; πάντα ὑμᾶς, "you all"), and v. 8 (πάντα ὑμᾶς, "you all"). But Paul is fond of wordplay and πᾶς and its cognates are easy: see 1 Cor 9:22 (τοῖς πᾶσιν γέγονα πάντα ἵνα πάντως κτλ., "I have become all things to all people that I might by all means . . ." [NRSV]); 2 Cor 9:8 (ἵνα ἐν παντὶ πάντοτε πᾶσαν αὐτάρκειαν ἔχοντες περισσεύητε εἰς πᾶν ἔργον ἀγαθόν, "so that by always having enough of everything you may share abundantly in every good work" [NRSV]). Further, Paul frequently uses some form of πᾶς in his letter introductions (e.g., Rom 1:7; 1 Cor 1:2; 2 Cor 1:1). It is not always clear why he does so. Perhaps it is to assert his reach as an apostle. But stylistic considerations are also a factor in Philippians, since in addition to the instances cited above, Paul uses πᾶς or a cognate three more times in 1:3-8, none of which refers to the Philippians: once in v. 3 (πάσῃ τῇ μνείᾳ, "every remembrance") and twice in v. 4 (πάντοτε, "always"; πάσῃ δεήσει, "every prayer"). For Dibelius (on Phil 1:1) this is simply a case of "Wortspiel." Alliteration in π may also be a factor: ποιούμενος ("making"; 1:4), πρώτης ("first"; 1:5), πεποιθώς ("confident"; 1:6), ἀπολογία ("defense"; 1:7), and ἐπιποθῶ ("long for"; 1:8). Perhaps Paul is attempting an introductory period (1:3-8), which he

concludes in 1:8 with a *clausula* in the form of an exclamation. See the discussion of Phil 1:3-8 below.

29 Some form of "in Christ" or "in the Lord" occurs in 1:1, 11 ("through Jesus Christ"), 13, 14, 26; 2:1, 5, 19, 24, 29; 3:1, 3, 9, 14; 4:1, 2, 4, 7, 10, 13 *v.l.*, 19, 21. Other relevant expressions occur in 1:8, 19, 21, 23, 29; 3:7, 8, 10, 18, 20-21; 4:22.

30 In addition to Phil 1:1; 4:21 (sg.) and 22, see Rom 1:7; 8:27; 12:13; 15:25, 26, 31; 16:2, 15; 1 Cor 1:2; 6:1, 2; 14:33; 16:1, 15; 2 Cor 1:1; 8:4; 9:1, 12; 13:12; and Phlm 5, 7. In 1 Thess 3:13 it is used of angels (cf. 2 Thess 1:10).

31 Deutero-Paulines and Pastorals: 13 times; Revelation: 14 times; otherwise only once in Matthew (27:52), four times in Acts (9:13, 32, 41; 26:10—all in the context of the Pauline mission), twice in Hebrews (6:10; 13:24), and once in Jude (14, which quotes *1 Enoch* 1:8, where it refers to angels).

32 Sanders, *Paul and Palestinian Judaism*, 452.

33 E.g., 1 Thess 4:5; Gal 2:15; 1 Cor 5:1; esp. Rom 1:18-32.

34 Rom 15:25, 26; 2 Cor 8:4; 9:1, 12.

35 The texts are given and discussed in C. H. W. Brekelmans, "The Saints of the Most High and Their Kingdom," *OTS* 14 (1965) 305–29; and Luc Dequeker, "The Saints of the Most High in Qumran and Daniel," *OTS* 18 (1973) 108–87; but now see Collins, *Daniel*, 313–17; Nickelsburg, *1 Enoch 1*, 140–41; Nickelsburg and VanderKam, *1 Enoch 2*, 98–100: "'the holy' is a designation of the righteous and chosen with a view to their destiny in the realm of the holy angels" (100).

64

because it reflected his belief in his converts' affiliation with the angels both in this life and in the next.[36] This explanation is supported by the term's use in Revelation, where it refers to believers whose prayers become incense offered by angels in the heavenly temple (8:3, 4; cf. 5:8).[37]

The phrase "in Christ [Jesus]" (ἐν Χριστῷ ['Ιησοῦ]) was coined by Paul to express his converts' relationship with the risen Christ.[38] Given its frequency—over one hundred times in Paul's authentic letters[39]—one might expect it to be a technical term. But Paul uses it in a variety of ways that defy easy classification.[40] A. J. M. Wedderburn calls "in Christ" one of Paul's most "characteristic and versa-

tile phrases," and he agrees with Udo Schnelle that to interpret it correctly one must look beyond the phrase itself to its place in Paul's thought.[41] Nevertheless, the phrase finds a near analogy in another characteristic Pauline phrase, "in the Spirit" (ἐν πνεύματι).[42] In the case of "in the Spirit," however, Paul is unambiguous about its meaning. Christ-believers are "in the Spirit" because the Spirit is "in them": "you are not in the flesh but in the Spirit [ἐν πνεύματι] *since* the spirit of God dwells in you [ἐν ὑμῖν]" (Rom 8:9a). To be "in the Spirit" means to be permanently possessed by the divine spirit: "since *we live in the Spirit* [ζῶμεν πνεύματι], let us also walk in the Spirit" (Gal 5:25).[43] By analogy, then, to be "in Christ"

---

36 At Qumran the emphasis shifted to the present life, as the sectaries imagined themselves to be already mingling with angels in worship (Collins, "Angelic Life," 296–302). Paul may have imagined something similar for his converts (1 Cor 11:10; cf. 1 Cor 14:12: "you are zealots for spirits [ζηλωταί ἐστε πνευμάτων]"; see Joseph A. Fitzmyer, "A Feature of Qumran Angelology and the Angels of 1 Cor 11:10," *NTS* 4 (1957–58) 48–58, reprinted in *Paul and the Dead Sea Scrolls*, ed. Jerome Murphy-O'Connor and James H. Charlesworth (Christian Origins Library; New York: Crossroad, 1990) 31–47. Paul believed that in resurrection his converts would receive angelic bodies (1 Cor 15:40-57; cf. Phil 3:21 and my comments there) and that this transformation begins even in this life (see Phil 2:15 and my comments there; cf. 2 Cor 3:18; 5:1-5). For Christ as angel, see my comments below on 2:6-11. See also the introduction, part 7: "Key Religious Topoi."

37 In Revelation it is the prayers of the "holy ones" as offered by angels that lead to judgment; cf. *1 Enoch* 47:1-2; 99:3.

38 Hans-Christoph Meier, *Mystik bei Paulus: Zur Phänomenologie religiöser Erfahrung im Neuen Testament* (TANZ 26; Tübingen: Francke, 1998) 27–39. Seminal studies include Adolf Deissmann, *Die neutestamentliche Formel "in Christo Jesu"* (Marburg: Elwert, 1892); Wilhelm Bousset, *Kyrios Christos: A History of the Belief in Christ from the Beginnings of Christianity to Irenaeus* (Nashville: Abingdon, 1970) 153–210; and Schweitzer, *Mysticism*, 101–40; see also Fritz Neugebauer, *In Christus: ἐν Χριστῷ: Eine Untersuchung zum paulinischen Glaubensbegriff* (Berlin: Evangelische Verlagsanstalt, 1961); Michel Bouttier, *En Christ: Étude d'exégèse et de théologie pauliniennes* (EHPhR 54: Paris: Presses universitaire de France, 1962). Udo Schnelle argues, unconvincingly in my view, on the basis of baptismal formulae that the expression

is pre-Pauline (*Gerechtigkeit und Christusgegenwart: Vorpaulinische und paulinische Tauftheologie* [GThA 24; Göttingen: Vandenhoeck & Ruprecht, 1983] 109–10).

39 These statistics include parallel expressions such as "in the Lord" or "in him"; see James D. G. Dunn, *The Theology of Paul the Apostle* (Grand Rapids: Eerdmans, 1998) 390–408, esp. 396–97; Udo Schnelle, *Apostle Paul: His Life and Theology* (Grand Rapids: Baker Academic, 2005) 481; Lars Klehn, "Die Verwendung von ἐν Χριστῷ bei Paulus: Erwägungen zu den Wandlungen in der paulinischen Theologie," *BN* 74 (1994) 66–79, here 68 (table 1). Other related phrases include "with Christ," "into Christ," and "through Christ."

40 A. J. M. Wedderburn, "Some Observations on Paul's Use of the Phrases 'in Christ' and 'with Christ'," *JSNT* 25 (1985) 83–97, here p. 87; cf. Friedrich Büchsel, "'In Christus' bei Paulus," *ZNW* 42 (1949) 141–58.

41 Wedderburn, "Some Observations," 83; Schnelle, *Gerechtigkeit*, 107–8. I think this approach is right as far as it goes, but I would also wish to maintain that, as one of Paul's stock phrases, "in Christ" is at times little more than a pious expression added by Paul for reasons that even he might not have been able to explain. The commentary tradition with its quest for theological meaning continues to attribute to Paul a precision he likely did not have.

42 Rudolf Bultmann, *Theology of the New Testament* (2 vols.; New York: Scribner; London: SCM, 1951, 1952) 1:311: "'in Christ' can interchange with 'in the Spirit.'"

43 It is a given for Paul that all Christ-believers "live in the Spirit." The expression "in the Spirit" was used differently by the author of Revelation: "I was in the Spirit [ἐν πνεύματι] on the Lord's day" (1:10), where

would mean to be permanently possessed by Christ.[44] This conclusion is supported by the fact (1) that for Paul Christ was himself now a "spirit" (1 Cor 15:45; cf. 2 Cor 3:17) and (2) that Paul often used "the spirit of God" and "the spirit of Christ" interchangeably.[45]

Paul believed that possession by Christ determined—or at least should determine—the whole of Christ-believers' lives: "I no longer live. Christ lives in me" (Gal 2:20).[46] This possession expressed itself most spectacularly in various altered states of consciousness such as prophetic inspiration, ritual ascents, visions of Christ, and ecstatic worship including glossolalia and healings.[47] But it was also responsible for more mundane things like Christ-believers' progress in righteousness, which Paul imagined as Christ taking shape within them.[48] Further, since Paul's assemblies were in effect spirit-possession cults, posses-

sion obviously determined Christ-believers' corporate life.[49] Whole congregations could therefore be referred to as "in Christ," as here in Phil 1:1.[50] The expression "in Christ" and related expressions such as "in the Lord" occur with greater frequency in Philippians than in any of Paul's other letters.[51]

Paul singles out among "all the saints in Christ Jesus in Philippi" certain functionaries of the church whom he designates ἐπίσκοποι καὶ διάκονοι, here translated "overseers and assistants."[52] Because these terms were subsequently used to denote the offices of "bishop" and "deacon," it has been suggested that the phrase containing them is a gloss reflecting a post-Pauline practice.[53] But there is no manuscript evidence to support this,[54] and the plural ἐπίσκοποι is inconsistent with the later monepisco-pacy.[55] The problem lies, instead, in assuming anachronis-

---

it signifies a temporary possession trance. Cf. Rev 4:2; 17:3; 21:10.

44 That Paul thought Christ possessed all Christ-believers is seen most clearly in Rom 8:9b: "if anyone does not have the spirit of Christ [πνεῦμα Χριστοῦ οὐκ ἔχει], this one does not belong to him." For the expression "to have a spirit" (πνεῦμα ἔχειν), see Mark 3:30; 7:25; 9:17; Luke 4:33; 11:6; Acts 8:7; 16:16.

45 E.g., Rom 8:9; cf. Gal. 4:6; Phil 1:19. See the introduction, part 7.b: "Paul's Spirit-Christ."

46 See John Ashton, *The Religion of Paul the Apostle* (New Haven/London: Yale University Press, 2000) 230 n. 23: "Paul's experience was ecstatic in nature."

47 Smith, "Pauline Worship"; Colleen Shantz, *Paul in Ecstasy: The Neurobiology of the Apostle's Life and Thought* (Cambridge: Cambridge University Press, 2009); see also Philip Esler, "Glossolalia and the Admission of Gentiles into the Early Christian Community," *BTB* 22 (1992) 136–42.

48 Gal 4:19 ("until Christ be formed [μορφωθῇ] within you"); cf. Rom 8:4; Gal 5:16.

49 Here see the incisive studies by Mount: "Spirit Possession"; idem, "Religious Experience"; and idem, "Gullibility." For this paragraph and the preceding one I have benefited greatly from an extended e-mail conversation with Professor Mount.

50 See Christian Strecker, *Die liminale Theologie des Paulus: Zugänge zur paulinischen Theologie aus kulturanthropologischer Perspektive* (FRLANT 185; Göttingen: Vandenhoeck & Ruprecht, 1999) 189–211, who understands the phrase to denote a "*Christus communitas*" in the context of which one experiences Christ.

51 I list these above in n. 30. Among the more interesting is 3:9: "that I might gain Christ and be found in

him." Here Paul imagines the believer's progress in actual righteousness ("the righteousness that is from God") as the process of becoming increasingly "in Christ." At the final judgment the sanctified person will be found to be fully "in him," possession by the spirit of Christ having had its full effect.

52 See Richard S. Ascough, *Paul's Macedonian Associations: The Social Context of Philippians and 1 Thessalonians* (WUNT 2/161; Tübingen: Mohr Siebeck, 2003) 71–162; and the essays in *Neutestamentliche Ämtermodelle im Kontext*, ed. Thomas Schmeller, Martin Ebner, and Rudolf Hoppe (QD 239; Freiburg im Breisgau: Herder, 2010). For "overseers," see Pilhofer, *Philippi*, 1:140–47, who notes a possible local parallel in the procurators of the so-called Thracian Rider cult; for "assistants," see John N. Collins, *Diakonia: Re-interpreting the Ancient Sources* (New York: Oxford University Press, 1990); Anni Hentschel, *Diakonia im Neuen Testament: Studien zur Semantik unter besonderer Berücksichtigung der Rolle von Frauen* (WUNT 2/226; Tübingen: Mohr Siebeck, 2007) 172–78.

53 Already by James Moffatt, *An Introduction to the Literature of the New Testament* (New York: Scribner, 1910) 171: a "catholicizing" gloss (citing earlier work by Brückner and Völter, *non vidi*).

54 T. C. Skeat argues on stoichometric grounds that lacunous 𝔭46 may have not included this phrase ("Did Paul Write to 'Bishops and Deacons' at Philippi? A Note on Philippians 1:1," *NovT* 37 [1995] 12–15), but he notes other possible explanations of the evidence and concludes "*non liquet*."

55 But see *Did.* 15:1.

tically that these terms specify established offices, rather than being simply descriptive terms applied to functionaries of the Philippian church.[56] Chrysostom assumes a hendiadys: "at that time *episkopoi* were also called *diakonoi*" (hom. 2.16.23 Allen).

Leadership within the Pauline churches emerged informally out of the house-church.[57] There was no set terminology,[58] and functionaries varied from place to place distinguished by such things as their dedication (1 Thess 5:12-13),[59] their gifts (1 Cor 12:28; Rom 12:6-8), and their social status (Rom 16:1-2). Displays of spirit possession may also have been key in some places.[60] It is likely that Paul's use of the terms ἐπίσκοπος and διάκονος here contributed to their wider usage and eventual technical meaning in the second and third centuries.[61] We can only speculate what the respective functions of these "overseers and assistants" might have been. Jürgen Roloff's proposal that "overseers" were heads of house-churches is not unreasonable,[62] at which point the plural would imply that there was more than one house-church at Philippi. Even so, it is not clear why only in Philippians Paul singles out "overseers and assistants." One plausible

explanation is that Paul mentions them in recognition of their work in collecting and sending the gift he recently received from the church.[63] A second possibility is that in his forced absence Paul is anxious to remind the Philippians that there are other leaders in the Christian movement on whom they can rely. These explanations are, of course, not mutually exclusive. The fact that significant local leadership had emerged in the Philippian assembly suggests an increase in number and a more conspicuous social presence in the city. This in turn would explain the rise of social hostility mentioned in 1:28-30, as for many residents the church will have become a more pronounced social and cultural threat.[64]

■ **2** The greeting "grace and peace to you" is first attested in Paul and is found in all his genuine letters.[65] It occurs without addition in 1 Thessalonians, the earliest of Paul's surviving letters, after which it is consistently modified by the prepositional phrase "from God our father and the Lord Jesus Christ."[66] This fuller form is imitated in the Deutero-Pauline and Pastoral Letters, though with occasional modifications.[67] 1 Peter, which has other Pauline

56 Reumann has suggested, plausibly, that these "offices" were ad hoc creations of the Philippians ("Contributions of the Philippian Community to Paul and to Earliest Christianity," *NTS* 39 [1993] 438–57; idem, "Church Office in Paul, especially in Philippians," in *Origins and Method: Towards a New Understanding of Judaism and Christianity*, ed. B. H. McLean [JSNTSup 86; Sheffield: JSOT Press, 1993] 82–91), a contention supported by Pilhofer, *Philippi*, 1:140–47.

57 Wayne A. Meeks, *The First Urban Christians: The Social World of the Apostle Paul* (New Haven: Yale University Press, 1983) 29–30, 75–77; see 1 Cor 16:15-16 for the "household of Stephanas," which is to enjoy authority ("you should submit to such") in the Corinthian church.

58 Tobias Nicklas, "Offices? Roles, Functions, Authorities and the Ethos in Earliest Christianity: A Look into the World of Pauline Communities," in *Rabbi – Pastor – Priest: Their Roles and Profiles through the Ages*, ed. Walter Homolka and Heinz-Günther Schöttler (Studia Judaica 64; Berlin: de Gruyter, 2013) 23–40, esp. 32–39.

59 Note also that the "household of Stephanas" is commended for its hard work (1 Cor 16:15-16).

60 Mount, "Spirit Possession." The traditional model of rigidly distinguishing between *charisma* (giftedness)

and *amt* (office) is romantic, and it is to be rejected in favor of a more nuanced approach in which giftedness, function, and office coexist and describe different aspects of the same phenomenon.

61 Reumann, pp. 86–89; idem, "Church Office."

62 Jürgen Roloff, *Der erste Brief an Timotheus* (EKK 15; Zurich: Benziger; Neukirchen-Vluyn: Neukirchener Verlag, 1989) 173.

63 For local church officers facilitating such financial matters, see Peter Lampe, *From Paul to Valentinus: Christians at Rome in the First Two Centuries* (Minneapolis: Fortress Press, 2003) 403–4.

64 See Acts 16:21: "they are promoting customs [ἔθη] that it is not lawful for us as Romans to accept or to perform."

65 Klaus Berger, "Apostelbrief und apostolische Rede: Zum Formular frühchristlicher Briefe," *ZNW* 65 (1974) 190–231, here 197–98; Franz Schnider and Werner Stenger, *Studien zum neutestamentlichen Brieffformular* (NTTS 11: Leiden: Brill, 1987) 26. I am not convinced by Berger's claim that the expression implies revealed knowledge.

66 The texts are 1 Thess 1:1; Rom 1:7; 1 Cor 1:3; 2 Cor 1:2; Gal 1:3; Phil 1:2; and Phlm 3.

67 Col 1:2 omits "and the Lord Jesus Christ," while 1 Tim 1:2 and 2 Tim 1:2 add "mercy" so as to read "grace, mercy, and peace" (cf. 2 John 3). The fuller

elements, shows the earlier formula—"grace and peace to you"—which is also reflected in 2 Peter.[68]

The double form of Paul's greeting has been explained as the combination of the familiar Greek greeting χαίρειν ("greetings," lit., "to rejoice") and Jewish greeting שלום ("peace"), with χάρις ("grace") being substituted for its near homonym χαίρειν.[69] But this is at best a partial explanation. The double form can itself be explained on entirely Jewish grounds;[70] and, where it can be demonstrated that Hellenistic-Jewish authors did in fact combine these greetings, the Greek infinitive was taken over without alteration: "Greetings . . . and good peace" (χαίρειν . . . εἰρήνην ἀγαθήν; 2 Macc 1:1). Further, χάρις was a central theological theme for Paul and therefore much more than a near homonym for χαίρειν. Finally, and per-

haps most importantly, the grace wish had for Paul both a liturgical and an epistolary function, as can be seen clearly in its repetition in his letter conclusions.[71] It is much more likely, then, that Paul crafted his characteristic greeting (1) from traditional Jewish sources (2) with an eye to its public reading to the assembled congregation.

The phrase "from God our father and the Lord Jesus Christ" indicates the source of "grace and peace." Christ often shares qualities and functions with God in Paul.[72] It is possible, however, that Paul is employing chiasmus, so that peace has its source primarily in God (cf. Phil 4:7: "the peace of God"; 4:9: "the God of peace")[73] and grace has its source in Jesus Christ (cf. Phil 4:23: "the grace of the Lord Jesus Christ be with your spirit").[74]

form also appears in Rev 1:4, where it has been modified to reflect the author's preferred way of referring to God: "grace to you and peace from the one who is etc."

68   1 Peter (followed by 2 Pet 1:2) adds the optative "may it be multiplied" (πληθυνθείη) in possible imitation of a Jewish model (e.g., *y. Sanh.* 18d; *t. Sanh.* 2.6). A similar greeting is found in Dan 4:1 (3:31 MT; cf. 6:36), for which see Collins, *Daniel*, 221, who cites Fitzmyer, "Aramaic Epistolography," in *Studies in Ancient Letter Writing*, ed. John L. White (*Semeia* 22; Chico, CA: Scholars Press, 1983) 25–57, here 34–35.

69   E.g., Vincent; cf. Johannes Weiss, *Der erste Korintherbrief* (KEK 5; Göttingen: Vandenhoeck & Ruprecht, 1910) 4–5 (on 1:3); Koskenniemi, *Studien*, 162. For similar expressions in the papyri, see Peter Arzt-Grabner, *Philemon* (Papyrologische Kommentare zum Neuen Testament 1; Göttingen: Vandenhoeck & Ruprecht, 1003) 109–23.

70   Taatz discounts the thesis altogether, arguing that Paul's pair "grace and peace" has its nearest analogue in the Jewish formula "mercy and peace" (*2 Bar.* 78:2), "grace" being Paul's preferred term

for "mercy" (*Frühjüdische Briefe*, 112; cf. 66–67). See also Doering, *Ancient Jewish Letters*, 247; Dieter Zeller, *Charis bei Philon und Paulus* (SBS 142; Stuttgart: Katholisches Bibelwerk, 1990) 132–33; cf. the remarks on the expression by Tertullian, *Adv. Marc.* 5.5.

71   See Rom 16:20b; 1 Cor 16:23; Gal 6:18; Phil 4:23; 1 Thess 5:18; Phlm 25; esp. 2 Cor 13:13. See Betz, *Galatians*, 40 n. 42 (on 1:3); cf. Malherbe, *Thessalonians*, 100.

72   See the discussion of this phrase by Malherbe, *Thessalonians*, on 2 Thess 1:2.

73   See Rom 15:33; 16:20; 1 Thess 5:23.

74   See Rom 16:20b; 1 Cor 16:23; 2 Cor 13:13; Gal 6:18; 1 Thess 5:18; Phlm 25. For a possible parallel case of chiasmus, see Phlm 5: "hearing of your love and faith, which you have toward the Lord Jesus and for all the saints," where the "Lord Jesus" is the object of "faith" and "all the saints" is the object of "love" (see Joseph A. Fitzmyer, *The Letter to Philemon: A New Translation with Introduction and Commentary* [AB 34C; New York: Doubleday, 2000] on v. 25).

II. Exordium[1] 1:3-11: Paul's Affection and Prayers for the Philippians

3/ I give thanks to my God[a] for every remembrance of you, 4/ always in every prayer of mine for you all praying with joy[b] 5/ over your partnership in the gospel from the first day until now, 6/ confident of this very thing: that he who began a good work within you will continue to perfect it until the Day of Christ Jesus;[c] 7/ and it is only right that I should feel this way about you all, given the place that you have in my heart as those who, both in these chains of mine and in[d] the defense and confirmation of the gospel, are my loyal partners in this grace[e]—8/ for God is[f] my[g] witness how I long for you all with the deepest affections of Christ! 9/ And here is what I am praying: that your love might increase[h] yet more and more in knowledge and all discernment, 10/ so that you can ascertain the things that really matter, to the end that you might be pure and blameless for the Day of Christ, 11/ having been filled with the fruit of righteousness[i] that is through Jesus Christ to God's glory and praise.[j]

a   A few witnesses (D* F G b; Ambst Cass^pt) read ἐγὼ μὲν εὐχαριστῶ τῷ κυρίῳ ἡμῶν, "I for my part give thanks to our Lord," an early interpretive paraphrase of the original, which simply reads εὐχαριστῶ τῷ θεῷ μου. The ἐγὼ μέν ("I for my part") would serve to single Paul out from the foregoing group (Timothy, overseers, assistants), while the plural "*our* Lord" is a common Paulinism (36 times, though never in Philippians).

b   Several witnesses (F G Ψ 2495 vg^mss sy^h) add καί ("also") after "joy": "praying with joy also" (i.e., *in addition to* giving thanks in 1:3). Without the καί "with joy" (μετὰ χαρᾶς) is epexegetical of "I give thanks" (εὐχαριστῶ): "I give thanks . . . praying for you all with joy."

c   As is often the case, the textual tradition here is split between Χριστοῦ Ἰησοῦ, "Christ Jesus" (p^46 B D L Ψ 630, 1241, Maj. lat; Ambst) and Ἰησοῦ Χριστοῦ, "Jesus Christ" (ℵ A F G K P 075, 0278, 33, 81, 104, 365, 614, 1175, 1505, 1739, 1881, 2464 ar vg^mss sy).

d   Some important witnesses (A D* F G vg^mss) omit the preposition ἐν ("in") before "defense." Since the preposition appears earlier in the sentence ("*in* my chains"), however, this would do little to change the sense, though the repetition of the preposition would lend a certain fullness to this important initial sentence.

e   Eberhard Nestle conjectured that χάριτος ("grace") should read χρείας ("need") on the basis of 4:16: "more than once you sent to my need [χρείαν]"; cf. 4:14. But in light of 1:29—"it has been given [ἐχαρίσθη] to you . . . to suffer for his sake"—χάρις presents no problem and should be retained.

f   The copulative ἐστίν ("is") is read in a number of witnesses (ℵ² A D K L P 075, 0278, 81, 104, 365, 630, 1175, 1241, 1505, 1881, 2464 Maj lat sy^h), while omitted in others (p^46 B F G Ψ 6, 33, 1739 d). In either case the sense is the same, though if read it again adds a certain fullness to Paul's initial period.

g   A number of witnesses (ℵ^3vid D F G Ψ 0278, 104, 326, 365, 1175, 1241) read μοι ("for me") for μου ("my"). The pronoun is omitted in p^46 and the Old Latin manuscript ar.

h   Several witnesses (B D Ψ 81, 2464, 2495) have the aorist subjunctive περισσεύσῃ instead of the present

---

1   While the point can be overemphasized, Paul's letters were written to be read aloud and have certain features in common with ancient public speeches. In describing Phil 1:3-11 it will be helpful, therefore, to imagine it as a kind of rhetorical *exordium* or προοίμιον ("introduction" or "opening"). Characteristic features of the *exordium* included an attempt to win the goodwill of the audience (the *captatio*

benevolentiae) as well as some indication of the theme or themes to be treated (the *propositio* or πρόθεσις; "thesis statement"). Paul's repeated insistence that he has fond memories of the Philippians and deep affections for them in 1:3-8 will have met the first requirement, while the prayer report of 1:9-11 will have met the second.

subjunctive $\pi\epsilon\rho\iota\sigma\sigma\epsilon\acute{\nu}\eta$. The sense is largely the same, though the present tense would presumably characterize the Philippians' acquisition of "knowledge and all discernment" as a learning process, a sense supported by the additional expression "still more and more."

i   A few manuscripts (P Ψ 365, 630, [1241], 1505, 1739^c 1881 Maj sy) read the plural $\kappa\alpha\rho\pi\hat{\omega}\nu\ \delta\iota\kappa\alpha\iota\sigma\acute{\nu}\nu\eta\varsigma\ \tau\hat{\omega}\nu\ \kappa\tau\lambda.$, "the fruits of righteousness which are etc." The singular $\kappa\alpha\rho\pi\grave{\nu}\ \delta\iota\kappa\alpha\iota\sigma\acute{\nu}\nu\eta\varsigma$, "fruit of righteousness" is read in 𝔓^{46} ℵ A B D F G I K L 048^{vid}, 075, 0278, 6, 33, 81, 104, 326, 1175, 1739*, 2464 lat co.

j   Most witnesses (ℵ A B D^2 I K L P Ψ 075, 0278, 33, 81, 104, 356, 630, 1175, 1241, 1505, 1739, 1881, 2464 Maj lat sy co) read $\epsilon\grave{\iota}\varsigma\ \delta\acute{o}\xi\alpha\nu\ \kappa\alpha\grave{\iota}\ \check{\epsilon}\pi\alpha\iota\nu\sigma\nu\ \theta\epsilon\sigma\hat{\nu}$, "to God's glory and praise." D* reads $\epsilon\grave{\iota}\varsigma\ \delta\acute{o}\xi\alpha\nu\ \kappa\alpha\grave{\iota}\ \check{\epsilon}\pi\alpha\iota\nu\sigma\nu$

$X\rho\iota\sigma\tau\sigma\hat{\nu}$, "to Christ's glory and praise" (possibly substituting XY for ΘY). F G and Ambst read $\epsilon\grave{\iota}\varsigma\ \delta\acute{o}\xi\alpha\nu\ \kappa\alpha\grave{\iota}\ \check{\epsilon}\pi\alpha\iota\nu\sigma\nu\ \mu\sigma\iota$, "to my glory and praise for me" (possibly reading MOI for ΘY). 𝔓^{46} reads $\epsilon\grave{\iota}\varsigma\ \delta\acute{o}\xi\alpha\nu\ \theta\epsilon\sigma\hat{\nu}\ \kappa\alpha\grave{\iota}\ \check{\epsilon}\pi\alpha\iota\nu\sigma\nu\ \acute{\epsilon}\mu\sigma\acute{\iota}$, "for God's glory and my praise" (presumably a conflation). Brent Nongbri has argued that F G and Ambst reproduce the original reading— "for my glory and praise"—of which 𝔭^{46} is then a conflation, and the reading adopted by *NTG*^{28} is an early theological correction ("Two Neglected Textual Variants in Philippians 1," *JBL* 128 [2009] 803–9). For the eschatological praise of the apostles of Christ by God, see 1 Cor 4:5b: "and then praise [$\check{\epsilon}\pi\alpha\iota\nu\sigma\varsigma$] will come to each one from God."

Analysis

Paul follows the prescript of 1:1-2 with the longest and most complex of his so-called introductory thanksgiving-periods (1:3-11).[2] Commentators frequently divide this section of the letter into three parts: the thanksgiving proper (1:3-6), a digression in which Paul affirms his affection for the Philippians (1:7-8), and an intercessory prayer report (1:9-11).[3] But since 1:7 continues the sentence begun in 1:3, and since Paul's affection for the Philippians is already the topic of 1:3-5, it is better to read all of 1:3-8 together as a single sentence concluding with a final exclamation or $\acute{\epsilon}\pi\iota\phi\acute{\omega}\nu\eta\mu\alpha$ at 1:8.[4] A new sentence does not begin, then, until the prayer report of 1:9-11, which recalls Paul's mention of his prayers for the Philippians in 1:4 and reveals his principal concern in writing.

Ancient consolers typically began their letters of consolation with a stronger than usual expression of affection for their readers. In cases of bereavement this included a reference to the writer's own grief. In lesser calamities a reference to the writer's grief might be omitted but not the warmth of expression. In Phil 1:3-8 Paul expresses his affection for the Philippians by declaring

how comforting his memories of them are: "I give thanks to my God for every remembrance of you . . . praying with joy over your partnership in the gospel." He flatters them that their present gift has made them partners in his suffering: "given the place that you have in my heart as those who, both in these chains of mine and in the defense and confirmation of the gospel, are my loyal partners." And he assures them in the strongest possible terms that, just as they are longing to see him, so he longs to see them: "God is my witness how I long for you all with the deepest affections of Christ!"[5]

Paul reports his prayers for the Philippians in 1:9-11. The fact that Paul keeps the Philippians in his prayers continues the theme of his affection for them from 1:3-8. Now, however, the focus shifts to the present letter and in particular to Paul's reason for writing.[6] In reflecting on the Philippians' grief over his imprisonment, Paul has concluded that their distress is due to the fact that they have failed to distinguish between "the things that really matter" ($\tau\grave{\alpha}\ \delta\iota\alpha\phi\acute{\epsilon}\rho\sigma\nu\tau\alpha$; 1:10a) and the things that do not, and he writes to remind them of this distinction and to urge them to observe it. He promises that if they will do this, they will be "filled with the fruit

---

2   See Rom 1:8-17; 1 Cor 1:4-9; 1 Thess 1:2-10; Phlm 4-7. For these periods in general, see the early work of Schubert, *Form and Function*; and O'Brien, *Introductory Thanksgivings*.

3   E.g., Gnilka, pp. 41–42; Collange, pp. 46–48.

4   For the figure $\acute{\epsilon}\pi\iota\phi\acute{\omega}\nu\eta\mu\alpha$, see below on 1:8.

5   Paul returns to this theme in 4:1: "much loved and longed for [$\acute{\epsilon}\pi\iota\pi\acute{o}\theta\eta\tau\sigma\iota$]."

6   For the notion that a prayer report might convey the central point Paul wishes to make, see Schubert, *Form and Function*, 62; Wiles, *Paul's Intercessory Prayers*, 156–229; O'Brien, *Introductory Thanksgivings*, 39 and passim; Meeks, "Man from Heaven," 333.

of righteousness" and be found "pure and blameless" in the Day of Christ.

Philippians 1:3-11 may be outlined as follows:

1:3-8 Thanksgiving
    1:3-5 Thanksgiving proper: Paul thanks God for the joy he derives from his fond memories of the Philippians' partnership in his gospel mission
    1:6 Warrant: Paul is confident that this partnership is not in jeopardy
    1:7-8 Warrant: Paul's affection for the Philippians is well deserved and only natural
1:9-11 Prayer report
    1:9 The Philippians' need for knowledge
    1:10a Paul's immediate objective: that the Philippians learn to discern the things that really matter
    1:10b-11 Paul's ultimate objective: that they be found pure and blameless at the parousia

Comment

■ **3-8** Of Paul's seven undisputed letters, five begin with a thanksgiving-sentence.[7] In four of these Paul variously thanks God for the readers' reception of the gospel.[8] But in Philippians, written while Paul was languishing in a Roman prison,[9] he takes a different approach, thanking God for his *memories* of the Philippians (1:3).[10] These memories center on the Philippians' enthusiastic reception of and subsequent "partnership" in the gospel (1:4-5). But Paul's immediate point is that his good memories are a source of consolation or "joy" in his imprisonment. Paul amplifies this claim with two rationale statements that explain why his memories of the Philippians are so comforting: first, because he fully expects the Philippians' partnership in the gospel to continue until the parousia (1:6), and, second, because their loyalty to him and his gospel, as witnessed by their willingness to identify with him in his imprisonment, has won them a special place in his affections (1:7-8). In beginning his letter in this manner, Paul introduces a number of its major themes, not the least of which is that his own happiness is closely linked to the Philippians' conduct in the gospel mission.[11]

■ **3** Paul's habit of beginning his letters with an expression of thanks is paralleled in a handful of other ancient Greek letters, and a number of commentators have therefore suggested that Paul is adapting a common epistolary cliché.[12] But the expression is not as common as has been assumed, and many of the texts cited are not true parallels.[13] At best Paul has appropriated a minor epistolary form for his own purposes, which include the public reading of his letters, where an introductory sentence beginning "I give thanks to my God" would have been particularly appropriate. In this regard it is noteworthy that, when in 2 Cor 1:3 Paul departs from his characteristic εὐχαριστῶ τῷ θεῷ ("I give thanks to God"), he employs another liturgical formula, εὐλογητὸς ὁ θεός, "Blessed be God." Both of these expressions were used interchangeably in Jewish liturgy at the time, and it is in this liturgy that Paul's usage finds its principal antecedent.[14] Paul's use of εὐχαριστῶ is therefore both

---

7   The others are Rom 1:8; 1 Cor 1:4; 1 Thess 1:2 (cf. 2:13); and Phlm 4 (cf. Col 1:3). 2 Corinthians 1:3 substitutes εὐλογητὸς ὁ θεός ("Blessed be God"; imitated in Eph 1:3 and 1 Pet 1:3). A notable exception is Gal 1:6, which famously begins with a disapproving θαυμάζω ("I am amazed!").

8   In Rom 1:8 Paul thanks God for his readers' faith; in Phlm 4, for his readers' faith and love; and in 1 Thess 1:3-5, for their faith, love, and hope; in 1 Cor 1:4 he thanks God for the grace the Corinthians have received.

9   Paul was in prison also when he wrote Philemon, but there his situation was rather different. Whereas in Philippians he has been in prison for a long time and is facing execution (1:20; 2:17-18), in Philemon Paul makes no mention of the dangers facing him but mentions his upcoming visit to Philemon as a matter of course (22).

10   For the translation problem here, see my "Thanks for the Memories" and the discussion on 1:3 below.

11   Paul returns to this theme in the digression of 1:27—2:16.

12   Following Schubert, *Form and Function*, 180.

13   Thus Arzt, "Epistolary Introductory Thanksgiving"; but see Reed, "Paul's Thanksgivings."

14   James M. Robinson, "Die Hodajot-Formel in Gebet und Hymnus des Frühchristentums," in *Apophoreta: Festschrift für Ernst Haenchen zu seinem siebzigsten Geburtstag am 10. Dezember 1964*, ed. W. Eltester and F. H. Kettler (BZNW 30; Berlin: Töpelmann, 1964) 194–235; cf. 1QH[a] 6:34; 10:22, 33; 11:20, 38; 12:6; 13:7; 15:9, 29, 37; 16:5; 19:6, 18: "I give thanks to you [אודכה], [my] God/Lord"; but 1QH[a] 7:12; 8:26; 18:16; 19:30: "Blessed [ברוך] are you, Lord." Note esp. 1QH[a] 13:22, where an original אודכה is rewritten ברוך.

epistolary and liturgical, reflecting the complex epistolary and liturgical settings of his letters.

Commentators are divided on how best to translate Phil 1:3, which in Greek reads εὐχαριστῶ τῷ θεῷ μου ἐπὶ πάσῃ τῇ μνείᾳ ὑμῶν. The problem lies with two terms: (1) the preposition ἐπί and (2) the genitive ὑμῶν. The most natural rendering of the Greek would interpret the preposition causally and the genitive objectively: "I give thanks to my God *for* every remembrance *of you*." But the commentary tradition has almost universally and without explanation rejected this interpretation, presumably because the idea of Paul's beginning a letter by thanking God for pleasant memories is too trivial to be considered.[15] Commentators have chosen instead one of two other options. The traditional and still majority view interprets the genitive objectively but renders the preposition temporally, producing a translation something like this: "I give thanks to my God *every time* I remember *you*."[16] An important minority view reverses this, interpreting the preposition causally and the genitive subjec-

tively, yielding a translation like this: "I give thanks to my God *for your* every remembrance [of me],"[17] the required objective genitive being supplied.

Neither of these interpretations is satisfactory. The first founders on the fact that, while ἐπί with the dative can be interpreted temporally,[18] in the expression εὐχαριστεῖν ἐπί τινι it functions causally: "to give thanks *for* something."[19] The second founders on the fact that verbs of remembering characteristically take their objects in the genitive,[20] so that when nouns like "remembrance" are modified by a genitive, that genitive is most naturally interpreted as objective.[21] We are left, then, with the natural sense of the Greek: "I give thanks to my God *for* every remembrance *of you*." Jerome glosses, "[Paul] celebrates with thanksgiving his memory [*memoriam*] of good things."[22]

However, this is not the embarrassment it is commonly imagined to be. Finding comfort in pleasant memories was a popular consolatory topos and had even been given philosophical rigor by Epicurus.[23] Further, it

---

15   But see Jerome on 1:3: *Bonorum memoriam cum gratiarum actione celebrat*, "He celebrates the memory of good things with an expression of thanks"; cf. Aquinas who quotes Prov 10:7: *memoria iusti cum laudibus*. The Vetus Latina according to Ambrosiaster and Pelagius translates unambiguously "I offer thanks to my God for [*super*] every memory of you."

16   So Lightfoot, Vincent, Lohmeyer, Beare, Gnilka, Collange, Müller, Wolfgang Schenk, *Die Philipperbriefe des Paulus: Kommentar* (Stuttgart: Kohlhammer, 1984).

17   Schubert, *Form and Function*, 74; discussed in detail by O'Brien. According to Vincent (p. 6), this translation was proposed as early as Harnack, *ThLZ* (1889) 419 (*non vidi*).

18   BDAG, s.v. ἐπί 18b. Paul does use ἐπί temporally in several of his εὐχαριστῶ-periods, but always with the genitive (e.g., Rom 1:10; 1 Thess 1:2; Phlm 4).

19   BDF §235.2. E.g., Philo, *Her.* 31; *Spec.* 1.67, 283, 284; 2.185; Josephus, *Ant.* 1.193; *T. Gad* 7.6 *v.l.*; *P. Lond.* 42 (= *UPZ* 59.9-10); *P. Vat.* 2289 (= *UPZ* 60.8); *IPerg* 224a.14; *SB* 3.7172.25. One does not have to look beyond Paul to see this point. This is the obvious sense of the expression in 1 Cor 1:4, which like Phil 1:3 introduces the letter's εὐχαριστῶ-period. It is also the sense of the related expression εὐχαριστίαν . . . ἀνταποδοῦναι . . . ἐπί τινι ("to return thanks for something") in 1 Thess 3:9. The causal translation is further confirmed for the Pauline corpus by the fact that the unambiguously causal εὐχαριστεῖν ὅτι ("to

give thanks *that*," or "*because*") is employed as the semantic equivalent of εὐχαριστεῖν ἐπί τινι in several Pauline and Deutero-Pauline εὐχαριστῶ-periods: Rom 1:8; 1 Thess 1:2-5; 2:13; 2 Thess 1:3; 2:13. The only difference between the two expressions is that ἐπί is used when the object is expressed in a noun clause (e.g., ἐπὶ τῇ χάριτι κτλ., "for the grace etc."), while ὅτι is required when the object is a verb clause (e.g., ὅτι . . . ἐβάπτισα κτλ., "that I baptized etc."); cf. *BGU* 2.423 (= *SelPap* 1.112; second century CE). Further, the expressions εὐχαριστεῖν ἐπί τινι and εὐχαριστεῖν ὅτι are used interchangeably in 1 Cor 1:4 and 14; cf. Hermas, *Sim.* 9.14.3. Here I depart from my earlier interpretation (*Consolation*, 88–89).

20   So the standard grammars (Goodwin, 1102; Smyth, 1356-59; BDF §175). Cf. BDAG, s.v. μιμνῄσκομαι 1a, b; 3b; s.v. μνήμη 1.

21   To my knowledge the commentary tradition has turned up only one exception to this rule in support of reading ὑμῶν as a subjective genitive, 1 Bar 5:5. But this is an exception that proves the rule, since 1 Baruch 5 is a poem and is arguably translation Greek. A better example of Pauline usage is 1 Thess 3:6; cf. *Odes Sol.* 9:22; *Sib. Or.* 5:486; Wis 5:14; 1 Bar 4:27; Rom 12:13 *v.l.*

22   *PL* 30:879.39-40.

23   See the following excursus.

makes perfect sense for Paul the prisoner to begin a letter of consolation to those grieved by his imprisonment by describing the consolation he himself derives from his pleasant memories of them. For one thing, it contributes substantially to the exordium's *captatio benevolentiae*. But it also adds to the Philippians' own consolation to learn that Paul himself is finding joy in his predicament and that they are in part at least responsible for that. The exiled Seneca offers his worried mother similar assurances in his letter of consolation to her,[24] as do the young recruits in their letters home to their parents that Loveday Alexander has called our attention to.[25]

Excursus: Epicurean Consolation

As a philosophical hedonist, Epicurus was constrained to take all forms of pain, including grief, at face value. His only recourse was distraction, which he sought in the memories of past pleasures.[26] He attempted to give philosophical precision to this technique by dividing it into two distinct mental operations. Cicero describes these in *Tusc.* 3.15.33:[27] "[Epicurus] places the alleviation of distress in two activities: calling the mind away from [*avocatione*] thinking about things that distress us, and calling the mind back to [*revocatione*] the contemplation of past pleasures." Epicurus's technique was popular with a broad range of consolers,[28] who were always eclectic in their methods.[29] In some cases his two-part process was followed closely.[30] In most cases, however, the method was imagined in less precise terms as a single act of recollection. Thus, the Stoic Seneca, writing to Marcia on the death of her son Metilius,

simply directs her to Metilius's happy "memory" (*memoriam*).[31]

Epicurus himself took this simpler approach in two letters that he wrote to former students on the day of his death, both of which sought to reassure the reader that his teacher had succeeded in finding comfort in his final afflictions.[32] The first letter was to Hermarchus of Mytilene, who would succeed Epicurus as head of the Garden. Cicero preserves it in Latin translation in *De fin.* 2.96. The relevant lines are the following: "I am suffering from diseases of the bladder and intestines that are of unsurpassable intensity. But all these are offset by the joy [*laetitia*] I lay hold of in my mind by the memory [*memoria*] of our theories and discoveries." The second letter was to Idomeneus of Lampsacus and is preserved in Diogenes Laertius, *Vit.* 10.22. Again the relevant lines: "Strangury and dysenteric pains afflict me with an unsurpassable intensity. But holding ground against all these discomforts is my heart's rejoicing [χαῖρον] over the memory [μνήμη] of the discussions we have had." In both of these letters Epicurus, like Paul in Phil 1:3-4, states that he is comforted by his memories (*memoria*, μνήμη), which are sources of joy (*laetitia*, τὸ χαῖρον) in his present distress. In the letter to Hermarchus, who would assume Epicurus's mantle as head of his philosophical school, these memories are of their philosophical discoveries. In the letter to Idomeneus, a former student and now friend, the memories are of a more personal nature, focusing on their relationship and the many conversations they have had.[33] The consoling memories Paul adduces in Phil 1:3, while pertaining to the Philippians' prior partnership in the gospel, also reflect on Paul's personal relationship with them as 1:7-8 will make plain.

24 Abel, *Bauformen*, 54.
25 Alexander, "Hellenistic Letter-Forms"; cf. *P. Yale* 42 discussed above in part 5.3 of the introduction.
26 I discuss this point in more detail in "Thanks for the Memories," portions of which are excerpted here.
27 See Cicero, *Tusc.* 3.31.76; 5.26.73–74; *De fin.* 1.57; Epicurus, *Sent. Vat.* 55; Philodemus, *De dis* 3 col. d (2) 23; *De mort.* 38.21. A slightly different view is espoused by Metrodorus in his consolatory letter to his sister (apud Seneca, *Ep.* 99.25).
28 Examples include Pseudo-Ovid, *Cons. ad Liv.* 377–416; Pseudo-Plutarch, *Ad Apoll.* 116a-b; Pliny, *Ep.* 8.5.2; and Julian, *Or.* 8.246c-248d. In early Christian literature, see Ambrose, *De exc. Sat.* 1.3; Jerome, *Ep.* 60.7.3; 108.1.2; 118.4.2; Basil, *Ep.* 5.2; 269.2; and Paulinus of Nola, *Ep.* 13.6; Scourfield, *Consoling Heliodorus*, 133–34.
29 Cicero, *Tusc.* 3.31.76; *Ad Att.* 12.14.3.
30 E.g., Plutarch, *Ad ux.* 610e; 608a-b; *De tran. an.* 468f–469d; *De exil.* 600d.
31 Seneca, *Ad Marc.* 4.3–5.6; *Ad Poly.* 10.6. Seneca also criticizes the method in *Ad. Helv.* 2.4–4.1; 17.2; *Ad Marc.* 1.2–5, 8. Elsewhere in Seneca, see *Ep.* 63.4 (Attalus); 99.3–5; *De ira* 3.39.4; *De brev. vit.* 10.2-4; *De vit. beat.* 6.1-2; *De benef.* 3.4.1; cf. Grollios, *Seneca's Ad Marciam*, 52–54; Johann, *Trauer und Trost*, 150–55; Abel, *Bauformen*, 26. The method also appears in Judaism in Sir 14:16 and 30:23, for which see Holloway, "'Deceive your soul' (Sir XIV:16; XXX:23): An Epicurean Theme in Ben Sira," *VT* 58 (2008) 1–16.
32 This will have been the ultimate validation of Epicurus's philosophy.
33 I will discuss Cicero's modification of this technique in a separate excursus at 4:8-9.

■ **4-5** If we depart from the commentary tradition in allowing the natural sense of the Greek in 1:3 to stand, then we must also reexamine that tradition's interpretation of 1:4-5, including the punctuation of these verses. Because most commentators do not interpret the ἐπί phrase in 1:3 as the object of εὐχαριστῶ, they are forced to look elsewhere for that object, which they find in the ἐπί phrase introducing v. 5: "I give thanks to my God . . . *for* [ἐπί] your partnership in the gospel." To make this reading plausible, they set off the intervening material in commas and interpret it as a parenthesis. Thus the NRSV: "I thank my God every time I remember you, constantly praying with joy in every one of my prayers for all of you, because of [ἐπί] your sharing in the gospel."[34]

This punctuation scheme makes sense if one adopts the majority translation of 1:3. But it is far from convincing if one interprets the ἐπί phrase in 1:3 as the proper object of εὐχαριστῶ. In this case there is no reason to insert a comma between v. 4 and v. 5, which can now be read together as a single participial phrase modifying v. 3. This allows the ἐπί phrase beginning v. 5 to find its natural antecedent in the more proximate μετὰ χαρᾶς ("with joy") of v. 4: "praying with joy *over* [ἐπί] your partnership in the gospel."[35] The reason Paul thanks God for his memories of the Philippians' prior partnership in his mission is that these memories bring him consolation or "joy."[36] We shall later see that not everything about the Philippians brings Paul joy (2:2; cf. 2:19).

Verses 4-5 specify both the occasion of Paul's memories: "always in every prayer [δεήσει] of mine for you all etc." And their content: "your partnership [κοινωνία] in the gospel from the first day until now." Paul is emphatic about his prayers for the Philippians—*always* [πάντοτε] in *every* [πάσῃ] prayer"—and he will return to these prayers in 1:9-11. But first he offers warrant for the consolation he draws from the Philippians' long-standing "partnership," or κοινωνία, in the gospel (1:6-8).[37] Κοινωνία ("partnership"), which may also be translated "fellowship," is a recurring theme in Philippians (1:5, 7; 2:1; 3:10; 4:14, 15). In 2:1 Paul speaks of a κοινωνία πνεύματος ("fellowship of spirit") and in 3:10 of κοινωνία παθημάτων αὐτοῦ ("fellowship of his [= Christ's] sufferings"). Here in 1:5 κοινωνία refers to the Philippians' continuing "partnership" with Paul in his gospel mission, which among other things has taken the form of repeated financial support, including the recent gift carried by Epaphroditus (4:14-18; cf. 2:25-30). In addition to the financial component of their partnership, Paul is anxious to emphasize the Philippians' sharing with him in his suffering (1:7; 4:14; cf. 1:29-30; 3:10). It is sometimes thought that Paul's κοινωνία language is used in a technical sense to refer to a specific financial arrangement between Paul and the Philippians.[38] It has also been read as part of the letter's friendship language.[39] Both interpretations are possible, but I would not want to press either, since κοινωνία and its cognates

---

34 The Nestle-Aland editors make a similar decision, although they parenthesize only the second half of 1:4 (μετὰ χαρᾶς τὴν δέησιν ποιούμενος, "praying with joy").

35 De Wette, following Calvin and Grotius (*Annotationes in Novum Testamentum*, vol. 2: *Annotationes in Acta Apostolorum et Epistolas Apostolicas* [Paris: Pelé, 1646]). Like εὐχαριστῶ, the noun χαρά ("joy") also commonly takes ἐπί plus the dative, as in Luke 15:7 and 10: χαρὰ . . . ἐπὶ ἑνὶ ἁμαρτωλῷ μετανοοῦντι, κτλ. ("joy . . . *over* one sinner repenting, etc."). In the Greek of 1:4-5 (μετὰ χαρᾶς τὴν δέησιν ποιούμενος ἐπί, κτλ.) the phrase μετὰ χαρᾶς has been moved forward for emphasis. Vincent's claim that for the phrase ἐπὶ τῇ κοινωνίᾳ ὑμῶν to serve as the object of χαρᾶς it needs to be preceded by the article (τῆς) is hard to explain. The substantive χαρᾶς is anarthrous, and even if it were not no subsequent article is required: "after verbal substantives denoting an *action* or a *state* an attributive prepositional

phrase is added without the article repeated" (Smyth, 1167a; emphases original).

36 For the collocation "thanksgiving," "joy," and "consolation," see 1 Thess 3:7-9.

37 Paul will return to this "partnership" in 4:15-16, where he again emphasizes the fact that it has been long-standing.

38 Most recently Julien M. Ogereau, *Paul's Koinonia with the Philippians: A Socio-Historical Investigation of a Pauline Partnership* (WUNT 2/377; Tübingen: Mohr Siebeck, 2014); see also Ulrike Roth, "Paul, Philemon, and Onesimus: A Christian Design for Mastery," *ZNW* 105 (2014) 102–30. (I am grateful to Timothy Barnes for bringing Roth's essay to my attention.)

39 See, e.g., the studies by Berry, Malherbe, and Fitzgerald in Fitzgerald, *Friendship*.

are common in Paul's letters (twenty-six times)[40] and should not be too narrowly interpreted.[41]

■ **6** Paul offers the first warrant for the "joy" he feels when he remembers the Philippians' partnership in the gospel in 1:6: "confident of this very thing, that he who began a good work within you will continue to perfect it until the Day of Christ Jesus."[42] Despite the Philippians' present discouragement, Paul is confident that their partnership will continue and will therefore remain a source of joy for him, since their commitment to the gospel is due ultimately to the benefaction or "good work" of God within them.[43] The phrase I have translated "within you" (ἐν ὑμῖν) might also be translated "among you."[44] It would then convey a corporate meaning, something like: "he who began a good work *at Philippi*." I have translated it as I have because of Paul's characteristic emphasis on the transformation of the individual.[45] Paul returns to this theme in 2:13: "for God is the one working within you [ἐνεργῶν ἐν ὑμῖν]."[46] The correlatives ἐναρξάμενος ("began") and ἐπιτελέσει ("will continue to perfect") reflect Paul's belief that God is involved in the Christ-believer's transformation from beginning to end.[47]

Paul uses the same language in Gal 3:3: "having begun [ἐναρξάμενοι] in the Spirit are you now to be made perfect [ἐπιτελεῖσθε] in the flesh?"[48]

■ **7-8** Paul offers a second warrant for his fond memories of the Philippians in 1:7-8: "and it is only right that I should feel this way about [= have such fond and comforting memories of] you all," he writes, "given the place you have in my heart as those who, both in these chains of mine and in the defense and confirmation of the gospel, are my loyal partners in this grace."[49] The Philippians' partnership with Paul in the gospel is extraordinary and deeply personal: not only have they partnered with him in his mission (1:5), but they have continued to partner with him even in his shameful condition as a prisoner (1:7; cf. 4:14).[50] Paul's affection for them is only "right." These verses present the interpreter with two problems: (1) the antecedent of the demonstrative pronoun τοῦτο in the expression τοῦτο φρονεῖν (lit., "to think *this*," or as I have translated "to feel *this way*"), and (2) the meaning of the clause τὸ ἔχειν με ἐν τῇ καρδίᾳ ὑμᾶς, which can be understood to mean either "the place you have in my heart" or "the place I have in your heart."

---

40   Κοινωνέω: Rom 12:13; 15:27; Gal 6:6; Phil 4:15; κοινωνία: Rom 15:26; 1 Cor 1:9; 10:16 (twice); 2 Cor 6:14; 8:4; 9:13; 13:13; Gal 2:9; Phil 1:5; 2:1; 3:10; Phlm 6; κοινωνός: 1 Cor 10:18, 20; 2 Cor 1:7; 8:23; Phlm 17; συγκοινωνέω: Phil 4:14; συγκοινωνός: Rom 11:17; 1 Cor 9:23; Phil 1:7.

41   2 Corinthians 8:4 may be relevant here, since there Paul uses κοινωνία to describe the Philippians' contribution to the Jerusalem offering in what is obviously not some sort of business agreement. There is a kind of quid pro quo, but it is a metaphor. In 2 Cor 8:23 Paul refers to Titus as his κοινωνός ("partner").

42   For "Day of Christ Jesus," see below on 1:10b-11; cf. 2:16.

43   Gundry Volf, *Perseverance*, 33–47.

44   Gnilka: "nicht 'in euch' . . . sondern 'bei euch'"; cf. Bonnard: "parmi vous."

45   E.g., Rom 8:9; 2 Cor 5:17; Gal 2:20; Phil 3:7-11.

46   Paul's treatment of divine versus human agency is largely rhetorical, fitted to the needs of the argument: in Phil 1:6 agency is simply attributed to God; in 2:13 both divine and human agency are asserted; in 3:13-14 Paul is running the race largely on his own, aided only by the "call of God." See further the essays collected in Barclay and Gathercole, *Agency*.

For a similar dialectic between "magic" (where human agency is emphasized) and "religion" (where divine agency is emphasized), see the astute observations and criticisms of Dorothy Hammond, "Magic: A Problem in Semantics," *American Anthropologist* 72 (1970) 1349–56.

47   With the addition of v. 6 Paul gives full scope to divine providence: from the foundation of the Philippian church ("from the first day"), through the present crisis ("until now"), until the promised parousia ("until the Day of Christ Jesus").

48   Paul holds that this inner working of the "spirit" distinguishes his gospel from that of his more Torah-observant opponents. In Rom 6:17 Paul even goes so far as to call his gospel a new "type of teaching," or τύπος διδαχῆς, for which see my "Commendatio," esp. 369–82.

49   The σύν- in συγκοινωνούς is redundant and should probably be read here as intensifying. Paul uses the participle συγκοινωνήσαντες in 4:14. In both instances the prefix seems to indicate a sympathetic or emotional attachment (cf. BDAG, s.v. συγκοινωνέω 1a).

50   For the role of shaming in Roman law, see my comments below at 1:20.

The antecedent of τοῦτο is uncertain. It has been interpreted to refer to all of vv. 3-6, to v. 6 only, or to vv. 3-5 only.[51] The first of these (a reference to all of vv. 3-6) makes the least sense: v. 6 is itself warrant for the feelings expressed in vv. 3-5. The second (to v. 6 only) is a little better: v. 7 would be further warrant to the warrant of v. 6, but this seems overly complicated. The third option (to vv. 3-5) makes the most sense, especially in light of v. 8, where it is clear that what Paul is emphatically reiterating is his affection for the Philippians, as indicated in vv. 3-5.[52] So, when Paul says in v. 7a, "and it is only right that I should feel this way about you all," the feelings he has in mind refer to the fond memories of vv. 3-5, memories that it is "right" for him to treasure given the fact that with their gift the Philippians have continued to identify with him even in his imprisonment and trial.[53] Paul is grateful that the Philippians have not abandoned him.

The ambiguity in the expression τὸ ἔχειν με ἐν τῇ καρδίᾳ ὑμᾶς is due to the fact that Greek infinitives such as ἔχειν take both their objects and their so-called subjects[54] in the accusative, which means that grammatically either με or ὑμᾶς can be the subject here. If the former, then taken by itself the expression might be translated: "I have you in [my] heart"; or in context: "given the place you have in my heart." If the latter, then: "you have me in [your] heart"; or: "given the place I have in your heart." Word order would favor taking the accusative immediately following the infinitive as the subject, and that is how I have interpreted it. But several commentators argue against this reading on the grounds that it makes better sense to see Paul's feelings about the Philippians as a response to their feelings toward him. This interpretation is reflected in the NRSV: "because you hold me in your heart." This is necessarily a subjective judgment, as the more natural rendering also makes good sense: Paul's fond memories (vv. 3-5) are an expression of his affections for the Philippians, made almost obligatory—"and it is only *right*"—by their extreme loyalty (vv. 7-8). On this reading it is not the Philippians' affection but Paul's affection that is in view, an interpretation supported by his emphatic restatement of that affection in 1:8: "for God is my witness how I long for you!" It is noteworthy that no less a native Greek speaker than Chrysostom interpreted the expression in this latter way (hom. 2.24.29 Allen).

Verses 7-8 make two substantive claims important to interpreting the letter. The expression "as those who, both in these chains of mine and in the defense and confirmation of the gospel, are my loyal partners," exegetes Paul's earlier references to the Philippians' "partnership" in the gospel in 1:5.[55] Paul recalls with joy the Philippians' partnership in the gospel mission, not least because they have continued to partner with him in his incarceration both through their prayers (Phil 1:19) and through their gift (Phil 2:25-30; 4:10-20). Of equal importance is Paul's reference to his suffering as "grace." One of the pillars of Jewish apocalyptic soteriology was that suffering is redemptive. This was also one of the pillars of Paul's theory of salvation, and it is key to his consolation in Philippians. Paul states this explicitly in 1:29, where suffering is imagined as a gift given by God: "it has been given [ἐχαρίσθη] to you . . . to suffer." Similarly in chap. 3 he celebrates the mystical and transformative "knowl-

---

51 Some commentators (Weiss, Vincent, Dibelius) understand the reference to be to the immediately preceding expression of confidence in 1:6; others (Lightfoot, Gnilka, Collange) see a reference to all of 1:3-6; yet others (e.g., Bonnard) take only 1:3-5 to be in view.

52 Note also that ὑπὲρ πάντων ὑμῶν ("about you all") in v. 7 recalls the identical expression in 1:4 (there translated "for you all"). The specific thought Paul seeks to justify in vv. 7-8 is, therefore, the joyful remembrance he claims in v. 4. For the expression δίκαιον φρονεῖν ("it is right to think/feel"), see Koskenniemi, *Studien*, 146, who cites *P. Cair. Zen.* 1.59076.3; see BDAG, s.v. δίκαιος. H. A. W. Meyer cites similar expressions in Herodotus, Plato, Thucydides, and Demosthenes (*Kritisch-exegetisches Handbuch über die Briefe Pauli an die Philipper, Kolosser*

und Philemon [KEKNT 9; Göttingen: Vandenhoeck & Ruprecht, 1859]).

53 Cf. Pelagius: *mihi memoriam vestri nec vis tribulationis nec sollicitudo defensionis auferrent*, "neither the intensity of my suffering nor the anxiety for my defense can take away from me your memory."

54 Strictly speaking, infinitives do not have subjects—otherwise they would be finite verbs—but express agency with an accusative of reference.

55 This twofold conception of imprisonment ("chains") and trial ("defense and confirmation of the gospel") organizes Paul's thoughts in 1:12-21, where he first speaks of his imprisonment (1:12-18b) and then of his anticipated appearance in court (1:18c-21).

edge of Christ" or γνῶσις Χριστοῦ (3:8) gained through suffering: "I want to know him [γνῶναι αὐτον] . . . and the fellowship of his sufferings [κοινωνίαν παθημάτων αὐτοῦ] . . . if somehow I might arrive at the resurrection from the dead" (3:10-11).

In v. 8 Paul concludes the sentence begun in 1:3 with what by ancient standards would have been read as an ἐπιφώνημα, or concluding exclamation,[56] here in the form of an oath.[57] Paul calls God as witness to his affections for the Philippians, which in one way or another has been the point since v. 3. Similar oaths assuring readers of a writer's strong feelings for them can be found at the beginning of other ancient letters of consolation.[58] Not surprisingly, Paul affirms his affections for the Philippians in language suggestive of spirit possession,[59] claiming that his longing for them is animated by Christ's own "deepest affections" (σπλάγχνοις, lit. "innards").[60] Verse 8 is both a forceful restatement of 1:7 and an apt conclusion to 1:3-8, which foregrounds Paul's strong feelings for and positive memories of the Philippians.

■ **9-11** The second part of the letter introduction is the prayer report of 1:9-11, which recalls Paul's earlier mention of his prayers for the Philippians in 1:4. Paul reports the content of his prayers in v. 9 and the objectives he wishes his prayers to accomplish in vv. 10-11. Rhetorically, the prayer report of 1:9-11 does two things: it expresses Paul's continuing investment in the Philippian Christ-believers, and it allows Paul to adumbrate his reasons for writing.[61]

■ **9** Commentators have traditionally balked at the plain meaning of v. 9, which is that Paul wished the Philippians to increase not in "love" but in "knowledge." The vast majority seem unaware of any problem; they simply proceed on the assumption that Paul always privileges "love" over "knowledge," often citing by way of example 1 Cor 8:1: ἡ γνῶσις φυσιοῖ, ἡ δὲ ἀγάπη οἰκοδομεῖ, "knowledge puffs up, love builds up."[62] A few like Karl Barth acknowledge the natural sense of the Greek but declare it too "difficult" (schwierig) to be Paul's meaning given his unambiguous love ethic.[63] But in the construction τινὰ περισσεύειν ἐν τινί ("something to abound in something"), it is not the subject of the verb that increases but the object of the preposition ἐν ("in").[64] Here is how Paul uses the construction elsewhere: "to increase *in* hope"

56 Philodemus, *Rhet.* 1.173(S); Dionysius of Halicarnassus, *Rhet.* 10.18; Quintilian, *Inst.* 8.5.11 (citing Virgil, *Aen.* 1.33, and Cicero, *Pro Mil.* 4.9); Hermogenes, *Inv.* 4.9; Sextus Empiricus, *Adv. math.* 2.57; Rufinus of Antioch, *De comp.* 29 (Halm): "a *sententia* at the end of a development expressed with feeling [*cum affectu*]."

57 For such oaths elsewhere in Paul, see Matthew V. Novenson, "'God Is Witness': A Classical Rhetorical Idiom in Its Pauline Usage," *NovT* 52 (2010) 355–75; contra Gustav Stählin, "Zum Gebrauch von Beteuerungsformeln im Neuen Testament," *NovT* 5 (1962) 115–43. The expression occurs elsewhere in Paul in Rom 1:9; 2 Cor 1:23; 1 Thess 2:5 and 10.

58 *PSI* 12.1248.3-5; *P.Congr.* 15.22.5.16.

59 Cf. Bengel, aptly citing Gal 2:20.

60 See Christopher A. Faraone, *Ancient Greek Love Magic* (Cambridge, MA: Harvard University Press, 1999) 43–44 for the physicality of desire. For "innards" (σπλάγχνα) in Greek love magic, see Robert W. Daniel and Franco Maltomini, *Supplementum Magicum* (2 vols.; Papyrologica Coloniensia XVI.1-2; Opladen: Westdeutscher Verlag, 1990–1992) 46.22–23 (cited by Matt Jackson-McCabe, "Women and Eros in Greek Magic and the Acts of Paul and Thecla," in *Women and Gender in Ancient Religions*, ed. Stephen P. Ahearne-Kroll, Paul A.

Holloway, and James A. Kelhoffer [WUNT 263; Tübingen: Mohr Siebeck, 2010] 270 n. 15.).

61 For the programmatic nature of Paul's so-called prayer reports, see Schubert, *Form and Function*, 62; Wiles, *Paul's Intercessory Prayers*, 175–229; cf. Meeks, "Man from Heaven," 333. That vv. 10-11 convey first Paul's penultimate and then ultimate purposes, see esp. Meyer.

62 E.g., Lohmeyer, Gnilka, Beare, Bockmuehl. Cf. Gal 5:6: πίστις δι' ἀγάπης ἐνεργουμένη, "faith working through love."

63 Karl Barth, *Epistle to the Philippians* (Richmond: John Knox, 1962) on 1:10. Similarly, Collange begins, "recognizing the readers' love . . . the apostle asks them to increase in knowledge and discernment [*de gagner en intelligence et en discernement*]." But then he strangely concludes, "And therefore love is the object of [Paul's] prayer [*l'agapè est l'objet de prière*]" (ET Heathcote, modified).

64 So Meyer. Περισσεύω occurs twenty-four times in the recognized letters of Paul (Rom 3:7; 5:15; 15:13; 1 Cor 8:8; 14:12; 15:58; 2 Cor 1:5 (twice); 3:9; 4:15; 8:2, 7 (twice); 9:8 (twice), 12; Phil 1:9, 26; 4:12 (twice), 18; 1 Thess 3:12; 4:1, 10; cf. Eph 1:8; Col 2:7). Twice it is transitive (2 Cor 9:8a; 1 Thess. 3:12); in its remaining twenty-two occurrences it is intransitive. Of these, it occurs eight times without

(Rom 15:13), "to increase *in* the work of the Lord" (1 Cor 15:58), "to increase *in* this grace [of benefaction]" (2 Cor 8:7). If Paul had considered the Philippians to be lacking in love, he would have written: "that your knowledge might abound in love." As it stands, however, his prayer commends their love and calls for an increase "in knowledge and all discernment."[65] This idea is not as foreign to Paul as the Christian theological tradition has imagined. For example, Paul offers a similar analysis of the condition of "Israel" in Rom 10:2: "they have a zeal for God but not according to knowledge [κατ᾽ ἐπίγνωσιν]." With the addition of καὶ πάσῃ αἰσθήσει ("and all discernment"),[66] Paul creates a hendiadys that specifies the kind of knowledge he believes the Philippians to need, a knowledge that would allow them to evaluate critically both his and their circumstances.

■ **10a** The first and more immediate reason Paul wants the Philippians to increase in knowledge and discernment is "so that you can ascertain τὰ διαφέροντα." At issue is the meaning of substantive τὰ διαφέροντα, which I leave untranslated for the moment. This expression has been a challenge to interpreters, who have sensed its programmatic importance but, hindered by the assumption that Paul's prayer in 1:9 calls for an increase in *love*, have struggled to interpret it in a way that fits with the rest of the letter.[67] The tradition offers two interpretations. On one side is Chrysostom, who assumes that love allows one to distinguish between Christian truth and pagan error[68] and therefore understands τὰ διαφέροντα to mean "things that differ." Theodore of Mopsuestia, on the other hand, assumes that love allows one to distinguish between things that are good and things that are best. Accordingly, he understands τὰ διαφέροντα to mean "things that are excellent."[69] Subsequent commentators have been satisfied to choose between these two options.[70]

There is a third option, however, that immediately recommends itself once we have correctly interpreted Paul's prayer in 1:9 to be a prayer not for love but for *knowledge*, and that is that what Paul wants for the Philippians is the "knowledge and discernment" required to ascertain "the things that really matter." On this reading, Paul is deploying the familiar cognitive distinction made popular by the Stoics between the things that do not matter (τὰ ἀδιάφορα) and the things that do (τὰ διαφέροντα).[71] This

---

further modification; three times it is modified by a noun in the dative; and thirteen times by a prepositional phrase: εἰς ("to" or "for," six times), ἐν ("in," six times), and πρός ("for," once). When the phrase begins with εἰς or πρός, it is typically the subject of the verb that is deemed lacking (e.g., Rom 5:15); an exception is 2 Cor 9:8 where εἰς is equivalent to ἐν (cf. 1 Cor 15:58). On the other hand, when περισσεύω is modified by a phrase beginning with ἐν, it is the object of the preposition that must be added or increased (Rom 15:33; 1 Cor 15:58; 2 Cor 8:7 [twice]; Phil 1:6; cf. 2 Cor 3:9 *v.l.*); the first three of these texts are cited in the next sentence.

65 Zahn comments insightfully: "[The Philippians] had acted with more goodwill and love than insight and discernment [*mehr guten Willen und Liebe als Einsicht und Unterscheidungsgabe*]" (*Introduction*, 1:528). Their error, he continues, "[was that] they believed not only that the apostle's life, but also the cause of the gospel, was in extreme peril." Thus Paul writes to correct this "unfounded opinion" (*unbegründeten Auffassung*) and "the feelings of deep depression" (*tief herabgedrückten Stimmung*) that it was causing (ET Trout, modified).

66 BDAG, s.v. πᾶς 3: "marker of the highest degree of something."

67 Following Lohmeyer, most commentators have also sensed that τὰ διαφέροντα is "an important philosophical term," though this is rarely reflected in their exegesis, in part because they discount Paul's philosophical culture; see Michaelis, Gnilka, Collange, Müller, Schenk; Camille Focant, *Les lettres aux Philippiens et à Philemon* (EtB n.s. 55; Paris: Gabalda, 2005). Troels Engberg-Pedersen warns against those who, under the rubric of *Popularphilosophie*, do not take Paul's philosophical language seriously ("Stoicism in Philippians," in *Paul in His Hellenistic Context,* ed. idem (Minneapolis: Fortress Press, 1995) 256–90, here 262 n. 10. He cites as an example Gnilka's treatment of τὰ διαφέροντα in Phil 1:10, as well as Gnilka's interpretation of Phil 4:11. See in general J. N. Sevenster, *Paul and Seneca* (NovTSup 4; Leiden: Brill, 1961); Adolf F. Bonhöffer, *Epiktet und das Neue Testament* (RVV 10; Giessen: Töpelmann, 1911); and Lightfoot, pp. 270–333, Appendix 2: "St. Paul and Seneca."

68 Hom. 3.38.10-14 Allen. See also Theophylact.

69 Likewise Theodoret.

70 But see Schenk, who interprets τὰ διαφέροντα generically as "the will of God" based on a partial verbal congruence with Rom 2:18 and 12:2.

71 BDAG, s.v. διαφέρω 4; cf. Müller, p. 45 n. 67:

is an especially attractive alternative since this distinction was central to Stoic consolation theory, which urged those suffering from grief to distinguish between the things that do and do not matter so as not to be distressed by the latter. This interpretation of τὰ διαφέροντα makes excellent sense of the consolation that follows in 1:12-26, where Paul (1) sets out to impart to the Philippians the "knowledge" they lack—"Now I want you *to know* [γινώσκειν], brothers"—and (2) argues that "the things that really matter" lie not in his present predicament—"*whether* in pretense *or* in truth" (1:18); "*whether* through life *or* though death" (1:20); "*whether* I come and see you *or* remain absent" (1:27)[72]—but the "progress of the gospel" and his own final "salvation."

Excursus: Seneca, *Epistulae morales* 107.1 and Philippians 1:9-10a

Seneca, *Ep.* 107.1 offers a number of illuminating parallels to the progression of Paul's thought in Phil 1:9-10a. Seneca has received word from Lucilius that several of Lucilius's most trusted slaves have run away. Lucilius feels deeply betrayed by this, and Seneca writes to console him. Seneca takes the position that his friend has lost sight of the fact that things like this do not really matter,[73] and he begins his letter with the following pointed questions:

Where is that practical knowledge of yours? Where is that facility of mind that allows you to make the necessary distinctions? Where is that ability to rise above circumstance? Does a matter of such insignificance affect you so much? (*Ubi illa prudentia tua? Ubi in dispiciendis rebus subtilitas? Ubi magnitudo? Tam pusilla te res tangit?*)

The progression of thought recalls Cleanthes's theory of consolation:[74] "practical knowledge" (*prudentia*), leading to a certain "facility of mind" (*subtilitas*), the objective of which is "to make the necessary distinctions" (*in dispiciendis rebus*), especially as regards matters of "insignificance" (*pusilla*), so as not to be unduly "affect[ed]" (*tangit*) by them. By reversing the order, it is easy to see how Seneca arrived at his analysis: Lucilius is distressed over what is in reality a matter of insignificance, which implies that he has failed to observe this distinction in his current circumstances, which in turn implies that he has faltered in his practical knowledge. Paul follows a similar line of though in Phil 1:9-10a: (1) he begins with a call for practical knowledge ("knowledge and discernment"),[75] (2) leading to a kind of situational awareness ("so that you can ascertain"), (3) which has as its objective distinguishing between "the things that really matter" and those that do not with the goal that the Philippians not be distressed by the latter.

"τὰ διαφέροντα ist stoischer Gegenbegriff zu τὰ ἀδιάφορα und dürfte aus der Popularphilosophie auch in die hellenistische Synagoge eingedrungen sein." Examples include Epictetus, *Diss.* 2.5.7: ὕλη οὐ διαφέρουσα ("stuff that does not really matter"); 4.7.27: οὐκέτι διαφέρομαι ("it matters nothing to me"; cf. 4.7.40); Stobaeus, *Ecl.* 2.80.8-9 (in Arius Didymus's synopsis of stoic ethics); Marcus Aurelius, *Med.* 9.10, 27; 11.16; cf. Bonhöffer, *Epiktet*, 298–99. For the term's wider philosophical usage, see Pseudo-Plato, *Eryx.* 394d5–6; Plutarch, *De rect. aud.* 12.43e. For the nonphilosophical use of the term, see Plutarch, *Caes.* 65; *Quom. adul.* 73a; *P. Oxy.* 9.1204 (299 CE); H. W. Waddington, *Inscriptions Grecques et Latines de Syrie* (Paris: Didot, 1870) 410.2. Paul uses the term in Gal 2:6 (οὐδέν μοι διαφέρει, "it matters nothing to me") and the exact expression (τὰ διαφέροντα) again in Rom 2:18, where he makes the Jewish teacher boast that he is able discern "the things that really matter" based on his knowledge of Torah; see Hans Lietzmann, *An die Römer* (4th ed.; HNT 8; Tübingen: Mohr Siebeck, 1993) 43, who sees the pagan philosophical connection. For the topos

of indifferent things in Hellenistic Judaism, see Philo, *Det.* 122; *Post.* 81; *Mos.* 2.40–41; *Leg.* 2.17; *Op.* 74; *Sac.* 99; *Fug.* 152; *Her.* 253; *Praem.* 70; *Spec.* 2.46; *Prob.* 61; 83 (collected by Betz, *Galatians*, 94 n. 351).

72 In each of these instances Paul uses the correlatives εἴτε ("whether") . . . εἴτε ("or") to indicate his indifference. See my discussion of these texts below.

73 See *Ep.* 42.5 and the comments by D. A. Russell, "Letters to Lucilius," in *Seneca*, ed. C. D. N. Costa (Greek and Latin Studies; London: Routledge & K. Paul, 1974) 72–79, here 76–77.

74 Cicero, *Tusc.* 3.31.76. See the introduction, part 1.c: "Greek and Roman Consolation," as well as my *Consolation*, 65–74.

75 See Leokadie Malunowiczówna, "Les éléments stoïciens dans la consolation grecque chrétienne," *StPatr* 13.2 (TU 116; Berlin: Akademie-Verlag, 1975) 35–45, here 36: "La manque de la vraie connaissance est la cause de notre tristesse"; cf. John Chrysostom, *In Epist. ad Thess.*, hom. 7.1 (PG 62:435); *Ad Stag.* 1.2 (PG 47:427).

There are at least two significant differences, however, between Seneca, *Ep.* 107.1 and Phil 1:9-10a. First, Paul is not as abrupt as Seneca. Although his point is basically the same, he does not indict the Philippians with a series of rhetorical questions but reports his prayers for them.[76] This gentleness will characterize the rest of letter.[77] Second, Paul's focus is more positive than Seneca's. He approaches his consolation not through things that do not matter (Seneca's *pusilla res*) but through the things that do (τὰ διαφέροντα). This second difference is particularly instructive for our understanding of Paul's overall consolatory strategy. By focusing on "the things that really matter" Paul anticipates his positive approach to consolation in the remainder of the letter, where he does not urge the Philippians to put aside their grief (Stoic apathy) so much as to "rejoice." Chrysostom outlines a similar positive objective in *Ep. ad Olymp.* 10.1.21–23 (Malingrey): "This is what we are seeking for you, not simply to rid you of your despondency, but to fill you with a great and lasting joy."[78] Paul's goal (and Chrysostom's) is much more ambitious than Seneca's.

■ **10b-11** If Paul's immediate concern is the consolation of the Philippians (1:10a), his ultimate concern is their eschatological salvation (1:10b-11).[79] This salvation depends on their being found "pure and blameless" at the final judgment or "Day of Christ," and it is accomplished over time as they are "filled with the fruit of righteousness."[80] This righteousness is produced "through Christ"[81] and redounds to the "glory and praise of God."[82] Like most of his contemporaries, Paul believed that grief was a destructive passion that, if left unaddressed, caused one to neglect one's duties,[83] which in the Philippians' case meant ceasing to make progress in righteousness. Paul's hope was that, once they were restored to their previous equanimity, the Philippians would begin again to make progress in the faith and thus progress toward their final salvation.[84]

Paul uses the expression "Day of Christ [Jesus]" to refer to the final judgment three times in Philippians (1:6, 10; 2:16) and its equivalent, "Day of [the/our] Lord [Jesus Christ]," four times elsewhere (1 Cor 1:8; 5:5; 2 Cor 1:14; 1 Thess 5:2 [cf. 5:4]).[85] He also refers to it as the παρουσία or "[second] coming" (1 Thess 2:19; 3:13; 4:15; 5:23; 1 Cor 15:23).[86] It is "a day of . . . righteous judgment" (Rom 2:5) "when God will judge persons' secrets" (Rom 2:16; cf. 1 Cor 3:13), and is therefore both a day of "wrath" and "destruction" for the wicked (Rom 2:5-6; Phil 1:29) and a day of "salvation" for the righteous (1 Cor 5:5; 1 Thess 1:10; Phil 1:29; 3:20-21). Paul expected this "day" to come suddenly and unexpectedly "like a thief in the night" (1 Thess 5:2). If on this day the Philippians are found "pure and blameless," "filled with

---

76 For this basic difference between Christian and pagan consolation, which Paul here initiates, see Scourfield, *Consoling Heliodorus*, 80–81; cf. Favez, *Consolation latine chrétienne*, 84–89.

77 Compare the *indirect* rebuke in 1:22-26.

78 J. N. D. Kelly, *Golden Mouth: The Story of John Chrysostom–Ascetic, Preacher, Bishop* (Ithaca, NY: Cornell University Press, 1995) 267: "[Chrysostom's] tireless insistence that experiences generally rated disastrous are really matters of indifference."

79 See introduction, part 7: "Key Religious Topoi."

80 Cf. Gal 5:5. The perfect tense of the participle beginning v. 11 implies that "having been filled [πεπληρωμένοι] with the fruit of righteousness" is the precondition of being "pure and blameless." The genitive "of righteousness" has been interpreted to mean either the fruit that is righteousness or the fruit that righteousness produces. The former is to be preferred, since Paul returns to the theme of the believer's righteousness in 3:9, where it is not something believers already possess but something they achieve over the course of their lives at the end of which, if successful, they are then "found" hav-

ing "the righteousness that is from God [ἐκ θεοῦ]." According to Phil 1:6, God has begun "a good work" in the Philippians that he is currently completing; according to Phil 2:12-13 God is currently "working" in the Philippians to achieve their "salvation."

81 For Christ's role in the sanctification of the believer, see Gal 2:20; 2 Cor 3:17-18; cf. Phil 3:21.

82 Along with eschatological sentences, and sometimes in conjunction with them, doxology is also a punctuating feature in Paul's letters: Rom 11:36; Gal 1:5; Phil 2:11; 4:20; cf. Gal 1:24; 1 Cor 10:31; 2 Cor 9:13-15. The sequence from Christ to God derives from Paul's apocalyptic theology: "for he must reign until he has put all enemies under his feet . . . then the son himself will be subjected to the one who has subjected all things to him, in order that God might be all in all" (1 Cor 15:25-28).

83 E.g., Cicero, *Ad Brut.* 1.9.2; Seneca, *Ep.* 94.39; *Ad Poly.* 5–6; *Ad Helv.* 18.7–8.

84 Here see esp. my comments below on 1:25–26.

85 BDAG, s.v. ἡμέρα 3.b.β.

86 BDAG, s.v. παρουσία 2.b.α.

the fruit of righteousness" (Phil 1:10b-11; cf. 1 Cor 1:8; 1 Thess 5:23), it will also be a day of boasting and joy for Paul (Phil 2:16; 4:1).

Rhetorically, Phil 1:10b-11 has been described as an "eschatological climax," a feature found at various points of transition in Paul's letters, especially at the end of his letter openings.[87] But that is only a partial explanation. Verses 10b-11 make a substantive claim that is essential to Paul's argument. For Paul, the eschaton will be a time when believers either realize or do not realize their "salvation" (Rom 2:6; 1 Cor 3:13-15; 4:4-5), and it is precisely with these ominous prospects in mind that he is writing.

---

87   J. T. Sanders, "Transition from Opening Epistolary Thanksgiving to Body in the Letters of the Pauline Corpus," *JBL* 81 (1962) 348–62; J. H. Roberts, "The Eschatological Tensions in the Pauline Letter Body," *Neot* 20 (1986) 29–36.

III. The Body of the Letter 1:12—4:1: Things That Really Matter and Other Consolatory Arguments

Ancient letters of consolation typically consisted of a series of *solacia*, or consolatory arguments. Paul offers six consolatory arguments in Phil 1:12—4:1: (1) that his imprisonment has actually furthered the "progress of the gospel" (1:12-18b); (2) that his imprisonment will also result in his "salvation" (1:18c-21); (3) that the Philippians may still hope to see him again, though should he be executed it will have been for the sake of the gospel (1:22-26 + 2:17-18);[1] (4) that he will soon send Timothy in his stead (2:19-24); (5) that Epaphroditus has completed his mission, recovered from a serious illness, and is now back at Philippi (2:25-30); and finally and most importantly (6) that the present suffering is producing in both Paul and the Philippians a mystical, transformative, and ultimately saving γνῶσις Χριστοῦ, or "knowledge of Christ" (3:1—4:1). Five of these arguments—all but (4)—explicitly mention "joy" as an outcome (1:18ab, 25; 2:17b-18, 28-29; 3:1).[2]

Each of these arguments is designed to console the Philippians, but in different ways.[3] The first two speak directly to the topic "the things that really matter" (1:10a), namely, the progress of the gospel and Paul's own salvation. The third argument continues with this topic, though now Paul raises the pressing question of his demise.[4] He sees two possible outcomes to his present ordeal: either he will survive and the Philippians

will see him again (1:22-26), or he will die a noble death in the service of the gospel (2:17-18). Both outcomes offer grounds for rejoicing.[5] The fourth and fifth arguments leave aside the topic of things that really matter, but they continue to speak to the current situation. The fourth tells of a plan to send Timothy as Paul's temporary replacement, while the fifth urges the Philippians to rejoice in the recovery and return of Epaphroditus. In the sixth and final argument, Paul returns to the topic of things that really matter, though now conceived more broadly as the one thing that matters above everything else, namely, the "knowledge of Christ" that suffering brings.[6]

It was typical of ancient consolation to include exhortation.[7] Sometimes the exhortation could be quite brief, a short sentence or two urging the reader to accept the consolation being offered. At other times the exhortation could be developed at length, in which case the focus was often on the various duties and obligations that the grieved person was in danger of neglecting.[8] Both of these patterns are present in Philippians. Paul inserts brief consolatory exhortations at 2:18, 29-30; 3:1, 15-16, 17; 4:1, 2-3, 4-9.[9] He inserts a long hortatory digression in the middle of the third consolatory argument in 1:27—2:16.

---

1. Paul's argument here is far from straightforward. I will discuss it at length below, but for now I note that Paul's profession of "confidence" that he will see the Philippians again in 1:25 is turned into what is essentially a *consolatio mortis* in 2:17-18. It is not at all clear that Paul expects to survive his current ordeal.

2. In the first two Paul registers his own joy (1:18a, b). In the third he speaks of the Philippians' "progress and joy in the faith" (1:25), and then of his and their joy should he be sacrificed in the service of the gospel (2:17-18). In the fifth and sixth arguments he mentions only the Philippians' joy (2:28-29; 3:1, but see 4:1).

3. Recall Zahn, *Introduction*, 1:529: "Paul uses every means in his power to dispel [the Philippians' grief] and to make the Church rejoice."

4. This question is raised near the end of the second argument when Paul dismisses his death as an *adiaphoron*: "whether by life or by death" (1:20).

5. Phil 1:25: "for your progress and joy [χαράν] in the faith"; 2:17b-18: "I rejoice [χαίρω] . . . rejoice with [συγχαίρετε] me."

6. In 3:1—4:1 Paul prescinds from what matters in the gospel mission and focuses on what matters in the religious life of the Christ-believer as such. This is the longest and most emotion-laden of Paul's arguments.

7. See, e.g., Chapa, *Letters of Condolence*, 38–43; Zimmermann, "Philosophie als Psychotherapie," 195–200; introduction, part 1.a: "Greek and Roman Consolation."

8. As when Seneca in the *Ad Polybium* urges the imperial secretary Polybius not to neglect his duties to Caesar, or in the *Ad Marciam* when he urges Marcia not to neglect her duties to her surviving loved ones.

9. Here note especially the exhortations to "rejoice" in 2:18, 29-30; 3:1; 4:4; the exhortations of 4:4-9 substitute "peace" for joy.

The letter body of Philippians may be outlined as follows:

A. First Consolatory Argument 1:12-18b: The Progress of the Gospel

12/ **Now I want you to know, brothers,[a] that my situation has in fact resulted in the progress of the gospel. 13/ For one thing,[b] it has become clear throughout the whole Imperial Guard and to all the rest that I am in chains because of Christ.[c] 14/ Further, the majority of the brothers[d] in the Lord, having been persuaded by my chains, increasingly dare to speak the word [of God][e] without fear. 15/ Some act out of jealousy and spite, but others preach Christ out of goodwill. 16/[f] The latter do so from love, knowing that I have been appointed for the defense of the gospel. 17/ The former openly proclaim Christ out of contentiousness, not sincerely, hoping to make[g] my imprisonment as hard as possible. 18a-b/ What does it matter?[h] Only that[i] in every way, whether in pretense or in truth, Christ is proclaimed. And[j] in this I rejoice.**

a   Paul writes "brothers" (ἀδελφοί) even though his letter is intended for both the women and the men in the Philippian assembly, as 4:2 ("I urge Euodia and I urge Syntyche") makes clear.

b   The construction ὥστε . . . γενέσθαι ("so that it has become . . .") indicates not the results of the gospel's progress so much as the developments that actually constitute that progress. I have attempted to indicate this by rendering ὥστε ("so that") idiomatically as "For one thing." This requires translating the καί ("and") beginning the next verse as "Further."

c   The Greek ὥστε τοὺς δεσμούς μου φανεροὺς ἐν Χριστῷ γενέσθαι is awkward. See my comments below on v. 13.

d   Paul writes "brothers" (ἀδελφοί), but this includes both men and women; for women in the Roman assemblies, see Rom 16:3-16.

e   A large number of witnesses (ℵ A B P Ψ 048^vid 075, 0278, 33, 81, 104, 326, 365, 629, 1175, 1241, 2464 lat sy^p,h** co; Cl) add τοῦ θεοῦ, "of God" (D* reads the genitive first: τοῦ θεοῦ τὸν λόγον, "God's word"). Uncials F and G add instead κυρίου, "of the Lord." Both of these additions appear to be later clarifications of τὸν λόγον, "the word" (p^46 D² K 630, 1505, 1739, 1881 Maj r vg^ms; Marcion according to Tertullian), the reading that best explains the others.

f   A few witnesses (D¹ Ψ 104, 630, 1505 Maj sy^h) reverse vv. 16 and 17.

g   Several witnesses (D² K Ψ 075, 0278, 630, 1505 Maj sy) read: ἐπιφέρειν, "to add." However, ἐγείρειν, "to raise up" or "to cause" is well attested (ℵ A B D* F G 33, 104, 326, 365, 1241, 1739, 1881, 2464 latt co); a few witnesses (D^1vid P 81, 1175) read the cognate verb ἐπεγείρειν.

h   BDAG, s.v. τίς, τί 1aβℶ.

i   The text (reading p^46 ℵ A F G P 048 075 0278 33 81 104 365 614 1175 1241 1739 2464) is πλὴν ὅτι, "only that." B simply has ὅτι, "that" or perhaps "because." D K L Ψ 630, 1505, 1881 Maj sy^h have πλήν, "only." It is possible that πλὴν ὅτι is a conflation, but the textual evidence suggests otherwise.

j   𝔓^46 bo^ms read ἀλλά, "but."

Analysis

The consolation of 1:12-18b trades on the familiar Stoic distinction between things that matter and things that do not (cf. 1:10a). Paul's imprisonment, as well as the spitefulness of certain local rivals, falls into the latter category (things that do not matter), while the gospel and its progress fall into the former (things that do matter). Without this distinction, Paul's imprisonment would be a source of legitimate grief both for himself and for the Philippians. With this distinction, however, things look different. Paul's imprisonment has not only failed to hinder the gospel; it has actually contributed to its "progress."[1] Far from being a source of grief, therefore, Paul's imprisonment is an occasion for rejoicing: "And in this I rejoice."

Paul's argument in 1:12-18b is easily outlined. It consists of a thesis, two supporting arguments, a short interpretive summary, and a statement of Paul's response inviting a similar response from the Philippians.[2] Paul states his thesis in 1:12: "my situation has in fact resulted in the progress of the gospel."[3] He follows with two supporting arguments in 1:13-17: (1) that his imprisonment has served to broadcast his reputation as a servant of Christ to outsiders (1:13), and (2) that it has also motivated other Christ-believers to be more bold in their witness (1:14-17). Paul has to admit that not all the Christ-believers in Rome are supportive of him. In fact, he accuses some of acting out of spite, hoping that their open proclamation will make things harder for him.[4] But even they are proclaiming the gospel, and so he concludes, "What does it matter? Only that in every way, whether in pretense or in truth, Christ is proclaimed" (1:18a). Adding by way of personal response: "And in this I rejoice" (1:18b).

The consolation of 1:12-18b operates on two levels. At one level, Paul is reassuring the Philippians that his spirits are high and that despite his predicament he can rejoice in "the progress of the gospel." At this level the fact that Paul is himself consoled serves to console the Philippians.[5] Paul hopes for a similar consolation from the Philippians in 2:19: "that I too might be comforted when I know how things are with you." In addition to this, however, Paul is offering the Philippians a model for enduring hardship in line with his larger thesis that grief can be avoided if one keeps in mind "the things that really matter." At this second level Paul invites the Philippians to follow him in discounting his imprisonment and finding consolation in the progress of the gospel. When Paul responds, "And in this I rejoice," he also means, "And you should too" (cf. 2:17-18).[6]

It is presumably with a view to this second level—that of an example to be imitated—that Paul mentions those who would "make [his] imprisonment as hard as possible," since he has received report of similar strife at Philippi (e.g., Phil 2:1-4). Even when faced with the "contentiousness" ($\epsilon\rho\iota\theta\epsilon\acute{\iota}\alpha$; 1:17; cf. 2:2) of other Christ-believers it is possible to find joy if, like Paul, one stays focused on what really matters, which is the progress of the gospel. The argument of 1:12-18b may be outlined as follows:

1:12 Thesis: Paul's imprisonment has led to the progress of the gospel

1:13 First supporting argument: Paul's reputation among outsiders

1:14-17 Second supporting argument: Paul's inspiring example to insiders

1:18a Concluding thought: the gospel is proclaimed and that is all that matters.

1:18b Personal response: Paul rejoices

Comment

■ **12** Paul introduces the body of his letter and thus his first consolatory argument with the epistolary cliché

---

1   2 Timothy 2:9 imitates our text: "[for the sake of the gospel] I suffer wrong, even to the point of being placed in chains [$\mu\acute{\epsilon}\chi\rho\iota\ \delta\epsilon\sigma\mu\hat{\omega}\nu$] as a criminal, but the word of God [$\acute{o}\ \lambda\acute{o}\gamma os\ \tauo\hat{\upsilon}\ \theta\epsilon o\hat{\upsilon}$] is not bound [$o\grave{\upsilon}\ \delta\acute{\epsilon}\delta\epsilon\tau\alpha\iota$]."

2   The exhortation to follow Paul in his response is left implicit here. It will become explicit in 2:17-18.

3   The passage $\epsilon\grave{\iota}s\ \ldots\ \grave{\epsilon}\lambda\acute{\eta}\lambda\upsilon\theta\epsilon\nu$ should be understood causally: "My situation has in fact *resulted in* the progress of the gospel." See my comment below on 1:12.

4   The reference to rivals in 1:15-17 may anticipate the rivalry between Euodia and Syntyche (4:2-3). The language of 1:15-17 is picked up again in 2:1-4, which in turn anticipates 4:2-3. See Nils Dahl, "Euodia and Syntyche and Paul's Letter to the Philippians," in *The Social World of the First Christians: Essays in Honor of*

Wayne A. Meeks, ed. L. Michael White and O. Larry Yarbrough (Minneapolis: Fortress Press, 1995) 3–15, here 7, 15. The subtext of 1:15-17 is that personal rivalry is a matter of indifference as long as Christ is proclaimed. Chrysostom (hom 3.44.7 Allen) glosses 1:18a: "what difference [$\tau\acute{\iota}\ \delta\iota\alpha\phi\acute{\epsilon}\rho\epsilon\iota$] does it make to me?" This sentiment obviously cuts against Paul's unity language elsewhere in the letter.

5   As I have already noted, Paul here is not unlike Seneca in the *Ad Helviam*, who was both his mother's consoler and her consolation (see Abel, *Bauformen*, 54: "nicht nur ihr *consolator*, sondern ihr *solacium*" [italics original]).

6   Antonio Pitta speaks of the letter's "etica della mimesi" (*Lettera ai Filippesi: Nuova versione, introduzione e commento* [Milan: Paoline, 2010] 276).

γινώσκειν δὲ ὑμᾶς βούλομαι, "Now I want you to know." Similar expressions appear throughout his surviving letter corpus: θέλω δὲ ὑμᾶς εἰδέναι, "I wish you to know" (1 Cor 11:3; cf. Col 2:1); οὐ θέλω (θέλομεν) ὑμᾶς ἀγνοεῖν, "I (we) do not wish you to be ignorant" (Rom 1:13; 1 Cor 10:1; 2 Cor 1:8; 1 Thess 4:13); and γνωρίζω (γνωρίζομεν) ὑμῖν, "I (we) make known to you" (1 Cor 15:1; 2 Cor 8:1; Gal 1:11).[7] None of these expressions, however, uses the verb γινώσκειν. Paul's use of the verb here, the placement of which is emphatic, recalls the prayer of 1:9: "that your love might increase yet more and more in knowledge [ἐπιγνώσει]." The implication is that Paul will now impart the knowledge the Philippians need to "ascertain the things that really matter" (1:10a).

At issue is how the Philippians should think about Paul's present circumstances, which Paul insists must be assessed in terms of the "progress of the gospel." The expression Paul uses to refer to his circumstances (τὰ κατ᾽ ἐμέ, "my situation") has legal overtones. It is used in Acts 25:14 to refer to "Paul's case" (τὰ κατὰ τὸν Παῦλον) pending before Festus.[8] Here, however, it must be more broadly construed to include his imprisonment, since it is his "chains" and not his trial as such that Paul claims are furthering the gospel.[9] When Paul returns to his circumstances in 2:23 he uses the more general expression τὰ περὶ ἐμέ ("how things are with me"), which he also uses in 1:27 and 2:19 to refer to circumstances at Philippi (τὰ περὶ ὑμῶν, "how things are with you").

"Progress" (προκοπή) was an important concept in ancient—especially Stoic—moral theory.[10] In Gal 1:14 Paul uses the cognate verb to describe his earlier efforts in Judaism: "and I was progressing [προέκοπτον] in Judaism

beyond many of my contemporaries." The notion also underlies the correlatives ἐνάρχεσθαι ("to begin") and ἐπιτέλεσθαι ("to perfect") in Phil 1:6: "he who began a good work within you will continue to perfect it."[11] Paul's reference to the "progress" (προκοπή) of the gospel in Phil 1:12 anticipates his use of the term again in 1:25, where he speaks of the Philippians' own "progress" (προκοπή) in faith, which he will imply has been stalled by their grief,[12] the conceit being that the gospel is still making progress while the Philippians are not.[13]

The expression εἰς . . . ἐλήλυθεν has a range of idiomatic meanings.[14] Here it implies not just coincidence but causality, and I have translated "has resulted in."[15] Paul's claim is not that things have simply turned out for the progress of the gospel but that his imprisonment has "actually" (μᾶλλον) caused the gospel to progress. This is a strong claim for which Paul must offer evidence.

■ 13 The first piece of evidence Paul offers in support of the claim that his imprisonment has furthered the gospel is the impact his "chains" are having on those who are not Christ-believers. The clause τοὺς δεσμούς μου φανεροὺς ἐν Χριστῷ γενέσθαι is difficult. The question is what to do with the phrase ἐν Χριστῷ ("in Christ"), which might easily be read with τοὺς δεσμούς μου ("my chains") were it not for the placement of φανερούς ("known"). Perhaps the simplest solution is to supply the infinitive εἶναι ("to be")—verbs of being are often omitted in Greek—and to render something like "my chains have become known *to be* in Christ,"[16] or, more idiomatically, "it has become clear . . . that I am in chains because of Christ," which is the translation offered here.[17]

7   See further Terence Y. Mullins, "Disclosure: A Literary Form in the New Testament," *NovT* 7 (1964) 44–50.
8   Cf. Col 4:7 and Eph 6:21, both of which are imitative of Phil 1:12; *P. Yale* 42.
9   Paul mentions his "chains" three times in Phil 2:13-17.
10   Geert Roskam, *On the Path to Virtue: The Stoic Doctrine of Moral Progress and Its Reception in (Middle-)Platonism* (Ancient and Medieval Philosophy 33; Leuven: Leuven University Press, 2005).
11   See esp. Gal 3:3, but also 2 Cor 7:1; 8:8; 12:9; Phil 3:12; similarly 2 Tim 4:7.
12   Paul imagines the sanctification of the people of God in the last days as a lengthy process in which it was essential for each believer to make progress.

This was especially necessary for gentile "sinners." As a Pharisee, Paul may have imagined Judaism in similar terms of personal progress (Gal 1:14).
13   Focant, pp. 73–78.
14   BDAG, s.v. ἔρχομαι 5.
15   Thus Wis 15:5: "whose appearance creates a craving [εἰς ὄρεξιν ἔρχεται] in the foolish."
16   One might reason that εἶναι was omitted so as not to introduce the confusion of another infinitive after ὥστε. If this was the case, then one possible confusion was traded for another!
17   This is the second appearance of the phrase ἐν Χριστῷ ("in Christ") in Philippians (cf. 1:1). In one form or another, including ἐν κυρίῳ ("in the Lord"), it occurs nineteen times in the letter and over one hundred times in Paul's authentic letters. Paul was

The meaning of the term πραιτώριον in the phrase ἐν ὅλῳ τῷ πραιτωρίῳ (here translated "throughout the whole Imperial Guard") is much debated. I discuss the term in more detail in the introduction, part 3.a: "Place of Writing." It transliterates the Latin *praetorium*, which originally referred to a Roman praetor's (i.e., general's) tent, and then to his staff, including his personal bodyguard. By the late Republic it could also refer to a Roman governor's provincial headquarters and its personnel. In the empire, the term came to be used of the Imperial Guard in Rome, after the establishment of which a governor's headquarters might still be called his *praetorium*, but his personal bodyguard began to be known as his *singulares*, with *praetorium* reserved for the emperor's men.[18] Thus, the phrase ἐν ὅλῳ τῷ πραιτωρίῳ refers either to a provincial governor's headquarters, as it does for instance in Acts 23:35,[19] or to the Imperial Guard in Rome. Arguing for the latter view is the full expression ἐν ὅλῳ τῷ πραιτωρίῳ καὶ τοῖς λοιποῖς πᾶσιν, where καὶ τοῖς λοιποῖς πᾶσιν ("and to all the rest"), given Paul's use elsewhere, is most naturally taken to refer not to other buildings but to other people, implying the same for ἐν ὅλῳ τῷ πραιτωρίῳ.[20] The Imperial Guard was responsible for political prisoners kept in the *castra praetoria*.[21] Since the Imperial Guard numbered approximately six thousand at this time, Paul's claim is hyperbolic. This hyperbole is continued in the second half of the expression: "and to *all* the rest."[22]

Excursus: *RPC* 1:1651[23]

RPC 1:1651[24] is a small copper coin (*semis*[25]) reading VIC(toria) AUG(usta) on the front and COHOR(s) PRAE(toria) PHIL(ippensis) on the back, an unusually large number of which (approx. 150 to date) continue to be recovered.[26]

---

undisciplined in his use of the phrase, however, and it is not always clear to the modern interpreter what he meant by it—judging from 2 Pet 3:16 it was not always clear to ancient interpreters either! Here I have translated "because of Christ," following Chrysostom, who glosses διὰ Χριστόν (3.40.20-21 Allen). This anticipates 1:29, where Paul describes his imprisonment as ὑπὲρ Χριστοῦ, "for Christ's sake."

18 See esp. Speidel, *Guards*.

19 Cf. Mark 15:16; Matt 27:27; John 18:28 (twice), 33; 19:9. A third logical possibility is that it might refer to some imperial structure in Rome. But there is no indication that any imperial building in Rome bore the name *praetorium*, which at any rate would have been highly unlikely since it would have implied some sort of military occupation, something Augustus was anxious to avoid after the assassination of Caesar (see Lightfoot, pp. 99–104, esp. 100).

20 For the adjective ὅλος used to circumscribe a group of people, see Rom 16:23; 1 Cor 14:23; cf. Matt 26:59 (par.); John 11:50; Acts 2:47; 5:11; 10:22; 15:22; 18:8; Heb 3:2, 5; 1 John 2:2; 5:19; Rev 12:9; 16:14.

21 Bingham, *Praetorian Guard*, 93–94. That Paul was a prisoner of the Guard supports Acts' claim that Paul was sent to Rome on political charges.

22 The expression "and to all the rest" is ambiguous. It must be a reference to other non-Christ-believers, since Paul does not adduce Christ-believers until the next verse. It may therefore be a reference to civilian members of the imperial service. Paul's intent is to include as impressive a number as possible.

23 The following excursus excerpts material from my paper "*Tab. Vind.* 2.154, *RPC* 1:1651, and the Provenance of Philippians," to be published in *First Urban Churches: Philippi*, ed. James Harrison and Larry Welborn (Polis and Ekklesia 4; Atlanta: SBL Press, forthcoming 2017).

24 Andrew Burnett, Michel Amandry, and Pere Pau Ripollès, eds., *Roman Provincial Coinage*, vol. 1: *From the Death of Caesar to the Death of Vitellius* (London: British Museum; Paris: Bibliothèque Nationale, 1992, reprinted with corrections 1998) pl. 81:1651.

25 Roman coins tended to decrease in nominal value by halves. The nominal unit was the *as*, half of which was the *semis* ("half"), and a quarter of which was the *quadrans* ("quarter"), not unlike the American dollar, half-dollar, and quarter-dollar. During the early Principate, two *asses* equaled a *dupondius*, two *dupondii* a *sesterius*, and four *sesterii* a *denarius*. The gold *aureus* was worth twenty-five *denarii*.

26 *RPC 1* lists eighty-five specimens held in various Western museums. Katerina Chryssanthaki-Nagle lists another forty-five found in Abdera (*L'histoire monétaire d'Abdère en Thrace (VIe s. avant J.-C.–IIe s. après J.-C.* (Meletēmata 51; Athens: National Hellenic Research Foundation, 2007) 795–98,; Sophia Kremydi-Sicilianou, *Multiple Concealments from the Sanctuary of Zeus Olympios at Dion: The Roman Provincial Coin Hoards* (Meletemata 35; Athens: Boccard [Paris], 2004) 85–89, lists 2 from Amphipolis 1998; 1 from Ierissos 1976; 7 from Dion 1999 (cat. nos. 1508-1514); 1 from Dion 1998 (cat. no. 77). Coins of this type have also been found in the agora

Photo. Forum Ancient Coins
(used with permission)

Collart (1937) dated this coin to the reign of Augustus and interpreted it as commemorating Augustus's victory over Antony in 31 BCE and his settlement at Philippi of a cohort of praetorians when he refounded the colony in 30 BCE, an interpretation consistent with the literary evidence but not required by it.[27] This interpretation went largely unchallenged until the publication of *RPC 1* (1992), which, based on the coin's copper composition, dated it no earlier than the reign of Claudius, though still allowing a reference to an early settlement of praetorians by Augustus.[28]

This redating has not been taken into account in subsequent interpretations of Philippians, which still rely exclusively on Collart, if they mention the coin at all.[29] If accepted, however, it casts considerable light on Paul's reference to the Imperial Guard in Phil 1:13. It not only dates the striking of the coin close to the time of Paul's letter but, more importantly, attests to Philippi's continuing pride in its praetorian foundations, a fact that Paul, now a prisoner of the Guard, would presumably to be alluding to.

Further evidence of the continuing importance of the Praetorian Guard for the civic self-understanding of the Philippians includes several military *diplomata* (official retirement papers) witnessed by one or more imperial guardsmen from Philippi,[30] as well as a number of inscriptions connected in one way or another to Philippi in which guardsmen are named.[31] Particularly intriguing is *CIPh* 2.1.6, a large dedicatory inscription honoring the imperial family datable to the reign of Claudius. *CIPh* 2.1.6 was commissioned by L. Atiarius Schoenias presumably on the occasion of his election to civic office. Unfortunately, the inscription is fragmentary and cannot be reconstructed with certainty, but one possible rendering identifies Schoenias not only as an important civic patron but also as a former "*tribunus cohortium praetoriarum VII et VIII.*"

Arguments for an even later dating of *RPC* 1:1651 have been proposed by Kremydi-Sicilianou.[32] Recent coin finds at Dion (1998), Amphipolis (1998), Ierissos (1976), and especially the large circulation hoard found at Dion in 1999, indicate that the coin, which appears in a variety of subtypes (Victoria standing on a globe, on a pedestal, or simply walking), continued in production as late as the reign of Antoninus Pius.[33] The content of these finds also suggests that the subtype in which Victoria is depicted standing on a globe marks the coin's earliest issue, since this iconography does not appear on any strikings datable to the second century.[34] On this basis, Kremydi-Sicilianou proposed that the Victoria on a globe was intended to evoke the Victoria (also on a globe) that Augustus placed in the renovated Curia in 29 BCE,

of Athens, J. H. Kroll, *The Athenian Agora*, vol. 26: *Greek Coins* (Princeton: American School of Classical Studies, 1993) 184, no. 476.

27 Collart, *Philippes*, 1:231–35; 2: pl. 30.8–11, whose arguments were accepted in subsequent *sylloges*: *SNG* Evelp., 1275–77; *SNG* ANS, 674–81; *SNG* Cop., 305–6; *SNG* Tüb., 1031 (Sophia Kremydi-Sicilianou, "*Victoria Augusta* on Macedonian Coins: Remarks on Dating and Interpretation," Τεκμήρια 7 [2002] 63–84, here 63 n. 1). The literary evidence includes Appian, *Bell. civ.* 5.1.3; Cassius Dio, *Hist.* 51.4.6.

28 *RPC 1*, pp. 288, 308. Marcel Durry had already dated the coin to the reign of Claudius ("Sur une monnaie de Philippes," *REA* 42 [1940] 412–16), while H. Gaebler simply dated it to "Imperial times" (*AMNG* 3.2:102–3 nos. 14–15).

29 New Testament scholars who still follow Collart include Oakes, *Philippians*, 13, 25; Bormann, *Philippi*, 22 n. 67; Laura S. Nasrallah, "Spatial Perspectives: Space and Archaeology in Roman

Philippi," in *Studying Paul's Letters: Contemporary Perspectives and Methods*, ed. Joseph Marchal (Minneapolis: Fortress Press, 2012) 53–74. Reumann, on the other hand, makes no mention of the coin.

30 Pilhofer, *Philippi*, index, s.v. *cohors*. See further: T. Sarikakis, "Des soldats Macedoniens dans l'armée romaine," *Ancient Macedonia* 2 (Thessalonica: Institute of Balkan Studies, 1977) 431–63; F. Papazoglou, "Quelques aspects d l'histoire de la province Macédoine," *ANRW* 2.7.1 (1979) 302–69, esp. 338–52.

31 Brélaz, *Corpus des inscriptions*, index, s.v. *cohors.*

32 Kremydi-Sicilianou, "*Victoria Augusta*"; eadem, *Multiple Concealments*; more generally, eadem, "'Belonging' to Rome, 'Remaining' Greek: Coinage and Identity in Roman Macedonia," in *Coinage and Identity in the Roman Provinces*, ed. Christopher Howgego, Volker Heuchert, and Andrew Burnett (Oxford: Oxford University Press, 2007) 95–106.

33 Kremydi-Sicilianou, "*Victoria Augusta*," 64, 67.

34 Ibid., 65–67 (based on the Dion 1999 evidence).

which became a widely circulated symbol of Roman imperial domination throughout the first century.[35] But as she goes on to observe, the Victoria in the Curia was initially called *Victoria Romana* and, so far as we know, began to be referred to as *Victoria Augusta* only in the reign of Claudius,[36] after which it became an important piece of imperial propaganda especially in the reign of Vespasian, who in an effort to establish a new dynasty was anxious to style himself as a new Augustus.[37] Kremydi-Sicilianou proposes that the coin was therefore first struck near the beginning of Vespasian's reign.[38] An issue in the reign of Claudius, however, also fits the evidence—especially if such a prominent civic figure as L. Atiarius Schoenias was a former tribune in the Guard.

A question raised by Kremydi-Sicilianou's proposed dating of the coin is whether the settlement of praetorians at Philippi referred to on the reverse of *RPC* 1:1651 might actually have taken place not in the reign of Augustus but early in the reign of Vespasian, when large numbers of soldiers were decommissioned after the civil wars that elevated him to emperor. This is possible, but if *RPC* 1:1651 was a commemorative issue linking Vespasian to Augustus, then a reference to an earlier settlement by Augustus—a point of continuing civic pride now exploited by Vespasian—still remains a plausible explanation, even if Vespasian himself also settled guardsmen there, which at this point, like most theories surrounding this fascinating coin, must remain uncertain.[39]

■ **14-17** A second positive outcome contributing to the progress of the gospel is the effect Paul's "chains" are having on other Christ-believers in Rome, many of whom have been "persuaded" by his imprisonment to be more daring in their proclamation of "the word" (1:14).[40] But Paul alleges that not all those proclaiming Christ are acting out of the same motive (1:15-17). One group is friendly toward Paul and acts out of "goodwill" and "love." They understand that calling attention to the faith might expose Paul to ridicule and abuse by his guards and might even prejudice his case.[41] But they also know that he has been "appointed for the defense of the gospel" and is prepared to suffer in its cause (1:15b-16; cf. 1:7).[42] There is, however, another group that is hostile to Paul. Paul claims that they are motivated by "jealousy and spite"[43] and that, although they too publicly proclaim[44] Christ, they do so out of "contentiousness," hoping "to make [Paul's] imprisonment as hard as possible" (1:15a, 17). It is clear from Paul's account of these groups that he received a very mixed reception among the Christ-believers in Rome, something he feared in his earlier letter to them.[45]

It is possible that Paul has accurately described the motives of both groups. He had a number of friends in Rome (Rom 16:3-16), but others would have interpreted his presence in the city as overreaching (Rom 15:20; cf. 1:11-12; 15:15). Moreover, there were theological differ-

---

35 Ibid., 69; cf. Paul Zanker, *Power of Images in the Age of Augustus* (Ann Arbor: University of Michigan Press, 1990) 79–85. A large statue of Victory on a globe was also set up in the Athenian agora. Vespasian also produced both an aureus and a silver denarius with similar iconography on the reverse.

36 Kremydi-Sicilianou, "*Victoria Augusta*," 73.

37 Ibid., 73.

38 Ibid., 75–76.

39 That Vespasian staffed the ranks of his army with recruits from Philippi is reasonable, and that at least some of these became part of his Imperial Guard is consistent with the military *diplomata* published by Pilhofer, three of which (items 030A, 202 [cf. 203], and 705) date from Vespasian's reign. One of these *diplomata* (item 705), however, can be dated to the first year of Vespasian's reign, making it likely that in at least this case we have a Philippian who was a member of the Guard before Vespasian came to power, a possibility made more likely if the Schoenias of *CIPh* 2.1.6 was also a retired guards-

man. For Kremydi-Sicilianou's claim that Vespasian renamed Philippi *colonia victrix* ("Victoria Augusta," 77) based on Philhofer's reconstruction of *CIL* 3.660, see Brélaz's alternative explanation at *CIPh* 2.1.151. (I wish to thank Prof. Brélaz for a private e-mail exchange regarding *CIPh* 2.1.151 in which he kindly shared his expertise with me.)

40 For Paul's use of the "the word" as shorthand for the gospel, see 1 Thess 1:6; Gal 6:6.

41 So Theodoret, Chrysostom (3.42.4-8, 21; cf. *Laud. Paul.* 4.15); Bengel on 1:17; see the excursus "Roman Attitudes toward Foreign Cults" below.

42 Paul's "appointment" here is no doubt a reference to his call to be an "apostle to the gentiles" (Rom 11:13; cf. 1:5; Gal 2:7-8).

43 Presumably jealousy and spite directed at Paul.

44 Paul's word choice here is interesting. He does not allow that his enemies "preach" (κηρύσσουσιν) Christ (v. 15), but that they "proclaim" (καταγγέλλουσιν) him (v. 17, repeated in the next verse).

45 See my "*Commendatio*."

ences in the Roman assemblies over such things as Jewish food laws and holy days that would have made Paul a controversial figure, though he had tried to play these down (Rom 14:1–15:13).[46] But whatever the nature of the conflict, by distinguishing these two groups Paul is able to offer a second example of how identifying the things that really matter has enabled him to endure difficult circumstances with equanimity: in this case to rise above the "contentiousness" (ἐριθεία) of other Christ-believers. In 2:1-4 Paul identifies "contentiousness" (ἐριθεία) as a disruptive force among the Christ-believers at Philippi.

Excursus: Roman Attitudes toward Foreign Cults

Roman attitudes toward foreign cults were a mixture of genuine religiosity, cultural chauvinism, and imperial pragmatism.[47] Romans were for the most part tolerant of the religions of their subject peoples.[48] At the same time they harbored an inherent distrust of foreign cults.[49] Some of these cults were given official recognition and a presence in the city,[50] but even their position remained tenuous.[51] Proselytism, for instance, was always opposed.[52] The Romans

certainly would not have welcomed the arrival of the new Christ cult, at the center of which was the valorization of a crucified criminal.[53]

Christ-belief came to Rome by way of the synagogue,[54] and Christ-believers initially would have been considered a Jewish sect (e.g., Acts 18:12–17),[55] which would have provided them with a degree of protection since Judaism was a recognized religion.[56] But disputes quickly arose in the synagogues over the claim that Jesus was the Messiah, and during the reign of Claudius Jewish Christ-believers were expelled from the city as troublemakers.[57] At this point gentile Christ-believers who had been attending synagogues as "God-fearers" would have begun to meet separately even if some among their members maintained ties to the parent religion, as Paul's letter to the Romans indicates they did.[58] Separated from the synagogue, these gentile Christ-believers could no longer claim the protection of a legal religion, and the time was ripe for a confrontation. According to Tacitus, this occurred dramatically and tragically during the reign of Nero, who brutally scapegoated the Christ-believers after the devastating fire of 64 CE.[59]

46　See John M. G. Barclay, "'Do We Undermine the Law?' A Study of Romans 14.1–15.6," in *Paul and the Mosaic Law*, ed. James D. G. Dunn (WUNT 89; Tübingen: Mohr Siebeck, 1996) 287–308.

47　Mary Beard, John North, and Simon Price, *Religions of Rome* (2 vols.; Oxford: Oxford University Press, 1998) 1:211–44.

48　Peter Garnsey, "Religious Toleration in Classical Antiquity," in *Persecution and Toleration: Papers Read at the Twenty-second Summer Meeting and the Twenty-third Winter Meeting of the Ecclesiastical History Society*, ed. W. J. Scheils (Studies in Church History 21; Oxford: Blackwell, 1984) 1–27.

49　So, e.g., the Bacchanal persecution in 186 BCE (*ILS* 18; also Beard, *Religions of Rome*, fig. 2.4, p. 94), which action was still authoritative for Livy, *Ab urb.* (39.8–19; cf. 39.29.8–10; 39.41.6–7; 40.19.9–10).

50　Beard, *Religions of Rome*, 1:249–60.

51　For example, the cult of Cybele or Magna Mater was officially brought to Rome in 204 BCE near the end of the Second Punic War (Livy, *Ab urb.* 39.10.4–11.8; Ovid, *Fasti* 4.247–348) but was famously kept under tight control (Dionysius of Halicarnassus, *Ant.* 2.19). For the ups and downs of the Isis cult in Rome, see Sharon Kelly Heyob, *The Cult of Isis among Women in the Greco-Roman World* (EPRO 51; Leiden: Brill, 1975) 1–36; in the early empire the cult was suppressed by Augustus (Cassius Dio, *Hist.* 53.2.4;

54.6.6 [Agrippa]) and Tiberius (Tacitus, *Ann.* 2.85; Suetonius, *Tib.* 36; cf. Josephus, *Ant.* 18.65–84).

52　Beard, *Religions of Rome*, 1:276, citing Origen, *Cel.* 3.55; and Justin, *2 Apol.* 2; cf. Robin Lane Fox, *Pagans and Christians* (New York: Knopf, 1986) 312–17.

53　Tacitus, *Ann.* 15.44; cf. Suetonius, *Ner.* 16.2; Pliny, *Ep.* 10.96.

54　By the time Paul wrote Romans in the mid-50s CE, Christ believers had been in Rome "for some years" (Rom 15:23). Acts 28:13 also mentions Christ-believers at Puteoli, the port of Rome in Paul's day, which suggests that Christ-belief came to Rome by traveling merchants. According to Suetonius, *Claud.* 25.4 (cf. Acts 18:2), Christ-believers originally existed as a group within the synagogues.

55　See Pervo, *Acts*, on this passage.

56　For Rome's uneasy acceptance of Judaism, see Tessa Rajak, "Was There a Roman Charter for the Jews?," *JRS* 74 (1984) 107–23; cf. James B. Rives, *Religion in the Roman Empire* (Blackwell Ancient Religions; Oxford: Blackwell, 2007) 193–96; more generally, see Peter Schäfer, *Judeophobia: Attitudes toward the Jews in the Ancient World* (Cambridge, MA: Harvard University Press, 1997).

57　Suetonius, *Claud.* 25.4; Acts 18:2; cf. Cassius Dio, *Hist.* 60.6.6–7; Lampe, *From Paul to Valentinus*, 11–16.

58　Holloway, "*Commendatio.*"

59　But see the reservations by Shaw, "Myth."

90

Recent scholarship on scapegoating has shown that only social groups previously stigmatized can be used as scapegoats.[60] This implies that for some time in advance of the pogrom of 64 CE gentile Christ-believers in Rome had become a recognizable social group and that they were already the target of significant social prejudice. Paul's arrival in the city as an imperial prisoner—Jesus had himself died a criminal—in the early 60s would have only made the group more visible and added to its stigmatization, while any increase in proselytism, which Paul claims credit for in Phil 1:15, would have further increased animosity toward the group and made its members, including Paul himself, all the more vulnerable to ridicule and abuse. Paul does not specify how the increased proselytizing by Christ-believers might have harmed him, but two possibilities come to mind: mistreatment by his guards, who would have shared any popular animus to the new cult, and a negative verdict at his upcoming trial. It is revealing that Paul does not feel the need to spell out for the Philippians the various ways in which he might be injured, possibilities they could well imagine.[61]

■ **18a-b** Paul highlights the theme of things that do and do not matter in the concluding summary of 1:18a.[62] He begins with the rhetorical question τί γάρ, the more usual form of which is τί οὖν (lit., "What then?").[63] The point of such questions in Paul and elsewhere is to invite the reader or hearer to identify what is salient in the preceding discussion or, in this case, to identify what really matters. I have translated: "What does it matter?" Paul answers the question himself: "Only that in every way, whether [εἴτε] in pretense or [εἴτε] in truth, Christ is proclaimed."[64] This is the first time that Paul uses the correlatives εἴτε . . . εἴτε, "whether . . . or," in the letter. He will use them again in 1:20 ("whether [εἴτε] by life or [εἴτε] by death") and in 1:27 ("whether [εἴτε] I come and see you or [εἴτε] remain absent"). In each instance they designate things that, on Paul's view, do not matter.[65]

Paul registers his personal response in 1:18b: "and in this I rejoice." Because he has evaluated his circumstances from the perspective of what really matters (in this case the "progress of the gospel" versus his "chains" and the "contentiousness" of others), he is consoled. Of the six consolatory arguments in Philippians, five explicitly list "joy" as the intended outcome. Here in 1:18b Paul simply reports his own "joy," as he will do again in 1:18c: "and I will rejoice." In 2:17-18 he reports his joy but invites the Philippians to join him ("I rejoice . . . likewise you rejoice"), an invitation he repeats in 2:28-29 ("Receive him . . . will all joy") and 3:1 ("rejoice in the Lord"). At the parousia the Philippians will be both Paul's "joy" and his "victory garland" (Phil 4:1).[66]

---

60   Here see esp. the work of Peter Glick, "Choice of Scapegoats," in *On the Nature of Prejudice: Fifty Years after Allport*, ed. John F. Dovidio, Peter Glick, and Laurie A. Rudman (Oxford: Blackwell, 2005) 244–61; idem, "Sacrificial Lambs Dressed in Wolves' Clothing: Envious Prejudice, Ideology, and the Scapegoating of Jews," in *Understanding Genocide: The Social Psychology of the Holocaust*, ed. Leonard S. Newman and Ralph Erber (New York: Oxford University Press, 2002) 113–42.

61   For the possibility that Paul was already being subjected to shaming treatment, see Phil 1:20; cf. 1 Pet 4:16 and my comments in *Coping with Prejudice*, 225–26.

62   A rhetorical "conclusion" (*conclusio*).

63   Rom 3:9; 6:15; 1 Cor 14:15, 26.

64   As in v. 17 Paul uses the verb καταγγέλλω ("proclaim") versus κηρύσσω ("preach"), which he used in v. 16. Only those with pure motives "preach" the gospel.

65   Cf. Musonius, frag. 38 (Hense); Epictetus, *Diss.* 3.22.1; Seneca, *Ep.* 74.26; 111.4 (*sive . . . sive*). Epictetus expresses "either . . . or" negatively as "neither . . . nor" (*Diss.* 4.7.4 μήτ᾽ ἀποθανεῖν μήτε ζῆν, "neither to die nor to live"; cf. 4.7.5: τὸ ἔχειν ταῦτα ἢ μὴ ἔχειν, "to have or not to have these things"). It is striking that Epictetus goes on to attribute this indifference to "Galileans" in 4.7.6. Pelagius glosses: *non curae mihi est.*

66   Already in this life the memory of the Philippians' partnership in the gospel brings "joy" to Paul (1:3-5).

B. Second Consolatory Argument 1:18c-21: Paul's Final Salvation

18c/ **But I also will rejoice, 19/ for**[a] **I know that this will lead to my salvation through your prayers for me and the provision of the spirit of Jesus Christ, 20/ in accordance with my eager expectation**[b] **and hope that in no way I shall be cowed but that with all boldness as always so now also Christ will be magnified in my body, whether through life or through death. 21/ For to me to live is Christ and to die is gain.**

a $\mathfrak{P}^{46}$ B 0278, 1175, 1739, 1881; Ambst read δέ ("but").
b   The text is ἀποκαραδοκίαν ("eager expectation"; cf. Rom 8:19); F G read καραδοκίαν.

Analysis

Paul introduces a second consolatory argument in 1:18c-21, where he identifies another positive outcome of his incarceration, namely, his "salvation" (σωτηρία; 1:19). Paul's argument continues to trade on the distinction between things that matter and things that do not. But this time the distinction is not between Paul's fate and that of the gospel (as in 1:12-18b) but between Paul's present predicament—here extended to include his possible execution—and his future salvation. What matters is not whether Paul's current imprisonment ends in his execution—"whether [εἴτε] through life or [εἴτε] through death"[1]—but whether it will result in his salvation, which requires that he continue to confess Christ "with all boldness" (ἐν πάσῃ παρρησίᾳ; 1:20). This will be no easy task, since Paul must now glorify Christ not only with his words but also, as the case may be, with his "body" (σῶμα). Yet he is confident that he will be successful, since he is supported in this task by the "prayers" of the Philippians and the "spirit of Christ Jesus," as well as by his own established pattern of "boldness."

Paul's argument in 1:18c-21 exhibits a similar structure to 1:12-18b. This time, however, he begins with his anticipated response: "But I also will rejoice" (ἀλλὰ καὶ χαρήσομαι; 1:18c). He then states his thesis: "for I know that this will lead to my salvation" (1:19a), followed by

three supporting arguments that explain his assurance: (1) the Philippians' prayers for him (1:19b); (2) the strength provided him by the spirit of Christ (1:19b); and (3) his long record of bold proclamation, which he expects to continue (1:20). Paul concludes with a striking clausular *sententia*: ἐμοὶ γὰρ τὸ ζῆν Χριστὸς καὶ τὸ ἀποθανεῖν κέρδος, "For to me to live is Christ and to die is gain" (1:21).[2]

The argument of 1:18c-21 may be outlined as follows:

1:18c Anticipated personal response: Paul also will rejoice in the future
1:19a Thesis: Paul's situation will result in his salvation
1:19b First supporting argument: the prayers of the Philippians will sustain Paul
1:19c Second supporting argument: the spirit of Christ will also sustain Paul
1:20 Third supporting argument: Paul's record of boldness will continue
1:21 Concluding thought: "to live is Christ and to die is gain"

Comment

■ **18c** Paul concluded his first consolatory argument in 1:12-18b with a personal response: "and in this I rejoice" (καὶ ἐν τούτῳ χαίρω; 1:18b). In 1:18c-21 he reverses that order and begins with his response, though in this case

1   We have seen this construction in 1:18a ("whether [εἴτε] in pretense or [εἴτε] in truth"); we will see it again in 1:27 ("whether [εἴτε] I come and see you or [εἴτε] remain absent"). In each case it indicates things that do not matter.

2   This concluding thought does not summarize the argument, as was the case in 1:18a, but simply serves to strengthen the third supporting argument. In this regard it is similar to the ἐπιφώνημα of 1:8, which offers direct support for 1:7.

it is his anticipated response: "But I also will rejoice" (ἀλλὰ καὶ χαρήσομαι; 1:18c). Paul here imagines further grounds for rejoicing to materialize in the future.[3] It was a common theme in both prophetic and apocalyptic Judaism that the future would bring consolation.[4]

■ **19a** Paul states a new thesis in 1:19a: "For I know that this will lead to my salvation."[5] Paul's imprisonment has resulted in the "progress" of the gospel. He is confident that it will also lead to his final "salvation" (σωτηρία).[6] Again it is knowledge—"for I know" (οἶδα γάρ)—that brings consolation, or in this case that allows Paul to anticipate consolation.[7] The verb ἀποβήσεται ("will lead to") corresponds to the expression εἰς . . . ἐλήλυθεν ("has resulted in") earlier in 1:12.

"Salvation" (σωτηρία) had yet to become a technical term in Christian theological vocabulary,[8] and Paul's use of the term here has been interpreted in a number of ways, from vindication in court, to deliverance from prison, to final salvation. Most commentators, however, rightly understand it to refer to Paul's final salvation.[9] Paul uses the term twice more in the letter: in 1:28, where he contrasts the "salvation" of Christ-believers with the "destruction" (ἀπώλεια) of their enemies, and in 2:12, where he urges the Philippians to "work hard" (κατεργάζομαι) to accomplish their "salvation." He uses the cognate agent noun σωτήρ ("savior") in an unambigu-

ously eschatological sense in 3:20: "for our citizenship is in heaven, from which we await a savior, the Lord Jesus Christ."

■ **19b-20** Paul's eschatological salvation is contingent on his continued "boldness" (1:20), but he has every reason to be hopeful, and in 1:19b-20 he offers three arguments why this is so. The first two arguments are stated briefly (1:19b):[10] the "prayers" of the Philippians and the "provision of the spirit of Christ Jesus." The term Paul uses for "prayer" here is δέησις ("entreaty," "petition"). It refers to the Philippians' prayers on Paul's behalf.[11] Paul has already mentioned his "prayer" (again δέησις) for the Philippians in 1:4.[12] In the expression "provision of the spirit" (ἐπιχορηγίας τοῦ πνεύματος) the genitive "of the spirit" (τοῦ πνεύματος) allows for two interpretations: either the provision that is Jesus's spirit, at which point the genitive is appositional, or the provision that is made by Jesus's spirit, at which point the genitive is subjective. Based on Gal 3:5—"the one therefore who provides [ἐπιχορηγῶν] to you the Spirit"—the former better fits Paul's idiom.[13]

The third supporting argument concerns the moral momentum of Paul's life. Based on his previous record of bold confession—"as always so now also"—Paul fully expects to continue to "magnify" Christ in his upcoming trial, even if it means physical torture or death: "whether

3 Paul expects to rejoice in his "salvation"; he also expects, though perhaps with a little less confidence, to rejoice in the Philippians' salvation (2:16; 4:1).

4 E.g., Hos 14:1-7; Amos 9:11-15; Mic 7:8-20; Dan 12:2; *1 Enoch* 98:12; cf. Isa 26:19. An important variation on this theme was that the rewards of the righteous and the punishments of the wicked had already been prepared and that the righteous were even now being preserved for their reward (*1 Enoch* 48:47; *2 Bar.* 52:7; 54:4; cf. 1 QHᵃ 17:32; 1 Pet 1:4-5).

5 For a possible allusion to Job 13:16 LXX ("Even this will turn out for my deliverance" [καὶ τοῦτό μοι ἀποβήσεται εἰς σωτηρίαν]), see Richard B. Hays, *Echoes of Scripture in the Letters of Paul* (New Haven: Yale University Press, 1993) 23–26.

6 Here I interpret the antecedent of τοῦτο ("this") to be τὰ κατ᾿ ἐμέ ("my situation") in 1:12, which in turn refers to Paul's imprisonment.

7 Cf. 1:12 ("I want you to know [γινώσκειν]"), following 1:9 ("increase still more and more in knowledge [ἐπιγνώσει]").

8 BDAG, s.v. σῴζω.

9 E.g., Lightfoot, Vincent, Gnilka, Collange, and others. Here I depart from my earlier interpretation (*Consolation*, 108–9). For Paul, the Christ-believer's final "salvation" is twofold. According to 1 Thess 1:10, it is deliverance "from the wrath to come." According to Phil 3:20-21, it is tantamount to resurrection: "a savior . . . who will transform the body of our humiliation to be conformed to his body of glory."

10 They are governed by the same preposition and article: διὰ τῆς ὑμῶν δεήσεως καὶ ἐπιχορηγίας τοῦ πνεύματος Ἰησοῦ Χριστοῦ, which might be paraphrased "*through the fact that* you are praying for me and the spirit of Jesus Christ is being supplied to me."

11 See also 2 Cor 1:11, where Paul imagines the prayers of the Corinthians as their "working together with" (συνυπουργούντων) him; cf. Phil 1:7.

12 In 4:6 he recommends prayer as a source of continued consolation.

13 So Chrysostom, hom. 4.60.3 Allen.

through life or through death." The term I have translated "I shall be cowed" is αἰσχυνθήσομαι (lit. "I shall be ashamed" or "made ashamed"). Chrysostom glosses: οὐ περιέσονται οὗτοι, "they shall not get the better of me" (4.60.18-19). Here "shame" is imagined as the antithesis of παρρησία ("boldness") in speaking.[14]

Speaking freely before a powerful magistrate was a common point of anxiety in the early Roman Empire, affecting even the senatorial class. Epictetus provided the young aristocrats who studied with him with numerous techniques—from mock dialogues, to memorable *sententiae*, and even scripted prayers to be said at the last minute—to prepare them for this possibility.[15] As always, Socrates was an example to be imitated: "Socrates does not save himself by some shameful act [αἰσχρῶς]. Indeed, it is impossible to save this man shamefully [αἰσχρῶς]. Rather it is in dying that he is saved" (*Diss.* 4.1.164–65). It was a common expectation among early Christ-believers that, should they ever be summoned to appear before a Roman magistrate, they would speak under the inspiration of the divine spirit,[16] which is no doubt the point of Paul's reference to "the spirit of Jesus Christ" in 1:19b.

■ **21** Paul ends his second consolatory argument with a concluding thought or *clausula*, a common feature of his prose style. Sometimes Paul's *clausulae* are simply neat turns of phrase that add a sense of closure. Here, however, he offers a substantial thought that further explains why he expects to continue his established practice of bold confession: "For to me to live is Christ and to die is gain." The latter half—"to die is gain"—was a popular expression meaning that death brings relief from life's toils.[17] There may be an element of that in Paul's use of the expression here, but that cannot be its primary sense since, as Paul will go on to say, "to depart" is to "be with Christ" (1:23). Paul has taken a popular expression and reinterpreted it in light of his own mythology: for the Christ-believer death's gain is not simply the absence of suffering but the presence of Christ. This leaves us with the first half of the sentence: "to live is Christ," which Paul has obviously crafted to correspond to "to die is gain." As is often the case, Paul has sacrificed clarity for point. At the very least Paul means that to live is to continue to "magnify" Christ (1:20) or to bear "fruit" for Christ (1:22). It is likely, however, that Paul is here also giving voice to his emerging Christ-mysticism. Later in chapter 3 he will describe his desire to "gain" Christ, "be found in him," "know him," and "lay hold of" him.

---

14 "Boldness" (παρρησία; Lat. *licentia*) had a history by Paul's day. It originally referred to the right of the citizen of a Greek city-state to speak his mind freely without fear of reprisal. In the Hellenistic period, with the rise of empire and the demise of the city-state and its citizen rights, the term was appropriated by various philosophical traditions to express the philosopher's characteristic frankness of speech, even before powerful political authorities. See esp. Ineke Sluiter and Ralph M. Rosen, *Free Speech in Classical Antiquity* (Mnemosyne Supplements 254; Leiden: Brill, 2004); Arnaldo Momigliano, "Freedom of Speech in Antiquity," in *Dictionary of the History of Ideas: Studies of Selected Pivotal Ideas* (5 vols.; New York: Charles Scribner's Sons, 1973–74) 2:252–63.

15 Robert J. Newman, "*Cotidie meditare*: Theory and Practice of the *meditatio* in Imperial Stoicism" *ANRW* 2.36.3 (1989)1473–1517; Chester G. Starr Jr., "Epictetus and the Tyrant," *CP* 44 (1949) 20–29.

16 Mark 13:11; cf. Matt 10:19-20; Luke 12:11-12. Contrast 1 Pet 3:15, which advised being "ready" (ἕτοιμοι) with a defense. Luke 21:14-15, on the other hand, specifically says "not to practice beforehand" (μὴ προμελετᾶν). Elite Roman officials like Pliny were not impressed by courtroom displays of the prophetic spirit, which they interpreted as impudence (*pertinaciam certe et inflexibilem obstinationem*; *Ep.* 10.96.3); see Holloway, *Coping with Prejudice*, 203–5; G. W. H. Lampe, "Martyrdom and Inspiration," in *Suffering and Martyrdom in the New Testament: Studies Presented to G. M. Styler by the Cambridge New Testament Seminar*, ed. William Horbury and Brian McNeil (Cambridge: Cambridge University Press, 1981) 118–35; David S. Potter, "Martyrdom as Spectacle," in *Theater and Society in the Classical World*, ed. Ruth Scodel (Ann Arbor: University of Michigan Press, 1993) 53–88.

17 See D. W. Palmer, "'To Die Is Gain' (Philippians 1:21)," *NovT* 17 (1975) 203–18; and *NW* 2.1 on this verse.

C. Third Consolatory Argument (Begun) 1:22-26: Paul's Acquittal and Return

22/ But if[a] it is to live on in the flesh—this will mean more fruit for my labors.[b] And yet what I shall choose I cannot say.[c] **23/** I am hard pressed by the two: having the desire to depart[d] and be with Christ, for that is much better by far,[e] **24/** but to stay on[f] in[g] the flesh is more necessary for your sakes. **25/** And being confident of this [necessity], I know that I shall stay on and be restored[h] to you all for your progress and joy in the faith,[i] **26/** that your boast in Christ might increase because of me by my presence again with you.

a   Two witnesses (p[46] D*) read εἴτε, "whether" (possibly after 1:20: εἴτε . . . εἴτε; cf. 1:18; 1:27).

b   Literally: "fruit of labor for me" (μοὶ καρπὸς ἔργου).

c   Translating the future (αἱρήσομαι). Several witnesses (p[46] B 2464) read the subjunctive τί αἱρήσωμαι, which can easily be interpreted as a question: "What should I choose?" that would then be answered, "I do not say." BDF §368 interprets the future αἱρήσομαι as a question: "What shall I choose?"

d   Several witnesses (p[46c] B F G) omit εἰς in the construction εἰς τὸ ἀναλῦσαι, "to depart."

e   The piling up of adverbial expressions here—πολλῷ γὰρ μᾶλλον κρεῖσσον—is largely unprecedented, a fact that I will return to below in my comments on 1:22b-23. Several witnesses (ℵ* D[2] K L Ψ 630, 1505, 2464 Maj lat syr[h]) omit γάρ, "for," though this does little to smooth the text. Others (D* F G) omit γάρ and read ποσῷ for πολλῷ ("so much more the better"). Yet others (p[46] 0278; Cl) keep γάρ and omit μᾶλλον, "for this is better by far." While it is often the case that the fuller text is a later conflation, here the changes seem to have gone in the other direction, starting with a fuller text and simplifying it to remove its strangeness. The fuller text is well attested in the manuscript tradition (ℵ[1] A B C 075, 6, 33, 81, 104, 326, 365, 1175, 1241, 1739, 1881 vg[mss]; Aug).

f   A number of witnesses (B 0278, 104, 365, 1175, 1241, 1505, 2464) read the aorist ἐπιμεῖναι for the present ἐπιμένειν. This does little to change the meaning.

g   The manuscript tradition is divided on whether to include the preposition ἐν ("in"). This does not affect the sense, though the expression ἐν [τῇ] σάρκι is by far the more common in Paul.

h   A few manuscripts (D[2] K L P 075, 0278[c], 365, 630, 1505, 2464 Maj) read συμπαραμενῶ for παραμενῶ ("continue"), probably a later attempt to overcome the near redundancy of the original, μενῶ καὶ παραμενῶ ("stay on and continue"). παραμενῶ is well attested (p[46] ℵ A B C D* F G Ψ 0278*, 6, 33, 81, 104, 323, 1175, 1739, 1181).

i   Gk. τῆς πίστεως, here interpreted as an objective genitive.

Analysis

Philippians 1:22-26 is one of the more challenging paragraphs in Paul's letters, both in terms of how it fits into the overall rhetoric of 1:12–2:18 and in terms of its own internal logic. Regarding the overall rhetoric of 1:12– 2:18, it is tempting to read 1:22-26 as simply the third in a series of consolatory arguments:[1] the gospel is making "progress" (1:12-18b), Paul's ordeal will result in his "salvation" (1:18c-21), *and* the Philippians will soon be bolstered by his "presence again" (1:22-26).[2] But there is more going on with this short text than its inclusion in a list of

---

1   The first consolatory argument is 1:12-18b; the second, 1:18c-21.

2   So Alexander, "Hellenistic Letter-Forms," 95.

otherwise straightforward consolatory arguments might suggest. To begin with, Paul prefaces his assurances with a deliberation of life and death in which he unhesitatingly states a preference for death (1:22-24). Second, when Paul eventually does get around to assuring the Philippians that they will see him again (1:25-26), it is only to introduce a long digression on how to respond to his continued "absence" (1:27–2:16).[3] Finally, no sooner does Paul finish this digression and return to the topic at hand than he reneges on his earlier promise, offering instead what amounts to a *consolatio mortis*: "But even if I am poured out on the sacrifice and service of your faith, I rejoice . . . likewise you rejoice" (2:17-18). At most, the consolation of 1:22-26 is a temporary calming offered in response to the possibility of Paul's death introduced in 1:20b and in anticipation of the harsh realities treated obliquely in 1:27–2:16 and then explicitly in 2:17-18.[4]

The internal logic of Phil 1:22-26, which is our immediate concern here, also calls for careful analysis. Philippians 1:22-26 is an instance of *dubitatio*, or "indecision" (Gk. ἀπορία), a figure well known from epic and tragedy.[5] Rather than simply reassure the Philippians that they will see him again—the assurance he will nominally offer in 1:25-26—Paul presents them with a dilemma (1:22-23a) and then invites them into his deliberations (1:23b-24). Paul must choose between what he personally wants to do: "having the desire to depart and be with Christ," and what he feels he must do for their sakes: "but to stay on in the flesh is more necessary for your sakes." He describes the first alternative, what he desires, in the strongest possible terms: "for that is much better by far," while he attributes the second, the necessity that has

been thrust upon him by Philippians, to their failure to continue to make "progress" in the faith and to "boast" in Christ (1:25-26). Without explicitly saying it, then, Paul leads the Philippians to see that the dilemma facing him is one of their own making.[6] This implicit rebuke provides the basis for his lengthy exhortation and warning in 1:27–2:16 that they change their behavior.

Philippians 1:22-26 may be outlined as follows:

1:22-23a Paul's dilemma: whether to choose life or death

1:23b-24 Paul's deliberations: what he desires to do versus what he feels he must do

1:25-26 Paul's decision: to choose life so that the Philippians will begin again to make progress in the faith.

Excursus: *Dubitatio*

The figure *dubitatio* is already attested in Homer, where it takes the form of a deliberative monologue placed in the mouth of a hero faced with a life-or-death dilemma.[7] It serves to dramatize the hero's decision making and in so doing reveal something of his character when it is finally expressed in his choice.[8] The figure falls into three parts: (1) the hero's acknowledgment of his dilemma, typically with a cry of despair ("Ah me!") that may be further dramatized with a desperate rhetorical question (e.g., "What is to become of me?"); (2) his impassioned deliberation of alternatives ("if . . . if"), all of which are bad; and finally (3) his decision to accept death with honor versus life with shame. The figure next appears in tragedy, where it quickly comes to characterize the genre.[9] The three-part form remains unchanged, except that the initial desper-

---

3   Cf. esp. 1:27 and 2:12.

4   Paul here is not unlike, say, a critically ill father assuring his children that "everything will be all right" (1:22-26), then urging them to be strong should things continue to go badly (1:27–2:16), and then, finally, offering what words of comfort he can if things turn out as he fears they might (2:17-18).

5   I describe this figure and its use here by Paul in more detail in my "Deliberating Life and Death: Paul's Tragic *Dubitatio* in Phil 1:22-26" (forthcoming in *HTR*).

6   The Philippians will attain to the putative consolation offered in 1:25-26 only if they follow Paul's reasoning regarding the constraints their failings are placing on him and how he will ultimately decide!

7   Homer, *Il.* 11.403-30 (Odysseus); 17.90-105 (Menelaus); 21.553-70 (Agenor); 22.98-130 (Hector). In writing this excursus I have benefited from the analyses of Max Bonnet, "Le dilemme de C. Gracchus," *REA* 8 (1906) 40–46; and R. L. Fowler, "The Rhetoric of Desperation," *HSCP* 91 (1987) 5–38. For Homer in particular, see C. Hentze, "Die Monologe in den homerischen Epen," *Philologus* 63 (1904) 12–30.

8   Cf. Aristotle's theory of προαίρεσις ("choice") defined in *EN* 3.2-3 (1111b4–1113a15) as voluntary action "preceded by deliberation [προβεβουλευμένον]."

9   E.g., Sophocles, *Ajax* 430–80; *Phil.* 1348–72;

ate question, which is now standard, is altered to emphasize the agency of the protagonist: "What shall I do?" "Where shall I turn?" Further, the dilemma no longer pertains simply to martial valor and cowardice but to such things as duty and desire, reason and passion, love and revenge, while possible outcomes include murder and suicide.[10] The *dubitatio* continued to be popular with comic playwrights, who used it to parody tragic dilemmas.[11] As part of this parody they frequently inserted a melodramatic self-description such as "I am being torn asunder!" after the protagonist's now largely stereotyped desperate question.[12] By the Roman-period *dubitatio* was appearing in a range of verse and prose genres,[13] including oratory, where speakers openly fretted over not only what course of action to take[14] but which word to use or where best to begin their speech.[15] By Paul's day, the figure had become so common that it

was even applied to inanimate objects[16] or used as a rhetorical conceit.[17]

Comment

■ **22-23a** Paul concluded 1:18c-21 with a clausular *sententia*: τὸ ζῆν Χριστὸς καὶ τὸ ἀποθανεῖν κέρδος, "to live is Christ and to die is gain." He begins a new thought in 1:22 by repeating the articular infinitive τὸ ζῆν ("to live").[18] To die is gain, but to live brings benefits too: "But if it is to live on in the flesh—this will mean more fruit for my labors."[19] Paul's dilemma, then, is whether to choose death or life,[20] which in the context may mean whether to commit suicide in prison,[21] though it is possible that Paul

---

Euripides, *Andr.* 384–420; *Hel.* 255–305; *Med.* 465–519; *Phoen.* 1595–1624; *Suppl.* 1094–1103.

10 On suicide, see esp. Euripides, *Her.* 1154–62, where, not unlike Paul, the distraught Heracles delays killing himself for the sake of his friend Theseus; cf. Plautus, *Mer.* 468–73; Virgil, *Aen.* 4.534–52.

11 Here see esp. the deliberations of the constipated Blepyrus in Aristophanes, *Eccles.* 375–77; cf. *Eq.* 71–83; for the figure in Menander, see Fowler, "Rhetoric," 36.

12 Plautus, *Mer.* 468–69. This self-description will continue in Roman tragedy. Thus Ovid's Medea: "I am carried here and there" (frag. 2 Ribbeck = Seneca Rhetor, *Suas.* 3.7), for which see Dan Curley, *Tragedy in Ovid: Theater, Metatheater, and the Transformation of a Genre* (Cambridge: Cambridge University Press, 2013) 42, 144–50. Elsewhere at Seneca, *Med.* 938–39: "anger pulls me in this direction, love in that"; *Agam.* 138: "I am driven by conflicting waves," for the latter of which see Gottfried Mader, "*Fluctibus variis agor*: An Aspect of Seneca's Clytemnestra Portrait," *AClass* 31 (1988) 51–70.

13 Ennius, *Med.* frag. 104 (Jocelyn) (= Cicero, *De orat.* 3.217); Catullus, *Carm.* 64.171–210; Virgil, *Aen.* 4.534–52 (Dido); Ovid, *Metam.* 8.113–18.

14 Gaius Gracchus, frag. 61 (Malcovati 1967) (= Cicero, *De orat.* 3.214); Cicero, *Mur.* 88–89; cf. Diodorus Siculus, *Bib. hist.* 13.28–33, esp. 31.1 (the speech of the Lacedaemonian general Gylippus).

15 This use of the figure has been described in detail by Clayton Croy, "'To Die Is Gain' (Philippians 1:19-26): Does Paul Contemplate Suicide?" *JBL* 122 (2003) 517–31; cf. Richard Volkmann, *Die Rhetorik der Griechen und Römer in systematischer Übersicht* (2nd ed.; Leipzig: Teubner, 1885; repr., Hildesheim:

Olms, 1987) 496–98; Heinrich Lausberg, *Handbuch der literarischen Rhetorik* (3rd ed.; Stuttgart: Franz Steiner, 1990) §§776–78. Quintilian discusses the figure in *Inst.* 9.2.19; cf. *Rhet. ad Her.* 4.40.

16 The texts are collected in R. J. Tarrant, *Seneca; Agamemnon: Edited with Commentary* (Cambridge: Cambridge University Press, 1976) 201.

17 E.g., Cicero, *Ad Att.* 8.7.2: *Habeo quem fugiam; quem sequar non habeo* (cited by Quintilian, *Inst.* 8.5.18 in a discussion of frivolous *sententiae*).

18 Paul adds "in the flesh" presumably because he imagines by way of contrast a non-flesh existence should he "depart and be with Christ" (1:23; cf. 1 Cor 15:50). He will repeat the phrase "in the flesh" in 1:24.

19 Cf. Rom 1:13.

20 Commentators have balked at the plain meaning of Paul's terms here, translating τί αἱρήσομαι "what I shall *prefer*" instead of "what I shall *choose*" (e.g., Betz, *Studies*, 128). Craig S. Wansink (*Chained in Christ: The Experience and Rhetoric of Paul's Imprisonments* [JSNTSup 130; Sheffield: Sheffield Academic Press, 1996] 97–102) has shown that this is a questionable translation of the verb αἱρήσομαι. But it is an impossible translation here, since Paul's *preference* is not in doubt: "having the desire to depart and be with Christ, which is much better by far." See further, Arthur Droge, "*Mori Lucrum*: Paul and Ancient Theories of Suicide," *NovT* 30 (1988) 262–86, esp. 279.

21 For suicide in prison see Krause, *Gefängnisse*, 302–3. For suicide in Roman antiquity more generally, see Yolande Grisé, *Le suicide dans la Rome antique* (Montreal: Bellarmin; Paris: Les Belles Lettres, 1982).

has something less direct in mind, such as a courtroom display of "boldness" (παρρησία; 1:20) that would almost certainly be fatal.[22] It should be noted that Paul does not say, "what I shall choose I do not *know*," but "what I shall choose I do not *say* [γνωρίζω]," or more idiomatically, "I cannot say." Paul actually does know what he will choose: "I know (οἶδα) that I shall stay on etc." (1:25), but he refuses to say so until he has walked the Philippians through his deliberations (1:23b-24). In other words, Paul poses the problem of what he should choose not to answer it but to show how he has already answered it.[23]

Verses 22-23a constitute the first part of Paul's *dubitatio*, his dilemma. Traditionally, this part of the *dubitatio* could contain as many as three elements: a cry of despair, a desperate question, and a dramatic self-description.[24] Paul omits the first element, the cry of despair,[25] and modifies the second and third: the desperate question ("What shall I do?") becomes the simple declaration "what I shall choose I cannot say," while the dramatic self-description ("I am being torn asunder!") becomes the comparatively prosaic "I am hard pressed between the two."[26] In rhetoric of his day, Paul presents himself in 1:22b-23 as calm and deliberative,[27] traits he will soon urge upon the "frightened" (1:28) and "anxious" (4:6) Philippians.

■ **23b-24** The second part of Paul's *dubitatio* is his deliberations. Paul is faced with two competing goods: to live on and bear "more fruit" for the gospel (v. 22a) or to depart and be "with Christ" (v. 23b). Were these the only two considerations, the choice would be easy. Paul's "desire" is to depart and be with Christ, which is "much better by far." But in v. 24 Paul introduces an additional consideration, the neediness of the Philippians: "to stay on in the flesh is more necessary for your sakes."[28] Paul does not say what this neediness is at this point. But it becomes clear in vv. 25-26 that he is worried that the Philippians have stopped making the required "progress" in the faith and are no longer "boast[ing] in Christ" to the degree that they should, and that only his "presence" again with them will reverse this. It is this second consideration, the Philippians' diffidence and inaction, that promises to tip the scales for Paul. Three items in 1:23b-24 call for further comment: (1) Paul's willingness to set aside his desire for death for the sake of the Philippians, (2) the thinly veiled complaint conveyed in his words, "this is much better by far," and (3) his expectation that when he dies he will go directly to be "with Christ."

In stating that he will forgo death out of his concern for the Philippians Paul deploys what had by his day become a common topos.[29] At *QFr.* 1.3, the exiled and

---

22 Cf. Pliny, *Ep.* 10.96.3: "such pertinacity and recalcitrant obstinacy must surely be punished"). The classic example of self-damning courtroom display is Xenophon's Socrates (*Apol.* 9; cf. Epictetus, *Diss.* 2.2.8–17). A roughly contemporary example can be found in the *Acta Alexandrinorm* (*CPJ* 2.156d.11-12; cf. Andrew Harker, *Loyalty and Dissidence in Roman Egypt: The Case of the* Acta Alexandrinorum [Cambridge: Cambridge University Press, 2008]). Focant proposes that Paul was contemplating simply not offering a defense (cf. Mark 15:4-5; Matt 27:13-14; Luke 23:9). For a discussion of the limited options facing Paul, see Samuel Vollenweider, "Die Waagschalen von Leben und Tod: Zum antiken Hintergrund von Phil 1,21-26," *ZNW* 85 (1994) 93–115, esp. 106–8.

23 This raises the question whether Paul had in fact contemplated suicide at some earlier point or simply posed it as a possibility to dramatize his deliberations. But that is a question we cannot answer.

24 See the above excursus.

25 The cry of despair had become largely passé in Paul's day and would at any rate have been melodramatic. See further my "Deliberating."

26 Contrast Plautus, *Mer.* 468-69; Ovid, *Med.* frag 2 Ribbeck (= Seneca Rhetor, *Suas.* 3.7); Seneca, *Med.* 938-39; *Agam.* 138, cited above. Cf. Tacitus, *Hist.* 1.76; Statius, *Ach.* 1.200.

27 Paul's self-presentation here and elsewhere in the letter was not lost on Chrysostom: "The great and philosophic soul is vexed by none of the grievous things of this life. Not feuds, not accusations, not slanders, not dangers or plots. . . . And such was the soul of Paul" (hom 4.58.7-11 Allen [on Phil 1:18]).

28 For the battle between "desire" (*cupido*) and such goods as duty (*pietas*) and modesty (*pudor*), see S. Georgia Nugent, "Passion and Progress in Ovid's *Metamorphoses*," in John T. Fitzgerald, ed., *Passions and Moral Progress in Greco-Roman Thought* (London: Routledge, 2008) 153–74. According to Nugent this topos derives from Aristotle's notion of ἀκρασία (*EN* 7.1-10.1145a–1152a). In Ovid desire typically wins; for Paul duty—what is "more necessary for your sake"—promises to win.

29 This feature of Phil 1:22-26 has been helpfully discussed by Wansink, *Chained*, 107–12.

despondent Cicero writes to his brother Quintus: "I shall go on living as long as you need me." And again at *QFr.* 1.4: "the tears of my family and friends forbade me to go to my death." At *Ep.* 1.22 Pliny writes admiringly of his friend Titius Aristo's similar decision: "to weigh calmly and deliberately the motives for life or death, and to be determined in our choice as reason counsels, is the mark of an uncommon and great mind." Seneca is characteristically grand: "Sometimes, even in spite of weighty reasons, the breath of life must be called back . . . for the sake of those whom we hold dear. For the good man will live not as long as he wants, but as long as he must" (*Ep.* 104). In his deliberations in Phil 1:23b-24 Paul presents himself as a model of just this kind of altruism, a further trait he wishes to see in the Philippians: "in humility considering others more important than yourselves, each not looking out for his or her own interests, but each for the interests of others" (2:3-4).

Paul assures the Philippians that he will postpone his death for their sake, but not before describing in the strongest possible terms his "desire [$\epsilon\pi\iota\theta\nu\mu\iota\alpha\nu$] to depart and be with Christ, for that is much better by far [$\pi o\lambda\lambda\hat{\omega} \ldots \mu\hat{\alpha}\lambda\lambda o\nu \ \kappa\rho\epsilon\hat{\iota}\sigma\sigma o\nu$]." Paul's three-fold $\pi o\lambda\lambda\hat{\omega} \ \mu\hat{\alpha}\lambda\lambda o\nu \ \kappa\rho\epsilon\hat{\iota}\sigma\sigma o\nu$ is exceedingly emphatic. Indeed, it is almost unprecedented,[30] so much so that later copyists thought it must surely be a mistake.[31] And so when Paul goes on to place over against it the simple comparative $\dot{\alpha}\nu\alpha\gamma\kappa\alpha\iota\dot{o}\tau\epsilon\rho o\nu$ ("more necessary") in the next clause, it

is hard not to see a complaint. Paul may decide to yield to the greater necessity thrust upon him by the Philippians' failure of nerve. But he makes it clear that this is an unwelcome necessity. Paul's subtle censure of the Philippians will become even more pointed in 1:25-26.

The third item in 1:22b-23 calling for comment is Paul's claim that after death he will go immediately to be "with Christ" ($\sigma\dot{\nu}\nu \ X\rho\iota\sigma\tau\hat{\omega}$).[32] In 1 Thess 4:13-18 Paul imagined things differently: those who die are not "with the Lord" ($\sigma\dot{\nu}\nu \ \kappa\nu\rho\iota\omega$) until his parousia, when they will fly up to meet him in the air (v. 17). Prior to that they are "sleeping" ($\kappa o\iota\mu\omega\mu\epsilon\nu\omega\nu$; v. 13).[33] Perhaps the prospect of his own demise has led Paul to change his view. But his developing theory of salvation, and in particular his so-called *Christusmystik* or "Christ-mysticism,"[34] will also have played a role. Whereas in 1 Thessalonians believers simply "await the son [$\dot{\alpha}\nu\alpha\mu\epsilon\nu\epsilon\iota\nu \ \tau\dot{o}\nu \ \nu\iota\dot{o}\nu$] from heaven, whom [God] raised from the dead" (1:10), in Philippians their objective is "to know him [$\gamma\nu\hat{\omega}\nu\alpha\iota \ \alpha\dot{\nu}\tau\dot{o}\nu$] and the power of his resurrection" even in this life (3:10). Paul presumably cannot imagine that intimacy being broken by death,[35] and so he reasons that Christ-believers who die remain in conscious communion with Christ.[36] Paul does not speculate further about any intermediate state when Christ-believers who have died but have not yet been raised are nevertheless "with Christ."[37] Nor does he indicate what changes if any his modified theory implies about when Christ-believers are judged "according to their deeds,"[38]

---

30 Lightfoot on 1:23.

31 See the manuscript evidence cited above in the textual notes on 1:23.

32 Cf. 2 Cor 5:8: "to be away from the body and at home with the Lord." For a similar theory of life-after-death in Judaism, see George W. E. Nickelsburg, "Judgment, Life-After-Death, and Resurrection in the Apocrypha and the Non-Apocalyptic Pseudepigrapha," in Alan J. Avery-Peck and Jacob Neusner, eds., *Judaism in Late Antiquity,* part 4: *Death, Life-After-Death, and the World-To-Come in the Judaisms of Antiquity* [Leiden: Brill, 2000] 141–62, here 149–51, who cites 2 Macc 7:36; 4 Macc 9:22; 10:21; 13:17; 16:13, 25; 17:18. It is noteworthy that Paul imagines his death as a leave-taking ($\dot{\alpha}\nu\alpha\lambda\hat{\nu}\sigma\alpha\iota$); cf. 2 Tim 4:16 ($\dot{o} \ \kappa\alpha\iota\rho\dot{o}\varsigma \ \tau\hat{\eta}\varsigma \ \dot{\alpha}\nu\alpha\lambda\dot{\nu}\sigma\epsilon\dot{\omega}\varsigma \ \mu o\nu$, "the time of my departure"), which echoes our text here.

33 Cf. 1 Thess 4:14: $\tau o\dot{\nu}\varsigma \ \kappa o\iota\mu\eta\theta\epsilon\nu\tau\alpha\varsigma$, "those who have fallen asleep."

34 The famous expression coined by Martin Dibelius,

Paulus, 87–91, and made popular by Albert Schweitzer, *Mysticism,* 3 and passim.

35 Cf. E. P. Sanders, *Paul: The Apostle's Life, Letters, and Thought* (Minneapolis: Fortress, 2015) 416–18.

36 The logic of Paul's argument actually implies that after death believers will be in even closer communion with Christ: if to live is to serve Christ (1:22), to die is to be with him (1:23).

37 He may imagine something like a disembodied soul, but he assiduously avoids that language in 1 Corinthians 15, speaking instead of a "spiritual body" and of the resurrected Christ as a "spirit."

38 E.g., Rom 2:6: "who will give to each according to his deeds [$\kappa\alpha\tau\dot{\alpha} \ \tau\dot{\alpha} \ \ddot{\epsilon}\rho\gamma\alpha$]." Some initial evaluation at the time of the individual Christ-believer's death would seem to be required. The options are rehearsed by Heikki Räisänen, *Rise of Christian Beliefs: The Thought World of Early Christians* (Minneapolis: Fortress, 2010) 98–102, 127.

though he is obviously not prepared to go as far as the gospel of John, which removes the final judgment for Christ-believers altogether (John 5:24). For Paul the final salvation of believers still hangs in the balance.

■ **25-26** This brings us to Paul's decision, which forms the third and final part of his *dubitatio*. Convinced of the Philippians' needs—"and being confident of this"[39]—Paul assures them that they will see him again, meaning that he will choose life.[40] He has known this all along: "I know [οἶδα] that, etc." But his objective has been to reveal the inner workings of his decision-making in order to register his concerns regarding the Philippians. He now further specifies those concerns as he explains the rationale for his decision: "for your progress and joy in the faith" (v. 25)[41] and "that your boast in Christ might increase because of me by my presence again with you" (v. 26). Paul is worried that the disconsolate Philippians have stalled in their faith and have grown diffident in their proclamation of Christ. In the words of v. 27, they are not "act[ing] in a manner worthy of the gospel."

Paul's linking "progress" and "joy" in his first rationale statement in v. 25 is significant. Like most of his contemporaries Paul believed that grief was a destructive passion that led to despondency and inaction[42] and that consolation not only brought a renewed "joy" but

allowed one to return to his or her duties,[43] what Paul here calls "progress." To Paul's mind, therefore, there will likely have been a causal relationship between "joy" and "progress": because the Philippians lack "joy"—which is to say, because they have remained unconsoled in their present grief—they have stopped making "progress" in the faith. Seneca displays a similar logic linking the ideas of progress and joy at *Ep.* 23.2: "He has made it to the top [*ad summa pervenit*] who knows how to rejoice [*gaudeat*]."[44] But even apart from these general considerations Paul's word choice is determinative since by this point in the letter "progress" and "joy" have acquired a particular salience.[45] In v. 12 Paul insists that the gospel is continuing to make "progress." In v. 18 he likewise insists that he is "rejoic[ing] and . . . will rejoice." Now in v. 25 he implies that the Philippians are doing neither! Paul has laid a rhetorical trap and in v. 25 he springs it. His language itself carries an implicit rebuke.[46]

This rebuke is carried forward in Paul's second rationale statement in v. 26: "that your boast in Christ might increase [περισσεύῃ] because of me by my presence again with you."[47] Far from discouraging the Christ-believers in Rome, Paul's chains have caused them to be even bolder in their proclamation: "having been persuaded by my chains, [they] increasingly [περισσοτέρως] dare to speak

---

39 The "this" (τοῦτο) of which Paul is confident is his immediately prior claim that "to stay on in the flesh is more necessary for your sakes" (v. 24).

40 This does not mean that the verdict will necessarily go in Paul's favor (2:17-18), but only that he will neither directly nor indirectly act to end his life.

41 Paul typically speaks of "faith" (πίστις = belief, trust), not "the faith" (ἡ πίστις = a body of beliefs, a religion); cf. 1:27: "the faith of the gospel" (ἡ πίστις τοῦ εὐαγγελίου). Paul has already used "the faith" in this sense in Gal 1:23; cf. 3:23. See further BDAG, s.v. πίστις.

42 Commenting on Phil 3:1, Chrysostom writes: "Despondency and anxiety, when they strain the soul beyond measure, rob it of its innate strength" (hom. 11.212.6-7 Allen); cf. Cicero, *Ad Brut.* 1.9.2; Seneca, *Ep.* 94.39; *Ad Poly.* 5-6; *Ad Helv.* 18.7-8.

43 For the relevant texts with commentary, see Valeria M. Hope, *Death in Ancient Rome: A Sourcebook* (London and New York: Routledge, 2007) 172-210, esp. 174-77.

44 Cf. Seneca, *Ep.* 59.14: "To the degree that you lack joy (*gaudio*), to that degree you lack wisdom."

45 Focant sees this.

46 For rebuke in consolation see the Introduction, part 1.1: "Greek and Roman Consolation." Examples of explicit rebuke include Seneca, *Ep.* 99.2; cf. 99.32; Cicero, *Ad Brut.* 1.9.1; *Ad fam.* 5.14.2; 5.16.6; *Ad Att.* 13.6.3; Cassius Dio, *Hist.* 38.18. For more subtle and indirect forms of rebuke, see: Seneca, *Ad Marc.* 2-3; Chrysostom, *Ep. ad Olymp.* 8.3.11–13; 17.4.32–43 Malingrey; Jerome, *Ep.* 39.3–4; Ambrose, *Ep.* 39. For the role shaming might play in consolation, see Wilcox, "Sympathetic Rivals."

47 Paul does not elaborate on the relationship between v. 25 and v. 26, but it is reasonable to read v. 26 as a further specification v. 25. In saying that the Philippians have stopped making "progress" in the faith, Paul is thinking primarily of their witness to or "boast" in Christ.

the word without fear" (v. 14). And Paul is himself praying for "boldness" to magnify Christ in his upcoming trial (v. 20), even if that boldness means his death. Scandalously, Paul's chains have had the opposite effect on the Philippians, who by contrast have faltered in their "boast in Christ."[48] Given their current state of mind, only Paul's "presence again" will reverse that.[49]

---

48   Similarly at Phil 3:3: "we are . . . those who serve in the spirit of God and boast in Christ"; cf. Rom 5:11, "boasting in God"; 1 Cor 1:31 and 2 Cor 10:17, "boast in the Lord" (quoting Jer 9:23). In Phil 1:27-28 Paul spells out what boasting in Christ looks like: "that you are standing fast in one spirit, contending side by side in one accord for the faith of the gospel, and are in no way frightened by your enemies, etc." According to Rom 2:23 those who promote Torah-observance "boast in the Law"; according to 1 Cor 3:21 those who align themselves with a particular teacher "boast in a human being"; cf. 2 Cor 7:4, 14; 9:2-3 (and possibly Gal 6:13), where to speak openly of someone is to "boast" in her or him.

49   Paul addresses the Philippians' insistence on seeing him again in 1:27–2:16, where he exhorts them to act in a manner worthy of the gospel—which is to say, act like the Roman Christ-believers and Paul himself—even in his "absence" (1:27; 2:12).

An informed reading of Phil 1:27–2:16 requires that we keep three things in mind. First—and this is easily missed—1:27–2:16 is a *request for consolation*. Chrysostom saw this clearly.[1] Paul has consoled the Philippians with news about his own situation (τὰ κατ᾽ ἐμέ, "my situation"; 1:12) and he now asks to be consoled with news about theirs: "that I might hear how things are with you [τὰ περὶ ὑμῶν]" (1:27; cf. 2:2). Or as he later says of his plan to send Timothy: "that I too might be comforted when I know how things are with you [τὰ περὶ ὑμῶν]" (2:19). In this regard the design of Paul's letter follows closely that of the so-called *Familienbriefe* or "family letters" identified by Heikki Koskenniemi and described in detail by Loveday Alexander: "reassurance about the sender" (1:12-26), followed by "request for reassurance about the recipients" (1:27–2:16).[2]

Second, in addition to being a request for consolation 1:27–2:16 is an extended *exhortation*.[3] This is where most commentators since at least Theodoret have focused, and with good reason, since Paul's stated aim in 1:27 is for the Philippians to "act in a manner worthy of the gospel."[4] The relationship between Paul's request for consolation and his exhortation of the Philippians is complex. Logically, Paul's consolation is the end to which his exhortation of the Philippians is the means. *If* the Philippians wish to console Paul, *then* they must heed his exhortation: "make my joy complete by being of the same mind, etc."

(2:2). Rhetorically, however, Paul's objective is to alter the Philippians' behavior. Paul couches his exhortation as a request for consolation—and how can the Philippians realistically refuse such a request—in order to be more persuasive.[5]

Finally, it is important to keep in mind that 1:27–2:16 is a *digression* embedded in the third of the letter's consolatory arguments (1:22-26 + 2:17-18).[6] In 1:22-26 Paul assures the Philippians that they will see him again. In 2:17-18 he withdraws this assurance, offering instead a kind of *consolatio mortis* in which he anticipates his own demise. To prepare the Philippians for this more frank assessment of his situation, Paul digresses in 1:27–2:16 to exhort them to "stand fast" in the faith "whether I come and see you again or else remain absent."

This leaves us with the question of disposition, the most obvious feature of which is the *exemplum* of 2:5-11, which divides the exhortation that precedes it in 1:27–2:4 from the exhortation that follows it in 2:12-16. The relation between 1:27-30 and 2:1-4 is less clear. There are certain verbal ties, such as the cognate expressions μιᾷ ψυχῇ ("in one accord") in 1:27 and σύμψυχοι ("of one accord") in 2:2. On the other hand, there is a significant change of topic, with 1:27-30 focusing on external "enemies" and 2:1-4 on interpersonal relationships within the Philippian assembly. There is also a characteristic rhetorical flourish in 1:30b suggesting the end of a thought.[7] On balance,

---

1   See esp. his comments at hom. 6:98.23-26 Allen.

2   Koskenniemi, *Studien*, 104–14; Alexander, "Hellenistic Letter-Forms," esp. 92–96.

3   Verbs in the imperative: πολιτεύεσθε ("live"; 1:27), πληρώσατε ("fill up"; 2:2), φρονεῖτε ("think"; 2:5), κατεργάζεσθε ("work to accomplish"; 2:12), ποιεῖτε ("do"; 2:14). These are in notable contrast to 1:12-26, where no imperative appears. The occasional imperative continues to appear in 2:17-30: χαίρετε καὶ συγχαίρετε ("rejoice and rejoice with [me]"; 2:18), προσδέχεσθε and ἔχετε ("welcome" and "hold"; 2:29), though the dominant mood is once again the indicative. See Theodoret on 1:27.

4   Paul has of course just received news about the Christ-believers at Philippi from Epaphroditus. What he now wants is news that they have heeded his exhortation; see Müller on 2:19.

5   See Chrysostom's astute remarks on 2:1, which I discuss in the commentary below on that verse.

6   Barth is admirably lucid here: he interprets 1:27–2:16 as a "hortatory digression" (*parenetische*

Zwischenrede) with which 2:17 "obviously has no relation" (*hat offenbar . . . keine Beziehung*) but instead picks up where 1:26 left off as both a "continuation and supplement" (*Fortsetzung und Überbietung*). Cf. Lohmeyer, who sees in 2:17-18 a "transition" (*Überleitung*) back to the topics of 1:25-26, which are then taken up in full in 2:19-30. Chrysostom is clear that Paul returns to consolation in 2:17: 1.4.15 Allen; 10.186.7-8..

7   See "A Note on Paul's Paragraphing" above in the introduction, part 6: "The Disposition of the Letter." The technical term is *clausula* (from Lat. *claudere* meaning "to close"). It is striking that each unit of exhortation in 1:27–2:16 ends with a similarly structured *clausula* based on the figure *geminatio*, or doubling: οἶον εἴδετε ἐν ἐμοὶ καὶ νῦν ἀκούετε ἐν ἐμοί ("that you saw me to have and now hear me to have"; 1:30b); μὴ τὰ ἑαυτῶν ἕκαστος σκοποῦντες ἀλλὰ τὰ ἑτέρων ἕκαστοι (lit., "each not looking to his affairs but each to others' affairs"; 2:4); ὅτι οὐκ εἰς κενὸν

then, the case for separating 1:27-30 and 2:1-4 is stronger. The result is two paragraphs of exhortation (1:27-30; 2:1-4), followed by an *exemplum* (2:5-11), followed by a third paragraph of exhortation (2:12-16).

A final question relating to the disposition of 1:27—2:16 is the status of 1:27a, which I have interpreted as a thematic exhortation summarizing the hortatory thrust of the whole digression (1:27b—2:16). If the "gospel" (τὸ εὐαγγέλιον) is what really matters—and that has been the point of 1:12-26—then the Philippians no less than Paul need to act like it: "I ask only that you act in a manner worthy of the gospel [ἀξίως τοῦ εὐαγγελίου]." What precisely this injunction means is the subject of the three more targeted exhortations in 1:27b-30; 2:1-4; and 2:12-

16. Taken together, the above considerations allow us to describe 1:27—2:16 as a *hortatory digression* presented as a request for *consolation*, which may be outlined as follows:

1:27a Thematic exhortation: to act in a manner worthy of the gospel

1:27b-30 First targeted exhortation: to stand firm against the enemies of the gospel

2:1-4 Second targeted exhortation: to work to preserve the unity of the group

2:5-11 *Exemplum:* Christ's self-humbling metamorphosis and reward

2:12-16 Third targeted exhortation: to patiently endure suffering without complaint

---

ἔδραμον οὐδὲ εἰς κενὸν ἐκοπίασα ("that I neither ran in vain nor labored in vain"; 2:16). For *clausulae* using *geminatio*, see Quintilian, *Inst.* 8.5.18.

27/ **I ask only that you act in a manner worthy** a
of the gospel of Christ, so that, whether I
come and see you or remain absent, I might
hear[a] **how things are with you: that you are**
standing fast in one spirit, contending side
by side in one accord for the faith of the
gospel, 28/ and are in no way frightened
by your enemies, which is to them[b] **a clear**
sign of destruction but of your[c] **salvation,**
and this from God; 29/ because it has been
given to you[d] **for Christ's sake, not only to**
believe in him but also to suffer for him,
30/ having the same sort[e] **of struggle that**
you saw me to have and now hear me to
have.[f]

a   Many witnesses (א[1] A C D[2] F G K L Ψ 0278, 33,
81, 104, 365, 630, 1175, 1505, 1739 1881 Maj) have
ἀκούσω (probably intended as an aorist subjunctive
but possibly a future indicative) instead of the present
subjunctive ἀκούω (p[46] א* B D* P 629, 1241, 2464).
There is no appreciable difference in meaning. 075
has mistakenly written the participle ἀκούων ("hearing") by attraction with the immediately prior participle ἀπών ("being absent").

b   A few witnesses insert μέν ("on the one hand") after
αὐτοῖς ("to them") to read ἥτις ἐστὶν αὐτοῖς μέν,
"which is to them, on the one hand" (D[1] P Ψ 075 104
1505); Maj reads μέν and improves the word order:
ἥτις αὐτοῖς μέν ἐστιν (cf. MVict Aug), though the sense
remains the same.

c   A few witnesses have the dative ὑμῖν ("to you") (D[1] K
L 075, 630 Maj lat co) to achieve parallelism with the
preceding αὐτοῖς ("to them"). Others (C* D* F G b
vg[ms]) read the first person plural ἡμῖν ("to us").

d   A few witnesses (A 1241) read ἡμῖν ("to us").

e   Translating the relative οἷον ("the sort that").

f   Two witnesses (p[46] 81) omit the second ἐν ἐμοί ("in
me," here translated "me to have").

Analysis

Philippians 1:27-30 constitutes the first paragraph—a
single sentence in the Greek—of a long hortatory digression that continues through 2:16. It begins in 1:27a with
a summary exhortation that announces the theme of the
whole digression: "I ask only that you act in a manner
worthy of the gospel of Christ." Paul has put the gospel
first (1:12-26), and the Philippians, their grief notwithstanding, must do the same, since to do anything less
would not be "worthy" of so great a cause. Paul follows
immediately with a brief motive clause: "so that, whether
I come and see you or remain absent, I might hear how
things are with you." This motive clause introduces a
conceit that will continue throughout 1:27—2:16, namely,
that Paul's exhortations are intended for his own consolation (2:1-2a; 2:16; cf. 2:19; 4:1).

Paul develops the general exhortation of 1:27a in
three more targeted exhortations in 1:27b-30; 2:1-4; and

2:12-16. We are here concerned with 1:27b-30, which may
be further divided into two parts. In the first part, the
exhortation proper (1:27b-28a), Paul urges the Philippians to be steadfast against the "enemies" of the gospel. In
the second (1:28b-30) he offers three supporting arguments,[1] the last of which also serves as a modest *clausula*
using the figure *geminatio*, or doubling: "having the same
sort of struggle that you saw me to have [εἴδετε ἐν ἐμοί]
and now hear me to have [ἀκούετε ἐν ἐμοί]."

Taken together, Phil 1:27-30 may be outlined as follows:

1:27a Thematic exhortation: to act in a manner worthy
    of the gospel
1:27b-28a First targeted exhortation: to stand firm
    against the enemies of the gospel
1:28b-30 Supporting arguments

---

1   It will be helpful to summarize these arguments
here. They are (1) that the Philippians' suffering
accomplishes their salvation and their enemies'

destruction, (2) that the suffering of Christ-believers
has been ordained by God, and (3) that others, in
this case Paul, have suffered similar hardships.

Comment

■ **1:27a** Paul introduces the digression of 1:27–2:16 with the improper adverb μόνον ("only"), which in the context must mean something like "I ask only." The expression is concessive. Paul concedes that the Philippians will not be restored to their former "progress and joy in the faith" short of his "presence" again with them. In the meantime, however, they must *at the very least* (μόνον) strive to "act in a manner worthy of the gospel of Christ."[2] Paul has found consolation in the continued "progress" of the gospel (1:12-18b) and his own good prospects for "salvation" (1:18c-21). But there is still one thing lacking, a good report from Philippi: "that I might hear how things are with you [ἀκούω τὰ περὶ ὑμῶν]."[3]

The expression "act in a manner worthy of the gospel" calls for comment. The verb translated "act" (πολιτεύεσθε) is unusual for Paul, whose preferred term is "walk" (περιπατέω).[4] It conveys the notion of "citizenship" (πολιτεία; cf. Phil 3:20) and the responsibilities that citizenship entails, which presumably would have struck a chord with the Philippians, whose social identity turned on being citizens of a Roman colony (*Colonia Iulia Augusta Philippensis*) and as such citizens of Rome.[5] Paul's point is that, like Roman citizenship, the "gospel"[6] carries not only privileges but also duties that it would be shameful to neglect.[7] Consolers were not above shaming their readers into accepting their advice,[8] and there is an element of that here. In his letter of consolation to Polybius, Claudius's secretary *a libellis*, Seneca charges Polybius "to do nothing unworthy [*indignum*] of his profession of sage and scholar" and cites Telamon[9] as one who bore his children's deaths in a manner "worthy [*dignam*] of a great man."[10] This shaming was often gendered, with male consolers accusing their grieving peers of acting like a woman or worse,[11] while pointing to themselves as those who had borne loss courageously,[12] something Paul does in 1:30. The parallel expression "to bear up nobly" (γενναίως φέρειν) appears frequently in papyrus letters of consolation.[13]

As in 1:12-26 Paul continues to draw a distinction between things that do and do not matter.[14] For Paul, the proclamation of the gospel is a calling that renders all other concerns insignificant.[15] His own life reflects this sense of vocation (1:12-26), and he wants the Philippians' lives to do so as well. At issue for the Philippians

---

2 The subtle rebuke begun in 1:22-26 continues.

3 Paul plans to send Timothy to Philippi in the near future "in order that I too might be comforted when I know how things are with you [τὰ περὶ ὑμῶν]" (2:19). Good news from Philippi, he says at 2:2, will "make my joy complete."

4 See 1 Thess 2:12: "to walk [περιπατεῖν] in a manner worthy of the Lord."

5 It is noteworthy in this regard that the author of Acts imagines the citizens of Philippi complaining that Paul was teaching religious customs "not lawful for us as Romans" (Acts 16:21). Sherwin-White sees here a reference to the Bacchanal Conspiracy of 186 BCE (*Roman Society and Roman Law*, 80).

6 Along with "joy" (χαρά), "gospel" (εὐαγγέλιον) is a leitmotif in Philippians, occurring nine times. The Philippians are Paul's partners in the gospel (1:5) and by their gift are sharing in his defense of it (1:7; cf. 2:16) in a Roman court. Paul takes comfort in the progress of the gospel (1:12), which is what really matters, and he speaks approvingly of those who struggle in the gospel alongside him (2:22; 4:3). In 4:15 he speaks of the "beginning of the gospel," by which it is clear that what he means by "gospel" is the gentile mission. Here in 1:27 he urges the Philip-

pians to act in a manner worthy of the gospel (1:27a) and to join him in struggling for it (1:27b).

7 Paul notes the privileges of heavenly "citizenship" in 3:20; here in 1:27b-28a he outlines its duties. On civic duties, see esp. Cicero, *Ad Brut.* 17.2.

8 Wilcox, "Sympathetic Rivals," 242: "Cicero [in *Ad fam.* 5.16] scolds Titius, flatters him, and shames him."

9 Similarly, Cicero, *Tusc.* 3.13.28, citing Ennius's tragedy *Telamon*.

10 Seneca, *Ad Poly.* 6.3 and 11.2, respectively. For the expression "worthy of a great man," see *Ep.* 107.7; cf. Cicero, *Ad fam.* 4.3.2; 4.5.6; *Ad Brut.* 1.9.2; Pseudo-Plutarch, *Ad Apoll.* 102d–103a; Jerome, *Ep.* 60.14.5–6.

11 Cassius Dio, *Hist.* 38.18.1; Seneca, *Ep.* 99.2; cf. Cicero, *Ad fam.* 5.16.6, with comments by Wilcox, "Sympathetic Rivals," 242–43.

12 Wilcox, "Sympathetic Rivals," 242–43.

13 Chapa, *Letters of Condolence*, 38–43, who cites *SB* 14.11646.9-10 (= *P. Yale* 663); *BGU* 3.801 (= *P. Berol.* 8636); and *PSI* 1248.11.

14 The exhortation of 1:27–2:16 builds on the consolation of 1:12-26.

15 E.g., 1:16: "I have been appointed [κεῖμαι]."

are Paul's continued imprisonment and possible execution. Paul signals the relative insignificance of these by euphemism ("absence"; 1:27; 2:12) and by the use once again of the correlatives εἴτε . . . εἴτε ("whether . . . or"; cf. 1:18, 20).

■ **1:27b-28a** To live in a manner worthy of the gospel means, first of all, showing courage against its enemies. The language Paul employs evokes the battlefield (cf. Eph 6:11, 13)[16] and, as such, stands at the head of a long tradition of martial imagery used to characterize the church's relationship to outsiders, what Tacitus called Christ-believers' *odium humani generis* ("hatred of the human race"; *Ann.* 15.44).[17] Paul's hostility toward non-believers is expressive of his apocalyptic heritage, one strand of which saw the last days as a time in which the righteous few were lethally opposed by the unrighteous many. Paul adduces this topos again in 2:15-16 when he demeans his contemporaries as "a crooked and perverse generation" among whom Christ-believers are to "shine like stars."[18]

To resist the gospel's enemies the Philippians must do two things. They must, as it were, fight as a unit: "that you are standing fast in one spirit, contending side by side in one accord for the faith of the gospel" (1:27b). And they must remain calm in the battle: "and are in no way frightened by your enemies" (1:28a). Paul is worried that the Philippians are in danger of failing at both of these tasks. Paul will develop the need for unity in a passionate appeal in 2:1-4, but three expressions in 1:27b adumbrate that need: "in one spirit" (ἐν ἑνὶ πνεύματι), "contending side by side" (συναθλοῦντες),[19] and "in one accord" (μιᾷ ψυχῇ).[20] A number of commentators have interpreted the first of these expressions ("in one spirit") to refer to the divine spirit rather than the human spirit.[21] To the degree that Paul would distinguish these two "spirits" in the Christ-believer, it is better to see a reference to the human spirit, since Paul continues μιᾷ ψυχῇ (lit., "in one soul").[22]

The expression "and are in no way frightened by your enemies" in 1:28a continues the battlefield imagery of 1:27b, most obviously in the term "enemies" (ἀντικείμενοι), but also in the term I have translated "frightened" (πτυρόμενοι), which was regularly used to describe the shock of first contact in battle.[23] Just as the

---

16 See further Edgar Krentz, "Military Language and Metaphors in Philippians," in *Origins and Method: Towards a New Understanding of Judaism and Christianity; Essays in Honour of John C. Hurd*, ed. Bradley H. McLean (JSNTSup 86; Sheffield: Sheffield Academic Press, 1993) 105–27; idem, "Paul, Games, and the Military," in *Paul in the Greco-Roman World: A Handbook*, ed. J. Paul Sampley (Harrisburg, PA: Trinity Press International, 2003) 344–83; cf. 3:17–18: "enemies [ἐχθρούς] of the cross of Christ."

17 This was originally a criticism of Jewish chauvinism, for which see John Granger Cook, *Roman Attitudes toward the Christians: From Claudius to Hadrian* (WUNT 261; Tübingen: Mohr Siebeck, 2010) 62–65.

18 One cannot speak of gentile prejudices against Christians (and Jews) without at the same time speaking of Christian (and Jewish) prejudice against gentiles.

19 The expression συναθλοῦντες τῇ πίστει τοῦ εὐαγγελίου is grammatically ambiguous. It can mean either "struggle alongside one another for the faith of the gospel" or "struggle alongside the faith of the gospel." The emphasis on unity requires the former. Lightfoot notes that συναθλοῦντες is an athletic metaphor picked up in 1:30 (ἀγῶνα, "struggle" or "contest"); see Martin Brandl, *Der Agon bei Paulus:*

Herkunft und Profil paulinischer Agonmetaphorik (WUNT 2/222; Tübingen: Mohr Siebeck, 2006) 246–408, esp. 337–44; and Uta Poplutz, *Athlet des Evangeliums* (HBS 43; Freiburg: Herder, 2004) 399–400 and passim, both of whom rightly emphasize the eschatological focus of the metaphor in Paul against Victor C. Pfitzner, *Paul and the Agon Motif: Traditional Athletic Imagery in the Pauline Letters* (NovTSup 16; Leiden: Brill, 1967). Philippians 1:30 is interpreted in 2 Tim 4:6: "I have struggled the noble struggle [τὸν καλὸν ἀγῶνα ἠγώνισμαι], I have finished the race [cf. Phil 3:12-14!], I have kept the faith."

20 Cf. Acts 4:32, where καρδία καὶ ψυχὴ μία ("one heart and soul") is taken to mean a community of goods. "With one soul" is a friendship cliché that is picked up in 2:2.

21 E.g., Bonnard, Gnilka, Müller, Reumann.

22 So Lightfoot, Lohmeyer.

23 Of horses frightened by the first clash of combat (Diodorus Siculus, *Bib. hist.* 2.19; Plutarch, *Fab.* 3; *Marc.* 6; *Phil.* 12). Philippians 1:28a probably lies behind *Act. Paul.* 4.33 (Hamburg). The term was also used more generally to describe an animal frightened by a loud noise: Philo Byblos apud Eusebius, *Praep. Ev.* 1.10.4 (= Jacoby, *FGrHist* 790 frag. 2,

calmness of seasoned troops in battle bodes ill for their enemies, so the refusal of the Philippians to be "frightened" by their enemies announces the eventual "destruction" of those enemies and the Philippians' own "salvation" (v. 28b). The battlefield imagery goes only so far, however, since Paul's horizon is eschatological and the victory consists in "salvation . . . from God."[24]

■ **1:28b-30** In the remainder of the paragraph Paul offers three consolatory arguments in support of the exhortation of 1:27b-28a. I have already alluded to the first of these: that the Philippians' equanimity before their enemies signals their enemies' destruction and their own salvation (1:28b). Underlying Paul's promise here is the familiar apocalyptic theme that in the last days the righteous will be persecuted by the wicked but that, in the process, they (the righteous) will be perfected while the wicked are simply confirmed in their wickedness.[25] For Christ-believers this theme will only have been confirmed by the fact that Jesus himself had suffered.[26] In describing the fate of the wicked as "destruction"[27] Paul expresses the putative Pharisaic belief that only the righteous would be raised from the dead and that the wicked would either be annihilated or doomed to a shadelike existence.[28]

Excursus: The Fate of the Wicked according to Paul

More than once Paul describes the fate of the wicked as "destruction" (ἀπώλεια) and the fate of the righteous as "salvation" (σωτηρία),[29] by which he means "resurrection" (ἀνάστησις), e.g., Phil 3:20-21. He does not speak of the resurrection of the wicked. It is not immediately evident what Paul means by the "destruction" of the wicked,[30] but 1 Cor 15:16-18 offers a clue: "if the dead are not raised, then Christ is not raised . . . and those who have fallen asleep in Christ have been destroyed [ἀπώλοντο]." Since it is the dead in Christ who are in view here, "destruction" can only mean a death from which there is no resurrection. Whether this means a shadelike existence in Sheol or Hades or annihilation cannot be determined. According to Josephus, the Pharisees believed that the righteous are raised and the souls of wicked are confined to an eternal prison.[31] According to the *Psalms of Solomon*, the righteous are raised and the wicked destroyed and forgotten: "the destruction [ἀπώλεια] of the sinner is forever, he will not be remembered . . . but those who fear the Lord shall rise [ἀναστήσονται] to everlasting life" (3:11-12).[32] Whatever the precise fate of the wicked—and Paul may not have settled on a particular view—under no circumstances are the wicked resurrected. Resur-

---

p. 807.5); Plutarch, *Praec. ger. reip.* 800c; cf. *Hom. Clem.* 2.39 (*PG* 2:104B); *P. Ness* 1.778 (6 CE), where it glosses *terreo*, which is used in the Vulgate of Phil 1:28. In Hippocrates, *Mul.* 1.25 it refers to a fright so severe that it may induce a miscarriage.

24 In the expression "and this from God," the pronoun "this" (τοῦτο) is neuter and encompasses both the "destruction" of Christ-believers' enemies and their own "salvation." For a similar vindication scene dramatically spelled out, see Wis 5:1-23 and comments by David Winston, *The Wisdom of Solomon: A New Translation with Introduction and Commentary* (AB 43; New York: Doubleday, 1979) on that passage.

25 See Dan 11:35; *Pss. Sol.* 3:3-4; 10:1-4; 13:6-11; *2 Bar.* 13:1-12; 4 Ezra 7:14; cf. Rev 7:14. For the general principle that God disciplines the godly in their sins while letting the wicked descend further into wickedness, see esp. 2 Macc 2:6-13. An opposite view of the divine patience is found in Rom 2:4. See further Holloway, *Coping with Prejudice*, 228–29.

26 This doctrine no doubt brought great comfort to those who were socially stigmatized and in some cases actively persecuted. Nevertheless, it produces significant difficulty for the historian, since it was in the very fabric of Judaism and especially that of

Christianity to see any opposition in exaggerated terms.

27 See Phil 3:19; Rom 2:12; 9:22; 14:15; 1 Cor 1:18; 8:11; 2 Cor 2:15; cf. 1 Cor 15:18; 2 Thess 2:10.

28 See the discussion in Heikki Räisänen, *The Rise of Christian Beliefs: The Thought World of Early Christians* (Minneapolis: Fortress, 2010) 117–18, 120–21. See also the following excursus and my comments on 3:11 below.

29 In addition to Phil 1:28b, see 1 Cor 1:18-19; 2 Cor 2:15.

30 For a range of possible meanings, see BDAG, s.v. ἀπόλλυμι, ἀπώλεια.

31 Josephus, *Ant.* 18.14; *Bell.* 2.163. See further Alan J. Avery-Peck and Jacob Neusner, eds., *Judaism in Late Antiquity*, part 4: *Death, Life-after-Death, Resurrection and the World-to-Come in the Judaisms of Antiquity* (Handbuch der Orientalistik 55; Leiden: Brill, 2000), esp. the essays by John J. Collins ("The Afterlife in Apocalyptic Literature," 119–39), George W. E. Nickelsburg ("Judgment," 141–62), and Lester L. Grabbe ("Eschatology in Philo and Josephus," 163–85).

32 Cf. *Pss. Sol.* 2:31; 13:11-12; 14:9-10; 15:6-13 and passim. The *Psalms of Solomon* were originally composed

rection is the exclusive reward of the righteous: "if somehow I might arrive at the resurrection from the dead" (Phil 3:11).[33]

The second and third consolatory arguments may be treated together.[34] They are that the suffering of Christ-believers has been ordained by God (1:29),[35] and that Paul himself stands as an example of one who both has suffered and continues to do so (1:30). Like the first argument, these arguments presuppose the eschatological suffering of the righteous. Taken together, they also gesture toward the familiar sentiment that suffering is common to all *and is therefore to be expected*. This popular remedy to grief was given technical expression in Cyrenaic consolation theory, which held that only unexpected misfortune was truly grievous and that, even after the fact, a reminder that misfortune should have been expected was calming. Paul has prepared for this argument in 1:28a with his use of the term "frighten" ($\pi\tau\acute{u}\rho\omega$), which, in addition to connoting the first fright of battle, was also commonly used to describe to the shock of any unexpected adversity.[36] In *Ep.* 107 Seneca develops a train of thought strikingly similar to Paul's. He first rebukes the grieving Lucilius for not having prepared himself for misfortune, since a person unprepared for misfortune will always be "frightened" (*expavit*) by it. He then points to the example of others who have suffered: "whatever misfortune you name, it has happened to many [*multis accidit*]" (*Ep.* 107.5).[37] Finally, he makes the theological claim that suffering has been ordained by God or, in this case, by divine law: "we should allow our mind to be conformed to this very law [*ad hanc legem*]" (*Ep.* 107.9).[38] Paul had offered a similar set of arguments in 1 Thess 3:2-4.[39]

Excursus: Cyrenaic Consolation—"Nothing unexpected has happened"[40]

Like Epicurus, the Cyrenaics were philosophical hedonists. They equated good and evil respectively with pleasure and pain, and they understood grief to be a special instance of the latter. But Cyrenaic hedonism differed from Epicurean hedonism in at least two significant ways. First, whereas Epicurean theory focused on "katastematic pleasure," that is, pleasure as a state of being,[41] the Cyrenaics understood both pleasure and pain to be types of motion, pleasure being a "smooth motion" ($\lambda\epsilon\hat{\iota}a$ $\kappa\acute{\iota}\nu\eta\sigma\iota\varsigma$) and pain being a "rough motion" ($\tau\rho\alpha\chi\epsilon\hat{\iota}a$ $\kappa\acute{\iota}\nu\eta\sigma\iota\varsigma$).[42] Second, whereas Epicurus held that pleasure and pain were contradictories, so that the absence of pain necessarily implied the presence of pleasure,[43] the Cyrenaics taught that

in Hebrew in the first century BCE and translated into Greek probably sometime in the first century CE and then later into Syriac. None of the original Hebrew survives. For the manuscript tradition, see Robert R. Hann, *The Manuscript History of the Psalms of Solomon* (SBLSCS 13; Chico, CA: Scholars Press, 1982); Joseph Trafton, *The Syriac Version of the Psalms of Solomon: A Critical Evaluation* (SBLSCS 11; Atlanta: Scholars Press, 1985); Robert B. Wright, *The Psalms of Solomon: A Critical Edition of the Greek Text* (Jewish and Christian Texts in Contexts and Related Studies 1; London/New York: T&T Clark, 2007).

33 See further my comments on Phil 3:10-11 below.

34 1 Thess 3:1-5; 1 Pet 5:6-9.

35 The form $\dot{\epsilon}\chi\alpha\rho\acute{\iota}\sigma\theta\eta$, "it has been given," constitutes a divine passive. For suffering as a "gift," see further Phil 1:7; cf. 2:17-18; 3:10.

36 In Pseudo-Plato, *Ax.* 370a, Axiochus is presented to Socrates as one "frightened" ($\pi\tau\nu\rho\epsilon\acute{\iota}\eta\varsigma$) by the sudden onset of a terminal illness (cf. *Ax.* 364b). Similarly, in *Med.* 8.45 Marcus Aurelius prays for a soul not "frightened" ($\pi\tau\nu\rho\rho\mu\acute{\epsilon}\nu\eta$) by unforeseen adversity.

37 Cf. *Ad Marc.* 2.1-5.6; *Ad Poly.* 14.1-17.6. See also Grollios, Τέχνη ἀλυπίας, 67-71; Kurth, *Senecas*

Trostschrift an Polybius, 26–34, 167–216; Abel, *Bauformen*, 88–91; Johann, *Trauer und Trost*, index, s.v. *exemplum*.

38 Seneca concludes the letter with his well-known translation of the final lines of Cleanthes's famous *Hymn to Zeus*, in which he pointedly expresses this law: *Ducunt volentem fata, nolentem trahunt*, "Fate leads the willing and drags the unwilling!"

39 "We sent Timothy to strengthen you and console you in your faith, so that you would not be shaken by these afflictions, for you yourselves know that we have been appointed [by God] to this . . . just as it has come to pass."

40 The following excursus epitomizes my early study "*Nihil inopinati accidisse.*"

41 Diogenes Laertius, *Vit.* 10.136 (Epicurus, frag. 1 Us); 2.87 (= Epicurus, frag 450 Us); cf. J. C. B. Gosling and C. C. W. Taylor, *The Greeks on Pleasure* (Oxford: Clarendon, 1982) 365–86.

42 Diogenes Laertius, *Vit.* 2.86-87; Athenaeus, *Deip.* 12.546e; Cicero, *De fin.* 2.18; Sextus Empiricus, *Pyrrh.* 1.215; *Suidas* 2.553.4.

43 Thus Cicero, *De fin.* 11.38; Erich Mannebach, *Aristippi et Cyrenaicorum Fragmenta* (Leiden: Brill, 1961) 109.

pleasure and pain were simply contraries and that there was a "middle state" (μέση κατάστασις) between the two that is "neither pleasant nor painful" (ἀηδονία καὶ ἀπονία) (Diogenes Laertius, *Vit.* 2.89–90).

From this general theory of pleasure and pain the Cyrenaics derived their special theory of grief and consolation. Cicero describes the Cyrenaic theory of grief in *Tusc.* 3.13.28: "The Cyrenaics believe that grief is not caused by every misfortune, but by misfortune that is unexpected and unanticipated [*insperato et necopinato*]." In other words, not all misfortunes produce the "rough" motion of grief, but only those that come about unexpectedly. Like the surprise attack of an enemy or a sudden storm at sea—two popular Cyrenaic analogies[44]—misfortune overwhelms us when it catches us off guard. But when misfortune is foreseen, or when we have adequately prepared ourselves for it, this is not the case. Such experiences are not pleasant; that is, they do not produce the smooth motion that is pleasure. But neither are they grievous in the proper sense of the term. Rather, they fall in the middle neutral state between pleasure and pain.

The Cyrenaics offered two practical remedies for grief, the first to be applied prophylactically before the advent of grievous circumstances, and the second after the fact. For those not currently experiencing misfortune they recommended the contemplation of future evil (*praemeditatio futuri mali*).[45] For those already afflicted with grief they sought to calm the violent motion produced by unexpected calamity with the reminder that "nothing unexpected has happened."[46] Cyrenaic consolation theory was obviously better suited to preventing grief than alleviating it.[47] Nevertheless, the reminder that misfortune ought to have been expected is found in a range of consolatory texts, including Pseudo-Plato, Pseudo-Ovid, Seneca, Plutarch, Pseudo-Plutarch, and Marcus Aurelius.[48] Early Christians also made frequent use of this consolatory strategy, which accorded well with their claim that, as the eschatological people of God, they were to expect suffering, just as Christ and his disciples had suffered.[49]

44 Cf. Cicero, *Tusc.* 3.22.52; cf. Pseudo-Plutarch, *Ad Apoll.* 112d; Seneca, *Ad Helv.* 5.3; *Ep.* 47.4; *De prov.* 4.6, 13; *De clem.* 1.7.3; John Chrysostom, *Ep. ad Olymp.* 15.1 (Malingrey). Cf. Malunowiczowna, "Les éléments stoïciens," 39.

45 Cicero, *Tusc.* 3.14.29; cf. Plutarch, *Ad Apoll.* 112 (= Nauck, *Trag. Graec. Frag.*, Euripides 964d). As a practical technique, the *praemediatio futuri mali* extended well beyond Cyrenaic consolation theory. Diogenes of Sinope taught it (Diogenes Laertius, *Vit.* 6.63), as did Chrysippus (Cicero, *Tusc.* 3.22.52), Panaetius (Plutarch, *De coh. ir.* 463d), Posidonius (Galen, *De plac.* 4.7.7-11), Carneades (Plutarch, *De tran. an.* 474e), Epictetus (*Diss.* 3.10.1-3; *Ench.* 21), Seneca (*Ad Helv.* 5.3; *De tran. an.* 11.6), and Plutarch (*De tran. an.* 465b); cf. Virgil, *Aen.* 6.103–5. See also Rabbow, *Seelenführung*, 160–79; Kassel, *Konsolationsliteratur*, 66; Johann, *Trauer und Trost*, 63–84.

46 Cicero, *Tusc.* 3.31.76: *nihil inopinati accidisse*; cf. 3.23.55: *nihil oportere inopinatum videri*, "Nothing should seem unexpected"; Epictetus, *Diss.* 3.24.104.

47 Kassel, *Konsolationsliteratur*, 66–67; Epictetus, *Diss.* 3.24.115; Cicero, *Tusc.* 3.13.28; 3.22.52–53; cf. Philo, *Spec.* 2.87.

48 Pseudo-Plato, *Ax.* 370a (cf. 364b); Pseudo-Ovid, *Cons. ad Liv.* 397–400; Seneca, *Ad Poly.* 11.1; *Ad Helv.* 5.3; *Ad Marc.* 9.2; *Ep.* 63.14; cf. *De brev. vit.* 9.4; *De vit. beat.* 8.6; Plutarch, *De vir. mor.* 449e; *De tran. an.* 476a, d; Pseudo-Plutarch, *Ad Apoll.* 112d; Marcus Aurelius, *Med.* 8.45.

49 See esp. 1 Pet 4:12-19; cf. 1 Thess 3:1-10; John 16:1-4. For 1 Pet 4:12-14, see my "*Nihil inopinati accidisse*"; for John 16:1-4, see my "Left Behind." For 1 Thess 3:1-10, see Abraham J. Malherbe, *Paul and the Thessalonians: The Philosophic Tradition of Pastoral Care* (Philadelphia: Fortress Press, 1987) 57–58; idem, "'Pastoral Care' in the Thessalonian Church," *NTS* 36 (1990) 375–91, here 387–88; idem, *Thessalonians*, 198; for the *praemeditatio futuri mali* more generally in Paul, see Malherbe, "Exhortation," 254–56; but note the criticism by Chapa, "Consolatory Patterns?" 220–28.

2

1/ **If there is therefore any[a] consolation in Christ, if any[a] comfort of love, if any[a] fellowship[b] of spirit, if any[a] deep affection or compassion, 2/ [then] make my joy complete by being of the same mind, having the same love, being of one accord, of one[c] mind; 3/ [doing] nothing based on selfish ambition, nor [anything] based on[d] empty conceit, but in humility considering[e] others[f] more important than yourselves, 4/ each[g] not looking out[h] for his or her own interests, but each[i] [also][j] for the interests of others.**

a   The manuscript tradition regarding these four instances of the indefinite adjective is difficult. In the first and third instances ("consolation" and "fellowship"), all the witnesses read the feminine adjective τις ("any") modifying the feminine nouns παράκλησις ("consolation) and κοινωνία ("fellowship"). In the second instance ("comfort") most witnesses read the neuter adjective τί ("any") modifying the neuter noun παραμύθιον ("comfort"), but a few manuscripts (D*,c L 33, 2495) read τις (apparently repeating the feminine form of the adjective from the preceding instance). Finally, in the fourth instance a number of witnesses (K Ψ 81, 323, 365, 614, 630, 945, 1241, 1739, 1881 vg[st,ww]) read the neuter singular τι, while a few witnesses (it vg[cl] Ambst Spec) read the more correct neuter plural τινα (modifying the neuter plural σπλάγχνα, here translated "deep affection," to which the masculine plural οἰκτιρμοί ["sympathy"] is added). Most manuscripts, however, read τις, which is also the more difficult reading, on which grounds it is to be preferred. Paul has therefore probably committed a "solecism" here, reflecting, perhaps, his intention that σπλάγχνα καὶ οἰκτιρμοί be interpreted as a hendiadys. Lightfoot proposes that in the fourth instance τι was original and that a scribe (or perhaps even the original secretary) misheard τις σπλάγχνα for τι σπλάγχνα. Blass (BDF §137[2]) argues that the neuter singular τι is intended throughout and that it is to be understood as an adverb, something like "if consolation in Christ amounts to *anything*, and so on." This reading requires conjectural emendations of the first and third instances, for which it is difficult to find a rationale.

b   One could translate "partnership" and this would fit nicely with Paul's use elsewhere in the letter, but the expression appears in 2 Cor 13:13, where "fellowship" is obviously the correct translation.

c   A number of witnesses read αὐτό, "same thing" (ℵ* A C I Ψ 33, 81, 1241, 2464 f vg) instead of ἕν, "one" (p[46] ℵ[2] B D F G K L P 075, 0278, 104, 365, 630, 1175, 1505, 1739, 1881 Maj it vg[ms] sy; Cl Hil Ambst). The latter is the better reading; the former reproduces the αὐτό in the earlier expression τὸ αὐτὸ φρονῆτε, "mind the same thing."

d   Most early manuscripts and a number of witnesses read μηδὲ κατά, "nor based on" (ℵ* A B C 0278, 33, 81, 104, 365, 1175, 1241, 1739, 1881 lat co; Ambst). A few read only μηδέ, "nor" (p[46] ℵ[2] pc), while others read only ἤ, "or" (D F G K L P Ψ 075, 630 Maj sy[h]), or ἢ κατά, "or based on" (629, 264 ar bo[mss]). The repetition μηδὲν κατ᾿ . . . μηδὲ κατά, "nothing based on . . . nor based on," adds fullness to Paul's statement. Cf. the repetition of ἕκαστος in the next verse: ἕκαστος . . . ἕκαστοι, "each . . . each."

e   A few manuscripts intensify ἡγούμενοι ("considering")

reading προηγούμενοι (𝔭⁴⁶ D*,c I K 075, 0278, 1175, 1505).

f   Two early manuscripts (𝔭⁴⁶ B) add the article τούς ("those"). The meaning is not changed, but the Greek would be a bit fuller if this reading were adopted.

g   The manuscript tradition is split between the singular ἕκαστος (𝔭⁴⁶ ℵ C D K L P 075, 104, 365, 630, 1241, 1505, 1739, 1881, 2464 Maj sy⁽ᵖ⁾; Hil Ambst Aug) and the plural ἕκαστοι (A B F G Ψ 0278, 33, 81, 1175 lat), both of which would be translated "each." Contemporary idiom preferred the singular, even with plural verb forms (BDAG, s.v. ἕκαστος). Paul uses the term in the plural at the end of the verse (see note below). It is possible that the plural is original here as well and that later scribes changed it to the singular to match contemporary idiom. But that would not explain why the plural is left to stand in the second instance. The repeated plurals would produce a simple doubling (geminatio), characteristic of Paul's clausulae (cf. the clausula at 1:30, where ἐν ἐμοί, "in me," is similarly repeated).

h   A few manuscripts change the well-attested plural participle σκοποῦντες (𝔭⁴⁶ ℵ A B C D F G P 075, 0278, 33, 81, 104, 365, 1175, 1241, 1739, 1881, 2464 latt) to the second person plural imperative σκοπεῖτε (L Ψ 630 Maj) or the third person singular imperative σκοπείτω (K 945, 1505 syʰ MVict) to form a separate sentence.

i   Most manuscripts repeat the pronoun "each," either in the plural ἕκαστοι (𝔭⁴⁶ ℵ A B D P Ψ 33 81 104 365 1175 1241ˢ 1739 1881 2464 pc MVict [C illeg.]) or the singular ἕκαστος (Maj d sy Hier). A few manuscripts, however, omit it (F G lat Ambst Pel). Several important manuscripts (ℵ[*] A C 33 pc) show a break before it so as to read it as the first word in v. 5, but this misses the doubling essential to the clausula of 2:4 (cf. 1:30 and 2:16) and is no doubt an attempt to improve Paul's prose style, which here suffers as a result of his striving for point. See my comment below.

j   The manuscript tradition favors reading καί, "also" (𝔭⁴⁶ ℵ A B C D¹ L P Ψ 075, 0278, 33, 81, 104, 365, 630, 1175, 1241, 1505, 1739, 1881, 2464 Maj vgˢᵗ,ʷʷ sy; Cass) though some manuscripts omit it (D*,c F G K it vgᶜˡ). Manuscript tradition notwithstanding, the "also" looks like a scribal addition intended to soften the exhortation: one may look out for one's own interests as long as one also looks out for the interests of others. The exemplum of Christ in 2:6-11 supports the more rigorous standard of setting aside one's own interests for the interests of others.

Analysis

Paul develops the general exhortation to "act in a manner worthy of the gospel" (1:27a) in a second targeted exhortation in 2:1-4. He has urged the Philippians to be steadfast against their "enemies" (1:27b-30). He now urges them to make every attempt to restore harmony in their group and to maintain a unified front. Formally, 2:1-4 is a long conditional sentence. The protasis comes in 2:1 and consists of four short motivational clauses deployed in staccato-like fashion: "If there is any . . . if any . . . if any . . . if any . . . ."[1] The apodosis comes in 2:2-4 and consists of a longer series of injunctions variously addressing the problem of disunity: "[then] make my joy complete by being of the same mind and so on." The last of these injunctions (2:4) doubles as a concluding rhetorical flourish or clausula after the example of 1:30.

Comment

■ **2:1** The protasis of 2:1 raises two questions for the interpreter. (1) What does the particle "therefore" (οὖν) tell us about the logical relationship between 2:1-4 and the material that precedes it in 1:27-30? And (2) when Paul goes on to speak of "consolation," "comfort," and so on, whose consolation and the like does he have in mind? The first question can be answered quickly. Since 2:1-4 is a conditional sentence, the "therefore" in 2:1 attaches most naturally to the apodosis of 2:2-4: "Therefore . . . make my joy complete by being of the same mind . . . ," which in turn continues the call to harmony in 1:27b.[2] Paul's reasoning is something like this: "Since standing fast against the enemies of the gospel is necessarily a group effort (1:27b), therefore (οὖν) strive for harmony in

---

1   Müller: "an almost singsong [beschwörenden] character."

2   Here note especially that "in one accord" (μιᾷ ψυχῇ) of 1:27b is echoed in σύμψυχοι (here translated "of one accord") of 2:2.

your assembly (2:2-4)." Harmony within his assemblies was an important ideal for Paul.[3]

This leaves us with the second and more difficult question: whose consolation? To answer this question we must consider both the specific rhetoric of 2:1 as well as the overall rhetoric of 1:27–2:16. The four short clauses in 2:1 are a clear instance of rhetorical amplification.[4] Paul's aim is not to produce a list of finely nuanced reasons for action but to create pathos, which he does by painting in very broad strokes: "consolation . . . comfort . . . love . . . fellowship . . . deep affection and compassion."[5] The language is more evocative than referential,[6] which means that its interpretation lies not in a close analysis of the sort New Testament scholars are wont to perform[7] but in the larger context, which brings us to the second consideration: the overall rhetoric of 1:27–2:16.

As I have already indicated, the rhetoric of 1:27–2:16 is determined by the conceit that Paul is not just urging the Philippians to follow his advice but to do so *in order to console him*. Paul the prisoner has consoled the Philippians (1:12-26), and now it is only fair that they console him (1:27–2:16; cf. 2:19). But, as Paul makes clear in 2:2-4, his consolation will be achieved only when harmony within the Philippian assembly has been reestablished. It seems likely, then, that *Paul's consolation* is in view in 2:1.[8] Here is Chrysostom's summary of the logic of 2:1-4: "Paul rep-resents concord among his disciples as if it were compassion toward himself."[9] Here is Chrysostom's paraphrase of 2:1: "If you wish to give *me* [μοι] any consolation in these trials, any encouragement in Christ, any comfort from love, if you wish to show any fellowship of spirit, if you have any deep affection or compassion, then make *my* joy complete. . . ."[10] Theodoret offers a similar paraphrase: "If you wish to offer me [ἐμοί] any consolation, any love, any comfort, any encouragement, then do it in the following way."[11]

■ **2:2-4** The apodosis of 2:2-4 consists of a main verb clause (v. 2a) followed by six explanatory injunctions (vv. 2b-4). The main clause conveys Paul's request for consolation: πληρώσατέ μου τὴν χαράν, "[then] make my joy complete." Paul is consoled in his incarceration by the joy he feels over the Philippians' "partnership in the gospel" (1:4-5), over the continued "progress of the gospel" (1:12-18b), and over the prospects of his own "salvation" (1:18c-21). But there is still something missing: harmony in the Philippian assembly. Paul's strategy so far has been to discount possible sources of grief (imprisonment, execution) as matters of indifference. But the strife at Philippi cannot be so easily set aside. For harmony in the Philippian assembly does matter, and until it is realized Paul's joy will remain incomplete.[12] In 2:2b-4 Paul explains what it will take to console him in this matter.

---

3   It is to this end that Paul deploys the letter's much-discussed friendship clichés: friends as it were share the same soul; friends think the same thing. In Greco-Roman culture, harmony was an important political virtue. For the topos see 1 Pet 3:8-12 and the comments by David L. Balch, *Let Wives Be Submissive: The Domestic Code of I Peter* (SBLMS 26; Atlanta: Scholars Press, 1981) 88–90, who cites among other texts Dio Chrysostom, *Or.* 38–41 on harmony and Aristides, *Or.* 42 and 44. Paul gives unity a theological rationale in 1 Corinthians 1–4, where it is used to suppress challenges to his authority; see Nils A. Dahl, "Paul and the Church at Corinth according to 1 Corinthians 1:10–4:21," in *Christian History and Interpretation: Studies Presented to John Knox*, ed. W. R. Farmer, C. F. D. Moule, and R. R. Niebuhr (Cambridge: Cambridge University Press, 1967) 313–35. Paul's unity language had a significant effect—not always salutary—on subsequent tradition (e.g., *1 Clem.* 22).
4   Pitta.
5   Beare is close to the mark when he writes, "Paul now appears to be casting around for any and every kind of thought, feeling, or Christian experience to which he may appeal, that may move them to respond to his plea for unity."
6   Calvin: "The exhortation here is full of emotion (*valde pathetica*)."
7   Reumann's analysis runs to seven pages; O'Brien's to twelve!
8   Cf. Aquinas: "The sense is as if he were saying, 'I wish to be consoled in you.'" Similarly, Calvin: "If there is 'any consolation in Christ' by means of which you may alleviate my grief [*meos dolores*]."
9   Hom. 6.98.26-27 Allen. The figure is metonymy: "have *compassion on me*, by which I mean *be at peace among yourselves*."
10   Hom. 6.98.23-26 Allen.
11   *PG* 82:569.4-7. Cf. Jerome: "If there is any consolation to be offered to me from you [*mihi a vobis*], etc." (*PL* 30:883.39-40).
12   Cf. 1 Thess 3:7-9: "we were consoled [παρεκλήθημεν], brothers, by you in all our distress and affliction through your faith, because we now

Of the six explanatory injunctions in 2:2b-4, the first four are in v. 2b. They are extremely brief (three words, four words, one word, and three words, respectively) and balance the four similarly short motivational clauses of 2:1. And like the clauses of 2:1, they also are an instance of rhetorical amplification, though this time the rhetoric is less successful.[13] Particularly transparent is Paul's almost verbatim repetition of the friendship cliché "to think the same thing" in the first and fourth injunctions: τὸ αὐτὸ φρονῆτε . . . τὸ ἓν φρονοῦντες (lit., "think the same thing . . . thinking the one thing"). This cliché also lies behind the second item in the list, τὴν αὐτὴν ἀγάπην ἔχοντες ("having the same love"). Like the parallel list in 2:1, this list does not merit close scrutiny.

The fifth and sixth injunctions in vv. 3-4, however, are longer and more substantial. Rhetorically, they bring a sense of fullness and closure to the list.[14] Each is developed by way of antithesis, one of Paul's favorite rhetorical figures, which will be echoed in the Christ-myth in 2:6-7. Verse 3 introduces the theme of "humility" (ταπεινοφροσύνη), which will appear again in 2:8 (ἐταπείνωσεν ἑαυτόν, "he humbled himself").[15] Similarly, the term translated "empty conceit" (κενοδοξία) anticipates the much-discussed expression "he emptied [ἐκένωσεν] himself" in 2:7.

Verse 4 contains several textual variants, two of which bear on its interpretation. The Greek reads: μὴ τὰ ἑαυτῶν ἕκαστος[16] σκοποῦντες, ἀλλὰ [καὶ] τὰ ἑτέρων ἕκαστοι, "each not looking out for his or her own interests, but each [also] for the interests of others." Most manuscripts favor the inclusion of "also" (καί), but a significant minority omit it. If included, it softens Paul's injunction: one may look out for one's own interests as long as one "also" looks out for the interests of others. But this reading does not fit with the first part of the clause, which does not read "each not looking out *only* for his or her own interests," but simply "each not looking out for . . . ." Further, it does not fit with the example of Christ that follows in 2:6-11, where Christ sets aside his interests *completely* for the sake of others.[17] The preference of the manuscript tradition notwithstanding, the "also" is likely an intentional scribal change and should be omitted.

A second textual variant has to do with punctuation. Several important manuscripts include a break before the second "each" (ἕκαστοι), reading it instead with what follows in v. 5. This is a tempting reading. It makes good sense of v. 5, which might then be translated "Let *each* of you have this attitude . . . ." It also avoids what would be the otherwise patent redundancy of v. 4. But it is a temptation that should be resisted. Like 1:30 and 2:16, v. 4 is Paul's attempt at a *clausula* using the figure *geminatio* (doubling). The result is awkward, and it apparently proved a point of embarrassment to later copyists who sought to correct it.[18]

---

live, if you stand fast in the Lord [στήκετε ἐν κυρίῳ]. Indeed, what gratitude can we render back to God for all the joy with which we rejoiced because of you [ἐπὶ πάσῃ τῇ χαρᾷ ᾗ χαίρομεν δι' ὑμᾶς]." See also 2 Cor 7:5-16.

13 Chrysostom makes the best of it: "How often he says that same thing [τὸ αὐτὸ λέγει] in order to express the depth of his feelings!" (hom. 6.100.12).

14 This is typical of such lists. Compare the immediately preceding list in 2:1, where the final item contains two elements. A similar pattern can be observed later in 3:9-10.

15 "Humility" was not deemed a virtue in antiquity, and Paul's promotion of it is unique and therefore something of a puzzle. It is probably a case of what social psychologists call "self-stigmatization," which occurs when a stigmatized group adopts the language of their detractors in an effort to change its valence from negative to positive. Early Christians will have done this on a number of levels, from the symbolism of the cross to the name "Christian" itself. See the excursus "Paul's 'Theology of the Cross'" below after the comment on 2:7-8.

16 For the singular ἕκαστος see the textual note above.

17 Cf. Troels Engberg-Pedersen, "Radical Altruism in Philippians 2:4," in *Early Christianity and Classical Culture: Comparative Studies in Honor of Abraham J. Malherbe*, ed. John T. Fitzgerald, Thomas H. Olbricht, and L. Michael White (NovTSup 110; Leiden: Brill, 2003) 197–214.

18 Quintilian would also have disapproved (*Inst.* 8.5.14, 20).

2

5/ **Have[a] this attitude[b] in yourselves, which
was[c] also in Christ Jesus,[d] 6/ who, although
he existed in the form of God, did not consider [his[e]] equality with God a possession
that he could not part with, 7/ but emptied
himself, taking the form of a slave, adopting[f] a human[g] likeness. And being found
in appearance as a human, 8/ he humbled
himself, becoming obedient to the point
of death, even death on a cross. 9/ And
therefore God more highly exalted him and
gave him the[h] Name that is above every
other name, 10/ in order that in the name
of Jesus every knee should bow, of those in
heaven and on earth and under the ground,
11/ and every tongue should confess[i] that
Jesus Christ is "Lord,"[j] to the glory of God
the Father.**

a A number of manuscripts (p[46] ℵ D F G K L P 075, 0278, 104, 365, 630, 1175, 1505, 1739, 1881, Maj lat sy[h]) read γάρ ("for"). Others (ℵ* A B C Ψ 33, 81, 1241, 2464, 2495 t vg[mss] co; Or Aug) omit it.

b Some manuscripts (C² K L P Ψ 075, 0278,104, 365, 630, 1175[c], 1241, 1505, 2464 Maj; Or) have the third person singular imperative φρονείσθω ("let this atti-tude be") instead of the second person plural impera-tive φρονεῖτε ("have this attitude"), which is read by p[46] ℵ A B C* D F G 33, 81, 1175, 1739, 1181 latt sy.

c The past tense of the supplied verb ("was") is implied by the narrative that follows which is told in the past tense; thus C. F. D. Moule, "Further Reflections on Philippians 2.5-11," in *Apostolic History and the Gospel: Biblical and Historical Essays Presented to F. F. Bruce on His 60th Birthday*, ed. W. W. Gasque and R. P. Martin (Exeter: Paternoster, 1970) 265–76, here 265.

d Literally, "Think this way in yourselves, which [way of thinking was] also in Christ Jesus."

e Interpreting the articular infinitive τὸ εἶναι ἴσα θεῷ as anaphoric, in effect: "the *aforementioned* equality with God." See BDF §399.1.

f Gk. ἐν ὁμοιώματι ἀνθρώπων γενόμενος (lit., "becoming in human likeness"; cf. v. 8: "becoming [γενόμενος] obedient"). For the expression γενόμενος ἐκ ("being born of"), see Gal 4:4; Rom 1:3; BDAG, s.v. γίνομαι 1. For the expression γενόμενος ἐν, see BDAG, s.v. γίνομαι 5c. In tales of metamorphosis, which is the context here, the verb γίνομαι commonly means "change into." See my comments below.

g Several witnesses (p[46] t vg[mss]; Mcion[T] Cyp) read the sin-gular ἀνθρώπου, "adopting the likeness of *a human*." Presumably this was to bring the plural into line with the singular in the next clause: "and being found in appearance as a human [ὡς ἄνθρωπος]."

h A number of manuscripts (D F G K L P Ψ 075, 0278, 81, 104, 365, 630, 1175[c], 1241, 1505, 1881, 2464 Maj; Clement[exThd]) omit the definite article: "gave him *a* name that is above every other name," possibly for idiomatic reasons but also implying that the name in question is "Jesus" not "Lord." The definite article, however, is better attested (p[46] ℵ A B C 33 629 1175* 1739) and correctly reflects Paul's less developed Christology that Jesus acquired the divine name "Lord" (YHWH) when he returned to his angelic form. See the discussion below.

i A number of manuscripts (A C D F* G K L P Ψ[vid] 075, 0278, 6, 33, 81, 104, 365, 630*, 1175, 1241, 1505, 1739, 1881, 2464; Ir[v.l.]) have the future ἐξομολογήσεται instead of the subjunctive ἐξομολογήσηται (p[46] ℵ B F[c] 323, 630[c] 2495; Ir Cl[exThd] Cl), though there is no appre-ciable difference in meaning.

j A few manuscripts ([A[c]] F G 1501* b g vg[ms] sa[ms]; Or[lat pl]) omit "Christ" and read simply "Jesus is Lord"; one manuscript (K) omits "Jesus," reading simply "Christ is Lord."

Analysis

Paul supports the exhortation to humility in 2:1-4 with an *exemplum* in 2:5-11, a metamorphic myth[1] in which Christ similarly "humbled himself" and was rewarded by God.[2] Throughout most of the last century, scholars interpreted this *exemplum* as an earlier prose hymn adapted by Paul for his own purposes, an interpretation that until recently went largely unchallenged.[3] This was part of a larger quest for sources that came to characterize much of New Testament studies, but which now appears to have run its course.[4] More and more scholars today are reading Phil 2:6-11 as a piece of encomiastic prose composed by Paul himself specifically for the present letter,[5] which is the view taken here.

Paul begins with a short exhortation urging the Philippians to accept the exhortation to humility in 2:1-4 on the grounds that humility was also characteristic of Christ: "Have this attitude in yourselves, which was also in Christ Jesus" (v. 5). He follows this with a metamorphic myth of Christ's self-humbling (vv. 6-11). The myth falls naturally into two parts: Christ's glorious pre-metamorphic existence and selfless assumption of a human "form," eventuating in his slavelike death on a cross (vv. 6-8), and his vindication and installation as God's even more glorious vice-regent who now bears the divine "Name" and will eventually rule the whole of creation (vv. 9-11).[6] Paul is careful to narrate not just the details of Christ's metamorphosis but the attitude it expressed: he "did not consider [ἡγήσατο] [his] equality with God a possession that he could not part with, but emptied himself, taking the form of a slave." It is precisely this attitude that God rewarded and that the Philippians are to imitate.[7]

In addition to providing support for the exhortation to "humility" in 2:1-4, Paul's Christ-myth also anticipates the exhortation to "obedience" in 2:12-16,[8] as well as the comments about Timothy in 2:19-24[9] and Epaphroditus in 2:25-30.[10] The myth's fit within its immediate epistolary context supports the thesis that Paul himself composed it.[11]

1   For a fuller discussion of Paul's metamorphic myths, see the introduction, part 7: "Key Religious Topoi."

2   The insistence by Ernst Käsemann ("Kritische Analyse von Phil. 2,5-11," *ZThK* 47 [1950] 313–60; ET "A Critical Analysis of Philippians 2:5-11," *JTC* 5 [1968] 45–88), followed by Ralph P. Martin (*Carmen Christi: Philippians 2:5-11 in Recent Interpretation and in the Setting of Early Christian Worship* [Cambridge: Cambridge University Press, 1967; 3rd ed.; Downers Grove, IL: InterVarsity Press, 1997]), that, contra Ernst Lohmeyer (*Kyrios Jesus: Eine Untersuchung zu Phil 2,5-11* [Heidelberg: Winter, 1928]), 2:6-11 is not an *exemplum* but a proclamation—the so-called "kerygmatic" versus "ethical" reading—on the grounds that Christ's incarnation cannot strictly be imitated is puzzling. Paul does not invite the Philippians to do what Christ did but to adopt his "attitude." Cf. Rom 15:3; 2 Cor 8:9. See the recent analysis by Heiko Wojtkowiak, *Christologie und Ethik im Philipperbrief: Studien zur Handlungsorientierung einer frühchristlichen Gemeinde in paganer Umwelt* (FRLANT 243; Göttingen: Vandenhoeck & Ruprecht, 2012).

3   For the history of scholarship, see Martin, *Carmen Christi*; Otfried Hofius, *Der Christushymnus Philipper 2:6-11: Untersuchungen zu Gestalt und Aussage eines urchristlichen Psalms* (WUNT 17; Tübingen: Mohr Siebeck, 1991).

4   Ralph Brucker, "'Songs', 'Hymns', and 'Encomia' in the New Testament," in *Literature or Liturgy? Early Christian Hymns and Prayers in Their Literary and Liturgical Context in Antiquity*, ed. Clemens Leonhard and Hermut Löhr (WUNT 2/363; Tübingen: Mohr Siebeck, 2014) 1–14.

5   See the excursus "On the Genre of Philippians 2:6-11" below.

6   Hofius, *Christushymnus*, 109–11; cf. Michael Lattke, *Odes of Solomon: A Commentary* (Hermeneia; Minneapolis: Fortress Press, 2009) 544–46.

7   Cf. Phil 2:3: "considering" (ἡγούμενοι); Wrede, *Paul*, 87.

8   Compare 2:12, "as you have always obeyed [ὑπηκούσατε]," with 2:8, "becoming obedient [ὑπήκοος]."

9   Compare 2:22, "he served as a slave [ἐδούλευσεν]," with 2:7, "the form of a slave [δούλου]."

10 Compare 2:30, "to the point of death [μέχρι θανάτου]," with 2:8, "to the point of death [μέχρι θανάτου]." Like Christ, Epaphroditus is explicitly cited as an example (2:29-30).

11 To be sure, the language of the myth at several points exceeds Paul's normal vocabulary, but that is also the case with other panegyric texts in Paul, such as 1 Corinthians 13.

Comment

■ **5** The exhortation of v. 5 is composed of two balanced clauses each ending with the prepositional phrase "in X." The first clause is relatively unambiguous: τοῦτο φρονεῖτε ἐν ὑμῖν, "Have this attitude in yourselves."[12] But the second clause is lacking a verb (ὅ καὶ ἐν Χριστῷ Ἰησοῦ; lit., "which also in Christ Jesus"), and scholars have struggled to know which verb to supply. A significant number of commentators repeat φρονεῖτε from the first half of the verse, retaining both the person and number but changing the mood from the imperative to the indicative: "Have this attitude in yourselves, which attitude you have also in Christ Jesus." This reading fits with Paul's use of "in Christ" elsewhere, but it is an odd way to introduce an *exemplum*.[13] A more likely solution is to supply some form of the verb εἶναι ("to be") which is often omitted in good Greek.[14] I have thus translated: "Have this attitude in yourselves, which *was* also in Christ Jesus."

Excursus: On the Genre of Philippians 2:6-11

Before turning to Phil 2:6-11 it will be helpful to say something about its genre. Philippians 2:6-11 con-

tains a number of poetic features, such as isocolon, antithesis, various forms of parallelism, chiasmus, homoioteleuton, climax, and a richer vocabulary than one typically finds in Paul's more conversational style. But it is not metered and so cannot be classified as a traditional lyric or epic hymn. Whether one classifies it as a prose hymn or an encomium is largely a matter of definition and perhaps prior use.[15] In general, panegyric when addressed to a god was called a "hymn" and when addressed to a human an "encomium."[16] Paul's Christ-myth renders this traditional distinction hard to apply. I will call 2:6-11 an encomium to distinguish my reading from earlier "hymnic" analyses.[17] For an analogous text with similar poetic features, one may compare Paul's earlier encomium to love in 1 Corinthians 13.

It is remarkable how well fitted Phil 2:6-11 is to its present context. Not only does it repeat the antithesis ("not . . . but") of 2:3-4, but it also illustrates precisely the attitude (humility) and behavior (obedience) enjoined respectively in 2:1-4 and 2:12-16.[18] This consideration, coupled with the fact that a similar logic—Christ-believers are to act as Christ himself acted—can be found in other undisputed Pauline texts (e.g., Rom 15:1-3; 2 Cor 8:7-9), makes a good case that 2:6-11 is a piece of elevated prose produced by Paul precisely for the exhortation of Phil 2:1-16.

---

12 The pronoun τοῦτο ("this") might refer to what precedes or what follows: "have *the above* attitude" or "have *the following* attitude." The meaning is roughly the same since in both cases the attitude is the same. Moule opts for the former ("Further Reflexions," 265). I have interpreted it to refer ahead to the second clause: "which (attitude) was also in Christ Jesus." The prepositional phrase ἐν ὑμῖν might also be understood in two senses: "in yourselves" (as I have translated) or "among yourselves." Both make good sense, but, given the parallel phrase "in Christ Jesus," the former is to be preferred (cf. the phrase in 1:6; 2:13).

13 This oddity lies behind Käsemann's so-called kerygmatic reading of the myth ("Kritische Analyse").

14 Given the fact that the myth that follows is told in the past tense, the past tense of the supplied verb should be used: "which *was* also in Christ Jesus."

15 Hermut Löhr, "What Can We Know about the Beginnings of Christian Hymnody?," in Leonhard and Löhr, *Literature or Liturgy?* 158–74.

16 Theon, *Prog.* 9 (Spengel 8); Hermogenes, *Prog.* 7; Aphthonius, *Prog.* 8; cf. Plato, *Resp.* 10.607a. See now Samuel Vollenweider, "Hymnus, Enkomion oder Psalm? Schattengefechte in der neutestamentlichen Wissenschaft," *NTS* 56 (2010) 208–31.

17 See esp. Ralph Brucker, *"Christushymnen" oder*

"epideiktische Passagen"? Studien zum Stilwechsel im Neuen Testament und seiner Umwelt (FRLANT 176; Göttingen: Vandenhoeck & Ruprecht, 1997) 350, who classifies Phil 2:6-11 as a rhetorical *epainos*. Klaus Berger classifies it as an encomium ("Hellenistische Gattungen im Neuen Testament," *ANRW* 2.25.2 (1984) 1031–1432, 1831–85, here 1173–91; and idem, *Formen und Gattungen im Neuen Testament* (UTB 2532; Tübingen: Franke, 2005) 401–3. Bockmuehl takes a somewhat middle ground and argues that whether one classifies Phil 2:6-11 as a "hymn" is in large part a matter of definition ("Form," 3). For a recent analysis of 2:6-11 as a Pauline composition, see Adela Yarbro Collins, "Psalms, Philippians 2:6-11, and the Origins of Christology" *BibInt* 11 (2002) 261–72. If one imagines Phil 2:6-11 as a "hymn" composed by Paul while in prison, it evokes the famous example of Socrates, who composed a hymn to God while in prison (*Phaedo* 60d; cf. Diogenes Laertius, *Vit.* 2.42), an act that Epictetus says shows one to be a philosopher (*Diss.* 4.4.23); cf. Acts 16:25, where Paul and Silas also compose a hymn while in prison in Philippi, for which see the comments in Pervo, *Acts*, 408–9, who cites Philostratus, *Vit. Apoll.* 4.36; Lucian, *Icar.* 1; *Act. Thom.* 108; Pr Azar 23–68; *T. Jos.* 8:5; *Mart. Pion.* 18.12.

18 Cf. also κενοδοξία, "empty conceit," in 2:3 and

Further evidence against 2:6-11 being the fragment of an earlier composition is that it is hard to imagine what might have come before 2:6 (Christ's initial angelic glory) or what might have come after 2:9-11 (Christ's postmortem promotion and promised eschatological dominion along with the final glorification of God). In other words, 2:6-11 seems to tell the whole story.[19] Indeed, if 2:6-11 relates any of the standard topics of encomia/prose hymns, it relates the *first* in the list, Christ's "divine" origins, and the *last*, his elevation because of exemplary virtue. The relative pronoun "who" (2:6) might seem to support the claim that Phil 2:6-11 is an independent prose hymn, since, as Eduard Norden has observed, the writers of ancient prose hymns sometimes deployed relative pronouns to structure their material.[20] But for this feature to count, other structurally significant relative pronouns would need to occur in 2:6-11, which is not the case. As it stands, the relative pronoun "who" in 2:6 simply identifies the subject of 2:6-11 as the "Christ Jesus" of 2:5.

■ **6-8** Verses 6-8 constitute the first half of the encomium of 2:6-11. They reproduce many of the ideas and expressions of 2:1-4, in light of which the solutions to their famous problems are to be sought. The overall logic is characteristically Pauline: the Philippians are to be humble (2:3-4) because Christ was humble (2:6-8). As already noted, a similar logic (and wordplay) can be found at Rom 15:1-3: "we ought not to please [ἀρέσκειν] ourselves . . . for Christ did not please [ἤρεσεν] himself," and 2 Cor 8:7-9: "you should abound in this benefaction [χάριτι] . . . for you know the benefaction [χάριν] of our Lord Jesus Christ." Verses 6-8 may be further divided into two parts: a brief description of Christ's pre-metamorphic existence (v. 6) and a longer account of his self-humbling metamorphosis (vv. 7-8).

■ **6** The expression ἐν μορφῇ θεοῦ ὑπάρχων in the first half of v. 6, here translated "although he existed in the form of God," raises two questions: (1) the meaning of μορφή ("form") and (2) the force of the participle ὑπάρχων (lit., "existing"). Commentators have balked at the plain meaning of μορφὴ θεοῦ ("form of God"), since μορφή denotes not "essence"[21] but "outward appearance"

ἐκένωσεν, "he emptied himself," in 2:7. It is one of the striking facts of the history of scholarship on Phil 2:6-11 that earlier scholars, convinced that they had uncovered an earlier hymn, identified a number of minor alleged divergences from the epistolary context and yet overlooked the rather glaring fact that the myth contained in 2:6-11 fits that context so remarkably well.

19   To be sure, there are elements omitted. But these are largely the elements Paul omits elsewhere regarding the historical Jesus. The claim that Phil 2:6-11 does not make explicit mention of the resurrection, certainly an important Pauline theme, is mooted by the fact that Christ's obedience results in death and ends in exaltation (a traditional encomiastic theme). Resurrection also has little place in a metamorphic myth, where the typical pattern is descent and ascent.

20   Eduard Norden, *Agnostos Theos: Untersuchungen zur Formengeschichte religiöser Rede* (Leipzig: Teubner, 1913) 383–87. The hymn fragment in 1 Tim 3:16 is sometimes cited in comparison, but there the relative pronoun finds no antecedent in the immediate epistolary context.

21   Numerous tortured attempts have been made to read the notion of an invisible "essence" back into the term, but none convinces. Lightfoot, for

example, notes the use of μορφή and σχῆμα (which appears in the next verse) in Aristotle, where μορφή denotes an outward appearance that is *unchanging* and σχῆμα denotes an outward appearance that *changes*. It is not clear what this approach gains, since in either case outward appearance is in view. Further, whatever one decides about Aristotle, for Paul μορφή and σχῆμα are synonymous, and the point of Phil 2:6-8 is that Christ precisely did change "form" (μορφή)! It might be objected that Christ did not change form so much as add a form: *taking* [λαβών] the form of a slave." But that is to read too much into the idiom. According to Euripides, *Hel.* 19, Zeus similarly "took" the form of a swan (μορφώματ' ὄρνιθος λαβών). Not all attempts are this sophisticated. Barth, with characteristic selectivity, avoids the problem altogether by limiting himself to the expression "equality with God," which he interprets absolutely; Bonnie Bowman Thurston simply translates "essence" without comment (Bonnie Bowman Thurston and Judith M. Ryan, *Philippians and Philemon* [Sacra Pagina 10; Collegeville, MN: Liturgical Press, 2005]). A handful of scholars have tried to skirt the theological problem altogether by interpreting the expression "form of God" (μορφὴ θεοῦ) as the equivalent of "image of God" (εἰκὼν θεοῦ) as predicated of the first man and woman in

or visible "shape,"[22] implying that Paul, a Jew, thought God could be "perceived by the senses."[23] To be sure, there is an important tradition in ancient Israelite and Jewish religion that God is beyond human perception.[24] But there is an equally prominent tradition that God or at least God's "Glory" (כבוד, *kābôd*; LXX δόξα) can be seen.[25]

According to Isa 6:1-3, God has a gigantic humanlike body: "I saw Yahweh sitting on a throne, high and lofty, and the hem of his robe filled the temple."[26] According to Ezek 1:26-28 this body is not God's per se but the luminous "image of the likeness of the Glory [כבוד] of Yahweh."[27] In *1 Enoch* 14:20, the figure seated on "the lofty throne" is identified as the "Great Glory" (ἡ δόξα ἡ μεγάλη), whose "raiment was like the appearance of the sun."[28] Angels were imagined to have similar humanlike

forms that increased in grandeur and radiance the closer they were stationed to God's throne.[29] To say then, as Paul does, that Christ existed in "the form of God" is simply to say that, prior to his self-humbling metamorphosis, Christ enjoyed a luminous appearance of the sort a powerful angel might possess.[30] Philo uses much the same language in his account of the burning bush in *Mos.* 1.66: "and at the center of the flame was a form [μορφή] that was supremely beautiful . . . an image most God-like in appearance [θεοειδέστατον] . . . but let it be called an angel [καλείσθω δὲ ἄγγελος]."[31]

C. F. D. Moule has proposed that the participle ὑπάρχων is causal rather than concessive, which is to say that Christ humbled himself "*because* he existed in the form of God" rather than "*although* he existed in the form of God."[32] This reading is grammatically possible, but

---

Gen 1:27. See Oscar Cullmann, *The Christology of the New Testament* (rev. ed.; Philadelphia: Westminster, 1963) 174–81; J. Murphy-O'Connor, "Christological Anthropology in Phil II,6-11," *RB* 83 (1976) 25–50; Morna D. Hooker, "Philippians 2.6-11," in *Jesus und Paulus: Festschrift für Werner Georg Kümmel zum 70. Geburtstag*, ed. E. Earle Ellis and Erich Grässer (Göttingen: Vandenhoeck & Ruprecht, 1978) 151–64; James D. G. Dunn, *Christology in the Making: A New Testament Inquiry into the Origins of the Doctrine of the Incarnation* (London: SCM, 1980) 174–81. Bockmuehl gives the main arguments against this position ("Form," 8–11). For the linguistic evidence, see David Steenburg, "The Case against the Synonymity of *morphé* and *eikôn*," *JSNT* 34 (1988) 77–86.

22 BDAG, s.v. μορφή.

23 Johannes Behm, "μορφή," *TDNT* 4 (1968) 745.

24 E.g., Deut 4:12: "Then Yahweh spoke to you out of the fire; you heard the sound of the words but saw no form [תמונה]," and 4:15: "you saw no form [תמונה] when Yahweh spoke to you out of the fire at Horeb"; cf. Exod 20:4; 33:20.

25 For the association of "glory" with "form" in the LXX, see Jarl Fossum, "Jewish-Christian Christology and Jewish Mysticism," *VC* 37 (1983) 260–87, here 263–64.

26 This motif is taken up in *2 Enoch* 13:3-10 and developed in later *Shi'ur Qomah* mysticism, for which see Schäfer, *Hidden*, 60, 99–102 and passim. For the motif in tannaitic midrash, see Michael Fishbane, "The 'Measurements' of God's Glory in the Ancient Midrash," in *Messiah and Christos: Studies in the Jewish Origins of Christianity Presented to David*

Flusser on the Occasion of the Seventy-Fifth Birthday, ed. Ithamar Gruenwald, Shaul Shaked, and Gedaliahu G. Stroumsa (TSAJ 32; Tübingen: Mohr Siebeck, 1992) 53–74; Benjamin D. Sommer, *Bodies of God and the World of Ancient Israel* (Cambridge/New York: Cambridge University Press, 2009). Cf. Jesus's gigantic size in *Gosp. Pet.* 40; *Book of Elchasai*, frag. 1 (apud Hippolytus, *Ref.* 9.13.1–3; cf. Epiphanius, *Pan.* 19.4.1; 30.17.6–7; 53.1.9).

27 This figure is encountered again in Ezek 8:2-3; cf. Dan 7:9; *L.A.E.* 25:3 *Vita*, for which see Nickelsburg, *1 Enoch 1*, 255–56.

28 Cf. *1 Enoch* 102:3; *T. Levi* 3:4, for which see George W. E. Nickelsburg, "Enoch, Levi, and Peter: Recipients of Revelation in Upper Galilee," *JBL* 100 (1981) 575–600; for *kābôd* elsewhere in *1 Enoch*, see 14:16, 20, 21; 40:1; 47:3; 60:2; 71:7; 103:1; 104:1 (Nickelsburg, *1 Enoch 1*, 255–56).

29 Dan 10:6; *Asc. Isa.* 7–8; 4QShirSabb passim.

30 Horbury, *Cult of Christ*, 199 n. 77: a "pre-existent angel-like figure." Bockmuehl has also pointed out that in the LXX "form" (μορφή) is frequently used in connection with "glory" (δόξα) ("Form," 8–10). According to Gen 1:26-27, it is not that God and angels have a humanlike form but that humans and angels have a godlike form, not divine "anthropomorphism" but human "theomorphism."

31 Bockmuehl, "Form," 15.

32 C. F. D. Moule, "The Manhood of Jesus in the NT," in *Christ, Faith, and History: Cambridge Studies in Christology*, ed. S. W. Sykes and J. P. Clayton (Cambridge: Cambridge University Press, 1972) 95–110, here 97.

it makes sense only if we force μορφή to mean Christ's essence instead of his appearance.[33] Otherwise we are left with the unintelligible claim that Christ humbled himself because he looked like God. The participle ὑπάρχων should therefore be interpreted as a concessive participle. An identical use of the participle is found in 2 Cor 8:9b: "*although* he was rich [πλούσιος ὤν], he impoverished himself for your sakes." Apollo's complaint in Euripides *Alc.* 2-7 displays a similar syntax and logic: "although a god [θεός περ ὤν] . . . my father [Zeus] compelled me to serve [θητεύειν]."[34]

The second half of v. 6—"did not consider [his] equality with God ἁρπαγμός"—also presents the interpreter with two problems: (1) the meaning of the expression "equality with God" (τὸ εἶναι ἴσα θεοῦ)[35] and (2) the meaning of the rare and difficult term ἁρπαγμός, which for the moment I leave untranslated. I will consider these problems in reverse order. According to its dictionary definition ἁρπαγμός is an abstract noun meaning the violent seizure of property, that is, "robbery." Nevertheless, it is often the case with abstract nouns that they carry a concrete sense as well, which in this instance would be "something stolen" and, by extension "something valuable or precious" (i.e., something worth stealing).[36] If this

item is not already in one's possession, then the term connotes "something precious *to be grasped*." If, however, the item is already in one's possession, then the connotation would be "something precious *to be held on to*."[37] This gives three possible meanings for the term: (1) "robbery," (2) "something precious to be grasped," and (3) "something precious to be held on to."[38]

The AV assumes the first meaning: "he did not consider equality with God robbery." This translation makes fine sense of the expression itself: Christ did not consider his equality with God something that was not rightly his.[39] But it destroys the parallelism with 2:3-4 and is generally rejected.[40] This leaves us with the concrete meaning of the term and its two connotations. But in order to decide between these connotations we need to solve the first problem, namely, the meaning of "equality with God." For if "equality with God" is something greater than being in the "form of God," then Christ did not initially possess it and ἁρπαγμός must connote "something precious to be grasped." If, on the other hand "equality with God" is just another way of saying "form of God," then Christ already possessed it and ἁρπαγμός must connote "something precious to be held on to."

---

33 The resultant sense would then be: "Because he shared in the *divine essence—and true divinity* is by its nature self-negating—Christ emptied himself . . . ." See Dieter Zeller, "New Testament Christology in Its Hellenistic Reception," *NTS* 47 (2001) 312–33, here 322 n. 54.

34 In this case, of course, Apollo does not humble himself but is humbled by Zeus.

35 Cf. Pseudo-Plato, *Ax.* 364a: "he [Herakles] was honored as equal with the gods [ἴσα θεοῖς]."

36 BDAG, s.v. ἁρπαγμός 2.

37 It is likely that in both of these concrete meanings the connotation is negative and Paul is registering disapproval of the conceived act: something to be *stolen* or something to be *greedily* held on to. This may be inferred from the generally negative connotations of the term, for which see Samuel Vollenweider, "Der 'Raub' der Gottgleichheit: Ein religionsgeschichtlicher Vorschlag zu Phil 2.6(-11)," *NTS* 45 (1999) 413–33, esp. 117–18. Not all instances, however, are negative (Ernest Moore, "ΒΙΑΖΩ, ΑΡΠΑΖΩ and Cognates in Josephus," *NTS* 21 [1975] 519–43, esp. 525); cf. BDAG, s.v. ἁρπάζω 2b.

38 A fourth idiomatic usage claimed for the whole expression "to consider something ἁρπαγμόν" is "to consider something a windfall" or "something to be exploited" (Werner W. Jaeger, "Eine stilgeschichtliche Studie zum Philipperbrief," *Hermes* 50 [1915] 537–53; Roy W. Hoover, "The *Harpagmos* Enigma: A Philological Solution," *HTR* 64 [1971] 95–119). But see the objections in Vollenweider, "Raub," 216–17.

39 Here see Norbert Baumert, "'Kein unrechtmäßiger Besitz' — eine Litotes in Phil 2,6," *ZNW* 56 (2012) 113–17.

40 There are actually two problems. The first regards the parallelism with 2:3-4. In v. 3a and v. 4a Paul urges the Philippians to do nothing out of selfishness. One expects some similar sentiment in v. 6. But if we translate "robbery," the resulting sense is that Christ did not think his equality with God illegitimate or undeserved. This is at best a poor analogy to 2:3a and 4a. A second problem is that it produces a strained meaning for ἀλλά ("but"), something more like ἀλλ' ὅμως ("but all the same" or "nevertheless"), as Lightfoot rightly notes.

The first thing to note is that, regardless of which way one understands "equality with God," it must be taken in a qualified sense, since even in 2:9-11 Christ's glory still serves the "glory of God the Father" (cf. 1 Cor 15:28). Strictly speaking, Christ is not "equal to God" either *before* his metamorphosis or *after* his exaltation. To interpret "equality with God" *sensu stricto* is therefore not an option. Nevertheless, both of the above ways of interpreting "equality with God"—as something greater than "form of God" or something roughly synonymous with it—make good sense in the larger context of 2:6-11. If "equality with God" is greater than being in "the form of God," then it refers ahead to Christ's further exaltation as God's vice-regent in 2:9. If, on the other hand, it is simply another way of saying "the form of God," then it refers back to Christ's luminous preexistence in 2:6a.

Two considerations point to the latter interpretation, that is, taking "equality with God" as roughly equivalent to "the form of God." The first consideration concerns the syntax of the Greek: τὸ εἶναι ἴσα θεοῦ (lit., "the state of being equal to God"). If, as some have argued, the article (τό) is anaphoric—this can be the case, but it need not be the case—then the expression refers back to "the form of God" in the preceding clause. A second, more compelling consideration in my view looks at the overall rhetoric of the passage and in particular at the parallelism between vv. 6 and 7. Just as in 2:6 "form of God" is followed by "equality with God," so also in 2:7 "form of a slave" is followed by "human likeness." Since in the latter case (v. 7) "human likeness" interprets "form of a slave,"[41]

it is reasonable to assume that when in the former case (v. 6) Paul wrote "equality to God" he meant it to interpret "form of God." On this reading "equality with God" would then be hyperbole, emphasizing the extraordinary extent of Christ's self-humbling and therefore of the exemplary nature of his humility. Returning to the connotation of ἁρπαγμός, if we accept the above arguments that "equality with God" is something *already* in Christ's possession, then ἁρπαγμός must mean "something precious to be held on to" or, as I have rendered it, "a possession that he could not part with."

■ **7-8** Paul imagines Christ's self-humbling to have occurred in two stages indicated respectively by the finite verbal expressions "he emptied himself" (ἑαυτὸν ἐκένωσεν) and "he humbled himself" (ἐταπείνωσεν ἑαυτόν). The first stage (2:7a-b) concerns Christ's initial assumption of a human form and might be called his metamorphosis proper. It contains a number of terms and expressions found in the metamorphic tradition: "*taking the form* [μορφήν . . . λαβών][42] of a slave, *adopting* [γενόμενος, lit., "becoming"][43] a human *likeness* [ὁμοιώματι]."[44] The second stage (2:7c-8) concerns Christ's death on a cross. It picks up where the first stage leaves off and continues to deploy metamorphic terminology: "and being found in *appearance* [σχήματι][45] as a human, he humbled himself, *becoming* [γενόμενος] obedient to the point of death, even death on a cross." Paul elsewhere attributes the agency behind Christ's mission to God.[46] Here he imagines the agency as Christ's— "he emptied himself . . . he humbled himself"—and thus

---

41 Theodoret.

42 Both the term μορφή ("form") and the expression μορφὴν λαβών ("taking the form" or "assuming the form") appear in the metamorphic tradition. The term appears frequently. For the expression μορφὴν λαβών, see Euripides, *Hel.* 19 (of Zeus) and *L.A.E.* 29:12 *Apoc.* (of Satan). I quote both of these texts below.

43 Γίνομαι is one of the most common verbs indicating change in metamorphic texts, for which see Buxton, *Forms of Astonishment*, 168–70; Forbes Irving, *Metamorphosis*, 171–94. Texts include Homer, *Od.* 4.454–59; 10.395–96; Euripides, *Bacch.* 1330; frag. 930 (Radt); Aristophanes, *Vesp.* 48–49; *Ran.* 289; Plato, *Resp.* 2.380d; *Phaedo* 82b; Callimachus, *Hym. Dem.* 57–58; *Hym. Dionys.* 44; Palaephatus, *Incred.* 8; Apollonius of Rhodes, *Argon.* 1430; Nicander,

Hetero. (apud Antoninus Liberalis, *Metam.* 1.5; 8.7; 10.4; 12.8; 14.3; 17.4–5 and passim); Boios, *Ornith.* (apud Antoninus Liberalis, *Metam.* 5.5; 7.7; 20.6–8); Moschus, *Eur.* 78; Pseudo-Apollodorus, *Bibl.* 3.13.5; Pausanias, 8.2.3; Philostratus of Lemnos, *Imag.* 1.18; Athenaeus, *Deip.* 8.334d.

44 Another term common in metamorphic myth, though typically in its verbal form: Diodorus Siculus, *Bib. hist.* 1.86.3; Aesop, *Fab.* 89 Perry (140 Halm); cf. Acts 14:11; Rom 8:3.

45 This is another common metamorphic term, though again frequently in its verbal cognate μετασχηματίζω; see *T. Reub.* 5:6; *T. Job* 6:4; 17:2; cf. 2 Cor 11:14 and later in Phil 3:20.

46 E.g., Rom 8:3: "God having sent his own son in the likeness [ὁμοιώματι] of sinful flesh"; cf. Gal 4:4: "And when the fullness of time came, God sent his son."

expressive of his humility and obedience. The repetition of the participle γενόμενος ("becoming") presents Christ's self-humbling as a process extending from this initial transformation to his death.[47] This metamorphic process will be reversed in 2:9-11 when Christ is restored to his angelic form.

Excursus: Metamorphosis in Greco-Roman and Jewish Myth

Greco-Roman myth with its frequent stories of both divine and human metamorphosis offers a rich context both conceptually and linguistically for interpreting Phil 2:6-11.[48] Thus Dionysus at the beginning of Euripides's popular *Bacchae*: "Here I am, having changed form [μορφήν] from that of a god to that of a human."[49] And then a few lines later: "I have taken in exchange a mortal image, I have changed my form [μορφήν] into that of a man."[50] Similarly, in *Hel.*

19 Zeus comes to Leda "taking the form of a swan" (μορφώματ᾽ ὄρνιθος λαβών), language very close to Phil 2:7a ("taking the form of a slave" [μορφὴν δούλου λαβών]). Zeus's metamorphosis at Moschus, *Eur.* 79, offers another striking parallel: just as Christ is said to have "emptied" (ἐκένωσεν) himself before "becoming" (γενόμενος) human, so Zeus "hid" (κρύψεν) his divinity before he "became" (γείνετο) a bull.[51]

By Paul's day metamorphic myths had also been incorporated into Jewish apocalyptic speculation, especially with regard to angelic metamorphoses.[52] I have already discussed this topic above in the introduction, part 7.c: "Paul's Metamorphic Myths," but here are a few representative texts. In *T. Reub.* 5:6, the Watchers of Genesis 6 "transform" (μετασχηματίζοντο) themselves into men, while in *T. Job* 6:4 Satan is "transformed" (μετασχηματισθείς) into a pauper, and then in 17:2 into a likeness of the Persian king.[53] In *L.A.E.* 29:12 *Apoc.*[54] Satan comes to Eve "taking the form of an angel (λαβών σχῆμα

---

47   For a similar play on γίνομαι, see Buxton, *Forms of Astonishment*, 130–34, commenting on Moschus, *Eur.* 165–66.

48   Dibelius, pp. 74–75; Müller, pp. 63–64; idem, "Der Christushymnus Phil 2,6-11," *ZNW* 79 (1988) 17–44, esp. 23–27; idem, *Die Menschwerdung des Gottessohn: Frühchristliche Inkarnationsvorstellungen und die Anfänge des Doketismus* (SBS 140; Stuttgart; Katholisches Bibelwerk, 1990) 20–26; Zeller, "Menschwerdung," 160–63; Thomas Söding, "Erniedrigung und Erhöhung: Zum Verhältnis von Christologie und Mythos nach dem Philipperhymnus (Phil 2,6-11)," *ThPh* 67 (1992) 1–28 (reprinted in idem, *Das Wort vom Kreuz: Studien zur paulinischen Theologie* [WUNT 93; Tübingen: Mohr Siebeck, 1997] 104–31); Vollenweider, "Metamorphose."

49   Euripides, *Bacch.* lines 4–5. The *Bacchae* continued to be performed well into the first centuries CE. With its anti-imperial themes, it may have been particularly popular in the Greek-speaking eastern provinces, as Michael Cover has recently argued in "The Death of Tragedy: The Form of God in Euripides' *Bacchae* and Paul's *Carmen Christi*" (forthcoming). I am grateful to Professor Cover for sharing the manuscript of his learned article with me in advance of its publication. The *Bacchae* was translated into Latin by Pacuvius and Accius by the second century BCE and forms the basis for Ovid, *Metam.* 3.511–733 (Courtney Friesen, *Reading Dionysus: Euripides' Bacchae and the Cultural Contestations of Greeks, Jews, Romans, and Christians* [STAC 95; Tübingen: Mohr Siebeck, 2015] 99). For the worship of Dionysus at Philippi, see Pilhofer,

Philippi, 1:100–107 (discussed by Cover, "Death of Tragedy"). For Dionysian themes in Acts, see Weaver, *Plots of Epiphany*; for Euripidean themes in Paul, see Stowers, *Rereading*, 260–72; for Dionysian themes in Second Temple Judaism, see Friesen, *Reading Dionysus*, 17–19, 36–39, 86–94 and passim.

50   Euripides, *Bacch.* lines 53–54. The verb translated "taken in exchange" (ἀλλάξας) is found in Paul in 1 Cor 15:51-52, where it is applied to the metamorphosis of the righteous at the parousia: "We shall not all sleep, but we shall all be changed [ἀλλαγησόμεθα] in a moment, in the blinking of an eye, with a last trumpet. For the trumpet will sound and the dead will be raised incorruptible, and we shall be changed [ἀλλαγησόμεθα]."

51   Translating κρύψεν and γείνετο as unaugmented or so-called Homeric aorists (Smyth §438c).

52   For human transformations, see, e.g., Mach, *Entwicklungsstadien*, 163–84.

53   Cf. *T. Sol.* 20:13, where the demon Ornias explains that demons are regularly "transformed" into men.

54   The Greek text of *L.A.E.* (commonly indicated by the suffix *Apoc.*, versus the somewhat different Latin version commonly indicated by the suffix *Vita*) is difficult. Here I follow the versification of Johannes Tromp, *The Life of Adam and Eve in Greek: A Critical Edition* (PVTG 6; Leiden: Brill, 2005). The versification of *L.A.E. Apoc.* in *OTP* 2 is slightly different. According to *OTP* 2 the text cited here is *L.A.E.*19:15 *Apoc.* (p. 261).

ἀγγέλου).[55] That Paul was familiar with these traditions is evident from 2 Cor 11:14: "for even Satan transforms himself [μετασχηματίζεται] into an angel of light."[56] According to the *Prayer of Joseph*, the patriarch Jacob was actually the angel Israel in human form, the implication being that, not unlike Paul's heavenly Christ, the angel Israel maintained his metamorphosed form over the course of a complete human life.[57]

In Greco-Roman myth, when a god changed form it was the god himself or herself that caused the change. When humans changed form, however, the change was not of their own doing but was effected by a god or some other agent of supernatural power such as a magician or witch.[58] Further, the self-transformation of a god in Greco-Roman myth was typically to conceal the god's identity, while the transformations of humans could be revelatory, showing something of the metamorphosed person's abiding character.[59] This feature of human metamorphosis is already present in Sophocles's lost *Tereus*.[60] We see it again, now as a leitmotif, in the *Ornithogonia* of the Hellenistic mythographer Boios.[61] It receives its fullest treatment in Ovid, where, for instance, the vicious Lycaon is changed into a wolf, while the inseparable Baucis and Philemon become trees that share a common trunk.[62] Joseph B. Sodolow calls this feature in Ovid "clarification."[63] At times divine transformations can also be revelatory.[64]

Not surprisingly, in Judaism, angels occupy a kind of halfway position: they have the power to transform themselves, but they can also be transformed by God

---

55 Again compare Phil 2:7a: "taking the form of a slave" (μορφὴν δούλου λαβών); see also Tatian, *Or.* 10.

56 See the discussion and texts cited by Hans Windisch, *Der zweite Korintherbrief* (KEK 6; Göttingen: Vandenhoeck & Ruprecht, 1924) on 2 Cor 11:14. See also Justin, *1 Apol.* 5.4: "the Word taking on form [μορφωθέντος] and becoming a human [ἀνθρώπου γενομένου]." On the postmortem Christ's continued metamorphosis, see the so-called longer ending of Mark (16:12), where he appears to the two on the road "in a different form" (ἐν ἑτέρᾳ μορφῇ).

57 Apud Origen, *In Ioann.* 2.31; cf. *PGM* 4.1716–870 ("The Sword of Dardanos"), esp. 1735–36. Cf. Horace, *Carm.* 1.2.41–48, which celebrates Augustus as the metamorphosed Mercury and prays that he remain with the Romans over the course of a long lifetime: "and may you, having changed form, assume the likeness of a youth [*mutata iuvenem figura . . . imitaris*] . . . and late return to heaven, pleased to dwell among the children of Quirinius for a long time [*serus in caelum redeas diuque laetus intersis populo Quirini*]." For other Greek and Roman deities who maintained their metamorphosed forms for lengthy periods, see Vollenweider, "Metamorphose," 13, who cites Euripides, *Alc.* 1–7 (Apollo), and Ovid, *Metam.* 11.202–3 (Apollo and Poseidon). These examples would seem to answer Zeller's objection that the "incarnation" cannot be viewed as an instance of metamorphosis since it took place over the course of a lifetime ("New Testament Christology," 322; cf. Reumann, p. 343). At any rate, all Christ-myths are by necessity hybrid myths since they must incorporate elements from the life of a historical person.

58 Examples are many: Homer, *Od.* 10.210–44; Apuleius, *Metam.* 3.24 and 11.13; Ovid, *Metam.* 6.135–45.

59 Cf. Caroline Walker Bynum, *Metamorphosis and Identity* (New York: Zone Books, 2001).

60 Here see Buxton, *Forms of Astonishment*, 57, who cites *TrGF* 4.435–36.

61 For a discussion, see Forbes Irving, *Metamorphosis*, 33–36.

62 Lycaon (Ovid, *Metam.* 1.237–39; cf. Hesiod, frag. 161–64); Baucis and Philemon (*Metam.* 8.707–20). Other examples include the foul-tongued Lycian shepherds, who are turned into frogs (Ovid, *Metam.* 6.374–76) and the hardhearted Anaxarete who becomes stone (*Metam.* 14.757–58; cf. 10.241–42).

63 Joseph B. Sodolow, *The World of Ovid's Metamorphoses* (Chapel Hill: University of North Carolina Press, 1988) 174–82. On the logic for the relationship between various types of transformation and characterization in Aristophanes, see M. S. Silk, *Aristophanes and the Definition of Comedy* (Oxford: Oxford University Press, 2000) 207–55. Even more to the point is the *Ornithogonia* of Boios, according to which various bird species arose when a human was metamorphosed into a bird that preserved one or more of its progenitor's traits. See Michael Kelly and Frank C. Keil, "The more things change . . . Metamorphoses and conceptual structure," *Cognitive Science* 9 (1985) 403–16.

64 In Homer, *Od.* 5.51–54, the messenger god Hermes takes the form of a seagull to travel across the sea, while in 5.352–53 the sea goddess Leukothea transforms herself into a shearwater; see Euripides, *Bacch.* 618 for Dionysos as a bull, indicative of his tauromorphic iconography but in this case possibly as a symbol of destruction as well as fertility (Walter Burkert, *Greek Religion* [Cambridge, MA: Harvard University Press, 1985] 64).

(e.g., Heb 1:7). Christ's metamorphosis in Phil 2:6-11 is of this mixed, angelic type. Christ initially effects his own transformation; however, his change back to a divine form is effected by God. Of particular relevance to the meaning of 2:6-11 in its larger context in the letter is the fact that Christ's metamorphosis "clarifies" (to use Sodolow's term) two key features of his character, namely, his humility and his obedience.[65] Paul's theory of the incarnation as metamorphosis may have found later expression in the gospels in the so-called transfiguration (Mark 9:2-8).[66]

Four expressions in vv. 7-8 call for separate comment: (1) "he emptied himself" (v. 7a); (2) "adopting a human likeness"; (3) "becoming obedient" (v. 8a); and (4) "even death on a cross" (v. 8b), the last of which I will treat in a separate excursus. The expression "he emptied himself" (ἑαυτὸν ἐκένωσεν) is important primarily because it became the basis for later christological theories of "kenosis," in the context of which it is then often overinterpreted. I will make three exegetical observations. First, as it stands in the letter, the verb "he emptied" (ἐκένωσεν) gestures to the earlier noun "empty conceit" (κενοδοξία) in 2:3a—just as the verb "he humbled" (ἐταπείνωσεν) in 2:8 references the earlier noun "humility" (ταπεινοφροσύνη) in 2:3b and the adjective "obedient" (ὑπήκοος), also in 2:8, anticipates the verb "obeyed" (ὑπηκούσατε) in 2:12. Paul chose the expression to produce a meaningful wordplay: rather than displaying "empty conceit" Christ "emptied himself." Second, the progression "he emptied himself, taking the form of a slave, adopting a human likeness" may reflect a two-step pattern found in other accounts of divine metamorpho-

sis, according to which a deity must first veil or set aside his or her divinity and its accoutrements before assuming a mundane form. We have already seen this in Zeus's metamorphosis in Moschus, *Eur.* 79: "he hid [κρύψεν] his divinity, transformed his body, and became [γείνετο] a bull."[67] Mercury follows a similar procedure in Ovid, *Metam.* 8.626, laying aside his wings (*positis alis*) before taking a human form.[68] Third and finally, the starkness of the claim "he *emptied* himself" neatly anticipates the hyperbole "taking the form of a slave," as well as Christ's slavelike death on a "cross."

The expression ἐν ὁμοιώματι ἀνθρώπων γενόμενος, which I have translated "*adopting* a human likeness," has also been translated "*being born* in human likeness" (NRSV). The latter may seem a better translation based on Gal 4:4: γενόμενος ἐκ γυναικός, "born of a woman," and Rom 1:3: γενόμενος ἐκ σπέρματος Δαυίδ, "born of the seed of David." But the expression used in Gal 4:4 and Rom 1:3 is γίνομαι ἐκ, whereas the expression used in Phil 2:7 is γίνομαι ἐν. According to BDAG γίνομαι ἐν indicates not coming to be in some absolute sense, such as, say, being born, but "entry into a new condition" or a new "state of being."[69] This is the language of change, not birth, and since in Phil 2:6 the new "condition" or "state" into which Christ enters is human "likeness" (ὁμοίωμα), the type of change in view is what Paul's contemporaries would have called metamorphosis.[70] I have already given numerous examples of metamorphic myths in which γίνομαι is used to mean "change into."[71] Here I simply cite *L.A.E.* 17:1 *Apoc*, where Eve uses the expression γίνομαι ἐν to describe Satan's metamorphosis in the Garden: "Then Satan adopted the appearance of an angel

65 For the eschatological "clarification" of the righteous and the wicked in Jewish apocalypticism, see *2 Bar.* 51:1-6; cf. Wisdom 1–6. For the relationship between the character of the righteous (and the wicked) and the form of their final transformation, see Liv Ingeborg Lied, "Recognizing the Righteous Remnant? Resurrection, Recognition and Eschatological Reversals in 2 Baruch 47–52," in *Metamorphoses: Resurrection, Body and Transformative Practices in Early Christianity*, ed. Turid Karlsen Seim and Jorunn Økland (Ekstasis 1; Berlin: de Gruyter, 2009) 311–35, esp. 330–31.

66 For the transfiguration as metamorphic myth, see Moss, "Transfiguration"; Adela Yarbro Collins,

Mark: A Commentary (Hermeneia; Minneapolis: Fortress Press, 2007) on 9:2-8; for the commentary tradition's reticence to use the language of metamorphosis, see Aichele and Walsh, "Metamorphosis."

67 It is noteworthy that, in commenting on Phil 2:7, Chrysostom (hom. 8.142.4-16 Allen) glosses "he emptied" (ἐκένωσεν) with "he hid" (ἔκρυψεν).

68 Zeller, "Menschwerdung," 163.

69 BDAG, s.v. γίνομαι 5, esp. 5c; contrast γίνομαι 1.

70 Collange (on 2:7) has also noted that γενόμενος in v. 8, where it clearly means "becoming," argues against taking γενόμενος in v. 7 to mean "born."

71 See n. 43 above.

[ἐγένετο ἐν εἴδει ἀγγέλου] . . . and I saw him bending over the wall."[72]

The expression "becoming obedient" anticipates the call to obedience in 2:12-16. In neither instance, however, does Paul indicate either the person to whom obedience is offered or the terms of that obedience (i.e., what command or what charge is being obeyed). It is reasonable to assume that the one whom Christ obeyed and whom the Philippians are to obey is God.[73] Less obvious are the terms of obedience. Paul uses the noun "obedience" (ὑπακοή) and its cognates eighteen times.[74] In a few instances the terms of obedience are specified, as in Rom 10:16, where Paul speaks of those who "do not obey the gospel" (cf. Rom 1:5). Frequently, however, obedience is used absolutely to refer to an attitude of submission to the divine will. This is the sense in 2:8, where Christ's submission is tested by extreme suffering. This will also be the sense in 2:12.[75]

Excursus: Paul's "Theology of the Cross"

The language of crucifixion occurs seventeen times in Paul's authentic letters.[76] Apart from references to Jesus's crucifixion in the Gospels, the noun "cross" and its cognates appear elsewhere in the New Testament only in later Pauline tradition (Eph 2:16; Col 1:20; 2:14) and in Heb 12:2 and Rev 11:8. We may with good reason therefore speak of Paul's theology of the cross. Roman law provided for the public shaming of convicted criminals.[77] The most extreme form of public shaming was crucifixion, which was so degrading that it turned its victim into an object of mocking and disgust, as can be seen from the various accounts of Jesus's crucifixion in the Gospels.[78] Paul's theology of the cross is remarkable in that it does not retreat from these social realities but embraces them in what is almost certainly an effort to subvert them by what social psychologists call self-stigmatization.[79] Paul insists that Christ's crucifixion was a source not of shame but of pride: "May it never be that I boast

---

72   I have already cited *L.A.E.* 29:12 *Apoc:* λαβὼν σχῆμα ἀγγέλου ("taking the form of an angel") in conjunction with the almost identical expression μορφὴν δούλου λαβὼν ("taking the form of a slave") in Phil 2:7. Taken together *L.A.E.* 17:1 *Apoc* and 29:12 *Apoc* argue strongly that the two expressions γίνομαι ἐν εἴδει/ὁμοιώματι and λαμβάνω σχῆμα/μορφήν are semantic equivalents. This is not to say, however, that at the time Paul wrote Phil 2:6-11 he no longer believed that Christ was "born of a woman" (Gal 4:4) or "born of the seed of David" (Rom 1:3), but only that, for Paul, Christ's birth was part of a larger *metamorphic* event. It was the means by which the angelic Christ assumed a human "form." For similar lifelong metamorphoses, see Origen, *In Ioann.* 2:31; *PGM* 4.1716–870, esp. 1735–36; Horace, *Carm.* 1.2.41–48; cf. Euripides, *Alc.* 1–7; Ovid, *Metam.* 11.202–3.

73   As this seems required by the logic of v. 9: "Therefore *God* highly exalted him . . ."; and by the statement in 2:13: "for *God* is the one working within you."

74   The noun occurs in Rom 1:5; 5:19; 6:16 (twice); 15:18; 16:19, 26; 2 Cor 7:15; 10:5, 6; Phlm 21; the verb occurs in Rom 6:12, 16, 17; 10:16; Phil 2:12; 1 Thess 1:8; 3:14.

75   For "obedience" to God as a willingness to accept suffering, see Epictetus, *Diss.* 2.6.16.

76   The noun σταυρός ("cross") occurs seven times (1 Cor 1:17, 18; Gal 5:11; 6:12, 14; Phil 2:8; 3:18), the verb σταυρόω ("to crucify") eight times (1 Cor 1:13,

23; 2:2, 3; 2 Cor 13:4; Gal 3:1; 5:24; 6:14), and the compound verb συνσταυρόω ("to crucify alongside of" or "to crucify together with") twice (Rom 6:6; Gal 2:19).

77   Jill Harries, *Law and Crime in the Roman World* (Cambridge: Cambridge University Press, 2007), index s.v. *infamia;* J. A. Crook, *Law and Life of Rome* (Aspects of Greek and Roman Life; Ithaca, NY: Cornell University Press, 1967) 83–85; A. H. J. Greenridge, *Infamia: Its Place in Roman Public and Private Law* (Oxford: Clarendon, 1894); cf. Donald G. Kyle, *Spectacles of Death in Ancient Rome* (London: Routledge, 1998).

78   See also Cicero, *Ver.* 2.5.66. More generally, Martin Hengel, *Crucifixion in the Ancient World and the Folly of the Message of the Cross* (Philadelphia: Fortress Press, 1977); John Granger Cook, *Crucifixion in the Mediterranean World* (WUNT 327; Tübingen: Mohr Siebeck, 2014).

79   Wolfgang Lipp, "Selbststigmatisierung," in *Stigmatisierung: Zur Produktion gesellschaftlicher Randgruppen,* ed. Manfred Brusten and Jürgen Hohmeier (Neuwied/Darmstadt: Luchterhand, 1975) 25–53; idem, *Stigma und Charisma: Über soziales Grenzverhalten* (Berlin: Reimer, 1985); cf. Götz Hartmann, *Selbststigmatisierung und Charisma christlicher Heiliger der Spätantike* (STAC 38; Tübingen: Mohr Siebeck, 2006). Lipp's theory has been insightfully and convincingly applied to the label "Christian" by David Horrell, "The Label Χριστιανός: 1 Peter 4:16 and the Formation of Christian Identity," *JBL* 126 (2007) 361–81; idem, "Leiden als Discriminierung und Mar-

in anything other than the cross of our Lord Jesus Christ" (Gal 6:14).

The evidence suggests that Paul came by this solution over time. He does not mention Christ's crucifixion in 1 Thessalonians, his earliest extant letter, even though it would have been relevant to his discussion of suffering in 3:1-5. But by the time he writes 1 Corinthians a few years later he can claim to preach nothing other than "Christ and him crucified" (2:2; cf. Gal 3:1).[80] Paul knows that Christ's crucifixion is a "scandal" (Gal 5:11) and that his message of the cross strikes many as "foolishness" (1 Cor 1:18). Nevertheless, he defiantly insists that for those who accept his gospel, the cross is "the power of God and wisdom of God" (1 Cor 1:24).[81] Paul incorporates his "theology of the cross" into the social identity of his assemblies through his theory of baptism as "co-crucifixion" with Christ (Rom 6:6; cf. Gal 2:19),[82]

and in his construction of his opponents as "enemies of the cross of Christ" (Phil 3:18; cf. Gal 6:14). Here in Phil 2:8 the cross becomes the dramatic turning point or *peripeteia* in Paul's Christ-myth. Paul's theology of the cross comes into the Gospel tradition through Mark, where it becomes the condition for the possibility of the first narrative account of Jesus's prophetic ministry and shameful death.[83]

■ **9-11** Verses 9-11 relate the second half of Paul's Christ-myth. As reward (διό, "therefore")[84] for the radical self-humbling and obedience of vv. 6-8, God grants Christ a kind of celestial promotion. Paul imagines this promotion taking place in two stages, both of which he derives from contemporary Jewish angel speculation. For the present Christ has been elevated to the rank of God's

tyrium: (Selbst-)Stigmatisierung und Social-Identität am Beispiel des ersten Petrusbriefes," in *Erkennen und Erleben: Beiträge zur psychologischen Erforschung des frühen Christentums*, ed. Gerd Theissen and Petra von Gemünden (Gütersloh: Gütersloher Verlagshaus, 2007) 119–32.

80   This marks a significant development in Paul's message and may have been due in part to social distance that existed between Paul and certain of the Corinthian Christ-believers, for whom Paul's lack of *urbanitas* was an embarrassment (cf. 2 Cor 10:10). Paul adduces the cross as evidence that God is in the process of subverting the social and cultural values that so significantly disadvantaged him (1:18-25). For the difference between Paul's missions to Thessalonica and Corinth, see John M. G. Barclay, "Conflict in Thessalonica," *CBQ* 55 (1993) 512–30; and esp. idem, "Thessalonica and Corinth: Social Contrasts in Pauline Christianity," *JSNT* 47 (1992) 49–74.

81   Here see esp. John M. G. Barclay, "Crucifixion as Wisdom: Exploring the Ideology of a Disreputable Social Movement," in *The Wisdom and Foolishness of God: First Corinthians 1–2 in Theological Exploration*, ed. Christophe Chalamet and Hans-Christoph Askani (Minneapolis: Fortress Press, 2015) 1–20.

82   For Paul's theory of baptism, see esp. Adela Yarbro Collins, "The Origins of Christian Baptism," *StudLit* 19 (1989) 28–46.

83   For Mark's theology of the cross as an expression of his Paulinism, see Joel Marcus, "Mark—Interpreter of Paul," *NTS* 46 (2000) 473–87, esp. 479–81; Troels Engberg Pedersen, "Biografisering: teologi og narration i Markusevangeliet kap. 8–10," in *Frelsens biografisering*, ed. Thomas L. Thompson and Henrik Tronier (Forum for Bibelsk Eksegese 13; Copenha-

gen: Museum Tusculanums Forlag, 2005) 177–89. Like Paul, Mark calls Jesus "the crucified one" (Mark 16:6; 1 Cor 1:23; 2:2; cf. Matt 28:5). It is also reasonable to assume that the allegedly dominical saying "let him take up his cross" (Mark 8:34; cf. Matt 16:24; Luke 9:3, which adds "daily") is of similar theological derivation. See Heikki Räisänen, "Jesus and the Food Laws: Reflections on Mark 7.15," *JSNT* 16 (1982) 79–100; Michael D. Goulder, "Those Outside (Mk. 4.10-12)," *NovT* 33 (1991) 289–302; Wolfgang Schenk, "Sekundäre Jesuanisierungen von primären Paulus-Aussagen bei Markus," in *The Four Gospels 1992: Festschrift for Frans Neirynck*, ed. Frans van Segbroeck, Christopher M. Tuckett, Gilbert Van Belle, and Joseph Verheyden (3 vols; BEThL 100; Leuven: Leuven University Press, 1992) 2:877–904.

84   This is the clear sense of διό, though the commentary tradition has steadfastly resisted it, for what appear to be wholly theological reasons; but see Photinus (bishop of Sirmium ca. 344) apud Aquinas: *hoc ponitur hic sicut praemium humilitatis Christi: et dicit, quod non est verus Deus, sed quod sit sibi data quaedam eminentia creaturae, et similitudo divinitatis* ["But Photinus says] that this is mentioned as a reward for Christ's humility: and he says that [Christ] is not true God but that he received a certain preeminence over creation and a likeness to divinity"; trans. Larcher modified). The tension between reward ("therefore") and grace ("he gave" [ἐχαρίσατο]) is characteristic of both Paul and more broadly Second Temple Judaism.

principal Name-bearing angel: "God more highly exalted him and gave him the Name that is above every other name" (v. 9). In the near future Christ will be made to rule over all creation as God's vice-regent: "in order that in the name of Jesus every knee should bow . . . and every tongue confess that Jesus Christ is 'Lord' to the glory of God the Father" (vv. 10-11).[85]

■ **9** The commentary tradition has focused on two items in v. 9: (1) the verb ὑπερύψωσεν, which I have translated "more highly exalted" and, to a lesser degree, (2) the expression τὸ ὄνομα τὸ ὑπὲρ πᾶν ὄνομα, which I have translated "the Name that is above every other name." In the first case a problem arises in terms of the prepositional prefix ὑπέρ. Does it retain its meaning as an independent preposition ("over and above")[86] or does it merely underscore the meaning of the root verb without substantially adding to it, a phenomenon common in Hellenistic Greek?[87] It is important to solve this problem, we are told,[88] because it determines whether we view the reward of vv. 9-11 as a restoration of the crucified Christ to his preexistent glory, or as his elevation to a status "over and above" what he initially enjoyed.

That the prepositional prefix retains something close

to its original meaning of "over and above" is made almost certain by its repetition in the immediately following expression "the Name that is above (ὑπέρ) every other name."[89] However, in terms of determining the overall meaning of the text, the precise connotation of the verb ὑπερύψωσεν is at best secondary. For in the expression ὁ θεὸς αὐτὸν ὑπερύψωσεν ("God more highly exalted him") the antecedent of the pronoun αὐτόν ("him") is the angelic Christ of v. 5, who retains his angelic identity throughout the metamorphosis of vv. 6-8,[90] just as, say, Zeus retains his divine identity when he "takes the form" of a swan in the Leda myth or "becomes a bull" in the rape of Europa, or as the great angel Satan retains his archangelic identity when he "transforms" himself first into a pauper and then into the king of Persia in the *Testament of Job*.[91] In other words, it is not the man Jesus allegedly[92] introduced in vv. 7-8 who is exalted in v. 9,[93] in which case a mere restoration to the status of v. 5 might legitimately be termed an "exaltation,"[94] but the angelic Christ, any exaltation of whom would necessarily mean an enhancement of his original status, regardless of how we understand the verb.[95]

---

85 This subjection has not yet taken place (Phil 3:21b; cf. 1 Cor 15:25-28).

86 BDAG, s.v. ὑπέρ B.

87 BDF §116.1.4.

88 E.g., Collange.

89 It is difficult to show this sense in a good English translation, but one might paraphrase: "Christ is exalted *over and above* (ὑπέρ-) by being given the Name that is *over and above* (ὑπέρ) etc."

90 Note that the pronoun "himself" (ἑαυτόν) in v. 7, repeated in v. 8, also has as its antecedent the Christ figure of v. 5.

91 Euripides, *Hel.* 19; Moschus, *Eur.* 79; *T. Job* 6.4 and 17.2. See the discussion of these texts above at 2:7-8. Presumably, in neither Zeus's case nor Satan's would a return to his pre-metamorphosed form have been considered an "exaltation." The same would thus hold true for Christ, whose "exaltation" must be more than a simple restoration.

92 Strictly speaking there is no human Jesus in vv. 7-8 but a heavenly being who has taken the "form" or "likeness" of a human; cf. Rom 8:3.

93 Beare: "it is in his *manhood* that Christ is now exalted" (emphasis original). Would the same hold

true, say, of Zeus's "bull-hood" upon his return to Olympus?

94 Zeller ("New Testament Christology") interprets Phil 2:9 as an instance of apotheosis on analogy with Ovid, *Metam.* 9.268–72 (Hercules) or *Metam.* 15.746–50 (Caesar). But this approach reifies the humanity of Jesus in a way not found in Phil 2:6-11. For Paul, Christ is here not a human who became a god but a god who took the "form" of a human and then returned to his divine form. This is not to say that other Christ-myths, such as that of Luke-Acts, might not be illuminated by the apotheosis model. Oddly, in his earlier "Menschwerdung" Zeller interprets Phil 2:6-8 as metamorphosis (or what he calls "epiphany").

95 These considerations return us to the larger question of how we are to understand the Christ-myth of 2:6-11. I have interpreted it as a straightforward metamorphic myth according to which a lesser divinity changes form to undertake a difficult mission and is rewarded with a kind of celestial promotion. Other models of the "incarnation" might place a greater emphasis on the human identity of Jesus, who, for example, following his martyrdom was

This brings us to the expression "the Name that is above every other name," which marks the first part of Christ's two-part reward. For a Jew like Paul, "the Name that is above every other name" would naturally have meant the divine name "Yahweh," which is why I have capitalized "Name" in the first instance. Most commentators readily allow this meaning, but a few like Moule point ahead to v. 10, where Paul writes "that in the name of Jesus [ἐν τῷ ὀνόματι Ἰησοῦ] every knee should bow," to argue that the name in question in v. 9 is not "Yahweh" but "Jesus."[96] There are at least two problems with Moule's interpretation. First, the phrase "in the name of Jesus" is an instance of the idiom "in the name of X," in which "X" does not so much indicate a name as a person, as in the phrase "in the name of the Lord."[97] Moule fails to discern this idiom, translating *at the name of Jesus*," as if it were when the name "Jesus" is announced that all creation will bow.[98] In answer to Moule, then, it is enough to observe that Paul is using "name" in two different senses, neither of which can be used to interpret the other.[99]

A second problem with Moule's interpretation is that it fails to recognize the emerging tradition of an exalted Name-bearing angel in contemporary Jewish apocalypticism. There was an established tradition in ancient Judaism about a מלך יהוה or "angel of Yahweh."[100] The imagined relationship of these angels to Yahweh is uncertain. They are often presented as distinct from Yahweh. At other times, however, their identity and Yahweh's are less clearly distinguished, since the individuals to whom they appear claim to have seen Yahweh himself. These texts are highly ambiguous—Benjamin D. Sommer has recently proposed that these angels are essentially "avatars" of Yahweh[101]—and there is usually no attempt to resolve that ambiguity in the surrounding narrative. An exception to this is Exod 23:20-21, where Yahweh explains to Moses that the angel assigned to lead Israel through the wilderness has "my *Name* [שמי] in him." This is presumably offered as an explanation of the way Yahweh is present in or with that angel, since the same language is used of Yahweh's presence at Shiloh and later in the Jerusalem temple: "I will cause my *Name* [שמי] to dwell there."[102]

Speculation about the nature and function of prominent angels increases greatly with the rise of apocalypticism.[103] I will say more about the role these angels played in my comment on 2:10-11 below. Here I simply note that in some instances these angels are described as bearing the divine Name. In the *Apocalypse of Abraham* a great angel named Yahoel appears to Abraham "in whom God's ineffable Name dwells."[104] The Babylonian Talmud (*b. Sanh.* 38b) preserves an early tradition attributed to Judah the Prince about an angel named Metatron who possesses a name "like the Name of his Master."[105] In *3 Enoch*, a much later mystical text, God calls the great angel Metatron "Little Yahweh"

"made both Lord and Christ" (Acts 2:36). But that is not the story Paul tells here, nor does it seem to have been Paul's view in general (see Rom 8:3, but cf. Rom 1:3-4). Christ adopts the "form" or "likeness" of a human, but he is thereby no more actually human than, say, Zeus is actually a swan or a bull or Satan a pauper or the king of Persia in the myths just cited. For Christ's earlier metamorphosis into a rock, see 1 Cor 10:4 ("the rock was [ἦν] Christ").

96   Moule, "Further Reflections," 264–76.

97   See, e.g., Jas 5:10, where prophets speak "in the name of the Lord"; see also BDAG, s.v. ὄνομα 1, d, γ, ב.

98   This misreading has been explicitly rejected already by Vincent: "'*in the name of Jesus*'; not '*at the name*.'"

99   This is not to say that Paul might not have been clearer.

100 Fridolin Stier, *Gott und sein Engel im alten Testament* (Alttestamentliche Abhandlungen 12.2; Münster: Aschendorff, 1934).

101 Sommer, *Bodies of God*, 40–44.

102 For the temple, see 1 Kgs 8:16, 29; 9:3; for Shiloh, Jer 7:12.

103 Mach, *Entwicklungsstadien*; Peter Schäfer, *Rivalität zwischen Engeln und Menschen: Untersuchungen zur rabbinischen Engelvorstellung* (Studia Judaica 8; Berlin: de Gruyter, 1975).

104 *Apoc. Abr.* 10:4-8; 11:1-3; cf. the *Ascension of Isaiah*, where each of the seven heavens is ruled by an angel whose name cannot be mentioned.

105 Perhaps assimilating the tradition about Yahoel, as initially suggested by Gershom G. Scholem, *Major Trends in Jewish Mysticism* (3rd rev. ed.; New York: Schocken, 1961; 1st ed. 1941) 68–69; see also idem, *Jewish Gnosticism, Merkabah Mysticism, and Talmudic Tradition* (New York: Jewish Theological Seminary, 1960) 41.

(יהוה הקטן).[106] In light of this developing tradition, it makes perfect sense for Paul to claim that, as reward for his humility and obedience, God promoted Christ to the rank of Name-bearing angel.[107]

■ **10-11** Verses 10-11 relate the second aspect of Christ's exaltation: his coming eschatological reign as God's vice-regent. One of the most intriguing features of Jewish angel speculation is the fact that it is not always God who sits on his throne and exercises world dominion. At the headwaters of this tradition is Ezekiel's vision of a human-like figure referred to as the "image of the likeness of the Glory of Yahweh" seated upon God's chariot-throne known in later tradition as the *merkābāh* (מרכבה, Ezek 1:26-28).[108] Similarly, in Daniel the angel Michael, who is described as "one like a son of man," is given "dominion and glory and kingship, that all peoples, nations, and languages should serve him" (Dan 7:14).[109] Particularly striking is the Messiah/Son of Man of the Parables of Enoch,

who as eschatological judge ascends to God's "throne of glory,"[110] an expression picked up in Matt 19:28; 25:31 to describe to Jesus's role as eschatological judge.[111] It is also noteworthy in this regard that the name of the exalted angel of later rabbinic-mystical tradition "Metatron" derives from the Greek *metathronos*. As it stands, the name means "one who stands behind the throne," but this name is commonly held to be a rabbinic reworking of Greek term *synthronos*, meaning something like "one who sits beside on the throne."[112] An Aramaic incantation bowl describes Metatron as איסרא רבא דכורסיה, "the great prince of [God's] throne."[113]

Christ's relationship to God is not spatially represented in Phil 2:10-11. Nevertheless, he is granted the divine Name "in order that[114] in the name of Jesus[115] every knee should bow, of those in heaven and on the earth and under the ground."[116] And his reign is on God's behalf: "to the glory of God the Father."[117] The

---

106 E.g., *3 Enoch* 10:3; cf. Peter Schäfer, *Synopse zur Hekaloth-Literatur* (TSAJ 2; Tübingen: Mohr Siebeck, 1981) §§15, 73, and 76.

107 See Samuel Vollenweider, "Zwischen Monotheismus und Engelchristologie: Überlegungen zur Frühgeschichte des Christusglaubens," in idem, *Horizonte neutestamentlicher Christologie: Studien zu Paulus und zur frühchristlichen Theologie* (WUNT 144: Tübingen: Mohr Siebeck, 2002) 3–27; and esp. idem, "'Der Name, der über jeden anderen Namen ist,' Jesus als Träger des Gottesnamens im Neuen Testament," in *Gott Nennen: Gottes Namen und Gott als Name*, ed. Ingolf U. Dalferth and Philipp Stoellger (RPT 35; Tübingen: Mohr Siebeck, 2008) 173–86.

108 See Schäfer, *Origins*, 34–52.

109 See Collins, *Daniel*, on this verse.

110 In *1 Enoch* 47:3 and 60:2 it is the "Lord of Spirits" who sits on his "throne of glory." Elsewhere it is the "Chosen One" or "Son of Man": 45:3; 55:4; 61:8; 62:2, 3, 5; 69:27, 29; 71:7; see Nickelsburg and VanderKam, *1 Enoch 2*, 261–63.

111 Nickelsburg, *Resurrection*, 94–95; and more recently, Leslie W. Walck, *Son of Man in the Parables of Enoch and in Matthew* (Jewish and Christian Texts in Contexts and Related Studies 9; London/New York: T&T Clark, 2011).

112 Saul Lieberman, "Metatron, the Meaning of His Name and His Functions," (Appendix) in Ithamar Gruenwald, *Apocalyptic and Merkavah Mysticism* (AGJU 14; Leiden: Brill, 1980; rev. ed., 2014) 235–41 (pp. 291–97 in the revised edition); supported

by Peter Schäfer, *Hidden*, 29 n. 70. In Rev 5:6 the phrase ἐν μέσῳ τοῦ θρόνου, "in the midst of the throne," is used of Christ; in 4:6 it is used of the τέσσαρα ζῷα, "four living creatures."

113 Cyrus H. Gordon, "Aramaic Magical Bowls in the Istanbul and Bagdad Museums," *Archiv orientálni* 6 (1934) 319–34, plates 10–15, here 328–29 (cited by Andrei A. Orlov, *The Enoch-Metatron Tradition* [TSAJ 107; Tübingen: Mohr Siebeck, 2005] 121).

114 Christ is given the divine Name "in order that" (ἵνα) he might rule. In other words, it is as the Name-bearing angel (v. 9) that Christ will eventually rule as God's vice-regent (vv. 10-11). This arrangement is expressive of Paul's famous already-not yet tension. Christ has *already* been granted the divine Name on the basis of which he will soon achieve universal dominion, but that dominion has *not yet* been realized.

115 The expression "in the name of Jesus" should be understood to mean that "those in heaven, etc." will soon bow their knees *to* Jesus; cf. Ps 62:5 LXX (MT 63:4; cited by Bockmuehl): "In your name [ἐν τῷ ὀνόματί σου] shall I raise my hands," where raising one's hands "in the name of" God means raising one's hands *to* God.

116 Revelation 5:13 equates a similar expression ("that which is in heaven and on the earth and under the earth and on the sea") with "all creation" (πᾶν κτίσμα). "Those under the ground" (καταχθονίων) presumably means both the dead and all chthonic deities; cf. Müller.

meaning of the confession that "Jesus Christ is Lord [κύριος]" is ambiguous.[118] It could simply mean Jesus Christ is one who exercises dominion.[119] But, given the reference to the divine Name in v. 9 and the fact that

κύριος typically translates the divine Name in the LXX, an allusion to Christ as the principal angel who now bears the divine Name seems more likely.

---

117 Cf. 1 Cor 15:28; for the characteristic Pauline phrase "for the glory of God," see Rom 15:7; 1 Cor 10:31; 2 Cor 1:20; 4:15.

118 See Isa 45:23 LXX for the similar expression "every knee bow and every tongue confess"; Paul quotes

the verse explicitly in Rom 14:11. The confession is compelled; cf. 1 Pet 2:12; *1 Enoch* 62:6; 63:2-3; Wis 5:4-13.

119 BADG, s.v. κύριος 2.

2

12/ **Therefore, my dearly loved ones, just as you have always obeyed—not as**[a] **in my presence only, but now so much the more in my absence—work hard to accomplish your own salvation with fear and trembling,** 13/ **for God, as an expression of his goodwill, is the one producing in you both the ability to will [what is right] and actually do [it].** 14/ **Do all things without grumbling and bickering,**[b] 15/ **so that you might become**[c] **blameless and pure, unblemished**[d] **children of God in the midst of "a crooked and perverse generation," among whom you "shine like stars" in the world,** 16/ **holding out the word**[e] **of life, so that I might have a boast in the Day of Christ, that I neither ran in vain nor labored in vain.**

a   "As" (ὡς) is omitted in several witnesses: B 33, 1241 vg^mss; Ambst.

b   The translation ("bickering") is Bockmuehl's.

c   Several important witnesses (p⁴⁶ A D* F G latt) read ἦτε ("that you might be") rather than γένησθε ("that you might become").

d   A number of witnesses (D F G K L P Ψ 075, 0278, 81, 104, 365, 630, 1739, 1881, 2462 Maj) have the variant spelling ἀμώμητα (cf. Deut 32:5 LXX) rather than ἄμωμα (p⁴⁶, ℵ A B C 33, 1241; Cl).

e   The Greek is ambiguous. The verb ἐπέχω (LSJ, s.v.) can either mean "to hold fast" or "to hold out" (as in to proffer), yielding either "holding fast to the word of life" or "holding out the word of life," both of which make good sense in the context. I have chosen the latter, for which see my comments below on 2:16.

Analysis

The exhortation of 2:12-16 is the third and final targeted exhortation of 1:27—2:16. According to the Christ-myth of 2:6-11, Christ is an example of one who "humbled" himself in the service of others, something Paul urged the Philippians to do in 2:1-4. But Christ is also an example of one who remained "obedient" (ὑπήκοος) even to the point of death. This kind of radical obedience in the face of suffering is the point of the exhortation of 2:12-16: "Therefore, my dearly loved ones, just as you have always obeyed [ὑπηκούσατε] . . . ." At stake is the Philippians' "salvation" (σωτηρία).

Formally, the exhortation of Phil 2:12-16 consists of two shorter exhortations (vv. 12-13 and vv. 14-16), each of which includes its own supporting rationale statement (vv. 13 and 15-16 respectively). Taken together these two shorter exhortations specify the nature of the "obedience" required of the righteous in the last days. Paul concludes 2:12-16—as he also concluded the earlier targeted exhortations of 1:27b-30 and 2:1-4—with a modest *clausula* that once again turns on the figure of doubling (*geminatio*): ὅτι οὐκ εἰς κενὸν ἔδραμον οὐδὲ εἰς κενὸν ἐκοπίασα, "that I neither ran in vain nor labored in vain."[1]

Philippians 2:12-16 may be outlined as follows:

First exhortation (2:12)
Rationale statement (2:13)
Second exhortation (2:14)
Rationale statement (2:15-16)

Comment

■ **12** The Christ-myth of 2:6-11 supports not only Paul's exhortation to "humility" in 2:1-4 but his exhortation to "obedience" in 2:12-16, where the inference is now explicit: "Therefore [ὥστε], my dearly loved ones . . . ." The prior conduct of the Philippians offers a further precedent: "*just as* [καθώς] you have always obeyed . . . ."[2] The verb "obeyed" (ὑπηκούσατε) occurs without an object, but so does the adjective "obedient" (ὑπήκοος) in the Christ-myth (2:8). Obedience to God is implied in both instances, but we should not imagine a specific command so much as a more general attitude of submission to God's will,[3] which in this case includes a willingness to suffer or even to die. Such "obedience" is prerequisite to the Philippians' final salvation (2:12), just as it was to Christ's final exaltation (2:9-11) and is to Paul's own salvation (1:18c-21).

---

1   Paul's repeated use of *geminatio* in all three *clausulae* in 1:27—2:16 is odd. Paul usually strives for more variety in his rhetorical flourishes.

2   Chrysostom: "I urge you to imitate not others but yourselves" (hom. 9.168.13-14). Cf. 1:20, where Paul deploys a similar logic: "that in no way I shall be

cowed but that with all boldness as always so now also [ὡς πάντοτε καὶ νῦν] . . . ."

3   In the first instance (2:8) it is a part of Christ's "attitude" that is to be imitated. For the "will" of God, see 2:13: "according to his goodwill [εὐδοκίας]."

After adducing the Philippians' prior obedience (2:12a), but before the exhortation proper (2:12c), Paul inserts a short parenthesis (2:12b): "not as in my presence only, but now so much the more in my absence."[4] Paul reminds the Philippians that their past obedience was carried out not only when he was with them but also when he was not, which is the case now.[5] The emphasis on absence—"so much the more [πολλῷ μᾶλλον] in my absence"—picks up the theme from 1:27,[6] which in turn continues the theme from 1:25-26,[7] where it is clear that what Paul here euphemistically calls his ἀπουσία, or "absence" (i.e., his imprisonment and possible execution), is the principal cause of the Philippians' distress and inaction: "that your boast in Christ might increase . . . by my presence [παρουσίας] again with you" (1:26).

Paul finishes the exhortation begun in 2:12a in 2:12c: "[just as . . . so now][8] work hard to accomplish [κατεργάζεσθε] your own salvation with fear and trembling." The imperative κατεργάζεσθε, which I have translated "work hard to accomplish," implies both effort and intention. Chrysostom glosses, "He did not say 'work' [ἐργάζεσθε] but 'work hard [κατεργάζεσθε],'" that is, with much earnestness and much attention [μετὰ πολλῆς τῆς σπουδῆς, μετὰ πολλῆς τῆς ἐπιμελείας]."[9] It is the first part

of an extended wordplay that Paul will finish in the next verse: "work hard to accomplish [κατεργάζεσθε] . . . for God . . . is the one producing [ἐνεργῶν] in you . . . both the ability to will [what is right] and to actually do [it] [ἐνεργεῖν]."[10] The adverbial phrase "with fear and trembling" is emphatic by word order and specifies the attitude of patient submission to the divine will that should characterize obedience in the last days.[11] Paul describes the salvation as "your own" (ἑαυτῶν) in contrast to "my [μοι] salvation" in 1:19, the point being that the Philippians must attend to their salvation just as Paul is attending to his.

■ 13 In v. 13 Paul offers a brief rationale statement supporting the exhortation of 2:12: "for [γάρ] God . . . is the one producing in you . . . ." Like the phrase "with fear and trembling" in v. 12, "God" here is emphatic by position.[12] The two emphases are linked: the Philippians are to endure suffering *with fear and trembling* because it is *God* who is at work in them. Also linking v. 13 to v. 12, as already noted, is the wordplay between κατεργάζεσθε ("work hard to accomplish") and ἐνεργῶν ("producing"): God is at *work* in the Philippians and so the Philippians must also *work*.[13] It is noteworthy that Paul senses no contradiction here between divine and human agency. This

4   The adverb "as" (ὡς) continues the comparison begun by "just as" (καθώς), which it now qualifies.

5   The antithesis "not as [μή ὡς] . . . but now [ἀλλὰ νῦν]" is drawn for rhetorical emphasis. Paul was fond of such antitheses. Here it also serves to continue to call attention to the problem of Paul's absence. The point not to be missed, however, is that the Philippians have been without Paul in the past, so the present situation is not wholly new.

6   Phil 1:27: "whether I come and see you or else remain absent [ἀπών]."

7   Phil 1:26: "by my presence [παρουσίας] again with you."

8   A comparison is introduced by the adverb καθώς ("just as"), which is often followed by the correlative οὕτως ("so") or ὁμοίως ("likewise"). The correlative is omitted here, presumably because of the intervening parenthesis in 2:12b.

9   Hom. 9.170.24 25 Allen.

10   Cf. 1 Thess 2:13, where it is the "word" of God that "works in" (ἐνεργεῖται) believers.

11   Paul uses the expression "fear and trembling" elsewhere to refer to his initial anxieties over preaching in Corinth (1 Cor 2:3) and to the Corinthians' recep-

tion of Titus (2 Cor 7:15). Here in Phil 2:12 God, the agent behind the Philippians' suffering, is the object: "for God is the one producing." The expression occurs in Exod 15:16; Deut 2:25; and 11:25 to refer to the fear of the Israelite armies by the inhabitants of the land. In *1 Enoch* 13:3 it marks the Watchers' response to Enoch's report of their pending judgment by God.

12   Paul has already claimed that suffering is from God in 1:29, where he uses the so-called *passiva divina* ("it has been given"). Here in 2:13 God's agency is both explicit and emphatic.

13   Bockmuehl sees here Paul's famous "indicative-imperative" or "is-ought" scheme, adducing Bultmann's dictum "Become what you are!" This does not quite fit, since here the subject of the "indicative" is God, while the subject of the "imperative" is the Philippians. The logic is not "you *are* this so *do* that" but "*God* is doing this so *you* do that." Further, Paul is not stipulating what the Philippians are to do so much as how they are to do it: "with fear and trembling" and, two verses later, "without grumbling and bickering." The sentiment finds a near analogy in Stoicism, where morality lies less in what one does

kind of unreflective "compatibilism" is typical of Paul,[14] for whom divine versus human agency—which was a live question already in his day,[15] even in Judaism[16]—is not so much a philosophical or theological problem as a rhetorical topos to be deployed as needed with the emphasis falling wherever it best suits his purpose.[17]

Paul claims that suffering is God's means of producing a change "within" (ἐν) the Christ-believer.[18] He describes this change as καὶ τὸ θέλειν καὶ τὸ ἐνεργεῖν, which I have translated "both the ability to will [what is right] and actually do [it]." The emphasis falls on the second element, καὶ τὸ ἐνεργεῖν, "and actually do [it]." To Paul's mind, the obstacle to right action lies not in willing what is right but in performing it. He wrote earlier to the Romans, "to

will [τὸ θέλειν] the good is present to me but to strive to accomplish [τὸ κατεργάζεσθαι] it is not" (Rom 7:18).[19] For a Stoic like Seneca, "willing" (velle) was all-important.[20] According to Paul, however, human action is complicated by "another law in my members [ἐν τοῖς μέλεσιν]" that overcomes "the law of my mind [νοός]" (Rom 7:23). Characteristically, the solution for Paul is spirit possession: the mind must be supplemented by the divine πνεῦμα or "spirit." Paul assures the Philippians that in their suffering the divine spirit is at work in them to produce right action,[21] and that all that has been happening to them (and him) is part of God's plan, God's "goodwill" (εὐδοκίας).[22] Suffering yields a similar result in Rom 5:3-5: "affliction produces endurance, and endurance produces

---

than in the attitude with which one does it, namely, complete submission to the divine will; "Father and master of the lofty heavens, lead wherever you wish. I will not hesitate to obey; I am ready and eager" (Seneca, *Ep.* 107.10).

14 Cf. the explicitly paradoxical Gal 2:20: ζῶ δὲ οὐκέτι ἐγώ . . . ὃ δὲ νῦν ζῶ, "I no longer live . . . that which I live."

15 Cf. David J. Furley, "Aristotle and Epicurus on Voluntary Action," in idem, *Two Studies in the Greek Atomists* (Princeton: Princeton University Press, 1967) 159–237; A. A. Long, "Freedom and Determinism in Stoic Theory of Human Action," in *Problems in Stoicism*, ed. A. A. Long (London: Athlone Press, 1971) 173–99.

16 E.g., *m. 'Abot* 3.15 (Akiva); Josephus, *Bell.* 2.163; *Ant.* 13.172–73; 18.13, 18, for which see Jonathan Klawans, "Josephus on Fate, Free Will, and Ancient Jewish Types of Compatibilism," *Numen* 56 (2009) 44–90; George Foot Moore, "Fate and Free Will in the Jewish Philosophies according to Josephus," *HTR* 22 (1929) 371–89; cf. Gerhard Maier, *Mensch und freier Wille nach den jüdischen Religionsparteien zwischen Ben Sira und Paulus* (WUNT 12; Tübingen: Mohr Siebeck, 1981); David Winston, "Freedom and Determinism in Philo of Alexandria," in idem, *The Ancestral Philosophy: Hellenistic Philosophy in Second Temple Judaism*, ed. Gregory E. Sterling (Brown Judaic Studies; Providence, RI: Brown Judaic Studies, 2001) 135–50; Philip Alexander, "Predestination and Free Will in the Theology of the Dead Sea Scrolls," in Barclay and Gathercole, *Agency*, 27–49; John M. G. Barclay, "Grace and the Transformation of Agency" in *Redefining First-Century Jewish and Christian Identities: Essays in Honor of Ed Parish Sanders*, ed. Fabian E. Udoh et al. (Christianity and

Judaism in Antiquity 16; Notre Dame, IN: University of Notre Dame Press, 2008) 372–89.

17 When Paul's purpose is to reassure, divine agency is emphasized (e.g., Phil 1:6); when his purpose is to exhort, human agency comes to the fore (e.g., Phil 1:12). Paul recognizes other agents as well, such as "sin" (Rom 7:8, 17, 20) and certain "elemental spirits" (Gal 4:8-9).

18 Cf. 1:6: "he who began a good work within you [ἐν ὑμῖν]."

19 Paul's abbreviated comments here no doubt reference that discussion. For Romans 7, see Stowers, *Rereading*, 251–84, esp. 260–64. For similar language elsewhere in Paul, see 2 Cor 8:10-12.

20 Seneca, *Ep.* 34.3: *itaque pars magna bonitatis est velle fieri bonum*, "And so the most important part of goodness is willing to be good"; *Ep.* 71.36: *Sed magna pars est profectus velle proficere*, "The most important thing for making progress is willing to make progress"; *Ep.* 80.4: *Quid tibi opus est ut sis bonus? Velle*, "What do you need to become good? The will!" For a nuanced discussion of the will in Seneca, see Brad Inwood, "The Will in Seneca," *CP* 95 (2000) 44–60, reprinted in idem, *Reading Seneca: Stoic Philosophy at Rome* (Oxford: Oxford University Press, 2005) 132–56.

21 Cf. Phil 1:19: "through your prayers for me and the provision of the spirit of Jesus Christ."

22 The prepositional phrase ὑπὲρ τῆς εὐδοκίας, which I have translated "as an expression of his [= God's] goodwill," modifies the participle "working." Paul has used the term εὐδοκία earlier (1:15) to mean "goodwill," and that is the sense I have given it here. The preposition ὑπέρ when used with the genitive carries the sense of "for the sake of." God's efforts to transform believers are "for the sake of" his

character," where God's goodwill or "love" is again adduced: "for God's love has been poured out into our hearts by virtue of the Holy Spirit that has been bestowed on us" (Rom 5:5).[23]

■ **14** Paul further specifies his call to obedience in a second exhortation in 2:14. His concern continues to be with the Philippians' patient submission to God's discipline: "do all things without grumbling and bickering [γογγυσμῶν καὶ διαλογισμῶν]."[24] Paul uses similar language in 1 Cor 10:10 in adducing the story of the "grumbling" of the exodus generation—"Do not grumble [γογγύζετε] as some of them grumbled [ἐγόγγυσαν] and were destroyed"[25]—and that is presumably the allusion here.[26] Paul sees in this story a lesson for the righteous in the last days: "These things happened to them as a type and were written down for our admonition, to whom the ends of the ages have come" (1 Cor 10:11).[27] Paul's point in Phil 2:14, then, is that just as the exodus generation failed to endure testing without "grumbling" and as a result did not reach the promised land, so Christ-believers who "grumble" will not achieve their final salvation. Commentators are divided on whether the grumbling that Paul has in view is directed toward others in the assembly[28] or toward God.[29] In the exodus story, the Israelites grumbled against Moses and God. The reference to "bickering" (διαλογισμός) might support the former (cf. 2:2; 4:2-3). But the warning in 2:13 that it is "God" who is at work in them indicates the latter.[30] The two are not mutually exclusive.[31]

■ **15-16** Paul follows the exhortation of 2:14 with a second rationale statement in 2:15-16. It is longer than the earlier rationale statement in 2:13, and it continues the reference to the story of the exodus generation. This time Paul looks not to divine agency as a motivation but to certain outcomes, both for the Philippians (2:15) and for himself (2:16). If the Philippians will submit to God's discipline "without grumbling and bickering," they will "become" (γένησθε) "blameless and pure" (ἄμεμπτοι καὶ ἀκέραιοι). Paul uses this language elsewhere to refer to the status of the righteous at the final judgment (1 Thess 3:13; 5:23; cf. Phil 1:10). Here, however, the present is in view, as v. 15 makes plain: "unblemished children of God in the midst of 'a crooked and perverse generation' among whom you 'shine like stars' in the world." Paul is imagining a two-stage process in which a Christ-believer's future status is determined by his or her present transformation. He imagines a similar process in 1:11-12, where being found "pure and blameless" in the Day of Christ depends on "having been filled" (πεπληρομένοι) with the fruit of righteousness in this life.[32]

Two items in 2:15 call for further comment: (1) the allusion to Deut 32:5 LXX in the expression "unblemished children of God in the midst of 'a crooked and perverse generation,'" and (2) the expression "'shine like stars' in the world." Paul's allusion to Deut 32:5 is far from straightforward. In Deuteronomy, the Israelites are condemned as "blemished [μώμετα] children" and a "crooked and perverse generation," while in Philippians

---

benevolent purposes, or as I have translated, "as an expression of." Cf. Phil 1:6, where Paul calls God's transformation of the Christ-believer a "good work" or benefaction, and 1:7, 29, where the suffering of the last days is called a gift expressive of divine favor.

23 See my comments on this key text in "*Commendatio*," 375–77.

24 For grumbling in persecution, see esp. *Pss. Sol.* 16:11: "grumbling and faintheartedness in affliction [γογγυσμὸν καὶ ὀλιγοψυχίαν ἐν θλίψει] remove far from me."

25 For the language of destruction and salvation earlier in Philippians, see 1:28 and my comments on that text above.

26 In the LXX, the Greek noun γογγυσμός and its cognate verb γογγύζω translate respectively the noun תלונה and the verb לון in Exod 16:7-12 (six times);

17:3; Num 14:27-29 (three times); 16:41; 17:5 (twice), 10.

27 This is one of the clearest statements of Paul's apocalyptic hermeneutic.

28 See, e.g., Collange; Bockmuehl.

29 See, e.g., Beare; Gnilka.

30 Cf. Exod 16:7, where it is explicitly stated that the complaining was not against Moses and Aaron but against Yahweh.

31 In the exodus story, the Israelites complain against Moses (Exod 16:2; cf. Num 17:5, 10), which is interpreted as complaining against God (Exod 16:7-12; cf. Num 11:1).

32 Cf. Phil 3:8c-9, where one must "gain" Christ in this life to be "found" in him in the final judgment; and 3:10-11, where one must "know" Christ in this life in order to "arrive at the resurrection from the dead."

Paul holds out to his readers the possibility of becoming "*un*blemished [ἄμωμα] children"[33] who exist "*in the midst of* [μέσον] 'a crooked and perverse generation.'" This has been interpreted as an early supersessionist statement: "the church takes over from Israel the privilege of being God's 'child,' but a child without reproach (*amōma*), not a bad, blameworthy child (*mōmēta*), and robbed of this privilege nothing remains for Israel but to melt away into the 'perverse and straying' mass of the world's (*en kosmō*) humanity."[34] Paul is not above such slurs.[35] The reference, however, is not to the Jews of Paul's day but to the *story* of the exodus generation, which stands as a warning to Christ-believers. Whereas these ancient Israelites had been judged to be "blemished" and a "crooked and perverse generation" because of their "grumbling," Paul hopes for an opposite set of outcomes for Christ-believers. On this reading "crooked and perverse generation" refers not to Jews but to the final generation of the unrighteous in the last days and is indicative of Paul's allegorizing, apocalyptic hermeneutic expressed in 1 Cor 10:11 quoted above.[36]

The second item in v. 15 calling for comment is Paul's promise that if the Philippians submit to God's discipline without grumbling they will "'shine like stars' in the world" (φαίνεσθε ὡς φωστῆρες ἐν κόσμῳ).[37] Paul's language here echoes almost identical promises in Dan 12:3 LXX: "and those who have understanding will shine like the stars of heaven [φανοῦσιν ὡς φωστῆρες τοῦ οὐρανοῦ]," and *1 Enoch* 104:2: "you will shine like the stars of heaven [ἀναλάμψετε ὡσεὶ φωστῆρες τοῦ οὐρανοῦ],"[38] but with one important difference. The promises in Daniel and *1 Enoch* speak to a future angelification of the righteous in the world to come,[39] whereas in Phil 2:15 the promise is that Christ-believers can begin to experience angelification already in this life, while they are still "in the midst of" (μέσον) the final generation, "among whom" (ἐν οἷς) even now they shine like stars "in the world" (ἐν κόσμῳ).[40] A similar development had already taken place at Qumran. Commenting on 1QHᵃ 11:20-22, John J. Collins writes, "The language here reflects the same understanding of resurrection we have seen in Daniel 12, except that the deliverance is already effected."[41]

---

33 Cf. Wis 2:18: "the righteous person is a son of God [υἱὸς θεοῦ]."

34 Collange.

35 See Rom 2:17-24, esp. v. 22 (cf. Josephus, *Ap.* 1.249 = *FGrH* 609, Manetho, frag. 10a.249, for which now see Gerald P. Verbrugghe and John M. Wickersham, *Berossos and Manetho, Introduced and Translated: Native Traditions in Ancient Mesopotamia and Egypt* [Ann Arbor; University of Michigan Press, 1996] Manetho, frag. 12.249), and 1 Thess 2:15-16 (if authentic).

36 A more specific reference may also be in view, namely, a reference to the Philippians' enemies, whose end, like that of the wilderness generation, is "destruction" (ἀπώλεια; Phil 1:28); cf. 1 Cor 10:10, "and were destroyed [ἀπώλοντο]."

37 See the discussion in Engberg-Pederson, *Cosmology*, 42–43.

38 For Dan 12:3, see Collins, *Daniel*, on that verse; for *1 Enoch* 104:2, see Nickelsburg and VanderKam, *1 Enoch 2*, on that passage, and Himmelfarb, "Ascent," 50; cf. M. David Litwa, *We Are Being Transformed: Deification in Paul's Soteriology* (BZNW 187; Berlin: de Gruyter, 2012) 140–51. For the notion of astral immortality in Greek and Latin religion and philosophy and its influence on Jewish eschatology, see Martin Hengel, *Judaism and Hellenism: Studies in Their Encounter in Palestine during the Early Hellenistic Period* (2 vols.; Philadelphia: Fortress Press, 1974) 1:196–202; cf. Franz Cumont, *Lux Perpetua* (Paris: Geuthner, 1949) 142–275, esp. 171–89. Texts include Cicero, *Resp.* 6.13–16; Seneca, *Ad Marc.* 25.3; 26.6–7; *Herc.* 1940–43, 1963, 1976–79; Porphyry, *Nymph.* 28; Proclus, *In Plat. Resp.* 2; and Macrobius, *In somn. Scip.*, 1.12.3.

39 See Himmelfarb, "Revelation"; Charlesworth, "Portrayal." Other texts include: *1 Enoch* 38:4; 39:76; *T. Mos.* 10:9; 4 Ezra 7:97; *2 Bar.* 51:10; 4 Macc 17:5; *2 Enoch* 66:7; Matt 13:43; cf. *Sifre Deut.* 47 (where the faces of the righteous in the future shine like the sun, moon, and stars.).

40 Cf. Gal 4:19: "until Christ is formed [μορφωθῇ] in you"; 2 Cor 3:18: "we are metamorphosed [μεταμορφούμεθα] . . . from glory to glory." For a fuller discussion, see the introduction, part 7.c: "Paul's Metamorphic Myths."

41 Collins, "Angelic Life," 304. Like Paul, the Qumran sectaries believed that the eschatological state of the righteous would in many ways be a continuation of the state already achieved in this life; cf. 1QS 4:18–19; 11:7–8; 1QM 12:1–3; 1QHᵃ 19:6–17.

Paul mentions a second outcome in v. 16. This outcome concerns not the Philippians but Paul: "holding out the word of life, so that I may have a boast in the Day of Christ."[42] The verb translated "holding out" is ἐπέχω. It can mean either "to hold fast" or "to hold out," as in "to offer." Both meanings make sense here, but given Paul's earlier criticism of the Philippians for not continuing to proclaim the gospel (see my comments above on 1:25-26), "to hold out" may be the better translation.[43] Supporting this interpretation is Paul's use of the expression "word of life" (λόγος ζωῆς), which echoes "word [of God]" (λόγος [τοῦ θεοῦ]) in 1:14, where Christ-believers

in Rome are praised for daring "to speak the word [of God] without fear." The content of Paul's eschatological "boast" would then be that his preaching of the gospel to the Philippians has been effective: "that I neither ran in vain nor labored in vain" (cf. Phil 4:1; 1Thess 2:19-20). If despite the current ordeal the Philippians will take a public stand for the gospel (cf. 1:27b-28a), then they like Paul will be saved (2:12; cf. 1:19), the gospel will have been advanced (cf. 1:12), and Paul's mission will have achieved a lasting result. As already noted, this statement forms a modest *clausula* that signals the end of Paul's present line of thought.[44]

---

42 For "Day of Christ," see my comment above at 1:10b-11; cf. 1:6.

43 But see 1 Cor 15:2, "by which you are saved, if you hold fast [εἰ κατέχετε] to the word preached to you, unless you have believed to no effect."

44 The figure Paul uses in his concluding *sententia* is *geminatio,* or "doubling"—"that I neither ran in vain [εἰς κενὸν ἔδραμον] nor labored in vain [εἰς κενὸν ἐκοπίασα]." This is the same figure he used in the *sententiae* ending 1:27b-30 and 2:1-4.

E. The Third Consolatory Argument (Concluded)
2:17-18: Paul's Noble Death

17/ **But even if I am poured out as a libation
on top of the sacrifice and service of your
faith, I rejoice [in my sacrifice] and rejoice
with you [in yours]; 18/ likewise you rejoice
[in your sacrifice] and rejoice with me [in
mine].**

Analysis

Paul followed the nominal assurance that he will survive his current ordeal in 1:22-26 with a lengthy digression in 1:27—2:16 on how the Philippians should behave in his continued absence. Now in 2:17-18 he returns to the topic of his survival but with a more frank assessment: "But even if I am poured out . . . ."[1] The result is that the initial, passing consolation of 1:22-26 is overwritten with what amounts to a *consolatio mortis*[2] in which Paul anticipates his own possible demise. Paul graciously imagines the Philippians' recent gift as a "sacrifice"[3] on top of which his death would be a kind of "libation." Should he be sentenced to death, Paul will rejoice with the Philippians in their offering, and he urges them to rejoice with him in his.

Comment

■ **17a** Although Codex Sinaiticus indicates a new paragraph at 2:17, both the Nestle-Aland and UBS texts include 2:17-18 in the paragraph beginning at 2:12. Most scholars today accept this paragraphing. This is not without problems, however, and commentators continue to struggle to explain how exactly 2:17-18 completes the thought of 2:12-16.[4] Barth sees things differently: "[2:17-18] has obviously no relationship to all that directly [2:12-16] or indirectly [1:27—2:16] precedes it." He recommends passing over "the hortatory digression" (*die parenetische Zwischenrede*) of 1:27—2:16 altogether and reading 2:17-18 as if it came directly after 1:22-26.[5] This reading is confirmed by the *clausula* of 2:16b—"that I neither ran in vain nor labored in vain"—which indicates that the thought begun 2:12 ends in 2:16.[6]

Paul describes his possible demise in figurative language: σπένδομαι, "I am being poured out."[7] The image is that of a libation or drink offering, which either could be offered by itself or poured out beside or, as in this case, on top of another sacrifice: ἐπὶ τῇ θυσίᾳ καὶ λειτουργίᾳ τῆς πίστεως ὑμῶν, "*on top of* the sacrifice and service of your faith." The reference is to Paul's possible execution, which Paul interprets positively as a sacrificial

---

1 In addition to the resumptive ἀλλὰ εἰ καί, "but even if," the πίστις ("faith") and χαίρω ("rejoice") of 2:17 reference the χαρά ("joy") and πίστις ("faith") of 1:25. For the expression ἀλλὰ εἰ καί, see 1 Cor 7:21: ἀλλ᾽ εἰ καὶ δύνασαι ἐλεύθερος γενέσθαι . . . , "But even if you can gain your freedom . . ."; and 2 Cor 4:16: ἀλλ᾽ εἰ καὶ ὁ ἔξω ἡμῶν ἄνθρωπος διαφθείρεται . . . , "But even if our outer nature is wasting away . . . ." Similarly, *Gosp. Pet.* 5: εἰ καὶ μή τις αὐτὸν ᾐτήκει, ἡμεῖς αὐτὸν ἐθάπτομεν, "even though no one asked for his body, we buried him." Cf. BDAG, s.v. εἰ 6e.

2 The *consolatio mortis* was by far the most common form of consolation. The standard arguments have been collected by Fern, *Latin* Consolatio Mortis; Evaristus, *Consolations of Death*; Hultin, "Rhetoric of Consolation." Underlying Paul's argument here is the consolatory topos that those who have died well in a noble cause (e.g., bravely in battle) are to be celebrated for their bravery and sacrifice, the classic example of which is Pericles's famous funeral oration (Thucydides, *Hist.* 2.34–46, esp. 44); cf. Teles, frag. 7.59.

3 See 4:18 for a similar description of their gift (cf. 2 Cor 8:5).

4 See, e.g., Gnilka's struggles.

5 Lohmeyer and de Wette take a similar view, and possibly so does Calvin; cf. Friedrich; Sigfred Pedersen, "'Mit Furcht und Zittern' (Phil. 2,12-13)," *ST* 32 (1978) 1–31.

6 See my comments above.

7 Cf. 2 Tim 4:18: "I am already poured out" (which no doubt interprets our text); Ignatius, *Rom.* 2.2. According to BDAG (s.v. σπένδω) an Apollo aretalogy preserved in *BGU* 11.517 (second cent. CE) refers to the martyrdom of a prophet of Apollo as a "libation" (σπονδή). Cf. Tacitus, *Ann.* 15.64; 16.35, where

libation.[8] Paul also describes the Philippians' "faith" in sacrificial terms: as both a θυσία and a λειτουργία, which are best read as a hendiadys meaning something like "sacrificial service" or even "priestly offering."[9] The primary reference here is to the money sent to Paul by way of Epaphroditus, which, if 2 Cor 8:1-6 is to be believed, would have been raised at considerable personal cost. Paul uses both terms to refer to the Philippians' gift later in the letter. In 2:30 he describes how Epaphroditus destroyed his health in supplying "what was lacking in your service [λειτουργίας] to me," while in 4:18 he calls the Philippians' gift an "acceptable sacrifice [θυσίαν]" to God. The genitive τῆς πίστεως ὑμῶν ("of your faith") could be interpreted as what grammarians call a genitive of source, "faith" being the impetus behind the Philippians' gift, or it could be in simple apposition, in which case "faith" would be a metonym meaning something like "the exercise of your faith."

■ **17b-18** The dual expressions χαίρω καὶ συγχαίρω and χαίρετε καὶ συγχαίρετε are difficult to translate in a way that does not strike the modern ear as odd. Their meaning is relatively straightforward. The Philippians have made a sacrifice and, should he be executed, Paul will too. If this turns out to be the case, Paul will "rejoice" in his offering and "rejoice with" the Philippians in theirs; while the Philippians must "rejoice" in their offering and "rejoice with" Paul in his.[10] The redundancy and repetition are best read as Paul's attempt at a rhetorical flourish wrapping up all of 1:22-26 + 2:17-18. At the same time, Paul is emphatic that his death is to be met with "joy." The theme of "joy" is thus resumed from 1:18b, 18c, and 25 and marks Paul's move back to consolation in 2:19—4:1 (cf. 2:28-29; 3:1).

Seneca uses similar language to refer to his forced suicide (cited by Bockmuehl).

8   For a noble death as a laudable sacrifice in Jewish tradition, see Wis 3:6; 2 Macc 7:38; 4 Macc 17:22; *T. Benj.* 3:8; 1QS 5:6; 8:3–4; cf. *T. Mos.* 9:6-7.

9   The same article governs both nouns.

10   For Paul's attitude toward his own death, see Phil 1:23.

19/ I hope in the Lord[a] Jesus to send Timothy to you shortly, in order that I too might be comforted when I know how things are with you. 20/ For I have no one so like myself who will genuinely care about how things are with you; 21/ for all pursue their own interests, not the interests of Jesus Christ.[b] 22/ But you know[c] his proven character, that he served with me in the gospel as a child with its father. 23/ I therefore hope to send him as soon as I better understand my own circumstances—24/ and I am confident in the Lord that I myself shall also come quickly.[d]

a   Several manuscripts (C D* F G 630, 1739, 1881 bo[pt]) read Χριστῷ instead of κυρίῳ: thus "in Christ Jesus" instead of "in the Lord Jesus," reflecting the more common Pauline expression "in Christ." Paul will use the phrase "in the Lord" again in 2:24, also with an expression of hope or confidence.

b   The order "Jesus Christ" is reversed in several witnesses (B L 0278, 104, 365, 630, 1175, 1241, 1505 Maj vg[st] sy[h]; Ambst Cass); two witnesses read only "Christ" (K; Cyp).

c   𝔓[46] reads οἴδατε for γινώσκετε, both of which mean "know." See further Moises Silva, "The Pauline Style as Lexical Choice: Γινώσκειν and Related Verbs," in *Pauline Studies: Essays Presented to Professor F. F. Bruce on His 70th Birthday*, ed. Donald A. Hagner and Murray J. Harris (Grand Rapids: Eerdmans, 1980) 184–207.

d   A number of authorities (ℵ* A C P 0282, 326, 629, 1241, 2464 lat sy[p] bo[mss]; Aug) add πρὸς ὑμᾶς ("to you"); others (p[46] ℵ[2] B D F G K L Ψ 075, 0278, 33, 81, 104, 365, 630, 1175, 1505, 1739, 1881 Maj b sy[h] sa[mss]; Ambst) omit the phrase. Since Paul omits the indirect object earlier in the same sentence in 1:25 ("I hope to send him"), one might expect an omission here as well, perhaps to achieve some type of *brevitas*. By this account πρὸς ὑμᾶς would then have been added following the example of 1:26: "through my presence again with you [πρὸς ὑμᾶς]."

Analysis

Paul offers a fourth consolation in 2:19-24.[1] He shifts the topic slightly from his current situation and its possible outcomes to his plans for the near future, at the center of which is his plan to send Timothy.[2] If Paul cannot come immediately, then at least he can send Timothy in his stead: "I have no one so like myself [ἰσόψυχον]."[3] Paul states his intent to send Timothy in 2:19a and then explains why in 2:19b-23: (1) that he himself might be consoled when Timothy brings back news from Philippi (2:19b), (2) that the Philippians might be consoled when they see Timothy (2:20-22), and (3) that Timothy might convey the latest news about Paul (2:23). Paul repeats

---

1   Gnilka, following Dibelius, sees 2:19-24 as a "letter of recommendation [*Empfehlungsbrief*] for Timothy." This is unlikely, since Timothy is not yet being sent. Paul's point is not to recommend Timothy (that will take place later) but to console the Philippians with a promise of his coming (Chrysostom, hom. 11.212.11-13 Allen on 3:1; cf. Calvin). It is noteworthy that news of Timothy's coming follows closely on the heels of Paul's frank admission in 2:17-18 that he (Paul) might be executed.

2   Omitting, then, the digression of 1:27–2:16, the line of thought for 1:12-26 + 2:17-30 runs something like this: Paul rejoices in the uninterrupted "progress" of the gospel and the prospect of sealing his "salvation"

and invites the Philippians to join him (1:12-21); he assures the Philippians that he will survive his present ordeal and be restored to the them for their own "progress and joy" (1:22-26); however, it is possible that he will not survive to see the Philippians again, at which point they can at least rejoice in his death in the service of the gospel (2:17-18); he promises to send Timothy soon, who in Paul's absence will care for the Philippians even as Paul himself does (2:19-24); he is now sending Epaphroditus who has recovered from his life-threatening illness and heroically completed his mission (2:25-30).

3   Chrysostom (hom. 10.188.16-17 Allen), Calvin; cf. Lohmeyer.

the nominal assurance of 1:25-26 that he will himself come soon (2:24).

Philippians 2:19-24 may be outlined as follows:

2:19a Paul's plan to send Timothy
2:19b-23 Paul's reasons for sending Timothy
  2:19b First reason: for Paul's own consolation
  2:20-22 Second reason: for the Philippians' consolation
  2:23 Third reason: to convey the latest news about Paul
2:24 Repeated assurance that Paul will come soon

Comment

■ **19a** Paul announces his plan to send Timothy "quickly" (ταχέως) in 2:19a. He repeats his intention in 2:23: "as soon as [ἐξαυτῆς] I better understand my own circumstances," after which he promises in 2:24 that he himself will also come "quickly" (ταχέως). There is a clear sense of urgency in Paul's words, as he considers what concrete steps he can take to assuage the Philippians' grief.[4]

■ **19b** The first reason Paul offers for sending Timothy is "that I too might be comforted when I know how things are with you." Several items call for comment. The expression I have translated "how things are with you" is τὰ περὶ ὑμῶν. It recalls the identical τὰ περὶ ὑμῶν of 1:27, which in turn echoes the τὰ κατ᾽ ἐμέ ("my situation") in 1:12.[5] Paul has told the Philippians how things are with him (1:12-26), and he has expressed his desire to hear how things are with them (1:27–2:16). He plans to send Timothy to Philippi to bring back that news. The verb εὐψυχῶ ("I might be comforted") was commonly used in grave inscriptions where the deceased is made to speak

words of consolation to the living.[6] It also appears in papyrus letters of consolation.[7]

Particularly helpful for the interpreter of Philippians is the contraction κἀγώ ("I too"). If Paul wants to learn how things are with the Philippians in order that *he too* might be consoled, the implication is that vice versa Paul's report on his own situation in 1:12-26 was intended for the consolation of the Philippians. Verse 19b is therefore implicit commentary on 1:12-26.[8] A further link to 1:12-26 is the participle γνούς ("when I know"), which recalls the opening words of Paul's report on his own situation in 1:12: "I want you to know [γινώσκειν] . . . ." Paul wanted the Philippians to "know" his situation, and now he wants to "know" theirs.

But 2:19b is also an implicit commentary on 1:27–2:16. In 1:27 Paul expresses his desire to "hear how things are with you [= the Philippians]." He does not explicitly give the reason, though the implication is that, having reassured the Philippians, he now wants similar reassurances about them. This is the pattern identified by Loveday Alexander in certain "family letters": "reassurance about the sender" followed by a "request for reassurance about the recipients."[9] Philippians 2:19b confirms this pattern: "that I too might be comforted."[10] In Paul's case, of course, what he wants to hear is not just that they are doing well but that they have heeded his exhortation to stand firm and to stand together. It is a common theme in Paul's letters that the religious well-being of his converts is a major source of comfort for him.[11]

■ **20-22** The second reason Paul gives for sending Timothy is that he might serve as his temporary replacement or stand-in. Paul here deploys a popular piece of advice offered to those mourning the death or absence of a close friend or loved one, namely, to find consolation

---

4 Cf. 2:26, where Epaphroditus is similarly "beside himself with worry" for the Philippians.
5 Cf. 2:23: τὰ περὶ ἐμέ (which I have translated "my own circumstances").
6 MM, s.v. εὐψυχέω. According to Chapa (*Letters of Condolence*, 36 n. 51) εὐψυχέω often replaces "do not grieve."
7 E.g., *P. Oxy.* 1.115; *BGU* 4.1097.15, for which see Chapa, *Letters of Condolence*, 62–63; cf. Hermas, *Vis.* 1.3.2.
8 The recent commentary tradition has failed to see this, though Chrysostom notes the implication of

2:19b for the interpretation of 1:12-26 (hom. 1.6.5-7; 10.186.17-23 Allen). See my discussion on genre in the introduction, part 5.
9 Alexander, "Hellenistic Letter-Forms," 92–93.
10 See further my comments above introducing 1:27–2:16, where I discuss the importance of this conceit for Paul's exhortation in these verses.
11 E.g., 1 Thess 3:6-10; 2 Cor 7:5-7. If Paul was both the Philippians' *consolator* and their *solacium*, the Philippians were also a major source of comfort for him (cf. 1:3-5; 2:2; 4:1).

in a surrogate.[12] The ideal replacement was the absent friend's child or sibling, especially if he or she had a similar disposition. Paul presents Timothy as fulfilling both of these criteria: he has apprenticed with Paul "as a child with its father" (ὡς πατρὶ τέκνον),[13] and Paul can think of no one else who is "so like myself" (ἰσόψυχος).[14] Paul reminds the Philippians that they themselves know Timothy's Paul-like "character" (δοκιμή) firsthand.

Excursus: Consolation for an Absent Loved One

It was a common practice in Greco-Roman antiquity for those having lost or having been separated from a close friend or loved one to seek some kind of replacement.[15] More often than not this was a realistic statue or portrait.[16] Thus Ovid's Laodamia writes to her husband Protesilaus: "While you are bearing arms in a far-off land, I keep for myself an image in wax that brings back your face . . . . I gaze upon it and press it to my breast in place of my true husband" (*Her.* 13.151–58).[17] When possible, however, another person might be sought out: "You have lost a loved one; seek another to love. Better to replace a friend than to mourn one" (Seneca, *Ep.* 63.12–13). An ideal replacement would be a close relative of the absent loved one, such as a sibling or even one of his or her children. This is what Dido longed for after the departure of Aeneas: "If only I had conceived a child of yours before your flight; if only there were a little Aeneas [*parvulus Aeneas*] to play here in my halls, who might bring you back to me in the features of his face—then I would not feel so entirely vanquished and abandoned" (Virgil, *Aen.* 4.327–30).[18] Similarly, Seneca to Marcia: "Substitute for [your dead son] Metelius his two surviving daughters. Fill the empty place with them . . . lighten your grief for one with the consolation of two" (*Ad Marc.* 16.8). Tacitus has the bereaved Agrippina console herself with the thought that her young son Britannicus was "a true portrait of his father" (*Ann.* 12.68). It is no doubt with this practice in mind that Menander Rhetor advises departing dignitaries to console their hosts with the promise that either they themselves would someday return or, if that was not possible, that they would send one of their children.[19] Paul's promise to send his like-minded "child" (τέκνον) Timothy to the Philippians

12 Lohmeyer comes close to this reading when he claims that Timothy would be sent "an Stelle des Paulus," though his thesis that the soon-to-be-martyred Paul was here appointing Timothy to be his successor is unnecessary; cf. Bockmuehl, who sees Timothy as Paul's "representative."

13 Cf. 1 Tim 1:2: "legitimate child in the faith" (γνήσιον τέκνον ἐν πίστει), which is almost certainly an interpretation of our text.

14 Collange, Aletti, Focant. Timothy's Paul-likeness is to "genuinely [γνησίως] care for" the Philippians. Paul's word choice here is not insignificant. The cognate adjective "genuine" (γνήσιος) was used to designate a "legitimate" child. BDAG, s.v. γνήσιος 1; citing *P. Flor.* 79.21 and 294.12: "legitimate children" (γνήσια τέκνα); *P. Oxy.* 10.1267.15: "legitimate son" (γνήσιος υἱός); Sir 7:18; Philo, *Mos.* 1.15: "legitimate child" (γνήσιος παῖς), etc.

15 I treat this topos in greater detail in "*Alius Paulus*," 544–49.

16 Maurizio Bettini, *The Portrait of the Lover* (Berkeley: University of California Press, 1999) 10: "the portrait is a substitute, a consolation."

17 Cf. *BGU* 2.423, a second-century papyrus letter from Apion, an Egyptian soldier in the Roman navy, to his father Epimachus, in which he describes a small portrait (εἰκόνιν) of himself that he has sent home (I would like to thank Troy Martin for calling this letter to my attention); cf. Libanius, *Ep.* 143.1–2. Chrysostom was well known for his devotion to a portrait of the apostle Paul (George of Alexandria, *Vit. Chrys.* 27 [147.1–6 Halkin]; Leo VI Philosophus, *Or.* 18.15 [*PG* 107:256D–257D]; Symeon Metaphrastes, *Vit. Chrys.* 23 [*PG* 114:1104B–1108B]). For erotic devotion to statues of the dead, see Euripides, *Alc.* 349–52; Hyginus, *Fab.* 104; Pseudo-Apollodorus, *Epitom.* 3.30; and the macabre parody in Xenophon of Ephesus, *Eph.* 5.1.11. According to Rabbi Nathan (*Mekh. Exod.* 12.30) the Angel of Death destroyed not the Egyptian firstborn but the funerary statues of those already dead. Similarly, according to the *scholia* on Aristides, Paris returns to Troy not with Helen herself but with her portrait (Wilhelm Dindorf, ed., *Aristides* [3 vols.; Leipzig: Reimer, 1829] 3:105; cf. Stesichorus, *Palin.* frag. 192; Herodotus, *Hist.* 2.112–20; Euripides, *Hel.* 29–36).

18 Cf. Chariton, *Chaer. et Call.* 3.8.7.

19 Menander Rhetor, Περὶ ἐπιδεικ. 2.15.431.22–30; 433.10–14 (D. A. Russell and N. G. Wilson, *Menander Rhetor* [Oxford: Clarendon, 1981]). Speeches of departure were generally understood to be consolatory (so Menander Rhetor, Περὶ ἐπιδεικ. 2.5.396.3–4; 2.15.430.10-11; cf. 2.15.431.31-432.2); for tears at separation in early Christianity, see Acts 20:37; 2 Tim 1:4.

is to be understood in this context. A variation on the theme appears at John 14:16 when the departing Jesus promises his soon-to-be-forlorn disciples: "I will ask the Father and he will give you another advocate [ἄλλον παράκλητον δώσει ὑμῖν]."[20]

In addition to being Paul-like, and thus a consolation, Timothy was also Christlike, and so an example to be followed.[21] For just as Christ took the form of a "slave" (δούλου; 2:7), so Timothy has "served [as a slave]" (ἐδούλευσεν) in Paul's gospel mission. Further, while some at Philippi are seeking "their own interests" (τὰ ἑαυτῶν), not "the interests of others" (τὰ ἑτέρων; 2:4), Timothy does just the opposite: "I have no one so like myself who will sincerely care about how things are with you [τὰ περὶ ὑμῶν], for all pursue their own interests [τὰ ἑαυτῶν], not the interests of Jesus Christ [τὰ Ἰησοῦ Χριστοῦ]."

■ 23 The third reason Paul offers for sending Timothy—or in this case *waiting* to send him—is so that the Philippians will have the latest news regarding Paul's case. The verb I have translated "I better understand" is ἀφίδω. It means "to know [more] precisely."[22] With it Paul further admits to a level of uncertainty in his situation.

■ 24 Verse 24 repeats the consolation of 1:25-26 that Paul

himself will come to Philippi. But it is linked syntactically to v. 23 by the use of μέν . . . δέ ("on the one hand . . . on the other hand"). These particles are often omitted in translation, and I have omitted them here. This linkage provides further evidence that Paul is offering Timothy to the Philippians as his surrogate. Paul's promise to send Timothy along with his assurance that he himself will come "quickly" (ταχέως) constitute his first response to the frank admission in 2:17-18 that he may in fact be executed. It is noteworthy that Paul does not say that he is confident he will come soon, but that he is "confident *in the Lord*" (πέποιθα ἐν κυρίῳ), suggesting that Paul's circumstances taken on their own (i.e., without divine intervention) are not that promising. Paul demurred in a similar fashion in 1:25, where again his "confidence" is not that he will see the Philippians again but that the Philippians are in need of seeing him again: "but to remain in the flesh is more needful for you, and being confident *of this* [τοῦτο πεποιθώς] . . . ." Paul's confidence "in the Lord" leaves open the realistic possibility that he will be "poured out as a libation" (2:17).

---

20 Cf. Statius, *Silv.* 2.6.103–4: *Fata alium tibi . . . Phileton . . . dabit* ("The Fates will give you another Philetos"), for which see Harm-Jam van Dam, *P. Paninius Statius, Silvae Book II: A Commentary* (Leiden: Brill, 1984) 391. The striking similarity with John 14:16 is identified by Friedrich Vollmer, *P. Papinii Statii Silvarum Libri* (Leipzig: Teubner, 1898) 372.

21 See Stephano Bittasi, *Gli esempi necessari per discernere: Il significato argomentative della struttura*

della lettera di Paolo ai Filippesi (AnBib 153; Rome: Pontifical Biblical Institute, 2003), 177–218, who proposes that, while Paul offers himself and Christ as examples to be imitated, it is Timothy (2:19-24) and Epaphroditus (2:25-30) who are the letter's most tangible *exempla*.

22 BDAG, s.v. ἀφοράω 2.

25/ I felt it necessary to send back to you Epaphroditus, my brother, fellow worker, and fellow soldier, and your apostle sent to minister to my need,ᵃ 26/ since he was longing for you allᵇ and beside himself with worry that you had heard that he was ill—27/ and indeed he was ill, close to dying,ᶜ but God had mercy on him, and not on him only but also on me, lest I have grief on top of grief. 28/ So I was all the more anxious to send him, that upon seeing him again you might rejoice,ᵈ and I might have one fewer cause for worry. 29/ Receive him therefore in the Lord with all joy and hold people like him in honor, 30/ since for the sake of the work of Christᵉ he came close to death, putting his life at riskᶠ in order to fill up what was lacking in your ministry to me.

a Here I follow Lightfoot in interpreting the Greek (ὑμῶν δὲ ἀπόστολον καὶ λειτουργὸν τῆς χρείας μου; lit., "but your apostle and minister to my need") as a hendiadys. For the language of "apostle," see 2 Cor 8:23.

b A significant number of manuscripts (ℵ* A C D Iⱽⁱᵈ 075, 0278, 33, 81, 104, 326, 365, 1175, 1241, 2495 sy bo) add ἰδεῖν ("to see"; thus: "longing to see you all"), perhaps on analogy with the common idiom found in Rom 1:11 and 1 Thess 3:6 (cf. 2 Tim 1:4). But see Phil 1:8: ὡς ἐπιποθῶ πάντας ὑμᾶς, "how I long for you all."

c A number of manuscripts (ℵ² B P Ψ 075, 0278*, 81, 104, 365, 1175, 2464, 2495) read the genitive θανάτου instead of the dative θανάτῳ. The preposition used here (παραπλήσιον) typically takes the dative, while its cognate (πλήσιον) typically takes the genitive.

d Or "on seeing him you might again rejoice." See my comment below.

e A number of manuscripts (ℵ A P Ψ 075, 33, 81, 104, 365, 1241, 1505 syʰ bo) read κυρίου ("of the Lord") instead of Χριστοῦ ("of Christ"; p⁴⁶ B F G 0278, 6, 1175, 1739, 1181, 2464 sa). A few (D K L 630 Maj) retain Χριστοῦ but add the article.

f Several manuscripts (C K L P Ψ 075, 33, 81, 104, 365, 630, 1241, 1505, 1739, 1881 Maj sy boᵖᵗ) read παραβουλευσάμενος ("having no concern for") instead of παραβολευσάμενος ("risking"; p⁴⁶ ℵ A B D F G 0278ⱽⁱᵈ, 1175 sa boᵖᵗ).

Analysis

Paul offers a fifth consolatory argument in 2:25-30: the recovery and return of the Philippians' emissary Epaphroditus. Both Paul and Epaphroditus have been concerned that news of the latter's illness had gotten back to Philippi and further discouraged the Christ-believers there. Paul is therefore sending Epaphroditus back with the present letter in hopes that the Philippians will be comforted by his return in good health: "that upon seeing him again you might rejoice." Paul urges the Philippians to console themselves with Epaphroditus's return and to see in him a further example of Christ's obedience "even to death."

Philippians 2:25-30 may be outlined as follows:

2:25 Paul's decision to send Epaphroditus
2:26-28 Paul's reason for sending Epaphroditus
2:29-30 How the Philippians should receive Epaphroditus

Comment

■ **25** Paul states that he is sending Epaphroditus back to Philippi out of necessity: "I felt it necessary [ἀναγκαῖον δὲ ἡγησάμην] to send back to you Epaphroditus." He makes it clear that this is in no way Epaphroditus's fault, whom Paul would have preferred to keep with him: "[he is] my brother, fellow worker, and fellow soldier,[1] and your apostle sent to minister to my need." The expres-

---

1 The term is συστρατιώτης. Paul uses it of Philemon in Phlm 2. It recalls the martial imagery of 1:27-28 (Bittasi, *Gli esempi*, 195). Epaphroditus is an example of one who is "standing fast," who is willing to risk his life (cf. 2:30) for the gospel mission. For military imagery elsewhere in Paul, see, e.g., Rom 7:23; 13:12; 1 Cor 9:7; 2 Cor 6:7; 10:3-5 (cf. Eph 6:11, 13; 2 Tim 2:4; Titus 1:18).

sion ἀναγκαῖον ἡγησάμην is an epistolary cliché used to explain why a writer has chosen to write at a particular point in time, the reason typically being the availability of a carrier.[2] Here, however, Paul is not explaining why he has taken the opportunity to write the Philippians a letter, but why he is returning their emissary. The adjective "necessary," which is emphatic by position, should therefore be given its full force: not "I had this *opportunity* and I thought I should take it" but "I felt *compelled* and so I acted." Paul's language recalls a similar complaint in 1:23-24: "having the desire to depart and be with Christ, for that is much better by far, but to stay on in the flesh is more necessary [ἀναγκαιότερον] for your sakes."

■ **26-28** In vv. 26-28 Paul explains why he has felt compelled to send Epaphroditus back. The journey from Philippi to Rome had been hard on Epaphroditus. He had fallen ill along the way but pressed on "putting his life at risk" to carry the Philippians' gift to Paul, who was languishing in a Roman prison. Epaphroditus was certain that news of his illness had gotten back to the Philippians and, given their already beleaguered mental state, this worried him: "he was . . . beside himself with worry that you had heard he was ill." Paul's solution was to send Epaphroditus back.

Barth also detects an element of complaint in Paul's language and assumes that it is directed at an overly anxious Epaphroditus: "'He was worried about your worry for him'—really? What a very strange motive for the behavior of a grown man!" But that one's equanimity could be dependent on another's was a common sentiment in antiquity[3] and seems to have been especially the case for Paul.[4] James Moffatt has uncovered a striking parallel to Phil 1:28 in a letter from a soldier to his mother (*P. Oxy.* 12.1481).[5] Someone had told the mother that her son was ill, and she believed it not least because her son had not written her for some time. But as the young soldier's letter explains, he has been slow in writing "not because of illness" but because he has been on maneuvers. "Do not be upset [μὴ λυποῦ]," he urges his mother, adding, "I was very upset when I heard that you had heard [λείαν δὲ ἐλυπήθην ἀκούσας ὅτι ἠκούσας] that I was ill." Like this soldier, and with equally good reason, Epaphroditus was "beside himself with worry" (ἀδημονῶν) that the Philippians had been further grieved by news of his illness. Paul shared this concern: "I was all the more anxious [σπουδαιοτέρως] to send him."

The expressions of grief, ἵνα μὴ λύπην ἐπὶ λύπην σχῶ, "lest I have grief on top of grief," and κἀγὼ ἀλυπότερος ὦ, which I have rendered "and I might have one fewer cause for worry" (lit., "and that I might be less grieved"), are difficult and call for comment. Both of these expressions imply that Paul is grieving, something he has thus far been loath to admit (e.g., 1:18; 2:17-18; cf. 4:11-13). Further, both imply at least two sources of grief: one that has been eliminated or otherwise averted and one that remains. In the first expression ("lest I have grief on top of grief") the source of grief that is averted is the death of Epaphroditus: "God had mercy on him, and not on him only but also on me." In the second expression ("and that I might have one fewer cause for worry") the source of grief that is eliminated—or "worry" as I have translated it—is the anxiety that Paul fears is gripping the already vulnerable Philippians concerning Epaphroditus's health, anxiety that will be relieved when they see him again: "that upon seeing him again you might rejoice and I might have one fewer cause for worry," where the "and" (καί) must mean something like "and *as a result*."[6]

---

2 Koskenniemi, *Studien*, 77–87; Bittasi, *Gli esempi*, 193 n. 38.

3 Cf. the common letter greetings "if you are well, so am I" (*si vales, valeo*) and "if you are well, I am happy" (*si vales, gaudeo*). Seneca discusses the former cliché and its philosophical implications in *Ep.* 15. For the latter expression, see Plautus, *Pers.* 511.

4 In 1 Thess 3:6-7 Paul reports that he and those with him "were consoled" (παρεκλήθημεν) to learn that the Thessalonians still think well of them. In 2 Cor 7:7 he "rejoices exceedingly" (μᾶλλον χαρῆναι) that the Corinthians still have fond memories of him, while in 2 Cor 7:13 he rejoices at Titus's joy: "we rejoiced even more [μᾶλλον ἐχάρημεν] at the joy [χαρᾷ] of Titus, because his spirit was put at ease by all of you."

5 James Moffatt, "Philippians II 26 and 2 Tim. IV 13," *JTS* 18 (1917) 311–12; cf. MM, s.v. λυπέω (p. 382).

6 BDAG, s.v. καί 1bζ: "to introduce a result that comes from what precedes." On this reading Paul's grief is due to the Philippians' worry over Epaphroditus, grief that will be removed when the Philippians see Epaphroditus again and "rejoice."

This leaves us with the grief that remains, for which there need be only one source. I see two possibilities. First, Paul could simply have let slip his true feelings about his current situation, which situation he now admits is a source of grief. But this seems unlikely. Even if Paul did find his situation distressing—and it is hard to imagine that he did not, at least at times—he has been at pains to claim otherwise. It is unlikely that he would suddenly forget that claim here in 2:27-28. The other, more likely alternative is that Paul's remaining source of grief was the Philippians' response to his incarceration, which he has already acknowledged to be a cause of concern: "that I too might be comforted when I know how things are with you" (2:19; cf. 2:2). On this reading the realities behind the above two expressions of grief would be as follows. First, Paul is grieved by the fact that his imprisonment has been so disruptive for the Philippians. This source of grief remains and will do so until Paul hears otherwise (2:19). Second, Paul was also grieved to think that news of Epaphroditus's illness had reached Philippi. This source of grief is alleviated by sending Epaphroditus back to Philippi healthy. Third and finally, Paul would have been grieved had Epaphroditus died, but God had mercy and this potential source of grief never materialized.

The adverb "again" (πάλιν) in v. 28 is ambiguous. It can modify either the verb that precedes it ("upon seeing him again you might rejoice") or the verb that follows it ("upon seeing him you might again rejoice").[7] Both make sense, though the former is to be preferred on analogy with 1:26: "by my presence again [τῆς ἐμῆς παρουσίας

πάλιν] with you." As in 1:25-26, where the Philippians' "progress and joy" is dependent on seeing Paul again (πάλιν), so here in 2:28 they will "rejoice" only when they see Epaphroditus again (πάλιν).

■ **29-30** Paul urges the Philippians to take comfort in Epaphroditus's return: "Receive him . . . with all joy [μετά πάσης χαρᾶς]" (v. 29a),[8] and to find in him a noble example to follow: "hold people like him in honor [ἐντίμους]" (vv. 29b-30). Just as Christ was obedient "to the point of death (μέχρι θανάτου)," so Epaphroditus "came close to death (μέχρι θανάτου)" in his efforts to complete his mission to Paul. As I have already indicated, the most natural way to read 2:30 is that Epaphroditus became ill in trying to bring the Philippians' gift to Paul and that he pressed on heroically "putting his life at risk in order to fill up what was lacking in your ministry to me." This, coupled with the fact that the Philippians were unaware of just how far Epaphroditus's illness had progressed (2:26-27), implies (1) that Epaphroditus fell ill early in his journey to Paul, (2) that by pressing on his illness was made worse to the point of being life threatening, and (3) that the report of Epaphroditus's illness told only of its initial phases, making it almost certain that that report was brought by someone who passed Epaphroditus going in the opposite direction at a time when his illness had still not been critical. The above also suggests that Epaphroditus's journey had been of some length and difficulty (i.e., not merely from Philippi to Ephesus but either from Philippi to Caesarea or, as I have argued, from Philippi to Rome).[9]

---

7   For the latter, see the comments by Lightfoot.
8   Paul's use of the imperative here is noteworthy. When Paul speaks directly of his "joy" (and only indirectly of the Philippians' joy) he uses the indicative (1:18b, c; 2:17). But when he speaks directly to the Philippians' "joy" he uses the imperative (here in 2:29 but also in 2:18 and 3:1). This is consistent with

contemporary consolation, where consolatory arguments were regularly augmented by exhortations to rejoice or be consoled. See the introduction, part 1: "Some Prefatory Remarks on Ancient Consolation."

9   See the introduction, part 3: "Date and Place of Writing."

Paul offers a sixth and final consolatory argument in 3:1—4:1. The argument is long, at times emotionally charged,[1] and considerably broadens the consolation of 1:12—2:30. It is easy to see why Paul saved it to the last. Because of its length, I will treat 3:1—4:1 differently than I have treated Paul's previous consolatory arguments. I will offer a short synopsis here, after which I will divide the argument into smaller units and comment on each of these separately.

Paul has thus far advised the Philippians where to find "joy" in the present situation:[2] in the "progress" of the gospel (1:12-18b); in his final "salvation" (1:18c-21); in his possible release from prison or, as the case may be, in his noble death in the cause of Christ (1:22-26 + 2:17-18); in the prospect of a visit from Timothy (2:19-24); and in the recovery and return of Epaphroditus (2:25-30). Now in 3:1—4:1 he adds a final reason for rejoicing: "Lastly, my brothers, rejoice *in the Lord*" (3:1a).[3] This takes Paul well beyond the range of things that matter in the gospel mission to the "one thing" (τὸ ἕν; 3:13) of supreme importance in the religious life of the individual Christ-believer, namely, his or her quest for γνῶσις Χριστοῦ or "knowledge of Christ" (3:8),[4] the "surpassing greatness"

of which knowledge renders all other accomplishments mere "table-scraps."[5] Since this γνῶσις, which is both mystical[6] and transformative and ultimately saving, is gained through precisely the kind of suffering that he and the Philippians are enduring, Paul offers it as the supreme source of consolation for Christ-believers in the last days.[7] To "know" (γνῶναι; 3:10) Christ remains Paul's central pursuit (3:12-16), and the Philippians should make it theirs too (3:17-21).

Although longer and more rhetorically sophisticated than his earlier arguments, the structure of Paul's argument in 3:1—4:1 is relatively clear. He begins in 3:1a with an introductory sentence announcing his new thesis that the Christ-believer's ongoing experience of the "Lord" is a further cause to "rejoice." He follows this immediately in 3:1b with an apology for repeating himself, for reminding the Philippians of something they already know.[8] After this he amplifies his thesis at length through a series of increasingly autobiographical remarks,[9] first by means of two rhetorical comparisons in 3:2-3 and 3:4-11, and then by self-correction in 3:12-16. The first comparison (3:2-3) contrasts two types of Christ-belief: one that places confidence in the "flesh" and one that boasts in

---

1   Commentators have often failed to distinguish clearly between the *vilification* of 3:2 and the *pathos* of Paul's overall argument. The opponents of 3:2 are foils and their vilification is brief, but Paul continues to write with pathos, although after 3:2 that pathos is largely positive and centers on his desire "to know" Christ. Conflating the vilification of 3:2 and the pathos of Paul's overall argument has led to two mistakes. If one observes, correctly, that the vilification of 3:2 ends quickly, then one is forced to deny that Paul continues to write with pathos. B. S. Mackay makes this mistake ("Further Thoughts," 163). If, on the other hand, one sees, again correctly, that Paul's pathos continues after 3:2, then one is forced to assume with Koester that Paul continues to write with "unrelenting harshness" ("Purpose," 319). Neither is the case: Paul's *harshness* is brief, but he writes with *pathos* throughout the chapter. See my comments below.

2   Phil 1:12: τὰ κατ᾽ ἐμέ ("my situation"); 2:23: τὰ περὶ ἐμέ ("how things are with me"). For "joy," see 1:18, 25; 2:17-18, 28-29.

3   Chrysostom, hom. 11.212.11-13 Allen.

4   See the excursus on γνῶσις below after my comments on 3:7-8a.

5   Paul here returns to the theme of the things that do and do not matter (cf. 1:10), though now it is the one thing that matters above all else.

6   The precise meaning of the term "mysticism" and its cognates continues to be debated (Schäfer, *Origins*, 1–33). Here I use the term to refer to an altered state of consciousness (ASC) interpreted as the direct experience of a deity. Whether this ASC is ritually induced—a central issue in the current debate—depends in large part on how broadly or narrowly one defines "ritual." For the role that ASC played in Paul's religion, see esp. Shantz, *Paul in Ecstasy*, and the review by Christopher Mount (*JR* 90 [2010] 599–601).

7   They will find joy in it (3:1) and he will find joy in their pursuit of it (4:1). For the Philippians as a source for Paul's "joy," see 2:2 and my comments on that text above.

8   This was a common technique among Hellenistic and Roman moralists that rendered frank moral instruction less offensive by flattering the recipients that they of course already knew what they were about to hear. See my discussion of 3:1b below.

9   Pitta, pp. 208–11.

"Christ."[10] The second (3:4-11) compares Paul's former values as a Pharisee with his current values as a Christ-believer whose overriding desire is to "know" Christ. In the self-correction of 3:12-16, Paul confesses that he has yet to achieve this knowledge, which remains a "calling" (κλῆσις) that he must continue to pursue. He finishes with a further exhortation to follow his example (3:17), supported by a third instance of rhetorical comparison in which he returns to the contrast of 3:2-3 but now expressed not in terms of the "flesh" but in terms of the "cross" (3:18-21).[11] A concluding sentence in 4:1 recalls the introductory sentence of 3:1a.

Philippians 3:1—4:1 may be outlined as follows:

3:1a Introductory sentence: "Rejoice in the Lord"

3:1b Apology: the Philippians already know what Paul is about to say

3:2-3 First comparison: "boasting in Christ" versus "having confidence in the flesh"

3:4-11 Second comparison: Paul's religious values before and after his vision of Christ

3:12-16 Self-Correction: Paul continues to pursue Christ

3:17-21 Exhortation: the Philippians should imitate Paul

4:1 Concluding sentence: "Stand fast in the Lord"

---

10   The figure "rhetorical comparison" was broad and included what we would call both comparisons and contrasts. See my comments on 3:2 below.

11   This final comparison highlights the respective eschatological outcomes of Paul's gospel and that of his competitors'.

1. Introductory Sentence 3:1
First Rhetorical Comparison 3:2-3

1/ **Lastly, my brothers,ᵃ rejoice in the Lord. To write the same things to you is not a burden for me and it will make you more steadfast [in your current distress].ᵇ 2/ Watch out for the dogs. Watch out for the depraved workers. Watch out for the mutilation. 3/ For we are the circumcision:ᶜ those who serve in the spirit of Godᵈ and boast in Christ Jesus and do not put confidence in the flesh.**

a   Paul writes "brothers" (ἀδελφοί) even though his letter is intended for both the women and the men in the Philippian assembly, as 4:2 ("I urge Euodia and I urge Syntyche") makes clear.

b   I discuss the translation of Greek ἀσφαλές ("safe," "steady," "secure") in the comments below.

c   For Paul to insist that his assemblies, which include both men and women (cf. Phil 4:2-3; Rom 16:1-16), are the "circumcision" is odd, but here at least Paul redefines the term so as largely to transcend sex, though the final reference to "flesh" is no doubt a derogative reference to physical circumcision.

d   A number of witnesses (א² D* P Ψ 075 365 1175 lat sy; Chr) read the dative θεῷ. Since the verb λατρεύω takes its object in the dative, the text might be translated as "worship God by the Spirit." This is almost certainly an attempt to remove the difficulty of the better-attested genitive θεοῦ, which does not allow for an object: "worship by the spirit of God." 𝔓⁴⁶ vgᵐˢˢ omit the noun θεός altogether.

Analysis

Paul introduces his sixth and final consolatory argument with a summary exhortation: "Lastly, my brothers, rejoice in the Lord" (Τὸ λοιπόν, ἀδελφοί μου, χαίρετε ἐν κυρίῳ; 3:1a). He repeats this exhortation in slightly different terms at 4:1: "Therefore my brothers . . . stand fast in the Lord" (Ὥστε, ἀδελφοί μου, . . . στήκετε ἐν κυρίῳ), from which it is clear (1) that Paul intends 3:1—4:1 to be read as a whole, and (2) that for Paul "rejoice in the Lord" (χαίρετε ἐν κυρίῳ) is roughly equivalent to "stand fast in the Lord" (στήκετε ἐν κυρίῳ; cf. Phil 1:27) and is there-

fore not a passing remark, and certainly not a cliché,[1] but a substantive exhortation that he will develop at length over the remainder of the chapter.[2]

Paul follows the exhortation of 3:1a with a short apology for repeating himself in 3:1b,[3] after which he launches into two συγκρίσεις,[4] or rhetorical comparisons (3:2-3, 4-11), that develop his initial exhortation. We are here interested in the first of these comparisons in 3:2-3. It is short and arresting and prepares for the considerably longer comparison in 3:4-11. The negative pole of the comparison comes in 3:2 and consists of a series of caustic warnings against Torah-observant missionaries of

---

1   Contra Goodspeed, *Problems*, 174–75; Rahtjen, "Three Letters," 171; Beare.

2   This exhortation encapsulates Paul's religious program, much as Seneca's similar exhortation *disce gaudere* ("learn to rejoice") in *Ep.* 23.3 encapsulates his understanding of the philosophical life; cf. *Ep.* 23.4; 59.14. I quote these texts below in my comments on 3:1a.

3   The fact that Paul is here covering familiar ground strongly suggests that material covered in 3:1—4:1 comes close to the heart of his message, a point made by Pelagius in his comments on this text. As we shall see, this confirms the classic judgment of

Albert Schweitzer that Paul was essentially a mystic, a judgment revived by E. P. Sanders under the rubric of the believer's "participation" in Christ (*Paul and Palestinian Judaism*, 502–8). See further Alan F. Segal, *Paul the Convert: The Apostolate and Apostasy of Saul the Pharisee* (New Haven: Yale University Press, 1992) 34–71; Ashton, *Religion*, 113–51; and esp. Mount, "Spirit Possession," 316–25; cf. Gunkel, *Influence*, 92–97.

4   I discuss the nature of this figure below at 3:2. Paul has already used it in the comparison of life and death in 1:22-24, for which see Vollenweider, "Waagschalen."

the sort that contradicted Paul's gospel in Galatia.[5] The positive pole comes in 3:3 and answers the warnings of 3:2.[6] Unlike in Galatians, however, Paul does not adduce the opponents of 3:2 because they insist that gentile Christ-believers keep Torah—they do but that is not Paul's point—but because in his view they espouse an inferior strategy for relating to God, a strategy that "put[s] confidence in the flesh" versus a strategy that "boast[s] in Christ."[7] It is the latter strategy that Paul espouses and it is in this strategy that Paul believes the Philippians will find both consolation and renewed progress.

Excursus: Paul's Opponents in Philippians 3

Though Paul mentions opponents only in 3:2 and probably again in 3:18-19, their identity has been the subject of considerable debate. Scholars have construed Paul's opponents in Philippians in a variety of ways: legalists, libertines, Gnostics, pneumatics, perfectionists.[8] They have also imagined Paul to be writing on as many as three different fronts.[9] Finally, scholars have disagreed on the level of threat that these opponents posed. Paul himself is partly to blame for this confusion. In speaking of his opponents he gives himself over to insult and vilification, which, while not completely impenetrable, nevertheless make his remarks more than a little ambiguous to modern readers, and especially challenging to those who take Paul, even when he is at his most

vituperative, to be a more or less objective source of information.

Part of the problem also lies in the rhetorical conventions of Paul's day. The rhetoric of Philippians 3 turns on two figures: σύγκρισις, or rhetorical comparison, and ἐπιδιόρθωσις, or self-correction.[10] As already noted, Paul uses the first of these figures (rhetorical comparison) three times in 3:2-3, 4-11, and 17-21, and the second (self-correction) once in 3:12-16. The impression that Paul is writing against an active threat comes from the rhetorical comparison of 3:2-3, where he inveighs against those who "put confidence in the flesh." But this is to read too much into Paul's rhetoric. Σύγκρισις was one of several techniques taught in the schools for amplifying a thesis.[11] This is clearly how Paul uses the figure in 3:4-11, and this is likely also the case in 3:2-3, on which account, then, the opponents he adduces in 3:2 need be little more than foils to his developing argument.[12] Recognizing the rhetorical nature of Paul's discourse also means that the shift between 3:4-11 and 3:12-16 need not indicate that he has changed opponents but only that he has changed figures from comparison to self-correction. The same holds true for the shift back to comparison in 3:17-21.[13]

This leads to the related observation that Paul's description of his opponents in 3:2 and again in 3:18-19 has been crafted to serve his own argument and tells us little if anything about his opponents: not how they might have appeared to a more neutral third party, and certainly not how they would

5   These Torah-observant missionaries are also Christ-believers. They are sometimes referred to as "Judaizers" on the basis of Gal 2:14. If we are following Paul's use of the term, however, "Judaizer" applies to gentile Christ-believers who "live as Jews" (Ἰουδαΐζειν).

6   The correspondence between 3:2 and 3:3 is more formal than material. It gives the appearance of a point-by-point comparison but does not actually provide this.

7   Here Paul restates his traditional contrast between "flesh" and "spirit" in christological terms suited to the rest of his argument, which revolves around the believer's mystical knowledge of "Christ."

8   The literature is extensive. For current bibliography, see Reumann, pp. 469–70. Important studies include Schmithals, "False Teachers"; Koester, "Purpose"; Robert Jewett, "Conflicting Movements in the Early Church as Reflected in Philippians," *NovT* 12 (1970) 362–90. Scholarly interest in Paul's opponents began with Ferdinand Christian Baur's influential essay "Die Christuspartei in der korinthischen Gemeinde,

der Gegensatz des petrinischen und paulinischen Christentums in der ältesten Kirche, der Apostel Petrus in Rom," *Tübinger Zeitschrift für Theologie* 4 (1831) 61–206.

9   E.g., Jewett, "Conflicting Movements."

10   I discuss these figures in my comments on 3:2-16 below; see esp. on 3:2 and 3:12.

11   The texts include Theon, *Prog.* 10 (Spengel 9); Hermogenes, *Prog.* 8; Libanius, *Prog.* 10; Aphthonius, *Prog.* 10; Nicolaus, *Prog.* 8. The standard treatment of the figure is still F. Focke, "Synkrisis," *Hermes* 58 (1923) 327–68.

12   Tacitus uses a similar technique in the *Agricola*, where his tendentious survey of early governors of Britain provides foils to his father-in-law; see B. C. McGing, "Synkrisis in Tacitus' Agricola," *Hermathena* 132 (1982) 15–25, here 15–18.

13   It is precisely on the basis of misunderstanding these shifts in rhetorical figure that a number of scholars assume Paul to be arguing on two or more fronts; see Jewett, "Conflicting Movements."

have described themselves. So, for example, when Paul says in 3:18 that his opponents "mind earthly things"—whatever that might mean—he is anticipating his claim to a "citizenship in the heavens" in the next sentence. Similarly, when in 3:3 he says that his opponents have confidence in the "flesh"[14]—presumably a demeaning reference to circumcision—he is bolstering his claim to serve in the "spirit" and to boast in "Christ." It is also doubtful that his opponents would have recognized themselves in his claim that their "god is the belly"[15] or that their "glory is in their shame."

When these considerations are taken into account, the following picture of Paul's opponents emerges. First, Paul need only have one set of opponents in mind. Second, these opponents may have been a distinct social group, but inasmuch as Paul says they are "many" (3:18), they may also have been an amorphous group existing as a unified front only in Paul's mind and for the purposes of his argument. Third, whatever their differences, these opponents practice circumcision ("mutilation"; 3:2) and are therefore Torah observant to a degree that Paul is not. Fourth, they also engage in some sort of missionary activity ("depraved workers"; 3:2).[16] Finally, although the opponents are themselves Christ-believers,[17] they do not embrace—at least not to Paul's satisfaction—Paul's apocalyptic theory of suffering as interpreted through the cross of Christ, of which "cross" they are "enemies" (3:18).[18] Paul assumes that they and their followers will not be saved in the final judgment: "their end is destruction" (3:19).[19] This picture is consistent with Paul's opponents in Galatia as well as those attacked in 2 Corinthians, especially when one takes into account the differences in Paul's

respective rhetorical agendas in these letters. It is not possible, in my view, to be more specific.

Comment

■ **1a** Paul introduces the sixth and final consolatory argument of the letter in 3:1a: "Lastly [Τὸ λοιπόν], my brothers, rejoice in the Lord."[20] He will repeat this exhortation (χαίρετε ἐν κυρίῳ) in slightly different terms in 4:1 (στήκετε ἐν κυρίῳ, "stand fast in the Lord") to form an *inclusio*. As I have already indicated, this means that, for Paul, 3:1a is no less substantive an exhortation than 4:1. It also means that there is no appreciable change in tone between 3:1a and the warnings that follow in 3:2, as commentators who partition the letter are wont to claim.[21] This continuity can readily be seen if we substitute the comparable exhortation of 4:1 for that of 3:1a, in which case Phil 3:1-2 would then read: "Stand fast in the Lord. . . . Watch out for the dogs, and so on."

This substitution is not necessary, however, if one attends to the seriousness with which Paul uses the language of "joy" in his letter. Seneca uses "joy" (*gaudium*) with similar earnestness in his consolatory writings. I have discussed these writings and related texts in the introduction to this commentary.[22] Here I simply note Seneca's substantive reflections on joy in *Ep.* 23.1–3: "Do you want to know what is the basis of a good mind? It is that you do not make your joy depend on unimportant things [*ne gaudeas vanis*]. Did I say basis? No, it is the pinnacle.

---

14 See the excursus "Paul's Language in Philippians 3:2-3" below.
15 On this last expression, see Karl Olav Sandnes, *The Belly and the Body in the Pauline Epistles* (SNTSMS 120; Cambridge: Cambridge University Press, 2002), as well as the apt remarks by Gnilka; cf. Rom 16:18. If Paul intended the expression to caricature the opponents' scruples about food laws, one can just as easily imagine them returning the insult and caricaturing Paul's permissive attitude to food as itself worshiping the belly rather than God. There is little to be gained here by closely parsing such insults.
16 Cf. 2 Cor 11:13; more generally: Matt 9:37-38; 10:10; Luke 10:2, 7; 13:27; 1 Tim 5:18; 2 Tim 2:15.
17 This can be inferred from their missionary practices alluded to in 3:2 and from the contrast drawn between them and exemplary believers in Phil 3:17-

18. Paul's statement "many walk about whom I have told you often" makes no sense if the reference is to Jews broadly.
18 Among other things this means that they do not see suffering as imitative and productive of a mystical experience that is transformative and ultimately saving, an interpretation of suffering that Paul elaborates upon at length in vv. 4-16.
19 Cf. 1:28, where Paul claims that a similar fate awaits the nonbelieving "enemies" of the Philippians.
20 So Chrysostom (hom. 11.212.11-13 Allen).
21 See the introduction, part 2.b: "Internal Evidence that Philippians 3:2–4:3 is a Letter Fragment."
22 See part 1.a: "Greek and Roman Consolation."

He has made it to the top who understands what is to be the proper object of joy [*quo gaudeat*]," adding, "This do before all else, my dear Lucilius, learn how to rejoice [*disce gaudere*]."

If Lucilius will learn to do this, he will be "lifted above all of life's calamities" to a joy that "never fails" (*Ep.* 23.4), something Paul also believes will be the case for the Philippians if they learn to "rejoice in the Lord." In *Ep.* 59 Seneca even claims that Lucilius can measure his progress in wisdom by how close he is to true joy: *tantum tibi ex sapientia, quantum ex gaudio deesse*, "to the degree that you lack joy, to that degree you lack wisdom," a point Paul will make mutatis mutandis in 3:15-16: "As many of us therefore as are perfect . . . ."[23] It is no wonder, then, that Seneca proclaims "true joy" (*verum gaudium*) to be a "serious matter" (*res severa*).[24] For Paul, of course, the basis for such joy lies not in one's moral self-sufficiency, as it does for the Stoic Seneca[25]—though Paul values that as well (Phil 4:11-13, but cf. 2 Cor 2:16)—but "in the Lord." What Paul means by rejoicing *in the Lord* will be the topic of 3:2—4:1.[26]

■ **1b** Before elaborating the exhortation of 3:1a, Paul pauses to apologize for repeating himself: "To write the same things to you . . . ." Paul's language is terse, and commentators have struggled to interpret it. Two items in 3:1b call for comment. The first is the expression "to write the same things to you" (τὰ αὐτὰ γράφειν ὑμῖν). The expression refers ahead to what Paul is about to write in 3:2—4:1. But in what sense is 3:2—4:1 "the same things"?[27] Is Paul referring to something he has written

to the Philippians in a prior letter?[28] Is he referring to something he has written earlier in the present letter? Or is he simply referring to something he has said before on one or more occasions and that the Philippians therefore already know?[29] The third option seems best, since Paul is here almost certainly employing a topos commonly used by contemporary moralists to make their teaching more acceptable, namely, to flatter one's hearers that they already know what they are about to hear and that the advice being offered does not imply any ignorance or major moral deficiency on their part but is simply by way of reminder.[30] The locus classicus for this topos in Paul is Rom 15:14-15: "I am quite confident, my brothers, that you are full of goodness, brimming with all knowledge, fully capable of admonishing yourselves. Nevertheless, I have written to you [ἔγραψα ὑμῖν] boldly on a few points by way of reminder [ὡς ἐπαναμιμνῄσκων], and so on." Paul uses the topos elsewhere in 1 Thess 4:9: "concerning brotherly love you have no need for me to write you [γράφειν ὑμῖν]"; 5:1: "concerning the times and seasons you have no need for someone to write you [ὑμῖν γράφεσθαι]"; and 2 Cor 9:1: "concerning the ministry to the saints it is superfluous for me to write you [γράφειν ὑμῖν]." A dynamic translation of 3:1b therefore might be: "I know you have heard me say these things before, but I don't mind repeating myself, and at any rate it will be good for you to hear them again."

The second item calling for comment in 3:1b is the expression ὑμῖν δὲ ἀσφαλές (lit., "but for you it is ἀσφαλές"). The Greek adjective ἀσφαλής[31] is a lot like the

---

23 Recall Paul's linking of "joy" (χαράν) and "progress" (προκοπήν) in 1:25.

24 Seneca, *Ep.* 23.4; cf. Philo, *Abr.* 156: "joy is the noblest of the good emotions" (ἡ εὐπαθειῶν ἀρίστη χαρά).

25 Seneca, *Ep.* 23.6: *ad verum bonum specta et de tuo gaude* ("Look to what is truly good and rejoice in what is your own").

26 Thus: "boast in Christ Jesus" (3:3); "on account of Christ" (3:7); "the knowledge of Christ Jesus my Lord" (3:8); "gain Christ" (3:8); "found in him" (3:9); "through faith in Christ" (3:9); "to know him . . ." (3:10); "laid hold of by Christ" (3:12); "the prize of the upward call of God in Christ Jesus" (3:14); "enemies of the cross of Christ" (3:18); "a savior, the Lord Jesus Christ" (3:20); and "stand fast in the Lord" (4:1).

27 It is possible to interpret τὰ αὐτά as emphatic by position.

28 This interpretation may lie in Polycarp's plural "letters" (ἐπιστολαί) in *Phil.* 3.2, for which see my discussion above in the introduction, part 2.a: "External Evidence that Philippians Is a Composite." Cf. 1 Cor 5:9.

29 These options are discussed in detail in Reumann, pp. 453–54.

30 For the topos see Abraham J. Malherbe, *Paul and the Thessalonians* (Philadelphia: Fortress, 1987) 70–72, who cites: Isocrates, *Nic.* 40; *Phil.* 105; Cicero, *Ad fam.* 1.4.3; 2.4.2; Seneca, *Ep.* 94.26; Dio Chrysostom, *Or.* 17.1-2.

31 Paul uses the neuter ἀσφαλές, since it modifies the infinitive "to write." The same thing is true for the adjective ὀκνηρόν (the neuter of ὀκνηρός), here translated as "is not a *burden* for me."

English adjective "secure" in that it can connote either safety or steadfastness.[32] Something is "secure" if it is well protected or safe; something is also "secure" if it is steadfast, fixed firmly in place and unlikely to be moved or to fall.[33] We are faced, then, with two options. If we interpret 3:1b with the warnings that follow in 3:2—something modern partition theories, which universally insert a break before 3:1b, require us to do—then ἀσφαλές may reasonably be understood to mean "safe." Thus the AV: "but for you it is safe," and the NRSV: "and for you it is a safeguard."[34] But if, as I have argued, we retain the connection between 3:1a and 3:1b and understand 3:2—4:1 to elaborate the exhortation to "rejoice" in the Lord in 3:1a, then another possibility immediately recommends itself, namely, that 3:1—4:1 constitutes the letter's final consolatory argument and that as such it is intended not to keep the Philippians "safe" but to make them "steadfast" ("secure" in the second sense) in their current distress and insofar as possible to return them to their former "progress and joy in the faith" (1:26). This is how I have interpreted Paul's expression, which I have translated periphrastically as "and it will make you more steadfast [in your current distress]." Paul expresses a similar concern in 1 Thessalonians: "We have sent Timothy . . . to make you steadfast [στηρίξαι] and console [παρακαλέσαι] you in the faith, lest any of you be shaken [σαίνεσθαι] by these oppressing hardships" (3:2-3). If the Philippians will learn to "rejoice in the Lord," then they will similarly be steadied and consoled in the faith or, in the words of Seneca, "lifted above life's calamites."

■ **2-3** I have already noted that it was common practice in Greco-Roman antiquity to amplify an argument with a rhetorical comparison, a figure called σύγκρισις (Lat. *comparatio*).[35] Typically, σύγκρισις took the form of a comparison that moved from good to better or from bad to worse. In the former case (from good to better) the comparison consisted of two encomiums; in the latter case (from bad to worse) it consisted two invectives.[36] At times, however, contraries could be "compared" (we would say contrasted), as in Cicero's comparison of the king with the tyrant in *De orat.* 3.117,[37] or Libanius's comparison of Demosthenes with Aeschines in *Prog.* 10.3.[38] In this case the comparison consisted of a mixture of invective and encomium. Thus Aphthonius: "*synkrisis* can be a double encomium, a double invective, or a speech made up of encomium and invective."[39] The σύγκρισις

32 LSJ, s.v. ἀσφάλεια.
33 The second meaning is especially common as the popular hendiadys ἀσφαλής τε καὶ βέβαιος ("steadfast and firm") readily attests. This hendiadys is used to describe an anchor in Heb 6:19; a solid financial investment in Plutarch, *Cato mai.* 21.5; a trustworthy author in Plutarch, *Comm. not.* 1061c; and divine wisdom in Wis 7:23. It is especially common in Philo: *Her.* 314 (of a mind in possession of divine wisdom); *Congr.* 141 (of true knowledge); *Conf.* 106 (of a mind fixed on permanent realities); and *Virt.* 216 (of a soul grasping the truth that God is one); see Harold W. Attridge, *The Epistle to the Hebrews: A Commentary on the Epistle to the Hebrews* (Hermeneia; Philadelphia: Fortress Press, 1989) on 6:19. Etymology also favors this connotation, since ἀσφαλής is formed by adding the α-privative to the second aorist σφαλεῖν, which forms from the verb σφάλλω and means "to cause to fall" or "to trip" as in wrestling.
34 The NRSV interprets the neuter adjective ἀσφαλές as a substantive. The same can be done for the adjective ὀκνηρόν ("causing hesitation" therefore "troublesome" or "onerous"), which I have translated as "burden." Cf. the British idiom "not a bother."
35 See the excursus "Paul's Opponents in Philippians 3" above. For Paul's use of this figure see Vollenweider, "Waagschalen," 103–11; Christopher Forbes, "Paul and Rhetorical Comparison," in *Paul in the Greco-Roman World*, ed. J. Paul Sampley (Harrisburg, PA: Trinity Press International, 2003) 134–71.
36 Hermogenes, *Prog.* 8; cf. Aphthonius, *Prog.* 10. The topics treated in encomium/invective and rhetorical comparison are the same (Theon, *Prog.* 9 [Spengel 8]-10 [Spengel 9]; Hermogenes, *Prog.* 7-8; Aphthonius, *Prog.* 8-10).
37 Cited by Vollenweider, "Waagschalen," 96 n. 15.
38 See also Hermogenes, *Prog.* 8; Aphthonius, *Prog.* 10; cf. McGing, "Synkrisis," 15.
39 George A. Kennedy, trans. and ed., *Progymnasmata: Greek Textbooks of Prose Composition and Rhetoric* (Writings from the Greco-Roman World 10; Atlanta: Society of Biblical Literature, 2003) 114 (trans. Kennedy modified).

in Phil 3:2-3 compares what Paul dismissively calls those who put confidence in the "flesh" with those who rely on the "spirit" or "Christ" (cf. Rom 2:28-29) and is obviously the third type (a mixture of encomium and invective), as will also be the case with the σύγκρισις of 3:18-21. The σύγκρισις of 3:4-11, on the other hand, is the first type: an encomium of what is *good* (Paul's life as a Pharisee) followed by an encomium of what is *better* (Paul's life as a Christ-believer).

Excursus: Paul's Language in Philippians 3:2-3

Nowhere is Paul's skill at invective more in evidence than in Phil 3:2, where in rapid succession he calls his opponents "dogs," "depraved workers," and "the mutilation."[40] Even in translation much of Paul's rhetorical art comes through: the use of short clauses of approximately equal length (isocolon) and the fact that each of these clauses begins with the same verb (anaphora). The Greek reveals other features. In each clause the direct object of the verb begins with the Greek letter kappa (κ): βλέπετε τοὺς κύνας ("dogs"), βλέπετε τοὺς κακοὺς ἐργάτας ("depraved workers"), βλέπετε τὴν κατατομήν ("mutilation"), while

the last term in this list (κατατομή) creates a stinging wordplay with περιτομή ("circumcision") in the next sentence.

Paul's strategy in 3:3 is more subtle. Here Paul claims for his new religious movement the ancient initiation rite of Judaism: "it is we who are the circumcision." Further, he labels the religious practices of his competitors as confidence in the "flesh," a debating term crafted to denigrate physical circumcision.[41] Scholars of early Christianity typically call "flesh" one of Paul's "anthropological terms," and in some instances this is justified.[42] But here in 3:3 the term is more evocative than descriptive.[43] In other words, Paul uses "flesh" here not to convey a stable meaning but to produce negative feelings.[44] Rhetoricians might call this a case of *pathos* versus *logos*. For social psychologists it is a parade example of stigmatization.

Failure to appreciate this has led to the all-too-common mistake of (1) assuming that Paul opposed certain practices because they were objectively of the "flesh" and then (2) trying to identify what precisely "flesh" might mean for Paul. But Paul's rhetoric worked the other way around: he *first* opposed these practices for other reasons—for example, that

---

40 For ancient invective, see Valentina Arena, "Roman Oratorical Invective," in *A Companion to Roman Rhetoric*, ed. William Dominik and Jon Hall (Oxford: Blackwell, 2007), 149–60; cf. Luke Timothy Johnson, "The New Testament's Anti-Jewish Slander and the Conventions of Ancient Polemic," *JBL* 108 (1989) 419–41.

41 The term appears ninety-one times in Paul's authentic letter corpus. It is deployed in a variety of contexts and draws upon a hodgepodge of traditions. It assumes a kind of crude Platonism in its discounting of the physical world in general and the physical body in particular—in this regard, "flesh" is not to be confused with "body," which according to 1 Cor 15:44 can be "spiritual." "Flesh" also incorporates notions of purity and defilement, since it is not only physical but contaminating, possessing what a social psychologist might call the "yuck!" factor. And in some contexts at least "flesh" looks a lot like the rabbinic notion of the "evil inclination," for which see Joel Marcus, "The Evil Inclination in the Letters of Paul," *Irish Biblical Studies* (1986) 8–21; cf. idem, "The Evil Inclination in the Epistle of James," *CBQ* 44 (1982) 606–21.

42 Jörg Frey, "Flesh and Spirit in the Palestinian Jewish Sapiential Tradition and in the Qumran Texts: An Inquiry into the Development of Pauline Usage," in *The Wisdom Texts from Qumran and the Development of*

Sapiential Thought, ed. C. Hempel, A. Lange, and H. Lichtenberger (BEThL 159; Leuven: Peeters, 2002) 367–404; idem, "The Notion of 'Flesh' in 4QInstruction and the Background of Pauline Thought," in *Sapiential, Liturgical, and Poetical Texts from Qumran: Proceedings of the Third Meeting of the International Organization for Qumran Studies, Oslo, 1998. Published in Memory of Maurice Baillet* (STDJ 35; Leiden: Brill, 2000) 197–226.

43 John M. G. Barclay, *Obeying the Truth: A Study in Paul's Ethics in Galatians* (Studies of the New Testament and Its World; Edinburgh: T&T Clark, 1988) 178–215, esp. 204: "for a skillful writer like Paul such a term [= σάρξ] also provides opportunities to link disparate entities by word-association and develop his polemic on this basis"; and 209: "Paul uses σάρξ as an 'umbrella term' under which he can gather such disparate entities as libertine behaviour, circumcision, a range of social vices and life under the law." See also idem, *Gift*, 427 n. 13.

44 One result of this is action, but another is the construction or maintaining of a new community of discourse; see Carol A. Newsom, *The Self as Symbolic Space: Constructing Identity and Community at Qumran* (STDJ 52; Leiden: Brill, 2004).

insisting on circumcision would hinder his gentile mission[45]—and *then* labeled them as pertaining to the "flesh" as part of his strategy to demean and ultimately reject them.[46] In this sense "flesh" is not unlike the American slang "bullshit." People do not reject something because it is objectively "bullshit"— whatever that might mean—but label something "bullshit" because they have already rejected it and wish others to do the same.[47] This is not to say that when Paul used the term "flesh" he was somehow being less than honest, since he himself presumably had the feelings he hoped to evoke by the term. Nor does this mean that modern readers must judge Paul's usage incoherent, since, properly understood, it is neither coherent nor incoherent but evocative. But it does mean that we need to see the expression for what it is—and what it seeks to do—and not over-interpret it. Scholars who read too much into Paul's polemical antitheses expose their own assumptions (often about Judaism) as much as they putatively describe his.

The rhetorical art that Paul deploys in vilifying his opponents in 3:2 scarcely supports claims that he has let his emotions get the better of him and that he is lashing out with "violent hysteria."[48] On the contrary, Paul has artfully crafted a rhetorical foil designed to produce aversion in the Philippians, which aversion he can then direct

toward their current behavior.[49] Paul's rhetorical strategy assumes that the Philippians will have agreed with him in rejecting the opponents of 3:2, from whose scheme for relating to God they will have wanted to distance themselves.

The various names Paul calls his opponents in 3:2 have drawn a lot of attention. None more so than the slur "dogs," which commentators have traditionally understood as Paul's inversion of a popular Jewish slur—that gentiles are unclean "dogs"—that Paul then throws back in the face of his Torah-observant opponents. This would make good rhetorical sense, and may be the case, but the evidence that Jews regularly called gentiles "dogs" is far from overwhelming,[50] so that if Paul is indeed inverting a Jewish slur it was by no means a common one, no more so than, say, the gentile slur that Jews were "temple robbers" that Paul deploys in Rom 2:22.[51] "Depraved workers" has generally been interpreted as an indication that Paul's opponents are carrying on their own mission to the gentiles, and that seems correct.[52] "Mutilation" is a clear reference to the practice of circumcision, as Paul's claiming "circumcision" for himself and his converts in next verse makes plain.[53]

The invective of 3:2 is the first part of a rhetorical comparison. As such it does not convey Paul's main

---

45 The author of Acts took this to be Paul's primary motive (e.g., Acts 15:19).

46 Here I am in complete agreement with E. P. Sanders (*Paul: The Apostle's Life, Letters, and Thought* [Minneapolis: Fortress Press, 2015] 28–30), who insists on distinguishing between prior and often unstated "reasons" and subsequent and explicit "arguments." See esp. his perceptive and charmingly frank comments on 1 Cor 6:13-20: "In my naïve and innocent youth, I thought that Paul first conceived the notion of union with Christ and then considered other unions [e.g., sex with prostitutes] that were inappropriate to it. . . . But I am now inclined to think that the argument about union with Christ and the temple of the Spirit is rationalization to support a point arrived at on another basis: he was a Diaspora Jew" (ibid., 302–3).

47 For a learned and humorous attempt to define this term, see Harry G. Frankfurt, *On Bullshit* (Princeton: Princeton University Press, 2005); cf. Phil 3:8!

48 J. L. Holden, *Paul's Letters from Prison: Philippians, Colossians, Philemon, and Ephesians* (Philadelphia: Westminster, 1977).

49 Paul's rhetoric says in effect, "Do you not realize that your response to the present situation is expressive of the values of these people!"

50 Mark Nanos, "Paul's Reversal of Jews Calling Gentiles 'Dogs' (Philippians 3:2): 1600 Years of an Ideological Tale Wagging an Exegetical Dog?" *BibInt* 17 (2009) 448–82.

51 Cf. Josephus, *Ap.* 1.311, for which see John M. G. Barclay, *Flavius Josephus: Translation and Commentary,* vol. 10: *Against Apion* (Leiden: Brill, 2007) on that passage.

52 Gnilka, Reumann; cf. Dieter Georgi, *The Opponents of Paul in Second Corinthians* (Philadelphia: Fortress Press, 1986) 40. For the term "worker" elsewhere in early Christian literature, see esp. 2 Cor 11:13 (where "deceitful workers" [ἐργάται δόλιοι] = "false apostles" [ψευδαπόστολοι]); cf. Matt. 9:37-38 (Luke 10:2); Matt 10:10 (Luke 10:7); Luke 13:27; 1 Tim 5:18; 2 Tim 2:15.

53 Cf. the reference to castration in Gal 5:12.

point. Rather, it serves to highlight the encomiastic claims of 3:3, which Paul believes should mark the social identity of all Christ-believers, including especially the Philippians: "For *we* are [ἡμεῖς γὰρ ἐσμεν] the circumcision, etc."[54] Koester argues that the items in v. 3 correspond in reverse order and point for point with the items in v. 2. Since there are four items in v. 3 and only three in v. 2, he combines items three and four. The result is that "circumcision" corresponds to "mutilation"; "who serve in the spirit of God" corresponds to "depraved workers"; and "[who] boast in Christ Jesus and do not put confidence in the flesh" corresponds to "dogs." This is not an unreasonable reading: "circumcision" obviously answers to "mutilation"; "serve" (λατρεύειν), like "workers," may well refer missionary activity (cf. Rom 1:9); and the antithesis "[who] boast in Christ Jesus and do not put confidence in the flesh" can easily be read as a single item, though here the connection with "dogs" is less than obvious.

A better reading in my view, and one that also attends more closely to the grammar, is to understand the expression "we are the circumcision" to govern the other three items in the list, which items then elaborate it.[55] Paul insists that his converts are now "the circumcision," *because* they "serve in the spirit of God and boast in Christ Jesus . . . ."[56] In other words, it is not physical circumcision but spirit possession that marks the people of God.[57] Possession by "the spirit of God," which for Paul is also "the spirit of Christ" (cf. Rom 8:9; Gal 4:6; Phil 1:19), animates Christ-believers' "service" or missionary activity[58] and thus their enthusiasm for or "boast[ing] in" Christ Jesus.[59] This, in turn, makes placing "confidence in the flesh"—understood as Torah observance, including circumcision ("mutilation")—irrational if not impossible. Presumably, possession by "the spirit of Jesus Christ" (1:19) is the basis for the mystical "knowledge of Christ" that will be the focus of the second rhetorical comparison in 3:4-11.

---

54 The "we" (ἡμεῖς) is emphatic.

55 Grammatically, "we are the circumcision" (ἡμεῖς γὰρ ἐσμεν ἡ περιτομή) is the independent clause on which the subsequent participial clauses ([οἱ] λατρεύοντες . . . καὶ καυχώμενοι . . . [καὶ] πεποιθότες) depend.

56 On this reading, serving in the spirit of God, boasting in Christ Jesus, and not placing one's confidence in the flesh are essentially the same thing.

57 For Paul's assemblies as spirit-possession cults, see Mount's incisive essays, "Spirit Possession" and "Religious Experience."

58 Earlier in Phil 1:19 Paul trusts that the "spirit of Jesus Christ" will enable him to speak boldly in his upcoming trial.

59 For the expression "who boast in Christ Jesus," see my comments above at 1:26.

3

4/ —although I also have [grounds for] confidence in the flesh. If anyone else thinks that he has reasons to be confident in the flesh, I have more: 5/ circumcised on the eighth day; of the people of Israel; the tribe of Benjamin; a Hebrew speaker raised by Hebrew speakers; regarding the law, a Pharisee; 6/ regarding zeal, persecuting the church;[a] regarding the righteousness prescribed in the law, blameless! 7/ But[b] what things were gains to me, these I have come to reckon a loss on account of Christ—8/ actually,[c] I consider all things to be a loss on account of the surpassing greatness of the knowledge of Christ[d] Jesus my lord, for whose sake I have suffered the loss of all things and consider them mere table-scraps![e]—in order that I might gain Christ 9/ and be found to be in him, not having my own righteousness that is from the law, but the one that is through faith in Christ,[f] the righteousness that is from God based on such faith; 10/ that I might know him and the power of his resurrection and [the] fellowship of his sufferings,[g] [even to the point of] being conformed to his death, 11/ if somehow I might arrive at the resurrection from the dead![h]

a   A few manuscripts (F G 0282 629 lat) add θεοῦ ("of God") possibly on analogy with Gal 1:13 and 1 Cor 15:9.

b   An impressive array of witnesses (א² B D F K L P Ψ 075, 104, 365, 630, 1175, 1505, 1739, 1881, 2464 Maj lat sy co) begin v. 7 with ἀλλά ("but") while an equally strong list (𝔭⁴⁶ 𝔭⁶¹ᵛⁱᵈ א* A G 0282 33 81 1241ˢ b d; Lcf Ambst) omit it. NA²⁸ prints it in brackets. The sense is clearly adversative whether ἀλλά is included or not, and it is certainly in keeping with Greek prose style to deploy asyndeton to mark a new and emphatic beginning (as the large number of manuscripts omitting it attest). It is perhaps easier to see a scribe intentionally adding ἀλλά for purposes of clarity. At any rate, good English prose style strongly invites an explicit contrast, and so I have included it.

c   The Greek is emphatic: ἀλλὰ μενοῦνγε καί. A number of manuscripts (𝔭⁴⁶ᵛⁱᵈ א* 6, 33, 1739, 1181 lat) reduce this slightly by omitting καί. BDF §448.6 suggests "not only this, but also"; BDAG, s.v. μενοῦν, translates "more than that."

d   Several older manuscripts (𝔭⁴⁶ 𝔭⁶¹ B) include the definite article before "Christ" perhaps on analogy with the preceding verse, where an article appears before "Christ."

e   A significant number of witnesses (𝔭⁶¹ᵛⁱᵈ א² A D² K L P Ψ 075, 81, 104, 365, 630, 1175, 1241, 1505, 1739, 1881, 2464 Maj vgᵐˢ; Aug) add the infinitive εἶναι ("to be") otherwise implied, no doubt on analogy with the preceding clause where the infinitive is expressed: "I consider all things *to be* (εἶναι) loss."

f   Gk. πίστις Χριστοῦ, which may be translated either "faith in Christ" or "Christ's faith[fullness]," for which see the excursus below.

g   Several important manuscripts (𝔭⁴⁶ א* A B 1241, 2464) lack a definite article before "fellowship," some of which (𝔭⁴⁶ א* B) also lack the article before "sufferings." A large number of witnesses include these articles (א² D F G K L P Ψ 075, 33, 81, 104, 365, 630, 1175, 1505, 1739, 1881 Maj before "fellowship"; א² A D F G K L P Ψ 075, 33, 81, 104, 365, 630, 1175, 1241, 1505, 1739, 1881 2464 Maj before "suffering"). It is difficult to say which is the better reading, though it is perhaps easier to explain a copyist adding the articles to bring the expression into line with the immediately preceding expression, "the power of his resurrection," where both "power" and "resurrection" have the definite article. This is exegetically significant, because if the latter expression ("fellowship of his sufferings") is anarthrous, then the article before "power" governs both expressions and thus links them closely together.

h   External evidence (𝔭⁴⁶ א A B D P Ψ 33, 81, 104, 365, 1175, 1505, 1739ᶜ lat sa; Irˡᵃᵗ Tert) strongly supports the reading translated here: τὴν ἐξανάστασιν τὴν ἐκ νεκρῶν, lit., "the resurrection that is out of the dead."

155

Several minor witnesses (K L 075, 630, 1241, 1739*, 1881, 2464, Maj bo; Hiet Aug) support the more typical expression τὴν ἐξανάστασιν τῶν νεκρῶν, "the resurrection of the dead," and two (F G) the garbled conflation τὴν ἐξανάστασιν τῶν ἐκ νεκρῶν, "the resurrection of those from the dead."

Analysis

Paul amplifies the exhortation to "rejoice in the Lord" with a second rhetorical comparison in 3:4-11.[1] In 3:2-3 he contrasted two types of Christ-belief, illustrating what were to his mind two strategies for relating to God: one whose practitioners "boast in Christ" and one whose practitioners "put confidence in the flesh." He continues this language in 3:4-11: "although I also have [grounds for] *confidence in the flesh*. If anyone else thinks that he has reasons to be *confident in the flesh*, I have more" (3:4). Now, however, the comparison Paul draws is not between two types of Christ-belief but between his earlier life as a Pharisee (3:5-6) and his present life as a Christ-believer (3:7-11). Philippians 3:4-11 is an important piece of Pauline autobiography.[2]

Paul lists seven social identity markers that describe his earlier religious life (3:5-6). The list reproduces the standard topics of an encomium and divides into two parts.[3] Those identity markers he possessed from childhood: "circumcised on the eighth day; of the people of Israel; the tribe of Benjamin; a Hebrew speaker raised by Hebrew speakers" (3:5a). And those identity markers he achieved later in life: "regarding the law, a Pharisee; regarding zeal, persecuting the church; regarding the righteousness prescribed in the law, blameless" (3:5b-6).[4] Paul contrasts these older markers with his new social identity marker as a Christ-believer: a consuming desire to "know" Christ (3:7-11).

In order to compare his past and present ways of life, Paul introduces the bookkeeping language of "loss" and "gain." This language is new and striking, and it is only with some difficulty that he manages to bring it into line with the letter's leitmotif of things that do and do not matter (1:10).[5] Even more important to Paul's developing argument is the fact that he imagines his new identity to reside not in things he presently possesses but in aspirations yet to be fully realized: "that I might gain Christ and be found in him . . . that I might know him and the power of his resurrection."[6] These aspirations revolve around what Paul calls ἡ γνῶσις Χριστοῦ or "the knowledge of Christ,"[7] a subjective experience that is at the same time mystical and transformative and ultimately saving.[8] Paul displays great pathos in describing this experience, insisting that its "surpassing greatness" renders all else "table-scraps" by comparison.

Readers must continue to tread carefully here, since the interpretive tradition surrounding Phil 3:4-11 is rife with caricatures of Judaism. These are due in part to the religious prejudices of Paul's Christian interpreters. But they are also due to what continues to be an insufficiently critical approach to Paul, whose pronouncements are often read as objective insights without taking into account that they are first and foremost polemical con-

---

1   Müller.

2   For Paul's autobiographical remarks in Galatians and 1 Thessalonians, see George Lyons, *Pauline Autobiography: Toward a New Understanding* (SBLDS 73; Atlanta: Scholars Press, 1985).

3   See my comments on 3:4-6 below.

4   So Chrysostom and most commentaries.

5   He manages to do this only in v. 8b, when he describes his past achievements not as "loss" but as meaningless "table-scraps," things that no longer matter to him in the least.

6   He will develop this point at length in 3:12-16, where he likens his new life as a Christ-believer to a race that is not yet finished and a "calling" (κλῆσις) to be continually pursued.

7   Cf. v. 10: "know him . . . and [the] fellowship of his suffering . . . being conformed to his death."

8   This γνῶσις is for Paul the subjective side of sanctification: it relates not the alleged *fact* of transformation so much as the Christ-believer's personal *experience* of it, which in the end is the experience of "joy" (cf. 3:1).

structions. I have already noted Paul's invective in 3:2-3 that Torah-observant Christ-believers practice a religion of the "flesh." To this may now be added Paul's presentation in 3:4-11 of Judaism as a static religion that looks to past achievements, whereas Christ-belief is dynamic and forward looking.[9]

Comment

■ **4-6** Paul now uses his past way of life as a Pharisee as a second foil to illustrate further the distinction between a religion of the "flesh" and a religion of the "spirit" that celebrates "Christ." He carries forward this distinction in 3:4, which taken together with 3:3—there is no major grammatical break between these verses—explicitly mentions "confidence in the flesh" three times. In keeping with current rhetorical practice, Paul uses a slightly different expression each time: ἐν σαρκὶ πεποιθότες . . . ἔχων πεποίθησιν καὶ ἐν σαρκί . . . πεποιθέναι ἐν σαρκί.[10]

Paul imagines himself beating his opponents at their own game. If they have grounds for confidence in the flesh, he has more. To demonstrate this claim he produces a brief encomium of his former life as a Pharisee (3:5-6).[11] Ancient encomiums were essentially lists of noteworthy traits and accomplishments variously organized and elaborated. The items on these lists differed depending on the specific person being praised, but common topics included birth, ethnic origin and tribe, family, education, vocation, notable virtues, and worthy deeds.[12] These topics were typically gathered into larger categories that served as a kind of outline. Theon proposes three groupings, as does Aphthonius; Nicolaus proposes five, and Hermogenes seven.[13] Paul's list divides naturally into two parts: external goods he possessed from childhood (3:5a) and accomplishments he achieved later in life (3:5b-6).

The first four of Paul's identity markers (3:5a) reflect the encomiastic topics of birth ("circumcised on the eighth day"),[14] ethnic and tribal origins ("of the people of Israel; the tribe of Benjamin") and upbringing ("a Hebrew speaker raised by Hebrew speakers").[15] Despite his Diaspora origins, Paul insists that he was born into a Torah-observant family, where ethnic and tribal affiliations were maintained and where from a child he learned

9   Apocalyptic Jews looked to the future no less than Paul did, while Paul placed no less confidence in the believer's past act of baptism (cf. Gal 3:27-29; Rom 6:1-11) than the Torah-observant placed in circumcision.

10   The shift from participle (πεποιθότες) to abstract noun (πεποίθησιν) to infinitive (πεποιθέναι) would have been much appreciated by his contemporary audience. See my "Paul's Pointed Prose," 41–42, 52.

11   That Paul uses encomium and not invective to treat his former life as a Pharisee is noteworthy; cf. Müller.

12   For the standard progression of encomiastic topics as taught in the schools, see Theon, *Prog.* 9 (Spengel, 8); Hermogenes, *Prog.* 7; Aphthonius, *Prog.* 8-9. A genre distinction was typically observed between praise of the dead (epitaphios), praise of the living (encomium), and praise of the gods (hymn). Virtues and other inanimate things could also be the subject of encomium (cf. Paul's encomium to love in 1 Corinthians 13).

13   Theon, *Prog.* 9 (Spengel 8): external goods, goods of the body, and ethical virtues and deeds (cf. Cicero, *Tusc.* 5.30.85: "there are three types of goods: first and foremost those of the mind [animi], then those of the body, and finally external things," following

Aristotle, *EN* 1.8.1098b13–17. Plato distinguished between the goods of the body and the goods of the soul, with the goods of the soul taking precedence [*Gorg.* 512a5-6]). Aphthonius, *Prog.* 8: origins, upbringing, and deeds. Nicolaus, *Prog.* 8: ethnic origins, birth, upbringing, youthful achievements, achievements as an adult. Hermogenes, *Prog.* 7: ethnic origins, birth, nurture, nature of mind and body, vocation, notable deeds, and external things such as friends and possessions.

14   Cf. Gen 21:4; Lev 12:3; cf. Luke 1:59; 2:21. Circumcision became an especially important identity marker in Judaism after the so-called Hellenistic crisis in the early second century BCE, when nude gymnastic exercising in Jerusalem caused certain Jewish youths to try to hide their circumcision through the surgical procedure known as epispasm (1 Macc 1:15; Josephus, *Ant.* 12.241; Soranus, *Gynaec.* 2.34; cf. 1 Cor 7:18: "Has anyone been called having been circumcised, let him not have it reversed [ἐπισπάσθω]").

15   For the translation "Hebrew speaker," see BDAG, s.v. Ἑβραῖος 2. In addition to 2 Cor 11:22, which I quote below, see Acts 6:1.

Hebrew.[16] Pilhofer has argued that Paul's claim to be of the tribe of Benjamin answers to the Philippians' membership in the Roman *tribus Voltinianus*,[17] but it is more likely a response to the imagined claims of his opponents. Paul had faced these claims at Corinth: "Are they Hebrews? So am I! Are they Israelites? So am I! Are they seed of Abraham? So am I!" (2 Cor 11:22).[18] And he had already drawn upon them to construct his public persona in his letter to the Romans: "I am myself also an Israelite, from the seed of Abraham, the tribe of Benjamin" (Rom 11:1).[19]

The last three identity markers on Paul's list (3:5b-6) pertain to his accomplishments as an adult and follow roughly the topics of vocation, moral character, and notable accomplishments. They all revolve around his relationship to the Jewish law: Paul approached the law with the carefulness of a "Pharisee";[20] he had an intense "zeal" ($\zeta\hat{\eta}\lambda o\varsigma$) for the law, which was demonstrated in his persecution of Christ-believers; and in his actual observance of the law he was "blameless" ($\check{\alpha}\mu\epsilon\mu\pi\tau o\varsigma$). Two items in 3:5b-6 call for comment. First, it should be noted that Paul attributes his early persecution of Christ-believers not to his Pharisaism but to his "zeal."[21] He offers a similar account of how he "persecuted the church of God beyond measure and attempted to destroy it" in Gal 1:13-14, where he describes himself as a "zealot [$\zeta\eta\lambda\omega\tau\acute{\eta}\varsigma$] for the traditions of the fathers." "Zeal" ($\zeta\hat{\eta}\lambda o\varsigma$; Heb. קנא) was a semitechnical term in Second Temple Judaism for an extreme form of religious devotion that lent itself to violence.[22] By modern Western standards such devotion would be considered fanaticism, and this seems to have been the view of the ancient Romans as well, who denied the term *religio* to extremism, calling it *superstitio* instead.[23] Many ancient Jews, however, regarded such "zeal" as an exemplary virtue.

Excursus: "Zeal" in Second Temple Judaism and Early Christianity

"Zeal" acquired its connotations of religious violence from the story of Phinehas, a Levite who in his "zeal" for God murdered an Israelite man along with his Midianite concubine in the belief that the man's relationship with a foreign woman had defiled Israel and brought about God's judgment (Num 25:6-13). In doing this, the story goes, he not only "atoned" for the sins of Israel and averted God's wrath[24] but also was rewarded with an "eternal priesthood" (Num 25:13; cf. Sir 45:24; 1 Macc 2:54). Psalm 106:31 (LXX

---

16 Cf. Acts 23:6: "I am a Pharisee, the son of Pharisees," which presumably derives from the author of Acts' exegesis of Phil 3:5.

17 Pilhofer, *Philippi* 1:121–27.

18 Note also the next verse: "Are they servants of Christ? (I speak as a fool!) I more [$\acute{v}\pi\grave{\epsilon}\rho \acute{\epsilon}\gamma\acute{\omega}$]"; cf. Phil 3:4: "I more" ($\acute{\epsilon}\gamma\grave{\omega} \mu\hat{\alpha}\lambda\lambda o\nu$).

19 Romans was written from Corinth (Rom 15:25-26; 16:1, 23; cf. Acts 19:29).

20 For the reputation of the Pharisees as interpreters of the law, see Acts 26:6; Josephus, *Ant.* 17.41; *Bell.* 2.162; *Vit.* 191. "Pharisee" may have become a negative term in the later Gospel tradition (esp. Matthew 23!), but it was not so in Paul. Acts 5:33-39 imagines the Pharisee Gamaliel as mild in his treatment of the emerging church. According to the Gospel of John, the Pharisee Nicodemus secretly believed in Jesus (3:1; 7:48-52) and honored him after his death (19:39).

21 Paul does not explicitly frame his zeal as pertaining to the law, but this is presumably how he is using the term, since the list of his adult accomplishments begins and ends with a reference to the law: "regarding the law . . . regarding the righteousness prescribed in the law" (cf. 1 Macc 2:26, where the

Hasmonean Mattathias kills a fellow Jew out of "zeal for the law"; Acts 21:20). When in Gal 1:13-14 Paul speaks of his zeal "for the traditions of the fathers," he means the law as interpreted by Pharisaic convention.

22 The standard discussion is still Martin Hengel, *Die Zeloten: Untersuchungen zur jüdischen Freiheitsbewegung in der Zeit von Herodes I. bis 70 n. Chr.* (Arbeiten zur Geschichte des Spätjudentums und Urchristentum 1; Leiden: Brill, 1961; 2nd ed., 1976; ET, *The Zealots: Investigations into the Jewish Freedom Movement in the Period from Herod I until 70 A.D.* [trans. David Smith; Edinburgh: T&T Clark, 1986]). But see Morton Smith, "Zealots and Sicarii: Their Origins and Relation," *HTR* 64 (1971) 1–19; and Richard A. Horsley, "The Zealots: Their Origin, Relationships and Importance in the Jewish Revolt," *NovT* 28 (1986) 159–92; see also John J. Collins, "The Zeal of Phinehas: The Bible and the Legitimation of Violence," *JBL* 122 (2003) 3–21.

23 See Beard, *Religions of Rome*, 1:217, citing *ILS* 8393.30–31 (the *Laudatio Turiae*): *religio sine superstitione*.

24 Num 25:11; cf. Ps 106:29; 1 Macc 3:8; 2 Macc 8:5.

105:31) adds that Phinehas's violent act, like Abraham's faith in Gen 15:6, was "reckoned to him for righteousness." In his famous Hymn to the Fathers, Ben Sira ranks Phinehas "third in glory" after Moses and Aaron "because he was zealous in the fear of the Lord" (Sir 45:23-24). In 1 Macc 2:23-28, the Hasmonean patriarch Mattathias is said to have "burned with zeal for the law just as Phinehas did" when he (Mattathias) slaughtered a Jewish man and a Seleucid official on the altar that the official had erected in Modein.[25] Later, in 4 Macc 18:12, Phinehas is identified as a "zealot" (ζηλωτής), a designation that by the First Jewish War implied militaristic nationalism and armed resistance against Rome.[26]

Other legendary figures were also assimilated to this tradition of "zeal." Elijah showed himself similarly "zealous for Yahweh" when he rounded up and killed the prophets of Baal, as did Jehu when he slaughtered the descendants of Ahab.[27] Levi was especially admired for his deception and killing of Hamor and Shechem in Gen 34:25-31. According to *Jub.* 30:18, "he was zealous to do righteousness and judgment and vengeance." According to the *T. Levi* 6:1, it was because of his "zeal" that Levi took the lead in the attack.[28] Judith finds in Levi's "zeal" an inspiration for her beheading of Holofernes (Jdt 9:2-4). "Zeal" was also an important concept at Qumran, where it produced "an everlasting hatred against all men of the pit" (1QS 9:21-23; cf. 1QHᵃ 6:25; 10:17). Finally, according to *2 Bar.* 66:3-5, it was because King Josiah "was zealous with the zeal of the Almighty with his whole heart" that he systematically tortured and killed those who worshiped gods other than Yahweh (cf. 1 Kgs 23:20).

Turning to early Christian sources, the Synoptic tradition reports that one of Jesus's disciples was called "Simon the Zealot,"[29] and in the Gospel of John Jesus's act of violence in the temple—his so-called Cleansing of the Temple—is interpreted as an expression of his "zeal": "the zeal for your house has consumed me."[30] According to Acts, James warned Paul during his final visit to Jerusalem that there were many Jewish Christ-believers in the city who remained "zealous for the law" (Acts 21:20). Shortly thereafter Paul tells a gathered crowd of Jews that he too had been "zealous for God just as all of you are today," and that as an expression of this zeal he had "persecuted this Way even to the point of death" (Acts 22:3-4).

As already noted, Paul attributes his persecution of Christ-believers to his "zeal" twice in his own letters. First in Gal 1:13-14: "I was violently persecuting the church of God and was trying to destroy it . . . (as) a zealot [ζηλωτής] for the traditions of my ancestors." And again in Phil 3:5-6, where this time his "zeal" is clearly imagined as something above and beyond his Pharisaism: "regarding the law, a Pharisee; regarding zeal [ζῆλος], persecuting the church. . . ." Paul expresses a continuing admiration for Jewish zeal in Rom 10:2, though he now feels that it has been misdirected because it has not resulted in devotion to Christ: "they have a great zeal for God, but it is not enlightened." In his own churches zeal could erupt with great force, as it did at Corinth regarding a man who had somehow offended Paul—"what indignation, what alarm, what passion, what zeal, what punishment!"—which zeal Paul had to try to quell (2 Cor 7:11-12; cf. 2:5-11).[31]

---

25 See Josephus, *Ant.* 12.271. This zeal continued to express itself in attacks on "sinners" and "lawless men" and in forced circumcisions (1 Macc 2:44-50).

26 E.g., Josephus, *Bell.* 2.651; 4.160.

27 Elijah: 1 Kgs 19:10, 14; 1 Macc 2:58; cf. Deut 13:1-5; Jehu: 2 Kgs 10:16-17.

28 In *Sifre Num.* 25 Phineas is called a "zealot, the son of a zealot," the latter being a reference to Levi, whose "zeal" was demonstrated in the dual murders of Genesis 34.

29 Mark 3:18; Matt 10:4; Luke 6:15; Acts 1:13. Mark and Matthew merely transliterate the Aramaic קנאן ("zealot"): Σίμων ὁ Καναναῖος (cf. *m. Sanh.* 9:6), while Luke translates into Greek: Σίμων ὁ ζηλωτής.

30 Citing Ps 69:9. As is well known, the author of John has moved this scene to the beginning of Jesus's prophetic career, where it serves to characterize Jesus's strident religious attitude, especially toward Judaism, a theme all too familiar in the Fourth Gospel.

31 Paul offered a model for this "zeal" with his vicarious ritual killing of the individual in 1 Cor 5:3-5: "When you are assembled, and my spirit is present with the power of our Lord Jesus, you are to hand this man over to Satan for the destruction of his flesh." For violence in early Christianity more generally, see Michael Gaddis, *There Is No Crime for Those Who Have Christ: Religious Violence in the Christian Roman Empire* (Transformation of the Classical Heritage 30; Berkeley: University of California Press, 2005); Thomas Sizgorich, *Violence and Belief in Late Antiquity: Militant Devotion in Christianity and Islam* (Divinations; Philadelphia: University of Pennsylvania Press, 2008); Brent D. Shaw, *Sacred Violence: African Christians and Sectarian Hatred in the Age of Augustine* (Cambridge: Cambridge University Press, 2011).

The second item in 3:5b-6 calling for comment is Paul's description of himself as "blameless" ($\mathring{a}\mu\epsilon\mu\pi\tau\sigma\varsigma$) before the Jewish law. Even from his new perspective as a Christ-believer Paul claims that he had succeeded in observing the law. This implies that—despite much previous scholarship to the contrary—Paul did not imagine the law to be impossible to keep. It further implies—again contrary to earlier scholarly opinion—that Paul did not convert to Christ-belief out of some sort of personal crisis stemming from his inability to keep the law.[32] Paul does not say here why he came to believe in Christ but only that what he once valued had changed and that he was now enamored of "the knowledge of Christ" (3:7-11). But in Gal 1:12 he claims to have come to believe "through a revelation [$\delta\iota'\ \mathring{a}\pi\sigma\kappa\alpha\lambda\acute{\upsilon}\psi\epsilon\omega\varsigma$] of Jesus Christ." Presumably, it was this initial experience of Christ that started him on his quest for a deeper $\gamma\nu\hat{\omega}\sigma\iota\varsigma\ X\rho\iota\sigma\tau\sigma\hat{\upsilon}$.

The above does not mean, however, that Paul was not critical of the law. He was. But his criticism lay not in the law's impossibility but in its limited efficacy. Even when fully kept, the law fails to effect the kind of radical transformation—"the righteousness which is from God [$\mathring{\epsilon}\kappa\ \theta\epsilon\sigma\hat{\upsilon}$]"—that is attainable by the Christ-believer (3:9).[33] This is the principal criticism of the law that Paul put forward in his letter to the Romans: "what the law was powerless [$\mathring{a}\delta\acute{\upsilon}\nu\alpha\tau\sigma\nu$] to do, because it was weakened [$\mathring{\eta}\sigma\theta\acute{\epsilon}\nu\epsilon\iota$] by the flesh" (8:3). Paul believed that the coming judgment would be exacting and impartial (Rom 2:11), and the law was at best a poor and uncertain preparation for this (cf. Rom 2:12-13, 25; Gal 5:2-5).

■ **7-11** Verses 7-11 form the second half of the rhetorical comparison begun in 3:4-6. They constitute a complex rhetorical climax, reaching a penultimate high point in 3:8b, "and I consider them mere table-scraps!," and the ultimate high point in 3:11, "if somehow I might arrive at the resurrection of the dead!" Because of this they divide naturally into two parts: vv. 7-8b, where Paul uses the language of "loss" and "gain" to explain the radical shift in values that took place when he became a Christ-believer, and vv. 8c-11, where in two parallel purpose clauses he specifies what, given his new values, he now hopes to "gain." Central to Paul's new values is what he calls $\mathring{\eta}$ $\gamma\nu\hat{\omega}\sigma\iota\varsigma\ X\rho\iota\sigma\tau\sigma\hat{\upsilon}$ or "the knowledge of Christ" (3:8), which knowledge now controls his aspirations: "that I might know [$\gamma\nu\hat{\omega}\nu\alpha\iota$] him" (3:10).

■ **7-8b** Paul may have inherited the bookkeeping language of "loss" ($\zeta\eta\mu\acute{\iota}\alpha$) and "gain" ($\kappa\acute{\epsilon}\rho\delta\sigma\varsigma$) from his earlier Pharisaism.[34] According to m. 'Abot 2.1, Judah the Prince taught his disciples to "reckon the loss [הפסד] incurred by the fulfillment of a precept against the gain [שכר] secured by its observance, and the gain [שכר] gotten by a transgression against the loss [הפסד] it involves."[35] In deciding a course of action, Judah's disciples were to perform two types of cost–benefit analysis. Positively, they were to weigh whatever "loss" might be incurred by observing a commandment against the greater "gain" the observance would bring. Negatively, they were to weigh

---

32 It is debated whether Paul's move to Christ-belief should be called a "conversion." In Gal 1:15-16 Paul presents his so-called Damascus road experience as a prophetic *call* (Krister Stendahl, "Paul and the Introspective Conscience of the West," *HTR* 55 [1963] 199–215; cf. Fredriksen, "Mandatory Retirement"). Here in Phil 3:4-11, however, where his point is not to establish apostolic independence but to distinguish as thoroughly as possible two strategies for relating to God, he presents his experience and the new interiority it produces as a kind of *conversion*. The classic study remains A. D. Nock, *Conversion: The Old and the New in Religion from Alexander the Great to Augustine of Hippo* (Oxford: Clarendon, 1933); but now see Segal, *Paul the Convert*; cf. Pierre Hadot's wide-ranging, "Conversio," *HWPh* (1971) 1:1033–36. Among its many ambiguities, the debate continues to labor under the assumption that autobiography offers a univocal and stable narrative.

33 For Paul, this righteousness was in large part God's work (Phil 1:6; 2:13).

34 The noun "loss" ($\zeta\eta\mu\acute{\iota}\alpha$) occurs twice and its cognate verb "to lose" ($\zeta\eta\mu\iota\acute{o}\omega$) once, while the noun "gain" ($\kappa\acute{\epsilon}\rho\delta\sigma\varsigma$) and the verb "to gain" ($\kappa\epsilon\rho\delta\alpha\acute{\iota}\nu\omega$) each occur once. Cf. Apuleius, *Metam.* 11.20, where Lucius twice speaks of the "gain" (*lucrum*) to be had from initiation into the mysteries of Isis. Troels Engberg-Pedersen sees a Stoic topos ("On Comparison: The Stoic Theory of Value in Paul's Theology and Ethics in Philippians," in Frey and Schliesser, *Philipperbrief*, 289–308, here 298).

35 As noted by Lohmeyer, citing Hermann Strack and Paul Billerbeck, *Kommentar zum Neuen Testament aus Talmud und Midrasch* (6 vols.; Munich: Beck, 1922–61) 1:749; cf. Collange.

whatever "gain" might be had by breaking a commandment against the greater "loss" incurred by doing so. In the first instance, the gain promises to outweigh the loss, while in the second it is the other way around. According to Mark 8:36, Jesus urged his disciples to perform the second (negative) type of analysis: "What does it profit a person to gain [κερδῆσαι] the whole world and lose [ζημιωθῆναι] his soul?" (cf. Luke 9:25; Matt 16:26). Any possible "gain" the disciples might get from denying Jesus is more than outweighed by the terrible loss they would eventually incur.

In Phil 3:7-8b Paul performs the first type of cost-benefit analysis, where gains outweigh losses. In this case, however, Paul's analysis is used not to decide on a course of action but to explain the results of an action already taken: "but what things were gains to me, these things I have come to reckon a loss on account of Christ."[36] Paul allows that, when viewed on its own terms, living as a committed Pharisee produces a net gain,[37] that any losses incurred by that lifestyle are more than matched by the "gains" accrued. But from Paul's new perspective as a Christ-believer, a very different analysis emerges. Any gains that came from being a good Pharisee are completely overshadowed by the "surpassing greatness [τὸ ὑπερέχον] of the knowledge of Christ," so much so that Paul now reckons them mere "table-scraps."[38] Paul had used this kind of reasoning earlier in 2 Corinthians. Speaking of the comparative "glory" (δόξα) of what he calls the "new covenant" versus the old, he writes, "for what had glory [τὸ δεδοξασμένον] turns out in this case not to have had glory [οὐ δεδόξασται] on account of the glory that now far surpasses it [τῆς ὑπερβαλλούσης δόξης]" (2 Cor 3:10). What was once glorious turns out not to have been glorious at all when viewed in light of what is surpassingly glorious.[39]

It is striking that in both Philippians and 2 Corinthians Paul's evaluative logic—"what was X is now not-X in light of what is surpassingly X"—results from an altered state of consciousness interpreted as a mystical experience of Christ that he calls γνῶσις: "the knowledge [γνώσεως] of the glory of God in the face of Jesus" (2 Cor 4:6), and "the knowledge [γνώσεως] of Christ Jesus my lord" (Phil 3:8). This gnosis is personal and intimate: according to the 2 Corinthians text it is found in the "face [προσώπῳ] of Jesus Christ,"[40] whereas in Philippians it is "of Christ Jesus my [μου] lord." It is also transformative: in 2 Cor 3:18 believers who achieve "γνῶσις of the glory of God [τῆς δόξης τοῦ θεοῦ]"[41] are "transformed from glory to

---

36 Formally, 3:7-8b is the first part of a complex rhetorical climax extending to 3:11. In vv. 7-8b Paul uses the figure of rhetorical climax to emphasize his change in values. In 3:7 he claims to reckon "what things were gains to me" a loss. In 3:8a he expands this to include "all things." Finally, in 3:8b he claims to "have [actually] lost all things" and yet still consider them "mere table-scraps." In designating his prior "gains" to be "mere table-scraps" Paul assimilates the metaphor of "loss" and "gain" to the letter's leitmotif of things that do and do not matter (cf. 1:10). The term I have translated "table-scraps" is typically used to refer to "refuse" or "excrement," which may well be its meaning here. *TDNT*, s.v. σκύβαλον, cites the *Suidas* s.v. σκυβαλίζεται which proposes κυσίβαλον (from "dog" and "throw") or τὸ τοῖς κυσὶ βαλλόμενον ("what is thrown to dogs") for an etymology (cf. *EM*, s.v. σκύβαλον; Melanchthon). This is almost certainly not the term's etymology, but such imaginative etymologies were popular, and if this one was known in Paul's day then Paul's use of the term here would be a reference to the "dogs" (κύνας) of 3:2.

37 It is noteworthy that Paul does not say "what things *I formerly reckoned gains* to me I have come to reckon a loss," but "what things *were gains* to me, I have come to reckon a loss." Paul does not dispute that the benefits of being a practicing Pharisee were real, but they have now been overshadowed.

38 "Table-scraps" is obviously hyperbolic, but so is "loss." It is not that Paul's former righteousness was actually a loss but that when viewed in light of "gaining Christ" it can be written off as such. Paul is forced by his antithesis to overstate his position.

39 In both of these texts (Phil 3:7-8b and 2 Cor 3:10) Paul's antithesis shades into oxymoron if not paradox. See Victor Paul Furnish, *II Corinthians: Translated with Introduction, Notes, and Commentary* (AB 32A; Garden City, NY: Doubleday, 1984) 204–5, 226–29.

40 Cf. 1 Cor 9:1: "Have I not seen [ἑόρακα] Jesus our lord?"; 15:8.

41 The *kābôd*, or "glory," of God was personified in ancient Judaism and could be imagined as a great angel (i.e., in human form; cf. Ezek 1:26-28). I take it that in 2 Cor 3:18 Paul is imagining the exalted Jesus as the "glory" of God. See my comments above on 2:9-11.

glory" (μεταμορφούμεθα ἀπὸ δόξης εἰς δόξαν),[42] while in Phil 3:10 Paul aspires to be "*conformed* [συμμορφιζόμενος] to [Christ's] death" and eventually to his resurrection when "[Christ] will *transform* [μετασχηματίσει] the body of our humiliation to be *conformed* [σύμμορφον] to the body of his glory [δόξης]" (3:20). The metamorphosis of the seer was a central element in emerging Jewish mysticism.[43] Paul's language of γνῶσις, however, finds an impressive parallel in "pagan" mysticism and magic.[44]

Excursus: *PGM* 3.591–611 and Paul's γνῶσις Χριστοῦ

PGM (Greek Magical Papyrus) 3.591–611[45] is an ancient prayer of thanksgiving. It contains a number of striking parallels to Paul's description of γνῶσις in Phil 3:7-11 and 2 Cor 3:18. Slightly different versions of the prayer appear in the Coptic *Prayer of Thanksgiving* (NHC VI.7)[46] and in the Hermetic *Asclepius* (41b),[47] which suggests (1) that it was an independent composition and (2) that it was popular in certain mystical circles.[48] The prayer expresses gratitude for the gift of γνῶσις and the transformation or "deification" that it brings. In *PGM* 3 the prayer comes at the

end of a larger "spell to establish a relationship with Helios."[49] In *Pr. Thank.* it is added as a kind of postscript to a dramatic dialogue depicting the ascent of a mystagogue and his initiation to the eighth and ninth (i.e., supraplanetary and therefore divine) spheres where a knowledge of God is acquired.[50] Here are the relevant lines (595–601):

> "[We give thanks to you for] having granted [χαρισάμενος] us understanding [νοῦν], speech [λόγον], and knowledge [γνῶσιν]: understanding, that we might understand you; speech that we might call upon you; knowledge, that we might know you [ἵνα σε ἐπιγνώσωμεν]. We rejoice that you have shown yourself to us [σεαυτὸν ἡμῖν ἔδιξας]. We rejoice that while we were still in bodies [ἐν πλάσμασιν; the Coptic reads "still in the body (σῶμα]"] you began to deify [ἀπεθέωσας] us by the knowledge of yourself [τῇ σεαυτοῦ γνώσει]."

The more obvious similarities to Paul include the following: (1) that γνῶσις is more than simple understanding or νοῦς; (2) that it has as its object a god and comes as a gift or χάρισμα of that god; (3) that it is obtained when a god or goddess shows himself or herself to the mystic;[51] (4) that it is transformative or

---

42   For the expression "from X to X," see Taylor, "From Faith to Faith."

43   See esp. Alan F. Segal, "Paul and the Beginning of Jewish Mysticism," in *Death, Ecstasy, and Other Worldly Journeys*, ed. John J. Collins and Michael Fishbane (Albany: State University of New York Press, 1995) 95–122; Morray-Jones, "Transformational Mysticism"; cf. *PGM* 3.600–601 discussed in the excursus below.

44   Dibelius, p. 89.

45   *P. Louvre* 2391 (Papyrus Mimaut), frag. 1, col. 18. The Greek text is difficult. The first reliable text was produced by Karl Preisendanz in *Papyri Graecae Magicae*, vol. 1 (Leipzig: Teubner, 1928). J. P. Mahé ("La Prière d'actions de graces du Codex VI de Nag-Hammadi et Le Discours parfait," *ZPE* 13 [1974] 40–60) produced a synoptic version of the Greek, Latin, and Coptic versions of the prayer, on the basis of which he was able to improve several of Preisendanz's readings. The Greek text cited here is that of Peter Dirkse and James Brashler ("The Prayer of Thanksgiving. VI,7:63,33–65,7," in *Nag Hammadi Codices V,2-5 and VI, with Papyrus Berolinensis 8501, 1 and 4*, ed. Douglas M. Parrott [NHS 11; Leiden: Brill, 1979] 378–87). An English translation by W. C. Grese can be found in *The Greek Magical Papyri in Translation, Including the Demotic Spells*, vol. 1: *Texts*, ed. Hans Dieter Betz (2nd ed.; Chicago: University

of Chicago Press, 1992) 33–34; Dirkse and Brashler also provide an English translation.

46   Mahé, "Prière"; Dirkse and Brashler, "Prayer" (with English translation).

47   A. D. Nock and A.-J. Festugière, *Corpus Hermeticum II* (Paris: Belles Lettres, 1945) 353–55; for an English translation see Brian P. Copenhaver, *Hermetica* (Cambridge: Cambridge University Press, 1995) 92.

48   Roelof van den Broek, *Gnostic Religion in Antiquity* (Cambridge: Cambridge University Press, 2013) 36; similarly, Dirkse and Brashler, "Prayer," 376.

49   The description is Betz's (*Greek Magical Papyri in Translation*, xi). The relevant lines of *PGM* 3 are 494–611.

50   See Douglas M. Parrott, "The Scribal Note: VI,7a:65,8-14," in idem, *Nag Hammadi Codices V,2–5 and VI*, 389–93.

51   For a goddess revealing herself to an initiate, see Isis's self-revelation to Lucius in Apuleius, *Metam.* 11.3–6, to her priest in 11.6, and multiple times to Lucius during his incubation in her temple in 11.19, 22. For Lucius's prayer of thanksgiving, see 11.24–25. For ecstatic gnosis in the cults of Isis and Osiris, see Plutarch, *De Is. et Os.* 2, 352a and comments by Hans D. Betz, "Ein seltsames mysterientheologisches System bei Plutarch," in *Ex orbe religionum: Studia Geo Widengren Oblata*, ed. S. G. F. Brandon, Claas

"deifying," or in Paul's case angelifying or perhaps "Christifying"; and (5) that the transformation it produces begins even in this life.

■ **8c-11** Verses 8c-11 consist of two lengthy purpose clauses (vv. 8c-9 and vv. 10-11), which begin respectively "that I might gain Christ" (ἵνα Χριστὸν κερδήσω) and "that I might know him" (τοῦ γνῶναι αὐτόν). The relationship between these two clauses is not immediately clear. Since, however, in 3:7-8b Paul insists that he has now replaced past "gains" with a desire for the "knowledge" of Christ, it is reasonable to assume that to "gain" Christ and to "know" him denote the same thing, though expressed from different points of view. Verses 8c-9 express Paul's desire to be objectively transformed, while vv. 10-11 express his desire for the subjective experience that accompanies and in a sense produces this metamorphosis.[52] In both cases the outcome is the same, namely, Paul's eschatological salvation: to "be found in him" (v. 9a), to "arrive at the resurrection from the dead" (v. 11).

■ **8c-9** The purpose clause beginning in vv. 8c-9 is governed by two finite verbs: "in order that I might gain [κερδήσω] Christ and be found [εὑρεθῶ] in him" (3:8c-9a).[53] The first verb looks back to the earlier antithesis of "loss" and "gain" in 3:7-8b, while the second introduces a new theme of eschatological salvation based on how one is "found" at the last judgment.[54] This new theme, the believer's standing in the final judgment, is then developed in a subordinate clause: "not having my own righ-

teousness that is from the law, but the one that is through faith in Christ, the righteousness that is from God based on such faith" (3:9b). The believer who *gains* Christ in this life will be *found* to be righteous in the next.

Verses 8c-9 raise three problems for the interpreter, which I will treat in the following order: (1) the precise nuance of "*my own* righteousness," (2) what Paul means by "the righteousness that is from God," and (3) what it might mean to gain "Christ" and be found in "him." Verse 9 also contains the much-discussed expression πίστις Χριστοῦ (here translated "faith in Christ"), which I will discuss in a separate excursus.

What does Paul mean when he speaks of "not having *my own* righteousness that is from the law"? Bultmann famously interpreted this to mean Paul's earlier *self*-righteousness as a law-observant Jew, a righteousness that Paul would later reject as having been arrogant and sinful.[55] But the juxtaposition here is not between Paul's former allegedly arrogant *self* and God (as Bultmann must maintain), but between the Jewish law and God: "the [righteousness] that is from the law [ἐκ νόμου]" and the "righteousness that is from God [ἐκ θεοῦ]."[56] The distinction, therefore, is simply between the righteousness that Paul was able to achieve as he earnestly sought to live by the law, a righteousness Paul imagines as being *without* divine enablement—thus the "my own"—and the righteousness he hopes to achieve as a Christ-believer, a righteousness produced at least in part by God's power in him.[57] Paul made the same point in Rom 10:3: "being

---

Jouco Bleeker, and Marcel Simon (2 vols.; SHR 21–22; Leiden: Brill, 1972) 1:347–54; Hans D. Betz and Edgar W. Smith, "De Iside et Osiride (Moralia 351C – 384C)," in *Plutarch's Theological Writings and Early Christian Literature*, ed. Hans D. Betz (SCHNT 3; Leiden: Brill, 1975) 36–84, esp. 40–41, with explicit reference to Phil 3:8, 10.

52 For both of these statements, see the commentary below.

53 The use of ἵνα ("[in order] that") in 3:8c calls for comment. It is parallel to the genitive articular infinitive in v. 10: to "gain Christ" is to come to "know him." A problem arises, however, when we attempt to specify the relationship of 3:8c to what precedes it. Some limit 3:8c to the expression in 3:8b "and consider [all things] table-scraps in order that . . . ." This is grammatically possible. But 3:8c continues the motif of loss and gain developed in 3:7-8b, and so it is probably better to interpret 3:8c as restating Paul's new set of values in terms of the objective or

goal ("in order that") to which those values point. Given "the surpassing greatness of the knowledge of Christ," Paul's aim is to "gain" him and to "know" him.

54 This is the result of a *cognitio*, or judicial examination/inquiry; cf. Herbert Preisker, "εὑρίσκω," *TDNT* 2 (1964) 769–70. In this regard it parallels 3:11: "if somehow I might arrive at the resurrection from the dead."

55 Rudolf Bultmann, *Theology of the New Testament* (2 vols.; New York: Scribner; London: SCM, 1951, 1952) 1:266–67.

56 The rhetoric of v. 9 makes this contrast plain. Here is a translation of v. 9 with what I take to be the correct emphasis: "not having my own righteousness that is *from the law*, but the one that is through faith in Christ, the righteousness that is *from God* based on such faith."

57 Cf. Phil 1:6: "he who began a good work *in you*"; 2:13: "for God is the one producing *in you*." This

ignorant of the righteousness of God and seeking to establish their own righteousness, they did not submit[58] themselves to the righteousness of God." Here again the criticism is not that Jews are arrogantly self-righteous but that they have failed to recognize Paul's gospel of divine empowerment according to which God produces righteousness in Christ-believers, who are therefore not left to "their own" resources. For Paul this failure is not a sin but a tragedy with far-reaching consequences (Rom 10:1). Most scholars today rightly reject Bultmann's reading for the theological imposition that it is.

This brings us to the second expression: "the righteousness that is from God." Scholars who, following Bultmann, interpret "my righteousness" as *self*-righteousness typically go on to interpret "the righteousness that is from God" as an *alien* righteousness that is fictively imputed to the Christ-believer—a righteousness that effects little or no change in the believer's person and that requires little or no effort on the believer's part. But this finds no support in Paul and certainly not in Philippians, where God "who began a good work within you will continue to perfect it until the Day of Christ" (1:6), and where the Philippians are urged to "work hard to accomplish your own salvation" (2:12). In other words, just as "my righteousness that is from the law" was an *actual* righteousness achieved by earnestly following Torah, so "the righteousness that is from God" is an *actual* righteousness produced over time as God now aids the believer in his or her own efforts at moral betterment.

The only difference is that, to Paul's mind, the righteousness achieved with God's help offers a better prospect of "resurrection" (3:11).[59]

To be fair, Paul could have been clearer. Judging from the letter of James (2:14-26), even Paul's contemporaries misunderstood him.[60] The principal point of confusion lies in Paul's repeated insistence that the righteousness of Christ-believers is through "faith," which he then neatly contrasts with the "works" of the law. Taken on its own, this antithesis between "faith" and "works" might seem to support the notion of an imputed versus an actual righteousness. But Paul is engaging in rhetorical shorthand in which both "faith" and "works" are metonyms for competing theories of how gentiles may join the eschatological people of God and prepare themselves for the final judgment.[61] The latter theory, which Paul designates "works," holds that gentiles become members of the people of God by submitting to the Jewish law and that they prepare themselves for judgment by following its sanctifying precepts. The former theory, which Paul designates "faith," claims that gentiles join simply by believing that Jesus was the Messiah and that they prepare themselves for the judgment by living out the demands of his spirit, which now possesses them *and aids in their transformation*.[62] As is often the case with Paul, clarity is sacrificed for rhetorical point.[63] It bears repeating that, as regards the Philippians, Paul is concerned that this process has been stalled and that they are no longer making "progress in faith" (1:25).

---

is not to imply that Paul's antithesis here is without caricature. He implies that Torah-observance is undertaken without divine enablement, a righteousness pursued in the "flesh" versus the "spirit." Many contemporary Jews would have disagreed (e.g., *1 Enoch* 5:8-9; 47:47; 1QS 3:21-24; 17:32; cf. Jer 31:33; Ezek 11:19-20; 18:31; 36:26-28). Geza Vermes, *The Complete Dead Sea Scrolls in English* (New York: Penguin, 1995) 74: "Not only is election itself owed to God's grace, but perseverance in the way of holiness cannot be counted on unless he offers his continuous help and support."

58   For similar language earlier in the letter, see Rom 1:5 "the obedience [ὑπακοήν] of faith"; cf. 2 Thess 1:8: "who do not obey (ὑπακούουσιν) the gospel."

59   At issue is God's ominous impartiality (Rom 2:6-13). Judging from Phil 3:4-11, Paul did not even believe that being "blameless" before the law was sufficient to guarantee that one would "arrive at the resurrec-

tion from the dead." To that end one is better served by the transformation produced over time by the inner workings of the divine spirit: "for we by the Spirit await in faith the hope [ἐλπίδα] of righteousness" (Gal 5:5). Cf. Gal 4:19: "until Christ is formed [μορφωθῇ] in you."

60   Martin Hengel, "Der Jakobusbrief als antipaulinische Polemik," in idem, *Paulus und Jakobus: Kleine Schriften III* (WUNT 141; Tübingen: Mohr Siebeck, 2002) 511–48. Cf. 2 Pet 3:15-16.

61   I discuss this briefly in the introduction, part 7.d: "Postscript: Justification."

62   E.g., Phil 1:19: "I know that this will lead to my salvation through your prayers for me and the provision of the spirit of Jesus Christ"; cf. 3:3.

63   It is possible that here in 3:9 Paul sought to clarify this by adding "the righteousness that is from God based on faith" after "but the one that is through faith in Christ."

Excursus: πίστις Χριστοῦ

In Phil 3:9 Paul speaks of having a righteousness that is διὰ πίστεως Χριστοῦ, which I have translated "through faith in Christ." Scholars debate how best to interpret this expression, which appears with slight variation elsewhere in Paul's authentic letters in Gal 2:16 (twice), 20; 3:22; and Rom 3:22, 26. At issue is the meaning of the genitive Χριστοῦ. It is often claimed that a "literal" English translation of πίστις Χριστοῦ would be "faith *of* Christ."[64] But such a translation already prejudices the case, since while Greek and English genitives have roughly the same range of meaning, the relative frequency with which these various meanings occur is significantly different for each language. As to the case in point, the Greek expression πίστις Χριστοῦ can readily mean either "faith in Christ" (an objective genitive) or "Christ's faith" (a subjective genitive), whereas the stilted English expression "faith of Christ" can realistically mean only the latter. A further ambiguity lies in the noun πίστις, which can either mean "faith" or "faithfulness," so that in the case of a subjective genitive the phrase might also be rendered "Christ's faithfulness."[65]

The principal argument in favor of a subjective genitive is that in all other instances where Paul uses πίστις with the genitive, the genitive is subjective.[66] This is not an insignificant observation, but it needs to be carefully evaluated.[67] In this case it is far from determinative, since πίστις Χριστοῦ is a technical expression in Paul's theological vocabulary and therefore must be treated on its own terms. In other words, given his distinctive theory of justification by faith—which is the context in which the expression πίστις Χριστοῦ first appears and afterwards always occurs—it would not have been unreasonable for Paul to expect his readers to understand the genitive in expressions like πίστις ὑμῶν ("your faith")[68] in one sense and the expression πίστις Χριστοῦ in another, which is of course precisely how many of Paul's interpreters have understood these expressions, not least the early Greek speakers Origen and Chrysostom, as we shall see below.

A second argument for the subjective genitive is that it avoids an unacceptable level of redundancy—or at least what certain proponents of the subjective genitive feel is an unacceptable level of redundancy.[69] For instance, if πίστις Χριστοῦ is read as an objective genitive in Gal 2:16, then Paul refers to faith "in" Christ three times in three consecutive clauses: twice as πίστις Χριστοῦ and once as εἰς Χριστὸν πιστεύειν ("believe in Christ"), a repetitiveness that, according to Leander Keck, yields an "un-Pauline, wooden redundancy."[70] Judgments regarding what constitutes an acceptable prose style are necessarily a matter of taste, and it is hard not to believe that there is some confusion here between normative judgments and historical ones, since among at least some of Paul's contemporaries varied repetition had become something of an art.[71] At any rate, Paul is certainly not

---

64 E.g., Bockmuehl, p. 210: "This is a literal translation of a much disputed Pauline phrase."

65 This is clearly the meaning of πίστις in Rom 3:3, which speaks of "God's faithfulness." Interpreted in this way πίστις Χριστοῦ would presumably be a reference to Paul's theory that Christ's death was an act of "obedience" (Phil 2:8; cf. Rom 5:19); cf. Richard B. Hays, *The Faith of Jesus Christ: The Narrative Substructure of Galatians 3:1–4:11* (2nd ed.; Grand Rapids: Eerdmans, 2002), 150–53; Luke Timothy Johnson, "Romans 3:21-26 and the Faith of Jesus," *CBQ* 44 (1982) 86.

66 E.g., George Howard, "Notes and Observations on the 'Faith of Christ,'" *HTR* 60 (1967) 459–84.

67 See esp. R. Barry Matlock, "Detheologizing the ΠΙΣΤΙΣ ΧΡΙΣΤΟΥ Debate: Cautionary Remarks from a Lexical Semantic Perspective," *NovT* 42 (2000) 1–24; James Barr, *The Semantics of Biblical Language* (Oxford: Oxford University Press, 1961) 161–205.

68 This expression occurs twelve times. Other instances of πίστις modified by a genitive include: πίστις ἡμῶν, "our faith" (once); πίστις σου, "your (sing.)

faith" (twice); πίστις αὐτοῦ, "his faith" (once); πίστις ἐμοῦ, "my faith" (once); ἡ πίστις τοῦ θεοῦ, which in the context must mean "God's faithfulness" (once); and πίστις [τοῦ πατρὸς ἡμῶν] Ἀβραάμ, "[our father] Abraham's faith" (twice).

69 This argument is addressed with insight by R. Barry Matlock, "The Rhetoric of πίστις in Paul: Galatians 2.16, Romans 3.22, and Philippians 3.9," *JSNT* 30 (2007) 173–203.

70 Leander Keck, "'Jesus' in Romans," *JBL* 108 (1989) 443–60, here 454; cf. S. K. Williams, "The 'Righteousness of God' in Romans," *JBL* 99 (1980) 273–74; I. G. Wallis, *The Faith of Jesus Christ in Early Christian Tradition* (SNTSMS 84; Cambridge: Cambridge University Press, 1995) 70–71; Morna Hooker, "ΠΙΣΤΙΣ ΧΡΙΣΤΟΥ," *NTS* 35 (1989) 321–42, 329. Further examples are collected in Matlock, "Rhetoric."

71 Ovid, for instance, was well known for this practice: H. Naumann, "Ovid und die Rhetorik," *AU* 11 (1968) 69–86; Bonner, *Declamation*, 149–56; see also the comments about Votienus Montanus in Seneca Rhetor, *Contr.* 9.5.15–17. For this and other features

above repeating himself, not least when sermonizing on the topic of the inclusion of the gentiles. In this case, this fact is pointedly demonstrated by Gal 2:16 itself, where alongside the three faith-expressions just noted the expression ἔργα νόμου, "works of the Law," appears verbatim three times. I will return to this fact below.

A third argument sometimes used in support of a subjective genitive is that it makes better theological sense.[72] It is not always clear what a particular interpreter means by this, but again it is hard not to believe that in at least some instances normative judgments are influencing historical ones.[73] Most interpreters, however, admit that Paul's theology, insofar as it can be historically reconstructed, will accommodate either the subjective or objective genitive.

In turning to arguments favoring an objective genitive, it bears repeating—especially for modern English speakers—that an objective genitive governing πίστις is a completely natural reading of the Greek,[74] as can readily be seen by the comments of such competent early Greek speakers as Origen and Chrysostom, who not only read Χριστοῦ in the expression πίστις Χριστοῦ as an objective genitive but felt no pressure to explain or justify that reading.[75] Origen, in his commentary on Romans, glosses the expression τὸν ἐκ πίστεως Ἰησοῦ (which I would translate "the one who has faith in Jesus," but which might also be rendered "the one who has Jesus's faith[fulness]") in Rom 3:26 unambiguously as "those who believe in Jesus [εἰς τὸν Ἰησοῦν]."[76] Similarly,

Chrysostom in *De incomprehensibili Dei natura*, hom. 2.419, commenting on the expression διὰ πίστεως Χριστοῦ in Phil 3:9, writes: "[Paul] then goes on to tell us what sort of faith he means, namely, the faith 'of knowing him and the power of his resurrection and the sharing in his sufferings.'"[77] Again, Christ is the object of faith. Though not a native Greek speaker, Augustine also takes it for granted that the genitive in the expression πίστις Χριστοῦ is objective: "the faith by which one believes in Christ" (*fidem qua creditur in Christum*; *Spir. et litt.* 9).

Proponents of the objective genitive also rightly note that, while Paul speaks of Christ as the object of faith in numerous places, nowhere does he unambiguously speak of Christ as the subject of faith.[78] Indeed, the principal evidence for the latter view is the phrase πίστις Χριστοῦ itself. So, for instance, Christ is never the subject of the verb πιστεύειν ("to believe") nor is he ever called πιστός ("believing" or "faithful") as, for instance, Abraham is.[79] Even in those contexts in which the expression πίστις Χριστοῦ is used, no unambiguous reference is made in the surrounding discussion to Christ's alleged "faith" or "faithfulness." What the ensuing discussion does develop, however, is Christ as the object of faith. Thus Gal 3:26: διὰ τῆς πίστεως ἐν Χριστῷ, "through faith *in* Christ," and Rom 3:25: διὰ πίστεως ἐν τῷ αὐτοῦ αἵματι, "through faith *in* his blood."[80] This is precisely what one would expect if an objective genitive were intended.

---

of Paul's prose style, see Holloway, "Paul's Pointed Prose."

72 E.g., J. Louis Martyn, *Galatians: A New Translation with Introduction and Commentary* (AB 33A; New York: Doubleday, 1997) 263–77; Hays, *Faith*, 150–53 and passim; but now see Barclay, *Gift*, 378–84.

73 Here see esp. Matlock ("Detheologizing," 22), who cites comments by Richard B. Hays, for whom the objective genitive borders on the "blasphemous," and Leander Keck, who finds that the subjective genitive offers "emancipation" from a kind of works salvation in which a person is saved by his or her own faith; cf. Barclay, *Gift*, 476: "behind a variety of linguistic and literary arguments, there often lurks a theological anxiety."

74 E.g., Mark 11:22: ἔχετε πίστιν θεοῦ, "have faith in God."

75 R. A. Harrisville III, "ΠΙΣΤΙΣ ΧΡΙΣΤΟΥ: The Witness of the Fathers," *NovT* 36 (1994) 233–41. To these may be added the witness of Eph 2:8-10 and Jas 2:14-26, for which see R. Barry Matlock, "Even the

Demons Believe: Paul and πίστις Χριστοῦ," *CBQ* 64 (2002) 300–318, here 306–7.

76 Jean Scherer, ed., *Le Commentaire d'Origène sur Rom III 5–V 7* (Cairo: L'Institut Français d'Archéologie Orientale, 1957) 162 (cited by Harrisville, "ΠΙΣΤΙΣ ΧΡΙΣΤΟΥ," 238).

77 Anne-Marie Malingrey, ed. and trans., *Jean Chrysostome: Sur l'incompréhensibilité de Dieu* (2nd ed.; SC 28; Paris: Cerf, 1970) 176; Eng. trans., Paul W. Harkins, *John Chrysostom: On the Incomprehensible Nature of God* (Fathers of the Church 72; Washington, DC: Catholic University of America Press, 1984) 88 (cited by Harrisville, "ΠΙΣΤΙΣ ΧΡΙΣΤΟΥ," 238–39).

78 Dunn, *Theology*, 381–85.

79 E.g., Gal 3:9. As already mentioned, when Paul does speak of Christ's earthly conduct he uses the language of "obedience" (Rom 5:19; Phil 2:8).

80 Cf. Gal 2:16: εἰς Χριστὸν Ἰησοῦν πιστεύειν ("to believe *in* Christ Jesus").

This raises the question why, if Paul meant "faith *in* Christ," he used the genitive in the first place, given its potential for misunderstanding—though that potential was considerably less likely for a native Greek speaker, as I have already indicated.[81] At this point it is important to say something more about Paul's prose style—not what we think it should have been but what it actually was—and to note in particular his penchant for balanced clauses characterized by such figures as isocolon, wordplay, paradox, and especially antithesis.[82] Nowhere is this penchant more in evidence than in Gal 2:14-21, where the expression πίστις Χριστοῦ first appears in Paul's letters, and where it may well have been coined, a possibility I will return to in the next paragraph. Paul's indictment of Peter in 2:14 trades on the antithesis of Jew and gentile: "If you, being a Jew, live as a gentile and not as a Jew, how is it that you compel the gentiles to live as Jews?"[83] Similarly, in 2:19 he deploys the double antithesis of dying to the law and living to God: "to the law [νόμῳ] I died [ἀπέθανον] in order that to God [θεῷ] I might live [ζήσω]," which is then followed immediately in 2:20a by the brilliant isocolon ζῶ δὲ οὐκέτι ἐγώ, ζῇ δὲ ἐν ἐμοὶ Χριστός, "I no longer live, but Christ lives in me," where antithesis shades into the paradox of spirit possession.

We are of course here concerned with the intervening material in Gal 2:15-16, where Paul continues the antithesis of Jew and gentile from 2:14 but adds a further antithesis—again a double antithesis—between ἔργα νόμου ("works of law") and our expression πίστις Χριστοῦ. This is the first appearance in Paul of πίστις Χριστοῦ, which is here clearly coined on analogy with ἔργα νόμου,[84] an expression already in use at Qumran and perhaps by Paul's law-observant opponents in Galatia.[85] Any ambiguity introduced by the genitive is immediately clarified in the next clause (2:16b)—καὶ ἡμεῖς εἰς Χριστὸν Ἰησοῦν ἐπιστεύσαμεν, "even we have believed *in* Christ Jesus"[86]—after which the conceit can be repeated without misunderstanding: ἐκ πίστεως Χριστοῦ καὶ οὐκ ἐξ ἔργων νόμου ("from faith [in] Christ and not from works of law" 2:16c). The expression appears again in slightly different terms in Gal 2:20, where Paul is wrapping up his argument and rehearsing key themes, and later in 3:22, where it stands in contrast to the abbreviated ἐκ νόμου, as it will also do in Phil 3:9. The expression appears two more times, in Rom 3:22 and 26, where it is again in contrast to ἔργα νόμου. In answer, then, to the question why Paul chose the genitive, it would appear that he coined the expression πίστις Χριστοῦ as a double antithesis to the

---

81 This question may be unavoidable in the present discussion, but it is not altogether apt, since all nominal cases and not only the genitive carry a range of potential meanings so that "ambiguity" is in a sense unavoidable, though rarely a problem for native speakers.

82 C. F. Georg Heinrici speaks of Paul's "Vorliebe für kühne und paradoxe Formulierungen und sentenziösen Ausdruck" ("Hellenismus," 454); cf. Bultmann, *Stil*, 94: "Paulus liebt es, in seine Erörterung scharf formulierte Sentenzen einzuflechten."

83 That Paul is striving for a point here is clear from the sophisticated wordplay he deploys: Ἰουδαῖος . . . Ἰουδαϊκῶς . . . Ἰουδαΐζειν; cf. 1 Cor 9:22: "to all men [πᾶσιν] I have become all things [πάντα] that by all means [πάντως] I might save some." See further Bonner, *Declamation*, 67–70; Eduard Norden, *Die antike Kuntsprosa, vom VI. Jahrhundert v. Chr. bis in die Zeit der Renaissance* (2 vols.; Leipzig: Teubner, 1898) 1:290.

84 So Dunn, "Once more ΠΙΣΤΙΣ ΧΡΙΣΤΟΥ," in *Pauline Theology*, vol. 4, *Looking Back, Pressing On*, ed. E. Elizabeth Johnson and David M. Hay (SBLSymS 4; Atlanta: Scholars Press, 1997) 72 n. 51, citing Brice L. Martin, *Christ and the Law in Paul* (NovTSup 62; Leiden: Brill, 1989) 116. It should be noted that

the parallels effected in Greco-Roman antitheses are structural and not semantic, which in this case means that we cannot look to the genitive νόμου to explain the genitive Χριστοῦ, anymore than, say, we can look to the dative νόμῳ ("to the law") to explain the dative θεῷ ("to God") in 2:19. At any rate, the genitive νόμου is neither objective nor subjective but means something like "works *prescribed* by the law" or "works *contained* in the law." In the context, the expression "works of the law" interprets "[to live] as a Jew" (Ἰουδαϊκῶς) in 2:14 (Barclay, *Gift*, 373).

85 Hays claims that πίστις Χριστοῦ is to be interpreted in light of the expression πίστις Ἀβραάμ ("Abraham's faith") in Rom 4:12 and 16 (*Faith*, 157). But it is better to interpret πίστις Χριστοῦ as arising from an intentional contrast with the expression ἔργα νόμου, since ἔργα νόμου is not only contextually more proximate—occurring three times in the same verse—but was clearly in view when the expression was first coined. For the expression "works of the law" in Judaism, see 4QFlor 1:1-7; 1QS 5:20-24; 6:18; and of course 4QMMT (*Miqṣat Maʿaśe ha-Torah*).

86 Cf. Gal 3:22 and Rom 3:22, where πίστις Χριστοῦ is again immediately clarified by the verb.

expression ἔργα νόμου in Gal 2:16, and that he afterwards repeated this antithesis to explain and defend his ideas on justification.[87]

This leaves us with the third problem confronting the interpreter of 3:8c-9, which for lack of a better term I will call Paul's "personalism":[88] "that I might gain *Christ* and be found in *him*."[89] For Paul all Christ-believers are possessed by the "spirit of Christ" (πνεῦμα Χριστοῦ; Rom 8:9; Gal 4:6; cf. 2:20) and are therefore already "in Christ" (ἐν Χριστῷ), one of Paul's most distinctive expressions.[90] Here, however, Paul allows that there is a further sense in which a Christ-believer may not yet be "in him" (ἐν αὐτῷ), a finding that will be made only at the final judgment. This takes us to the heart of Paul's gospel, which is radically Christ-centered.[91] Paul claims that Christ-believers are not only *possessed* by Christ ("in Christ" in the first sense) but that as a result of this possession they can be progressively *transformed* into his image ("in him" in the second sense): "my children, for whom I labor in birth *a second time* [πάλιν] until Christ is formed [μορφωθῇ] in you" (Gal 4:19; cf. 1 Cor 4:15).[92] This process of transformation is completed in resurrection: "just as we bore the image [εἰκόνα] of the earthly one, so we will bear the image [εἰκόνα] of the heavenly one" (1 Cor 15:49).[93]

But it is begun in earnest now: "we all with unveiled face beholding the glory of the Lord reflected [in Christ] are metamorphosed [μεταμορφούμεθα] into that same image [τὴν αὐτὴν εἰκόνα] from glory to glory." To put this in the language of Phil 3:8c-9, "to gain Christ" means to be transformed into Christ's image in this life, while "to be found in him" means to be judged righteous (i.e., fully [sufficiently?] transformed) in the final judgment.

■ **10-11** Verses 10-11 constitute a second purpose clause that repeats and interprets the earlier purpose clause of vv. 8c-9,[94] though now from the viewpoint of the Christ-believer's subjective experience: whereas vv. 8c-9 spoke of *gaining* Christ, vv. 10-11 speak of *knowing* him. This allows Paul to amplify the theme of knowing Christ introduced at 3:8a. Formally, 3:10-11 is a graded list consisting of five items: "that I (1) might know him (2) and the power of his resurrection (3) and fellowship of his sufferings, (4) [even to the point of] being conformed to his death, (5) if somehow I might arrive at the resurrection from the dead!" It is generally agreed that the first item is explicated by items 2 to 5.[95] A problem arises, however, when we seek to understand how items 2 to 5 are related to each other. A common solution is to see a chiasm, with item 2 corresponding to item 5 and item 3 to item 4.[96] But this gives too much weight to form

---

87 Matlock comes to a similar conclusion ("Detheologizing," 21–23), opting, as he puts it, for "rhetoric" over "theology." A similar antithesis is deployed in Gal 3:3 and 5, where twice ἐξ ἔργων νόμου, "by the works of the law," is contrasted with ἐξ ἀκοῆς πίστεως, "by the hearing/message of faith."

88 I struggle with language here. Paul's mythology of salvation might also be described as a type of "relationalism," and Paul's many compound verbs beginning with the preposition σύν ("with") might seem to justify this. But the effective collapse of "relation" in the new interiority of spirit possession ("I no longer live, but Christ lives in me"; Gal 2:20) clearly shows the limits of this kind of language.

89 Paul's language here carries forward the personalism of 3:8a: "the knowledge of *Christ Jesus my lord*," to which he will return in 3:10: "that I might know *him*"; cf. 3:1: "rejoice in the *Lord*." For a similar progression, cf. *Corp. Herm.* 13.8-9, where "knowledge" (γνῶσις) leads to "joy" (χαρά) and to moral transformation and being "made righteous" (δικαιοῦσθαι).

90 I discuss "in Christ" and similar expressions in my comments on 1:1b above.

91 A full account of the personalism of Paul's gospel remains a desideratum in New Testament studies.

92 For possession leading to transformation, see esp. Gal 5:5; Rom 8:11 (12:1); cf. Col 1:27.

93 Cf. Rom 8:29: "whom he foreknew, these he also predestined to be conformed [συμμόρφους] to the image [εἰκόνος] of his son"; Phil 3:20-21.

94 Just as one *gains* Christ and is *found* in him in the final judgment (3:8c-9), so one comes to *know* Christ and thereby *arrives* at resurrection (3:10-11); cf. 2 Pet 1:3-8, which is possibly an early interpretation of our text.

95 Reumann. The "and" (καί) joining items 1 and 2 functions epexegetically (BDF §442.9: "explicative"). The "and" (καί) joining items 2 and 3 is a true coordinating conjunction, though in this case the emphasis in each item is slightly different. In the second item the emphasis falls on the accusative "power" (cf. 4:13), while in the third the emphasis falls on the genitive "sufferings" (cf. 1:29).

96 Schenk, Reumann; cf. Koester, "Purpose," 323 n. 4.

over substance and ignores the list's obvious emotional crescendo in item 5. Paul is writing with great pathos, and his words both here and earlier in vv. 8c-9 are driving toward an eschatological conclusion, which he now explicitly presents as a quest: "if somehow *I might arrive at* [κατάντήσω] the resurrection from the dead." It is better, therefore, to allow for a linear progression of some sort, even if the result is not so tidy.

I will first comment on the syntax of vv. 10-11. Items 2 and 3 continue to be governed by the infinitive "know" (γνῶναι) expressed in item 1: "that I might know him *and* the power of his resurrection *and* fellowship of his sufferings." Item 4 carries its own verbal form, the participle συμμορφιζόμενος, "being conformed to," while item 5 is a purpose clause expressed dramatically as the conditional "if somehow [εἴ πως] I might arrive at . . . ." A final syntactical observation concerns the textual problem in v. 10. I have already indicated in the textual notes above that the manuscript tradition is unclear whether Paul repeats the definite article before "fellowship" ("the power of his resurrection and *the* [τήν] fellowship of his sufferings") or omits it ("the power of his resurrection and fellowship of his sufferings"). If the latter is the case—and internal evidence points in that direction—then items 2 and 3 are further linked by the fact that they share the same article.

Perhaps the most natural way to read vv. 10-11 is as a kind of "curriculum" for knowing Christ (item 1) and thereby achieving resurrection from the dead (item 5), with the curriculum proper coming in items 2 to 4. The first element in the curriculum (item 2 in the overall list) is to know "the power [δύναμιν] of [Christ's] resurrection." In his evolving criticism of the Jewish law, Paul eventually settled on the problem of empowerment. According to Romans, the law is correct in naming sin (3:20; 7:7) but

"powerless" (ἀδύνατος) to overcome it (8:3; cf. Gal 3:21). Paul's gospel, on the other hand, conveys "the power [δύναμις] of God for salvation for all who believe" (1:16; cf. 1 Cor 1:18, 24; Rom 15:13).[97] Through the gospel, believers come to be possessed by the "spirit" of the resurrected Christ (Rom 8:9; cf. Gal 4:6), who as a "life-giving [ζωοποιοῦν] spirit" (1 Cor 15:45) now conveys the power of God for their transformation: "the one who raised Christ from the dead will *give life to* [ζωοποιήσει] your dead bodies through his spirit that inhabits you" (Rom 8:11).[98] When, therefore, in Phil 3:10 Paul describes the first element in his curriculum as knowing the "power of Christ's resurrection," he is presumably referring to the experience of sensing oneself possessed by Christ: "I no longer live, but Christ lives in me" (Gal 2:20). The most obvious channel for this experience was ecstatic worship.[99] But Paul also encouraged his followers to cultivate this experience on a more routine basis by variously "walk[ing] according to/in the Spirit" (Rom 8:4; Gal 5:16), "mind[ing] the things of the Spirit" (Rom 8:5), "[being] led by the Spirit" (Gal 5:18; Rom 8:14), "follow[ing] the Spirit" (Gal 5:25), and thereby "put[ting] to death the deeds of the body by the Spirit" (Rom 8:13).

The second element in Paul's curriculum (item 3 in the overall list) is to know the "fellowship [κοινωνίαν] of [Christ's] sufferings [παθημάτων]." Christ-believers gain their initial experience of Christ in baptism when the spirit of Christ comes to possess them: "God sent the spirit of his son into our hearts, crying 'Abba!' which means father" (Gal 4:6). They deepen that "fellowship" through suffering: "it has been given to you . . . not only to believe [πιστεύειν] . . . but also to suffer [πάσχειν]" (Phil 1:29).[100] It is difficult to be more precise about the relationship in Paul's mind between believers' possession

---

97 For Paul the gospel is a new τύπος διδαχῆς or "type of teaching" (Rom 6:17) that brings not just illumination but empowerment (for which see my "*Commendatio*," esp. 369–82).

98 According to Rom 6:3-4, this experience begins at baptism: "as many of us as were baptized into Christ were baptized into his death . . . in order that just as Christ was raised from the dead by the glory of the Father, we too might walk in newness of life." Cf. Col 2:12: "having been buried with him in baptism, in which you were also raised with him."

99 Here see esp. 1 Corinthians 12 and 14; cf. 1 Thess 5:19-20.

100 As an apocalyptic Jew, Paul expected the people of God to suffer in the last days and to be purified by that suffering (already in 1 Thess 3:3-4, 12-13; 5:23; Rom 5:3-4; Phil 2:12-13; 4:13; cf. Dan 11:35; *Pss. Sol.* 3:3-10; 10:1-3; 13:8-10; *2 Bar.* 13:1-2; 4 Ezra 7:14; cf. Jas 1:2-4; Rev 7:14; for the principle in general, see 2 Macc 6:12-17). As an apostle of Christ he came to believe that this suffering also brought believers into a deepening "fellowship" or mystical communion with Christ in his sufferings: "we suffer with [συμπάσχομεν] him in order that we might also be glorified with [συνδοξασθῶμεν] him" (Rom 8:17).

by Christ and their suffering with him. One possibility is that the power that comes from possession makes the endurance of suffering possible. Another possibility is that possession by the spirit of Christ is made even more palpable—one senses a "fellowship" with Christ—through belief that one is suffering with him (2 Cor 12:9; cf. 4:7; Rom 8:23-27). Needless to say, these possibilities (and there may be others) are not mutually exclusive. The complex psychosomatic relationship between possession, suffering, and symbolic death in the experience of many shamans offers a possible heuristic analogy.[101]

This leads to the third and final element in Paul's curriculum (the fourth item in the list): "[even to the point of] being conformed to his death." The language here is metaphorical and hyperbolic, but the hyperbole is that of religious enthusiasm, and for Paul, at least, the superlative experience it seeks to describe was real, as the language of metamorphosis ("being conformed"; συμμορφιζόμενος) makes clear.[102] Paul uses similar imagery and a similar progression from empowerment to suffering to death in 2 Cor 4:8-10: "Now we have this treasure [the spirit of Christ?] in earthen pots, in order that it might be seen that the power which is beyond com-parison [ἡ ὑπερβολὴ τῆς δυνάμεως] belongs to God and not to us. In every way we are afflicted, but not crushed; despairing, but not utterly desperate; persecuted, but not forsaken; struck down, but not destroyed; always carrying about in the body the death of Jesus [τὴν νέκρωσιν τοῦ Ἰησοῦ]" (trans. Furnish).

The fifth and final item in Paul's list is climactic: "if somehow I might arrive at the resurrection from the dead!"[103] Paul's tentativeness regarding his resurrection—"if somehow"—calls for comment. According to Josephus, the Pharisees believed that, while all the dead would be judged, only the righteous would experience resurrec-tion,[104] by which account "resurrection" is equivalent to final salvation. This seems to be the way Paul is using the term here, and his usage elsewhere is consistent with this: he uses "resurrection" when speaking of the fate of the righteous (including, of course, Jesus) and "destruc-tion" when speaking of the fate of the unrighteous.[105] The point of v. 11, then, is that Paul's continuing efforts to "know" Christ are tantamount to his ongoing quest for salvation, which quest the Philippians must imitate (Phil 1:19; 2:12). Paul will develop this theme further in 3:12-16.

For Paul, then, apocalyptic suffering had become "christological" suffering.

101 See Ioan M. Lewis, *Ecstatic Religion: A Study in Shamanism and Spirit Possession* (3rd ed.; London: Routledge, 2003); Ashton, *Religion*, 127; and even more incisively, Mount, "Spirit Possession"; idem, "Gullibility." Cf. the deathlike experience of Lucius during his initiation into the mysteries of Isis in Apuleius, *Metam.* 11.21: "the very rite of dedication itself was performed in the manner of a voluntary death"; ibid. 11.23: "I approached the boundary of death and treading on Proserpine's threshold . . ." (trans. Griffiths).

102 Speaking of Phil 3:10, Ashton writes, "there remained the continuous transformation [into Christ] . . . that gave Paul grounds for hope in an eventual resurrection" (*Religion*, 126).

103 Expressive of its placement as the final element in a list, item 5 is pleonastic. Paul's typical expression is ἀνάστασις νεκρῶν (Rom 1:4; 1 Cor 15:12, 13, 21, 52) or simply ἀνάστασις (Rom 6:5). Here he writes τὴν ἐξανάστασιν τὴν ἐκ νεκρῶν, repeating both the article (τήν) and the preposition (ἐξ-/ἐκ). The meaning remains the same, however, since even in its shorter form the genitive νεκρῶν is partitive. We have already encountered pleonasm in the last element in a list in 2:1: "If there is any consolation in Christ, if any comfort in love, if any fellowship of the Spirit, *if any tender mercy or compassion* . . . ." We will encounter it again in the list of consolatory exhorta-tions in 4:4-9, for which see my comments below.

104 Josephus, *Ant.* 18.14; *Bell.* 2.163; cf. *Pss. Sol.* 3:10-12.

105 See my comments above at 1:28b-30 and the excur-sus "The Fate of the Wicked according to Paul" there.

3

12/ Not that I have already received [the prize][a] or have already been perfected, but I race on if by any means[b] I may lay hold of that for which[c] I was myself also laid hold of by Christ Jesus.[d] 13/ Brothers,[e] I do not[f] consider myself to have laid hold of [this prize], but there is one thing [I have laid hold of]: forgetting the things that lie behind me, and straining toward what lies ahead, 14/ I race[g] toward the goal, toward[h] the prize of the upward calling[i] of God in Christ Jesus.[j] 15/ Let as many of us, therefore, who are "perfect"[k] think this way, and if in anything you think otherwise, this too God will reveal to you. 16/ Only let us be diligent to persist[l] in whatever progress we have already made.[m]

a I supply "the prize" (Gk. βραβεῖον) here on analogy with 1 Cor 9:24 (εἷς δὲ λαμβάνει τὸ βραβεῖον, "but only one receives the prize") and in anticipation of the term in 3:14, for which see the comments by Chrysostom. Several witnesses add at this point ἢ ἤδη δεδικαίωμαι, "or have already been justified" (𝔭46 D*·c F G ar; Ambst), or ἢ ἤδη δικαίωμαι, "or am already justified" (F G b; Irlat), possibly to clarify ἔλαβον, "I have already received," which is ambiguous due to the fact that it has no direct object.

b Several witnesses (א* D* F G 326, 2464, 2495 lat syp) omit καί, simply reading εἰ ("if") instead of εἰ καί (lit., "if indeed"). I have translated "if by any means," carrying forward the sense of 3:11: "if somehow" (εἴ πως).

c The Greek expression ἐφ᾽ ᾧ here is difficult. It is found later in Philippians in 4:10 and elsewhere in Paul in Rom 5:12 and 2 Cor 5:4. For a discussion, see Joseph A. Fitzmyer, "The Consecutive Meaning of Ἐφ᾽ Ὧ in Romans 5:12," NTS 39 (1993) 321–39. It is commonly interpreted as the equivalent of the conjunction διότι ("since," "because") following the comments of Photius, the ninth-century scholar and patriarch of Constantiople, and Thomas Magister, a fourteenth-century grammarian (both cited by Fitzmyer). This, however, is not the sense given by early patristic commentators, who typically take it to introduce a relative clause (Stanislas Lyonnet, "Le sens ἐφ᾽ ᾧ en Rom 5,12 et l'exégèse des Pères grecs," Bib 36 [1955] 436–56), which is how I have interpreted it here.

d Several witnesses (B D F G 33 b; Tert Cl Ambst) omit "Jesus."

e Paul writes "brothers" (ἀδελφοί) even though his letter is intended for both the women and the men in the Philippian assembly, as 4:2 ("I urge Euodia and I urge Syntyche") makes clear.

f A number of important witnesses (א A D* P 075, 33, 81, 104, 365, 614, [629], 1175, 1241 ar vgmss shh** bo; Cl) read οὔπω ("not yet") in a misguided attempt to clarify the original οὐ ("not"), which makes perfectly good sense as a simple negation of λογίζομαι ("consider").

g Two witnesses (I Ψ) read the participle διώκων for the finite verb διώκω, presumably on analogy with the participles in v. 13.

h Several witnesses (D F G K L P 075, 104, 630 Maj) read ἐπί instead of εἰς ("toward") with little change in meaning.

i Two witnesses (1739v.l.; Tert) read ἀνεγκλησίας ("irreproachability") instead of ἄνω κλήσεως ("upward calling").

j The reading τοῦ θεοῦ ἐν Χριστῷ Ἰησοῦ, "of God in Christ Jesus," is well attested (𝔭16vid א A B D1 I Ψ 075 33 1739 1881 Maj lat sy(p) co; Or). There are, however, a number of weakly attested variants: θεοῦ, "of God" (𝔭46; Ambst); ἐν Χριστῷ Ἰησοῦ, "in Christ Jesus" (Cl);

ἐν κυρίῳ Ἰησοῦ Χριστοῦ, "in the Lord Jesus Christ" (F G); τοῦ θεοῦ ἐν κυρίῳ Ἰησοῦ Χριστοῦ, "of God in the Lord Jesus Christ" (D*); τοῦ θεοῦ ἐν Ἰησοῦ Χριστοῦ, "of God in Jesus Christ" (p16).

k Given the fact that Paul has explicitly denied perfection in v. 12 (οὐχ ὅτι ἤδη . . . τετελείωμαι, "not that I have already been perfected"), I have placed "perfect" (τέλειοι) here in quotation marks.

l The Greek is difficult and the manuscript tradition convoluted. The reading adopted here is τῷ αὐτῷ στοιχεῖν, lit., "to persist in the same" (p16, 46 ℵ* A B Ivid 6, 33, 1739 b co; Hil Aug). A number of witnesses variously add the dative κανόνι (cf. Gal 6:16) and τὸ

αὐτὸ φρονεῖν, or substitute φρονεῖν for στοιχεῖν: (1) τῷ αὐτῷ στοιχεῖν κανόνι, τὸ αὐτὸ φρονεῖν, "to persist in the same rule, to think the same thing" (ℵ2 K L Ψ 075, 630, 1505, 2464 Maj sy(p)); (2) τὸ αὐτὸ φρονεῖν, τῷ αὐτῷ [συσ]στοιχεῖν κανόνι, "to think the same thing, to persist in the same rule" (D [F G] 81, 104, 365, 629, 1175, 1241 [vg]). One manuscript substitutes φρονεῖν for στοιχεῖν: τὸ αὐτὸ φρονεῖν, "to think the same thing" (1881).

m 𝔓16vid samss read the second person plural ἐφθάσατε, "you have already made."

Analysis

Paul continues to argue through personal example for the thesis of 3:1 that the Christ-believers at Philippi must learn to "rejoice in the Lord,"[1] by which he means take consolation in an ever-increasing "knowledge of Christ." Paul argued this in 3:2-11 by way of rhetorical comparison (σύγκρισις). Now in 3:12-16 he employs a new figure, ἐπιδιόρθωσις or self-correction (3:12-14), followed by a short exhortation (3:15-16). Paul's specific objective in these verses is to highlight the claim adumbrated in 3:7-11 that for the Christ-believer the knowledge of Christ remains a relentless quest. To illustrate this mind-set— "Let as many of us, therefore, who are 'perfect' *think* this way, and if in anything you *think* otherwise . . . ."—Paul introduces the image of a runner in the final stretch of a race when all of his or her[2] attention is focused on the finish line.[3] Consistent with the figure of self-correction Paul

1   That is, to find consolation in the deepening "knowledge of Christ" that their current "fellowship in his sufferings" is making possible.

2   Women did not compete in the Olympic games, which they originally were not even allowed to attend (Pausanias 5.6.7–8; 6.20.9), but there was a separate festival (the *Heraia*) held at Olympia in honor of the goddess Hera in which girls and young women did participate. According to Pausanias (5.15.1–6) the Heraean games included four different footraces for "virgins." Here see esp. the well-known bronze statuette of a young female runner (British Museum, bronze no. 208; GR inv. no. 1876.0510.1), whose attire matches perfectly the attire of the young female runners described by Pausanias, as well as the similarly attired Palermo runner (Palermo Museo Nazionale, inv. no. 8265 [42]). See Nancy Serwint, "The Female Athletic Costume at the Heraia and Prenuptial Initiation Rites," *AJA* 97 (1993) 403–22; Thomas F. Scanlon, "The Footrace of the Heraia at Olympia," *AncW* (1984) 77–90; idem, *Eros and Greek Athletics* (Oxford: Oxford University Press, 2002) 98–120. In Sparta, young women famously trained and competed alongside young men; see Stephen G. Miller, *Ancient Greek Athletics* (New Haven: Yale University Press, 2004) 150–59. For women in Roman sports, see Donald G.

Kyle, *Sport and Spectacle in the Ancient World* (2nd ed.; Malden, MA: Wiley Blackwell, 2015) 209–21, who cites the following inscriptional evidence: *SEG* 11.830, which tells of a footrace for girls at a festival in honor of Livia established in Sparta either by Tiberius or Cladius; J. H. Kent, *Corinth*, vol. 8.3: *The Inscriptions, 1926–1950* (Princeton: Princeton University Press, 1966) no. 153 (= Corinth museum inv. no. 1952), which tells of a certain *agōnothetēs* in the reign of Claudius who established a sporting event (probably a footrace) for young girls at Corinth in honor of Livia; and *SIG*3 802, in which a certain Hermesianax of Trelles celebrates the athletic feats of his daughters Tryphosa (who won the *stadion* for "virgins" twice in the Pythian games and once in the Isthmian games), Hedea (who won the *stadion* in the Nemean games and at Sikyon), and Dionysia (who won the *stadion* again at the Isthmian games and in games in honor of Asclepius at Epidaurus). According to *IG* 14.755 the *Augustalia* at Naples also appears to have included a *stadion* for daughters of magistrates, while according to Suetonius (*Dom.* 4.4; cf. Cassius Dio 67.8.1) the Capitoline Games established by Domitian included a race by girls.

3   The quest of 3:11 ("if somehow I might arrive at") now becomes a sprint ("I race on . . . I race toward the goal"). See Chrysostom on this image (hom.

adopts a more conversational style that includes direct address as well as several instances of ellipsis.[4] Formally, the self-correction of 3:12-14 consists of two antithetical sentences (v. 12 and vv. 13-14), while the exhortation of 3:15-16 doubles as a *conclusio* to all of 3:2-16.[5]

Philippians 3:12-16 may be outlined as follows:

3:12-14 Rhetorical self-correction
    3:12 First antithetical sentence
    3:13-14 Second antithetical sentence
3:15-16 Concluding exhortation

Comment

■ **12** Verse 12 is an antithetical sentence consisting of a negative assertion or denial (v. 12a) and a positive assertion or affirmation (v. 12b). Paul begins v. 12a with an expression signaling rhetorical self-correction: *"Not that [οὐχ ὅτι] I have already received . . . ."*[6] In Rom 9:6 he uses this expression to introduce a new topic: *"Not that [οὐχ . . . ὅτι] the word of God has failed . . . ."* In 2 Cor 3:5 he uses it to amplify a topic already being discussed: *"Not that [οὐχ ὅτι] we are competent of ourselves . . . ,"*[7] which

is how the figure functions here in Phil 3:12. In neither of these other occurrences is an actual opponent implied and so there is little basis for seeing a new set of opponents behind 3:12-16.[8] The positive assertion in v. 12b continues the quest language of 3:11: διώκω δέ (lit., "but I press on"), which, given the racecourse imagery developed in vv. 13-14, I have translated "but I race on."

The first verb in v. 12, ἔλαβον ("I have received"), requires an object, but none is given and so one must be supplied. The next two verbs, τετελείωμαι and διώκω ("I have been perfected" and "I race on"), offer little clue to what this object might be, since they do not require an object, while the next verb after that, καταλάβω ("I may lay hold of"), has as its object an equally ambiguous circumlocution: "that for which [ἐφ' ᾧ] I was myself also laid hold of [κατελήμφθην] by Christ."[9] Since, however, Paul has used λαμβάνω and καταλαμβάνω together elsewhere to evoke the image of the racetrack,[10] and since that image is explicitly adduced in the next sentence, a natural reading would be to supply "prize" (βραβεῖον) from 3:14. This is how Chrysostom completes the sense of v. 12,[11] and it is how I have translated it: "Not that I have already received [the prize] . . . ."

12.242.15-20 Allen). Cf. 2 Tim 4:7: "I have finished the race, I have kept the faith."

4   Müller observes this but attributes it to Paul's penchant for the diatribe style, citing Thomas Schmeller, *Paulus und die "Diatribe": Eine vergleichende Stil-Interpretation* (NTAbh, n.F. 19; Münster: Achendorff, 1987). The standard treatment of Paul's use of the diatribe style remains Bultmann, *Stil*, as updated and corrected by Stowers (*The Diatribe and Paul's Letter to the Romans* [SBLDS 57; Chico, CA: Scholars Press, 1981; repr., 2008]).

5   Verse 15 returns to the first person plural of 3:3. There is also a neat wordplay between τετελείωμαι ("I have been perfected"; 3:12) and τέλειοι ("perfect"; 3:15) typical of Paul's terminal *sententiae*. Here see the comments by Chrysostom below. Of course, the summary exhortation of 3:15-16 not only concludes the autobiographical remarks of 3:2-16 but neatly anticipates the more sustained exhortation of 3:17—4:1, which returns to the thematic exhortation of 3:1a. See my comments on both of these texts (3:15-16 and 3:17—4:1) below.

6   He uses this expression again in 4:11 and 17.

7   Lightfoot, Müller.

8   Contra Jewett, "Conflicting Movements."

9   The result is one of Paul's characteristic conceits: "if by any means *I may lay hold of* [καταλάβω] that for which *I was myself also laid hold of* [κατελάμφθην] by Christ." Here as elsewhere Paul begins with a verb in the active voice and then repeats the same verb in the so-called divine passive. Thus Gal 4:9: "but now knowing [γνόντες] God, or rather being known [γνωσθέντες] by God." Similarly 1 Cor 13:12: "then I will know [ἐπιγνώσομαι] even as I was known [ἐπεγνώσθην]"; cf. 1 Cor 8:2-3: "If anyone appears to know [ἐγνωκέναι] anything, he does not yet know [ἔγνω] as he should; but if anyone loves God, this one is known [ἔγνωσται] by him." See the comments by Dibelius and Müller, as well as by Betz, *Galatians*, on 4:9.

10   Cf. esp. 1 Cor 9:24: "Do you not know that in a race . . . only one receives [λαμβάνει] the prize [βραβεῖον]? Run in such a way that you may lay hold of it [καταλάβητε]."

11   So Chrysostom (hom. 12.242.3 Allen; cf. Bengel, Beare. This reading is confirmed by the repetition of διώκω ("I race [on]") in vv. 12 and 14, the second instance of which has "the prize [βραβεῖον] of the upward calling of God in Christ" as its stated objective.

This solves the basic translation problem in 3:12, but we must still determine what this "prize" is. Here we are helped a little by the second verbal expression, "I have been perfected," which implies that receiving the prize entails achieving some sort of perfection (cf. 1:6). Verse 14, however, is again determinative: "the prize of the upward calling of God in Christ Jesus," which presumably means that the prize is in some sense Christ himself, in keeping with the earlier expressions, "that I might gain *Christ* and be found in *him*," and "that I might know *him*," and so on. This must also be the sense of the circumlocution at the end of v. 12, "that for which I was laid hold of by Christ."[12] This reading fits nicely with Paul's larger myth of salvation, where salvation consists in the believer's transformation into Christlikeness, a metamorphosis begun in this life and completed in the next.[13]

■ **13-14** Paul clarifies the antithetical sentence of 3:12 in a second, longer antithetical sentence in 3:13-14. He uses direct address ("Brothers") to signal his earnestness, after which he repeats the negative assertion of 3:12a but with a new psychological element: "I do not *consider* myself to have laid hold of [the prize]" (3:13a). As in 3:4-11,[14] Paul's concern in 3:12-16 is to exemplify a proper mind-set: Paul "reckons" (ἡγέομαι) all things table-scraps compared to the surpassing greatness of knowing Christ (3:8b), but he does not "consider" (λογίζομαι) himself to have fully attained that knowledge (3:13a). He illustrates his mind-set in the positive assertion of 3:13b-14. Here is the centerpiece of Paul's argument: "but there is one thing [I have laid hold of[15]]: forgetting the things that lie behind me, and straining toward what lies ahead." Paul may not have laid hold of the prize yet, but he has as it were laid hold of the *mind-set* of continuing to focus on the prize. Indeed, if we take Paul's racetrack imagery seriously, his claim in vv. 13-14 is not simply that he continues to focus on the prize but that he does so with increasing intensity as he sees the finish line come into view (cf. 3:20; 4:5).

Paul's language is realistic in 3:13b-14, bordering on what ancient literary critics called "vivid description," or ἔκφρασις.[16] Paul pictures himself as a runner nearing the end of a race. He does not look back over the distance he has covered but stays focused on the finish: "forgetting [ἐπιλανθανόμενος] the things that lie behind,[17] and straining toward [ἐπεκτεινόμενος] what lies ahead, I race toward the goal [κατὰ σκοπόν]." Lucian paints a similar picture of a runner in *Cal.* 12: "the good runner thinks only of what is in front of him and, stretching [ἀποτείνας] his mind toward the *terma* and putting his hope of victory

---

12 Cf. Rom 8:28-30, where believers are defined as those who have been "called" to be "conformed to the image of [Christ]."

13 Cf. Chrysostom, hom. 12.240.5-6 Allen: "we become christs" (χριστοὶ γινόμεθα).

14 "I have come to reckon [ἥγημαι] a loss . . . I consider [ἡγοῦμαι] all things to be a loss . . . and I consider [ἡγοῦμαι] them mere table-scraps."

15 The Greek is again elliptical and a second verb needs to be supplied. Translators typically supply some form of "to do." "I do not consider myself to have laid hold of. But one thing [I do]." A better option, in my view, is to repeat the verb "to lay hold of": "I do not consider myself to have laid hold of. But one thing [I have laid hold of]."

16 This technique was also taught in the schools: Theon, *Prog.* 7 (Spengel 11); Hermogenes, *Prog.* 10; Libanius, *Prog.* 12; Aphthonius, *Prog.* 12; Nicolaus, *Prog.* 11. See the discussion in Bradley Arnold, *Christ the* Telos *of Life: Moral Philosophy, Athletic Imagery and the Aim of Philippians* (WUNT 2/371; Tübingen: Mohr Siebeck, 2014) 124–41.

17 Here see *ABV* 68.2 (C.C. 648), a fifth-century black-figure cup in the inside of which is a runner looking back over his right shoulder (for a photograph of this figure, see John Boardman, *Athenian Black Figure Vases* [New York: Oxford University Press, 1974] fig. 43, p. 38); cf. British Museum bronze 208 (= Greece and Rome 1876.0510.1), the small bronze statuette already noted of a young women runner from the Heraean games at Olympia similarly glancing back over her right shoulder (for a photograph, see Scanlon, *Eros*, fig. 4.1, p. 102; Kyle, *Sport*, fig. 11.1, p. 213). Running figures (both human and divine) in this posture appear in a number of red-figure vases, for which see John Boardman, *Athenian Red Figure Vases in the Archaic Period* (New York: Oxford University Press, 1979) figs. 59, 60, 61, 67, 91, 93, 110, 236; Philip F. Esler, "Paul and the Agon: Understanding a Pauline Motif in Its Cultural and Visual Context," in *Picturing the New Testament*, ed. Annette Weissenrieder, Friederike Wendt, and Petra von Gemünden (WUNT 2/193; Tübingen: Mohr Siebeck, 2005) 371, fig. 3.

in his feet, does not . . . even consider his competitors."[18] A number of Greek vase paintings show runners in the short sprint, or *stadion*, running stretched out toward the finish line.[19] The *Greek Anthology* 16.54 vividly describes a bronze statue by the sculptor Myron of an athlete named Ladas straining for the finish line: "As you were in life, Ladas, flying before wind-foot Thymos barely touching the ground with the tips of your toes, just so did Myron cast you in bronze engraving all over your body expectation of the crown of Pisa."[20]

The expression τὸ βραβεῖον τῆς ἄνω κλήσεως τοῦ θεοῦ ἐν Χριστῷ Ἰησοῦ ("the prize of the upward calling of God in Christ Jesus") calls for further comment. The genitive κλήσεως is best read as a genitive of apposition: "the prize *which is* the upward calling of God."[21] "Calling" would then mean not the act of calling itself—as if the prize were to be called—but the condition or state to which the Christ-believer is called.[22] This condition can be described as residing "in Christ Jesus" inasmuch as the believer's aim is to be "found in him [ἐν αὐτῷ]" (3:9) and to be resurrected with a body like "his [αὐτοῦ] body of glory" (3:21; cf. Rom 8:29). And it is "upward" (ἄνω), since, as Paul will say in 3:20, the believer's true citizenship is "in the heavens" (ἐν οὐρανοῖς), which is also the present location of Christ: "from which also we eagerly await a savior." Whether Paul imagined "the heavens" also to be the final location of believers themselves is unclear, but in 1 Thess 4:16-17 he imagines believers

being caught up "into the clouds" for a rendevouz with Christ "in the air."[23] It bears repeating that, for Paul, this eschatological "prize" is presently experienced as a divine κλῆσις or "calling," an objective strived for in this life but not fully realized until the next.[24]

■ **15-16** Paul concludes with a short exhortation in 3:15-16 that continues to focus on the believer's mind-set: "Let as many of us, therefore, who are 'perfect' think this way."[25] Several commentators read vv. 15-16 with the exhortation that follows in 3:17–4:1.[26] But these exhortations are not the same: in vv. 15-16 Paul is addressing the "perfect"—those who might be tempted to think that they have already "laid hold of" the prize—and in 3:17–4:1 he is addressing the whole assembly. Further, the conceit that the "perfect" (3:15) are precisely those who view themselves as *not* having been "perfected" (3:12) produces a neat *clausula* and forms an obvious *inclusio*.[27] I have therefore interpreted 3:15-16 as a brief hortatory *conclusio*.[28]

At issue in 3:15-16 is the mind-set (φρονεῖν, "think") that Paul exemplifies in his autobiographical remarks in 3:2-11 and especially in 3:12-14. In 2:5-11 Paul urged the Philippians to adopt Christ's humble and obedient mind-set: "Have this attitude [φρονεῖτε] in yourselves which was also in Christ Jesus." Now in 3:15-16 he urges them to adopt his own "quester's" mind-set: "Let as many of us . . . who are 'perfect' think [φρονῶμεν] this way."[29] Paul's words here could be interpreted as a sarcastic rebuke to

18 Cited by Arnold, *Christ as the* Telos, 199, from the translation of Stephen G. Miller, *Arete: Greek Sports from Ancient Sources* (3rd expanded ed.; Berkeley: University of California Press, 2004) 21.

19 E.g., MMA 14.130.12 (= *ABV* 322.6); MMA 1978.11.13 (for both of these amphorae, see Mary B. Moore, "'Nikias Made Me': An Early Panathenaic Prize Amphora in the Metropolitan Museum," *Metropolitan Museum Journal* 34 [1999] 37–56); *ABV* 120; 322.4; 408.4 (= Boardman, *Black Figure Vases*, figs. 295, 298, and 302, respectively). Other examples are cited in Donald G. Kyle, *Athletics in Ancient Athens* (2nd ed.; Mnemosyne Supplement 95; Leiden: Brill, 1993) 179 n. 3. The *stadion* was the original and always the principal Olympic event, the winner of which was proclaimed the victor of the games and had his name given to that Olympiad.

20 Cited by Arnold, *Christ as* Telos, 200 (again after the translation of Miller, *Arete*, 254.)

21 BDF §167.
22 BDAG, s.v. κλῆσις 2.
23 Cf. Heb 3:1: "heavenly calling."
24 Cf. Epictetus, *Diss.* 3.22 for the Cynic's "calling."
25 The NRSV incorrectly translates "think the same" recalling the friendship idiom (τὸ αὐτὸ φρονεῖν) in 2:2, which is repeated in 4:2. The expression here, however, is τοῦτο φρονεῖν, to think in the preceding manner or as I have translated "[to] think this way."
26 E.g., Bockmuehl.
27 Cf. Chrysostom: "It belongs to the perfect [τελείου] not to think himself perfect [τέλειον]" (hom. 13.254.28 Allen).
28 It is unclear whether Paul intended the *conclusio* of 3:15-16 to include 3:2-11, but the mind-set that he recommends is already the topic of 3:3 (e.g., "who boast in Christ Jesus").
29 Christ is an example of humility while Paul is an example of the continued pursuit of Christ. This is

those in Philippi who arrogantly consider themselves to be "perfect," but since Paul includes himself among the mature ("let as many of *us* . . . who are 'perfect' think this way"), it seems better to understand his wordplay not as sarcasm but as an attempt at point.[30]

Paul softens the exhortation of 3:15a with a double concession in vv. 15b-16: (1) "and if in anything you think [φρονεῖτε] otherwise, this too God will reveal[31] to you," and (2) "Only let us be diligent to persist in whatever progress we have already made."[32] The first concession is relatively straightforward. It expresses confidence in the Philippians' ability to continue to make progress on their own without Paul (but with God's help). The second concession is more difficult. Its relationship to what comes before it is not specified (πλήν, "only"), and the Greek is sententious and terse: εἰς ὃ ἐφθάσαμεν, τῷ αὐτῷ στοιχεῖν. The verb φθάνω in the first clause means to "precede" or "come first" (cf. Lat. *praevenire*) and is often used in the sense of "overtake" or "outstrip" in a race.[33] It continues Paul's racecourse imagery. Paul used φθάνω earlier in Rom 9:31, also with διώκω: "But Israel, who chased after [διώκων] the law of righteousness, did not catch [ἔφθασεν] it." Here in Phil 3:16 it implies that, while complete perfection remains an eschatological hope, the Philippians have *already* achieved an element of it. I have translated, "in whatever progress we have already made." The Greek in the second clause is defective: στοιχεῖν ("to

proceed in a line") is a complementary infinitive but the verb that it complements, most likely δεῖ ("it is binding" in the sense of a moral obligation), is omitted and must be supplied. I have translated, "let us be diligent to persist."[34]

Excursus: φρονεῖν in Philippians

The verb φρονεῖν, which I have variously translated as "feel," "have the attitude," "be of a mind" or "be mindful," and "think," occurs ten times in Philippians,[35] rivaling χαίρειν ("rejoice") and its cognates, which occur sixteen times.[36] Neither φρονεῖν nor its cognate noun φρόνημα appears in 1 Thessalonians, while in the Corinthian letter archive the verb appears only two times and in Galatians only once.[37] But this changes dramatically in Romans where over the course of sixteen chapters φρονεῖν and φρόνημα appear thirteen times.[38] Paul uses φρονεῖν even more frequently in Philippians (ten times in only four chapters). Paul's use of φρονεῖν in Philippians varies widely, suggesting that he allowed himself to fall into a kind of verbal rut.[39] At times, however, Paul places considerable weight on the term, especially when writing about what might be called the mechanics of salvation: to mind (φρονεῖν) the same things as Christ in 2:5, to mind (φρονεῖν) the same things as Paul in 3:15 (cf. 3:19).

Paul begins to think seriously about the mechanics of salvation in his letter to the Galatians, where he must defend his non-Torah-observant gospel against the charge that it does not adequately address the

---

not quite the same as "be imitators of me as I am of Christ" (1 Cor 11:1); contra Peter Wick, "'Ahmt Jesus Christus mit mir zusammen nach!' (Phil 3,17): *Imitatio Pauli* und *imitatio Christi* im Philipperbrief," in Frey and Schliesser, *Philipperbrief*, 309–26.

30 Quintilian might have called this a *sententia ex inopinato* (*Inst.* 8.5.15), a sentence with an element of "surprise" or paradox in it. If anything, Paul's wit here blunts the force of his admonition. For similar attempts at point in Paul, see Rom 3:26; 8:13; 1 Cor 1:25; 3:18-19; 9:6, 19, 30-31; 14:16; 2 Cor 8:9; 12:10.

31 Paul seems to assume here that the Philippians' present knowledge is due in part at least to revelation.

32 The Greek is defective (τῷ αὐτῷ στοιχεῖν; lit., "to persist in the same"), and some verb taking a complementary infinitive must be supplied, most likely δεῖ ("it is necessary"; so Barth; cf. Rom 12:15), yielding lit., "it is necessary to persist," or as I have translated "let us be diligent to persist etc."

33 LSJ s.v. φθάνω I.

34 For the infinitive στοιχεῖν, see LSJ, s.v. στοιχέω II.

35 Phil 1:7; 2:2 (twice), 5; 3:15 (twice), 19; 4:2, 10 (twice). The cognitive component of Paul's advice in Philippians has repeatedly been emphasized (largely correctly in my view) by Troels Engberg-Pedersen. See, e.g., his *Paul and the Stoics*; idem, "Complete and Incomplete Transformation in Paul—a Philosophical Reading of Paul on Body and Spirit," in Seim and Økland, *Metamorphoses*, 123–46; cf. idem, "Self-Sufficiency and Power: Divine and Human Agency in Epictetus and Paul," in Barclay and Gathercole, *Agency*, 117–39.

36 Phil 1:4, 18 (twice), 25; 2:2, 17 (twice), 18 (twice), 28, 29; 3:1; 4:1, 4 (twice), 10.

37 1 Cor 13:11; 2 Cor 13:11; Gal 5:10.

38 Verb: Rom 8:5; 11:20; 12:3 (twice), 16 (twice); 14:6 (twice); 15:5; noun: 8:6 (twice), 7, 27.

39 For a similar undisciplined use of a favorite expression, compare Paul's use of the phrase "in Christ" and its equivalents.

problem of gentile sinfulness.[40] Paul's response is that even Torah does not combat "the flesh," for which one needs what he calls "the Spirit"[41] or "the spirit of [God's] son," which spirit God sends into the bodies of all believers at baptism (4:4). But possession by the spirit of Christ (cf. Gal 2:20) only partially addresses the problem of gentile sinfulness: it is the condition for the possibility of defeating the flesh but not its actual defeat. For this one must go a step further and harness the power of the Spirit, bring it to bear in one's daily life and upon one's behavior. This further step constitutes what I am here calling the *mechanics* of salvation.

Not surprisingly, Paul struggles to find the words for this. In Galatians he can only speak metaphorically: one "walks" in the Spirit (5:16, 25), is "led" by the Spirit (5:18), "sows" to the Spirit (6:8), with the result that one bears the "fruit" of the Spirit (5:22). Paul continues to use these metaphors in Romans

(e.g., 8:4, 14), but he also attempts to translate them into more concrete psychological terms, as when he explains in 8:5: "for those who live according to the flesh *mind* [$\phi\rho\nu\sigma\hat{\nu}\sigma\iota\nu$] the things of the flesh and those who live according to the Spirit [*mind*] the things of the Spirit," adding in 8:6: "for the *mind* [$\phi\rho\acute{o}\nu\eta\mu\alpha$] of the flesh is death, but the *mind* [$\phi\rho\acute{o}\nu\eta\mu\alpha$] of the Spirit is life and peace" (8:6). Paul uses this psychological language almost exclusively in Philippians. However, in Philippians there is a further development, at least in emphasis. The focus is less on the "Spirit" than on Christ himself: having the mind of Christ (2:5), seeking to gain Christ (3:8), seeking to know Christ (3:10), wanting to lay hold of Christ (3:12).[42] Here the mechanics of salvation are absorbed into Paul's emerging Christ-mysticism. They have become, to borrow a phrase from Mircea Eliade, "les techniques de l'extase."[43]

---

40 It is striking to think how much of subsequent Christian theology had its origins in Paul's and his contemporaries' prejudice against gentiles as "sinners."

41 See esp. the antithesis between the "flesh" and the "spirit" in Gal 5:16-25.

42 See esp. 3:3, where to serve by the "spirit of God" is immediately interpreted as boasting "in Christ Jesus." But see 1:19 ("spirit of Jesus Christ").

43 Mircea Eliade, *Shamanism: Archaic Techniques of Ecstasy* (London: Routledge & Kegan Paul, 1964) 4. In Phil 3:1-16 Paul offers himself as a model of these techniques.

3

17/ **Become imitators together of me, brothers,**[a]
and take note of those who walk accord-
ingly as you have us for a pattern. 18/ For
many walk, about whom I have spoken
to you often and now say even weeping
that they are[b] **enemies of Christ's cross,**
19/ whose end is destruction, whose god is
the belly and whose glory is in their shame,
they who mind earthly things! 20/ For our
citizenship exists in the heavens, from
which we also eagerly await a savior, the
Lord Jesus Christ, 21/ who will transform
the body of our humiliation to be[c] **con-**
formed to the body of his glory in exer-
cise of his power to subject all things to
himself.[d]

a Paul writes "brothers" (ἀδελφοί) even though his letter
is intended for both the women and the men in the
Philippian assembly, as 4:2 ("I urge Euodia and I urge
Syntyche") makes clear.

b 𝔓[46] adds βλέπετε ("watch out for") on analogy with
3:2.

c The copulative ("to be") is supplied. Several witnesses
(D[1] K L Ψ 075, 33, 104, 365, 630, 1505, 2464 Maj sy;
Ir Ambr) insert εἰς τὸ γένεσθαι αὐτό, "that it might
become."

d A number of witnesses (ℵ[2] D[2] L Ψ 6, 81[vid], 104, 326,
630, 1175, 1241 *pm* lat) read ἑαυτῷ instead of αὐτῷ,
both of which in the context mean "himself."

e A few witnesses (D* ar b vg[mss]) omit "beloved," while
others (B 33 sy) add "my."

4

1/ **Therefore, my brothers,**[a] **much loved and**
longed for, my joy and victory garland, thus
stand fast in the Lord, beloved.[e]

Analysis

In 3:17-21 Paul broadens the exhortation to the perfect
of 3:15-16 to include the whole assembly. All the Christ-
believers at Philippi are to follow Paul's example of
seeking "to know Christ" above all else. Formally, 3:17-21
consists of a short exhortation (3:17), followed by two
rationale statements (3:18-19, 20-21), which rationale
statements, taken together, produce a third rhetorical
comparison, or σύγκρισις.[1] As in 3:2-3 Paul compares two
types of Christ-believers: those who embrace his apocalyptic theory of suffering and those who do not and are
therefore "enemies of Christ's cross." Presumably these
"enemies" whose "god is the belly" are the "dogs" and the
like of 3:2 who seek to relate to God through the "flesh,"
but again Paul's vituperative rhetoric makes their identification difficult. The second rationale statement (3:20-21)
doubles as an eschatological climax signaling the end of
Paul's argument. Paul adds a concluding exhortation in
4:1 that mirrors the introductory exhortation in 3:1a. It

is indicative of Paul's penchant for closure that 3:20—4:1
also effectively concludes the letter body (1:12—4:1).[2]

Comment

■ **3:17** In 3:17 Paul exhorts all the Philippian Christ-
believers to "become imitators together [συμμιμηταί] of
me." The noun συμμιμηταί ("imitators *together*") is not
attested prior to Paul and may be a Pauline coinage.[3]
But whether a neologism or not, Paul's word choice will
have made his point hard to miss: the *whole* assembly is to
join *together* in following his example.[4] Paul's readiness to
suffer in order "to know Christ" is to become part of the
church's corporate self-understanding or social identity. If some at Philippi have lost sight of this—Paul has
asserted this ideal before (3:1b)—Paul insists that others
have not (e.g., Epaphroditus), and they too, like Paul, are
to be imitated: "and mark those who walk accordingly as
you have us for a pattern."

---

1 The earlier instances of the figure are 3:2-3 and 3:4-
11.

2 See my comments on 3:20-21 and 4:1 below; cf. Rom
8:31-39; 11:33-36.

3 Cf. BDAG, s.v. συμμιμητής; but see Lightfoot for the
compound verb in Plato in *Polit.* 274d.

4 Collange.

■ **3:18-19** Paul supports the exhortation of 3:17 with two rationale statements in 3:18-19 and 20-21.[5] Together they form a third rhetorical comparison. As in the earlier comparisons in 3:2-3 and 3:4-11, Paul begins with the position he rejects (3:18-19). His rhetoric is again abusive (cf. 3:2), so much so that it is now impossible to identify its targets without appealing to context.[6] But since Paul has remained on topic since 3:1, it is reasonable to assume that he has returned to the group adduced in 3:2, namely, Torah-observant Christ-believers whose faith is no less evangelistic than his own but whose theory of salvation focuses on what Paul calls the "flesh" rather than "Christ."

Paul has warned the Philippians against these evangelists before: "for many walk, about whom I have spoken to you often [πολλάκις]."[7] He does so now "even weeping."[8] It is possible that Paul's emotion is due to the presence of these other teachers at Philippi, but it is more likely that it simply continues his religious pathos and reflects his concern for the Philippians themselves, in whom he discerns an alarming misunderstanding of the role suffering plays in the salvation of the Christ-believer (cf. 1:29; 2:12; 3:10-11). Assuming they ever fully agreed with Paul, it would seem that the Philippians' experience of actual suffering—both Paul's and theirs—has led them to question his theology of suffering. Paul warns that this

effectively puts them in the company of the Torah-observant whose strategy for relating to God he has taught them to eschew.

The list of insults that follows merits only brief scrutiny.[9] "Enemies of the cross of Christ" reflects the fact that Paul's competitors do not share his theory of suffering as presaged in the "cross" of Christ (cf. 2:8). "Whose end is destruction" reminds that the outcome of his competitors' religious practices is not salvation but judgment.[10] "Whose god is the belly and whose glory is in their shame" may be references to food practices[11] and circumcision,[12] respectively, but it is impossible to say with any certainty.[13] Both are strikingly paradoxical. The first, "whose god is the belly," renders even more pointed a sentiment from Paul's earlier letter to the Romans—"people like this do not serve our Lord Jesus Christ but their own belly!" (Rom 16:18)[14]—while the second, "whose glory is in their shame," was no doubt chosen at least in part to contrast with "body of glory" in 3:21. Similarly, "who mind earthly things,"[15] anticipates by way of antithesis "for our citizenship exists in the heavens" in 3:20.

■ **3:20-21** The second part of the rhetorical comparison comes in 3:20-21.[16] The difference is straightforward and stark.[17] The "enemies" of 3:18-19 are occupied with "earthly things" (ἐπίγεια), while Paul and the Philippians possess a citizenship in "the heavens" (οὐρανοί).[18] The

---

5   "For [γάρ] many walk, about whom I have spoken to you often . . ." (3:18); and "For [γάρ] our citizenship exists in the heavens . . ." (3:20).

6   Gnilka, Collange.

7   Paul commonly uses the verb "to walk" to refer to the way a person conducts his or her life (BDAG, s.v. περιπατέω 2), so much so that it becomes noteworthy when he departs from this (e.g., Phil 1:27, where he uses the verb πολιτεύομαι; cf. 3:20, πολίτευμα).

8   For similar displays of pathos in Paul, see 2 Cor 2:4; Rom 9:1-5; 10:1; cf. Phil 1:8.

9   See my comments on 2:1 above.

10 Paul imagines them sharing the same fate ("destruction") as nonbelievers (1:28). For the "destruction" of the wicked, see the excursus at 1:28b. Cf. 2 Cor 11:15.

11 Theodoret; Gnilka equates "belly" with "flesh" (3:3-4).

12 Jerome; Chrysostom (hom. 14.268.28 Allen) comments, "some say this is a reference to circumcision, but I do not think so." Cf. Bengel, Barth, Edart.

13 For a full discussion, see Sandnes, *Belly and Body*.

14 For this type of rhetorical improvement elsewhere in Paul, see my "Paul's Pointed Prose."

15 The mind-set (φρονεῖν) of the enemies here explicitly contradicts the mind-set (φρονεῖν) of the perfect in 3:15.

16 There are a number of linguistic parallels between 3:20-21 and 2:6-11. This has led some to imagine that 3:20-21, like 2:6-11, is a hymnic fragment. This assumes, of course, that 2:6-11 is a hymn, which I do not believe to be the case. It seems more likely that 3:20-21 purposefully reproduces terminology from 2:6-11 in order to link the two passages, the exaltation of Christ anticipating the exaltation of the Christ-believer.

17 The contrast is both spatial and temporal. This is characteristic of Jewish and early Christian apocalypticism, of which Paul offers no clearer expression.

18 For "citizenship," see my comment above on 1:27. John M. G. Barclay rightly cautions against too political a reading of this text, noting that the contrast here is not with "Rome" but with the "world" (*Pauline Churches and Diaspora Jews* [WUNT 275;

enemies' end is "destruction" (ἀπώλεια), while Paul and the Philippians await "a savior" (σωτήρ) (cf. 1:28; 1 Thess 1:10).[19] The enemies' "glory" (δόξα) is shameful (v. 19), while Paul and the Philippians stand to have their bodies transformed to be like Christ's "body of glory" (σῶμα τῆς δόξης).

Verses 20-21 constitute one of the clearest statements of Paul's mythology of salvation as metamorphosis: "who will transform [μετασχηματίσει] the body of our humiliation to be conformed [σύμμορφον] to his body of glory." Believers who are *conformed* to Christ's death in this life (3:10; συμμορφιζόμενος) will have their bodies *transformed* to be *conformed* to his supremely glorious angelic body in the next.[20] In 2:9-11 it is God who subsumes all things to Christ; here it is Christ's own power that does so: "in exercise of his power to subject all things to himself."[21]

The expression "the body of his glory" (τὸ σῶμα τῆς δόξης αὐτοῦ; cf. 1 Cor 15:40) may indicate that Paul imagined the glorified Christ to be not only God's Name-bearing angel (2:10) but also the angel who carried the divine "glory" or *kābôd*.[22]

■ **4:1** Paul restates the introductory summary exhortation of 3:1a ("rejoice in the Lord"; χαίρετε ἐν κυρίῳ) in slightly different terms in 4:1a: "stand fast in the Lord" (στήκετε ἐν κυρίῳ).[23] Recalling earlier themes, he reminds the Philippians that they are his "joy" (χαρά; cf. 2:2) and will be his "victory garland" (στέφανος; cf. 2:16). He refers to them affectionately as those "longed for" (ἐπιπόθητοι; cf. 1:8), and twice he calls them his "much loved ones" or "beloved" (ἀγαπητοί; cf. 2:12). Philippians 4:1 forms both an *inclusio* with 3:1a and an apt concluding sentence to all of 1:12–4:1.

Tübingen: Mohr Siebeck, 2011] 379). Philo, *Conf.* 77–78 speaks of the heavenly citizenship of the wise. Paul's language is picked up in *1 Clem.* 2.8; 3.4; 21.1; 44.6; 51.2; 54.5. Pilhofer's suggestion (*Philippi*, 1:127–34) that Paul's opponents are offering the Philippians the protection of a legal *politeuma* is unnecessarily speculative.

19 Paul uses the term "eagerly await" (ἀπεκδέχομαι), which seems to be a semitechnical term in Paul for awaiting the parousia and its benefits (see 1 Cor 1:7;

Gal 5:5; Rom 8:19, 23, 25). For the notion of a savior from heaven, see 1 Thess 4:13-18.

20 This is the logic of the "cross" established in 2:6-11.

21 Cf. 1 Cor 15:26-28, where, contrary to much current interpretation, it strikes me that some sort of messianic interregnum is in view.

22 Segal, *Paul the Convert*, 10; cf. 2 Cor 2:8; 3:18; 4:6; Heb 1:3; Ezek 1:26-28.

23 For "stand fast," cf. 1:27.

4

2/   **I urge Euodia and I urge Syntyche to be of the same mind in the Lord. 3/ And I ask you, my true comrade,[a] help these women who contended in the gospel alongside me and Clement and the rest of my co-workers[b] whose names are in the book of life.**

4/   **Rejoice in the Lord at all times. I will say it again: rejoice!**

5/   **Let your graciousness be known to all people. The Lord is near.**

6/   **Do not be anxious for anything, but in every matter through prayer and petition, along with thanksgiving, let your requests be known to God, 7/ and the peace of God[c] that defies all understanding will guard your hearts and minds[d] in Christ[e] Jesus.**

8/   **Finally, brothers,[f] whatever things are true, whatever noble, whatever just, whatever pure, whatever pleasing, whatever admirable, if there is any virtue and if there is anything deserving of praise,[g] think on these things; 9/ and the things that you have learned and received and heard and seen in me, practice these things, and the God of peace will be with you.**

a   Various modern commentators have proposed that the Greek σύζυγε ("comrade") be understood as a proper name. This would be an elegant solution to the problem of the identity of this person, were it not for the fact that there is no evidence that Σύζυγος was a proper name, and no ancient commentator has interpreted the term this way, though all seem to be aware of the problem and try to solve it (e.g., Victorinus understands it as a reference to Epaphroditus; Clement of Alexandria and Origen as a reference to Paul's wife; see Reumann).

b   Two early witnesses (𝔓[16vid], ℵ*) read συνεργῶν μου καὶ τῶν λοιπῶν ("my co-workers and the rest") perhaps as an attempt to distinguish between Euodia, Syntyche, and Clement, and Paul's "co-workers."

c   Several witnesses (A t vg[mss] sy[hmg]) read Χριστοῦ ("Christ").

d   Several witnesses (F G ar d MVict Pel) read σώματα ("bodies"), presumably on the assumption that "hearts and minds" is redundant. 𝔓[16vid] reads νοήματα καὶ τὰ σώματα ("minds and bodies"), a conflation that, interestingly, pushes the above minority reading (σώματα, "bodies") back to at least the late third century.

e   𝔓[46] reads κυρίῳ, "Lord," no doubt in imitation of the expression "in the Lord" that appears multiple times in the immediate context: 4:1 (cf. 3:1), 2, 4, and 10.

f   Although Paul writes "brothers" (ἀδελφοί) here, he includes women, for his letter is intended for both the women and the men in the Philippian assembly, as 4:2 ("I urge Euodia and I urge Syntyche") makes clear.

g   A number of witnesses (D* F G ar vg[cl] Ambst) add ἐπιστήμης ("of knowledge"), apparently confused at the unusual use of ἔπαινος ("praise") for "praise-worthy."

Analysis

Nowhere is the oratorical dimension of Paul's letters more evident than in the hortatory peroration that typically draws the large central argumentative portion of his letters to a close.[1] In Philippians this peroration comes in 4:2-9. Older scholarship used to imagine these exhortations as largely unrelated to the rest of the letter.[2] That view has now changed, and it is generally admitted that these exhortations support Paul's purpose(s) in writing,[3] which is the case here. Paul has written with two objectives in mind: to console the Philippians in their grief and

---

1   Similar perorations can be found in 1 Thess 5:12-22 and Gal 5:25—6:10. For the peroration as an essential part of oratorical composition and performance, see Heinrich Lausberg, *Handbook of Literary Rhetoric: A Foundation for Literary Study* (Leiden: Brill, 1998) §§431–42.

2   E.g., Martin Dibelius, *From Tradition to Gospel* (New York: Scribner, 1965) 238–39 (cited by Malherbe, *Thessalonians*, 81–82). The term scholars commonly apply to this material is "parenesis" (from the Gk. παραίνεσις, "advice, counsel"), defined as a loosely arranged series of stock exhortations that have little to do with the larger context. This misunderstands both the ancient practice and the nature of the material itself. See further James Starr and Troels Engberg-Pedersen, eds., *Early Christian Paraenesis in Context* (BZNW 125; Berlin, de Gruyter, 2004).

3   Malherbe, *Thessalonians*, 80–84, 308–9.

to urge them to work together in his gospel mission. In 4:2-9 he takes these up in reverse order. In 4:2-3 he urges two people in particular, Euodia and Syntyche, to "be of the same mind," while in 4:4-9 he gathers together several final pieces of consolatory advice on how to overcome "anxiety" and find "peace."[4]

Comment

■ **4:2-3** The exhortation to unity in 4:2-3 raises a host of questions that cannot be answered with any degree of probability. It concerns a disagreement between two members of the Philippian assembly, Euodia and Syntyche, who have not yet been mentioned but whose disagreement is presumably included in if not central to the general exhortations in 1:27 and 2:2 to "be of the same mind." We know nothing of them or of their disagreement except what Paul writes here.[5] Paul identifies them as "co-workers" who "contended in the gospel alongside me and Clement,"[6] indicating that they have played a prominent role in his mission.[7] It is not clear whether "Clement" is a member of the Philippian assembly, a member of Paul's missionary team no longer in Philippi, or even an independent missionary similar to Apollos.[8]

It is also possible that Clement has now died and that Paul is utilizing the Philippians' fond memories of him to motivate reconciliation.

Even more enigmatic is the reference to the "true comrade" whom Paul urges to "help" (συλλαμβάνου), i.e., to be a peacemaker between, Euodia and Syntyche. Not even the name of this individual is known, unless it is a reference to Epaphroditus, which it may well be. It has also been suggested that Σύζυγος (the word translated "comrade") is a proper name and the Paul is punning on the name,[9] but this name is not otherwise attested and σύζυγος was a common expression indicating partnership.[10] It is likely that Paul chose the sobriquet σύζυγος (lit., "yoke-fellow") to highlight the need for shared effort in the gospel mission.

■ **4:4-9** The consolatory exhortations in 4:4-9 are neatly structured. They increase in length, complexity, and rhetorical intensity.[11] Formally, each is in two parts. In the second, third, and fourth exhortations the second part is a motive clause; in the first there is simple repetition.

■ **4:4** The first consolatory exhortation continues the letter's leitmotif of "joy" especially as expressed in 3:1, which it repeats verbatim, though now adding the adverb πάντοτε: "Rejoice in the Lord *at all times*." By repeating

---

4   Chrysostom (15.284.16-18, 288.13 Allen) is especially clear on the consolatory elements in vv. 4-9.

5   Several scholars (e.g., Cynthia Briggs Kittredge, *Community and Authority: The Rhetoric of Obedience in the Pauline Tradition* [HTS 45; Harrisburg, PA: Trinity Press International, 1998] 105–8) have proposed that Euodia and Syntyche's disagreement was not with each other but with Paul. This understands "to be of the same mind" to mean "to be of the same mind *with me*" and to refer to 3:15-16, where the verb φρονεῖν twice occurs. This is not an unreasonable interpretation, but the expression "to be of the same mind" (τὸ αὐτὸ φρονεῖν) finds its exact parallel in 2:2 (τὸ αὐτὸ φρονῆτε), where harmony among members of the assembly itself is in view. That Paul interpreted at least certain types of disorder in his assemblies as a threat to his dominance is clear from 1 Corinthians 1–4. Given their names, it is possible that Euodia and Syntyche were slaves or freedwomen (*NewDocs*, 4:178–79, citing *IG* 5.2.277 and *CIJ* 1.1391).

6   Lightfoot reads μετὰ καὶ Κλήμεντος κτλ with "true comrade." On this reading, Paul urges his comrade along with Clement and his other co-workers to help with the reconciliation of Euodia and Syntyche.

7   Cf. Tryphaena and Tryphosa in Rom 16:12a, who seem to have been a missionary team ("workers in the Lord").

8   Origen (*In Ioann.* 1.29) identifies this Clement with Clement of Rome, the author of *1 Clement* and an early bishop of Rome.

9   Much as he does the slave name "Onesimus" in Phlm 11.

10   It has also been suggested that Paul is here referring to his wife (see the text note a above). It is likely, however, that Paul is referring to another teacher (Joachim Jeremias, "Paarweise Sendung im Neuen Testament," in *New Testament Essays: Studies in Memory of Thomas Walter Manson 1893-1958*, ed. A. J. B. Higgins [Manchester: Manchester University Press, 1959] 136–43, reprinted in idem, *Abba: Studien zur neutestamentlichen Theologie und Zeitgeschichte* [Göttingen: Vandenhoeck & Ruprecht, 1966] 132–39, notes that in contemporary Judaism two teachers made a "yoke").

11   A similar progression can be found in the peroration of Gal 5:25–6:10. The peroration in 1 Thess 5:12-22 is structured differently, with short staccato maxims coming at the end. In both cases Paul strives for variety and a sense of closure.

3:1 Paul further emphasizes the letter's principal piece of advice developed at length in 3:1—4:1, while the addition of "at all times" has the effect of turning that advice into a general maxim: like the Stoic sage, though for different reasons, the Christ-believer was to maintain a joyful disposition "at all times."[12] Judging from 3:1b Paul had offered this advice to the Philippians before. In 4:4b he explicitly repeats himself: "I will say it again [πάλιν ἐρῶ]: rejoice!"

■ **4:5** The second consolatory exhortation looks to the promise of vindication in the near future as grounds for maintaining a "gracious spirit" now.[13] It reiterates the exhortation to harmony in 2:3-4. The consolation lies in the second clause (4:5b), which conveys a common apocalyptic motivation: "the Lord is at hand [ἐγγύς]."[14] The nearness of the end promises that any self-sacrifice will be brief.[15]

■ **4:6-7** The consolation of the third exhortation is explicit: "Be anxious for nothing. . . ." Ancient consolers often spoke of grief in terms of anxiety.[16] The solution to anxiety that Paul recommends is prayer to God: "with all[17] prayer and petition [τῇ προσευχῇ καὶ τῇ δεήσει], with

thanksgiving, let your requests be known to God" (4:6b). Aesop offers similar advice in *Fab.* 288: "Pray to God [εὔχου τῷ θεῷ] and do not grieve."[18] Paul specifies that prayer be offered "with thanksgiving" (μετὰ εὐχαριστίας). Continued gratitude to the gods for life and its various goods was a common theme in ancient consolation.[19] Chrysostom comments, "Here is another consolation, a medicine that heals grief and hardship and all that is painful. And what is it? To pray, to offer thanks in all things."[20] Paul promises that the result of prayer will be a divine tranquillity: "the peace of God . . . will guard your hearts and minds in Christ Jesus" (4:7).[21] He adds the further comforting thought that God's peace is always greater than one might reasonably expect: "that defies [ὑπερέχουσα; lit., "surpasses"] all understanding."[22]

■ **4:8-9** The final exhortation in 4:8-9 is the most developed of the four and forms a neat conclusion to the peroration of 4:2-9 (cf. 2 Cor 13:11). The exhortation proper (4:8-9a) is in two parts, both of which are lists. The first ends "think on these things" (ταῦτα λογίζεσθε; 4:8), and the second "practice these things" (ταῦτα πράσσετε;

---

12   Paul elsewhere adds a kind of universalizing sentiment to his concluding maxims (esp. 1 Thess 5:16-22; cf. Col 4:6). For "joy" as the characteristic disposition (εὐπάθεια; "good emotion") of the Stoic sage, see the introduction part 1a.

13   The Greek τὸ ἐπιεικές is a neuter adjective serving as a noun. The noun ἐπιείκεια was sometimes used for political clemency (cf. 2 Cor 10:1; Donald Dale Walker, *Paul's Offer of Leniency [2 Cor 10:1]* [WUNT 152; Tübingen: Mohr Siebeck, 2002]).

14   That the eschaton was soon to arrive was a traditional piece of apocalyptic consolation. It is evident in virtually every instance of *vaticinium ex eventu*, which places events current with the actual audience just before the end. In Paul, see 1 Thess 5:1-11.

15   That suffering is typically brief was a familiar Epicurean consolation (e.g., *Sent. Vat.* 4).

16   Seneca, *Ad Helv.* 17.5; 18.5, 9; *Ad Marc.* 24.4; *De tran. an.* 7.3; 16.1; Plutarch, *De tran. an.* 477e; Cassius Dio, *Hist.* 38.20.1; Pseudo-Plutarch, *Ad Apoll.* 109e; Cyprian, *De mort.*

17   The force of "all" (παντί) is not clear. It could mean all types of prayer. More likely it means praying "always" on analogy with 1 Thess 4:17: "Pray unceasingly" (ἀδιαλείπτως προσεύχεσθε).

18   Ed. Hausrath; cf. Plutarch, *Cor.* 35.2 (230e).

19   Johann, *Trauer und Trost*, 85–92. Texts include Epicurus, *Sent. Vat.* 55; Lucretius, *De re. nat.* 3.957

(Cyrus Bailey, *Lucretius on Nature of Things* [Oxford: Oxford University Press, 1910], commenting on this text also cites Epicurus, *Sent. Vat.* 14; fr. 490 Usener, Democritus, frag. B 202 Diels and Kranz, and Lucretius, *De re. nat.* 3.1082–83); Cicero, *De fin.* 1.57, 62; Seneca, *Ad Marc.* 10.2; 12.1–2; *Ad Poly.* 3.1; 10.2; *Ep.* 99.4; Plutarch, *Ad ux.* 610e–611b; Marcus Aurelius, *Med.* 2.2–3; Fronto, *De nep. am.* 2.2.

20   Hom. 15.284.16-18 Allen; cf. idem, *Ep. ad Olymp.* 7.3.4–5 (Malingrey). See further Gesa Schenke, "Die Trauer um ein kleines Mädchen: Eine Bitte um Trost," *ZPE* 127 (1999) 117–22.

21   Paul's language here recalls the topos *de tranquilitate animi*; cf. Col 3:15 ("peace of Christ"). "Peace" is also a common theme in Paul's letter conclusions (Rom 15:33; 16:20; 2 Cor 13:11; 1 Thess 5:23; cf. Gal 6:16). The expression "will guard your hearts and minds" likely means "protect you from becoming discouraged and falling away" (cf. 1 Thess 5:23: "May the God of peace himself make you completely holy, and may your whole spirit, soul, and body be kept [τηρηθείη] blameless, etc."; 1 Pet 1:5). Bockmuehl sees in the verb "guard" (φρουρέω) a possible allusion to a military garrison at Philippi guarding the famous *Pax Romana*.

22   Cf. *1 Enoch* 82:2 ("this wisdom that surpasses their thought") and comments by Nickelsburg, *1 Enoch 1*, on this passage.

4:9a). These lists are attempts at rhetorical amplification and as always should not be overinterpreted. The motive clause in 4:9b—"and the God of peace will be with you"—again promises tranquillity and indicates that consolation is still in view.

The first list (v. 8) contains a series of positive thoughts that Paul urges the Philippians to "think on": "whatever things are true, whatever noble . . . if there is any virtue [ἀρετή], and so on."[23] This is the second time in the letter that Paul deploys Epicurus's famous *avocatio*, or consolation by distraction. In 1:3-4 Paul used the *avocatio* in its traditional form of distraction by pleasant memories: "I give thanks to my God for every remembrance of you . . . with joy over your partnership in the gospel from the first day until now." Here in 4:8 Paul adopts a modified version of the technique developed, it would seem, by Cicero, who recommended not the recollection of pleasure but the disciplined contemplation of virtue.[24] It is noteworthy that Phil 4:8 contains the only occurrence of "virtue" (ἀρετή) in Paul's surviving letter corpus.[25]

For Cicero the only goods worthy of contemplation are the goods of virtue. He therefore proposed a modified technique based not on the recollection of pleasure but on the contemplation of virtue: "But if, Epicurus, you call me back [*revocas*] to these goods [= the virtues], I obey" (*Tusc.* 3.17.37).

Seneca deploys Cicero's modified technique twice, in *Ad Poly.* 18.7-8 and *Ad Marc.* 24.1-4. Jerome makes similar use of it in *Ep.* 60.7.3. Remarkably, Paul deploys precisely this modified version in Phil 4:8-9 and in language that smacks of contemporary values: "whatever things are *true*, whatever *noble*, whatever *just* . . . if there is any *virtue*, and if there is *anything deserving of praise*, think on these things [ταῦτα λογίζεσθε] . . . and the God of peace will be with you." The focus here is not on pleasant memories as was the case in 1:3-4 but on the contemplation of "virtue" and its associated goods.[28] Paul promises the Philippians that they will find "peace" (εἰρήνη) in their current distress, if they direct their minds (ταῦτα λογίζεσθε; cf. Cicero's *bona cogitare*) to whatever is virtuous and good in their current situation.[29]

Excursus: Epicurean Consolation (as modified by Cicero)

Cicero accepted in principle Epicurus's technique of consolation through distraction.[26] However, he rejected Epicurus's focus on pleasure:[27]

> You bid me to reflect on good things [*bona cogitare*] and to forget evil things. There would be something in what you say and something worthy of a great philosopher, were you mindful that those things are good that are most worthy of a human being. . . . But you are turning my thoughts towards pleasures.

The second list (4:9a) is a series of four verbs denoting the various ways the Philippians have received instruction from Paul: "the things you have learned and received and heard and seen in me." It repeats the cadence of v. 8 and is another instance of amplification that should not be overinterpreted. The last two verbs ("heard and seen") carry forward the theme of imitating Paul from 3:17 (cf. 1:30; 2:18), while the imperative πράσσετε ("practice") suggests a way of life and forms a neat complement to λογίζεσθε ("think on") in v. 8. The motive clause in 4:9b repeats with slight variation the motive clause in the third exhortation—"the peace of God [ἡ εἰρήνη τοῦ θεοῦ; 4:7] . . . the God of peace [ὁ θεὸς τῆς εἰρήνης; 4:9b]"[30]—and is the peroration's final rhetorical flourish.

23   Cf. Müller. For a similar *Tugendkatalog* or "list of virtues," see Cicero, *Tusc.* 5.23.67; Plutarch, *De tran. an.* 468f–469d.

24   Jerome (*PL* 30:891.18) summarizes: *haec tantummodo cogitate* ("reflect on these things only").

25   Paul typically avoids such common "pagan" moral terms (e.g., φίλος, "friend"). That he includes "virtue" in his list here would seem to indicate that he is drawing on a somewhat fixed topos; cf. Seneca, *Ad Marc.* 24.3 (*virtus*); Pseudo-Phalaris, *Ep.* 103.1–2 (ἀρετή); Jerome, *Ep.* 60.7.3 (*virtus*). Cf. 2 Pet 1:5.

26   For an account of Epicurus's method, see part 1 of the introduction and the excursus at 1:3.

27   Cicero, *Tusc.* 3.16.35–3.17.37.

28   The verb λογίζομαι can mean "calculate" or "reckon," but here it means "think about" or "let your mind dwell upon" (BDAG, s.v. λογίζομαι 2). Chrysostom (hom. 15.290.16-17 Allen) paraphrases: "busy yourself with these things, be anxious for them, contemplate them"; cf. *Ep. ad Olymp.* 1.1.9; 7.5.33–34 (Malingrey); similarly, Seneca, *Ep.* 99.4.

29   I discuss this more fully in "*Bona Cogitare*"; now see also von Gemünden, "Freude," 250–51.

30   Cf. Rom 15:33; 16:20; 1 Cor 14:33; 2 Cor 13:11 ("God of love and peace"); 1 Thess 5:23; imitated in 2 Thess 3:16: "Lord of peace."

4

10/ I rejoiced in the Lord greatly that now at last you revived your mindfulness[a] of me, though of course[b] you were mindful of me but did not have the opportunity to show it. 11/ Not that I speak out of a sense of lack, for I have learned to be self-sufficient in my circumstances—12/ I know how to be abased and I know how to abound; in any and all circumstances I have found out how to be full and to hunger, how to abound and to suffer lack: 13/ I have the strength to deal with all things in him[c] who empowers me.

14/ Nevertheless you have done well to have partnered so closely with me in my affliction. 15/ You[d] yourselves know as well as I, Philippians, that in the beginning of the gospel, when I came out from Macedonia, no church partnered with me to pay back what they received except you alone, 16/ and that even in Thessalonica you more than once sent to me what I needed.[e] 17/ Not that I am desiring the gift, but I am desiring fruit abounding to your account. 18/ I am in receipt of all that you sent and it is more than enough. Indeed[f], I am completely sated having received from Epaphroditus the items from you: a sweet fragrance, an acceptable sacrifice, [an offering] pleasing to God. 19/ And my God will satisfy[g] your every need according to his riches in glory in Christ Jesus. 20/ To our God and Father be glory forever and ever! Amen!

a F and G read the gentive τοῦ with the infinitive φρονεῖν instead of the accusative τό, an apparent case of parablepsis by a scribe directly copying a manuscript written in *scriptio continua* and repeating the initial upsilon of the following ὑπέρ. The genitive articular infinitive would soften Paul's implicit criticism of the Philippians: "you have at last been revived *so as to be able* to think of me again."

b The expression here (ἐφ᾽ ᾧ) is difficult, but the logic of the text is simple enough. Paul has essentially accused the Philippians of having forgotten him and he now wishes to soften that rebuke with a modest self-correction: he did not mean that they had stopped caring about him but only that they did not have the opportunity to show it. For the difficulties surrounding the expression, see Fitzmyer, "Ἐφ᾽ Ὧ," and my comments above at 3:12. In addition to here and in 3:12, Paul uses the expression in 2 Cor 5:4 and most famously in Rom 5:12.

c A number of witnesses (ℵ² D² [F G] K L P Ψ 075, 81, 104, 365, 630, 1175, 1241, 1505, 1881, 2464 Maj sy; Hier) add Χριστῷ to read "Christ who strengthens me." This is possibly a scribal emendation to reflect 1 Tim 1:12.

d A few witnesses (p⁴⁶ D* 1505 vgᵐˢ syʰ) omit δέ as redundant before καί.

e The text printed by Nestle-Aland (following ℵ B F G K Ψ 33, 365, 1505, 1739, 1881 Maj lat) reads εἰς τὴν χρείαν μοι ἐπέμψατε (lit., "sent to me for [my] need"). A significant number of witnesses (p⁴⁶ A 81, 104, 326, 1175, 1241, 2464) omit εἰς ("for" in the literal translation in the preceding sentence). This would involve understanding χρείαν to mean "what is needful" (BDAG, s.v. χρεία 3) versus "need" (BDAG, s.v. χρεία 2) and would yield a literal translation like "sent to me what was needful." Other witnesses (D¹ L P 323, 614, 629, 630 gᵗˣᵗ; [Ambst]) change the dative μοι to the genitive μου ("my need"). A few witnesses (D* 075 [ar gᵛ·ˡ·]) change to the genitive and omit εἰς.

f 𝔓⁴⁶ 2495 vgᵐˢ add δέ to avoid asyndeton. Here, however, asyndeton lends weight to Paul's words (BDF §462) as the sense of the passage would seem to require.

g A number of witnesses (D* F G Ψ 075, 6, 33, 81, 104, 326, 365, 1175, 1241, 1505, 1739, 1881 latt) read the optative πληρώσαι ("*may* my God supply").

Analysis

It was customary in Greek and Roman antiquity for the recipient of goods carried by a third party to acknowledge receipt of those goods. The principal purpose of such an acknowledgment was not to express the recipient's gratitude—although that too was expected—but to assure the sender that the goods indicated had been delivered. Paul follows this practice in Philippians, appending to his letter a note, possibly in his own hand,[1] acknowledging the Philippians gift: ἀπέχω πάντα, "I am in receipt of all that you sent" (4:18).[2]

Paul's acknowledgment of the Philippians' gift is complicated, however, by the fact that it is postscripted to a much longer letter of consolation in which Paul's principal argument has been that his present hardship is really a matter of indifference, an argument that makes duly acknowledging the Philippians' gift a rhetorical challenge. On the one hand, if Paul's suffering does not really matter, as he has repeatedly insisted, then the Philippians' attempt to alleviate that suffering would appear not to matter either. On the other hand, if the Philippians' gift provided needed relief, then Paul's suffering must be more significant that his argument has allowed. Paul is faced with a dilemma of his own making. Paul's solution to this problem is ingenious if not altogether successful: Paul himself did not need the gift, but it was pleasing to God and will add to the Philippians' "account." Paul has already made several appreciative references to the gift (1:6, 8; 2:25-30).

Formally, 4:10-20 consists of two expressions of thanks (vv. 10-13 and vv. 14-17), each of which contains a substantial self-correction (vv. 11-13 and 17 respectively). These are followed in v. 18 with a formal acknowledg-

ment of the gift, which is now reimagined as "a sweet fragrance, an acceptable sacrifice, [an offering] pleasing to God." Paul concludes with a promise that God can and will reward the Philippians' generosity (4:19-20).

Comment

■ **4:10-13** The expression "I rejoiced . . . greatly" (ἐχάρην . . . μεγάλως) can be used to introduce a separate letter.[3] Here it introduces a postscripted note acknowledging the receipt of goods.[4] It carries forward the letter's leitmotif of "joy" and may indicate a pleasant surprise. The Philippians had been slow to send to Paul's aid[5] and Epaphroditus had no doubt conveyed their apologies. Paul responds on two levels. On one level, he acknowledges that delay ("now at last") and graciously excuses it as due to a lack of "opportunity."[6] On another level, however, Paul appears to lodge yet another tactful rebuke (cf. 1:22-26; 2:2, 25-30). For he does not say that now at last the Philippians have sent to his need, but that now at last they have begun to think of him again: "that now at last you have revived your mindfulness of me [ἀνεθάλετε τὸ ὑπὲρ ἐμοῦ φρονεῖν]," a statement that stands in stark contrast to Paul's unwavering "mindfulness" of the Philippians emphatically affirmed at the beginning of his letter: "I give thanks to my God for every remembrance of you, always in every prayer of mine for you all praying with joy . . . and it is only right that I should feel this way about you all [φρονεῖν ὑπὲρ πάντων ὑμῶν] . . . for God is my witness how I long for you all with the deepest affections of Christ!" (1:3-8).[7] The Philippians' grief had even caused them to neglect Paul! Even so Paul is comforted by their current efforts.

1   For the possibility that 4:10-20 is a so-called epistolary autograph, see Gamble, *Textual History*, 94, 145–46; and Jeffrey A. D. Weima, *Neglected Endings: The Significance of Pauline Letter Closings* (JSNTSup 101; Sheffield: JSOT Press, 1994) 123–24, who cites *BGU* 1.183; 2.5.26; 3.910; *P. Giss.* 97; *P. Princ.* 2.71; Cicero, *Att.* 11.24; 12.28; 12.32; see also Gordon J. Bahr, "Subscriptions in the Pauline Letters," *JBL* 87 (1968) 29.

2   BDAG, s.v. ἀπέχω 1.

3   Koskenniemi, *Studien*, 74–76. Similar expressions include ἐχάρην λίαν and ἐχάρην πολλά.

4   Cf. Rom 16:1, where Paul uses a formula often used to introduce a separate letter of recommendation ("I commend to you so and so . . .") in what is clearly a continuation of his letter.

5   Chrysostom, hom. 1.6.7-8; 16.296.25.

6   For the topos "lack of opportunity," see Seneca, *De benef.* 2.32.2; 4.40.3.

7   Cf. Brian J. Capper, "Paul's Dispute with Philippi: Understanding Paul's Argument in Phil 1–2 from his Thanks in 4.10-20," *ThZ* 49 (1993) 193–214.

Paul follows the appreciative comments of 4:10 with an extended self-correction in 4:11-13: "not that [οὐχ ὅτι] . . ." (cf. 3:12; 4:17).[8] His concern is that in thanking the Philippians for their gift[9] he might be seen to compromise his earlier claim that his material circumstances are matters of indifference. Paul insists that what he has just said is not due to a sense of "lack" (ὑστέρησις), for he has learned to be indifferent to his situation (αὐτάρκης, "self-sufficient") whatever it might be (cf. 1:10).[10] He makes the strong claim that he maintains his indifference "in any and all circumstances" (ἐν παντὶ καὶ ἐν πᾶσιν), and he amplifies this claim rhetorically in a series of antitheses: "I know how to be abased and I know how to abound . . . how to be full and how to hunger, how to abound and to suffer lack [ὑστερεῖσθαι]." As elsewhere in the letter Paul's amplification borders on redundancy: "to abound [περισσεύειν] . . . to abound [περισσεύειν]"; "lack [ὑστέρησιν] . . . to suffer lack [ὑστερεῖσθαι]."

Paul's initial claim is that he has "learned" (ἔμαθον) to be self-sufficient. In v. 12, however, he changes the verb to μεμύημαι ("I have found out"), which carries the connotation of religious initiation, in particular of being initiated into the mysteries.[11] Paul's self-sufficiency has been acquired not through practice[12] but by religious insight, and it is sustained by the inner strengthening that the spirit of Christ provides: "I have the strength to deal with all things in him who empowers me" (cf. 1:19).[13]

■ **4:14-17** Paul expresses appreciation for the Philippians' gift a second time in vv. 14-16, followed again by self-correction in v. 17. In v. 10 he spoke of the Philippians "mindfulness" of him. Now he speaks of their active "partnership," both in the present (v. 14) and, by way of further amplification, in the past (vv. 15-16): "you have done well to have partnered with [συγκοινωνήσαντες] me in my affliction . . . in the beginning of the gospel, when I came out from Macedonia, no church partnered [ἐκοινώνησεν] with me . . . except you alone." He commends them for not having been embarrassed by his present "affliction" (i.e., imprisonment; cf. 1:7),[14] and he praises their past support as unprecedented ("you alone"), immediate ("even in Thessalonica"),[15] and generous ("more than once"). This is what he meant in 1:5 when he said he found consolation in the memory of their "partnership [κοινωνίᾳ] in the gospel from the first day until now."

Excursus: The Philippians' "Partnership" with Paul

Paul uses the noun κοινωνία ("partnership," "fellowship") and its cognates six times in Philippians,[16] and nineteen times in his remaining letters.[17] The word-group derives from the adjective κοινός and in each of its forms carries the notion of two or more parties holding something in "common." It can be used of friendship: friends were defined as those

8   See my comments on 3:12 above.
9   Strictly speaking, Paul does not in v. 10 actually thank the Philippians for their gift but "rejoices" in their renewed "mindfulness" of him.
10 Audrey N. M. Rich, "The Cynic Conception of αὐτάρκεια," *Mnemosyne* 9 (1956) 23–29; but now esp. Daniele Pevarello, "Paul and the Philosophical Concept of Self-Sufficiency," in *Paul's Graeco-Roman Context*, ed. Cilliers Breytenbach (BEThL 277; Leuven: Peeters, 2015) 501–23.
11 E.g., BDAG, s.v. μνέω.
12 Contrast Cynic and Stoic ἄσκησις ("exercise"); cf. Gnilka. More generally, Sevenster, *Paul and Seneca*; B. L. Hijmans, ἈΣΚΗΣΙΣ: *Notes on Epictetus' Educational System* (Assen: Van Gorcum, 1959).
13 For the spirit of Christ strengthening Paul in his ordeal, see Phil 1:19: "through your prayers and the supply of the spirit of Jesus Christ [τοῦ πνεύματος Ἰησοῦ Χριστοῦ]." Cf. 1:6; 2:12.
14 Shaming was a common feature in the Roman penal system: "do not be ashamed [ἐπαισχυνθῇς] . . . of me the prisoner" (2 Tim 1:8). See Chrysostom's remarks here as well as in 1:19 (hom. 4.60.18-19; 16.302.13 Allen), for which see also my comments on that passage (cf. 1 Pet 4:16; 2 Tim 4:16).
15 According to Acts 16:11–17:9, Paul's mission to Thessalonica came right after his mission to Philippi; cf. 1 Thess 2:2.
16 Κοινωνία: 1:5; 2:1; 3:10; κοινωνέω: 4:15; συγκοινωνέω: 4:14; συγκοινωνός: 1:7.
17 Κοινωνία: Rom 15:26; 1 Cor 1:9; 10:16 (twice); 2 Cor 6:14; 8:4; 9:13; 13:13; Gal 2:9; κοινωνέω: Rom 12:13; 15:27; Gal 6:6; κοινωνός: 1 Cor 10:18, 20; 2 Cor 1:7; 8:23; Phlm 17; συγκοινωνός: Rom 11:17; 1 Cor 9:23. For a recent detailed analysis, see Ogereau, *Paul's Koinonia*.

who hold things in common.[18] It can also be used of a formal partnership: partners share a common project and typically a set of common resources.[19] In early Christianity the word group also came to denote the camaraderie Christ-believers had with one another and with Christ, a camaraderie especially prominent in Pauline circles, where each believer was thought to be possessed by Christ.[20] The challenge to interpreting Paul's κοινωνία language in Philippians is that it draws upon each of the above domains: Paul writes to console and thus as a friend;[21] he writes to thank the Philippians for their financial support and thus as a partner; and he writes as a Christ-mystic anxious to restore their sense of camaraderie with Christ and with each other.

Central to the interpretation of Paul's κοινωνία language in Philippians is 4:15: "in the beginning of the gospel, when I came out from Macedonia, no church partnered [ἐκοινώνησεν] with me εἰς λόγον δόσεως καὶ λήμψεως except you alone."[22] The phrase I have left untranslated, εἰς λόγον δόσεως καὶ λήμψεως, is Paul's attempt[23] to render in Greek the Latin expression *ratio dati et accepti*, which will have been familiar to the Philippians as members of a Roman *colonia*.[24] The meaning of the expression is relatively clear: "an account or ledger of monies, goods, and services given and received." What the expression refers to in Philippians is another matter.[25]

It has been suggested that Paul is here referring to an account maintained by the Philippians into which they collected funds to be released to him as he conducted his mission, and that they paid out in coin what Paul returned in kind through his missionary efforts.[26] This interpretation has two components: (1) that the Philippians funded an account from which to support Paul's mission, and (2) that Paul was as it were under contract with the Philippians. The first component is quite plausible. It resembles the advice Paul gave the Galatians and the Corinthians for collecting monies for the gift to Jerusalem in 1 Cor 16:1-2. The second component, however—that Paul was under contract with the Philippians and needed to keep up his end of the bargain—is less certain. A slightly different reading, and one that I favor, is that Paul had *already* done his part when he initially evangelized the Philippians and that they were now (by way of repayment) supporting him in his work, with the additional hope that this would result not only in the "progress of the gospel" (1:12) but in "fruit" accruing to their own "account" (Phil 4:17). This way of construing the Philippians' partnership with Paul fits neatly with Paul's earlier reference to material support in 1 Cor 9:11: "for if we have sown spiritual things among you is it too much if we reap material things?"[27] It also reflects the logic and to a degree the language of Rom 15:27: "For if the gentiles have shared [ἐκοινώνησαν] in their [= the Jews'] spiritual things, then they [the gentiles] ought to minister [λειτουργῆσαι] to them [the Jews] in material things" (Rom 15:27).[28] On this reading, Paul's κοινωνία with the Philippians was an arrangement that left the Philippians invested in Paul's mission but did not place Paul under continued contractual obligation. It is difficult to convey this in a word-for-word translation of 4:15, so I have adopted the following, more dynamic translation: "no church partnered with me to pay back what they received except you alone."

In v. 17 Paul again qualifies his expression of appreciation with a self-correction: "not that [οὐχ ὅτι] I seek a

---

18 Thus the cliché κοινὰ τὰ φίλων ("common are the possessions of friends"), for which see Plato, *Lys.* 207c; Cicero, *De off.* 151; Diogenes Laertius, *Vit.* 8.10; cf. Acts 4:32.

19 Ogereau, *Paul's Koinonia*; J. Paul Sampley, *Pauline Partnership in Christ: Christian Community and Commitment in Light of Roman Law* (Philadelphia: Fortress, 1980).

20 For the word group's range of meaning see the various entries in BDAG, s.vv.

21 E.g., Euripides, *Alc.* 369–70; *Iph. Aul.* 408; cf. Rom 12:15.

22 Paul uses financial terms throughout 4:14-17, for which see Betz, *Studies*, 124–30, and Ogereau, *Paul's Koinonia*.

23 I say "Paul's attempt" because the expression does not occur elsewhere in Greek, though its component parts do.

24 E.g., Cicero, *De amic.* 15.58 (*NW*). Discussed by Ogereau, *Paul's Koinonia*, 270–89.

25 Cf. Ogereau, *Paul's Koinonia*, 104: "whether, in the context of Philippians 4:10-20, it is best taken figuratively as an expression evoking gift-exchange within the context of friendship or social reciprocity, or whether it should be understood, in a more literal sense, as referring to a financial account that Paul and the Philippians kept in common."

26 Ogereau, *Paul's Koinonia*; cf. Betz, *Studies*, 124–30.

27 Thus Chrysostom, hom 16.304.2-6.

28 For the Philippians' gift to Paul as λειτουργία, see Phil 2:17, 30; cf. 2:25, where Epaphroditus is called their λειτουργός.

gift" (cf. 4:11). It is not the material "gift," or δόμα, as such that Paul desires, but the "fruit" (καρπός) that will be credited to the Philippians' "account" (λόγος).[29] The reference is presumably to the last judgment. Paul uses similar language in 1:11: "that you might be pure and blameless for the Day of Christ, having been filled with the fruit [καρπόν] of righteousness" (cf. 1:22).

■ **4:18** With the expression ἀπέχω πάντα, "I am in receipt of all that you sent," Paul formally acknowledges the Philippians' gift. He underscores the adequacy of the gift: "it is more than enough . . . I am completely sated." He mentions Epaphroditus by name and thus further commends him for fulfilling his mission. In keeping with his indiffer-

ence to the material goods themselves, Paul describes the Philippians' gift not in economic but in religious terms: "a sweet fragrance, an acceptable sacrifice, [an offering] pleasing to God."

■ **4:19-20** Paul assures the Philippians that God has accepted their sacrifice and will begin to show them favor even now. God's resources are more than sufficient: "according to his riches in glory."[30] Paul concludes with a short doxology that not only neatly continues the theme of "glory" from v. 19 but as it were pours out on the Philippians' "acceptable sacrifice" his libation of praise: "To our God and Father be glory forever and ever (cf. 2:17-18).

---

29 Paul does not necessarily mix metaphors here, since καρπός can mean "profit"; but this is not his normal usage (e.g., 1:11).

30 It is sometimes argued that, since Paul is in prison and cannot keep up his end of his alleged "contract" with the Philippians, God is paying Paul's part. But this makes no sense at this point in the letter, since according to 1:12 the gospel is still progressing and so Paul has in fact kept up his end of any assumed bargain.

4

21/ Greet every saint in Christ Jesus. The brothers[a] who are with me greet you. 22/ All the
saints greet you, especially those of the
household of Caesar. 23/ May the grace of
the Lord Jesus Christ be with your spirit.[b]
[Amen.][c]

a   Paul writes "brothers" (ἀδελφοί) even though his letter
is intended for both the women and the men in the
Philippian assembly, as 4:2 ("I urge Euodia and I urge
Syntyche") makes clear.

b   Several witnesses (ℵ² K L Ψ 630, 1505, 2464 Maj sy)
replace τοῦ πνεύματος ("spirit") with παντῶν ("all") so
as to read "with you all."

c   A number of important authorities (p⁴⁶ ℵ A D K L P
Ψ 33, 81, 104, 365, 630, 1175, 1241, 1505, 1739ᶜ, 2464
Maj lat sy bo) add ἀμήν ("Amen").

Analysis

Paul typically concludes his letters with mixture of exhortation,[1] greetings, and prayer. In Philippians he confines
exhortation to the peroration of 4:2-9 and–following the
postscripted note of 4:10-20–concludes with only three
short greetings (4:21-22) and a prayer (4:23). The mention of the so-called *domus* or *familia Caesaris* is striking
and was no doubt included to further encourage the
Philippians that the gospel was indeed progressing. The
final prayer is formulaic and appears with slight variation in each of Paul's authentic letters. In each instance
the meaning is the same: that God would provide for the
continued transformation of Christ-believers.

Comment

■ **4:21-22** Paul concludes his letter to the Philippians with
three greetings. His own greeting is conveyed by means
of an imperative urging those present at the reading of
his letter to greet one another and the rest of the assembly for him: "Greet every saint in Christ."[2] He then conveys greetings from the members of his missionary team
present in Rome: "the brothers who are with me greet
you" (cf. Rom 16:21-23; 1 Cor 16:9b; Phlm 23).[3] Finally,
he conveys the greetings of "all the saints"–by which he
presumably means the members of the various Roman
assemblies–"especially those of the household of Caesar
[οἱ ἐκ τῆς Καίσαρος οἰκίας]" (cf. Rom 16:16; 1 Cor 16:19a;
2 Cor 13:12b).

The expression οἱ ἐκ τῆς Καίσαρος οἰκίας calls for comment. A relatively minor problem is the meaning of οἰκία,
which can refer either to a physical dwelling ("house") or,
by extension, to the people who live there ("household").[4]
Here it almost certainly means "household": "those of
[ἐκ = "out of," i.e., "counted among"] the household of
Caesar." A more difficult problem is whether Paul means
by the expression members of Nero's family or members of the imperial bureaucracy. The expression most
naturally refers to members of Nero's family,[5] though
by Roman standards "family" (*familia*, *domus*) included
dependent kin of any degree of relationship as well as

---

1   E.g., 1 Thess 5:25: "pray for us!"
2   Cf. 1 Thess 5:26; 1 Cor 16:20; 2 Cor 13:12; Rom
16:3-16 (sixteen times!). The only first person greeting in Paul's letters is Rom 16:22 and is by Tertius
the amanuensis. The reference to Christ-believers as
"saints" is characteristic of Paul's letter prescripts (cf.
1:1) and final greetings. For the expression, see my
comments on 1:1.
3   The mention of this group is surprising since Paul
appears to dismiss them in 2:19-21: "I hope in the
Lord Jesus to send Timothy . . . for I have no one so
like myself . . . for all seek their own things, not the
things of Christ."

4   BDAG, s.v. οἰκία. That the two meanings were
not always clearly delineated can be seen from
Matt 10:12: "and entering into the house [οἰκίαν
= dwelling], greet it [αὐτήν = those who live in the
house]."
5   F. C. Baur considered its use here in 4:22 an anach-
ronism and for that and other reasons famously concluded that Philippians was a later forgery not unlike
Ephesians (*Paul, the Apostle of Christ, His Life and
Work, His Epistles and His Doctrine* [2 vols.; London:
Williams & Northgate, 1875–76] 2:59–60).

household slaves and various retainers, which in the case of a Roman emperor would have been a very large group. That at least some of these had been attracted to Judaism and through it to Christ-belief is entirely possible. But it was also the case that emperors used various slaves and freedmen to staff their bureaucracies, especially in Rome.[6] Nero's predecessor, Claudius, was infamous for this. Lightfoot therefore argued that the expression referred more broadly to members of the imperial service and that perhaps even some of those with servile names listed in Romans 16 (e.g., Ampliatus, Hermes, Nereus, Persis) were members of this service.[7] This too is possible, but it is unclear whether "household of Caesar" (Lat. *familia Caesaris*) had become a technical expression by Paul's day and so its reference here must remain uncertain.[8] Whichever the case, whether members of Nero's extensive *domus* or members of the imperial service, Paul includes a greeting from "those of the household of Caesar" as further evidence of the progress of the gospel at Rome (cf. 1:13).

■ **4:23** Each of Paul's authentic letters concludes with the following formulaic prayer, sometimes called the grace benediction: "The grace of [the/our] Lord Jesus [Christ] be with you[r spirit]."[9] In terms of consistency of expression it compares with the greeting formula found in each of Paul's letter prescripts: "Grace to you and peace [from God our father and the Lord Jesus Christ]."[10] It is doubtful whether the addition of "spirit" here (also in Gal 6:18 and Phlm 25) changes the prayer's meaning. The point is the same: that the grace of Christ is present realistically in his spirit and is actively transforming Christ-believers. This is a leitmotif of Paul's theology, and it is revealing that it is with this prayer that he ends each of his letters.[11]

---

6   Here see esp. Weaver, *Familia Caesaris*; and, more generally, Leonhard Schumacher, *Sklaverei in der Antike: Alltag und Schicksal der Unfreien* (Munich: Beck, 2001) esp. 265–75; Henrik Mouritsen, *The Freedman in the Roman World* (Cambridge: Cambridge University Press, 2011).

7   Lightfoot, pp. 171–78. Cf. Lampe, *From Paul to Valentinus*, 170–83.

8   Standhartinger, "Letter," 129–30 n. 90. For *liberti Augusti* at Philippi, see *AÉ* 1935 (1936) 46 (= *BCH* 58 [1934] 449–53); cf. Pilhofer, *Philippi*, 2:282; Bormann, *Philippi*, 198–99; Collart, *Philippes*, 314 n. 1. The likelihood that the terminology was not yet fixed in Paul's day is suggested by the fact that, as already noted, it was Nero's immediate successor Claudius who first made extensive use of imperial freedmen in his administration.

9   In addition to here, see Rom 16:20; 1 Cor 16:23; 2 Cor 13:13; Gal 6:18; 1 Thess 5:28; and Phlm 25. 2 Corinthians 13:13 is unique in that it adds "and the love of God and the fellowship of the Holy Spirit" to "the grace of the Lord Jesus Christ."

10   Only 1 Thessalonians omits "from God our father and the Lord Jesus Christ."

11   The "grace of the Lord Jesus Christ" is presumably "the spirit of Jesus Christ" possessing and transforming the believer (cf. Phil 1:19). For the Spirit as the "love of God poured out in our hearts," see Rom 5:5.

The following is a selective list of critical or otherwise historically significant commentaries and studies.

1. Selected Critical and Historically Significant Commentaries

a. Patristic

Ambrosiaster
In Epistolam ad Philippenses, PL 17:425–44; CSEL 81.3:127–63; ET: Gerald Bray, trans. and ed., *Commentaries on Galatians–Philemon. Ambrosiaster* (Ancient Christian Texts; Downers Grove, IL: IVP Academic, 2009).

Jerome
Commentarii in Epistolam Philippenses, PL 30:879–92.

John Chrysostom
In Epistolam ad Philippenses, PG 62:177–298. Frederick Field, ed., *Ioannis Chrysostomi Interpretatio omnium Epistolarum Paulinarum* (7 vols.; Oxford: Parker, 1859–62) 5:1–171, 499–530 (notes). ET: Pauline Allen, *John Chrysostom, Homilies on Paul's Letter to the Philippians* (SBLWGRW 36; Atlanta: Society of Biblical Literature, 2013).

Marius Victorinus
In Epistolam Pauli ad Philippenses, CSEL 83.2:174–229.

Pseudo-Oecumenius
Commentarius in Epistolam ad Philippenses, PG 118:1259–1326.

Pelagius
Expositio in Philippenses, in Alexander Souter, *Pelagius's Expositions of Thirteen Epistles of St. Paul* (2 vols.; Texts and Studies 9; Cambridge: Cambridge University Press, 1922–26) 2:387–416.

Theodore of Mopsuestia
In Epistolam B. Pauli ad Philippenses, in H. B. Swete, *Theodori Episcopi Mopsuesteni in Epistolas B. Pauli Commentarii: The Latin Version with Greek Fragments* (2 vols.; Cambridge: Cambridge University Press, 1880) 1:197–252. ET: Rowan A. Greer, *Theodore of Mopsuestia: The Commentaries on the Minor Epistles of Paul* (SBLWGRW 26; Atlanta: Society of Biblical Literature, 2010) 290–361.

Theodoret
In Epistolam ad Philippenses, PG 82:557–590. See Charles Marriott, ed., *Theodoreti Episcopi Cyri Commentarius in omnes B. Pauli Epistolas,* completed by Philip E. Pusey (2 vols.; Oxford: Parker, 1870) 2:45–67. ET: Robert C. Hill, *Theodoret of Cyrus: Commentary on the Letters of St. Paul* (2 vols.; Brookline, MA: Holy Cross Orthodox Press, 2001) 2:64–83.

b. Medieval

Hugo of St. Victor
Quaestiones in Epistolam ad Philippenses, PL 175:575–80.

Peter Lombard
Collectanea in Epistolam ad Philippenses, PL 192:221–58.

Photius
Fragments in Karl Staab, *Pauluskommentare aus der greichischen Kirche* (Munster: Aschendorff, 1984) 621–30.

Rhabanus Marus
Expositio in Epistolam ad Philippenses, PL 112:477–508.

Theophylact
Commentarius in Epistolam ad Philippenses, PG 124:1139–1204.

Thomas Aquinas
Commentaria in omnes D. Pauli Apostoli Epistolas (Paris: Larouse, 1874) 2:318–55; ET: Fabian R. Larcher and Michael Duffy, trans., *Commentary on St. Paul's First Letter to the Thessalonians and the Letter to the Philippians* (Aquinas Scripture Series 3; Albany: Magi Books, 1969).

c. Renaissance and Reformation

Calvin, John
Commentarius in Epistolam ad Philippenses, Corpus Reformatorum, *Joannis Calvini opera quae supersunt omnia,* 52:5–76; ET: *The Epistles of Paul the Apostle to the Galatians, Ephesians, Philippians, and Colossians* (Edinburgh: Oliver & Boyd, 1965) 225–95.

Erasmus, Desiderius
Adnotationes in Epistolam Pauli ad Philippenses, in *Opera Omnia* (Basel: Froben, 1518) 6:861–80; facsimile reprint, Anne Reeve, ed., *Erasmus' Annotations on the New Testament: Galatians to the Apocalypse* (Leiden: Brill, 1993) 619–32.

Idem
Paraphrases in Epistolam Pauli ad Philippenses, in *Opera Omnia* (Basel: Froben, 1518) 7:991–1004.

Lapide, Cornelius a
Commentaria in Sacram Scripturam (Antwerp: Verdussen, 1614) 461–506.

Melanchthon, Philip
Argumentum Epistolae Pauli ad Philippenses, Corpus Reformatorum, *Philippi Melanchthonis opera quae supersunt omnia,* 15:1283–94.

Zwingli, Ulrich
In Epistolam ad Philippenses Annotationes, in *Opera H. Zwinglii* (Zurich: Schulthess, 1838) 6.2:209–19.

d. Eighteenth Century

Bengel, Johann Albrecht
Gnomon Novi Testamenti (1742; 3rd ed.; Stuttgart: J. F. Steinkopf, 1855). ET: 5 vols.; Edinburgh: T&T Clark, 1858.

Grotius, Hugo
Annotationes in Novum Testamentum, vol. 2: *Annotationes in Acta Apostolorum et Epistolas Apostolicas* (Paris: Pelé, 1646) 599–622.

Wettstein, Johann Jakob
Η ΚΑΙΝΗ ΔΙΑΘΗΚΗ. *Novum Testamentum Graecum* (2 vols.; Amsterdam: Dommer, 1751–52; repr., Graz: Akademische Druck- und Verlagsanstalt, 1962).

e. Nineteenth Century

De Wette, W. M. L.
Kurze Erklärung der Briefe an die Colosser, an Philemon, an die Ephesier und Philipper (Leipzig: Weidmann, 1847).

Lightfoot, Joseph Barber
St. Paul's Epistle to the Philippians: A Revised Text with Introduction, Notes, and Dissertations (London: Macmillan, 1868, rev. 1913).

Lipsius, R. A.
Briefe an die Galater, Römer, Philipper (HThKNT 2.2; Freiburg im Breisgau: Mohr, 1892).

Meyer, H. A. W.
Kritisch-exegetisches Handbuch über die Briefe an die Philipper, Kolosser und an Philemon (KEK 9; Göttingen: Vandenhoeck & Ruprecht, 1859).

Vincent, Marvin R.
A Critical and Exegetical Commentary on the Epistles to the Philippians and to Philemon (ICC; Edinburgh: T&T Clark, 1897).

Weiss, Bernhard
Der Philipper-Brief ausgelegt und die Geschichte seiner Auslegung kritisch dargestellt (3rd ed.; Berlin: Hertz, 1859).

f. Twentieth Century

Barth, Karl
Epistle to the Philippians (Richmond: John Knox, 1962).

Beare, F. W.
A Commentary on the Epistle to the Philippians (3rd ed.; BNTC; London: A. & C. Black, 1973).

Bockmuehl, Marcus
The Epistle to the Philippians (BNTC; London: A. & C. Black; Peabody, MA: Hendrickson, 1998).

Bonnard, Pierre
L'épître de saint Paul aux Philippiens (CNT 10: Neuchâtel: Delachaux et Niestlé, 1950).

Bruce, F. F.
Philippians (NICNT; San Francisco: Harper & Row, 1983).

Collange, Jean-François
The Epistle of Saint Paul to the Philippians (translated from the 1st French edition by A. W. Heathcote; London: Epworth, 1979).

Dibelius, Martin
An die Thessalonicher II: An die Philipper (3rd ed.; HNT 11; Tübingen: Mohr Siebeck, 1937).

Ewald, P.
Der Brief des Paulus an die Philipper (Kommentar zum Neuen Testament 11; Leipzig: Deichert, 1908).

Ewald, P., and G. Wohlenberg
Der Brief des Paulus an die Philipper (4th ed.; Kommentar zum Neuen Testament 11; Leipzig: Deichert, 1923).

Gnilka, Joachim
Der Philipperbrief (3rd ed.; HThKNT 10.3; Freiburg: Herder, 1980).

Hawthorne, Gerald F.
Philippians (WBC 43; Waco, TX: Word, 1983; rev. and expanded by Ralph P. Martin [Nashville: Nelson Reference & Electronic, 2004]).

Hooker, Morna D.
"The Letter to the Philippians," in *The New Interpreter's Bible*, ed. Leander E. Keck (12 vols.; Nashville: Abingdon, 2000) 11:469–549.

Lohmeyer, Ernst
Die Briefe an die Philipper, an die Kolosser und an Philemon (1930; rev. ed.; KEK 9.1; Göttingen: Vandenhoeck & Ruprecht, 1953).

Michaelis, Wilhelm
Der Brief des Paulus an die Philipper (ThHKNT 11; Leipzig: Deichert, 1935).

Müller, Ulrich B.
Der Brief des Paulus an die Philipper (ThHKNT 11.1; Leipzig: Evangelische Verlagsanstalt, 1993).

O'Brien, Peter T.
The Epistle to the Philippians: A Commentary on the Greek Text (NIGTC; Grand Rapids: Eerdmans, 1991).

Pesch, Rudolf
Paulus und seine Lieblingsgemeinde: Paulus—neu gesehen: Drei Briefe an die Heiligen von Philippi (Freiburg: Herder, 1985).

Schenk, Wolfgang
Die Philipperbriefe des Paulus: Kommentar (Stuttgart: Kohlmanner, 1984).

Walter, N., E. Reinmuth, and P. Lampe
Die Briefe an die Philipper, Thessalonicher und an Philemon (NTD 8.2; Göttingen: Vandenhoeck & Ruprecht, 1998).

g. Twenty-First Century

Aletti, Jean-Noël
Saint Paul, Épître aux Philippiens (EB n.s. 55; Paris: Gabalda, 2005).

Focant, Camille
Les lettres aux Philippiens et à Philemon (CNT 11; Paris: Cerf, 2015).

Pitta, Antonio
Lettera ai Filippesi. Nuova versione, introduzione e commento (Milan: Paolini, 2010).

Reumann, John
Philippians: A New Translation with Introduction and Commentary (AYB 33B; New Haven: Yale University Press, 2008).

2. Selected Studies on or Closely Related to Philippians

Abel, Karlhans
Bauformen in Senecas Dialogen: Fünf Strukturanalysen: dial. 6, 11, 12, 1 und 2 (Bibliothek der klassischen Altertumswissenschaften 18; Heidelberg: Winter, 1967).

Aichele, George, and Richard Walsh
"Metamorphosis, Transfiguration and the Body," *BibInt* 19 (2011) 253–75.

Alexander, Loveday
"Hellenistic Letter-Forms and the Structure of Philippians," *JSNT* 37 (1989) 87–101.

Anger, Rudolf
Über den Laodicenerbrief: Eine biblisch-kritische Untersuchung (Leipzig: Gebhardt & Reisland, 1843).

Arband, S., W. Macheiner, and C. Colpe
"Gefangenschaft," *RAC* 9:318–45.

Arnold, Bradley
Christ the Telos of Life: Moral Philosophy, Athletic Imagery and the Aim of Philippians (WUNT 2/371; Tübingen: Mohr Siebeck, 2014).

Arzt, Peter
"The 'Epistolary Introductory Thanksgiving' in the Papyri and in Paul," *NovT* 36 (1994) 29–46.

Ascough, Richard S.
Paul's Macedonian Associations: The Social Context of Philippians and 1 Thessalonians (WUNT 2/161; Tübingen: Mohr Siebeck, 2003).

Ashton, John
The Religion of Paul the Apostle (New Haven/London: Yale University Press, 2000).

Aspan, P. F.
"Toward a New Reading of Paul's Letter to the Philippians in Light of a Kuhnian Analysis of New Testament Criticism" (Ph.D. diss., Vanderbilt University, 1990).

Avery-Peck, Alan J., and Jacob Neusner, eds.
Judaism in Late Antiquity, part 4: *Death, Life-After-Death, Resurrection and the World-to-Come in the Judaisms of Antiquity* (Handbuch der Orientalistik 55; Leiden: Brill, 2000).

Bahr, Gordon J.
"Subscriptions in the Pauline Letters," *JBL* 87 (1968) 27–41.

Baillet, Jules
Inscriptions grecques et latines des tombeaux des rois ou syringes à Thèbes (MIFAO 42; Cairo: L'Institut français d'archéologie orientale du Caire, 1926).

Balz, Horst
"Philipperbrief," *TRE* 26:504–13.

Barclay, John M. G.
"Believers and the Last Judgment in Paul: Rethinking Grace and Recompense," in *Eschatologie – Eschatology: The Sixth Durham-Tübingen Research Symposium. Eschatology in the Old Testament, Ancient Judaism, and Early Christianity (Tübingen, September 2009),* ed. Hans-Joachim Eckstein, Christof Landmesser, and Hermann Lichtenberger, eds. (WUNT 272; Tübingen: Mohr Sibeck, 2011) 195-208.

Idem
"Grace and the Transformation of Agency," in *Redefining First-Century Jewish and Christian Identities: Essays in Honor of Ed Parish Sanders,* ed. Fabian E. Udoh (Notre Dame, IN: University of Notre Dame Press, 2008) 372–89.

Idem
"Believers and the Last Judgment in Paul: Rethinking Grace and Recompense," in Hans-Joachim Eckstein, Christof Landmesser, and Hermann Lichtenberger, eds., *Eschatologie-Eschatology* (WUNT 272; Tübingen: Mohr Siebeck, 2011) 195–208.

Idem
Paul and the Gift (Grand Rapids: Eerdmans, 2015).

Idem
Pauline Churches and Diaspora Jews (WUNT 275; Tübingen: Mohr Siebeck, 2011).

Barclay, John M. G., and Simon J. Gathercole, eds.
Divine and Human Agency in Paul and His Cultural Environment (LNTS; London/New York: T&T Clark, 2006).

Bauer, Karl Ludwig
Rhetoricae Paullinae (2 vols.; Halae: Impensis Orphanotrophei, 1782).

Baumert, Norbert
"'Kein unrechtmäßiger Besitz'—eine Litotes in Phil 2,6," *ZNW* 56 (2012) 113–17.

Beard, Mary, John North, and Simon Price
Religions of Rome (2 vols.; Oxford: Oxford University Press, 1998).

Becker, Jürgen
Paul: Apostle to the Gentiles (Louisville: Westminster John Knox, 1993).

Behm, Johannes
"μορφή," *TDNT* 4 (1968) 742–46.

Beker, J. Christiaan
Paul the Apostle: The Triumph of God in Life and Thought (Philadelphia: Fortress, 1980)

Berger, Klaus
"Apostelbrief und apostolische Rede: Zum Formular fruhchristlicher Briefe," *ZNW* 65 (1974) 190–231.

Idem
Formen und Gattungen im Neuen Testament (UTB 2532; Tübingen: Franke, 2005).

Idem
Formgeschichte des Neuen Testaments (Heidelberg: Quelle & Meyer, 1984).

Idem
"Hellenistische Gattungen im Neuen Testament," *ANRW* 2.25.2 (Berlin: de Gruyter, 1984) 1031–1885.

Berry, Ken L.
"The Function of Friendship Language in Philippians 4:10-20," in *Friendship, Flattery, and Frankness of Speech: Studies on Friendship in the New Testament World*, ed. John T. Fitzgerald (NovTSup 82; Leiden: Brill, 1996) 111–16.

Betz, Hans Dieter
Galatians: A Commentary on Paul's Letter to the Churches in Galatia (Hermeneia; Philadelphia: Fortress Press, 1979).

Idem, ed.
The Greek Magical Papyri in Translation, Including the Demotic Spells, vol. 1: *Texts* (2nd ed.; Chicago: University of Chicago Press, 1992).

Idem
Studies in Paul's Letter to the Philippians (WUNT 343; Tübingen: Mohr Siebeck, 2015).

Bingham, Sandra
The Praetorian Guard: A History of Rome's Elite Special Forces (London: I. B. Tauris, 2013).

Bitassi, Stephano
Gli esempi necessari per discernere: Il significato argomentativo della struttura della lettera di Paolo ai Filippesi (AnBib 153; Rome: Pontifical Biblical Institute, 2003).

Idem
"'Per scegliere ciò che conta di più' (Fil 1.10): Il criterio cristologico dello scegliere nella lettera di san Paolo ai Filippesi," *RasT* 47 (2006) 831–49.

Black, D. A.
"The Discourse Structure of Philippians: A Study in Text Linguistics," *NovT* 37 (1995) 24–25.

Blenkinsopp, Joseph
Isaiah 56–66: A New Translation with Introduction and Commentary (AB 19B; New York: Doubleday, 2003).

Boardman, John
Athenian Black Figure Vases (New York: Oxford University Press, 1974).

Bockmuehl, Marcus
"'The Form of God' (Philippians 2:6): Variations on a Theme of Jewish Mysticism," *JTS* n.s. 48 (1997) 1–23.

Boer, Martinus C. de
"Paul and Apocalyptic Eschatology," in Collins, ed., *Encyclopedia*, 345–83.

Bonhöffer, Adolf F.
Epiktet und das Neue Testament (RVV 10; Giessen: Töpelmann, 1911).

Bonner, Stanley
Roman Declamation in the Late Republic and Early Empire (Liverpool: University Press of Liverpool, 1949).

Bormann, Lukas
Philippi: Stadt und Christengemeinde zur Zeit des Paulus (NovTSup 78; Leiden: Brill, 1995).

Bornkamm, Günther
"Der Philipperbrief als paulinische Briefsammlung," in *Neotesamentica et Patristica: Eine Freundesgabe Herrn Professor Dr. Oscar Cullmann* (NovTSup 6; Leiden: Brill, 1962) 192–202.

Bousset, Wilhelm
Kyrios Christos: A History of the Belief in Christ from the Beginnings of Christianity to Irenaeus (Nashville: Abingdon, 1970; German original, 1921).

Bouttier, Michel
En Christ: Étude d'exégèse et de théologie pauliniennes (EHPhR 54; Paris: Presses universitaires de France, 1962).

Brandl, Martin
Der Agon bei Paulus: Herkunft und Profil paulinischer Agonmetaphorik (WUNT 2/222; Tübingen: Mohr Siebeck, 2006).

Brélaz, Cédric
Corpus des inscriptions grecques et latines de Philippes, vol. 2: *La colonie romaine*, part 1: *La vie publique de la colonie* (Études Épigraphiques 6; Athens: École française d'Athènes, 2014).

Breytenbach, Cilliers
Versöhnung: Eine Studie zur paulinischen Soteriologie (WMANT 60; Neukirchen-Vluyn: Neukirchener Verlag, 1989).

Idem
"'Christus starb für uns': Zur Tradition und paulinischen Rezeption der sogenannten 'Sterbeformeln,'" in idem, *Grace, Reconciliation, Concord: The Death of Christ in Graeco-Roman Metaphors* (NovTSup 135; Leiden: Brill, 2010) 95–126.

Brown, Raymond E.
An Introduction to the New Testament (ABRL; New York: Doubleday, 1997).

Bruce, F. F.
"St. Paul in Macedonia 3: The Philippian Correspondence," *BJRL* 63 (1981) 260–84.

Brucker, Ralph
"'Songs,' 'Hymns,' and 'Encomia' in the New Testament," in *Literature or Liturgy? Early Christian Hymns and Prayers in Their Literary and Liturgical Context in Antiquity*, ed. Clemens Leonhard and Hermut Löhr (WUNT 2/363; Tübingen: Mohr Siebeck, 2014) 1–14.

Idem
"Christushymnen" oder "epideiktische Passagen"? Studien zum Stilwechsel im Neuen Testament und seiner Umwelt (FRLANT 176; Göttingen: Vandenhoeck & Ruprecht, 1997).

Buchanan, C. O.
"Epaphroditus' Sickness and the Letter to the Philippians," *EvQ* 36 (1964) 158–60.

Büchsel, Friedrich
"'In Christus' bei Paulus," *ZNW* 42 (1949) 141–58.

Bultmann, Rudolf
Der Stil der paulinischen Predigt und die kynisch-stoische Diatribe (FRLANT 13; Göttingen: Vandenhoeck & Ruprecht, 1910, repr., 1984).

Buresch, Carl
"Consolationum a Graecis Romanisque scriptarum historia critica," *Leipziger Studien zur classischen Philologie* 9 (1886) 1–170.

Buxton, Richard
  Forms of Astonishment: Greek Myths of Metamorphosis (Oxford: Oxford University Press, 2009).

Capper, Brian J.
  "Paul's Dispute with Philippi: Understanding Paul's Argument in Phil 1–2 from His Thanks in 4.10-20," *ThZ* 49 (1993) 193–214.

Carroll, Robert P.
  When Prophecy Failed: Reactions and Responses to Failure in the Old Testament Prophetic Traditions (New York: Seabury, 1979).

Chapa, Juan
  "Consolatory Patterns? 1 Thes 4,13.18; 5,11," in *The Thessalonian Correspondence*, ed. Raymond F. Collins (BEThL 87; Leuven: Leuven University Press, 1990) 220–28.

Idem
  Letters of Condolence in Greek Papyri (Papyrologica Florentina 29; Florence: Gonnelli, 1998).

Charlesworth, James H.
  "The Portrayal of the Righteous as an Angel," in *Ideal Figures in Ancient Judaism: Profiles and Paradigms*, ed. George W. E. Nickelsburg and John J. Collins (SBLSCS 12; Chico, CA: Scholars Press, 1980) 135–51.

Collart, Philippe
  Philippes, ville de Macédoine, depuis ses origins jusqu'à la fin de l'époque romaine (2 vols.; Paris: Boccard, 1937).

Collins, John J.
  "The Angelic Life," in *Metamorphoses: Resurrection, Body, and Transformative Practices in Early Christianity*, ed. Turid Karlsen Seim and Jorunn Økland (Ekstasis 1; Berlin/New York: de Gruyter, 2009) 291–310.

Idem
  "Apocalyptic Eschatology and the Transcendence of Death," *CBQ* 36 (1974) 21–43.

Idem
  Daniel: A Commentary on the Book of Daniel (Hermeneia; Minneapolis: Fortress Press, 1993).

Idem, ed.
  The Encyclopedia of Apocalypticism, vol.1: *The Origins of Apocalytpicism in Judaism and Christianity* (New York: Continuum, 2000).

Idem
  "From Prophecy to Apocalypticism: The Expectation of the End," in *The Encyclopedia of Apocalypticism*, vol.1: *The Origins of Apocalypticism in Judaism and Christianity* (New York: Continuum, 2000) 129–61.

Idem
  "The Heavenly Representative: The 'Son of Man' in the Similitudes of Enoch," in *Ideal Figures in Ancient Judaism: Profiles and Paradigms*, ed. George W. E. Nickelsburg and John J. Collins (SBLSCS 12; Chico, CA: Scholars Press, 1980) 111–33.

Collins, John N.
  Diakonia: Re-interpreting the Ancient Sources (New York: Oxford University Press, 1990).

Cook, David
  "Stephanus Le Moyne and the Dissection of Philippians," *JTS* 32 (1981) 138–42.

Cover, Michael
  "The Death of Tragedy: The Form of God in Euripides' *Bacchae* and Paul's *Carmen Christi*" (forthcoming in *HTR*).

Croy, N. Clayton
  "'To Die Is Gain' (Philippians 1:19-26): Does Paul Contemplate Suicide?" *JBL* 122 (2003) 517–31.

Cullmann, Oscar
  The Christology of the New Testament (rev. ed.; Philadelphia: Westminster, 1963).

Dahl, Nils
  "Euodia and Syntyche and Paul's Letter to the Philippians," in *The Social World of the First Christians: Essays in Honor of Wayne A. Meeks*, ed. L. Michael White and O. Larry Yarbrough (Minneapolis: Fortress Press, 1995) 3–15.

Dalton, W. J.
  "The Integrity of Philippians," *Bib* 60 (1979) 97–102.

Deissmann, Adolf
  Die neutestamentliche Formel "in Christo Jesu" (Marburg: Elwert, 1892).

Idem
  "Zur ephesinischen Gefangenschaft des Apostel Paulus," in *Anatolian Studies presented to Sir William Mitchell Ramsey*, W. H. Buckler and W. M. Calder (Manchester: Manchester University Press, 1923) 121–27.

Dessau, H.
  "Der Name des Apostels Paulus," *Hermes* 45 (1910) 347–68.

Dibelius, Martin
  Paulus: Eine kultur- und religionsgeschichtliche Skizze (Tübingen: Mohr Siebeck, 1911).

Dirkse, Peter, and James Brashler
  "The Prayer of Thanksgiving. VI,7:63,33–65,7," in *Nag Hammadi Codices V,2-5 and VI, with Papyrus Berolinensis 8502*, ed. Douglas M. Parrott (NHS 11; Coptic Gnostic Library; Leiden: Brill, 1979) 378–87.

Doering, Lutz
  Ancient Jewish Letters and the Beginnings of Christian Epistolography (WUNT 298; Tübingen: Mohr Siebeck, 2012).

Droge, Arthur J.
  "*Mori lucrum*: Paul and Ancient Theories of Suicide," *NovT* 30 (1988) 263–86.

Duncan, G. S.
  St. Paul's Ephesian Ministry: A Reconstruction with Special Reference to the Ephesian Origin of the Imprisonment Epistles (London: Hodder & Stoughton, 1930).

Dunn, James D. G.
  Christology in the Making: A New Testament Inquiry into the Origins of the Doctrine of the Incarnation (London: SCM, 1980) 174–81.

Idem

The New Perspective on Paul (rev. ed.; Grand Rapids: Eerdmans, 2008).

Idem

"Once more ΠΙΣΤΙΣ ΧΡΙΣΤΟΥ," in *Pauline Theology*, vol. 4: *Looking Back, Pressing On*, ed. E. Elizabeth Johnson and David M Hay (SBLSymS 4; Atlanta: Scholars, 1997).

Idem

The Theology of Paul the Apostle (Grand Rapids: Eerdmans, 1998).

Durry, Marcel

"Sur une monnaie de Philippes," *REA* 42 (1940) 412–16.

Edart, Jean-Baptiste

L'Épître aux Philippiens: Rhétorique et Composition Stylistique (EB 45; Paris: Gabalda, 2002).

Engberg-Pedersen, Troels

"Complete and Incomplete Transformation in Paul—a Philosophical Reading of Paul on Body and Spirit," in *Metamorphoses: Resurrection, Body, and Transformative Practices in Early Christianity*, ed. Turid Karlsen Seim and Jorunn Økland (Ekstasis 1; Berlin/New York: de Gruyter, 2009) 123–46.

Idem

Cosmology and Self in the Apostle Paul: The Material Spirit (Oxford: Oxford University Press, 2010).

Idem

"On Comparison: The Stoic Theory of Value in Paul's Theology and Ethics in Philippians," in *Der Philipperbrief des Paulus in der hellenistisch-römischen Welt*, ed. Jörg Frey and Benjamin Schliesser (WUNT 353; Tübingen: Mohr Siebeck, 2015) 289–308.

Idem

Paul and the Stoics (Edinburgh: T&T Clark, 2000).

Idem

"Radical Altruism in Philippians 2:4," in *Early Christianity and Classical Culture*, ed. John T. Fitzgerald, Thomas H. Olbricht, and L. Michael White (NovTSup 110; Leiden: Brill, 2003) 197–214.

Idem

"Self-Sufficiency and Power: Divine and Human Agency in Epictetus and Paul," in *Divine and Human Agency in Paul and His Cultural Environment*, ed. John M. G. Barclay and Simon J. Gathercole (LNTS; London/New York: T&T Clark, 2006) 117–39.

Idem

"Stoicism in Philippians," in *Paul and His Hellenistic Context*, ed. idem (Minneapolis: Fortress Press, 1995) 256–90.

Eschner, Christina

Gestorben und hingegeben "für" die Sünder: Die griechischen Konzeption des Unheil abwendenden Sterbens und deren paulinische Aufname für die Deutung des Todes Jesu Christi (2 vols.; WMANT 122; Neukirchen-Vluyn: Neukirchener Verlag, 2010).

Esler, Philip F.

"Glossolalia and the Admission of Gentiles into the Early Christian Community," *BTB* 22 (1992) 136–42.

Idem

"Paul and the Agon: Understanding a Pauline Motif in Its Cultural and Visual Context," in *Picturing the New Testament: Studies in Ancient Visual Images*, ed. Annette Weissenrieder, Friederike Wendt, and Petra von Gemünden, eds. (WUNT 2/193; Tübingen: Mohr Siebeck, 2005) 356–84.

Esteve-Forriol, José

Die Trauer- und Trostgedichte in der römischen Literatur (Munich: Schubert, 1962).

Evaristus, Mary

The Consolations of Death in Ancient Greek Literature (Washington, DC: National Capital Press, 1917).

Fairweather, Janet

Seneca the Elder (Cambridge Classical Studies; Cambridge: Cambridge University Press, 1981).

Favez, Charles

La consolation latine chrétienne (Paris: J. Vrin, 1937).

Idem

L. Annaei Senecae Dialogorum liber XII Ad Helviam matrem de consolatione, texte latin publié avec une commentaire explicatif (Lausanne/Paris: Payot, 1918).

Feine, Paul

Die Abfassung des Philipperbriefes in Ephesus mit einer Anlage über Röm 16,3-20 als Epheserbrief (BFCTh 20; Gütersloh: Bertelsmann, 1916).

Fern, Mary E.

Latin Consolatio Mortis *as a Literary Type* (St. Louis: Saint Louis University Press, 1941).

Fitzgerald, John T., ed.

Friendship, Flattery, and Frankness of Speech: Studies on Friendship in the New Testament World (NovTSup 82; Leiden: Brill, 1996).

Idem

"Philippians, Epistle to the," *ABD* 5:218–26.

Fitzmyer, Joseph A.

"The Consecutive Meaning of Ἐφ' Ὧ in Romans 5:12," *NTS* 39 (1993) 321–39.

Idem

"Philippians," in *Jerome Biblical Commentary*, ed. Raymond E. Brown, Joseph A. Fitzmyer, and Roland E. Murphy (Englewood Cliffs, NJ: Prentice Hall, 1968) 2:247–53.

Idem

"A Feature of Qumran Angelology and the Angels of 1 Cor 11:10," in *Paul and the Dead Sea Scrolls*, ed. Jerome Murphy-O'Connor and James H. Charlesworth (New York: Crossroad, 1990) 31–47.

Flanagan, Neal

"A Note on Philippians 3:20-21," *CBQ* 18 (1956) 8–9.

Fletcher-Louis, Crispin

"4Q374: A Discourse on the Sinai Tradition: The Deification of Moses and Early Christology," *DSD* 3 (1996) 236–52.

Forbes Irving, P. M. C.
  Metamorphosis in Greek Myths (Oxford: Oxford University Press, 1990).
Fossum, Jarl E.
  "Jewish-Christian Christology and Jewish Mysticism," *VC* 37 (1983) 260–87.
Idem
  "The Magharians: A Pre-Christian Jewish Sect and Its Significance for the Study of Gnosticism and Christianity," *Henoch* 9 (1987) 303–44.
Frede, Hermann Josef
  Altlateinische Paulus-Handschriften (Freiburg: Herder, 1964).
Idem, ed.
  Epistulae ad Philippenses et ad Colossenses (Vetus Latina: Die Reste der altlateinischen Bibel 24.2; Freiburg: Herder, 1966–71).
Idem
  Ein neuer Paulustext und Kommentar (2 vols.; Vetus Latina: Aus der Geschichte der lateinischen Bibel 7–8; Freiburg: Herder, 1973–74).
Fredriksen, Paula
  "Mandatory Retirement: Ideas in the Study of Christian Origins Whose Time Has Come to Go," *SR* 35 (2006) 231–46.
Eadem
  "Why Should a 'Law Free' Mission Mean a 'Law Free' Apostle?" *JBL* 3 (2015) 637–50.
Frey, Jörg
  "Flesh and Spirit in the Palestinian Jewish Sapiential Tradition and in the Qumran Texts: An Inquiry into the Development of Pauline Usage," in *The Wisdom Texts from Qumran and the Development of Sapiential Thought*, ed. C. Hempel, A. Lange and H. Lichtenberger (BEThL 159; Leuven: Peeters, 2002) 367–404.
Idem
  "The Notion of 'Flesh' in 4QInstruction and the Background of Pauline Thought," in *Sapiential, Liturgical, and Poetical Texts from Qumran: Proceedings of the Third Meeting of the International Organization for Qumran Studies, Oslo, 1998. Published in Memory of Maurice Baillet*, ed. Daniel K. Falk, Florentino García Martínez, and Eileen M. Schuller (STDJ 35; Leiden: Brill, 2000) 197–226.
Frey, Jörg, and Benjamin Schliesser, eds.
  Der Philipperbrief des Paulus in der hellenistisch-römischen Welt (WUNT 353; Tübingen: Mohr Siebeck, 2015).
Friesen, Courtney
  Reading Dionysus: Euripides' Bacchae and the Cultural Contestations of Greeks, Jews, Romans, and Christians (STAC 95; Tübingen: Mohr Siebeck, 2015).
Funk, Robert
  Language, Hermeneutic, and Word of God: The Problem of Language in the New Testament and Contemporary Theology (New York: Harper & Row, 1966).
Gamble, Harry
  The Textual History of the Letter to the Romans (Grand Rapids: Eerdmans, 1977).

Garland, David
  "The Composition and Unity of Philippians: Some Neglected Literary Features," *NovT* 27 (1985) 141–73.
Gemünden, Petra von
  "Der 'Affekt' der Freude im Philipperbrief und seiner Umwelt," in *Der Philipperbrief des Paulus in der hellenistisch-römischen Welt*, ed. Jörg Frey and Benjamin Schliesser (WUNT 353; Tübingen: Mohr Siebeck, 2015) 223–253.
Gieschen, Charles A.
  Angelomorphic Christology: Antecedent and Early Evidence (AGJU 42; Leiden: Brill, 1998).
Goodspeed, Edgar J.
  Problems of New Testament Translation (Chicago: University of Chicago Press, 1945).
Gregg, Robert C.
  Consolation Philosophy: Greek and Christian Paideia in Basil and the Two Gregories (PMS 3; Cambridge, MA: Philadelphia Patristic Foundation, 1975).
Grollios, Constantin
  Seneca's Ad Marciam: *Tradition and Originality* (Athens: Christou, 1956).
Idem
  Τέχνη ἀλυπίας: κοινοὶ τόποι τοῦ Πρὸς Πολύβιον τοῦ Σενέκα καὶ πηγαὶ αὐτῶν (Ἑλληνικά, παράρτημα 10; Athens: Christou & Son, 1956).
Gundry Volf, Judith M.
  Paul and Perseverance: Staying In and Falling Away (WUNT 2/34: Tübingen: Mohr Siebeck, 1990).
Gunkel, Hermann
  The Influence of the Holy Spirit: The Popular View of the Apostolic Age and the Teaching of the Apostle Paul (Philadelphia: Fortress Press, 1979; German original, 1888).
Hani, Jean
  "La consolation antique," *REA* 75 (1973) 103–10.
Harrer, G. A.
  "Saul Who Is Also Called Paul," *HTR* 33 (1940) 19–33.
Harrisville, R. A., III
  "ΠΙΣΤΙΣ ΧΡΙΣΤΟΥ: The Witness of the Fathers," *NovT* 36 (1994) 233–41.
Hays, Richard B.
  Echoes of Scripture in the Letters of Paul (New Haven: Yale University Press, 1993).
Idem
  The Faith of Jesus Christ: The Narrative Substructure of Galatians 3:1–4:11 (2nd ed.; Grand Rapids: Eerdmans, 2002).
Heinrici, C. F. Georg
  "Zum Hellenismus des Paulus," in idem, *Der zweite Brief an die Korinther* (KEK 6.8; Göttingen: Vandenhoeck & Ruprecht, 1900) 436–58.
Hemer, C. J.
  "The Name of Paul," *TynBull* 36 (1985) 179–83.

Hengel, Martin
  "Der Jakobusbrief als antipaulinische Polemik,"
  in idem, *Paulus und Jakobus: Kleine Schriften III*
  (WUNT 141; Tübingen: Mohr Siebeck, 2002)
  511–48.
Idem
  The Pre-Christian Paul (London: SCM, 1991).
Idem
  "Sit at My Right Hand!" in idem, *Studies in
  Early Christology* (Edinburgh: T&T Clark, 1995)
  119–225.
Hentschel, Anni
  *Diakonia im Neuen Testament: Studien zur Semantik
  unter besonderer Berücksichtigung der Rolle von Frauen*
  (WUNT 2/226; Tübingen: Mohr Siebeck, 2007).
Himmelfarb, Martha
  Ascent to Heaven in Jewish and Christian Apocalypses
  (New York/Oxford: Oxford University Press,
  1993).
Eadem
  "Revelation and Rapture: The Transformation
  of the Visionary in the Ascent Apocalypses," in
  *Mysteries and Revelations: Apocalyptic Studies after the
  Uppsala Colloquium*, ed. John J. Collins and James
  H. Charlesworth (JSPSup 9; Sheffield: JSOT Press,
  1991) 79–90.
Hofius, Otfried
  *Der Christushymnus Philipper 2:6-11: Untersuchungen
  zu Gestalt und Aussage eines urchristlichen Psalms*
  (WUNT 17: Tübingen: Mohr Siebeck, 1991).
Holloway, Paul A.
  "*Alius Paulus*: On Paul's Promise to Send Timothy
  in Phil 2.19-24," *NTS* 54 (2008) 542–56.
Idem
  "The Apocryphal *Epistle to the Laodiceans* and
  the Partitioning of Philippians," *HTR* 91 (1998)
  321–25.
Idem
  "*Bona Cogitare*: An Epicurean Consolation in Phil
  4:8-10," *HTR* 91 (1998) 89–96.
Idem
  "*Commendatio aliqua sui*: Reading Romans with
  Pierre Bourdieu," *EC* 2 (2011) 356–83.
Idem
  "Consolation: II. Greco-Roman Antiquity; III. New
  Testament; IV. Judaism: Second Temple and Hel-
  lenistic Judaism," *EBR* 5:669–73.
Idem
  *Consolation in Philippians: Philosophical Sources and
  Rhetorical Strategy* (SNTSMS 112; Cambridge: Cam-
  bridge University Press, 2002).
Idem
  *Coping with Prejudice: 1 Peter in Social-Psychological
  Perspective* (WUNT 244; Tübingen: Mohr Siebeck,
  2009).
Idem
  "Deliberating Life and Death: Paul's Tragic *Dubita-
  tio* in Philippians 1:22-26" (forthcoming in *HTR*).

Idem
  "The Enthymeme as an Element of Style in Paul,"
  JBL 120 (2001) 329–39.
Idem
  "Left Behind: Jesus' Consolation of His Disciples in
  John 13–17," *ZNW* 96 (2005) 1–34.
Idem
  "*Nihil inopinati accidisse*–'Nothing unexpected has
  happened': A Cyrenaic Consolatory Topos in 1 Pet
  4:12ff.," *NTS* 48 (2002) 433–48.
Idem
  "Paul as Hellenistic Philosopher: The Case of
  Philippians," in *Paul and the Philosophers*, ed. Ward
  Blanton and Hent de Vries (New York: Fordham
  University Press, 2014) 52–68.
Idem
  "Paul's Pointed Prose: The *Sententia* in Roman
  Rhetoric and Paul," *NovT* 40 (1998) 32–53.
Idem
  "Thanks for the Memories: On the Translation of
  Phil 1.3," *NTS* 52 (2006) 419–32.
Holmes, Michael W.
  "The Text of the Epistles Sixty Years After: An
  Assessment of Günther Zuntz's Contribution to the
  Text-Critical Methodology and History," in *Trans-
  mission and Reception: New Testament Text-Critical
  and Exegetical Studies*, ed. J. W. Childers and D. C.
  Parker (Piscataway, NJ: Gorgias, 2006) 89–113.
Hooker, Morna D.
  "Philippians 2.6-11," in *Jesus und Paulus: Festschrift
  für Werner Georg Kümmel zum 70. Geburtstag*,
  ed. E. Earle Ellis and Erich Grässer (Göttingen:
  Vandenhoeck & Ruprecht, 1978) 151–64.
Eadem
  "ΠΙΣΤΙΣ ΧΡΙΣΤΟΥ," *NTS* 35 (1989) 321–42.
Hoover, Roy W.
  "The *Harpagmos* Enigma: A Philological Solution,"
  HTR 64 (1971) 95–119.
Horbury, William
  Jewish Messianism and the Cult of Christ (London:
  SCM, 1998).
Horst, Pieter W. van der
  *Ancient Jewish Epitaphs: An Introductory Survey of a
  Millennium of Jewish Funerary Epigraphy (300 BCE–
  700CE)* (CBET 2; Kampen: Kok Pharos, 1991).
Howard, George
  "Notes and Observations on the 'Faith of Christ,'"
  HTR 60 (1967) 459–84.
Hultin, N.
  "The Rhetoric of Consolation: Studies in the Devel-
  opment of the 'Consolatio Mortis'" (Ph.D. diss.,
  Johns Hopkins University, 1965).
Jaeger, Werner W.
  "Eine stilgeschichtliche Studie zum Philipperbrief,"
  Hermes 50 (1915) 537–53.
Jewett, Robert
  "Conflicting Movements in the Early Church as
  Reflected in Philippians," *NovT* 12 (1970) 362–90.

Idem

"The Epistolary Thanksgiving and the Integrity of Philippians," *NovT* 12 (1970) 40–53.

Johann, H. T.

Trauer und Trost: Eine quellen- und strukturanalytische Untersuchung der philosophischen Trostschriften über den Tod (STA 5; Munich: Fink, 1968).

Johnson, Luke Timothy

"The New Testament's Anti-Jewish Slander and the Conventions of Ancient Polemic," *JBL* 108 (1989) 419–41.

Jongkind, Dirk

"The Text of the Pauline Corpus," in *The Blackwell Companion to Paul*, ed. Stephen Westerholm (Oxford: Blackwell, 2011).

Käsemann, Ernst

"Kritische Analyse von Phil. 2,5-11," *ZThK* 47 (1950) 313–60; ET: "A Critical Analysis of Philippians 2:5-11," *JTC* 5 (1968) 45–88.

Kassel, Rudolf

Untersuchungen zur griechischen und römischen Konsolationsliteratur (Zetemata 18; Munich: Beck, 1958).

Kilpatrick, G. D.

"ΒΛΕΠΕΤΕ in Phil 3:2," in *In Memoriam P. Kahle*, ed. Matthew Black and Georg Fohrer (BZAW 103; Berlin: Töpelmann, 1968) 146–48.

Kittredge, Cynthia Briggs

Community and Authority: The Rhetoric of Obedience in the Pauline Tradition (HTS 45; Harrisburg, PA: Trinity Press International, 1998).

Klehn, Lars

"Die Verwendung von ἐν Χριστῷ bei Paulus: Erwägungen zu den Wandlungen in der paulinischen Theologie," *BN* 74 (1994) 66–79.

Kleinknecht, K. T.

Der leidende Gerechtfertige: Die alttestamentlich-jüdische Tradition vom "leidenden Gerechten" und ihre Rezeption bei Paulus (WUNT 2/13; Tübingen: Mohr Siebeck, 1984).

Koester, Helmut

"1 Thessalonians—Experiment in Christian Writing," in *Continuity and Discontinuity in Church History*, ed. F. F. Church and T. George (SHCT 19; Leiden: Brill, 1979) 33–44.

Idem

"The Purpose of the Polemic of a Pauline Fragment (Philippians III)," *NTS* 8 (1961–62) 317–32.

Koperski, Veronica

"The Early History of the Dissection of Philippians," *JTS* 44 (1993) 599–603.

Koskenniemi, Heikki

Studien zur Idee und Phraseologie des griechischen Briefes bis 400 n. Chr. (Helsinki: Kirjakauppa; Wiesbaden: Harrassowitz, 1956).

Koukouli-Chrysanthaki, Chaido

"Colonia Iulia Augusta Philippensis," in *Philippi at the Time of Paul and after His Death*, ed. Charalambos Bakirtzis and Helmut Koester (Harrisburg, PA: Trinity Press International, 1998) 5–35.

Krause, Jens-Uwe

Gefängnisse im Römischen Reich (HABES 23; Stuttgart: Franz Steiner, 1996).

Kremydi-Sicilianou, Sophia

Multiple Concealments from the Sanctuary of Zeus Olympios at Dion: The Roman Provincial Coin Hoards (Meletemata 35; Athens: Boccard [Paris], 2004).

Eadem

"*Victoria Augusta* on Macedonian Coins: Remarks on Dating and Interpretation," Τεκμήρια 7 (2002) 63–84.

Krentz, Edgar

"Military Language and Metaphors in Philippians," in *Origins and Method: Towards a New Understanding of Judaism and Christianity*, ed. Bradley H. McLean (JSNTSup 86; Sheffield: Sheffield Academic Press, 1993) 105–27.

Idem

"Paul, Games, and the Military," in *Paul in the Greco-Roman World: A Handbook*, ed. J. Paul Sampley (Harrisburg, PA: Trinity Press International, 2003) 344–83.

Kurth, Thomas

Senecas Trostschrift an Polybius, Dialogue 11: Ein Kommentar (BAK 59: Stuttgart: Teubner, 1994).

Kyle, Donald G.

Sport and Spectacle in the Ancient World (2nd ed.; Malden, MA/Oxford: Wiley Blackwell, 2015).

Lake, Kirsopp

"Critical Problems of the Epistle to the Philippians," *The Expositor* 8, no. 7 (1914) 485.

Lampe, Peter

From Paul to Valentinus: Christians at Rome in the First Two Centuries (Minneapolis: Fortress Press, 2003).

Lattimore, Richard

Themes in Greek and Latin Epitaphs (Illinois Studies in Language and Literature 28.1-2; Urbana: University of Illinois Press, 1942).

Leary, T. J.

"Paul's Improper Name," *NTS* 38 (1992) 467–69.

Leonard, Clemens, and Hermut Löhr, eds.

Literature or Liturgy? Early Christian Hymns and Prayers in Their Literary and Liturgical Context in Antiquity (WUNT 2/363; Tübingen: Mohr Siebeck, 2014).

Levison, John R.

Filled with the Spirit (Grand Rapids: Eerdmans, 2009).

Lieu, Judith M.

"'Grace to You and Peace': The Apostolic Greeting," *BJRL* 68 (1985) 161–78.

Lightfoot, J. B.

St. Paul's Epistle to the Colossians and to Philemon (London: Macmillan, 1892).

Lillo Redonet, Fernando

Palabras contra el dolor: La consolación filosófica latina de Cicerón a Frontón (Madrid: Ediciones Clásicas, 2001).

Litwa, M. David
We Are Being Transformed: Deification in Paul's Soteriology (BZNW 187; Berlin: de Gruyter, 2012).

Lohmeyer, Ernst
Kyrios Jesus: Eine Untersuchungen zu Phil 2,5-11 (Heidelberg: Winter, 1928).

Löhr, Hermut
"What Can We Know about the Beginnings of Christian Hymnody?" in *Literature or Liturgy? Early Christian Hymns and Prayers in Their Literary and Liturgical Context in Antiquity*, ed. Clemens Leonhard and Hermut Löhr (WUNT 363; Tübingen: Mohr Siebeck, 2014) 158–74.

Lyonnet, Stanislas
"Le sens ἐφ' ᾧ en Rom 5,12 et l'exégèse des Pères grecs," *Bib* 36 (1955) 436–56.

Lyons, George
Pauline Autobiography: Toward a New Understanding (SBLDS 73; Atlanta: Scholars Press, 1985).

Mach, Michael
Die Entwicklungsstadien des jüdischen Engelglaubens in vorrabbinischer Zeit (TSAJ 34; Tübingen: Mohr Siebeck, 1992).

Mackay, B. S.
"Further Thoughts on Philippians," *NTS* 7 (1961) 161–70.

Mahé, J. P.
"La Prière d'actions de graces du Codex VI de Nag-Hamadi et Le Discours parfait," *ZPE* 13 (1974) 40–60.

Malherbe, Abraham J.
"Exhortation in First Thessalonians," *NovT* 25 (1983) 238–56.

Idem
The Letters to the Thessalonians: A New Translation with Introduction and Commentary (AB 32B; New York: Doubleday, 2000).

Idem
"Paul's Self-Sufficiency (Philippians 4:11)," in *Friendship, Flattery, and Frankness of Speech: Studies on Friendship in the New Testament World*, ed. John T. Fitzgerald (NovTSup 82; Leiden: Brill, 1996) 125–39.

Malingrey, Anne-Marie, ed. and trans.
Jean Chrysostome: Lettres à Olympias; vie d'Olympias (2nd ed.; SC 13; Paris: Cerf, 1968).

Malunowiczówna, Leokadia
"Les éléments stoïciens dans la consolation grecque chrétienne," *StPatr* 13.2 (TU 116; Berlin: Akademie-Verlag, 1975) 35–45.

Marcus, Joel
"The Evil Inclination in the Letters of Paul," *Irish Biblical Studies* (1986) 8–21.

Idem
"Mark—Interpreter of Paul," *NTS* 46 (2000) 473–87.

Martin, Dale B.
Slavery as Salvation: The Metaphor of Slavery in Pauline Christianity (New Haven: Yale University Press, 1990).

Martin, Ralph P.
Carmen Christi: Philippians 2:5-11 in Recent Interpretation and in the Setting of Early Christian Worship (SNTSMS 4; Cambridge: Cambridge University Press, 1967; 3rd ed., Downers Grove, IL: InterVarsity, 1997).

Marxsen, Willi
Introduction to the New Testament: An Approach to Its Problems (trans. G. Buswell; Oxford: Blackwell, 1968).

Matlock, R. Barry
"Detheologizing the ΠΙΣΤΙΣ ΧΡΙΣΤΟΥ Debate: Cautionary Remarks from a Lexical Semantic Perspective," *NovT* 42 (2000) 1–24.

Idem
"Even the Demons Believe: Paul and πίστις Χριστοῦ," *CBQ* 64 (2002) 300–318.

Idem
"The Rhetoric of πίστις in Paul: Galatians 2.16, Romans 3.22, and Philippians 3.9," *JSNT* 30 (2007) 173–203.

McGing, B. C.
"Synkrisis in Tacitus' Agricola," *Hermathena* 132 (1982) 15–25.

Meeks, Wayne A.
"The Man from Heaven in Philippians," in *The Future of Early Christianity: Essays in Honor of Helmut Koester*, ed. Birger A. Pearson (Minneapolis: Fortress Press, 1991) 329–36.

Idem
The First Urban Christians: The Social World of the Apostle Paul (New Haven: Yale University Press, 1983).

Meier, Hans-Christoph
Mystik bei Paulus: Zur Phänomenologie religiöser Erfahrung im Neuen Testament (TANZ 26; Tübingen: Francke, 1998).

Meinel, Peter
Seneca über seine Verbannung: Trostschrift an die Mutter Helvia (Bonn: Habelt, 1972).

Metzger, Bruce M.
A Textual Commentary on the Greek New Testament: A Companion Volume to the United Bible Societies' Greek New Testament (Fourth rev. ed.) (2nd ed.; Stuttgart: United Bible Societies, 1994).

Michaelis, Wilhelm
"Die Gefangenschaftsbriefe des Paulus und antike Gefangenenbriefe," *NKZ* 36 (1925) 586–606.

Miller, Arthur
"Rhetorical Exigence," *Philosophy & Rhetoric* 5 (1972) 111–18.

Mitchell, Alan C.
"'Greet the Friends by Name': New Testament Evidence for the Greco-Roman *Topos* on Friendship," in *Greco-Roman Perspectives on Friendship*, ed. John T. Fitzgerald (SBLRBS 34; Atlanta: Scholars Press, 1997) 225–62.

Mitchell, Jane F.
"Consolatory Letters in Basil and Gregory Nazianzen," *Hermes* 96 (1968) 299–318.

202

Moffatt, James
"Philippians II 26 and 2 Tim. IV 13," *JTS* 18 (1917) 311–12.

Mommsen, Theodor
"Die Rechtsverhältnisse des Apostels Paulus," *ZNW* 2 (1901) 81–96.

Montefiore, C. G.
Ancient Jewish and Greek Encouragement and Consolation (Bridgeport, CT: Hartmore House, 1971).

Moore, Ernst
"ΒΙΑΖΩ, ΑΡΠΑΖΩ and Cognates in Josephus," *NTS* 21 (1975) 519–43.

Morray-Jones, Christopher
"Transformational Mysticism in the Apocalyptic-Merkabah Tradition," *JJS* 43 (1992) 1–31.

Moss, Candida R.
"The Transfiguration: An Exercise in Markan Accommodation," *BibInt* 12 (2004) 69–89.

Moule, C. F. D.
"Further Reflections on Philippians 2.5-11," in *Apostolic History and the Gospel: Biblical and Historical Essays Presented to F. F. Bruce on His 60th Birthday*, ed. W. W. Gasque and R. P. Martin (Exeter: Paternoster, 1970) 265–76.

Mount, Christopher
"1 Corinthians 11:3-16: Spirit Possession and Authority in a non-Pauline Interpolation," *JBL* 124 (2005) 313–40.

Idem
"Belief, Gullibility, and the Presence of a God in the Early Roman Empire," in *Credible, Incredible: The Miraculous in the Ancient Mediterranean*, ed. Tobias Nicklas and Janet E. Spittler (WUNT 321; Tübingen: Mohr Siebeck, 2013) 85–106.

Idem
"Religious Experience, the Religion of Paul, and Women in the Pauline Churches," in *Women and Gender in Ancient Religions: Interdisciplinary Approaches*, ed. Stephen P. Ahearne-Kroll, Paul A. Holloway, and James A. Kelhoffer (WUNT 263; Tübingen: Mohr Siebeck, 2010) 23–47.

Müller, Ulrich
"Der Christushymnus Phil 2,6-11," *ZNW* 79 (1988) 17–44.

Idem
Die Menschwerdung des Gottessohn: Frühchristliche Inkarnationsvorstellungen und die Anfänge des Doketismus (SBS 140; Stuttgart; Katholisches Bibelwerk, 1990).

Müller-Bardorff, J.
"Zur Frage der literarischen Einheit des Philipperbriefes," *WZJena* 7 (1957–58) 591–604.

Mullins, Terence Y.
"Disclosure: A Literary Form in the New Testament," *NovT* 7 (1964) 44–50.

Idem
"Formulas in the New Testament Epistles," *JBL* 91 (1972) 380–90.

Murphy-O'Connor, Jerome
"Christological Anthropology in Phil II,6-11," *RB* 83 (1976) 25–50.

Nanos, Mark
"Paul's Reversal of Jews Calling Gentiles 'Dogs' (Philippians 3:2): 1600 Years of an Ideological Tale Wagging an Exegetical Dog?" *BibInt* 17 (2009) 448–82.

Nasrallah, Laura S.
"Spatial Perspectives: Space and Archaeology in Roman Philippi," in *Studying Paul's Letters: Contemporary Perspectives and Methods*, ed. Joseph Marchal (Minneapolis: Fortress Press, 2012) 53–74.

Neugebauer, Fritz
In Christus, ἐν Χριστῷ: Eine Untersuchung zum paulinischen Glaubensbegriff (Berlin: Evangelische Verlagsanstalt, 1961).

Nicklas, Tobias
"Offices? Roles, Functions, Authorities and the Ethos in Earliest Christianity: A Look into the World of Pauline Communities," in *Rabbi–Pastor–Priest: Their Roles and Profiles through the Ages*, ed. Walter Homolka and Heinz-Günther Schöttler (Studia Judaica 64; Berlin: de Gruyter, 2013) 23–40.

Nickelsburg, George W. E.
1 Enoch 1: A Commentary on 1 Enoch, Chapters 1–36; 81–108 (Hermeneia: Minneapolis: Fortress Press, 2001).

Idem
"Judgment, Life-After-Death, and Resurrection in the Apocrypha and Non-Apocalyptic Pseudepigrapha," in *Judaism in Late Antiquity*, Part 4: *Death, Life-After-Death, Resurrection and the World-to-Come in the Judaisms of Antiquity*, ed. Alan J. Avery-Peck and Jacob Neusner (Handbuch der Orientalistik 55; Leiden: Brill, 2000) 141–62.

Idem
"Religious Exclusivism: A World View Governing Some Texts Found at Qumran," in *Das Ende der Tage und die Gegenwart des Heils: Begegnungen mit dem Neuen Testament und seiner Umwelt. Festschrift für Heinz-Wolfgang Kuhn zum 65. Geburtstag*, ed. Michael Becker and Wolfgang Fenske (AGJU 44; Leiden: Brill, 1999) 45–67.

Idem
Resurrection, Immortality, and Eternal Life in Intertestamental Judaism and Early Christianity (HTS 56; expanded ed.; Cambridge, MA; Harvard University Press, 2007).

Nickelsburg, George W. E., and James C. VanderKam
1 Enoch 2: A Commentary on 1 Enoch, Chapters 37–82 (Hermeneia: Minneapolis: Fortress Press, 2011).

Nock, A. D.
Conversion: The Old and the New in Religion from Alexander the Great to Augustine of Hippo (Oxford: Clarendon, 1933).

Noth, Martin
  "The Holy Ones of the Most High," in idem, *The Laws of the Pentateuch and Other Studies* (London: Oliver & Boyd, 1966) 215–28.

Novenson, Matthew V.
  "'God Is Witness': A Classical Rhetorical Idiom in Its Pauline Usage," *NovT* 52 (2010) 355–75.

Oakes, Peter
  Philippians: From People to Letter (SNTSMS 110; Cambridge: Cambridge University Press, 2001).

O'Brien, Peter T.
  Introductory Thanksgivings in the Letters of Paul (NovTSup 49; Leiden: Brill, 1977).

Ogereau, Julien M.
  Paul's Koinonia with the Philippians: A Socio-Historical Investigation of a Pauline Partnership (WUNT 2/377; Tübingen: Mohr Siebeck, 2014).

Ollrog, Wolf-Henning
  Paulus und seine Mitarbeiter: Untersuchungen zu Theorie und Praxis der paulinischen Mission (WMANT 50; Neukirchen-Vluyn: Neukirchener Verlag, 1979).

Parrott, Douglas M., ed.
  Nag Hammadi Codices V,2-5 and VI, with Papyrus Berolinensis 8502 (NHS 11; Coptic Gnostic Library; Leiden: Brill, 1979).

Pedersen, Sigfred
  "'Mit Furcht und Zittern' (Phil. 2,12-13)," *ST* 32 (1978) 1–31.

Pervo, Richard I.
  Acts: A Commentary (Hermeneia; Minneapolis: Fortress Press, 2009).

Peterlin, Davorin
  Paul's Letter to the Philippians in Light of the Disunity in the Church (NovTSup 79; Leiden: Brill, 1995).

Pevarello, Daniele
  "Paul and the Philosophical Concept of Self-Sufficiency," in *Paul's Graeco-Roman Context*, ed. Cilliers Breytenbach (BEThL 277; Leuven: Peters, 2015) 501–23.

Pfitzner, Victor C.
  Paul and the Agon Motif: Traditional Athletic Imagery in the Pauline Letters (NovTSup 16; Leiden: Brill, 1967).

Pilhofer, Peter
  Philippi, vol. 1: *Die erste christliche Gemeinde Europas*; vol. 2: *Katalog der Inschriften von Philippi* (WUNT 87, 119; Tübingen: Mohr Siebeck, 1995, 2001).

Pollard, T. E.
  "The Integrity of Philippians," *NTS* 13 (1967) 57–66.

Poplutz, Uta
  Athlet des Evangeliums (HBS 43; Freiburg: Herder, 2004).

Rabbow, Paul
  Seelenführung: Methodik der Exerzitien in der Antike (Munich: Kösel, 1954).

Rahtjen, B. D.
  "The Three Letters of Paul to the Philippians," *NTS* (1959–60) 167–73.

Räisänen, Heikki
  The Rise of Christian Beliefs: The Thought World of Early Christians (Minneapolis: Fortress Press, 2010).

Rankov, Boris
  "The Governor's Men: The *Officium Consularis* in Provincial Adminstration," in *The Roman Army as a Community, Including Papers of a Conference Held at Birkbeck College, University of London, on 11–12 January 1997*, ed. Adrian Goldsworthy and Ian Haynes (JRASup 34; Portsmouth, RI: Journal of Roman Archaeology, 1999) 15–34.

Rapske, Brian
  The Book of Acts and Paul in Roman Custody (Grand Rapids: Eerdmans; Carlisle: Paternoster, 1994).

Reed, Jeffrey T.
  "Are Paul's Thanksgivings 'Epistolary'?" *JSNT* 61 (1996) 87–99.

Reumann, John
  "Church Office in Paul, Especially in Philippians," in *Origins and Method: Towards a New Understanding of Judaism and Christianity*, ed. B. H. McLean (JSNTSup 86; Sheffield: JSOT Press, 1993) 82–91.

Idem
  "Contributions of the Philippian Community to Paul and to Earliest Christianity," *NTS* 39 (1993) 438–57.

Idem
  "Philippians 3.20-21—a Hymnic Fragment?" *NTS* 30 (1986) 593–609.

Idem
  "Philippians, Especially Chapter 4, as a 'Letter of Friendship': Observations on a Checkered History of Scholarship," in *Friendship, Flattery, and Frankness of Speech: Studies on Friendship in the New Testament World*, ed. John T. Fitzgerald (NovTSup 82; Leiden: Brill, 1996) 83–106.

Roberts, J. H.
  "The Eschatological Tensions in the Pauline Letter Body," *Neot* 20 (1986) 29–36.

Robinson, James M.
  "Die Hodajot-Formel in Gebet und Hymnus des Frühchristentums," in *Apophoreta: Festschrift für Ernst Haenchen*, ed. W. Eltester and F. H. Kettler (BZNW 30; Berlin: Töpelmann, 1964) 194–235.

Rolland, P.
  "La structure littéraire et l'unité de l'Epître aux Philippiens," *RevSR* 64 (1990) 213–16.

Roller, Otto
  Das Formular der paulinischen Briefe (BWANT 4.6; Stuttgart: Kohlhammer, 1933).

Samply, J. Paul
  Pauline Partnership in Christ: Christian Community and Commitment in Light of Roman Law (Philadelphia: Fortress Press, 1980).

Sanders, E. P.

Paul: The Apostle's Life, Letters, and Thought (Minneapolis: Fortress Press, 2015).

Idem

Paul and Palestinian Judaism: A Comparision of Patterns of Religion (Philadelphia: Fortress Press, 1977).

Idem

Paul, the Law and the Jewish People (Philadelphia: Fortress Press, 1983).

Sanders, J. T.

"Transition from Opening Epistolary Thanksgiving to Body in the Letters of the Pauline Corpus," *JBL* 81 (1962) 348–62.

Sandnes, Karl Olav

The Belly and the Body in the Pauline Epistles (SNTSMS 120; Cambridge: Cambridge University Press, 2002).

Sass, Gerhard

"Zur Bedeutung von δοῦλος bei Paulus," *ZNW* 40 (1941) 24–32.

Scanlon, Thomas F.

Eros and Greek Athletics (Oxford: Oxford University Press, 2002).

Schäfer, Peter

The Hidden and Manifest God: Some Major Themes in Early Jewish Mysticism (Albany: State University of New York Press, 1992).

Idem

The Origins of Jewish Mysticism (Princeton: Princeton University Press, 2011).

Idem

Rivalität des Engeln und Menschen: Untersuchungen zur rabbinischen Engelvorstellung (Berlin: de Gruyter, 1975).

Schmeller, Thomas, Martin Ebner, and Rudolf Hoppe, eds. *Neutestamentliche Ämtermodelle in Kontext* (QD 239; Freiburg: Herder, 2010).

Schmithals, Walter

"Die Irrlehrer des Philipperbriefes," *ZThK* 54 (1957) 297–341; revised for idem, *Paulus und die Gnostiker: Untersuchungen zu den kleinen Paulusbriefen* (ThF 35; Hamburg-Bergstedt: Herbert Reich, 1965) 47–87; ET: "The False Teachers of the Epistle to the Philippians," in idem, *Paul and the Gnostics* (Nashville: Abingdon, 1972) 65–122.

Schnelle, Udo

Apostle Paul: His Life and Theology (Grand Rapids: Baker Academic, 2005).

Idem

Gerechtigkeit und Christusgegenwart: Vorpaulinische und paulinische Tauftheologie (GThA 24; Göttingen: Vandenhoeck & Ruprecht, 1983).

Idem

The History and Theology of the New Testament Writings (Minneapolis: Fortress Press, 1998).

Schnider, Franz, and Werner Stenger

Studien zum neutestamentlichen Briefformular (NTTS 11; Leiden: Brill, 1987).

Schoonhoven, Henk

The Pseudo-Ovidian AD LIVIAM DE MORTE DRUSI (Consolatio ad Liviam, Epicedium Drusi): A Critical Text with Introduction and Commentary (Groningen: Forsten, 1992).

Schubert, Paul

Form and Function of the Pauline Thanksgivings (BZNW 20; Berlin: Töpelmann, 1939).

Schweitzer, Albert

The Mysticism of Paul the Apostle (Baltimore: Johns Hopkins University Press, 1998; orig., 1930).

Scourfield, J. H. D.

Consoling Heliodorus: A Commentary on Jerome 'Letter 60' (Oxford: Clarendon, 1993).

Segal, Alan F.

"Paul and the Beginning of Jewish Mysticism," in *Death, Ecstasy, and Other Worldly Journeys*, ed. John J. Collins and Michael Fishbane (Albany: State University of New York Press, 1995) 95–122.

Idem

Paul the Convert: The Apostolate and Apostasy of Saul the Pharisee (New Haven: Yale University Press, 1992).

Seim, Turid Karlsen, and Jorunn Økland, eds.

Metamorphoses: Resurrection, Body and Transformative Practices in Early Christianity (Ekstasis 1; Berlin/New York: de Gruyter, 2009).

Sellew, Philip

"*Laodiceans* and the Philippians Fragments Hypothesis," *HTR* 87 (1994) 17–28.

Idem

"*Laodiceans* and Philippians Revisited: A Response to Paul Holloway," *HTR* 91 (1998) 327–29.

Sevenster, J. N.

Paul and Seneca (NovTSup 4; Leiden: Brill, 1961).

Shantz, Colleen

Paul in Ecstasy: The Neurobiology of the Apostle's Life and Thought (Cambridge: Cambridge University Press, 2009).

Shaw, Brent

"The Myth of the Neronian Persecution," *JRS* 105 (2015) 73–100.

Sherwin-White, A. N.

Roman Society and Roman Law in the New Testament (Oxford: Clarendon, 1963).

Silva, Moises

"The Pauline Style as Lexical Choice: Γινώσκειν and Related Verbs," in *Pauline Studies: Essays Presented to Professor F. F. Bruce on His 70th Birthday*, ed. Donald A. Hagner and Murray J. Harris (Grand Rapids: Eerdmans, 1980) 184–207.

Skeat, T. C.

"Did Paul Write to 'Bishops and Deacons' at Philippi? A Note on Philippians 1:1," *NovT* 37 (1995) 12–15.

Smith, Morton
  "Pauline Worship as Seen by Pagans," *HTR* 73
  (1980) 241–49; reprinted in *Studies in the Cult of
  Yahweh*, ed. Shaye J. D. Cohen (2 vols.; SBLRGRW
  130, 131; Leiden: Brill, 1996) 2:95–102.
Söding, Thomas
  "Erniedrigung und Erhöhung: Zum Verhältnis
  von Christologie und Mythos nach dem Philipper-
  hymnus (Phil 2,6-11)," *ThPh* 67 (1992) 1–28;
  reprinted in idem, *Das Wort vom Kreuz: Studien zur
  paulinischen Theologie* (WUNT 93; Tübingen: Mohr
  Siebeck, 1997) 104–31.
Sommer, Benjamin D.
  Bodies of God and the World of Ancient Israel
  (Cambridge: Cambridge University Press, 2009).
Sorensen, Eric
  *Possession and Exorcism in the New Testament and
  Early Christianity* (WUNT 2/157; Tübingen: Mohr
  Siebeck, 2002).
Speidel, Michael
  *Guards of the Roman Imperial Armies: An Essay on
  the Singulares of the Provinces* (Antiquitas 1; Bonn:
  Habelt, 1978).
Stählin, Gustav
  "Zum Gebrauch von Beteuerungsformeln im
  Neuen Testament," *NovT* 5 (1962) 115–43.
Standhartinger, Angela
  "Letter from Prison as Hidden Transcript: What It
  Tells Us about the People at Philippi," in *The People
  beside Paul: The Philippian Assembly and History from
  Below*, ed. Joseph A. Marchal (ECL; Atlanta: SBL
  Press, 2015) 107–40.
Starr, James, and Troels Engberg-Pedersen, eds.
  Early Christian Paraenesis in Context (BZNW 125;
  Berlin: de Gruyter, 2004).
Steenburg, David
  "The Case against the Synonymity of *morphé* and
  eikôn," *JSNT* 34 (1988) 77–86.
Stegemann, W.
  "War der Apostel Paulus ein römischer Bürger?"
  ZNW 78 (1987) 200–229.
Stendahl, Krister
  "Paul and the Introspective Conscience of the
  West," *HTR* 55 (1963) 199–215.
Still, Todd D.
  "More than Friends? The Literary Classification
  of Philippians Revisited," *Perspectives in Religious
  Studies* 39 (2012) 53–66.
Stowers, Stanley K.
  "Friends and Enemies in the Politics of Heaven:
  Reading Theology in Philippians," in *Pauline Theol-
  ogy*, vol. 1, ed. Jouette M. Bassler (Minneapolis:
  Fortress Press, 1991) 105–21.
Idem
  "Paul and the Terrain of Philosophy," *EC* 6 (2015)
  141–56.
Idem
  A Rereading of Romans: Jews, Justice, and Gentiles
  (New Haven: Yale University Press, 1994).

Strecker, Christian
  *Die liminale Theologie des Paulus: Zugänge zur
  paulinischen Theologie aus kulturanthropologischer
  Perspektive* (FRLANT 185; Göttingen: Vandenhoeck
  & Ruprecht, 1999).
Taatz, Irene
  *Frühjüdische Briefe: Die paulinische Briefe im Rahmen
  der offiziellen religiösen Briefe des Frühjudentums*
  (NTOA 16; Fribourg: Universitätsverlag; Göttingen:
  Vandenhoeck & Ruprecht, 1991).
Taylor, John W.
  "From Faith to Faith: Romans 1.17 in the Light of
  Greek Idiom," *NTS* 50 (2004) 337–48.
Theissen, Gerd
  "Paulus — der Unglücksstifter: Paulus und die
  Verfolgung der Gemeinden in Jerusalem und
  Rom," in *Biographie und Persönlichkeit des Paulus*, ed.
  Eve-Marie Becker and Peter Pilhofer (WUNT 187;
  Tübingen: Mohr Siebeck, 2005) 228–44.
Vollenweider, Samuel
  "Hymnus, Enkomion oder Psalm? Schattengefechte
  in der neutestamentlichen Wissenschaft," *NTS* 56
  (2010) 208–31.
Idem
  "Die Metamorphose des Gottessohns," in *Das
  Urchristentum in seiner literarischen Geschichte: Fest-
  schrift für Jürgen Becker zum 65. Geburtstag*, ed. Ulrich
  Mell and Ulrich B. Müller (BZNW 100; Berlin: de
  Gruyter, 1999) 109–31.
Idem
  "'Der Name, den über jeden anderen Namen ist,'
  Jesus als Träger des Gottesnamens im Neuen Testa-
  ment," in *Gott Nennen: Gottes Namen und Gott als
  Name*, ed. Ingolf U. Dalferth and Philipp Stoellger
  (RPT 35; Tübingen: Mohr Siebeck, 2008) 173–86.
Idem
  "Der 'Raub' der Gottgleichheit: Ein religions-
  geschichtlicher Vorschlag zu Phil 2.6(-11)," *NTS* 45
  (1999) 413–33.
Idem
  "Die Waagschalen von Leben und Tod: Zum anti-
  ken Hintergrund von Phil 1,21-26," *ZNW* 85 (1994)
  93–115.
Idem
  "Zwischen Monotheismus und Engelchristologie:
  Überlegungen zur Frühgeschichte des Christus-
  glaubens," in idem, *Horizonte neutestamentlicher
  Christologie: Studien zu Paulus und zur frühchristlichen
  Theologie* (WUNT 144; Tübingen: Mohr Siebeck,
  2002) 3–27.
Wachtel, Klaus, and Klaus Witte, eds.
  *Das Neue Testament auf Papyrus, II: Die paulinischen
  Briefe, Teil 2: Gal, Eph, Phil, Kol, 1 u. 2 Thess,
  1 u. 2 Tim, Tit, Phlm, Hebr* (ANTF 22; Berlin: de
  Gruyter, 1994).

Waddell, James A.
The Messiah: A Comparative Study of the Enochic Son of Man and the Pauline Kyrios (Jewish and Christian Texts in Context 10; London: Bloomsbury T&T Clark, 2011).

Wallis, I. G.
The Faith of Jesus Christ in Early Christian Tradition (SNTSMS 84; Cambridge: Cambridge University Press, 1995).

Walter, Nikolaus
"Die Philipper und das Leiden: Aus den Anfängen einer heiden-christlichen Gemeinde," in *Die Kirche des Anfangs*, ed. Rudolf Schnackenburg, Josef Ernst, and Joachim Wanke (EThSt 38; Freiburg: Herder, 1978) 417–43.

Wansink, Craig S.
Chained in Christ: The Experience and Rhetoric of Paul's Imprisonments (JSNTSup 130; Sheffield: Sheffield Academic Press, 1996).

Wasserman, Emma
Death of the Soul in Romans 7: Sin, Death, and the Law in Light of Hellenistic Moral Philosophy (WUNT 2/256; Tübingen: Mohr Siebeck, 2008).

Watson, Duane F.
"A Rhetorical Analysis of Philippians and Its Implications for the Unity Question," *NovT* 30 (1988) 57–88.

Watson, Francis
Paul, Judaism, and Gentiles: Beyond the New Perspective (rev. and expanded ed.; Grand Rapids: Eerdmans, 2007).

Weaver, P. R. C.
Familia Caesaris: A Social Study of the Emperor's Freedmen and Slaves (Cambridge: Cambridge University Press, 1972).

Wedderburn, A. J. M.
"Some Observations on Paul's Use of the Phrases 'in Christ' and 'with Christ,'" *JSNT* 25 (1985) 83–97.

Weima, Jeffrey A. D.
Neglected Endings: The Significance of Pauline Letter Closings (JSNTSup 101; Sheffield: JSOT Press, 1994).

Weiss, Johannes
"Beiträge zur paulinischen Rhetorik," in *Theologische Studien: Herrn Wirkl. Oberkonsistorialrath Professor D. Bernhard Weiss zu seinem 70. Geburtstag*, ed. C. R. Gregory et al. (Göttingen: Vandenhoeck & Ruprecht, 1897) 165–247.

White, John L.
"Introductory Formulae in the Body of the Pauline Letter," *JBL* 90 (1971) 91–97.

Idem
Light from Ancient Letters (Philadelphia: Fortress Press, 1986).

Idem
"Saint Paul and the Apostolic Letter Tradition," *CBQ* 45 (1983) 433–44.

White, L. Michael
"Morality between Two Worlds: A Paradigm of Friendship in Philippians," in *Greeks, Romans, and Christians: Essays in Honor of Abraham J. Malherbe*, ed. D. L. Balch, E. Ferguson, and Wayne A. Meeks (Minneapolis: Fortress Press, 1990) 201–15.

White, Peter
Cicero in Letters: Epistolary Relations of the Late Republic (Oxford: Oxford University Press, 2010).

Wick, Peter
"'Ahmt Jesus Christus mit mir zusammen nach!' (Phil 3,17): *Imitatio Pauli* und *imitatio Christi* im Philipperbrief," in *Der Philipperbrief des Paulus in der hellenistisch-römischen Welt*, ed. Jörg Frey and Benjamin Schliesser (WUNT 353; Tübingen: Mohr Siebeck, 2015) 309–26.

Idem
Der Philipperbrief: Der formale Aufbau des Briefs als Schlüssel zum Verständnis seines Inhalts (BWANT 7.15; Stuttgart: Kohlhammer, 1994).

Wilcox, Amanda
"Sympathetic Rivals: Consolation in Cicero's Letters," *AJPh* 126 (2005) 237–55.

Wiles, Gordon P.
Paul's Intercessory Prayers (SNTSMS 24; Cambridge: Cambridge University Press, 1974).

Wojtkowiak, Heiko
Christologie und Ethik im Philipperbrief: Studien zur Handlungsorientierung einer frühchristlichen Gemeinde in paganer Umwelt (FRLANT 243; Göttingen: Vandenhoeck & Ruprecht, 2012).

Wrede, William
Paul (London: Green, 1907).

Yarbro Collins, Adela
"Psalms, Philippians 2:6-11, and the Origins of Christology" *BibInt* 11 (2002) 261–72.

Yarbro Collins, Adela, and John J. Collins
King and Messiah as Son of God: Divine, Human, and Angelic Messianic Figures in Biblical and Related Literature (Grand Rapids: Eerdmans, 2008).

Zahn, Theodor
Introduction to the New Testament (trans. John Moore Trout et al. from 3rd German ed.; 3 vols.; Edinburgh: T&T Clark, 1903).

Zeller, Dieter
Charis bei Philon und Paulus (SBS 142; Stuttgart: Katholisches Bibelwerk, 1990).

Idem
"Die Menschwerdung des Sohnes Gottes im Neuen Testament und die antike Religionsgeschichte," in *Menschwerdung Gottes – Vergöttlichung von Menschen*, ed. Dieter Zeller (NTOA 7; Freiburg: Universitätsverlag; Göttingen: Vandenhoeck & Ruprecht, 1988) 141–76.

Idem
"New Testament Christology in Its Hellenistic Reception," *NTS* 47 (2001) 312–33.

Zimmermann, Bernhard
  "Philosophie als Psychotherapie: Die griechisch-römische Consolationsliteratur," in *Stoizismus in der europäischen Philosophie, Literatur, Kunst und Politik: Eine Kulturgeschichte von der Antike bis zur Moderne*, ed. Barbara Neymeyr, Jochen Schmidt, and Bernhard Zimmermann (2 vols.; Berlin: de Gruyter, 2008) 1:193–213.

Zuntz, Günther
  The Text of the Epistles: A Disquisition upon the Corpus Paulinum (The Schweich Lectures of the British Academy 1946; London: British Academy/Oxford University Press, 1953).

12.241	157^{14}	2.40-41	79^{71}	*y. Sanh.*			
12.271	159^{25}	2.288	50^{399}	18d	68^{68}		
13.172-73	132^{16}	*Op.*					
17.41	158^{20}	74	79^{71}	**f / New Testament**			
18.13	132^{16}	*Plant.*					
18.14	$46^{365}, 107^{31},$	138	3^{15}	Matthew			
	170^{104}	*Post.*		5:33-39	158^{20}		
18.18	132^{16}	81	79^{71}	9:37-38	$149^{16}, 153^{52}$		
18.65	90^{51}	*Praem.*		10:4	159^{29}		
Ap.		32	3^{15}	10:19-20	94^{16}		
1.249	134^{35}	70	79^{71}	10:10	$149^{16}, 153^{52}$		
Bell.		*Prob.*		10:12	190^{4}		
2.162	158^{20}	61	79^{71}	11:18	47^{379}		
2.163	$46^{365}, 107^{31}, 132^{16},$	83	79^{71}	13:43	134^{39}		
	170^{104}	*Q. Gen.*		16:26	161		
2.651	159^{26}	1:92	46^{367}	19:28	$45^{360}, 48^{386}, 128$		
3.120	23^{175}	*Sac.*		22:30	50^{397}		
4.160	159^{26}	99	79^{71}	23	158^{20}		
Vit.		*Spec.*		25:31	$45^{360}, 48^{386}, 128$		
191	158^{20}	1.67	72^{19}	26:59	$22^{172}, 87^{20}$		
		1.283	72^{19}	27:13-14	98^{22}		
Philo		1.284	72^{19}	27:27	87^{19}		
Abr.		1.285	72^{19}	27:52	64^{31}		
156	$3^{15}, 150^{24}$	2.46	79^{71}	28:5	125^{83}		
Conf.		2.87	109^{47}				
106	151^{33}	*Virt.*		Mark			
146	48^{385}	216	151^{33}	1:33	22^{172}		
Congr.				3:16	62^{16}		
141	151^{33}	**e / Rabbinic Writings**		3:18	159^{29}		
De cher.				3:22	47^{379}		
26	47^{378}	*b. Sanh.*		3:30	$47^{379}, 66^{44}$		
De migr. Abr.		38b	$48^{385}, 127$	5:15	47^{379}		
35	47^{378}			7:25	$47^{379}, 66^{44}$		
Det.		*m. 'Abot*		8:36	161		
122	79^{71}	2.1	160	9:2-8	49^{390}		
135	3^{15}	3.15	132^{16}	9:17	$47^{379}, 66^{44}$		
Fug.				11:22	166^{74}		
152	79^{71}	*m. Sanh.*		13:11	94^{16}		
Her.		9.6	159^{29}	13:19-20	27^{215}		
31	72^{19}			15:1	22^{172}		
253	79^{71}	*Mekh. Exod.*		15:4-5	98^{22}		
314	151^{33}	12:30	140^{17}	15:16	87^{19}		
315	$3^{15}, 29^{226}$			16:6	125^{83}		
Jos.		*Sifre Num.*					
81-84	26^{206}	25	159^{28}	Luke			
Leg.				1:59	157^{14}		
2.17	79^{71}	*Sifre Deut.*		2:21	157^{14}		
Mos.		47	134^{39}	4:33	$47^{379}, 66^{44}$		
1.15	140^{14}			6:15	159^{29}		
1.66	49^{391}	*t. Sanh.*		6:22	45^{360}		
		2.6	68^{68}				

214

2:12-13	160	7:23	132, 142[1]	12:2	78[70]	
2:12	53[416], 107[27]	7:24	42[327]	12:3	176[38]	
2:13	54	7:25b	40[310]	12:6-8	67	
2:16	45[360], 80	8:3	120[44, 46], 126[92],	12:13	64[30], 75[40], 187[17]	
2:17-24	134[35]		127[95], 160, 169	12:13 *v.l.*	72[21]	
2:18	78[70], 79[71]	8:4	52[404], 66[48], 169,	12:15	3[13], 32[246], 176[32],	
2:22	134[35], 153		177		188[21]	
2:23	101[48]	8:5	169, 176[38], 177	12:16	176[38]	
2:25	160	8:6	176[38], 177	12:21	40[310], 41[320]	
2:28-29	40[310], 152	8:7	176[38]	13:12	142[1]	
3:3	165[65]	8:9	28, 28[216, 218], 47,	14:6	176[38]	
3:9	91[63]		47[377], 48[380], 54,	14:10	50[396]	
3:20	40[310], 169		66[45], 75[45], 154,	14:10 *v.l.*	45[360]	
3:22	165, 167[86]		168, 169	14:11	129[118]	
3:26	41[319], 165-66,	8:9a	65	14:15	107[27]	
	176[30]	8:9b	66[44]	14:23	40[310]	
3:27	77[64]	8:11	168[92]	15:1-3	116-17	
4:12	167[85]	8:13	169, 176[30]	15:3	115[2]	
4:16	167[85] 4:25	8:14	52[404], 169, 177	15:5	176[38]	
	41[320]	8:17	46[364], 169[100]	15:7-13	27[213]	
5–8	48[381]	8:18	27[215]	15:7	129[117]	
5:1	54[419]	8:19	180[19]	15:13	77[64], 78, 169	
5:1b-2	54	8:23-27	170	15:14-15	150	
5:3-5	132	8:23	180[19]	15:16	42[332]	
5:3-4	46[364], 169[100]	8:25	180[19]	15:18	124[74]	
5:5	54, 133, 191[11]	8:27	64[30], 176[38]	15:22-29	13	
5:9	54[418-19]	8:28-30	174[12]	15:20	20[158]	
5:10-11	54	8:29	175	15:23	90[54]	
5:10	54[419]	8:31-39	9, 178[2]	15:24	23	
5:11	101[48]	8:29	52	15:24b	23[180]	
5:12-21	48[381]	9:1-5	179[8]	15:25-28	21[164]	
5:15	77[64], 78[64]	9:22	53[416], 107[25]	15:25-26	158[19]	
5:19	124[74], 165[65],	9:30-31	41[321]	15:25	64[30], 64[34]	
	166[79]	9:31	176	15:26	64[30], 64[34], 75[40],	
6:3-4	46[363], 169[98]	10:1-15:13	90		187[17]	
6:4	46	10:1	164, 179[8]	15:27	75[40], 187[17], 188	
6:5	46, 170[103]	10:2	78, 159	15:28-29	23[180]	
6:6	124[76], 125	10:3	163	15:28	23	
6:12	124[74]	10:13	40[310]	15:31	64[30]	
6:15	91[63]	10:16	124, 124[74]	15:33	68[73], 78[64], 183[21],	
6:16	124[74]	10:17	40[310], 41[322]		184[30]	
6:17	75[48], 124[74], 169[97]	11:1	62[13], 158	16:1-2	67	
6:23	40[310]	11:7	22[170]	16:1	158[19], 186[4]	
7	132[19]	11:13	27[212], 45[355], 89[42]	16:2	64[30]	
7:7	169	11:17	75[40], 187[17]	16:2a	182[7]	
7:8	132(17	11:20	176[38]	16:3-16	190[2]	
7:17	132[17]	11:33-36	178[2]	16:8	179	
7:18	132	11:33	41[325]	16:15	64[30]	
7:20	132[17]	11:36	41[325], 80[82]	16:16	190	
7:22	52	12:1	168[92]	16:19	124[74]	

---

1   The principal treatment of passages from Philippians is in the commentary *ad locum*. These references are not listed in this index. Other references to passages from Philippians are noted in the index.

1 Timothy (*continued*)
2:4	142[1]
3:16	117[20]
5:18	149[16], 153[52]

2 Timothy
1:1	62[9]
1:2	67[67]
1:4	140[19]
1:8	187[14]
2:3	46[364]
2:9	85[1]
2:15	149[16], 153[52]
4:6	106[19]
4:7	86[11], 173[3]
4:16	99[32], 187[14]
4:18	136[7]

Titus
1:1	62[9]
1:11	22[172]
1:18	142[1]

Philemon
1	62[9], 63[24]
2	142[1]
3	67[66]
4-7	70[2]
4	71[7-8], 72[18]
5	64[30], 68[74]
6	75[40]
7	3[13], 64[30]
9	62[9]
11	182[9]
17	75[40], 187[17]
19	62[9]
21	124[74]
22	13, 71[9]
23	190
25	68[71, 74], 191[9]

Hebrews
1:3	180[22]
1:7	49
3:2-5	22[172]
3:1	175[23]
3:2	87[20]
3:5	87[20]
6:10	64[31]
6:19	151[33]
12:2	124
13:2	49
13:24	64[31]

James
1:1	61[3]
1:2-4	43[342], 169[100]
2:14-26	166[75]
2:14-16	164
5:10	127[97]

1 Peter
1:1-12	9
1:3	71[7]
1:4-5	93[4]
1:5	55[425], 183[21]
1:6	27[215]
2:12	129[118]
3:8-12	112[3]
3:15	94[16]
4:12–5:23	9
4:12-19	109[49]
4:12-14	109[49]
4:12	9
4:13	46[363]
4:16	91[61], 187[14]
4:17	27[215]
5:1	61[a]
5:10	27[215]
5:12	9, 55[425]

2 Peter
1:2	68[68]
1:3-5	168[94]
1:5	184[25]
3:15-16	164[60]
3:15	62[9]
3:16	87[17]

1 John
2:2	22[172], 87[20]
2:28	27[215]
5:19	22[172], 87[20]

2 John
3	67[67]
4	17[137]
12	13[104]

3 John
3	17[137]
13-14	13[104]

Jude
14	64[31]
24	55[425]

Revelation 9
1:4	68[67]
1:10	51[403], 65[43]
2:22	27[215]
3:10	22[172]
4:2	51[403], 66[43]
4:6	128[112]
5:6	128[112]
5:8	65
5:13	128[116]
7:14	27[215], 43[342], 107[25]
7:14	169[100]
8:3	65
8:4	65
11:8	124
12:9	22[172], 87[20]
16:14	87[20]
17:3	51[403], 66[43]
21:1	51[403]
21:10	66[43]

g/ Early Christian Writings

1 Clem.
2.8	180[18]
3.4	180[18]
5.5	23[186]
21.1	180[18]
22	112[3]
44.6	180[18]
51.2	180[18]
54.5	180[18]

Act. Paul. et Thecl.
3	52

Act. Paul.
3.3	52
4.33	106[23]
14	24[186]

Act. Thom.
108   116^{17}

Ambrose
De exc. Sat. 7^{51}
1.3 3^{12}, 5^{37}, 73^{28}
Ep.
15   7^{51}
39   4^{25}, 7^{31}, 100^{46}
Hexam.
5.6 12^{95}
Obit. Theod. 7^{51}
Obit. Valent. 7^{51}

Ambrosiaster
In Phil.
On 1:3 72^{15}

Augustine
Ep.
79   12^{95}
92   7^{51}
259   7^{51}
263   7^{51}
In Psalm.
67.32.4 12^{95}
Serm.
172   7^{51}
173   7^{51}
Spir. et litt.
7.12 62^{15}
9   166

Basil
Ep.
5   7^{51}
5.2 5^{37}, 73^{28}
6   7^{51}
28   7^{51}
29   7^{51}
31   7^{51}
140   7^{51}
238   7^{51}
247   7^{51}
256   7^{51}
257   7^{51}
269.2 5^{37}, 73^{28}
301   7^{51}
302   7^{51}

Book of Elchasai
frag. 1 118^{26}

Catalogus Sinaiticus
   11, 11^{88}

Cyprian
De mort. 7^{51}, 183^{16}

Did.
3.9 66^{55}
16.5 55^{425}

Epiphanius
Pan.
19.4.1 118^{26}
30.17.6-7 118^{26}
53.1.9 118^{26}

Eusebius
Hist. eccl.
2.25.8 24^{186}
Praep. Ev.
1.10.4

Gosp. Pet.
5   136^{1}
40   118^{26}

George of Alexandria
Vit. Chrys.
27(147.1-6 Halkin) 140^{17}

Georgius Syncellus
Chronographia   11
12.651 11^{89}

Gregory Nazianzen
Ep.
31.4 2^{6}
165   2^{9}, 4^{23}
Or.
7   7^{51}
18   7^{51}

Gregory of Nyssa
Melet. 7^{51}
Pulch. 7^{51}
Flac. 7^{51}

Gregory Thaumaturgus
Pan. Orig.
16–19 6^{50}

Hermas
Sim.
9.14.3 72^{19}
Vis.
1.3.2 34^{259}, 139^{7}

Hippolytus
Ref.
9.13.1-3 118^{26}

Hom. Clem.
2.39 107^{23}

Ignatius of Antioch
Eph.
1.1 62^{16}
Mag.
1.1 62^{16}
Rom.
2.2 136^{7}
Smyrn.
10.1-2 16^{126}
Trall.
1.1 62^{16}

Jerome
Ep.
23   7^{71}
39   7^{51}
39.3-4 4^{25}, 100^{46}
60   7^{51}
60.7 3^{12}
60.7.3 $5^{37, 38}$, 73^{28}, 184^{25}
60.14.5-6 105^{10}
66   7^{51}
75   7^{51}
76.2 2^{6}
77   7^{51}
79   7^{51}
108   7^{51}
108.1.2 5^{37}, 73^{28}
118   7^{51}
118.4.2 5^{37}, 73^{28}
127   7^{51}

---

2   Cited by homily, page, and line number(s) in Allen.

3   Homily 1 is prefatory. The MS tradition variously calls it a ὑπόνημα ("summary account") or a ὑπόθεσις ("argument"). It briefly summarizes the letter, the proper exposition of which begins in homily 2. Allen's numbering differs from *PG* 62 in that she lists this summary as homily 1, while PG 62 treats it as a separate *praefatio.*

2 Apol.
2   90[52]

Laodiceans   12-13, 13[97]
6   12[95]
7   12[95]
9   12[95], 12[96]
13   12
15-16   12[95]

Leo VI Philosophus
Or.
18.5   140[17]

Martin (Martinus I, papa)
Narr. de exil.
30   35[275]

Mart. Pion.
18.12   116[17]

Origen
Cel.
3.55   90[52]
In Ioann.
1.29   182[8]
2:31   50[393], 122[57], 124[72]
In Rom.
3:26   166

Paulinus of Nola
Carm.
31   7[51]
33   7[51]
Ep.
13   7[51]
13.6   5[37], 73[28]

Pelagius
In Phil.
on 1:3   72[15]
on 1:7   76[53]
on 1:18   91[65]
on 3:1   147[3]

Polycarp
Ad Phil.
3:2   11, 11[90], 150[28]

Prayer of Thanksgiving
(Coptic/NHC VI.7)
    162
595-601   162

Pseudo-Jerome
Ep.
5   2[6]

Symeon Metaphrastes
Vit. Chrys.
23   140[17]

Tatian
Or.
10   122[55]

Tertullian
Ap.
1.7   27[210]
37.4   27[210]
Scap.
2.10   27[210]

Theodoret
In Phil.
on 1:12-13   33[256]
on 1:13   22[171]
on 1:17   89[41]
on 2:1   112, 112[11]
on 2:17-18   33[256]
on 3:1   11[90]
3:19   179[11]
on 4:22   33[256]

Vetus Latina
Phil 1:3   72[15]

h / Greek/Latin/Coptic/Syriac Writings

Aelianus
Var. hist.
7.3   2

Aesop
Fab.
89 (Perry)   120[44]
288 (Hausrath)   183

Anth. Graec.
16.54   175

Antoninus Liberalis
Metam.
1.5   120[43]
5.5   120[43]
7.7   120[43]
8.7   120[43]
10.4   120[43]
12.8   120[43]
14.3   120[43]
17.4-5   120[43]
20.6-8   120[43]

Aphthonius
Prog.
4.67-72   41[314]
8-9   151[36], 157[12]
8   116[16], 157[13]
10   148[11], 151[36, 38]
12   174[16]

Apollonius of Tyana
Ep.
55   6[46]
58   6[46]

Appian
Bell. civ.
4.105-38   26
5.1.3   87[27]

Apollonius of Rhodes
Argon.
1430   120[43]

Apuleius
Metam.
3.24   51[400], 122[58]
11.3-6   162[51]
11.6   162[51]
11.13   51[400], 122[58]
11.19   162[51]
11.20   160[34]
11.21   170[101]
11.22   162[51]
11.23-24   52[404]
11:23   170[101]
11.24-25   162[51]

Aristides
Or.
31   6[49]
42   112[3]

226

3.31.76	4, 4[30], 29[228], 36[285], 73[27, 29], 79[74], 109[46]
3.32.77	37[288]
3.34.81	2
4.7.14	5[33]
4.16.35	3[21]
4.38.82	5[33]
5.23.67	184[23]
5.26.73-74	5[35], 73[27]
5.30.85	157[13]
Ver.	
2.5.66	124[78]

Corp. Herm.

4.11b	52[404]
13.8-9	168[89]\13.8 3[12]

Demetrius
Eloc.

2.106	42[326]
9	41[314]

Democritus

frag. B 202 (Diels and Kranz)	183[19]

Dio Chrysostom
Or.

13.8	5[34]
17.1-2	150[30]
27.9	4
28	6[49]
29	6[49]
30	6[50], 35[277]
30.6	35[277]
38-41	112[3]

Diodorus Siculus
Bib. hist.

1.86.3	120[44]
2.19	106[23]
13.28.33	97[14]
13.31.1	97[14]

Diogenes Laertius
Vit.

2.34	2[6]
2.42	26[202], 116[17]
2.86-87	108[42]
2.87	108[41]
2.89-90	109
5.24	2[6]
6.63	109[45]
8.10	188[18]
9.20	2[6]
10.22	6[50], 35[272, 277], 73
10.136	108[41]

Dionysius of Halicarnassus
Ant.

2.19	90[2.19]
Rhet.	
10.18	77[56]

EM (Etymologicum Magnum)

s.v. σκύβαλον	191[36]

Ennius
Med.

frag. 104	97[13]

Epictetus
Ench.

5	5[33]
21	109[45]
Diss.	
2.2.8-17	98[22]
2.5.7	79[71]
2.6.16	124[75]
2.6.27	26[202]
3.10.1-3	109[45]
3.22	175[24]
3.22.1	91[65]
3.24.104	109[46]
3.24.115	109[47]
4.1.164	94
4.4.23	116[17]
4.7.4	91[65]
4.7.5	91[65]
4.7.6	91[65]
4.7.27	79[71]
4.7.40	79[71]

Epicurus
frag. (Usener)

1	18[41]
122	35[271]
138 (= Arrighetti frag 52)	35[272]
450	108[41]
490	1183[19]
Sent. Vat.	
4	183[15]
14	183[19]
55	5[35], 73[27], 183[19]
66	2[9]

Euripides
Alc.

1-7	122[57], 124[72]
2-7	119
349-52	140[17]
369-70	6[45], 32[246], 61[7], 188[21]
Andr.	
384-420	97[9]
Bacch.	121
4-5	121[49]
53-54	121[50]
618	122[64]
1330	120[43]
frag.	
930	120[43]
964d	109[45]
Hec.	
445-83	6[50]
Hel.	
19	117[21], 120[42], 121, 126[91]
29-36	140[17]
255-305	97[9]
Her.	
1154-62	97[10]
Iph. Aul.	
408	6[45], 32[246], 188[19]
Med.	
465-519	97[9]
Phoen.	
625-35	6[50]
1595-1624	97[9]
Suppl.	
1094-1103	97[9]

Favorinus
De exil.

96.2	3[19]
frag. (Barigazzi)	
9-17	2[6]
22.22.44-48	5[34]

Rutilius Namatianus

De red.

1-164	6[50]

Scholia on Aristides

3:105 Dindorf	140[17]

Seneca

Ad Helv. 6[47], 33, 34, 37[289]

1.2	33, 35
2:4-4:1	73[31]
2-3	34[261]
4-5	3, 5[32]
4.1	15, 34
4.2-13.8	33, 34[262]
4.2	15
5.1	5[34], 15, 34
5.3-5	35[268]
5.3	5[39], 6[42], 109[44-45], 109[48]
10-13	2[6]
14.1-19.1	33
17.2	73[31]
17.5	183[16]
18-19	5[37]
18.1-19.7	35[268]
18.5	183[16]
18.7-8	4[26], 80[83], 100[42]
18.9	183[16]

Ad Marc. 6[47], 37[289], 82[8]

1.2-5	73[31]
1.8	73[31]
2.1-5.6	6[43], 108[37]
2-4	3[20]
2-3	4[25], 100[46]
2.3-4	5[37]
3.4	3[12]
4.3-5.6	5[37], 73[31]
9.2	6[42], 109[48]
10.2	4[27], 183[19]
12.1-2	183[19]
16.8	140
21.1-4	5[37, 38]
24.1-4	184
24.3	184[25]
24.4	183[16]
25.3	134[38]
26.6-7	134[38]

Ad Poly. 6[47], 82[8]

2.2	4[27]
3.1	183[19]
4.1	4[27]
5-8	5[37]
5-6	4[26], 80[83], 100[42]
5.4	3[20]
5.5	34[263]
6.3	105[10]
10.2	183[19]
10.6	3[12], 73[31]
11.1	6[42], 109[48]
11.2	105[10]
12-13	5[37]
14.1-17.6	6[43], 108[37]
14.1-16.3	3[20]
17.3-6	3[20]
18.7-8	184
18.8	5[38]

Agam.

138	97[12], 98[26]

De benef.

2.32.2	186[6]
3.4.1	5[37], 73[31]
4.40(3)	186[6]

De brev. vit.

9.4	109[48]
10.2-4	5[37], 73[31]

De clem.

1.7.3	5[39], 109[44]

De ira

3.39.4	5[37], 73[31]

De prov.

4.6	5[39], 109[44]
13	5[39], 109[44]

De tran. an.

7.3	183[16]
11.6	109[45]
16.1	183[16]

De vit. beat.

6.1-2	5[37], 73[31]
8.6	109[48]

Ep.

13.4	5[32]
15	143[3]
17	2[6]
21	2[6]
23.1-3	149
23.1	4, 15, 15[114]
23.2	3, 15, 29[226], 100
23.3	3[15], 147[2]
23.4	15[118], 147[2], 150, 150[24]
23.6	15[115], 150[25]
24	2[6]
34.3	132[20]
42.5	79[93]
47.4	5[39], 109[44]
59	150
59.14	3, 29[226], 100[44], 147[2]
60.7.3	184
63	6[46]
63.4	5[37], 73[31]
63.12-13	140
63.14	6[42], 109[48]
66.5	3[15], 29[226]
71.36	132[20]
74.26	91[65]
75	61[8]
80.4	132[20]
81	2[6]
91.9	2[6]
93	6[46]
94.26	150[30]
94.39	4, 4[26], 80[83], 100[42]
99	6[46]
99.2	4, 100[46], 105[11]
99.3-5	5[37], 73[31]
99.3	3[12]
99.4	183[19], 184[28]
99.25	73[27]
99.32	4, 100[46]
104	99
107	2[6], 1-8
107.1	79, 80
107.2-9	6[43]
107.4	6[42]
107.5	108
107.7	105[10]
107.9	4[27], 108
107.10	132[13]
111.4	91[65]

Herc.

1940-43	134[38]
1963	134[38]
1976-79	134[38]

Med.

938-39	97[12], 98[26]

Seneca Rhetor
Contr.
3 pr. 7   40[312]
9.5.15-17   165[71]
Suas.
3.7   97[12], 98[26]

Sextus Empiricus
Adv. math.
2.57   77[56]
Pyrrh.
1.215   108[42]

Sophocles
Ajax
430-80   96[9]
Phil.
1348-72   96[9]
1452-71   6[50]

Soranus
Gynaec.
2.34   157[14]

Statius
Ach.
1.200   98[26]
Silv.
2.1   6[48]
2.4   6[48]
2.6   6[48]
2.6.103-4   141[20]
2.7   6[48]
3.3   6[48]
5.1   6[48]
5.3   6[48]
5.5   6[48]

Stesichorus
Palin.
frag. 192   140[17]

Stobaeus
Ecl.
2.80.8-9   79[71]
Flor.
4.48.16-31   2[7]
4.51.1-32   6[43]

Suetonius
Aug.
50   19[147]
Claud.
25.4   90[54, 57]
Dom.
4.4   172[2]
Ner.
16.2   90[53]
Tib.
36   90[51]
37.1   23[177]

Suidas
2.553.4   108[43]

Tacitus
Agr.
46.1   6[50], 35[277]
Ann.
2.85   90[51]
4.2   23[177]
12.68   140
15.44   90[53], 106
15.60-64   6[50], 35[277]
15.64   136[7]
16.35   136[7]
Dial.
20   41
Hist.
1.76   98[26]
2.93.2   23[177]

Teles
frag.
3   5[34]
7.59   136[2]
8   6[47]
22.1-2   5[34]
29.2-3   5[34]

Themistius
Or.
20   6[49]

Theognis
El.
11–14   6[50]

Theon
Prog.
7   174[16]
9-10   151[36]
9   116[16], 157[12-13]
10   148[11]

Thucydides
Hist.
2.34-46   136[2]
2.44   2, 39[303], 136[2]

Tibullus
El.
1.10   6[50]

Virgil
Aen.
1.33   42, 77[56]
4.327-30   140
4.333-61   6[50]
4.534-52   97[10, 13]
6.103-5   109[45]

Xenophon
Apol.
9   98[22]
27-28   6[50], 35[277]
Cyropaed.
7.6-28   6[50], 35[277]
Mem.
2.4.6   32[246]

Xenophon of Ephesus
Eph.
5.1.11   140[17]

i/ Papyri/Inscriptions/Ostraca/Coins etc.

ABV
68.2   174[17]
120   175[19]
322.4   175[19]
322.6   175[19]
408.4   175[19]

AÉ
1922.33   22[175]
1933.56   22[175]
1935(1936).46   191[8]
1937.250   22[175], 23[175]

2. Greek Terms and Expressions

μορφὴν/μόρφωμα λαμβάνειν (see also
   σχῆμα λαμβάνειν)
   117[21], 120, 120[42], 121, 122[55],
   124[72]
μνεία
   72
μνήμη
   73
μυέω
   187

νοῦς
   162

ὁ ἔσω ἄνθρωπος
   52
οἶδα
   93, 98, 100
οἰκεῖν ἐν
   47[377]
οἰκία (see also familia Caesaris,
   "household of Caesar")
   23, 190, 190[4]
ὁ/ἡ καί (see also qui/quae et)
   62, 62[16]
ὀκνηρός
   150[31], 151[34]
ὅλος
   21, 22[172], 87[20]
ὁμοίωμα
   49, 120, 120[46], 123, 124[72]
ὄνομα (see also τὸ ὄνομα τὸ ὑπὲρ πᾶν
   ὄνομα, ἐν τῷ ὀνόματι)
   18, 48[385]
οὐρανός (see also ἐπουράνιος)
   18, 134, 175, 179
οὐσία
   46[367]
οὐχ ὅτι
   173, 187–88

πάθημα
   74, 77, 169
πάθος
   3[14]
παράδειγμα
   3[19]
παράδοξος
   41[321]

παραμυθέω/παραμυθία/
   παραμυθητικός
   1, 33, 39[304]
παρακαλέω/παράκλησις
   1, 3, 15[117], 18[137], 34[259], 112[12], 143,
   151
παρουσία
   30[232], 80, 80[86], 131, 131[7], 144
παρρησία
   92, 94[14], 98
πᾶς
   64[28], 74, 78[6]
πάσχω (see also συμπάσχω)
   169
πείθω
   64[28], 141, 154[55], 157, 157[10]
πένθος
   1
πεποίθησις
   157, 157[10]
περιπατέω
   105, 105[4], 179[7]
περισσεύω/περισσοτέρως (see also
   τινὰ περισσεύειν ἐν τινί)
   77, 77[64], 78[64], 100, 187
περιτομή
   152, 154[55]
πιστεύω/πίστις/πίστος
   3, 19, 39, 77[62], 100[41], 106[19], 136,
   136[1], 137, 140[13], 165, 165[68], 166,
   169
πιστεύω εἰς
   166, 166[80], 167
πίστις ἐν
   166
πίστις θεοῦ
   166[74]
πίστις Χριστοῦ
   55[426], 163, 165–67, 167[85, 86]
πνεῦμα
   19, 28, 46, 47[372], 65[36], 74, 93
πνεῦμα ἔχειν
   47, 66[44]
πνεῦμα θεοῦ/Χριστοῦ
   47[377], 187[13]
πνευματικός
   46, 46[367], 47
πολιτεύομαι/πολίτευμα
   19, 102[3], 105, 179[7]
πολλῷ μᾶλλον κρεῖσσον
   99

πραιτώριον
   21, 21[166, 167], 22–23, 87
πράσσω
   183–84
προαίρεσις
   96[8]
προκόπτω/προκοπή
   3, 86, 150[23]
προπέμπω
   23[180]
προσεύχομαι/προσευχή (see also
   εὔχομαι)
   183, 183[17]
πτύρω
   30, 106, 108, 108[36]

σάρξ
   152[43], 157
σινγουλαρίος
   23[175]
σκοπός
   174
σκύβαλον
   161[36]
σπένδω
   136
σπλάγχνα
   77, 77[60]
σπονδή
   136[7]
σταυρόω/σταυρός
   18, 124[76]
στέφανος
   180
στήκω
   19, 113[12], 147, 149
στοιχέω
   176, 176[32, 34], 177[42]
συγκοινωνέω/συγκοινωνός
   17[133], 19[145], 75[40, 49], 187, 187[16, 17]
συγχαίρω (see also χαίρω)
   19[145], 82[5], 102[3], 137
σύζυγος
   182
συλλαμβάνω
   182
συμμιμητής
   178

3. Latin Terms and Expressions

colonia victrix
89[39]

Colonia Victrix Philippensium
26

consolator
34, 85[5], 139

consolor
33

consolatio mortis
39, 82[1], 96, 102, 136, 136[2]

cupido
98[27]

dignus
105

diploma
88, 89[39]

disputatio
37[289]

dolor
1, 112[8]

domus
23, 190

expaveo
108

familia
23, 190

familia Caesaris
23, 190–91

fides qua creditur in Christum
166

gaudeo
3[15], 12, 15, 15[115], 29[226], 34[264], 41[323], 100, 143[3], 147, 149, 150[25]

gaudium
2–3, 3[15], 15, 100[44], 149

indignus
105

inopinatus
41[321], 109[46], 176[30]

laetitia
2, 73

liberti Augusti
191[8]

licentia
94[14]

meditatio
94[16]

memoria
72, 72[15], 73, 76[53]

molliter
4

nihil mali
15

odium humani generis
106

praecaveo
12, 12[95]

praemeditatio futuri mali
5, 109, 109[45, 49]

praemeditatio mortis
39[303]

praetorianus
22[175]

praetorium
21, 21[166], 87

primum bonum
29[226]

princeps praetorii
22[175]

prudentia
79

pusilla res (*see also res severa*)
79

qui/quae et
62[16]

ratio dati et accepi (*see also λόγος δόσεως καὶ λήμψεως*)
188

religio
158, 158[23]

res severa
3[15], 15, 15[118], 150

revocatio/revoco
5, 73, 184

salutem (plurimam) dicit
61[4]

schola
37[289]

singularis
22, 87

sive . . . sive
91[65]

solacium
1, 34, 85[5], 139

solicitudo
76[53]

stationarius
22[175]

supernomen
62[16], 63, 63[18]

superstitio
24, 158, 158[23]

tranquilitas
183[21]

tribunus cohortium praetoriarum
88

volo
132, 132[20]

video
12[95]

virtus
184[26]

4. Modern Authors

Abel, K.
34, 34[263, 265], 37[288], 73[24, 31], 85[5], 108[37]

Aichele, G.
49[390], 123[66]

Aland, B.
57[437]

Aland, K.
55[428], 56[430]

Aletti, J.-N.
18[141], 140[14]

Alexander, L.
18[137], 29[230], 32, 32[249], 33, 33[251], 35, 35[276], 36, 36[282], 38, 38[295–98], 73, 73[25], 95[2], 102, 102[2], 139, 139[9]

Alexander, P.
132[16]

Allenbach, J.
56[430]

Amandry, M.
87[24, 26], 88[28]

Anger, R.
12[92-93, 95]

Aquinas, T.
72[15], 112[8], 125[84]

Arband, S.
19[151], 26[206]

Arena, V.
152[40]

Arnold, B.
174[16], 175[18, 20]

Arzt, P.
18[137], 71[13]

Arzt-Grabner, P.
68[69]

Ascough, R. S.
66[52]

Ashton, J.
66[46], 147[3], 170[101-2]

Aspan, P. F.
14[113]

Attridge, H. W.
151[33]

Aune, D. E.
32[244]

Austin, N. J. E.
22[175]

Avery-Peck, A. J.
107[31]

Bagnall, R. S.
36[279]

Bahr, G. J.
186[1]

Bailey, C.
183[19]

Balch, D. L.
112[3]

Baillet, J.
22[175], 23[175]

Balz, H.
10[80]

Barclay, J. M. G.
42[330], 46[369], 53[414], 54[425], 75[46], 90[46], 125[80-81], 132[16], 152[43], 153[51], 166[72-73], 167[84], 179[18]

Barr, J.
165[67]

Barth, K.
39[302], 77, 77[63], 102[6], 117[21], 136, 143, 179[12]

Bassler, J. M.
54[424]

Bauer, K. L.
42[327]

Bauer, W.
11[90]

Baumert, N.
119[39]

Baur, F. C.
148[8], 190[5]

Beard, M.
90[47, 49-50, 52]

Beardsley, M.
25[191]

Beare, F. W.
10[79], 13[100], 14[110], 72[16], 77[62], 112[5], 126[93], 133[29], 147[1], 158[23], 173[11]

Becker, J.
11[83]

Behm, J.
118[23]

Beker, J. C.
42[335]

Bengel, J. A.
14[113], 15[115], 34[264], 77[59], 173[11], 179[12]

Berger, K.
9[75], 67[65], 116[17]

Berry, K. L.
17[130], 70[39]

Bettini, M.
140[16]

Betz, H. D.
10[82], 32[243], 39[303], 47[378], 52[404], 79[71], 97[20], 162[45, 49, 51], 173[9], 188[22, 26]

Betz, H. D.
163[51]

Biesecker, B. A.
25[190]

Billerbeck, P.
160[35]

Bingham, S.
21[167], 23[175], 87[21]

Bittasi, S.
141[21], 142[1], 143[2]

Bitzer, L.
24[189], 25[190]

Black, D. A.
17[133]

Blenkinsopp, J.
8[64], 43[344]

Boardman, J.
174[17], 175[19]

Boccaccini, G.
44[346]

Bockmuehl, M.
10[81], 21[162], 23[177, 179], 77[62], 116[17], 118[21, 30-31], 128[115], 133[28], 140[12], 165[64], 175[26]

Boer, M. C. de
44[349]

Bohnenblust, G.
32[246]

Bonhöffer, A. F.
78[67], 79[71]

Bonnard, P.
18[138], 75[44], 76[51], 106[21]

Bonner, S.
40[311], 165[71], 167[83]

Bonnet, M.
96[7]

Bormann, L.
10[82], 11[86], 13[102], 25[193], 88[29], 191[8]

Bornecque, H.
41[313]

Bornkamm, G.
13[102], 14[112]

Boudon-Millot, V.
2[6]

Bousset, W.
51[401, 404], 65[38]

Bouttier, M.
65[38]

Brandl, M.
106[19]

Brashler, J.
162[45-46, 48]

Braund, S. M.
5[41]

Brekelmans, C. H. W.
64[35]

Brélaz, C.
25[193], 88[31], 89[39]

Breytenbach, C.
53[417], 54[419]

Broek, R. van den
162[48]

Bronwen, N.
35[275]

Brown, R. E.
10[80]

Bruce, F. F.
11[85], 16[125], 22[175]

Brucker, R.
115[4], 116[17]

Bruyne, D. de
12[95], 57[441]

Buchanan, C. O.
16[125]

Büchsel, F.
65[40]

Bultmann, R.
40[311], 65[42], 163, 163[55], 164,
167[82], 173[4]

Buresch, C.
1[2]

Burkert, W.
52[405], 122[64]

Burnett, A.
87[24, 26], 88[28]

Buxton, R.
48[387], 120[43], 121[47], 122[60]

Bynum, C. W.
122[59]

Calderini, R.
62[16]

Calvin, J.
33[254], 39[302, 307], 74[35], 112[6, 8],
136[5], 138[1, 3]

Capper, B. J.
186[7]

Carroll, R. P.
7[56], 8[63], 43[337]

Cassidy, R. J.
19[151]

Chapa, J.
3[22], 6[46], 7[51], 34[259], 82[7], 105[13],
109[49], 139[6-7]

Charles, R.
21[164]

Charlesworth, J. H.
50[397], 134[39]

Chester, S.
52[408]

Chryssanthaki-Nagle, K.
87[26]

Collange, J. F.
14[106, 112], 16[122-23], 70[3], 72[16], 76[51],
77[63], 78[67], 93[9], 123[70], 126[88],
133[28], 134[34], 140[14], 160[35], 178[4],
179[6]

Collart, P.
25[193], 88, 88[27], 191[8]

Collins, J. J.
7[53], 8[64], 9[70], 28[224], 42[337-38], 43[345],
44[352-53], 45[356, 357, 361], 46[370],
50[397-98], 51[402], 64[35], 65[36], 68[68],
107[31], 128[109], 134, 134[38, 41], 158[22]

Collins, J. N.
66[52]

Colpe, C.
19[151], 26[206]

Conzelmann, H.
47[372]

Cook, D.
10[79]

Cook, J. G.
106[17], 124[78]

Cook, S. L.
8[64]

Copenhaver, B. P.
162[47]

Cortès, E.
35[277]

Cousin, J.
40[313]

Cover M.
121[49]

Crenshaw, J. L.
7[54]

Cribiore, R.
36[279]

Crook, J. A.
21[169], 124[77]

Croy, C.
97[15]

Cullman, O.
118[21]

Cumont, F.
134[38]

Curley, D.
97[12]

Dahl, N.
20[156], 85[4], 112[3]

Dalton, W. J.
17, 17[133], 18, 18[141, 143]

Dam, H.-J. van
141[20]

Daniel, R. W.
77[60]

Deissmann, A.
20[160], 65[38]

Dequeker, L.
64[35]

Dessau, H.
62[15]

De Wette, W. M. L.
39[302], 74[35], 136[5]

Dibelius, M.
16[130], 21[167], 47[376], 64[28], 76[51], 99[34],
121[48], 138[1], 162[44], 173[9], 181[2]

Dindorf, W.
11[89]

Dirkse, P.
162[45-46, 48]

Doering, L.
61[4], 68[70]

Doty, W. G.
13[100]

Douglas, A. E.
37[289]

Droge, A. J.
97[20]

Duncan, G. S.
20[160]

Dunn, J. D. G.
43[340], 53[413, 415], 65[38], 118[21], 166[78],
167[84]

Durry, M.
21[167], 88[28]

Ebner, M.
66[52]

Edart, J.-B.
10[82], 179[12]

Egger, R.
22[175]

Eliade, M.
177, 177[43]

Engberg-Pedersen, T.
46[369], 78[67], 113[17], 125[83], 134[37],
160[34], 176[35], 181[2]

Eschner, C.
53[417]

Esler, P. F.
66[47], 174[17]

Harnack, A. von
12[93], 72[17]

Harrer, G. A.
63[18]

Harries, J.
124[77]

Harrisville III, R. A.
166[75]

Hartmann, G.
124[79]

Hawthorne, G.
10[81]

Hays, R. B.
93[5], 165[65], 166[72-73], 167[85]

Heinrici, C. F. G.
40, 40[311], 167[82]

Hemer, C. J.
63[18]

Hengel, M.
48[386], 50[394], 53[417], 62[17], 124[78], 134[38], 158[22], 164[60]

Hentschel, A.
66[52]

Hentze, C.
96[7]

Henze, M.
46[370]

Heyob, S. K.
90[51]

Hijmans, B. L.
187[12]

Himmelfarb, M.
49[389], 50[397], 51[401], 134[38-39]

Hofius, O.
115[3, 6]

Hofmann, J. C. K. von
15[120]

Høgenhaven, J.
8[62]

Holden, J. L.
153[48]

Holloway, P. A.
1, 1[3], 5[35], 6[50], 9[71, 73, 76-77], 10[78-79], 12[94], 23[180], 24[185], 29[227], 31[240], 34[260], 35[268, 277], 36[283], 37[289, 293], 39[305], 40[309], 41[315, 320], 53[418], 61[5], 71[10], 72[19], 73[26, 31], 75[48], 79[74], 87[23], 89[45], 90[58], 91[61], 94[16], 96[5], 98[25], 107[25], 109[49], 133[23], 140[15], 157[10], 166[71], 169[97], 179[14], 184[29]

Holmes, M. W.
55[428]

Hooker, M. D.
118[21], 165[70]

Hoover, R. W.
119[38]

Hope, V.
100[43]

Hoppe, R.
66[52]

Horbury, W.
49[391], 118[30]

Horner, G. W.
56[435-36]

Horrell, D.
124[79]

Horsley, R. A.
158[22]

van der Horst, P.
1[3], 50[393]

Howard, G.
165[66]

Hultin, N.
6[44], 136[2]

Hutchinson G. O.
25[191]

Inwood, B.
132[20]

Jackson-McCabe, M.
77[60]

Jaeger, W. W.
119[38]

Jedan, C.
2[8]

Jeremias, J.
182[10]

Jewett, R.
17[133], 19, 19[145], 23[180], 63[27], 148[8-9, 13], 173[8]

Johann, H. T.
5[41], 73[31], 108[37], 109[45], 183[19]

Johnson, L. T.
152[40], 165[65]

Jones, M.
18[138]

Jongkind, D.
56[434]

Jouanna, J.
2[6]

Juckel, A.
57[437]

Kajanto, I.
62[10, 16], 63[18]

Kaplan, B.
9[74]

Käsemann, E.
42[335], 115[2], 116[13]

Kassel, R.
1[2], 27, 5[35, 41], 109[45, 47]

Keck, L.
165, 165[70]

Keil, F. C.
122[63]

Kelly, J. N. D.
80[78]

Kelly, M.
122[63]

Kennedy, G. A.
31[240], 151[39]

Kent, J. H.
172[2]

Kerschensteiner, J.
56[437]

Kilgour, R.
56[437]

Kilpatrick, G. D.
14[108]

Kim, Y. K.
56[432]

Kittredge, C. B.
182[5]

Klawans, J.
132[16]

Klehn, L.
65[39]

Kleinknecht, K. T.
27[215]

Koester, H.
10[79, 82], 32[242], 145[1], 148[8], 154, 168[96]

Koperski, V.
10[79]

Koskenniemi, H.
17[137], 33[250], 68[69], 76[52], 102, 102[2], 143[2], 186[3]

Koukouli-Chrysanthaki, C.
25[193-94]

Miller, S. G.
172[2], 175[18, 20]

Missitzis, L.
25[195]

Mitchell, A. C.
32[246]

Mitchell, J. F.
4[23]

Mitchell, M. M.
23[180], 55[427]

Mitchell, S.23[176]

Moffatt, J.
66[53], 143, 143[5]

Momigliano, A.
94[14]

Mommsen, T.
62[17]

Montefiore, C. G.
1[3]

Moore, E.
119[37]

Moore, G. F.
132[16]

Moore, M. B.
175[19]

Moos, P. von
1[2]

Morin, G.
57[442]

Morray-Jones, C.
50[397], 163[43]

Moss, C. R.
49[390], 123[66]

Moule, C. F. D.
118, 118[32], 127, 127[96]

Mount, C.
28[216, 222], 51[403], 66[49], 67[60], 145[6],
147[3], 154[57], 170[101]

Mouritsen, H.
191[6]

Muenchow, C. A.
1[3]

Müller, U. B.
14[112], 35[279], 72[16], 78[67, 71], 102[4],
106[21], 111[1], 121[48], 128[116], 156[1],
157[11], 173[4], 173[7, 9], 184[23]

Müller-Bardorff, J.
10[79], 13[99, 101], 14, 14[106, 112]

Mullins, T. Y.
13[100], 18[137], 86[7]

Münzer, F.
62[10]

Murphy O'Connor, J.
11[84], 118[21]

Myers, K. S.
48[387]

Nanos, M.
153[50]

Nasrallah, L. S.
88[29]

Naumann, H.
165[71]

Nesselrath, H.-G.
2[6]

Neugebauer, F.
65[38]

Neusner, J.
107[31]

Newman, R. J.
94[15]

Newsom, C. A.
1[3], 152[44]

Nickelsburg, G. W. E.
7[53], 8[61], 9[70], 43[339], 44[346, 354],
45[358, 360], 46[362, 370], 50[400], 64[35],
99[32], 107[31], 118[27-28], 128[110, 111],
134[38], 183[22]

Nicklas, T.
67[58]

Nock, A. D.
160[32], 162[47]

Nongbri, B.
70[j]

Norden, E.
117, 117[20], 167[83]

Nordheim, E. von
35[277]

North, J.
90[47, 49-50, 52]

Novenson, M. V.
77[57]

Nugent, S. G.
98[28]

Oakes, P.
25[193], 88[29]

O'Brien, P. T.
10[81], 16[128], 70[2, 6], 72[17], 112[7]

Ogereau, J. M.
74[38], 187[17], 188[19, 22, 25-26]

Ollrog, W.-H.
63[20]

Orlov, A. A.
128[113]

Palmer, D. W.
94(17

Papazoglou, F.
25[193], 88[30]

Parker, D. C.
55[428]

Parrott, D. M.
162[50]

Parsenios, G.
9[76]

Patton, J. H.
25[190]

Pedersen, S.
136[5]

Pervo, R. I.
20[157], 26[200, 206], 62[14], 63[22], 90[55],
116[17]

Peterlin, D.
29[229], 64[28]

Pevarello, D.
187[10]

Pfitzner, V. C.
106[19]

Pietrobelli, A.
2[6]

Pilhofer, P.
25[193], 66[52], 67[56], 88[30], 89[39], 121[49],
158, 158[17], 180[18], 191[8]

Pink, K.
12[95]

Pinkerton, J.
56[437]

Pitta, A 85[6], 112[4], 145[9]

Pollard, T. E.
18[138]

Poplutz, U.
106[19]

Potter, D. S.
94[16]

Preisendanz, K.
162[45]

Preisker, H.
163[54]

Price, S.
90[47, 49-50, 52]

5. Subjects

metamorphosis (*continued*)
48[387], 49[388], 121–22; in Jewish apocalypticism: 121, 121[52]; Incarnation as: 49, 115, 117–18, 120, 121, 126, 126[94, 95]; into stars (astral immortality): 28[224], 50, 52, 106, 133, 134, 134[39]; "kenosis" as part of: 123, 123[67]; of Adam: 50[399]; of angels: 48–49, 121, 121[53]; of Christ into a rock: 127[95]; of Enoch: 50[399]; of Mercury into Augustus: 122[57]; of Moses: 50, 50[399]; of Noah: 50, 50[399]; of Satan: 48, 121–24, 126, 126[91]; of the angel Israel into Jacob: 122; of the apocalyptic seer: 50, 162; of the Jewish patriarchs: 50[399]; of the righteous: 50, 52, 52[404]; of the unrighteous: 123[65]; resurrection as: 9, 28, 46[368], 52, 93[9], 121[50], 162, 174, 180; sanctification/salvation as: 9, 28–29, 43, 47, 48[381], 51, 51[404], 52, 52[406, 407], 54, 65[36], 75–76, 82, 133, 134[40], 145, 149[18], 160–63, 164[59], 168–69, 170[102], 174, 180, 190; shape-shifting: 49, 49[389]; subjective experience of: 50[399, 400], 156, 156[8], 161, 163, 168, 170; terms used to describe: 120, 120[42, 43, 44, 45], 121, 121[50], 123–24, 124[72]; through ascent: 49[389], 50, 50[399, 400], 51[401], 162; through gnosis: 9, 76, 82, 145, 156, 156[8], 161–62, 168[89]; through possession: 43, 47–48, 51, 54, 164, 164[59], 168, 168[92], 169, 191, 191[11]; Transfiguration as: 49[390], 123, 123[65]; visible in this life: 52, 52[406]

Metatron
48[385], 127–28

Michael (angel)
45

monepiscopacy
66

myth
27, 42, 42[224], 43, 43[338], 44, 47, 94, 115[1, 11], 116[13, 14], 117[18], 122, 122[57], 126, 127[95], 168[88], 174, 180

Christ-myth: 46, 49[393], 113, 115–16, 122[57], 125, 126[94, 95], 130; metamorphic myth: 48, 115, 117[19], 120[44], 121, 123, 123[66], 126[95]; mythological thinking: 42[334], 52

Name
28, 48[385], 49–50, 114[h], 126–28, 128[114], 129

oath
42, 77, 77[57]

obedience
8, 30[232], 49, 115, 115[8], 116, 117[19], 120–21, 123–24, 124[75], 125, 128, 130, 131, 132[13], 133, 142, 144, 164[58], 165[65], 166[79], 175

orator, Paul as
42

overseers and assistants (*see also* ἐπίσκοπος, διάκονος)
27[210], 62, 64, 66, 66[52], 67

paradox of spirit possession
167

parenesis
4[24], 14, 181[2]

Paul (name)
62–63

perfection
7[55], 8–9, 15, 27, 29[226], 43, 44[348], 46[364], 52, 75, 86, 107, 148, 150, 164, 172–73, 173[5], 174–75, 175[27], 176, 178, 179[15]

peristasis catalogue
17, 17[134]

persecution
8[65], 24[186], 43, 90[49], 107, 107[26], 133[24], 156, 158–59, 170

"personalism," Paul's
168, 168[89, 91]

Pharisees
42, 42[335], 86[12], 107, 146, 152, 156–57, 157[11], 158[16, 20, 21], 159–61, 161[37], 170

Philippi
battle of: 26; civic pride at: 88; distance from place of Paul's imprisonment: 20, 20[154], 21[162], 23, 142–44; early history: 25–26;

Imperial guardsmen from: 88–89; *liberti Augusti* at: 191[8]; Paul's imprisonment at: 26, 116[17]; Roman colony: 26, 26[203], 89, 105[5]; Vespasian possibly recruited troops from: 89; worship of Dionysius at: 121[49]

Popularphilosophie
78[67], 79[61]

possession (*see also* in Christ; in the Spirit; altered states of consciousness)
28[216], 47[378], 51, 51[403, 404], 67, 77, 132, 168[88, 92], 170; by a demon (*see also* τὸ πνεῦμα ἔχειν): 47, 47[379]; by the spirit of Christ (*see also* in Christ): 9, 28, 28[223], 47, 47[378], 48[380], 54, 66, 66[44, 51], 77, 154, 164, 167–68, 168[88], 169–70, 177, 188, 191[11]; by the spirit of God (*see also* in the Spirit): 48[380], 65, 66[43], 132, 154; Paul's assemblies as spirit possession cults: 66, 154, 154[57]

power (*see also* δύναμις; ἀδύνατος)
28, 28[217], 29, 43[338], 46, 48[381], 51, 54, 99, 118, 122, 125, 156, 159[31], 160, 163–64, 166, 168, 168[95], 169, 169[97], 170, 177, 180, 185

praemeditatio futuri mali
5, 109, 109[49]

praemeditatio mortis
39[303]

Praetorian Guard (*see* Imperial Guard)

prejudice
45[355], 64, 89, 91, 106[18], 156, 165, 177[40]

prison/imprisonment
5, 11, 11[84, 85], 12, 12[96], 13, 13[102], 15, 15[117], 19, 19[151], 20, 20[157, 160], 21, 21[165], 22–24, 26, 26[202, 206], 27, 29, 29[230], 30, 33, 33[254, 258], 34–35, 35[273, 278, 279], 36, 36[279], 42, 63[24], 70–71, 71[9], 73, 75–76, 76[55], 82, 84–87, 87[17, 21], 88–89, 91–93, 93[6], 97, 97[21], 106–7, 112, 116[17], 131, 143–45, 187, 187[14], 189

prize (*see also* βραβεῖον)
150[26], 173[10, 11], 174–75

In the design of the visual aspects of *Hermeneia*, consideration has been given to relating the form to the content by symbolic means.

The letters of the logotype *Hermeneia* are a fusion of forms alluding simultaneously to Hebrew (dotted vowel markings) and Greek (geometric round shapes) letter forms. In their modern treatment they remind us of the electronic age as well, the vantage point from which this investigation of the past begins. The Lion of Judah used as visual identification for the series is based on the Seal of Shema. The version for *Hermeneia* is again a fusion of Hebrew calligraphic forms, especially the legs of the lion, and Greek elements characterized by the geometric. In the sequence of arcs, which can be understood as scroll-like images, the first is the lion's mouth. It is reasserted and accelerated in the whorl and returns in the aggressively arched tail: tradition is passed from one age to the next, rediscovered and re-formed.

"Who is worthy to open the scroll and break its seals. . . ."

Then one of the elders said to me

"weep not; lo, the Lion of the tribe of David, the Root of David, has conquered, so that he can open the scroll and its seven seals."

Rev. 5:2, 5

To celebrate the signal achievement in biblical scholarship which *Hermeneia* represents, the entire series will by its color constitute a signal on the theologian's bookshelf: the Old Testament will be bound in yellow and the New Testament in red, traceable to a commonly used color coding for synagogue and church in medieval painting; in pure color terms, varying degrees of intensity of the warm segment of the color spectrum. The colors interpenetrate when the binding color for the Old Testament is used to imprint volumes from the New and vice versa.

Wherever possible, a photograph of the oldest extant manuscript, or a historically significant document pertaining to the biblical sources, will be displayed on the end papers of each volume to give a feel for the tangible reality and beauty of the source material.

The title page motifs are expressive derivations from the *Hermeneia* logotype, repeated seven times to form a matrix and debossed on the cover of each volume. These sifted-out elements will be seen to be in their exact positions within the parent matrix.

Horizontal markings at gradated levels on the spine will assist in grouping the volumes according to these conventional categories.

The type has been set with unjustified right margins so as to preserve the internal consistency of word spacing. This is a major factor in both legibility and aesthetic quality; the resultant uneven line endings are only slight impairments to legibility by comparison. In this respect the type resembles the handwritten manuscripts where the quality of the calligraphic writing is dependent on establishing and holding to integral spacing patterns.

All of the typefaces in common use today have been designed between AD 1500 and the present. For the biblical text a face was chosen which does not arbitrarily date the text, but rather one which is uncompromisingly modern and unembellished so that its feel is of the universal. The type style is Univers 65 by Adrian Frutiger.

The expository texts and footnotes are set in Baskerville, chosen for its compatibility with the many brief Greek and Hebrew insertions. The double-column format and the shorter line length facilitate speed reading and the wide margins to the left of footnotes provide for the scholar's own notations.

Kenneth Hiebert

Category of biblical writing,
key symbolic characteristic,
and volumes so identified.

1
Law
(boundaries described)
 Genesis
 Exodus
 Leviticus
 Numbers
 Deuteronomy

2
History
(trek through time and space)
 Joshua
 Judges
 Ruth
 1 Samuel
 2 Samuel
 1 Kings
 2 Kings
 1 Chronicles
 2 Chronicles
 Ezra
 Nehemiah
 Esther

3
Poetry
(lyric emotional expression)
 Job
 Psalms
 Proverbs
 Ecclesiastes
 Song of Songs

4
Prophets
(inspired seers)
 Isaiah
 Jeremiah
 Lamentations
 Ezekiel
 Daniel
 Hosea
 Joel
 Amos
 Obadiah
 Jonah
 Micah
 Nahum
 Habakkuk
 Zephaniah
 Haggai
 Zechariah
 Malachi

5
New Testament Narrative
(focus on One)
 Matthew
 Mark
 Luke
 John
 Acts

6
Epistles
(directed instruction)
 Romans
 1 Corinthians
 2 Corinthians
 Galatians
 Ephesians
 Philippians
 Colossians
 1 Thessalonians
 2 Thessalonians
 1 Timothy
 2 Timothy
 Titus
 Philemon
 Hebrews
 James
 1 Peter
 2 Peter
 1 John
 2 John
 3 John
 Jude

7
Apocalypse
(vision of the future)
 Revelation

8
Extracanonical Writings
(peripheral records)